Hospitality Strategic Management

CONCEPTS *and* CASES

SECOND EDITION

CATHY A. ENZ

WILEY

JOHN WILEY & SONS, INC.

Library of Congress Cataloging-in-Publication Data

Enz, Cathy A., 1956-
    Hospitality strategic management : concepts and cases / Cathy A. Enz. — 2nd ed.
        p.   cm.
    Includes bibliographical references.
    ISBN 978-0-470-08359-8 (cloth)
        1. Hospitality industry—Management.   2. Strategic planning.   I. Title.
    TX911.3.M27E56 2009
    647.94'068—dc22
                                                                    2008021438
Printed in the United States of America

10   9   8   7   6   5   4   3   2

*Dedicated to my
parents Richard and Betty Enz,
two remarkable people*

CONTENTS

CASES

PREFACE

My goal in writing this second edition of **Hospitality Strategic Management, Second Edition** is to provide students, hospitality professors, and practitioners with an up-to-date, thorough, and rigorous treatment of strategic management in a hospitality context. In this edition, the text continues to provide a comprehensive treatment of strategy concepts and ideas, while illustrating important ideas with numerous new and relevant examples from the hospitality industry. Since the last edition, the business landscape in the hospitality industry has changed dramatically. Consolidation, mergers, new entrants, and new brand introductions continue, while tourism and brand expansion is growing rapidly in emerging nations. In this edition, new concepts and business initiatives, along with shifting trends and evolving strategies, are reflected through all-new examples and cases.

Not only does this text cover strategic management from the perspective of hospitality professionals, but it is also based on what strategic managers actually do, making it a practical guide. On one hand, they acquire, develop, and manage internal *resources* such as people, knowledge, financial capital, and physical assets. Of equal importance, they acquire, develop, and manage *relationships* with external stakeholders such as guests, suppliers, owners, franchisors, venture partners, and governmental agencies. **Hospitality Strategic Management, Second Edition** provides a realistic, balanced view of the field. It draws heavily from the resource-based perspective that firms can develop competitive advantages through the acquisition, development, and management of resources. It also uses stakeholder theory to help explain when firms should form partnerships, the form they should take, and how to manage them.

This book also contains the most relevant theory and models from what might be called the traditional approach to strategic management. Consequently, combining the resource-based view and the stakeholder view with traditional theory and models provides a comprehensive and managerially useful perspective of strategic management. The focus of this book is on the translation of strategic ideas into hospitality contexts. Using a diverse set of examples and new cases, the book seeks to link useful strategies and strategic issues to actions and activities of hospitality firms. Furthermore, this text introduces theories, recent research, and models in key areas that fit the hospitality context better than ideas found in the general strategy literature.

WHO SHOULD READ THIS BOOK?

After teaching hospitality strategy for 20 years, I know the struggles that hospitality faculty have had in finding a book that focuses on the industry while also adequately handling the ideas and theories within the field of strategic management. General strategy textbooks often focus on theories and ideas that are more appropriate in manufacturing contexts, while this hospitality-based text works to illustrate key ideas as they apply to or affect the management of an array of travel and hospitality firms. Application and illustration of key concepts within the hospitality industry is a major feature of this second edition.

The text focuses on concepts and ideas that contribute to a practical understanding of strategic issues from a general management perspective. General managers within the industry have the responsibility for guiding their organization, whether they lead a small hotel, restaurant, or travel agency or manage a multiunit operation or portfolio of hotels. This book is designed to give managers who are engaged in trying to solve strategic problems a foundation. The text can be used in executive education courses that explore issues of competitive analysis and positioning, as well as undergraduate and graduate courses in strategic management or strategic issues and leadership. The typical hospitality program may use the book in a senior-level or masters-level core course that examines strategic problems with the aid of case analyses. The book is also well suited as a supplement in any general management course. In executive education courses, this text is particularly useful for senior managers or aspiring managers because it takes the perspective of the general manager who is responsible for the entire enterprise.

TEACHING AND LEARNING FEATURES IN THE SECOND EDITION

The organization and style of the second edition continues to focus on essential material without all the "fluff." Principles and theories are explained with brief examples that get right to the point. The treatment of models and theories is comprehensive, and yet the book continues to rely on brevity and emphasizes hospitality examples. Several valued characteristics of the first edition have been retained, with enhancements as follows:

- **Featured Story:** All-new opening cases introduce each chapter. The opening stories help direct students and include discussion questions to stimulate student thinking and class discussion.

- **Hospitality Focus Boxed Illustrations:** Hospitality illustrations and profiles are made more evident in this edition by having them featured in boxed sections of the text called "Hospitality Focus." Many more industry examples and mini-profiles are used in this edition throughout each chapter to show how various concepts and ideas are put into practice or operate in various hospitality businesses. The expanded number of these hospitality-relevant examples in each chapter help to link theory and practice.

- **Key Points Summary:** Key ideas presented in the chapters are summarized in a bulleted list at the close of each chapter. These summaries make it easy for students to review the critical ideas contained in each chapter.

- **Review Questions:** Each chapter concludes with a set of questions that focus on the main concepts and most important ideas covered in the chapter.

- **Enhanced Support Materials:** The book is supported by an instructor's manual that includes suggestions for teaching each chapter, suggested activities or cases, answers to review questions, and suggested additional readings. In addition, a user-friendly companion web site contains special features for students and instructors, including additional readings from the Cornell Center for Hospitality Research. Please visit www.wiley.com/college for instructor's resources, and www.hotelschool.cornell.edu/research/chr/ for up-to-date industry research.

NEW TO THIS EDITION

Thanks to feedback from students and instructors, this edition has several new features to enhance the value of this popular textbook.

Features

- **New Chapter Content:** In each chapter, the materials have been revised and expanded to reflect new theories or studies within service firms, and the shifting of corporate ownership and performance within the hospitality industry. All chapters have been edited to retain readability and brevity. Some topics have been reordered to accommodate new material or improve the flow of the subject matter for teaching purposes.

- **Learning Objectives:** Each chapter begins with a set of learning objectives.

- **Key Terms:** Important terms are italicized throughout the chapters to highlight their importance.

- **Critical Thinking and Application Questions:** To help students develop critical thinking skills and apply important ideas in the hospitality context, these questions focus on experimentation, research, and application of key concepts.

- **All-New Cases:** Eight new hospitality cases were developed by various faculty members for inclusion in this edition. The exciting cases selected for the text include a variety of firms from various segments of the hospitality industry. The cases are current and illustrate key issues of concern in the industry. In addition, the cases are shorter than the cases featured in the first edition to facilitate student engagement while still offering comprehensive coverage of important strategic problems and opportunities.

• **A Case Matrix:** A Case Matrix is included in this edition, which correlates each case to the appropriate chapters and highlights the topics and industry segment covered in each of the eight cases. This mapping tool is useful in guiding both instructors and students in identifying the focus of various cases.

Chapter Content

The text discusses strategic management in 10 chapters, beginning with an introduction to the various perspectives on strategy and the global competitiveness of the industry in Chapter 1. A simple model of the strategic management process (see figure that follows) begins with a situational analysis of the broad and operating environments, including internal resources, and both internal and external stakeholders. Chapter 2 deals with the external environment, which includes groups, individuals, and forces outside of the traditional boundaries of the organization that are significantly influenced by or have a major impact on the

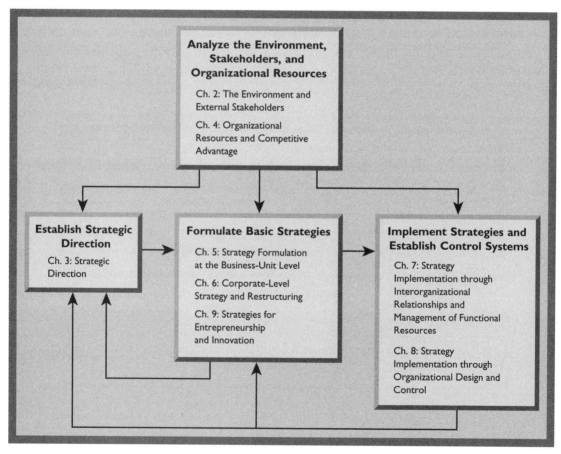

FIGURE 1 **Chapter content and the strategic management process**

organization. The internal organization discussed in Chapter 4 includes all of the stakeholders, resources, knowledge, and processes that exist within the boundaries of the firm. Establishing strategic direction is reflected in mission statements and organizational visions. Strategic direction pertains to the longer-term goals and objectives of the organization and is the central topic of Chapter 3.

The process of planning strategies is often divided into two levels: business and corporate levels. Chapter 5 is concerned primarily with business-level strategies such as low-cost leader, differentiator, and best value and how to competitively position. Chapter 6 contains a detailed discussion of the corporate-level strategies of concentration, vertical integration, and diversification. Strategy implementation involves managing stakeholder relationships and organizational resources in a manner that moves the business toward the successful execution of its strategies, consistent with its strategic direction. These topics are discussed in Chapter 7.

Implementation activities also involve creating an organizational design and organizational control systems to keep the company on the right course. Organizational control refers to the processes that lead to adjustments in strategic direction, strategies, or the implementation plan, when necessary. Chapter 8 deals with organizational design and organizational control systems. Chapter 9 focuses on entrepreneurship in both independent companies and corporations, and the book concludes with a discussion in Chapter 10 of global strategies and the future of hospitality management. The aforementioned figure and the structure of the textbook reflect the progression of activities in the strategic management process—from situation analysis and strategic direction to strategy formulation and implementation.

WHAT'S UNIQUE ABOUT THIS BOOK?

In addition to the balanced approach found in this book, it also contains several other features that are a direct result of current trends in strategic management:

1. *International flavor.* The hospitality industry is a pioneer in globalization; hence, global strategic management theory is woven into many of the chapters and discussed in a separate international chapter.

2. *Section on strategic thinking.* Strategic thinking is different from other aspects of strategic management. In fact, some strategists have argued that strategic planning processes can stifle strategic thinking. The perspective taken in this book is that strategic thinking is an essential, creative aspect of the strategy process.

3. *Chapter on entrepreneurship and innovation.* Innovation and entrepreneurship are vital to strategic success, particularly in the foodservice and lodging industries. The entrepreneurship chapter contains elements of starting a business (such as what a business plan contains), franchising, and entrepreneurship within existing organizations (organizational entrepreneurship or "intrapreneurship").

4. *Section on competitive dynamics.* Firms do not create strategies in a static environment. They need to account for the dynamic elements of industry competition. This book reflects the reality of a dynamic environment in every chapter.

5. *Innovative and comprehensive treatment of implementation and control.* Consistent with the balanced theme of the book, implementation is treated from the perspective of managing

internal processes as well as external relationships. A careful treatment of organizational design and a fully integrated strategic control model pull the implementation process together.

6. *Size is not overwhelming.* Despite all this coverage, the book is only 10 chapters. The smaller size of the book allows instructors to use more cases, simulations, exercises, or readings.

ACKNOWLEDGMENTS

First, I am grateful to many of my former students, who offered their insights and suggestions as a result of reading the first edition. I would also like to acknowledge the special contributions of the following organizations: InterContinental Hotels and Resorts, Tata Group, Starwood Hotels and Resorts, Four Seasons Hotels and Resorts, Starbucks, YUM! Brands, Marriott Hotels and Resorts, Darden Restaurants, Banyan Tree Hotels, and McDonald's Corporation. I am grateful to several senior managers within these and many other hospitality organizations for their interest in this project, supportive input, and wonderful conversations. To my executive education students, thank you for sharing your own stories and strategic challenges.

I have benefited from thoughtful and supportive faculty reviewers, who provided excellent insights and observations that have substantially improved this edition of the book. Many thanks to David Corson, University of Denver; Robert H. Woods, University of Nevada at Las Vegas; Jerrold Leong, Oklahoma State University; Bo Hu, San Francisco State University; Renata Kosova, Cornell University; David Chang, University of South Florida; and Michael G. Brizek, University of South Carolina. I am appreciative of the expertise and guidance provided by Rachel Livsey at John Wiley & Sons, Inc., in the process of writing this book. I am also most profoundly thankful for the love and support of my family, who tolerated evenings and days spent working on this book. To my husband and children, I owe my gratitude for their constant encouragement and understanding.

Finally, I would like to acknowledge an extraordinary leader: Lewis G. Schaeneman, Jr., former CEO of Stop and Shop Groceries. Lew was a great man and served as a model of leadership and innovation. He and his family have, for the last decade, generously provided for the endowed professorship that I hold.

—Cathy A. Enz

ABOUT THE AUTHOR

Cathy A. Enz holds the Lewis G. Schaeneman, Jr. Professorship of Innovation and Dynamic Management and is a full professor at the School of Hotel Administration at Cornell University. Dr. Enz received her Ph.D. from the Fisher College of Business at The Ohio State University, and taught on the faculty of the Kelley School of Business at Indiana University before arriving at Cornell in 1990.

Cathy has published more than 80 journal articles, book chapters, and three books in the areas of strategic management and hospitality best practices. Her research interests include competitive dynamics, innovation and change management, and intangible asset investment strategies. Her research has been published in a wide variety of prestigious academic and hospitality journals, such as *Administrative Science Quarterly, The Academy of Management Journal, The Journal of Service Research, The Journal of Travel Research*, and *The Cornell Hospitality Quarterly*. Her book *American Lodging Excellence: The Key to Best Practices in the U.S. Lodging Industry*, co-authored with three marketing professors, was the winner of an excellence award from the American Hotel and Lodging Association.

Dr. Enz is the recipient of both outstanding teaching and research awards. She was the recipient of the Cornell Center for Hospitality Research Industry Relevance award in 2006, 2007, and 2008 for her research on competitive pricing in hotels. In addition to teaching graduates and undergraduates, she presents in numerous executive programs in Europe, Asia, and Central America. Dr. Enz consults extensively in North America and serves on the Board of Directors of two privately owned hotel companies.

Before commencing her academic activities, Dr. Enz held several industry positions, including strategy development analyst in the office of corporate research for a large insurance organization and operations manager responsible for Midwestern U.S. customer service and logistics in the dietary foodservice division of a large U.S. health-care corporation.

CHAPTER 1

STRATEGIC MANAGEMENT

YOU SHOULD BE ABLE TO DO THE FOLLOWING AFTER READING THIS CHAPTER:

1. Describe the key elements in the strategic management process.

2. Discuss the three different perspectives or approaches used in understanding strategy, including the traditional perspective, the resource-based view, and the stakeholder view.

3. Understand strategy formulation at the corporate, business, and functional levels.

4. Explain the difference between strategic thinking and strategic planning.

5. Characterize and explain the key players in the lodging and foodservice industries.

FEATURED STORY

MCDONALD'S PLAN TO WIN

After 50 years of operation, McDonald's is revitalizing its products, and pushing innovation through a variety of initiatives. This foodservice giant with more than 30,000 restaurants in 100 countries provides food to nearly 50 million customers each day, but decades of expansion, sales growth, and profits made the burger giant complacent. By focusing on getting bigger, not better, the company stumbled in 2002, recording its first losing quarter. By 2003, U.S. sales had flattened, as many consumers were turning to healthier options and restaurants with more upscale menu items, a segment sometimes referred to as "fast-casual". Morgan Spurlock's film *Super Size Me*, released in 2004, also seriously diminished the public image of the quick-service chain, as moviegoers watched Spurlock become ill and gain 25 pounds after eating only McDonald's food for one month.

With pressure to get back on track, it was time for McDonald's to rethink the business. The chain devised a recovery strategy that included new menu items, redesigned restaurants, and a focus on the consumer experience. Through a program titled "Plan to Win," McDonald's focused on making a deeper connection with customers through the five business drivers of people, products, place, price, and promotion. Using its own five P's, the company is developing and refining new strategies to deliver value, offering product variety, developing updated and contemporary stores, balancing the delivery of value pricing with more expensive items, and marketing through bold and innovative promotions.

Execution of this strategy has included mystery shoppers and customer surveys, along with grading restaurants to help the company deliver on its people goals. New menu items like the Fruit & Walnut Salad in the United States and deli sandwiches in Australia are part of the commitment to serve high-quality products to satisfy customer demand for choice and variety. Restaurants are staying open longer, accepting credit and debit cards, enabling wireless Internet access, and even providing delivery service in parts of Asia. As part of the program, franchisees and suppliers are asked to provide their opinions and ideas on facility design, while the company benchmarks retail leaders, such as Crate & Barrel, to help produce cleaner and smarter restaurants. The company is testing small handheld devices to use on what it calls "travel paths," a process for checking operational failures such as the temperature inside the refrigerators. Experiments with a new grilling concept from Sweden, which grills burgers vertically instead of horizontally, offers space-saving possibilities for the chain. Product offerings like the McCafé, a concept developed in the Australian market that provides gourmet coffee inside 500 existing restaurants, are proving to be successful.

The trouble experienced in the early part of the millennium has abated, and executives at McDonald's have declared success after several years of progress under the Plan to Win.

Company revenues are up, and the firm plans to remain focused on its core business. One indication of its commitment to fast food was the divestiture of its seven-year ownership stake in Chipotle Mexican Grill, a highly successful fast-casual burrito chain. With the sale of around 5 million shares of Chipotle stock, the burger maker is now refocusing on Brand McDonald's.

Attracting more customers to McDonald's remains its goal for growth. In the U.S. market, the strategy is to leverage menu innovation; in Europe, upgrading the customer experience and enhancing local relevance have driven management efforts; and the Asia/Pacific, Middle East, and Africa markets have focused on building sales through extended hours. The question remains whether focusing on the core business will yield maximum return. At McDonald's, the executives are betting on the core brand and hoping that this strategy will pay off.[1]

DISCUSSION QUESTIONS:

1. Will the decision to focus on Brand McDonald's yield the best returns?

2. Why divest shares in the popular fast-casual Chipotle Mexican Grill concept just as it begins to take off?

3. Can the premium coffee McCafé concept expect to compete seriously with Starbucks? Or will McDonald's, like the market leaders in many other industries in the past, struggle?

4. How many times can McDonald's reinvent itself and continue to grow?

INTRODUCTION

The hospitality business is fiercely competitive. When McDonald's began its rapid expansion in the middle of the 20th century, there were few fast-food alternatives. McDonald's did more than any other company to shape the fast-food market, picking up new rivals at every stage. As domestic growth began to level off, the company increased its investments outside of the United States. However, other American companies followed, and foreign rivals began to develop and expand in their home markets. At the turn of the millennium, the company faced some of its most difficult problems as the domestic U.S. markets neared saturation and consumers' tastes began to change. This giant of the foodservice industry made a remarkable recovery by reinventing itself and returning to the basics of focusing on the customer experience.

Why are some companies successful, while so many other businesses fail? Some organizations may just be lucky. They may have the right mix of products and/or services at the right time. But even if luck leads to success, it probably will not last. Most companies that are highly successful over the long term effectively acquire, develop, and manage resources and capabilities that provide competitive advantages. For example, McDonald's enjoys outstanding brand recognition and a world-class operating system. Marriott enjoys these same benefits in the lodging industry.

Successful companies have also learned how to develop and manage relationships with a wide range of organizations, groups, and people that have a stake in their firms. The emergence of a fiercely competitive global economy means that firms have to expand their networks of relationships and cooperate with each other to remain competitive.[2] McDonald's investment in Chipotle was a cooperative venture. As Steve Ells, Founder, Chairman, and CEO of Chipotle noted, "We've enjoyed our relationship with McDonald's since the beginning and appreciate the support they've shown in funding Chipotle's growth over the last seven years. Still, we've always operated independently, and that won't change as McDonald's continues to reduce its investment in Chipotle and focuses on its core business."[3]

This book explores how organizations can grow and prosper through successful execution of the strategic management process. *Strategic management* is a process through which organizations analyze and learn from their internal and external environments, establish strategic direction, create strategies that are intended to move the organization in that direction, and implement those strategies, all in an effort to satisfy key stakeholders. *Stakeholders* are groups or individuals who can significantly affect or are significantly affected by an organization's activities.[4] An organization defines who its key stakeholders are, but they typically include customers, employees, and shareholders or owners, among others. Although larger companies tend to use the strategic management process, this process is also a vital part of decision making in smaller companies.

Firms practicing strategic planning processes tend to outperform their counterparts that do not.[5] In fact, executives have reported higher levels of satisfaction with strategic management tools and ideas than with most other management tools. Furthermore, 81 percent of companies worldwide reported doing strategic planning. In North America, the figure was even higher (89 percent).[6] Hospitality firms also benefit from strategic planning, as suggested by a recent study of hotels in the United Kingdom, which found that business performance was positively associated with the thoroughness, sophistication, participation, and formality of strategic planning processes.[7] An example of how strategic analysis can help guide business strategy is shown in Starwood Hotels & Resorts' efforts to launch a new product.

This book also recognizes that there is a difference between the strategic planning process and strategic thinking, and that both are a part of effective strategic management. The strategic planning process tends to be a rather rigid and unimaginative process in many organizations. Strategic thinking, however, leads to creative solutions and new ideas like Starwood Hotel's launch of the Heavenly Bed. As illustrated in the Heavenly Bed example, a firm that injects strategic thinking into the strategic planning process has the best of both worlds.

STRATEGIC THINKING AT STARWOOD

HOSPITALITY FOCUS

The "Heavenly Bed," first launched by the Westin brand of Starwood Hotels & Resorts, has transformed the bed, a basic feature of any hotel room, into a luxurious object of desire, enhancing the revenues of the chain and leaving many hotel operators to follow suit with copycat linens and custom bedding of their own.

The strategic process at Starwood began with consumer analysis and product testing. First, Westin commissioned a study involving 600 business executives who travel frequently. The results showed that 84 percent said a luxurious bed would make a hotel room more attractive to them. What is more, 63 percent said a good night's sleep is the most important service a hotel can provide. Half of those surveyed said they sleep worse in hotels than at home. After testing 50 beds from 35 lodging chains, *Westin* developed its prototype all-white *Heavenly Bed* with a custom-designed pillow-top mattress, goose down comforters, five pillows, and three crisp sheets ranging in thread count from 180 to 250.

Once the product was designed and tested, the firm introduced the bed with a carefully planned marketing strategy. *USA Today* ran a story on the front page of its business section. The same day, 20 pristine white *Heavenly Beds* lined Wall Street up to the New York Stock Exchange in New York City. Inside the Stock Exchange, Barry Sternlicht, the then Chairman and CEO of Starwood Hotels & Resorts rang the opening bell and threw out hats proclaiming, "Work like the devil. Sleep like an angel." Meanwhile, at New York's Grand Central Station, 20 more beds graced one of the rotundas there, and commuters disembarking the trains were invited to try them out. Similar events were staged the same day at 38 locations across the United States, tailored to each city. Savannah's event featured a bed floating on a barge down the river with a landing skydiver. Seattle's event took place atop the Space Needle. And to reinforce the message, a concurrent advertising campaign asked, "Who's the best in bed?"[8]

THE ORIGIN OF STRATEGIC MANAGEMENT

The increasing importance of strategic management may be a result of several trends. Increasing competition in most industries has made it difficult for some companies to compete. Modern and cheaper transportation and communication have led to increasing global trade and awareness. Technological development has led to accelerated changes in the global economy. Regardless of the reasons, the past two decades have seen a surge in interest in strategic management. Many perspectives on strategic management and the strategic management process have emerged. This book's approach is based predominantly on three of these perspectives: (1) the traditional perspective, (2) the resource-based view of the firm, and (3) the stakeholder approach, which are outlined in Table 1.1.

TABLE 1.1 Three Perspectives on Strategic Management

	TRADITIONAL PERSPECTIVE	RESOURCE-BASED VIEW	STAKEHOLDER VIEW
ORIGIN	Economics, other business disciplines, and consulting firms	Economics, distinctive competencies, and general management capability	Business ethics and social responsibility
VIEW OF FIRM	An economic entity	A collection of resources, skills, and abilities	A network of relationships among the firm and its stakeholders
APPROACH TO STRATEGY FORMULATION	Situation analysis of internal and external environments leading to formulation of mission and strategies	Analysis of organizational resources, skills, and abilities Acquisition of superior resources, skills, and abilities	Analysis of the economic power, political influence, rights, and demands of various stakeholders
SOURCE OF COMPETITIVE ADVANTAGE	Best adapting the organization to its environment by taking advantage of strengths and opportunities and overcoming weaknesses and threats	Possession of resources, skills, and abilities that are valuable, rare, and difficult to imitate by competitors	Superior linkages with stakeholders leading to trust, goodwill, reduced uncertainty, improved business dealings, and ultimately higher firm performance

The Traditional Perspective

As the field of strategic management began to emerge in the latter part of the 20th century, scholars borrowed heavily from the field of economics. For some time, economists had been actively studying topics associated with the competitiveness of industries. These topics included industry concentration, diversification, product differentiation, and market power. However, much of the economics research at that time focused on industries as a whole, and some of it even assumed that individual firm differences did not matter. Other fields also influenced early strategic management thought, including marketing, finance, psychology, and management. Academic progress was slow in the beginning, and the large consulting firms began to develop their own models and theories to meet their clients' needs. Scholars readily adopted many of these models into their own articles and books.

Eventually, a consensus began to build regarding what is included in the strategic management process. The traditional process for developing strategy consists of analyzing the internal and external environments of the company to arrive at organizational strengths, weaknesses, opportunities, and threats (SWOT). The results from this "situation analysis," as this process is sometimes called, are the basis for developing missions, goals, and strategies.[9] In general, a company should select strategies that (1) take advantage of organizational strengths and environmental opportunities or (2) neutralize or overcome organizational weaknesses and environmental threats.[10] After strategies are formulated, plans for implementing them are established and carried out. Figure 1.1 presents the natural flow of these activities.

The model contained in Figure 1.1 provides a framework for understanding the various activities described in this book. However, the traditional approach to strategy development also brought with it some ideas that strategic management scholars have had to reevaluate. The first of these ideas was that the environment is the primary determinant of the best strategy. This is called *environmental determinism*. According to the deterministic view, good management is associated with determining which strategy will best fit environmental, technical, and human forces at a particular point in time, and then working to carry it out.[11] The most successful

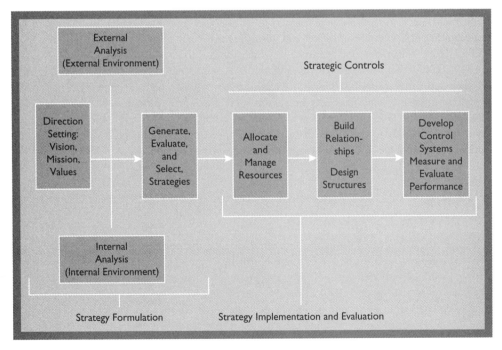

FIGURE 1.1 **The strategic management process**

organization best adapts to existing forces. Some evidence suggests that the ability to align the skills and other resources of the organization with the needs and demands of the environment can be a source of competitive advantage.[12] However, after a critical review of environmental determinism, a well-known researcher once argued:

> There is a more fundamental conclusion to be drawn from the foregoing analysis: the strategy of a firm cannot be predicted, nor is it predestined; the strategic decisions made by managers cannot be assumed to be the product of deterministic forces in their environments. On the contrary, the very nature of the concept of strategy assumes a human agent who is able to take actions that attempt to distinguish one's firm from the competitors.[13]

Basically, a large firm may decide not to compete in a given environment. Or, as an alternative, the firm may attempt to influence the environment to make it less hostile and more conducive to organizational success. This process is called *enactment*, which means that a firm can influence its environment.

THE PRINCIPLE OF ENACTMENT

The principle of enactment assumes that organizations do not have to submit to existing forces in the environment; they can, in part, create their environments through strategic alliances with stakeholders, investments in leading technologies, advertising, political lobbying, and a variety of other activities.[14] Of course, smaller organizations are somewhat limited in their ability to influence some components of their environments on their own. For example, a small restaurant firm may have a difficult time influencing national government agencies and administrators. However, smaller organizations often band together into trade groups, such as the National Restaurant Association, to influence government policy on pressing issues like minimum wage, immigration policy, and health-care costs. Also, they may form alliances with other entities. The Global Hotel Alliance is one example, in which Omni Hotels, Kempinski Hotels & Resorts, Pan Pacific Hotels and Resorts, Rydges Hotels & Resorts, Marco Polo Group, Dusit Hotels & Resorts and Landis Hotels & Resorts have joined forces to compete against the mega chains.[15] In addition, even a small firm may be able to exert a powerful influence on its local operating environment. The key to enactment is understanding that a firm does not necessarily have to adapt completely to the forces that exist in its operating environment. It can at least partly influence certain aspects of the environment in which it competes.

DELIBERATE STRATEGY VERSUS EMERGENT STRATEGY

The traditional school of thought concerning strategy formulation also supported the view that managers respond to the forces discussed thus far by making decisions that are consistent with a preconceived strategy. In other words, strategy is deliberate. Deliberate strategy implies that managers plan to pursue an intended strategic course. In some cases, however, strategy simply emerges from a stream of decisions. Managers learn as they go. An emergent strategy is one that was not planned or intended. According to this perspective, managers learn what will work through a process of trial and error.[16] Supporters of this view argue that organizations that limit themselves to acting on the basis of what is already known or understood will not be sufficiently innovative to create a sustainable competitive advantage.[18] Despite the strength

AN EMERGING RETAIL STRATEGY FOR THE HEAVENLY BED

In the first week of launching the Westin Heavenly Bed, 32 guests called to ask where they could buy the bed. A light bulb went on. Westin executives put order cards with a toll-free number in every room. Then they started placing catalogs by bedsides and desks and set up a web site. By June of 2004, Westin had sold 20,000 pillows—$75 for the king-sized version—and 3,500 bed/bedding combos, at $2,965 each, enough to spread the idea throughout Starwood, with the Sheraton, St. Regis, and W lines all turning into retailers. The unanticipated success of the Heavenly Bed has spawned a new business—companies that help hotels run their retail arms. Boxport, a spin-off of San Francisco–based hotel procurer Higgins Purchasing Group, operates web sites and catalogs for several chains that now sell bedding.[17]

of this example of emergent strategy, it is not a good idea to reject deliberate strategy either. One of the strongest advocates of learning and emergent strategy recently confessed, "We shall get nowhere without emergent learning alongside deliberate planning."[19] Both processes are necessary if an organization is to succeed. When Starwood first launched the concept of the Heavenly Bed in 1999, the strategy was a deliberate effort, but the opportunity to provide retail sales was an unintended outcome, and this unforeseen opportunity led to an emergent and highly successful retail strategy, as the above example shows.

EFFECTIVE STRATEGIC PLANNING

In summary, scholars have determined that both adaptation and enactment are important to organizations. They should adapt to environmental forces when the costs of enacting (influencing) the environment exceed the benefits. However, they should be proactive in creating their own opportunities. In addition, organizations should engage in deliberate strategic planning processes, but they should also be willing to make mistakes and learn from them as they chart a strategic course. In other words, strategy should be both deliberate and emergent, and firms should both adapt to and enact their environments, with the situation determining which option to choose. Westin learned these lessons by paying attention to their customers.

The Organization as a Bundle of Resources: The Resource-Based View

In recent years, another perspective on strategy development has gained wide acceptance. The resource-based view of the firm has its roots in the work of the earliest strategic management theorists.[20] It grew out of the question, "Why do some firms persistently outperform other firms?" An early answer to that question was that some firms are able to develop distinctive competencies in particular areas.[21] One of the first competencies identified was general management capability. This led to the proposition that firms with high-quality general managers will outperform their rivals. Much research has examined this issue. Clearly, effective leadership is important to organizational performance, but it is difficult to specify what makes an effective leader. Also, although leaders are an important source of competence for an organization, they are not the only important resource that makes a difference.

Economic thought also influenced development of the resource-based view. Nearly two centuries ago, an economist named David Ricardo investigated the advantages of possessing superior resources, especially land.[22] One of Ricardo's central propositions was that the farmer with the most-fertile land had a sustained performance advantage over other farmers. More recently, another economist, Edith Penrose, expanded on Ricardo's view by noting that various skills and abilities possessed by firms could lead to superior performance. She viewed firms as an administrative framework that coordinated the activities of numerous groups and individuals, and also as a bundle of productive resources.[23] She studied the effects of various skills and abilities possessed by organizations, concluding that a wide range of skills and resources could influence competitive performance.

A common thread of reasoning in the distinctive competency literature and the arguments of Ricardo and Penrose is that organizational success can be explained in terms of the resources and capabilities possessed by an organization. Many modern scholars have contributed to this perspective of the firm.[24] According to this view, an organization is a bundle of resources, which fall into the general categories of:

1. *Financial resources*, including all of the monetary resources from which a firm can draw

2. *Physical resources*, such as land, buildings, equipment, locations, and access to raw materials

3. *Human resources*, which pertains to the skills, background, and training of managers and employees, as well as the way they are organized

4. *Organizational knowledge and learning*

5. *General organizational resources*, including the firm's reputation, brand names, patents, contracts, and relationships with external stakeholders[25]

The organization as a bundle of resources is depicted in Figure 1.2.

Envisioning the firm as a bundle of resources has broad implications. For example, the most important role of a manager becomes that of acquiring, developing, managing, and discarding resources. Also, much of the research on the resource-based perspective has demonstrated that firms can gain competitive advantage through possessing "superior resources."[26] Superior resources are those that have value in the market, are possessed by only a small number of firms, and are not easy to substitute. If a particular resource is also costly or impossible to imitate, then the competitive advantage may be sustainable. A sustainable competitive advantage may lead to higher-than-average organizational performance over a long period.[27] Marriott is an example of a corporation that has successfully capitalized on its resources to gain a competitive advantage over other hotels. (See the "Hospitality Focus" boxed section on page 12.)

Many strategy scholars believe that acquisition and development of superior organizational resources is the most important reason that some companies are more successful than

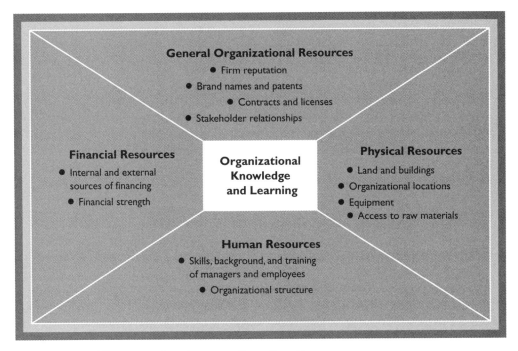

FIGURE 1.2 **The organization as a bundle of resources**

others.[28] Most of the resources that a firm can acquire or develop are directly linked to its stakeholders. For example, financial resources are closely linked to establishing good working relationships with financial intermediaries. Also, the development of human resources is associated with effective management of organizational stakeholders. Finally, organizational resources reflect the organization's understanding of the expectations of society and the linkages it has established with stakeholders.

The Organization as a Network of Stakeholders

A *Fortune* magazine cover story described modern business in these terms: "Business already is moving to organize itself into virtual corporations: fungible modules built around information networks, flexible workforces, outsourcing, and webs of strategic partnerships."[29] Negotiating and contracting have always been important to business. However, the trend in business is toward more strategic alliances, joint ventures, and subcontracting arrangements with stakeholders. The fact is that some of a firm's most valuable resources may extend beyond the boundaries of a firm.[30] Consequently, business organizations are becoming a tangled web of alliances and contracts.

The hotel business contains many examples of the network approach, such as the variety of strategic alliances and cross-branding partnerships formed by Starwood. Nordstrom, the

Seattle-based retailer, sells the Westin Heavenly Bed At Home Collection, becoming the first national retail chain to offer the furnishings of a major hotel company.[32] The hotel chain's other partners include American Express, MasterCard, PepsiCo, Amazon.com, BMW, Nestlé, eMusic, Yahoo, and Seattle's Best Coffee. Alliances between major competitors are also a hallmark of the hotel industry. It is not uncommon for a company to own a hotel property that is managed by one of its competitors. Nor is it uncommon to share brand affiliations. For example, Starwood Lodging owns the Princeton Marriott, a 294-room hotel in Plainsboro, New Jersey. A third party to the venture, Princeton University, leases the land upon which the Marriott is built.[33]

THE EMERGENCE OF THE STAKEHOLDER APPROACH

In the mid-1980s, a stakeholder approach to strategic management began to emerge. It was developed as a direct response to the concerns of managers who were being buffeted by increasing levels of complexity and change in the external environment.[34] The existing strategy models were not particularly helpful to managers who were trying to create new opportunities during a period of such radical change. The word *stakeholder* was a deliberate play on the word *stockholder*. Much of the strategy literature at the time was founded, either explicitly or implicitly, on the idea that stockholders were the only important constituency of the modern for-profit corporation. Stakeholder theory contradicted this idea by expanding a company's responsibility to groups or individuals who significantly affect or are significantly affected by the company's activities; including stockholders.[35]

Figure 1.3 contains a typical stakeholder map. A firm has internal stakeholders, such as employees, who are considered a part of the internal organization. In addition, the firm has frequent interactions with stakeholders in what is called the operating (or task) environment. The firm and stakeholders in its operating environment are influenced by other factors, such as society, technology, the economy, and the legal environment. These other factors form the broad environment.

This section has laid a foundation on which the rest of this book will be built. The three perspectives that will be incorporated are the traditional, the resource-based, and the stakeholder views of strategic management and the firm. Now the strategic management process will be introduced in more detail.

FIGURE 1.3 **A typical stakeholder map**

THE STRATEGIC
MANAGEMENT PROCESS

Three perspectives on strategic management have been discussed so far: the traditional model, the resource-based view, and the stakeholder approach. In this book, these three approaches are combined (see Table 1.2). The basic strategic management process is most closely related to the traditional model. However, each of the stages of this process is heavily influenced by each of the three approaches.

The key activities in the strategic management process are shown in Figure 1.4 and begin by providing:

1. A situation analysis of the broad and operating environments of the organization, including internal resources and both internal and external stakeholders

2. The establishment of strategic direction, reflected in mission statements and organizational visions

TABLE 1.2 A Combined Perspective of Strategic Management

PROCESS	Firms conduct external and internal analysis (situation analysis), both of which include analysis of stakeholders. On the basis of information obtained, they create strategic direction, strategies, and tactics for implementing strategies and control systems.
ORIGIN	Traditional, resource-based, and stakeholder perspectives
ADAPTATION VS. ENACTMENT	Influence the environment when it is economically feasible to do so. Take a proactive stance with regard to managing external stakeholders. Monitor, forecast, and adapt to environmental forces that are difficult or costly to influence.
DELIBERATE VS. EMERGENT	Firms should be involved in deliberate strategy-creating processes. However, they should learn from past decisions and be willing to try new things and change strategic course.
SOURCE OF COMPETITIVE ADVANTAGE	Firms can obtain competitive advantage from superior resources, including knowledge-based resources, superior strategies for managing those resources, and/or superior relationships with internal or external stakeholders (which are another type of resource).
CREATION OF STRATEGIC ALTERNATIVES	Firms develop strategies to take advantage of strengths and opportunities or overcome weaknesses or threats. They arise as organizations conduct resource analysis, analyze organizational processes, and analyze and partner with external stakeholders.

3. A formulation of specific strategies

4. Strategy implementation, which includes designing an organizational structure, controlling organizational processes, managing relationships with stakeholders, and managing resources to develop competitive advantage

While these activities may occur in the order specified, especially if a firm is engaging in a formal strategic planning program, they may also be carried out in some other order or even simultaneously. For example, it is not uncommon for a strategic direction to serve as a foundation for the situation analysis.

The feedback loops at the bottom of Figure 1.4 indicate that organizations often cycle back to earlier activities during the strategic management process, as new information is gathered and assumptions change. For instance, a company may attempt to develop strategies

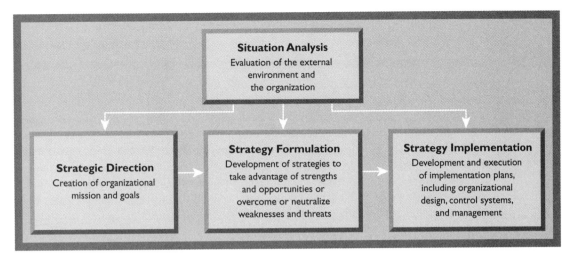

FIGURE 1.4 **The strategic management process**

consistent with its strategic direction and, after a trial period, discover that the direction was not reasonable. Also, an organization may discover rather quickly (or over a longer period of time) that a proposed strategy cannot be implemented feasibly. As a result, the firm may have to cycle back to the formulation stage to fine-tune its strategic approach. In other words, organizations may learn from their own past actions and from environmental forces, and they may modify their behavior in response.

However, not all organizations engage in all of the processes depicted in Figure 1.4: entrepreneurial start-up firms rarely do. They often begin with an entrepreneur who has an idea for a product or service that he or she believes will lead to market success. Venture capital is raised through a variety of public or private sources, and a new business is born. The entrepreneur may establish an informal sense of direction and a few goals, but the rest of the formal strategy process may be overlooked. If the organization is successful, it will typically expand in both sales and personnel until it reaches a critical point at which the entrepreneur feels a loss of control. At this point, the entrepreneur may attempt to formalize various aspects of strategic planning, by either hiring outside consultants, creating planning positions within the firm, or involving other managers in planning activities. This same process is typical of nonprofit start-ups as well, except that the nature of the cause (i.e., humanitarian or educational) may place tighter constraints on the way the firm is financed and organized.

Consequently, the model in Figure 1.4 is not intended to be a rigid representation of the strategic management process in all organizations as they currently operate. Nevertheless, the progression of activities—from analysis to planning to action and control—provides a logical way to study strategic management. Furthermore, the activities relate equally well to for-profit, nonprofit, manufacturing, and service entities, although some of the differences in the way these organizations approach strategic management will be described throughout the text.

Now that the strategic management process has been introduced, each of its components—situation analysis, strategic direction, strategy formulation, and strategy implementation—will be described in more detail.

Situation Analysis

Many of the stakeholders and forces that have the potential to be most important to companies are presented in Figure 1.3. All of the stakeholders inside and outside of the firm, as well as the major external forces, should be analyzed at both the domestic and international levels. The external environment includes groups, individuals, and forces outside of the traditional boundaries of the organization that are significantly influenced by or have a major impact on the organization.[36] External stakeholders, part of a company's operating environment, include competitors, customers, suppliers, financial intermediaries, local communities, unions, activist groups, and local and national government agencies and administrators. The broad environment forms the context in which the company and its operating environment exist, and includes sociocultural, economic, technological, political, and legal influences, both domestically and abroad. One organization, acting independently, may have very little influence on the forces in the broad environment; however, the forces in this environment can have a tremendous impact on the organization. The internal organization includes all of the stakeholders, resources, knowledge, and processes that exist within the boundaries of the firm.

SWOT ANALYSIS

Analyzing the environment and the company can assist the company in all of the other tasks of strategic management.[37] For example, a firm's managers should formulate strategic direction and specific strategies based on organizational strengths and weaknesses and in the context of the opportunities and threats found in its environment. A *SWOT analysis* is a tool strategists use to evaluate Strengths, Weaknesses, Opportunities, and Threats. Strengths are company resources and capabilities that can lead to a competitive advantage. Weaknesses are resources and capabilities that a company does not possess, to the extent that their absence places the firm at a competitive disadvantage. Opportunities are conditions in the broad and operating environments that allow a firm to take advantage of organizational strengths, overcome organizational weaknesses, and/or neutralize environmental threats. Threats are conditions in the broad and operating environments that may impede organizational competitiveness or the achievement of stakeholder satisfaction.

Strategic Direction

Strategic direction pertains to the longer-term goals and objectives of the organization. At a more fundamental level, *strategic direction* defines the purposes for which a company exists and operates. This direction is often contained in *mission* and *vision statements*. An organization's mission is its current purpose and scope of operation, while its vision is a forward-looking statement of what it wants to be in the future. Unlike shorter-term goals and strategies, mission and vision statements are an enduring part of planning processes within the company. They are often written in terms of what the organization will do for its key stakeholders. For example, the philosophy, vision, mission, and guiding principles of Shangri-La Hotels and Resorts are:

Our Philosophy: Shangri-La hospitality from caring people

Our Vision: The first choice for customers, employees, shareholders, and business partners

Our Mission: Delighting customers each and every time

Our Guiding Principles (Core Values):

We will ensure leadership drives for results.

We will make customer loyalty a key driver of our business.

We will enable decision making at customer contact point.

We will be committed to the financial success of our own unit and of our company.

We will create an environment where our colleagues may achieve their personal and career goals.

We will demonstrate honesty, care, and integrity in all our relationships.

We will ensure our policies and processes are customer and employee friendly.

We will be environmentally conscientious and provide safety and security for our customers and our colleagues.[38]

A well-established strategic direction provides guidance to the stakeholders inside the organization who are largely responsible for carrying it out. A well-defined direction also provides external stakeholders with a greater understanding of the company and its activities. The next logical step in the strategic management process is strategy formulation.

STRATEGY DEFINED

A *strategy* can be thought of in either of two ways: (1) as a pattern that emerges in a sequence of decisions over time, or (2) as an organizational plan of action that is intended to move a company toward the achievement of its shorter-term goals and, ultimately, its fundamental purposes. In some organizations, particularly those in rapidly changing environments and in small businesses, strategies are not planned in the formal sense of the word. Instead, managers seize opportunities as they come up, but within guidelines or boundaries defined by the firm's strategic direction or mission. In those cases, the strategy reflects the insight and intuition of the strategist or business owner, and it becomes clear over time as a pattern in a stream of decisions. Strategies as plans are common in most organizations, as the following business strategy for FelCor Lodging Trust illustrates.

STRATEGIC PLANS AT FelCor LODGING TRUST

For FelCor Lodging Trust, one of the largest hotel real estate investment trusts (REITs) in the United States, a strategic planning exercise led the company to rethink its strategy. Calling itself the "New FelCor," the firm has made dramatic steps toward repositioning itself. The firm's business strategy is to dispose of nonstrategic hotels, including all of its Holiday Inn Hotels located in secondary and tertiary markets. After the sale, it will have lower exposure to markets with low barriers to entry.

Other elements of the new business strategy are (1) to acquire hotels in high-barrier-to-entry markets; (2) to improve the competitive positioning of core hotels through aggressive asset management and the judicious application of capital; and (3) to pay down debt through a combination of operational cash flow and the sale of nonstrategic hotels. The company will become a lower-leveraged company with a stronger and fully renovated portfolio of hotels.[39]

Strategy Formulation

Strategy formulation, the process of planning strategies, is often divided into three levels: corporate, business, and functional. One of the most important roles of *corporate-level strategy* is to define a company's domain of activity through selection of business areas in which the company will compete. *Business-level strategy* formulation pertains to domain direction and navigation, or how businesses should compete in the areas they have selected. Sometimes business-level strategies are also referred to as *competitive strategies*. *Functional-level strategies* contain the details of how functional resource areas, such as marketing, operations, and finance, should be used to implement business-level strategies and achieve competitive advantage. Basically, functional-level strategies are for acquiring, developing, and managing organizational resources. These characterizations are oversimplified, but it is sometimes useful to think of corporate-level strategies as "where to compete," business-level strategies as "how to compete in those areas," and functional-level strategies as "the functional details of how resources will be managed so that business-level strategies will be accomplished."

Another way to distinguish among the three levels—perhaps a more accurate one—is to determine the level at which decisions are made (see Figure 1.5), as follows:

- *Corporate-level decisions* are typically made at the highest levels of the organization by the CEO and/or board of directors, although these individuals may receive input from managers at other levels. If an organization is involved in only one area of business, then business-level decisions tend to be made by these same people.

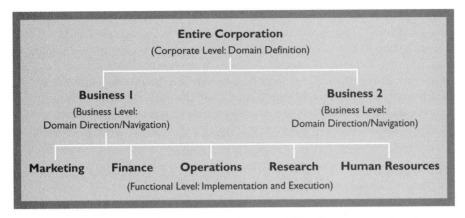

FIGURE 1.5 **Strategy formulation in a multibusiness organization**

- *Business-level decisions* in organizations that have diversified into multiple areas, which are represented by different operating divisions or lines of business, are made by division heads or business-unit managers.

- *Functional-level decisions* are made by functional managers, who represent organizational areas such as operations, finance, personnel, accounting, research and development, or information systems.

Figure 1.5 shows the levels at which particular strategy decisions are made within a multibusiness firm. To illustrate these three levels of decision making, the Tata Group, one of India's largest conglomerates, has more than 96 companies in seven business sectors. One company in the portfolio is the Taj Hotels Resorts and Palaces, which consists of 59 hotels at locations across India and internationally. In this very complex company, corporate-level decisions are made for all 96 businesses, but business strategy decisions are made at the firm level. Hence, business-level decisions that concern the Taj Hotels company are made by senior management of the hotel chain, while functional leaders, such as those who lead human resources, purchasing, and development, guide functional-level decisions.

Strategy Implementation

Strategy formulation results in a plan of action for the company and its various levels, whereas *strategy implementation* represents a pattern of decisions and actions that are intended to carry out the plan. Strategy implementation involves managing stakeholder relationships and organizational resources in a manner that moves the business toward the successful execution of its strategies, consistent with its strategic direction. Implementation activities also involve creating an organizational design and organizational control systems to keep the company on the right course.

Organizational control refers to the processes that lead to adjustments in strategic direction, strategies, or the implementation plan, when necessary. Thus, managers may collect information that leads them to believe that the organizational mission is no longer appropriate or that its strategies are not leading to the desired outcomes. A strategic-control system may conversely tell managers that the mission and strategies are appropriate, but that they have not been well executed. In such cases, adjustments should be made to the implementation process.

In summary, the four basic processes associated with strategic management are:

1. Situation analysis

2. Establishment of strategic direction

3. Strategy formulation

4. Strategy implementation

Morrison Restaurants is among many hospitality firms that fully use these processes. The company, with more than $1 billion in revenues, developed and implemented "an integrated strategic plan for each of its divisions and concepts."[40] Based on a strategic analysis, the company developed its strategies on the basis of its strengths, weaknesses, opportunities, and threats (SWOT). Its plan and goals, which are widely used and understood by managers and team members, support its mission of "feeding America for under $10."

GLOBAL COMPETITIVENESS IN THE HOSPITALITY INDUSTRY

Most successful organizations eventually find that their domestic markets are becoming saturated or that foreign markets offer opportunities for growth and profitability that often are not available domestically. Many forces are leading firms into the international arena.[41] For example, global trends are leading to a more favorable environment for foreign business involvement. Trade barriers are falling in Europe (e.g., the European Union) and North America (e.g., the North American Free Trade Agreement). Also, newly industrialized countries, such as South Korea, Taiwan, and Brazil, are leading to increasing global competition and new marketing opportunities. There is a worldwide shift toward market economies, as in China and Vietnam, and financial capital is now readily exchanged in global markets. In addition, communication is easier due to satellites, the Internet, and cellular phones, and English is becoming a universally spoken business language, particularly in Asia, Latin America, and Central Europe. Finally, technical standards have started to become uniform in industrialized countries around the world.

The strategic management implications of increasing globalization are profound. Managers cannot afford to ignore opportunities in foreign markets. However, business methods and customs differ from country to country. These differences make stakeholder analysis and management even more important. Analysis of broad environmental forces, such as society, technology, and political influences, must also be expanded to each of the areas in which an organization conducts business. People also differ greatly from country to country. They cannot be managed in the same way. For example, when China opened its doors to foreign hotel investments in the early 1980s, the Chinese workers had no understanding of career advancement; for these employees, the first job held was believed to be the one the person would do for many years, if not for life.[42] This is still largely the case in Japan. In a study of cultural differences in Chinese and British hotels, the authors reported that expatriate managers in China found that employees were reluctant to take initiative and make decisions or propose suggestions.[43]

Variables Affecting Strategic Management

The tools, techniques, and models found in this book apply well to strategic management in a global environment. The methods and theories are used by top strategic planners in business situations around the globe. However, there are differences between strategic management in a domestic setting versus an international one. Each of the four basic parts of the strategic management process (i.e., situation analysis, strategic direction, strategy formulation, and implementation) is different when applied to an international environment.

1. Analysis of the environment associated with a situation analysis is complicated by the fact that the organization is involved in multiple environments with varying characteristics.

2. Strategic direction must consider stakeholders with a much broader range of needs.

3. The number of alternative strategies is greatly increased as a firm considers options arising from foreign environments.

4. The specific details associated with implementing strategies will be very different from country to country because of differences in laws, customs, resources, and accepted business practices.

The challenges of an increasingly competitive global marketplace can be addressed through a well-devised strategic management process. However, strategic planning does not always lead to the kinds of changes that are necessary to remain competitive over the long term. Ineffective strategic planning is often the result of a missing ingredient—strategic thinking.

STRATEGIC THINKING

What does it take for a company to be on the cutting edge in its industry? Organizational leaders can learn a great deal from studying the strategies of competitors. Clearly, an organization can learn things from competitors that will lead to improvements in performance. However, by the time a firm develops the skills and acquires the resources that are necessary to imitate industry leaders, those leaders probably will have moved on to new ideas and strategies. Consequently, industry leaders break out of traditional mind-sets and defy widely accepted industry practices.

Gary Hamel, a well-known strategic management author and consultant, calls these firms Industry Revolutionaries. He says that revolutionaries do not simply seek incremental improvements to existing business systems to increase efficiency, nor do they focus exclusively on individual products or services. Instead, they invent new business concepts. According to Hamel, "Industry revolutionaries don't tinker at the margins; they blow up old business models and create new ones."[44] For instance, Southwest Airlines decided to reject the hub-and-spoke operating model that is so prevalent in the airline industry in favor of a point-to-point system, which led other airlines such as JetBlue to do the same.

Bill Gates, CEO of Microsoft, has said that his company is "always two years away from failure."[45] At any time, a competing firm may develop a software product that is perceived to be superior to whatever version of Windows® Microsoft is selling, and, within a couple of years, become the market leader. Indeed, Microsoft almost missed a huge opportunity with the Internet and had to play catch-up to Netscape. Strategic thinking does not mean that a firm should randomly try new things until something works. Instead, it allows creative thought to emerge, which should then be accompanied by systematic analysis to determine what should actually be done.

Much will be said in this book about the importance of innovation and how to foster organizational entrepreneurship. An excellent way to start this discussion is with the topic of strategic thinking, since such thinking runs parallel to both innovation and entrepreneurship. It is important to understand from the outset that strategic thinking is not a replacement for the strategic planning process. Certain aspects of the process, such as analysis of the external environment, foster strategic thinking. Also, parts of the strategic planning process should be done systematically, such as the evaluation of alternatives and the development of control systems. However, strategic thinking helps organizations move beyond what is tried and proven. Effective strategic management includes both strategic thinking and strategic planning.

Strategic Planning Can Drive out Strategic Thinking

The term *strategic thinking* is used in so many ways that it is difficult to determine what people mean when they use it. In fact, most people probably do not know exactly what they mean: they may use the word to mean "thinking about strategy" or use it interchangeably with "strategic management" or "strategic planning."[46] According to a well-known strategist, Henry Mintzberg, *strategic planning* is an analytical process aimed at carrying out strategies that have already been identified. Strategic planning results in the creation of a plan. On the other hand, *strategic thinking* involves intuition and creativity. It is a way to synthesize stimuli from the internal and external environments to create "an integrated perspective of the enterprise."[47] According to Mintzberg, strategic planning is so rigid that it tends to drive out creative-thinking processes. The following true story illustrates this point. However, many companies, especially larger ones, have strategic planning processes that mirror the ones described in this example.

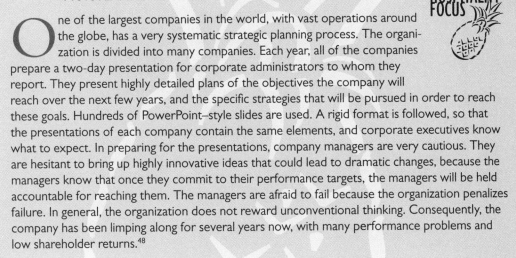

A SYSTEMATIC APPROACH TO STRATEGIC PLANNING

HOSPITALITY FOCUS

One of the largest companies in the world, with vast operations around the globe, has a very systematic strategic planning process. The organization is divided into many companies. Each year, all of the companies prepare a two-day presentation for corporate administrators to whom they report. They present highly detailed plans of the objectives the company will reach over the next few years, and the specific strategies that will be pursued in order to reach these goals. Hundreds of PowerPoint–style slides are used. A rigid format is followed, so that the presentations of each company contain the same elements, and corporate executives know what to expect. In preparing for the presentations, company managers are very cautious. They are hesitant to bring up highly innovative ideas that could lead to dramatic changes, because the managers know that once they commit to their performance targets, the managers will be held accountable for reaching them. The managers are afraid to fail because the organization penalizes failure. In general, the organization does not reward unconventional thinking. Consequently, the company has been limping along for several years now, with many performance problems and low shareholder returns.[48]

This kind of approach to strategic planning can be referred to as "strategy as form filling," whereas strategic thinking is "crafting strategic architecture."[49] The next section provides more detail on the essential elements of strategic thinking.

Characteristics of Strategic Thinking

When Arlington Hospitality began the search for a new CEO, it asked candidates to draft "strategic white papers" presenting their opinions on the future direction of the company.[50] Candidates who did not have an intellectual focus or vision for the firm or who presented status quo thinking were eliminated. The company was in search of a strategic thinker, who possesses the six characteristics of strategic thinking:

1. Intent-focused
2. Comprehensive
3. Opportunistic
4. Long-term oriented
5. Built on the past and the present
6. Hypothesis-driven

TABLE 1.3 Elements of Strategic Thinking

INTENT FOCUSED	Built on a managerial vision of where the firm is going and what it is trying to become. This is called strategic intent.
COMPREHENSIVE	A "systems" perspective. Envisions the firm as a part of a larger system of value creation. Understands the linkages between the firm and the other parts of the system.
OPPORTUNISTIC	Seizes unanticipated opportunities presented to the firm.
LONG-TERM ORIENTED	Goes beyond the here and now. Looks several years into the future at what the firm will become, based on its strategic intent.
BUILT ON PAST AND PRESENT	Does not ignore the past or present. Instead, learns from the past and builds on a foundation of the realities of the present.
HYPOTHESIS DRIVEN	A sequential process in which creative ideas are then critically evaluated. Is willing to take a risk. Learns from mistakes.

Source: This table was strongly influenced by J. M. Liedtka, "Strategy Formulation: The Roles of Conversation and Design," in *The Blackwell Handbook of Strategic Management,* ed. M. A. Hitt, R. E. Freeman, and J. S. Harrison (Oxford: Blackwell Publishers, 2001), 70–93.

A summary of these characteristics is found in Table 1.3.[51]

INTENT-FOCUSED

Strategic thinking is not a random process of trial and error. Instead, it involves *strategic intent*, which is a vision with regard to where an organization is or should be going. Strategic intent

> *implies a particular point of view about the long-term market or competitive position that a firm hopes to build over the coming decade or so. Hence, it conveys a sense of direction. A strategic intent is differentiated; it implies a competitively unique point of view about the future. It holds out to employees the promise of exploring new competitive territory. Hence, it conveys a sense of discovery. Strategic intent has an emotional edge to it; it is a goal that employees perceive as inherently worthwhile. Hence, it implies a sense of destiny. Direction, discovery, and destiny. These are the attributes of strategic intent.*[52]

A recently announced signing of a letter of intent between Trump Entertainment Resorts and Diamondhead Casino Corporation to form a joint venture partnership to develop, build, and operate a destination casino resort is a formal statement of intent. However, behind this statement of intention is the strategic thinking that leads to this proposed venture.

DIAMONDHEAD AND TRUMP: A JOINT VENTURE

HOSPITALITY FOCUS

Deborah A. Vitale, the Chairman, CEO, and President of Diamondhead, makes the case for the venture by stating:

We believe a partnership with Trump Entertainment Resorts for this venture adds up to an ideal combination because of their experience, the value of the Trump brand, the location of our site on Interstate 10, and the vitality of the Gulf Coast market. We have the land, the location, and the desire to pursue a master plan for the entire tract that should not only enhance long-term shareholder value, but which should significantly enhance the surrounding economy.

James B. Perry, President and CEO of Trump Entertainment Resorts, Inc., explains his firm's views on the proposed joint venture as follows:

As we renovate and re-brand our Atlantic City properties, we are also focused on our corporate development initiatives and expanding the Trump brand into new markets. We are excited about the prospect of bringing the Trump brand to the Gulf Coast, and we hope to join private and public entities in redeveloping the region. We believe that this is a great opportunity to create value for our company, our shareholders and the citizens of Mississippi.[53]

COMPREHENSIVE

Strategic thinking is based on a systems perspective that envisions the firm as a part of a complete end-to-end system of value creation. Furthermore, strategic thinking means that decision makers are aware of the interdependencies in the system.[54] This type of thinking fits within the stakeholder view of the organization, which is one of the important perspectives on which our model of strategic management is based. Organizational managers each possess a "mental model," which is a view of "how the world works."[55] Mental models should include an understanding of both the internal and external organization. An industry-based model of the external environment has dominated for many years.[56] However, a more promising model views the company not as a member of a single industry, but as a part of a larger business system that crosses a variety of industries. Companies co-evolve around innovations, and they work both in competition and cooperatively to satisfy the demands of a wide variety of stakeholders, including customers, suppliers, and broader society and its governments, as well as to create or absorb the next round of innovation.[57] Organizations are a part of one or more value chains, to which they can contribute in many ways.

Managers who want to think strategically must also understand and appreciate the internal pieces that make up the whole of their companies. The role of each person within the larger system must be identified, as well as the effect of that role on other people and groups within the organization and on the outcomes of the organization. It is impossible to optimize an organizational system in, for example, satisfying customer needs, without understanding how individuals fit into the system.[58] So the strategic thinker observes and understands the connections between and among the various levels of a business, as well as the linkages between the business and stakeholders in the external environment.

OPPORTUNISTIC

Although strategic thinking is based on strategic intent, there has to be room for what might be called "intelligent opportunism."[59] *Intelligent opportunism* can be defined as the ability of managers at various levels of the organization to take advantage of unanticipated opportunities to further an intended strategy or even redirect a strategy. For example, Marriott saw an opportunity for growth in the lower-priced segment of the lodging industry when Courtyard was introduced. Of course, the company has a long history of bold entrepreneurship, beginning with a root beer stand started in 1927 by John and Alice Marriott. They added hot food, incorporated, and expanded their Hot Shoppes into a regional chain. The next major move was Marriott's first hotel, the Twin Bridges Marriott Motor Hotel, which opened in Arlington, Virginia, in 1957. With the increase in airline travel, Marriott built several hotels at airports during the 1970s. Each of these ventures was in response to an opportunity, and each was a vital part of building the Marriott that exists today. Intelligent opportunism is consistent with the traditional strategic planning model. According to that model, strategies often come from taking advantage of opportunities that arise in the external environment.

LONG-TERM ORIENTED

Managers, especially in America, are often accused of making shortsighted decisions.[60] Perhaps a renovation or expansion plan is canceled because the payoff looks too far away, or employees are laid off when occupancies drop, only to be rehired within a few months. In contrast, strategic thinking is long-term oriented. Actions that a firm must make now should be linked to a vision of what the firm should become, based on the strategic intent of its top managers. This type of thinking is driving many hoteliers into international markets on a much larger scale.

BUILT ON PAST AND PRESENT

Although strategic thinking is long-term oriented, it does not ignore the present or the past. In fact, it might be referred to as "thinking in time":

> *Thinking in time (has) three components. One is recognition that the future has no place to come from but the past, hence the past has predictive value. Another element is recognition that what matters for the future in the present is departures from the past, alterations, changes, which prospectively or actually divert familiar flows from accustomed channels . . . . A third component is continuous comparison, an almost constant oscillation from the present to future to past and back, heedful of prospective change, concerned to expedite, limit, guide, counter, or accept it as the fruits of such comparison suggests.*[61]

Strategic thinkers need to consider the past. The past forms a historical context in which strategic intent is created. Learning from past mistakes helps the firm avoid making them again. Also, analysis of the past behaviors of important stakeholders, such as customers, competitors, unions, or suppliers, can help a firm anticipate how the stakeholders will react to new ideas and strategies.

The present is also important to strategic thinking, because it places constraints on what the organization is able to accomplish. Strategic thinking is a creative process, but it is also a well-reasoned process. Although it may lead firms to consider unconventional ideas, the ideas that are actually pursued are selected based on rational analysis, including consideration of the organization's current resources, knowledge, skills, and abilities.

HYPOTHESIS-DRIVEN

Organizations should test their decisions to see if they are appropriate or likely to be successful. This process is similar to the scientific method, in which hypotheses are developed and tested. *Hypothesis development* is a creative process built on brainstorming, whereas *hypothesis testing* is an analytical process. A typical process begins as managers suggest ideas regarding what the firm might want to do. Those that are considered reasonable are then subjected to rigorous analysis of potential using a well-developed methodology. After analysis, managers determine which of the ideas are worthy of implementation. However, the company may decide not to make a full commitment to each of them at first. Instead, it may allocate enough resources to implement the ideas on a trial basis, so that the company will be able to tell whether the ideas are going to work out. The ideas that are successful are given additional resources. In this description, hypothesis testing occurred twice. The first test was the rigorous analysis conducted by managers in the organization. The second test occurs as the company tries the ideas in the marketplace.

If you combine all six of the elements of strategic thinking, what you have is a long-term thinker who builds a vision for the future on the foundation of the present and the past. It is someone who understands how the organization fits within its external environment, and who has a firm grasp of relationships with external stakeholders. Furthermore, it is someone who is willing to break out of traditional mind-sets and to seize opportunities, but who uses a rational approach to test ideas to prevent the organization from moving indefinitely in an inappropriate direction.

Motivating Managers and Employees to Think Strategically

Organizations can encourage strategic thinking in several ways. First, managers and employees can receive training that describes strategic thinking and how to do it. Second, an organization can encourage and reward employees who generate new ideas (hypotheses). For example, Disney allows some of its employees an opportunity each year to present new ideas to top managers. With a similar philosophy, Virgin, well known for its unconventional airline, created a one-stop bridal-services company because one of its flight attendants was having a difficult time lining up those services for a friend's wedding.[62] Virgin Bride, the name of the venture, is now Britain's largest bridal emporium. Third, a company can actually implement a strategic planning process that incorporates the elements of strategic thinking. Such a process would include a thorough evaluation of the external environment, with a special emphasis on relationships with stakeholders. It would also include the generation of new ideas and facilitate their testing. Finally, to encourage strategic thinking, an organization has to be willing to take risks. It was risky for Kemmons Wilson to develop the first Holiday Inn back in 1952, after returning from a family vacation disheartened at the lack of family and value-oriented lodging, but the strategy worked so well that Holiday Inn developed into a trusted name along the emerging interstate highway system.[63]

STRATEGIC MANAGEMENT IN THE HOSPITALITY INDUSTRY

Hotels and restaurants are among the most competitive businesses in the world. The hospitality industry primarily consists of businesses that provide accommodation, food and beverage, or some combination of these activities. Hospitality businesses provide services, which differ from tangible products because they are immediately consumed and require a people-intensive creation process. They differ from other service establishments by providing for those who are in the process of traveling away from home in contrast to local residence, although restaurants often serve both travelers and local guests. The offering of an experience is also becoming an important component of hospitality. In addition, a wide range of business structures exist in hospitality, such as direct ownership by chains, franchising, asset management, and consortia. Today, the hospitality industry has become more complex and sophisticated, with a movement away from the "mine host" (i.e., a view of hospitality in which the host personally and socially entertains visiting guests) and the cost-control frameworks of the past to a more strategic view of the business, in both investment and operations domains.

"Travel and tourism" is a broad term used to capture a variety of interrelated businesses that provide services to travelers. Tourism is the largest industry worldwide, the second largest services export industry, and the third largest retail sales industry in the United States.[64] It is the first, second, or third largest employer in 30 of the 50 states. Besides the traditional hospitality businesses of hotels and restaurants, the tourism industry includes a broad range of businesses, such as airlines, cruise lines, car rental firms, entertainment firms, travel agents, tour operators, and recreational enterprises. The focus of this textbook will be on those hospitality businesses primarily engaged in providing food and lodging to traveling guests. However, we will also include discussions of other travel-related businesses, such as casinos, airlines, cruise lines, time-shares, travel agents, tour operators, and governmental tourism institutions.

The Foodservice Industry—The Players

The foodservice industry consists of a wide variety of different businesses, including institutional providers and food contractors such as Aramark Corp., Sodexho Alliance, Autogrill SpA's, HMS Host, and Compass Group. Institutional foodservice and military foodservice are small segments of the industry and consist of noncommercial institutions that operate their own foodservice. Contractors operate for-profit services to commercial, industrial, university, school, airline, hospital, nursing home, recreation, and sports centers. Management is provided by the contractor of restaurant services, but the institution may provide the facilities and personnel for these operations.

Contract companies are highly consolidated after aggressive merger and acquisition activities that gave them strong positions in the various on-site segments (e.g., school, corporate, and health care). Compass Group's Americas Division, for example, is the largest contract foodservice company, with $7.5 billion in revenues. Its purchase of Bon Appetit Management Company, a $300 million provider of upscale foodservice for corporations and universities, is one example of its expanded coverage in various key segments.[65] Its parent company, Compass Group PLC, has worldwide revenues of $21 billion, with more than 400,000 associates working in more than 90 countries. Sodexho Alliance is the second-largest provider of foodservice worldwide, with operations in 79 countries employing 324,500 people.[66] In the latest rankings, Aramark is the leading contract chain in U.S. systemwide sales ($5.53 billion) and market share (28.8 percent share of aggregate sales of contract chains in top 100), followed by Canteen Services and Sodexho.[67]

The restaurant industry is the largest private-sector employer in the United States, and consists of commercial dining and drinking establishments, such as restaurants, bars, cafeterias, ice cream parlors, and cafés. It dominates the foodservice industry. Within foodservice, the restaurant industry is by far the largest segment, with 935,000 restaurants in the United States, sales of around $537 billion in 2007, and an annual growth rate of around 8.4 percent.[68]

Common convention is to split the restaurant industry into two main segments: quick-service and full-service. Quick-service, commonly called fast-food or fast-service, restaurants are defined as eat-in or take-out operations with limited menus, low prices, and fast service. This segment of the industry is further broken down into sandwiches (e.g., hamburgers and tacos), pizza, and chicken. Leaders in market share in the sandwich segment are McDonald's, Burger King, Wendy's, Subway, and Taco Bell, while the chicken segment is led by KFC (Kentucky Fried Chicken), Chick-fil-A, and Popeye's Chicken and Biscuits.[69] The pizza segment is led by two strong players: Pizza Hut with 43 percent of the market and Domino's Pizza with a 27 percent market share.[70]

Full-service restaurants offer eat-in service, with more expansive menus, and prices that range from low to high. In providing annual comparisons, *Nation's Restaurant News* divides full-service restaurants into family, grill-buffet, and dinner house segments. Family chains include players like Denny's and IHOP(International House of Pancakes), and grill-buffet segment leaders include Golden Corral, Ryan's Family Steak House, and Ponderosa Steakhouse.[71] Finally, the large dinner house segment is aggressively focusing on value-oriented menu items, advertising, and improved execution in operations, with several major players including Applebee's Neighborhood Grill and Bar, Chili's Grill and Bar, Outback Steakhouse, Olive Garden, Red Lobster, and T.G.I. Friday's.[72]

Other key players in this segment are the multiconcept operators and franchisors like Darden and Brinker. Large companies in the restaurant industry, such as Yum! Brands (which owns many of the aforementioned brands such as Pizza Hut and Taco Bell), are aggressively developing portfolios of restaurants, and international expansion continues to serve as a viable growth strategy for firms like Starbucks. Small operators and independent restaurants compete with the large chains in an industry known for its low barriers to entry and entrepreneurial opportunities.

The Lodging Industry—The Players

Lodging in the United States is a $113.7 billion industry, with more than 47,000 hotels and around 4.4 million guest rooms.[73] Like the foodservice industry, consolidation has been a theme for the last decade, with most of the largest companies being publicly owned. Hyatt

FAMILY-OWNED CARLSON COMPANIES

Carlson Companies began as the Gold Bond Stamp Company, providing consumer incentive programs for grocery stores, when founder Curtis L. Carlson started the business in 1938 with a loan of $55. When the trading stamp business reached its peak in the late 1960s, the company entered the hospitality industry, changing its name in the 1970s to reflect its transition into a marketing, travel, and hospitality leader. The company currently employs more than 171,000 people in more than 145 companies, owns 5,300 travel agencies, an incentive travel and marketing company, plus more than 1,700 hotels, resorts, restaurants, and cruise ships. Current brands and services include: Regent International Hotels®; Radisson Hotels & Resorts®; Park Plaza Hotels & Resorts; Country Inns & Suites By Carlson; Park Inn® hotels; Regent Seven Seas Cruises®; T.G.I. Friday's® and Pick Up Stix® restaurants; Carlson Wagonlit Travel; Cruise Holidays; All Aboard Travel; Cruise Specialists; Fly4Less.com; CruiseDeals.com; Results Travel; Carlson Destination Marketing Services; Carlson Leisure Travel Services; SeaMaster Cruises®; SinglesCruise.com®; CW Government Travel; Carlson Marketing®; Peppers & Rogers Group®; and Gold Points Reward Network®, an online/offline consumer loyalty program.[74]

Hotels, owned by the Pritzker family, and Carlson Companies are exceptions to this rule, with Carlson being one of the largest privately held companies in the United States. (See the "Hospitality Focus" boxed section above.)

SEGMENTATION

Providing a bed, bathroom, television, and phone are hotel basics, but additional amenities and services are common. *Segmentation* is a strategy that distinguishes properties on the basis of price, service, function, style, offerings, and type of guest served. Hotel chains have been utilizing segmentation, particularly since the 1980s, to enable growth, expand their customer base, and leverage corporate resources and expertise. A widely used approach to classifying segments of the lodging industry was devised by Smith Travel Research and Bear Stearns and includes five segments: luxury (upper upscale), upscale, midscale with food and beverage services, midscale without food and beverage services, and economy. Extended-stay hotels are also included in many classifications as either upper or lower tier, depending on the range of services they offer. Many of the largest hotel chains have developed brands in a variety of segments, from luxury to economy. Accor Hotels, for example, has the Sofitel brand in the upper upscale segment; Novotel, Mercure, and Suitehotel in the upscale and midscale segments; Ibis in the economy segment; and Etap, Motel 6, and Formula 1 in the budget segment.[75]

OWNERSHIP STRUCTURES

A hotel may be owned by one company, franchised by another, and operated by a third, or any combination of these situations. This complex web of business relationships often makes the question of business identity confusing for those who do not understand the structure of the industry. Companies that choose to own hotels can select from a variety of different forms, including corporations, partnerships, and real estate investment trusts (REITs). A company that owns hotels may also be part of a franchise.

Management companies run the operation of a hotel and may also be franchisors. These companies may actually own the hotels they manage or operate hotels that others own. Table 1.4 lists the companies managing the most hotels worldwide based on a recent *Hotels* survey. As

TABLE 1.4 Large Hotel Players

Company	Hotels Managed	Total Hotels	Company	Hotels Franchised	Total Hotels
Marriott International	947	2,832	Wyndham Hotel Group	6,441	6,473
Extended Stay Hotels	681	681	Choice Hotels International	5,376	5,376
Accor	525	4,065	InterContinental Hotel Group	3,204	3,741
InterContinental Hotel Group	512	3,741	Hilton Hotels Corp.	2,241	2,935
Starwood Hotels & Resorts Worldwide	426	871	Marriott International	1,784	2,832
Tharaldson Enterprises	351	351	Accor	1,121	4,121
Hilton Hotels Corp.	343	2,935	Carlson Hospitality Worldwide	905	945
Societe du Louvre	292	840	Vantage Hospitality Group (Americas Best Value Inn)	699	699
Interstate Hotels	219	223	Global Hyatt Corp	425	749
Global Hyatt Corp.	186	749	Starwood Hotels & Resorts Worldwide	360	871

Source: Hotels' Giants Survey 2007, *Hotels* magazine, a Reed Business Information publication.

the rankings in Table 1.4 suggest, Marriott Accor, InterContinental, and Starwood are also franchisors and owners of hotels. Based on Table 1.4, the top five franchise hotels worldwide are Wyndham Worldwide, Choice Hotels International, InterContinental Hotels Group, Hilton Hotels Corporation, and Marriott International.[76] Overall, the top players based on the number of rooms they hold around the world are, in that order: InterContinental Hotels Group, Wyndham Worldwide (formerly Cendant Hotel Group), Marriott International, Hilton Hotels Corporation, Choice Hotels International, Accor, Best Western International, Starwood Hotels & Resorts Worldwide, Carlson Hospitality Worldwide, and Global Hyatt Corporation. As this list suggests, 80 percent of the largest chains are headquartered in North America, although this percentage drops to half when the list includes the top 50 corporations. Best Western International is the largest chain with independently owned and operated hotels, which explains why it has no managed or franchised hotels. Starwood also has 130 owned hotels and 19 vacation ownership resorts in addition to its managed and franchised hotels.

As firms in the industry have evolved and transitioned into more consolidated international operations, so too has the mind-set of managers moved to a more strategic way of thinking about the business. Many of the assumed differences between hospitality firms and other businesses have disappeared, being replaced with a clear understanding of business practice. Although differences still exist between hospitality firms and firms of other types, in most ways hospitality firms are not that different. From one perspective, hotels and restaurants are a big assembly operation, much like a manufacturing operation. However, they are seldom studied in this manner. Also, all hospitality firms can be studied in terms of their cash flows, just like other types of firms. They also all rely on markets for capital, human resources, customers, and supplies. They are subject to economic, sociocultural, technological, and political influences and trends. They have competitors. In summary, there are more similarities than differences between hospitality firms and firms of other types.

Consequently, the general strategic management process does not require substantial modifications to be applicable to hospitality firms. Similar to the manufacturing industry, the process begins with analysis of the firm and its environment, which forms the foundation for development of strategic direction, strategies, and implementation plans. The outcomes from this process are different for each hospitality firm, because results depend on the specifics of the situation. In addition, certain ideas require modification to understand their use and application in services.

The most unique aspect of this book compared to general strategic management texts is the translation of these ideas into service contexts through the use of hospitality industry examples. These examples should help you as you learn the strategic management process. Also, they will help you become more aware of strategies and strategic issues in the industry. However, the most up-to-date theories and ideas of strategic management are also contained here. Nonhospitality examples will occasionally be used when they better illustrate a point.

One of the most important strategic issues facing the hospitality industry today is the ability to leverage human capital.[77] In particular, managers are concerned about human resource activities, such as attracting, retaining, and developing the workforce. Although human resources are an area of concern in every business, the hospitality business faces particularly great challenges because of relatively low wage rates and a large percentage of routine jobs. Managers are also very interested in effective use of capital, aligning the interests of stakeholders such as employees, customers, and owners, understanding their customers better, and applying information technology. Because of their importance to the industry, these issues will receive special attention in this book.

KEY POINTS SUMMARY

This chapter emphasized the important role of the strategic management process in modern organizations.

- The strategic management process includes (1) analysis of the external environment and the organization, (2) establishment of a strategic direction, (3) formulation of a strategy, and (4) implementation of the strategy and development of a system of controls.

- Organizations seldom begin with a thorough strategic management process. Instead, they usually begin with basic financial planning or forecasting. Over time, they develop methods that are more closely associated with what we refer to as strategic management.

- The traditional approach to strategy development is that firms should adapt to their environments. According to this deterministic view, good management is associated with determining which strategy will best fit environmental, technical, and human forces at a particular point in time, and then working to carry out that strategy.

- The principle of enactment assumes that organizations need not submit to existing forces in the environment; they can, in part, create their environments through strategic alliances with stakeholders, investments in leading technologies, advertising, political lobbying, and a variety of other activities.

- The traditional strategy formulation model supports the view that managers create strategies deliberately; however, a more reasonable approach may be to suggest that, through trial and error, managers can also learn as they go.

- The resource-based view of the firm explains that an organization is a bundle of resources, which means that the most important role of a manager is that of acquiring, developing, managing, and discarding resources. According to this view, firms can gain competitive advantage through possessing superior resources.

- Most of the resources that a firm can acquire or develop are directly linked to an organization's stakeholders, which are groups and individuals who can significantly affect or are significantly affected by an organization's activities. A stakeholder approach depicts the complicated nature of the management task.

- Many trends and forces are leading firms into global markets at increasing rates, which have led to a high level of global economic interconnectedness. While the tools, techniques, and models of strategic management apply well to a global environment, there are differences between managing in domestic and international arenas.

- Industry leadership is often associated with breaking out of traditional mind-sets and defying widely accepted industry practices. Strategic planning results in the creation of a plan. Strategic thinking involves intuition and creativity.

- Strategic thinking is intent-focused, comprehensive, opportunistic, long-term oriented, built on the past and the present, and hypothesis-driven. Organizations can encourage strategic thinking through training, rewards systems, integrating elements of strategic thinking into the strategy-making process, and by encouraging risk taking.

REVIEW QUESTIONS

1. Explain each of the component activities in the definition of the strategic management process. Which of these activities do you think is most important to the success of an organization? Why?

2. Summarize the traditional, resource-based, and stakeholder perspectives of strategic management.

3. What are some of the considerations motivating companies to go global?

4. What is the difference between the strategic planning process and strategic thinking?

5. Which of these is essential to effective strategic management?

6. What are the important characteristics associated with strategic thinking? How can an organization encourage this sort of thinking?

7. Who are the key players in the restaurant industry? Lodging industry? How did you arrive at your lists?

CRITICAL THINKING AND APPLICATION QUESTIONS

1. Identify deliberate and emerging strategies for various hotel companies. You may find the following industry news web sites useful in your search for examples of strategies:

   www.globalhotelnetwork.com

   www.hotelinteractive.com

   www.hotel-online.com

2. Name several hospitality firms that you think outperform others. Why are they higher performers? What would the traditional perspective have to say about these high performers?

3. List an industry revolutionary. What makes this person or company revolutionary?

4. Research McDonald's "Plan to Win" initiative. Will the focus on "Brand McDonald's" yield maximum return? Why or why not? You can start your efforts at www.mcdonalds.com.

5. China has been criticized for its unsafe products recently. There appears to be a backlash in the United States, a movement against buying Chinese products. Consumers are avoiding products made in China and questioning providers about the origin of products. In light of this, should hospitality companies take steps to eliminate Chinese products; should they institute a system to ensure the safety of Chinese products for their guests; or should such external environmental issues be ignored?

CHAPTER 2

THE ENVIRONMENT AND EXTERNAL STAKEHOLDERS

YOU SHOULD BE ABLE TO DO THE FOLLOWING AFTER READING THIS CHAPTER:

1. Identify the most important elements of the broad environment, including the sociocultural, economic, political, and technological contexts.

2. Know the difference between a trend and a fad.

3. Understand Porter's five forces model and the nature of industry structure.

4. Explain the difference between the operating environment and the broad environment.

5. List and explain the various tactics managers can use to influence stakeholders.

FEATURED STORY

THE AFRICAN CHALLENGE

Africa in the 21st century is a continent of possibilities. With 53 independent and sovereign countries, Africa is home to the largest desert and savanna plains, jungles, and the pyramids. The adventure capital of the world leaves travelers awestruck, providing affordable luxury, prize-winning wines, friendly people, and a rich culture. Even with all of these natural resources, Africa is also one of the poorest and most underdeveloped regions of the world. With a history that includes a slave trade, corrupt governments, despotism, genocide, civil wars, and colonialism, these issues have all contributed to the economic and political challenges of this vast and beautiful continent. Ongoing armed conflicts, food shortages, and the AIDS pandemic are but a few of the challenges that plague this part of the world. Almost half of Ethiopia's children are malnourished, resulting in a stunted and weak workforce that still operates on manual labor. Sixty percent of all people living in sub-Saharan Africa (approximately 25.8 million) have HIV, with 2.1 million deaths resulting from AIDS coming from this region. South Africa alone has one of the highest AIDS infection rates in the world, with approximately 1,000 people dying daily from the disease, leaving a staggering number of orphans.

One of the worst human rights violations in recent history is taking place in Darfur, a region in Western Sudan. The Sudanese government, with the support of an Arab militia, the Janjaweed, began mounting a campaign of mass killing, looting, and systematic rape of the non-Arab population of Darfur, in response to a rebellion initiated in 2003 by two local rebel groups: the Justice and Equality Movement (JEM) and the Sudanese Liberation Army (SLA). In 2004, the United Nations Security Council called for a Commission of Inquiry on Darfur, and by May 2006, the main rebel group (Sudanese Liberation Movement) agreed to a draft peace agreement with the government. By May 2007, 400,000 Darfurians had died as a result of genocide, while more than 2.5 million surviving inhabitants had fled to refugee camps.

Despite these tumultuous events, restaurants and hotels in the capital city of Khartoum continue to serve patrons, but often without Sudanese workers. The manager of Mo'men, a popular Egypt-based fast-food chain, believes that the Sudanese people don't like to work as hard as others do, so he hires Egyptians and Ethiopians. This view is voiced by others who hire servers from the Philippines despite having to pay for their visas, airfare, and housing. Another explanation offered is that the Sudanese lack the necessary training. A third reason offered by some is that employers are reluctant to hire black Sudanese women because of long-standing cultural divisions that exist between northern Arabs and southerners of African descent. Finally, Islamic expectations view it as unsuitable for women to serve people in public in Sudan. The impact of political crisis, as well as cultural and religious expectations, all shape the way in which business is conducted in this and all parts of the world.[1]

DISCUSSION QUESTIONS:

1. What opportunities and threats do you see for hospitality firms that may wish to establish businesses in Africa?

2. Why would the managers of local hospitality establishments have difficulty taking advantage of the Sudanese workforce displaced by war and languishing in poverty?

INTRODUCTION

The staffing challenges faced by the hospitality industry in Khartoum illustrate the complex connection between political, religious, and cultural factors. Successful organizations stay abreast of changes in their external environments to anticipate concerns, predict trends, and generate ideas. These activities lead to the identification of external opportunities and threats, which are then considered by managers as they develop strategic direction and formulate and implement organizational strategies.[2] The lack of qualified local service staff in Khartoum may create an opportunity for an entrepreneur to consider the development of a hospitality training program to fulfill the needs of local businesses.

The external environment can be divided into the broad and operating environments. The operating environment is different for each firm, although similarities may exist among firms in the same industries. The broad environment is not firm specific or industry specific. In other words, the major trends and influences that occur in the broad environment impact many firms and industries, although the type and level of influence may be different from one industry to the next. For example, the AIDS epidemic is felt strongly in the African travel and lodging sectors; however, virtually every industry has been affected in some way.

The major components of the broad and operating environments are displayed in Figure 2.1. An organization can have a much more significant influence on events that transpire in its operating environment than it can in its broad environment. In fact, this is one way to distinguish between the two environments. For example, it would be difficult for a firm, working independently, to dramatically influence societal views on genocide, the role of women, AIDS, or malnutrition. However, an organization can have a profound impact on the attitude of its customers or suppliers, competitive rivalry, or even government regulations (assuming proactive political activities). Because organizations typically can have only a minimal influence on forces in the broad environment, the emphasis in the first section will be on analyzing and adapting to those forces.

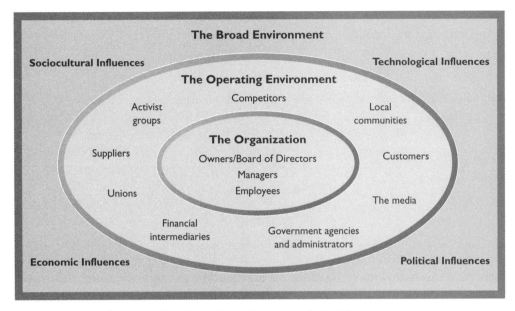

FIGURE 2.1 The organization, its primary stakeholders, and the broad environment

ASSESSMENT OF THE BROAD ENVIRONMENT

This section describes many of the most important forces in the broad environment and how some organizations respond to them. The emphasis in this section will be on scanning, monitoring, forecasting, and adapting to broad environmental influences. Figure 2.2 provides a brief description of the ways in which you can analyze the broad environment, moving from the most general scanning of many factors in the environment, to more focused and precise monitoring, projecting, and adapting of particularly important trends.

The broad environment forms the context in which the firm and its operating environment exist. The key elements in the broad environment, as it relates to a business organization and its operating environment, are:

1. Sociocultural influences

2. Global economic influences

3. Political influences

4. Technological influences

These four areas will now be described, as well as examples of successful and unsuccessful organizational responses.

Scanning: General indicators—Looking for early warning signals from many trends.

Monitoring: Following specific indicators—An ongoing observation of key important trends.

Projecting: Forecasting the impact of key trends on the organization based on monitored specific changes over time.

Adapting: Determining what requires change in the organization based on an assessment of the timing, influence, and importance of specific trends. The key question is how the trends will affect firm strategy.

FIGURE 2.2 **Broad environmental analysis**

The Sociocultural Context

Society is composed of the individuals who make up a particular geographic region. Some sociocultural trends are applicable to the citizens of an entire country. For example, a few of the major social issues currently facing the United States are:

- Role of government in health care and elder care
- Terrorism and levels of violent crime
- Security of travel and public places
- Global warming
- War and role of the military
- Declining quality of education
- Financial market failures
- Quality and health levels of various imported and manufactured food products
- Pollution and disposal of toxic and nontoxic waste

Attitudes and beliefs can also relate to geographic areas that are larger or smaller than individual countries. For example, people refer to the South, which alludes to the southern states of the United States; to Western culture (globally speaking); or to Latin American countries. These sociocultural groups have meaning to most well-educated people, because of the widely held beliefs and values that are a part of the culture in these areas.

ANALYSIS OF SOCIETAL TRENDS

The value of watching social trends is that it helps firms to understand preferences, strengthen ties with existing customers, and create innovative products. The rising popularity of green hotels and restaurant menus with organic foods are two examples of how broader social trends can shape the industry. Hospitality firms that pay attention to social trends are able to:

- Recognize opportunities
- Identify unique generational and cultural differences
- Enhance corporate reputation
- Avoid unwanted legislation

The following sections discuss each of these benefits in turn.

OPPORTUNITY CREATION

First, broader societal influences can create opportunities for organizations. For example, societal interest in wellness has led to the development of state-of-the-art spas as a differentiating feature in upscale hotels and resorts. Also, many baby-boomer couples had babies later in life than did past generations, causing a demographic trend toward older couples with children. The higher income levels of these more established parents means that they are more likely to travel with their children, which has led to the development of programs that cater to their special interests. One outgrowth of this trend is the creation of family-friendly cruises such as the Disney Cruise Lines, and kid-friendly spas such as Phantom Horse spa in Phoenix, Arizona. The health and wellness trends in the industry have evolved a host of intriguing concept ideas such as airport spas, while treatments have ranged from the typical Swedish massage to exotic snake and cactus massages, bird-dropping facials, and toxin-reducing suction-cupping treatments.

Population characteristics, or demographics, are often used in marketing research to understand subgroups or segments and the behaviors of a typical member of a segment. Demographic trends, such as the average age of a population, ethnic mix, migration patterns, income levels, and literacy rates, can help in the development of strategy. The impact of the post-war baby-boomer population bulge (born 1946 to 1964) may have increased demand for stocks, fueling the bull market of the 1990s, when members of this group began to save for retirement. As this population group becomes elderly and retires, they will continue to shape the hospitality industry in new ways, providing opportunities for companies in recreation and nursing homes. Companies in many industries are taking advantage of this trend by offering special services and discounts to senior citizens. For example, the failing eyesight of the large group of baby boomers has been identified and accommodated in restaurants such as Romano's Macaroni Grill, a nationwide chain of Italian restaurants, which provides reading glasses and large-print menus on request.[3]

GENERATIONAL COHORTS IN AMERICA

1. Depression cohort
   (born from 1912 to 1921)

   Memorable events: The Great Depression, high unemployment, poverty, and financial uncertainty

   Key characteristics: risk adverse, desire for financial security, and strive for comfort

2. World War II cohort (born from 1922 to 1927)

   Memorable events: men going to war and many not returning, the personal experience of the war, women working in factories, and a focus on defeating a common enemy

   Key characteristics: the nobility of sacrifice for the common good, patriotism, and team players

3. Post-war cohort (born from 1928 to 1945)

   Memorable events: sustained economic growth, social tranquility, The Cold War, and McCarthyism

   Key characteristics: conformity, conservatism, and traditional family values

continues...

GENERATIONAL AND CULTURAL AWARENESS

Culture is defined as an evolving set of shared beliefs, values, and attitudes that help shape how a social group thinks, sees, acts, and reacts to various events and situations.[4] A generation may shape its identity or distinctive beliefs and views as a result of social, political, and economic events that occur during the preadult years. These groups are called generational cohorts, because they experience the same events at the same time. For example, the Republican Era (1911–1949) in China was a period of extreme poverty, war, and political instability culminating in the Civil War of 1945–1959.[5] The next two generational eras were under Chinese Communist rule (i.e., the Consolidation Era 1950–1965 and the Great Cultural Revolution 1966–1976) and stressed a classless society, conformity, and self-sacrifice. The Social Reform Era in China (1978–present) encourages individual achievement, materialism, and entrepreneurship.

In the United States, Generation Y is one of several terms, including Echo Boomers, Millennials, the Second Baby Boom, and the Internet Generation to describe a group born roughly between 1980 and the present.[6] A comprehensive study of Americans, linking world events to their importance for various individuals, revealed seven distinct cohorts as described following, along with the memorable events that define them and the key characteristics of the cohort.[7] (See the "Hospitality Focus" boxed section above which continues on page 43.)

4. Baby Boomer cohort 1 (born from 1946 to 1954)

   Memorable events: assassinations of John F. Kennedy and Martin Luther King Jr., political unrest, putting a man on the moon, Vietnam War, antiwar protests, social experimentation, sexual freedom, civil rights movement, environmental movement, women's movement, protests and riots, and experimentation with various intoxicating drugs

   Key characteristics: experimentation, individualism, free-spirited, and social cause oriented

5. Baby Boomer cohort 2 (born from 1955 to 1964)

   Memorable events: Watergate, Nixon resigns, the Cold War, the oil embargo, inflation, and gasoline shortages

   Key characteristics: distrust of government, pessimism, and general cynicism

6. Generation X cohort (born from 1965 to 1983)

   Memorable events: Challenger explosion, Iran-Contra, social malaise, Reaganomics, AIDS, safe sex, fall of Berlin Wall, and single-parent families

   Key characteristics: quest for emotional security, entrepreneurial, and informal

7. Generation Y cohort, also called N Generation (born from 1984 to present)

   Memorable events: rise of the Internet, September 11th attacks, cultural diversity, and two wars in Iraq

   Key characteristics: quest for safety and security, heightened fears, acceptance of change, technically savvy, and environmentally conscious

CORPORATE REPUTATION

A positive organizational reputation among stakeholders such as customers and suppliers may increase demand for products or lead to increased business opportunities. Awareness of and compliance with the attitudes of society can also help an organization avoid problems associated with being perceived as a "bad corporate citizen." For example, Denny's was known for many years as one of America's most racist companies. However, Ron Petty, Denny's CEO, introduced initiatives that turned the company into a model of multicultural sensitivity.[8] In general, the public is becoming increasingly distrusting of larger corporations, a part of the aftermath of the Enron, WorldCom, and Tyco scandals.

The distrust of corporations goes hand in hand with greater confidence in the views and opinions of consumers, particularly the views of other travelers. Social media web sites and blogs, for example, have become an important tool for prospective hotel guests who visit these sites to read comments and reviews about the hotels at their destination before they make a reservation. Online buzz is a powerful way for customers to discover both bad and good information about travel businesses. (See the "Hospitality Focus" boxed section on page 44.)

ONLINE BUZZ

The challenge for the industry in dealing with social media web sites and blogs is to know what the buzz is and how to add positive buzz about your own business. More than 40 percent of all online travel shoppers visit web sites and blogs to read comments and reviews about a hotel or destination before making a reservation. According to Richard Walsh, Vice President of Lodging Interactive:

In our months of research prior to launching Chatter Guard, our online service to help hotels capture, analyze, report, and respond to user-generated media, we found that online buzz is available on thousands of web sites, and whether the comment is good or bad or even whether it is accurate or not, it will affect a hotel's business. So it is infinitely important that you manage your online reputation, and that is done by being responsive to any type of online chatter. The social media web sites and blogs are replacing the office water cooler. They are where people are finding out about travel services and deciding which service they will purchase and which ones they will not.[9]

Companies such as Four Seasons, Marriott, and McDonald's go to great lengths to present themselves in a positive light. Each year, *Fortune* magazine rates corporations on the basis of their reputations. One of these issues began with the following introduction: "Each year we hear of more companies that have made an explicit corporate goal of improving their performance in *Fortune*'s annual survey of corporate reputations."[10] Four Seasons, Starbucks, and Marriott are hospitality favorites on the Fortune 100 best companies to work for list. A corporate reputation can be a very important organizational resource, because it cannot be imitated completely. The value of this resource will be discussed further in Chapter 3.

SOCIAL RESPONSIBILITY

Finally, correct assessment of social trends can help businesses avoid restrictive legislation, which can be a threat to organizational success. Industries and organizations that police themselves are less likely to be the target of legislative activity, while being perceived as socially responsible. *Social responsibility* is when a firm takes a proactive stance in its social role, going beyond what is called for by law. Legislative activity is often generated in response to a public outcry against the actions of firms or industries. A socially responsible firm not only refrains from acting unethically, but also voluntarily seeks to improve society. Important legislative and regulatory issues that affect the restaurant industry include obesity lawsuits, health and safety regulations, immigration reform, business meal deductibility, trans-fat bans, and minimum-wage regulations. A complex social issue facing the restaurant industry is its role in influencing a healthy lifestyle for diners. (See the "Hospitality Focus" boxed section on page 45.)

Correct evaluation of societal forces can help direct organizational planning. For instance, understanding trends and fads can help an organization forecast industry demand for new products and services and their staying power. *Trends* usually capture long-term changes or

SOCIAL RESPONSIBILITY AND HEALTHY FOODS

New York City became the nation's first city to ban artificial trans fats at restaurants. Trans fats are frequently used in frying and baking, and are formed when hydrogen is added to liquid oils to make them solid fats. The health concern is based on numerous studies that have revealed that trans fats raise the risk of heart disease by increasing bad cholesterol while lowering the good high-density lipoprotein (HDL) cholesterol. These human-made fats are considered much worse for you than any other natural fat, even the saturated fats found in butter and beef, according to experts. Despite the health concerns, the restaurant industry views the ban as unnecessary and burdensome. Dan Fleshler of the National Restaurant Association (NRA) noted, "We don't think that a municipal health agency has any business banning a product the Food and Drug Administration has already approved." Before passage of the ban, the NRA argued that the city's approach was too narrow and did not address the much larger health issue. They further observed that the supply of trans fat–free oils is in short supply, which would pose a problem for some chains for years to come. The association urged the city to focus on the larger health picture and work to educate citizens and the business community on the importance of a healthy lifestyle.[11]

movements that are substantial to the society and last. In contrast, a *fad* is a cultural blip, it's what's hot, but fades fast and doesn't return. While a trend might begin with a few people, the trendsetters, it becomes central to the broader culture. For example, many people considered hip-hop music to be an urban fad of the early 1980s. More than 20 years later, hip-hop is deeply rooted in popular culture from fashion to advertising jingles.

Distinguishing long-term food trends from fads is not always an easy task. Evolving consumer food preferences and dining habits considered to be trends will impact menu research and development for an extended time. Experts suggest that ethnic foods (Asian, Pan-Asian, Mediterranean, Latin), premium products (bottled water, upscale coffees, exotic mushrooms), products perceived to have healthful benefits (organic, grass-fed and free-range, pomegranates, bite-size desserts), flavorful foods (fresh herbs, salt, pan searing and grilling), and convenience foods (specialty sandwiches) all have staying power.[12] The popularity of television chefs has raised the profile of the culinary profession influencing food trends, while diet fads can shift the focus of menu design in the short term. Table 2.1 shows the results of a survey of chefs from the American Culinary Federation ranking items that are "hot" and "cool" (passé).[13] Food fads may come and go, but dining out is here to stay as an integral part of our lifestyles, with Americans spending 47.9 percent of their food dollars away from home.[14] A senior manager of a cookware chain makes the following prediction about cooking in the future:

It's headed toward easier and more convenient cooking. I don't think people will let their favorite dishes disappear, but the kind of cooking done by our grandmothers will. People just don't have the time and there are too many alternatives. People used to cook three meals a day because they had to, even if they did not like to cook. Now there are other options. People today cook on weekends and to entertain.[15]

TABLE 2.1 Top 20 Culinary Trends

Hot Items	Cool Items (passé)
Bite-size desserts	Fruit/flavored wine
Locally grown produce	Starfruit
Organic produce	Tofu
Small plates/tapas/mezze	Kosher wine
Specialty sandwiches	Low-carb dough
Craft/artisan/microbrew beer	Mezcal
Sustainable seafood	Vermouth
Grass-fed items	Chai
Energy drink cocktails	Dried fruits
Salts (e.g., sea, smoked, colored, kosher)	Prickly pear/cactus pear/cactus
Ethnic fusion cuisine	Foie gras
Flatbreads	Kosher items
Martinis/flavored martinis	Indonesian cuisine
Mojito	Barley
Asian entrée salad	Low-fat/nonfat sauces and dressings
Pomegranates	Lychee/litchi
Asian appetizers	Crêpes (sweet/savory)
Microdistilled/artisanal liquors	Guava
Organic wine	Cakes/layered cakes
Specialty beer (e.g., seasonal, fruit, spice/herb, beer cocktails)	Cobb entrée salad

Source: What's Hot and What's Not Chef Survey of 1,282 members of the American Culinary Federation, National Restaurant Association, 2007 (*www.restaurant.org*).

The Economic Context

Economic forces can have a profound influence on organizational behavior and performance. Economic forces that create growth and profit opportunities allow organizations to take actions that satisfy many stakeholders simultaneously, particularly owners, employees, and suppliers. When economic trends are negative, managers face tremendous pressures as they balance potentially conflicting stakeholder interests, often between employees and owners.

Economic growth, interest rates, the availability of credit, inflation rates, foreign exchange rates, and foreign-trade balances are among the most critical economic factors (see Table 2.2). Many of these forces are interdependent. Organizations should constantly scan the economic environment to monitor critical but uncertain assumptions concerning the economic future, and then link those assumptions to the demand pattern and profit potential for their products and services. These assumptions often form the base on which strategies and implementation plans are built.

Economic growth can have a large impact on consumer demand for hospitality services. Consequently, hospitality organizations should consider forecasts of economic growth in determining when to make critical resource-allocation decisions such as expansion and new market entry. The economy of India is a case in point of fast growth, with the signs of rising prices that could set off an inflationary spiral, although their inflation remains much lower than in many developing countries.[16] Nevertheless, prices in India are rising more than twice as fast as in China, and faster than those in industrialized countries.

Rising food prices in India are attributed to a wide range of global factors, including poor harvests in Australia, the growing use of crops to produce ethanol, and a higher cost of diesel fuel for tractors. The government policy of encouraging futures trading in agricultural

TABLE 2.2 A Few of Many Global Economic Forces to Monitor and Predict

FORCE	POTENTIAL INFLUENCES
Economic Growth	Consumer demand, cost of factors of production, availability of factors of production (especially labor and scarce resources)
Interest Rates	Cost of capital for new projects, cost of refinancing existing debt, consumer demand (due to customer ability to finance purchases)
Inflation	Interest rates, cost of factors of production, optimism or pessimism of stakeholders
Exchange Rates	Ability to profitably remove profits from foreign ventures, government policies toward business
Trade Deficits	Government policies, incentives, trade barriers

commodities is cited as an explanation for higher prices. Wholesale price inflation has accelerated to 6 percent, with the consumer price index rising nearly 7 percent in urban areas over the period 2006–2007, and almost 9 percent in rural areas, where more than two-thirds of the population lives and where higher food prices are having the biggest effect.[17]

Inflation and the availability of credit, among other factors, influence interest rates that organizations have to pay. High interest payments can constrain the strategic flexibility of firms by making new ventures and capacity expansions prohibitively expensive. Conversely, low interest rates can increase strategic flexibility for organizations and also influence demand by encouraging customers to purchase goods and services on credit. For example, the Wynn Macau casino resort refinanced a $744 million loan to secure a lower interest rate.[18] Strong cash flows and earnings success of their casinos enhanced the ability of the firm to negotiate better terms for the loan to construct its downtown Macau casino hotel.

Volatile inflation and interest rates, such as those experienced in the United States in the 1970s and in South American and Eastern European countries, increase the uncertainty associated with making strategic decisions. Therefore, inflation and interest rates are worthy of monitoring or forecasting efforts in most organizations, but especially in those that are highly dependent on debt or have customers who finance their purchases.

Foreign-exchange rates are another major source of uncertainty for global organizations. Companies sometimes earn a profit in a foreign country, only to see the profit turn into a loss due to unfavorable currency translations. Furthermore, the organization may have billings in one currency and payables in another. Foreign-trade balances are relevant to both domestic and global organizations, because they are an indication of the nature of trade legislation that might be expected in the future. For example, the United States has run a trade deficit since the mid-1970s, while China has a strong trade surplus with no indication of reductions in demand for their products, despite rising costs and greater consumer concerns about quality after a series of recalls of tainted products from pet food and toothpaste to toys.[19] Finally, several economic variables may be interesting to specific types of firms. For example, gasoline price fluctuations have been found to influence U.S. lodging demand.[20]

Executives involved in strategic planning should develop their own sets of economic variables to track and forecast. The variables discussed here are just examples. Unexpected shocks to the world economy, such as wars, terrorist attacks, or an epidemic such as SARS (Severe Acute Respiratory Syndrome), can have serious implications for hospitality organizations; however, these situations are almost impossible to predict. The coordinated bomb attacks on the Grand Hyatt Hotel, the Radisson SAS Hotel, and the Days Inn in Amman, Jordan, in 2005 killed 60 people and injured 115 others. The Glasgow International Airport attack in 2007 occurred when a car loaded with propane canisters crashed through the main terminal entrance. Both of these incidents were impossible to anticipate. In general, the increasing frequency of such jolts has made hospitality firms extremely sensitive to complex global political issues and their impact on the industry.

The Political Context

Political forces, both at home and abroad, are among the most significant determinants of organizational success. Governments provide and enforce the rules by which organizations operate. These rules include laws, regulations, and policies.

Governments can encourage new-business formation through tax incentives and subsidies, or through direct intervention. For example, several U.S. cities have directly financed the development of hotels intended to serve local convention centers. Governments can also restructure companies, as in the case of the American Telephone and Telegraph (AT&T) breakup, or totally close firms that do not comply with laws, ordinances, or regulations. Alliances among governments provide an additional level of complexity for businesses with significant foreign operations. Also, some countries have established independent entities to counsel them on government policy. For example, the Australian government uses task forces to help devise policy.[21] They are independent of both business and government. Recently, these task forces have examined technological progress and the needs of various industries to evolve in order to become more competitive.

Some organizations find themselves in a situation in which they are almost entirely dependent on government regulators for their health and survival. In many countries, tight regulatory controls are found in a wide variety of industries. In countries such as China or Cuba, the government has significant control over the actions of firms. In the United States, utilities are a good example of a highly regulated environment; however, hospitality firms tend to be less regulated than firms in other businesses are.

Although all organizations face some form of regulation, there is a trend toward deregulation and privatization (transfer of government productive assets to private citizens) of industries worldwide. In Italy, for example, the government plans to sell Alitalia Airlines, the national airline carrier that has not posted a profit since 1998 and has net debt of more than 1 billion euros.[22] In Eastern Europe, many industries are struggling to survive and prosper in an emerging market economy. While Central and Eastern Europe initiated privatization programs to transition their economies after 1989, developed countries such as New Zealand and the United Kingdom have also engaged in comprehensive efforts. Privatization has been viewed as successful in the telecommunications industry in Europe, although some question the success of these efforts in the Republic of Ireland. In the United States, the past 20 years have brought the deregulation of the airline, banking, long-distance telephone, and trucking industries. With deregulation, existing industry competitors face turbulence and unpredictability. The highly volatile airline industry is an excellent example. However, deregulation can provide new opportunities for firms to enter the market. JetBlue, a relative newcomer, is thriving amid the struggles of other air carriers.

Monitoring and complying with laws and regulations is a good idea from a financial perspective. Involvement in illegal activities can result in a significant loss of firm value.[23] Failure to operate responsibly can often lead to new legislation. The accounting scandals that cost investors in corporations like Enron, Tyco International, and WorldCom billions of dollars resulted in the creation of the Sarbanes–Oxley Act of 2002. This piece of legislation was established to oversee and regulate issues of auditor independence, internal control assessment, and financial disclosure. While some see the law as enhancing corporate accountability, others view it as an intrusion into corporate management. The "Hospitality Focus" boxed section on page 50 demonstrates what can happen when an organization mishandles or ignores government regulation.

Lawmakers often pursue legislation in response to requests and pressures from constituents. Regulatory agencies and revenue-collection agencies develop the specifics of the regulations needed to carry out new laws, and they serve an enforcement role as well. The courts handle disputes, interpret laws as needed, and levy fines and penalties. Although one organization may not be able to alter major political forces as a whole, it may have considerable impact within its own specific industries and operating domain. Consequently, major political

MISHANDLING GOVERNMENT REGULATION

Buying California's most famous, most beautiful, most historic golf course—the one where Bing Crosby kidded Bob Hope and knocked out ashes from his pipe against the cypress trees—must have seemed the coup of coups to Minoru Isutani, owner of Cosmo World, a Japanese golfing conglomerate. True, the price he paid in September 1990—said to be somewhere between $800 million and $1 billion—seemed high, but Isutani had a plan. He would transform Pebble Beach into a private club, with memberships (at $740,000 each) sold primarily to wealthy Japanese. Golfers of lesser means protested. Under existing rules, anybody willing to endure a waiting list and pay a $200-per-person greens fee could play the course. But if Pebble Beach went private, the best hours would be reserved for members. Enter the California Coastal Commission, all-powerful in matters of coastal access: Did the new owners have a commission permit for this conversion? No, they didn't. They didn't think they needed one. The commission ruled they did, and withheld it.[24]

forces are considered a part of the broad environment, while government agencies and administrators are considered a part of the operating environment. Political strategies for dealing with government within industries will be described later in this chapter.

The Technological Context

Technological change creates new products, processes, and services, and, in some cases, entire new industries. It also can change the way society behaves and what society expects. Notebook computers, compact discs and MP3 players, direct satellite systems, and cellular telephones are technological innovations that have experienced extraordinary growth in the last decade, leaving formerly well-established industries stunned, creating whole industries, and influencing the way many people approach work and leisure. Computers and telecommunications technologies, for example, have played an essential role in creating the increasingly global marketplace. The Internet, in particular, added a new communications and marketing tool that has led to many new global business threats and opportunities. Organizations that don't embrace technological change may live to regret it. (See the "Hospitality Focus" boxed section on page 51.)

Technology refers to human knowledge about products and services and the way they are made and delivered. This is a fairly broad definition of technology. Typically, technology is defined in terms of such things as machinery, computers, and information systems. However, technologies don't have to be technically sophisticated. For example, there is a technology associated with cooking or with cleaning a room. Just because these technologies are simple does not mean that technological opportunities do not exist. There is still room for innovation and improvement. Industry consultant Grace Leo-Andrieu, in an interview with *Travel+Leisure* magazine, paints a picture of the future in which hotels offer "services that may not necessarily

THE USE OF TECHNOLOGY: ONLINE TRAVEL

Use of online Internet sites for hotel bookings has exploded. Originally envisioned as an online alternative to "brick-and-mortar" travel agencies, these sites have now evolved into online merchants, while putting pressure on room prices. In response, Travelweb LLC, originally launched as Hotel Distribution System LLC in February 2002, was formed and is currently backed by Hilton Hotels Corporation, Hyatt Corporation, Marriott International, InterContinental Hotels Group, Six Continents Hotels, Starwood Hotels, and travel technology provider Pegasus Solutions, Inc. Travelweb pioneered the seamless merchant distribution model, which some believe returned yield and revenue management capabilities back to hoteliers, while broadening their distribution options.[25]

be performed by humans. Food and drinks could be dispensed by machines or robots, rooms could be cleaned by built-in vacuum and disinfecting systems, and a quick back-and-foot massage could be provided by a robotic apparatus."[26]

Technological innovations can take the form of new products or processes, such as high-definition televisions and cellular phones. When an innovation has an impact on more than one industry or market, it is referred to as a basic innovation. Examples include the microprocessor, the light bulb, superconductors, and fiber optics. Basic innovations reverberate through society, transforming existing industries and creating new ones. The hospitality industry has the challenge of selecting appropriate technologies for consumers, whether they be three-dimensional holographic teleconferencing or smart cards embedded with microchips that allow the hotel to personalize the guest experience, from checking in automatically to remembering guest preferences. An industry study reported that although in-room fax machines and cell phone rentals were not popular hotel technologies, Internet reservation systems, management e-mail systems, in-room modems, and voice mail were.[27] The challenge for many hospitality managers is determining which technology innovations are appropriate, particularly as the growth in bandwidth demand increases. Bandwidth is a particularly challenging issue as guests continue to require more bandwidth to download video, watch TV (e.g., Slingbox), use VoIP (Voice-over-Internet Protocol) like Skype or Vonage, and use a VPN (Virtual Private Network) to conduct business.

Technological change is difficult, but not impossible, to predict. An understanding of the three characteristics of innovation can help an organization develop a plan for monitoring technological change. They are:

1. Innovations often emerge from existing technologies.

2. A dominant design will eventually be widely adopted.

3. Radical innovations often come from outside of the industry group.

These three characteristics will now be discussed.

INNOVATION: THE COMPCIERGE

To efficiently and quickly respond to the increasing number of guest requests for assistance concerning computer-related problems, several companies, including the Ritz-Carlton Hotels and the InterContinental Hotels, have created a staff position within the MIS department. The "compcierge," technology-butler, or technology concierge is a position designed to handle the array of unanticipated computer problems that can plague a traveler. Can't open a document? Can't connect to the Internet? Don't worry, computer whizzes are on call day and night to solve guest problems. As Michael D'Anthony, the developer of Ritz-Carlton's companywide program noted, "Everyone's on the Internet now, and everyone needs their e-mail. When they travel, they run into problems. Either they can't plug in their computer, or they don't know how to change the settings on their computer, or they can't figure out how to get their e-mail, or whatever." These technology experts are a combination of technician and diplomat as they calm frustrated and tense guests. "If it's 3 in the morning, we'll be there," says Victor Martinez, who works at the Boca Raton Resort and Club. "We'll get it working." The tech crew at the Biltmore Hotel in Coral Gables once helped a business group set up their entire network at the hotel's conference center so it was a live extension of their New York office, giving them e-mail and data access.[28]

INNOVATIONS FROM EXISTING TECHNOLOGIES

As James Utterback pointed out in his book *Mastering the Dynamics of Innovation,* most innovations draw from the existing technologies of the time, but, through a new configuration of some type, they fulfill a new need or fulfill an existing need better.[29] For example, the first personal computers were sold as do-it-yourself kits for electronics enthusiasts and used existing electronics technology. It was only after Apple Computer provided a user-friendly interface and appearance, and software designers provided applications, that the personal computer (PC) began to gain legitimacy as a home and office machine. With the entry of IBM into the market, which further signaled the importance of the innovation, the market for personal computers exploded. Since then, innovations in semiconductor and microprocessor manufacturing have lead to smaller, less-expensive components, which has improved affordability and design flexibility. Now business travelers and even tourists often travel with an array of technological toys and tools. A recent survey of visitors to the Hostelworld.com web site found that 21 percent travel with a laptop, 54 percent with an MP3 player, 83 percent with a mobile phone, and 86 percent with a digital camera.[30] The evolving technologies for travelers provide both opportunities and challenges to hoteliers as they try to determine the staying power of various network and infrastructure investments, and as consumers continue to demand fast, wireless, and free.

ADOPTION OF A DOMINANT DESIGN

Innovations in the PC industry illustrate a second characteristic of technological innovation. Just like the invention process, commercial innovations tend to evolve through predictable stages—from chaotic efforts to develop variations on the innovation to the emergence of a dominant design as customer needs become clear.[31] The emergence of a dominant design has strategic implications for firms in the industry and for firms considering entering the industry. A *dominant design* suggests that the industry may evolve as a commodity—with customers comparing prices and businesses finding fewer ways to create differences that customers will pay for.

For example, when the PC was first emerging, many companies entered the market. They each had different target applications, different keyboard configurations, different operating systems, different microprocessor capabilities, and different overall appearances. Each manufacturer was struggling to create a computer that would appeal to a largely unknown target market. Over time, however, the PCs began to converge toward a dominant design: operating systems with pull-down menus and user-friendly icons, a standard keyboard, standard word-processing/spreadsheet/graphics applications, and a standard microprocessor. Although computers made by different companies are not identical, they are now so similar that few people have trouble moving from model to model. This standardization of computers has made it possible for hotels to provide computer-related services efficiently, one of the latest being a technology concierge. (See the "Hospitality Focus" boxed section on page 52.)

RADICAL INNOVATIONS FROM OUTSIDE THE INDUSTRY

A third characteristic of the innovation process is that radical innovations usually originate outside of the industry boundaries, which makes monitoring of trends outside the immediate competitive group so important. For example, it was not the existing office-machine companies that developed the PC, although office machines were ultimately displaced by PCs. Many innovations in electronics, telecommunications, and specialty materials originated with space and military projects and were adopted by other industries for use in commercial applications. In general, when the rate of improvements with an existing technology begins to slow down, the likelihood of a substitute innovation increases.

Hospitality firms should monitor the technological developments in industries other than their own, conducting brainstorming sessions about the possible consequences for their own services and markets. Recently, for example, seven European rail companies and their high-speed subsidiaries announced plans to link their reservations system and create a new seamless network that will compete with air and road travel over international borders. Railteam, the new railway network, will include Deutsche Bahn, SNCF, SNCB, NS Hispeed, SBB, Eurostar U.K., and others in an airline-style alliance that will provide business travelers with value-added services, including a rewards program.[32] Early innovators with new technologies enjoy first-mover advantages with regard to winning over and keeping customers.

DEALING WITH TECHNOLOGICAL CHANGE

To help identify trends and anticipate their timing, companies may participate in several kinds of technological-forecasting efforts. In general, organizations may:

- Monitor trends by surfing the Web, studying journals, and staying current with the latest reports.

- Solicit the opinion of experts outside of the organization. This is a more formal method of technological forecasting, and these experts may be interviewed directly or contacted as part of a formal survey, such as a Delphi study.

- Develop scenarios of alternative technological futures, which capture different rates of innovation and different emerging technologies. Scenarios allow an organization to conduct "what-if" analyses and to develop alternative plans for responding to new innovations.

In addition to forecasting, some organizations establish *strategic alliances* with universities to engage in joint research projects, which allow them to keep abreast of trends. For example, the Center for Hospitality Research at Cornell University has research collaborations with numerous hospitality firms as well as reports available for downloading.[33] Other hospitality programs have similar programs.

Change and Interdependence among the Broad Environmental Forces

Although each of the broad environmental forces has been discussed separately, in reality they are interdependent. For example, social forces are sometimes intertwined with economic forces. In the United States, birthrates (a social force) are low, and, because of improved health care and lifestyles (another social force), people are living longer. This demographic shift toward an older population is influencing economic forces in society. For instance, the older population means that there are shortages of young workers to fill the service jobs in hospitality, while demand for premium services by older consumers is increasing.

To assess the effect of broad environmental forces, including those that are interdependent, organizations often create models of their business environments using different scenarios. The scenarios are composed of optimistic, pessimistic, and best-case assumptions and interpretations of various economic, social, political, and technological data gleaned from an organization's business-intelligence system. Continuing the example of the aging population, a firm providing services for the elderly might develop different demand and wage-rate scenarios as a way of considering several possible future business environments.

Information about broad environmental forces and trends is often available through public and private, published and unpublished sources, but organizations must take deliberate steps to find and use the information. For example, industry surveys, information about consumer trends, demographic patterns, economic trends, investment patterns, technological advances, and even societal views are widely available through published sources and government reports in libraries and on the Internet. Mintel publications, available in many university libraries, produces more than 600 reports covering an extensive number of industry sectors and focusing on European, UK-specific, and U.S. consumer intelligence reports. Mintel offers a host of travel and leisure reports that analyze market sizes and trends, market segmentation, consumer attitudes, and purchasing habits.

Table 2.3 contains a chart that can help organizational managers track trends in their broad environments. It can also be used to generate strategic alternatives. On the left, a manager should describe the nature of each trend. The column in the middle can be used to identify each trend

TABLE 2.3 **Assessment of the Broad Environment**

	IMPLICATION FOR ORGANIZATION			
TRENDS, CHANGES, OR FORCES	OPPORTUNITY	THREAT	NEUTRAL	ORGANIZATIONAL RESPONSE, IF ANY
Sociocultural Influences • Attitude changes • Demographic shifts • Sensitive issues • New fads • Public opinions • Emerging public-opinion leaders				
Global Economic Forces • Economic growth • Unemployment • Interest rates • Inflation • Foreign-exchange rates • Balance of payments • Other (depending on business)				
Technological Forces • New production processes • New products/product ideas • Current process-research efforts • Current product-research efforts • Scientific discoveries that may have an impact				
Political/Legal Forces • New laws • New regulations • Current administrative policies • Government stability wars • International pacts and treaties				

CONSUMER TRENDS: MASSCLUSIVITY

HOSPITALITY FOCUS

Massclusivity, or giving the masses exclusive access to high quality, was exploited by Fergus McCann, a Scottish-American
entrepreneur, when he created a new business called
LimoLiner. This entrepreneur, who made his fortune in the golf vacation industry, considered the frequent delays, long lines, lost luggage,
and overcrowded terminals of typical airline and train travel an opportunity to provide a
28-passenger, state-of-the-art, luxury bus. Offering service between New York and Boston,
LimoLiner provides services such as leather seats with 41 inches of leg room (typical buses,
by comparison, have 27 inches), seat-side power outlets, flat-panel televisions tuned to
either news or a movie, clear and constant cell phone reception, sandwiches and coffee, a
10-seat conference center, clean bathrooms (with flowers), and wireless Internet access,
all for the low price of $79 one way. This luxurious bus is now a threat to short-distance
train and airline routes. LimoLiner hopes to take passengers from airline shuttles like those
of Delta Air Lines and US Airways, and from Amtrak's Acela Express trains. LimoLiner is
cheaper than either taking the train or plane (a one-way ticket on Acela starts at $99, and
the airline shuttles start at about $250 for a walk-up fare), and its amenities were designed
to compete with the shuttles' first-class cabins and Acela Express's business-class service. "I
started LimoLiner because I believe that traveling well is not a privilege, but a right—every
traveler's right," notes McCann.[34]

as an opportunity, a threat, or as neutral to the organization. The third column should list possible actions the firm could take to respond to the opportunities and threats, if appropriate. Opportunities and threats are conditions in the broad environment that help or hinder, respectively, a firm's efforts to achieve competitiveness.[35] Key opportunities and threats may come from unlikely sources, and very often can be viewed as two sides of the same coin, meaning that an opportunity that competitors exploit can become a threat. An Amsterdam-based company called Trendwatch.com scans worldwide to locate consumer trends, such as exclusivity for the masses, a trend they have coined as "Massclusivity" or "Five Star Living," a term they use to refer to the emerging market for combining the luxury of five-star hotels or cruise ships with residences or other real estate development.[36] (See the "Hospitality Focus" boxed section above.)

Gathering Information on International Environments

Collecting information on the broad environment in an international setting can be a significant challenge. Although most industrialized nations have similar sources of trend data, developing nations will not. Consequently, organizations often rely on a local firm to provide the kinds of broad environmental insights necessary for good strategic decision making, or turn to organizations such as the World Tourism Organization (WTO), which provides statistics and market reports for a wide variety of countries and regions of the world. In the lodging industry, Smith Travel Research and The Bench provide a comprehensive database of hotel performance information, while HVS (Hospitality Valuation Services) makes available a wide array of articles about all aspects of hospitality, including hotel investments, lending, operations, asset management, sales and marketing, and public relations.[37]

As an organization becomes involved in or even interested in international business opportunities, the amount of data that must be collected and analyzed increases dramatically. The economic, social, and political environments of various countries and continents can be very different. Africa, for example, must work with serious issues of hunger and poverty. As David DeVilliers, WTO deputy secretary-general, noted, "Passion for Africa and a belief in the power of tourism as a change agent can be major factors in responding to the challenges of poverty and inequity."[38] China faces the challenges of stress on tourism infrastructure as tourism accelerates. Beijing, home of the 2008 Summer Olympics, is tied with Venice on the list of top vacation destinations.[39] European travelers are directing their attention to Croatia, the Czech Republic, Poland, Istanbul, and even Albania, as these Eastern European countries begin to offer higher-quality hotels and tourist amenities in comparatively less expensive locations. Key environmental factors to any hospitality firm are:

1. The openness of a country's borders

2. The tourism infrastructure

3. The availability of tourism support systems

4. Frequency of airline routes

Of all the elements in the broad environment, perhaps societal differences are the most difficult to analyze, monitor, predict, and integrate into the strategic plan. For example, the explosion of immigrants from southern and southeastern Asia, Pakistan, Thailand, and India will shape any analysis of the global tourism environment. To illustrate the impact of population growth, Malcolm Gladwell, author of *The Tipping Point* and *Blink*, shows in a recent *New Yorker* article how dependency ratios—or the relationship between the number of people who aren't of working age (the young and the old) to those who are—can shape the social and economic future of a country. (See the "Hospitality Focus" boxed section on page 58.)

Differences also exist within the technological environment; however, they tend to be a little less severe because of global information sharing and standardized technologies in many industries. The primary differences stem from the fact that some countries are more advanced in certain technologies than are others. Consequently, the global technological environment also deserves attention. In particular, organizations should try to identify where the most-advanced technologies exist so that they can be learned and applied to internal firm processes. As will be discussed later, one of the best ways to do this is through joint ventures with firms that possess the best technologies.

This section has been a discussion of the broad environment and the importance of collecting information on broad environmental trends. The emphasis in this section has been on scanning, monitoring, predicting, and adapting to trends in the sociocultural, economic, political, and technological environments. Attention will now turn to an analysis of the operating environment.

HOSPITALITY FOCUS

SOCIETAL FACTORS IN IRELAND

According to Malcolm Galdwell, "Dependency ratios are best understood in the context of countries. In the past two decades, for instance, Ireland has gone from being one of the most economically backward countries in Western Europe to being one of the strongest: its growth rate has been roughly double that of the rest of Europe. There is no shortage of conventional explanations. Ireland joined the European Union. It opened up its markets. It invested well in education and economic infrastructure. It's a politically stable country with a sophisticated, mobile workforce.

But, as the Harvard economists David Bloom and David Canning suggest in their study of the "Celtic Tiger," of greater importance may have been a singular demographic fact. In 1979, restrictions on contraception that had been in place since Ireland's founding were lifted, and the birth rate began to fall. In 1970, the average Irish woman had 3.9 children. By the mid-1990s, that number was less than two. As a result, when the Irish children born in the 1960s hit the workforce, there weren't a lot of children in the generation just behind them. Ireland was suddenly free of the enormous social cost of supporting and educating and caring for a large dependent population. It was like a family of four in which, all of a sudden, the elder child is old enough to take care of her little brother and the mother can rejoin the workforce. Overnight, that family doubles its number of breadwinners and becomes much better off." Ireland's dependency ratio hit an all-time low in 2005, which corresponds precisely with the country's extraordinary economic surge.[40]

ANALYSIS OF EXTERNAL STAKEHOLDERS AND THE OPERATING ENVIRONMENT

The operating environment consists of stakeholders with whom organizations interact on a fairly regular basis, including customers, suppliers, competitors, government agencies and administrators, local communities, activist groups, unions, the media, and financial intermediaries. Not all stakeholders are equally important to firm success, nor do any of them play the same roles. Furthermore, stakeholders have varying levels and types of power to influence an organization.

This section will briefly explore the characteristics that determine the nature of an industry, as well as relationships that exist between an organization and its external stakeholders. It will discuss the power particular stakeholder groups have to influence firm behavior and success. To begin, three of these stakeholder groups will be discussed with regard to economic power in an industry: customers, suppliers, and competitors. Other factors determining the dynamics of industry competition will also be presented. Methods for managing external stakeholders and the operating environment will be presented. In particular, joint ventures and other cooperative relationships will be discussed, as well as political and economic strategies firms might pursue. Relationships with stakeholders and involvement in interorganizational relationships can be sustainable sources of competitive advantage.

Porter's Five Forces, Economic Power, and Industry Characteristics

The first step in any type of industry analysis is to determine the boundaries of the industry to be analyzed. Hospitality can be divided into several major industries, as illustrated in the following list:[41]

- Hotels
- Resorts
- Bed and Breakfasts (B&Bs)
- Inns
- Golf and country clubs
- Restaurants
- Foodservice
- Cruise lines
- Airlines
- Gaming/casinos
- Travel and tourism operators
- Online and regular travel agencies
- Global reservation distribution systems
- Trade associations
- Nightclubs
- Meeting and convention planners
- Time-share/vacation ownership
- Theme parks
- Spas
- Ski industry
- Real estate development for these enterprises
- Franchise development for these enterprises
- Consultants, attorneys and accountants, and vendors to all of these sectors
- Hospitality trade media

Of course, there is a lot of overlap. A big hotel in Reno, Nevada, may compete in the lodging, gaming, time-share, and restaurant industries. Many restaurant and lodging companies are involved in other types of food services. Time-shares are combined with regular lodging in the same resorts. In addition, although resorts are typically included in lodging, they may be better classified as a separate segment. Finally, the broad tourism industry is not well defined at all; it includes travel agencies, Web-based travel services, vacation planning, and outdoor services and activities.

Industries are often difficult to define, but in general they refer to a group of organizations that compete *directly* with one another to win customers or sales in the marketplace. Consequently, before an analysis is conducted, managers need to define precisely who they consider to be a part of the relevant industry group. Levels are also important. For example, a regional hotel chain may consider all hotels in a specific part of the world, say Central America, as its competitors. However, a single private resort may only consider other hotels in the same location when conducting an analysis of competitors. In contrast, another property may view resorts on the other side of the world in similar tropical settings to be competitors. The right definition of industry is the one that best fits the needs of the firm conducting the analysis.

Michael Porter, one of the most significant scholars in strategic management, developed a model that helps managers evaluate industry competition.[42] Porter described how the economic power of customers and suppliers influences the ability of a firm to achieve economic success. He reviewed factors that lead to high levels of competition among direct competitors. He also noted how entry barriers and the strength of substitute products increase or decrease the level of competition. These five areas of competitive analysis, referred to as the *five forces of competition*, are presented in Figure 2.3. According to Porter, the five forces largely determine the type and level of competition in an industry and, ultimately, the industry's profit potential.[43]

An analysis of the five forces is useful from several perspectives:

- First, by understanding how the five forces influence competition and profitability in an industry, a firm can better understand how to position itself relative to the forces, determine any sources of competitive advantage now and in the future, and estimate the profits that can be expected.

- For small and start-up businesses, a five forces analysis can reveal opportunities for market entry that will not attract the attention of the larger competitors.

- An organization can also conduct a five forces analysis of an industry before entry to determine the sector's attractiveness.

- If the firm is already involved in the industry, a five forces analysis can serve as a basis for deciding to leave it.

- Finally, company managers may decide to alter the five forces through specific actions.

Examples of such actions will be presented later in the chapter.

ECONOMIC POWER OF CUSTOMERS

Customers provide demand for products and services, without which an organization would cease to exist. Because customers can withhold demand, they have bargaining power, a form

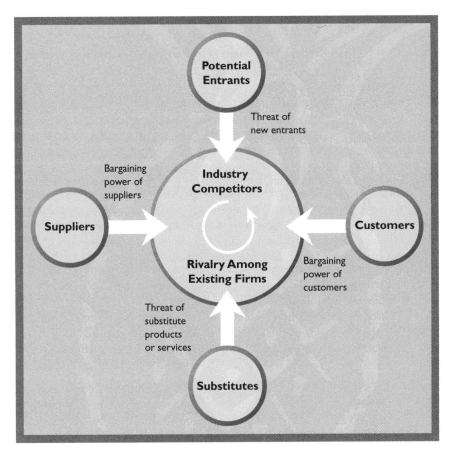

FIGURE 2.3 Porter's five forces model of industry competition
Source: Reprinted with the permission of The Free Press, a division of Simon & Schuster
Adult Publishing Group, from *Competitive Advantage: Creating and Sustaining Superior
Performance* by Michael E. Porter, p. 5. Copyright 1985, 1998 by Michael E. Porter. All
rights reserved.

of economic power. They can influence a firm's behavior. However, not all customers have the
same amount of bargaining power. For example, a tour operator who buys 60 percent of rooms
inventory of a given hotel has substantial influence over that operation. According to Porter,
customers tend to exhibit greater bargaining power under the following conditions:[44]

- *They are few in number.* This creates a situation in which an industry competitor can't afford to lose a customer. The number of customers to hospitality
  firms tends to be large, so this typically is not much of a factor.

- *They make high-volume (regular) purchases.* High-volume purchasers in the hospitality industry can often dictate contract terms, force price concessions,
  or demand special services, for example, when a corporate client books
  many room nights per year.

- *The products they are buying are undifferentiated (also known as standard or generic) and plentiful.* This means that customers can find alternative suppliers. Higher-end hotels tend to focus on creating differentiated elements to retain guests, while budget or economy hotels focus on efficient operation. All hotels worry about their products and services being too similar to those of their competitors, what is called *competitive convergence.*

- *They are highly motivated to get good deals.* This happens when they earn low profits or when a lot of what they buy comes from the same industry. Terms of a deal may greatly influence whether they will be successful in the next year. It is interesting to note that airlines are asking for concessions from the airports they use because they are making such low profits.[45]

- *They can easily integrate backward and thus become their own suppliers.* Vertical integration means that a firm moves forward to become its own customer or, in this case, backward to become its own supplier. TUI (Touristik Union International), the giant German company, owns hotels, airlines, travel agencies, and cruise ships.

- *They are not concerned about the quality of what they are buying.* This happens when the products or services don't influence the quality of the buyers own products or services. Because quality is not affected, customers will be interested primarily in obtaining the lowest possible price. For example, office supplies don't influence the quality of services provided by a high-quality hotel or restaurant.

- *They have an information advantage when compared to the firms from which they buy products and services.* Information creates bargaining power. If customers know a lot about the cost and profit structure of firms from whom they are buying, they can use this information to their advantage. For instance, Web-based discount hotel retailers have substantial information about the lodging companies from whom they buy inventory. This puts them at a relative advantage at the bargaining table.

- *They are well organized.* Sometimes weaker customers come together to increase their bargaining power. For example, tourists may join clubs or associations to increase their ability to get relevant information or to obtain discounts.

In combination, these forces determine the bargaining power of customers—that is, the degree to which customers exercise active influence over pricing and the direction of product-development efforts. Powerful customers must be given high priority in strategic management activities.

ECONOMIC POWER OF SUPPLIERS

Powerful suppliers can raise their prices and therefore reduce profitability levels in the buying industry. They can also exert influence and increase environmental uncertainty by threatening to raise prices, reducing the quality of goods or services provided, or not delivering supplies when needed. Many of the factors that give suppliers power are similar to the factors that give customers power, only in the opposite direction. In general, supplier power is greater under the following conditions:[46]

- *Suppliers are few in number, or, in the extreme case, there is only one supplier for a good or service.* This limits the ability of buying organizations to negotiate better prices, delivery arrangements, or quality. In the hospitality industry, this often applies to landowners at popular destinations and airline or cruise ship builders.

- *They sell products and services that cannot be substituted with other products and services.* If there are no substitutes, the buying industry is compelled to pay a higher price or accept less-favorable terms. Exotic, but popular, foods are often sold at very high prices, even to restaurants, because they are not substitutable.

- *They do not sell a large percentage of their products or services to the buying industry.* Because the buying industry is not an important customer, suppliers can reduce shipments during capacity shortages, ship partial orders or late orders, or refuse to accept orders at all, all of which can create turbulence for the buying industry, reduce profits, and increase competition.

- *They have a dependent customer.* In other words, the buying industry must have what the suppliers provide in order to provide its own services. In a literal way, restaurants must have the foods they prepare in order to remain in business; however, in most markets, the abundance of potential suppliers offsets this factor.

- *They have differentiated their products or in other ways made it costly to switch suppliers.* For example, smaller hotel companies sometimes contract with a reservation service to handle their bookings. If the company later chooses to purchase these services from a different supplier, it must remove the reservation system, purchase or contract for a new system, and retrain employees to use it.

- *They can easily integrate forward and thus compete directly with their former buyers.* This happened when PepsiCo. acquired several quick-service restaurants, including Taco Bell, KFC, and Pizza Hut.

- *They have an information advantage relative to the firms they are supplying.* If a supplier knows a lot about the cost and profit structure of firms to which it is selling, the supplier can use this information to its advantage. For instance, if a supplier knows that a buyer is making high profits, a more attractive sales price can probably be negotiated.

- *They are well organized.* Sometimes suppliers form associations to enhance their bargaining power. In a sense, employees who organize into a union are an example of increasing supplier power.

These forces combine to determine the strength of suppliers and the degree to which they can exert influence over the profits earned by firms in the industry.[47]

COMPETITION, CONCENTRATION, AND MONOPOLY POWER

Competitive moves by one firm affect other firms in the industry, which may incite retaliation or countermoves. In other words, competing firms have an *economic stake* in one another. Examples of competitive moves and countermoves include:

- Advertising programs
- Sales force expansions
- New-service introductions
- Capacity expansion
- Long-term contracts with customers

In most segments of the hospitality industry, competition is so intense that profitability may suffer. Some of the major forces that lead to high levels of competition include the following:[48]

- *There are many competitors in the industry, and none of them possess a dominant position.* Economists sometimes call this pure competition. In a situation of pure competition, organizations must work hard to maintain their positions, because customers have so many options. Consider how many lodging options a tourist has in one of the larger cities of the world.

- *The industry is growing slowly.* Slow industry growth leads to high levels of competition, because the only way to grow is through taking sales or market share from competitors. For example, the U.S. lodging industry reported a growth rate of around 5.1 percent in revenue per available room (RevPAR), a leading financial indicator for hotels.[49]

- *Products in the industry are not easily differentiated* (i.e., they are standard or generic). Lack of product differentiation puts a lot of pressure on prices and often leads to price-cutting strategies that appeal to customers but reduce the profitability of industry participants. High-end hotels try to differentiate, but they often appear to offer similar products and services, which can lead to pricing pressure.

- *High fixed costs exist*, such as those associated with large hotel properties, airlines, cruise lines, or theme parks. High fixed costs mean that firms are under pressure to increase sales to cover their costs and eventually earn profits. It is not easy to cut back on the inventory of rooms in the short term, so hoteliers will cut prices or increase marketing expenses to increase demand.

- *High exit barriers exist.* When exit barriers are high, firms may lose all or most of their investments in the industry when they withdraw from it. Therefore, they are more likely to remain in the sector even if profits are low or nonexistent. Some consider the hotel industry to be "under-demolished" because it is so difficult to take these high fixed-cost assets out of service.

The relative size of firms in an industry has a great deal to do with competitive dynamics. The first item in the previous list describes pure competition as a situation in which sales are spread out over many companies without a dominant firm or firms in the industry. This type of situation fosters competitive rivalry, which in theory is good for consumers, because it keeps prices at relatively low levels. At the other extreme are *monopoly* situations, in which one company dominates all others in a sector. Monopolists may misuse their dominant positions through activities such as engaging in unfair practices that limit the ability of competitors to compete, erecting entry barriers to keep new competitors out of the industry, or charging too much for products or services. Consequently, some governments intervene to break up monopolies or penalize them for unfair practices. This is why AT&T was broken up, and why Microsoft has struggled with litigation.

Most segments of the hospitality industry are composed of a multitude of competitors. In the lodging industry, even the giants like InterContinental Hotel Group, Accor, Starwood, Hilton Hotels, and Marriott, despite their market power, could not be classified as monopoly players. However, some industries are often characterized by the existence of a few very large firms. These industries are called *oligopolies*. The theme park and cruise industries are good examples of oligopolies. Some analysts might classify the airline industry as an oligopoly. This is probably an accurate classification if major geographic regions are considered separately. For example, the airline industries in the United States, the European Union, and Asia are dominated by a few large carriers.

Firms in oligopolies may informally cooperate with each other by not pursuing radical departures from existing pricing. They do this because they have learned that price wars hurt the profitability of the entire industry. Formal price-fixing, which is illegal in several countries, is called collusion. For example, British Airways colluded with rival Virgin Atlantic to fix prices on long-haul routes, resulting in fines of millions of pounds. Conversely, some oligopolies are known for severe price-cutting and high levels of competition. The U.S. airline industry has struggled for many years as a result of price wars. If firms in an oligopoly sell products that are difficult to differentiate, they are especially prone to a high level of competitive rivalry.

One of the global factors resulting in the creation of increasingly dominant companies and oligopolies is industry consolidation. Competitors in most industrialized countries are merging together to form larger companies with more market power. The major lodging, airline, and restaurant companies have engaged in many consolidating acquisitions. The acquisition of Hilton Hotels Corporation by the private equity firm Blackstone Group is one example. (See the "Hospitality Focus" boxed section on page 66.)

Richard D'Aveni has identified industries that experience what he calls *hypercompetition*, a condition of rapidly escalating competition based on price, quality, first-mover actions, defensive moves to protect markets, formation of strategic alliances, and reliance on wealthy parent companies.[50] Short product life cycles, international competitors, global market opportunities, and deep pockets are causing some industries to stay in turmoil. The results of efforts to differentiate are not sustainable, because competitors match each other move for move. Competitive practices are forcing profits to lower and lower levels. Airlines are clearly hypercompetitive.

Some managers might argue that the lodging industry also has characteristics of hypercompetition. In a recent study of competitive hotel pricing, efforts to drop prices led to small increases in hotel market share, but did not result in increased sales revenue, suggesting that demand for lodging products may be price inelastic.[51] In light of this research, defensive moves that lead to price discounts appear to harm all players in the industry, as they move away from differentiation and toward commodity pricing—hence a hypercompetitive condition of escalating competition.

INDUSTRY CONSOLIDATION: BLACKSTONE GROUP ACQUIRES HILTON HOTELS CORP.

HOSPITALITY FOCUS

The estimated $26 billion dollar acquisition of Hilton Hotels Corp. follows a series of acquisitions made by the Blackstone Group, provider of financial advisory services and a leading global alternative asset manager. In recent years, the firm has acquired Wyndham International, MeriStar Hospitality, and Travelport, the parent of the Orbitz online travel management company and Galileo global distribution system. The firm views Hilton as an "important strategic investment." Before the Hilton acquisition, Blackstone owned more than 100,000 hotel rooms in the United States and Europe, including La Quinta Inns and Suites and LXR Luxury Resorts and Hotels. The company's alternative asset management businesses include the management of corporate private equity funds, proprietary hedge funds, senior debt funds, mezzanine funds, and closed-end mutual funds.[52]

Figure 2.4 contains an abbreviated example of a five forces analysis for the U.S. airline industry. In addition to the three forces just described, the figure also includes the similarity of substitute products, as well as barriers that keep new competitors from entering an industry. These forces will now be discussed.

ENTRY BARRIERS AND SUBSTITUTES

Several forces determine how easy it is to enter an industry, and therefore how many new entrants can be expected. New entrants increase competition in a sector, which may drive down prices and profits. The new entrants may add capacity, introduce new products or processes, and bring a fresh perspective and new ideas—all of which can drive down prices, increase costs, or both. Forces that keep new competitors out, providing a level of protection for existing competitors, are called entry barriers. Examples of entry barriers found in many industries include:

Economies of scale. Economies of scale occur when it is more efficient to provide a service at higher volume. For example, the larger hotels enjoy economies of scale because standard features such as the front desk and communications systems can service multiple rooms simultaneously. If a new entrant will be at a substantial cost disadvantage because of size, few firms will enter.

Capital requirements. Also known as start-up costs, high capital requirements can prevent a small competitor from entering an industry. High capital requirements are sometimes associated with economies of scale, because new entrants need to invest in a large facility to be cost competitive. However, high capital requirements also result from research-and-development costs, start-up losses, or expenses associated with extending credit to customers. In the hospitality industry, high capital requirements tend to be closely linked to economies of scale.

Product differentiation. Established firms enjoy a loyal customer base, which comes from many years of past advertising, customer service, loyalty programs,

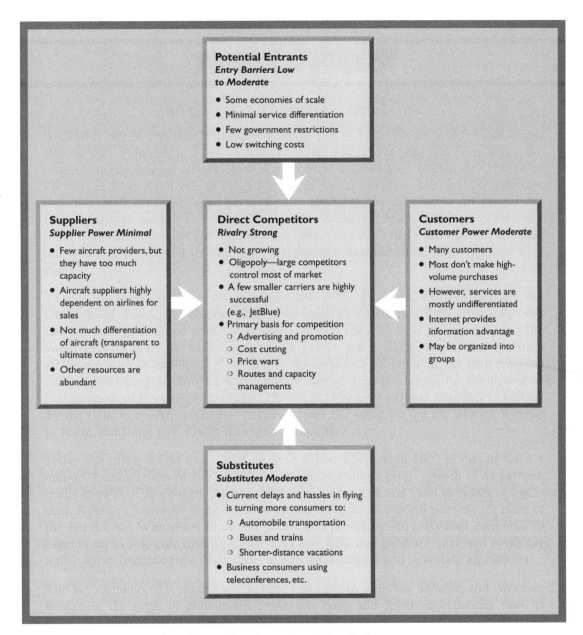

Potential Entrants
*Entry Barriers Low
to Moderate*

- Some economies of scale
- Minimal service differentiation
- Few government restrictions
- Low switching costs

Suppliers
Supplier Power Minimal

- Few aircraft providers, but they have too much capacity
- Aircraft suppliers highly dependent on airlines for sales
- Not much differentiation of aircraft (transparent to ultimate consumer)
- Other resources are abundant

Direct Competitors
Rivalry Strong

- Not growing
- Oligopoly—large competitors control most of market
- A few smaller carriers are highly successful (e.g., JetBlue)
- Primary basis for competition
  - Advertising and promotion
  - Cost cutting
  - Price wars
  - Routes and capacity managements

Customers
Customer Power Moderate

- Many customers
- Most don't make high-volume purchases
- However, services are mostly undifferentiated
- Internet provides information advantage
- May be organized into groups

Substitutes
Substitutes Moderate

- Current delays and hassles in flying is turning more consumers to:
  - Automobile transportation
  - Buses and trains
  - Shorter-distance vacations
- Business consumers using teleconferences, etc.

FIGURE 2.4 **Porter's five forces for the U.S. airline industry**

word of mouth, or simply being one of the first competitors in a particular market. These factors make it very difficult for a new entrant to compete.

High switching costs. Switching costs were mentioned earlier in our discussion of supplier and buyer power, but they can also serve as an entry barrier to protect competing firms. Switching costs are generally low in hospitality firms, as customers can select a new firm with each stay, flight, or meal. Loyalty and frequent flyer programs might increase the cost of switching for some buyers.

Access to distribution channels. In industries where supply networks are strong and competition is intense, access to distribution channels may effectively thwart new entry. Distribution channels in the hospitality industry tend to be open to new competitors. However, existing hotels or restaurants in a market can put pressure on suppliers not to extend the same services or prices to newcomers.

Inimitable resources. Resources that are possessed by industry participants but are difficult or impossible to duplicate completely may include patents, favorable locations, proprietary service technology, government subsidies, or access to scarce raw materials such as land. Because these types of advantages are difficult or impossible for new entrants to duplicate in the short term, they often discourage entry.

Government policy. Sometimes governments limit entry into an industry, effectively preventing new competition. For instance, many Native American tribes enjoy exclusive rights to open casinos on their reservations, while developers in the surrounding communities do not enjoy the same privilege.[53] For many years, airlines enjoyed a protected status, with their routes and prices protected from competitive pressures. However, when the airline industry became deregulated, many new competitors entered, and existing competitors greatly expanded their routes. These forces resulted in fare wars and lower profitability for all of the firms in the industry. Currently, airline companies are consolidating to build competitive strength.[54]

Taken together, these forces can result in high, medium, or low barriers. Examples of industries that traditionally are associated with high barriers to entry are aircraft manufacturing (technology, capital costs, reputation) and automobile manufacturing (capital costs, distribution, brand names). Medium barriers are associated with industries such as household appliances, cosmetics, and books. Low entry barriers are found in most service industries, such as lodging, restaurants, and even airlines.[55]

Substitute products are another force outside of the industry that can influence the level of industry competition. If organizations provide goods or services that are readily substitutable for the goods and services provided by an industry, these organizations become indirect competitors. Close substitutes serve the same function for customers and can place a ceiling on the price that can be charged for a good or service.[56] In the service sector, credit unions are substitutes for banks, and rapid rail travel is a substitute for airline travel. Close substitutes also set new performance standards.

Whether a product or service qualifies as a substitute depends on how the boundaries of the industry are drawn. For example, there are few substitutes for the lodging industry in general. Perhaps staying with friends or relatives or camping would qualify. However, it may be more helpful to analyze a particular segment of the lodging industry, such as the midscale segment. If the industry is defined as the midscale segment, then the other segments would become substitutes. This is relevant because the lower segment may improve its services to the extent that consumers would be unwilling to pay the price differential to stay in a midscale hotel. Consequently, midscale hotels need to be aware of and stay ahead of what is happening in the budget segment.

For example, Jinjiang Inn, China's largest budget hotelier, along with Home Inn and Motel 168, are expanding rapidly. A relatively new concept in China, experts define these budget hotels as having "a two-star lobby, three-star rooms, and four-star beds."[57] Regardless of how industries are defined, organizations should pay close attention to the actions of the producers of close substitutes when formulating and implementing strategies.

External Stakeholders, Formal Power, and Political Influence

The emphasis throughout this section so far has been on economics and bargaining power. Economic analysis is important to strategic management. However, economic power is not the only type of power available to stakeholders, nor do economic factors completely determine the competitiveness of organizations. Figure 2.5 demonstrates that stakeholders can be classified based on their stakes in the organization and the type of influence they have. Such an analysis can help managers understand both the needs and the potential power of their key stakeholders. Internal stakeholders are included in Figure 2.5 for completeness, although our focus in this section will be on external stakeholders.

In Figure 2.5, groups and individuals can have an ownership stake, an economic stake, or a social stake. An *ownership stake* means that a stakeholder's own wealth depends on the value of the company and its activities. For example, a hotel holding company depends on the operating units for income. Stakeholders also can be *economically dependent* without ownership. For example, employees receive a salary, debtholders receive interest payments, governments collect tax revenues, customers may depend on what they purchase to produce their own products, and suppliers receive payments for goods and services provided to the company. Finally, a social stake describes groups that are not directly linked to the organization but are interested in ensuring that the organization behaves in a manner that they believe is *socially responsible*. These are the watchdogs of our modern social order, such as Greenpeace and The Sierra Club.

On the influence side, groups and individuals may enjoy formal power, economic power, or political power. *Formal power* means stakeholders have a legal or contractual right to make decisions for some part of the company. Regulatory agencies have formal power. *Economic power* is derived from the ability to withhold services, products, capital, revenues, or business transactions that the firm values. The discussion of Porter's five forces was largely a discussion of economic power. Finally, *political power* comes from the ability to persuade lawmakers, society, or regulatory agencies to influence the behavior of organizations. Notice that some stakeholders have more than one source of power. For example, creditors sometimes have both economic and formal influence because they have formal contracts and may also have a seat on the company's board of directors.

In general, powerful stakeholders should be given more attention during strategy formulation and implementation. The most important external stakeholders are those with the greatest impact on the firm's ability to survive and prosper. In for-profit organizations, the most important external stakeholders are typically customers.[58] For example, Four Seasons envisions everything it does as a means to "satisfy the needs and tastes of our discriminating customers."[59] At Four Seasons, satisfaction of customers is the key to satisfying other stakeholders. Tourism operations must take into consideration residents' attitudes and perceptions in any effort to plan and implement a destination attraction. This social stakeholder group is often the key

		Formal (Contractual or Regulatory)	Economic	Political
Stake in the organization	**Ownership**	Managers and directors who own stock in organization Stockholders in general Sole proprietors Alliance or joint venture partners	Other companies that own stock in the organization	Governments with ownership stake
	Economic	All paid managers and directors of for-profit and nonprofit firms Joint venture partners Creditors Internal revenue service	Employees Customers Suppliers Creditors Competitors	Competitors Foreign governments Local communities
	Social	Regulatory agencies Unpaid trustees or managers of nonprofit organizations	Financial community at large (e.g., large brokerage houses, fund managers, and analysts)	Activist groups (e.g., Green peace International) Government leaders The media Residents

Influence on Behavior

FIGURE 2.5 Typical roles of various stakeholders
Source: Adapted from R. E. Freeman, *Strategic Management: A Stakeholder Approach* (Boston: Pittman, 1984), p. 63.
Copyright 1984 by R. Edward Freeman. All rights reserved.

to achieving intelligent development. Hence, the key to effective stakeholder management is that while some stakeholders are given more attention, none of the important stakeholders is ignored. In fact, consideration of a wide range of stakeholders can sometimes lead to creative strategies through partnerships and alliances.

MANAGING THE OPERATING ENVIRONMENT

The operating environment may seem overwhelming to many managers. Powerful customers or suppliers can limit organizational success and profitability. Powerful competitors can make it difficult to remain competitive. Substitute products put pressure on prices and other product features. When entry barriers are low, new competitors enter the industry on a regular basis. Finally, external stakeholders can be powerful and difficult to deal with, based not only on

TABLE 2.4 **Tactics for Managing External Stakeholders**

ECONOMIC ACTIONS	POLITICAL ACTIONS	PARTNERING ACTIONS
Increasing advertising	Trade associations	Joint ventures
New-product launches	Industry panels	Networks
Cost-reduction efforts	Lobbying	Consortia
New service methods	Local business organizations (e.g., Chamber of Commerce)	Trade associations
Quality improvements		Alliances
		Interlocking directorates

economic power, but on formal or political power as well. However, responding to challenges such as these defines the success of a manager. Fortunately, organizations can pursue a variety of actions to make their operating environments less hostile and thus increase the likelihood of organizational success. These actions tend to fall into three broad categories: economic actions, political actions, and partnering actions (see Table 2.4).

Economic Actions

Firms may take a variety of economic actions to offset forces in the operating environment. For example, if entry barriers are low, companies may work to erect new entry barriers that prevent other firms from entering, thus preserving or stabilizing industry profitability. Although a difficult task, the erection of entry barriers can be accomplished through actions such as increasing advertising to create product differentiation or by constructing larger facilities to achieve economies of scale. For example, large lodging companies set up centralized reservation centers or purchasing departments that process large numbers of transactions somewhat more efficiently than do small-volume companies. Similarly, multiunit restaurant chains can afford more elaborate advertising campaigns. As another entry barrier, some firms make it unattractive for customers to switch. For example, hotels and airlines set up consumer loyalty programs that encourage repeat consumption. InterContinental Hotels boasts more than 33 million members in its Priority Club Rewards program, considered to be the first, largest, and fastest-growing guest loyalty program in the hotel industry.[60] Nevertheless, some have suggested that airline mileage programs are losing much of their value due to more fees, higher award prices, fewer available seats, and complex redemption rules.[61] Clearly, how a firm implements its strategic efforts to reduce switching can make all the difference.

Competitive Tactics

Industry rivals apply a variety of competitive tactics in order to win market share, increase revenues, and increase profits at the expense of rivals. Competitive tactics include advertising, new-product launches, cost-reduction efforts, new service methods, and quality improvements, to name a few. Typically, a particular industry can be characterized by the dominance of one or more of these tools. For example, the chain restaurant industry is characterized by high levels of advertising as a competitive weapon. In addition, the entrance of international competitors into national and regional hospitality markets has placed an increasing emphasis on product differentiation through high levels of quality. Other common competitive tactics include providing high levels of customer service and achieving economies of scale (which can lead to lower costs, thus allowing lower prices to customers). Notice that some of these competitive tactics can also lead to the erection of entry barriers, as previously discussed.

Competitive benchmarking is a popular technique for keeping up with competitors. *Benchmarking* is a tool for assessing the best practices of direct competitors and firms in similar industries, then using the resulting stretch objectives as design criteria for attempting to change organizational performance.[62] Xerox pioneered competitive benchmarking in the United States upon discovering that competitors were selling products at prices that were equal to Xerox's costs of producing them. The company responded by establishing benchmarks as a fundamental part of its business planning.[63] In the lodging industry, a wide variety of consulting firms and universities perform benchmarking activities for governments and associations. One example of this type of industry benchmarking was a study conducted by Cornell University with the financial support of American Express and the American Hotel Foundation.[64]

While benchmarking may help a company improve elements of its operations, it will not help a firm gain competitive advantage. Benchmarking is a little like shooting at a moving target. While a firm is shooting, the target is moving. If an organization benchmarks against an industry leader, that leader will probably have moved on by the time the benchmark is achieved. Marriott International, for example, created a systemwide leadership development program that has since moved beyond building talented managers to considering the ways in which the organization can be developed and improved to make the best use of its human talent.[65] Strategic thinking, described in Chapter 1, can help an organization move beyond what competitors are doing to set new standards and pursue new strategies.

Political Strategies

Political strategies include all organizational activities that have as one of their objectives the creation of a friendlier political climate for the organization. Many large organizations hire lobbyists to represent their views to political leaders. While lobbying can be part of a political strategy, it is only a small part of the bigger political picture. Companies may donate to political causes or parties, special-interest groups, or charities. They may pursue community-relations efforts or

COLLECTIVE EFFORTS BY THE TRAVEL INDUSTRY ASSOCIATION (TIA)

The TIA has as its mission to represent the entire U.S. travel industry by promoting and facilitating increased travel to and within the United States. The organization seeks to develop a unified travel industry identity and gain support from policy makers at all levels of government. Key objectives of the association include:

Objectives

Promote a wider understanding of travel and tourism as a major industry that contributes to the economic, cultural, and social well-being of the nation.

- Improve domestic and international travelers' experiences, including gaining access to, arriving in, traveling within, and departing the United States.
- Develop, coordinate, and implement the industry's umbrella marketing efforts to promote travel to and within the U.S.
- Enhance TIA's position as the authoritative source for travel industry information and research.
- Promote travel industry cohesion and provide communications forums for industry leaders.
- Pursue and influence policies, programs and legislation that are responsive to the needs of the industry as a whole.[66]

become involved in community service. Most large organizations have public-relations officers, and many do public-relations advertising.

Some scholars have suggested that individual firm lobbying efforts are often ineffective. Fragmented involvement, in which each company represents its own interests, has resulted in a free-for-all, and the collective interests of business have been the real loser.[67] One suggestion for fixing this problem is increased efforts to strengthen collective institutions such as the Travel Industry Association (TIA) or the National Restaurant Association (NRA). (See the "Hospitality Focus" boxed section above.)

Collective activity, as exhibited by TIA's objectives, may include membership in trade associations, chambers of commerce, and industry and labor panels. Firms join associations to have access to information and to obtain legitimacy, acceptance, and influence.[68] Trade associations, although not as powerful in the United States as in Japan and Europe, often serve an information-management and monitoring purpose for member firms. They provide information and interpretation of legislative and regulatory trends, may collect market research, and sometimes provide an informal mechanism for exchanging information about competitors. Companies may also join industry and labor panels to manage negotiations with activist groups and unions. In addition, competitors may form alliances of many types in an effort to influence stakeholders, such as activist groups, unions, the media, or local communities.

Partnering with External Stakeholders

Organizations may partner for political reasons; however, many other types of partnerships exist. Often firms partner to obtain complementary technologies or knowledge. As mentioned previously, a firm's most valuable resources may extend beyond the boundaries of the company.[69] Table 2.5 lists and describes common forms of *interorganizational relationships*, which is a term that includes many types of organizational cooperation,[70] including the following:

TABLE 2.5 Common Forms of Interorganizational Relationships

INTERORGANIZATIONAL FORM	DESCRIPTION
Joint Venture	An entity that is created when two or more firms pool a portion of their resources to create a separate, jointly owned entity.
Network	A hub-and-wheel configuration with a local firm at the hub organizing the interdependencies of a complex array of firms.
Consortia (Cooperative Partnerships)	Specialized joint ventures encompassing many different arrangements. Consortia are often a group of firms oriented toward problem solving and technology development, such as R&D consortia.
Alliance	An arrangement between two or more firms that establishes an exchange relationship but has no joint ownership involved.
Trade Association	Organizations (typically nonprofit) that are formed by firms in the same industry to collect and disseminate trade information, offer legal and technical advice, furnish industry-related training, and provide a platform for collective lobbying.
Interlocking Directorate	Occurs when a director or executive of one firm sits on the board of a second firm or when two firms have directors who also serve on the board of a third firm. Interlocking directorates serve as a mechanism for interfirm information sharing and cooperation.

Source: Adapted from *Journal of Management*, Vol. 26, B. B. Barringer and J. S. Harrison, "Walking a Tightrope: Creating Value Through Interorganizational Relationships," p. 383, Copyright 2000, with permission from Elsevier.

- Joint ventures
- Networks
- Consortia
- Trade associations
- Alliances
- Interlocking directorates

A *joint venture* is created when two or more firms pool their resources to create a separate, jointly owned organization.[71] Joint ventures are often formed to gain access to international markets or to pursue projects that were not mainstream to the organizations involved.[72] For example, Britain's Hilton Group PLC and India's Blue Coast Hotels formed a joint venture to develop first-class and luxury hotels and resorts in India.[73] They are also used to pursue a wide variety of strategic objectives, including combining operations to gain scale economies or developing new services.[74]

Networks are constellations of businesses that organize through the establishment of social, rather than legally binding, contracts.[75] Typically, a focal organization sits at the hub of the network and facilitates the coordination of business activities for a wide array of other organizations. Each firm focuses on what it does best, allowing for the development of distinctive competencies. A special type of network form, common in Japan, is called a *keiretsu,* which is organized around an industry and works in much the same way as other networks; however, firms in a keiretsu often hold ownership interests in one another. Lodging firms in other countries are often linked in elaborate networks in which property ownership, branding, and management of operations are shared among competitors. They are not as large as the Japanese keiretsu, but they accomplish many of the same purposes.

Consortia or *cooperative partnerships* consist of a group of firms that have similar needs and band together to create an entity to satisfy those needs. By banding together, these firms are able to accomplish much more research more affordably than any one or a small group of firms could accomplish on its own. Similar in many ways to consortia, *trade associations* typically are nonprofit organizations formed within industries to collect and disseminate information, offer legal or accounting services, furnish training, and provide joint lobbying efforts.[76] Cruise Lines International Association (CLIA) is an example of an association dedicated to the promotion and growth of the cruise industry. CLIA focuses on industry issues like safety, public health, environmental responsibility, security, medical facilities, passenger protection, and legislative activities.[77] The primary advantages of belonging to a trade association are collective lobbying, learning, and cost savings through combining efforts in certain areas.

Alliances are agreements among two or more firms that establish some sort of exchange arrangement but involve no joint ownership.[78] They are sometimes informal and do not involve the creation of a new entity. A typical *Fortune* 500 company has 60 strategic alliances.[79] Walt Disney Company and Kellogg Company, the world's leading producer of cereals, formed an alliance in which Mickey Mouse and other Disney characters will show up on everything from cereal boxes to toothbrushes.[80] In the lodging industry, Fairmont Hotels and Resorts teamed up with the luggage forwarder Virtual Bellhop to create a program in which its guests have their luggage picked up for them at their homes and delivered to their destinations.[81] Fairmont also teamed up with Porsche in a cross-marketing program that provides high-end consumers with a Porsche driving experience.[82]

Interlocking directorates occur when an executive or director of one firm sits on the board of directors of another firm, or when executives or directors of two different companies sit on the board of a third company.[83] In the United States, the *Clayton Antitrust Act of 1914* prohibits competitors from sitting on each other's boards. However, they are allowed to sit on the board of a third company. The primary advantage of interlocking directorates is the potential for what is referred to as *co-optation*, defined as drawing resources from other firms to achieve stability and continued existence.[84] For example, if a firm develops a new technology, the interlocking director would have access to this information. Also, an organization may add to its board a director from a financial institution in an effort to facilitate financing.

The common characteristic behind all of these forms of interorganizational relationships is that they are an effort to combine resources, knowledge, or power to benefit each participant. They involve partnering and resource sharing. While the emphasis in much of this chapter has been on analysis of the environment in order to formulate strategy, the notion of partnering will be a common theme throughout the rest of this book. Successful interorganizational relationships can be an important source of sustainable competitive advantage.

Information collected during environmental analysis is used in every aspect of strategic planning, including the creation of strategic direction, formulation of strategies, and creation of implementation plans and control systems. Organizations can pursue a variety of economic, political, and partnering actions to make their operating environments more hospitable. The next chapter will explore internal aspects of organizations and the ability of firm resources to provide other sources of sustainable competitive advantage.

KEY POINTS SUMMARY

- The most important elements in the broad environment are sociocultural influences, economic influences, technological influences, and political influences. The broad environment can have a tremendous impact on a firm and its operating environment; however, individual firms typically have only a marginal impact on this environment.

- The distinction between a trend and a fad is important when examining the broad environment. Trends are long-term changes or patterns that are substantial to the society and last, whereas a fad is a short-term cultural moment. Fads fade fast while a trend becomes central to the broad culture.

- Analysis of society is important, because broad societal changes and trends can provide opportunities for organizations and enhance a firm's awareness of the attitudes of society. A positive organizational reputation among stakeholders, such as customers and suppliers, and the avoidance of restrictive legislation can also be obtained by maintaining an awareness of shifting social trends.

- Economic forces such as economic growth, interest rates, availability of credit, inflation rates, foreign-exchange rates, and foreign-trade balances are among the most critical economic factors. Economic forces play a key role in determining demand patterns and cost characteristics within industries.

- Organizations should also track political forces, particularly as they relate to increases and decreases in the degree of regulation and privatization. Governments can encourage new business in a variety of ways.

- Most industrialized nations have comparable government entities. Involvement in more than one country further increases the number of relevant government forces.

- Although one organization may not be able to alter dramatically major political forces, it may have considerable impact within its own specific industries and operating domain. Consequently, major political forces are considered a part of the broad environment, while government agencies and administrators are considered a part of the operating environment.

- Technological forces in the broad environment have the power to create and destroy entire industries. In general: (1) innovations usually arise from existing technologies; (2) most products and processes evolve toward a dominant design; and (3) radical innovations tend to come from outside the established group of competitors. An understanding of these characteristics can help a manager develop a system for monitoring technology trends.

- The operating environment includes stakeholders such as customers, suppliers, competitors, government agencies and administrators, local communities, activist groups, the media, unions, and financial intermediaries.

- One important distinction between the operating and broad environments is that the operating environment is subject to a high level of organizational influence, while the broad environment is not.

- The nature and level of competition in an industry is dependent on competitive forces that determine rivalry, such as the number of competitors and the growth rate of the industry, as well as the strength of customers and suppliers, the height of entry barriers, and the availability of substitute products or services. These competitive forces are known collectively as the five forces of competition.

- Tactics for influencing stakeholders and the operating environment often involve interorganizational relationships, including joint ventures, networks, consortia, alliances, trade associations, and interlocking directorates.

- Other important tactics include contracting, various forms of stakeholder involvement in organizational processes and decisions, and exercising political influence to promote favorable regulations.

- Analysis of external stakeholders and the broad environment can result in the identification of opportunities and threats, which are then considered by managers as they establish a strategic direction and develop and implement strategies.

• At this point, you should begin to appreciate that stakeholder analysis and management is a difficult and comprehensive management task. The themes, tools, and ideas contained in this chapter will be applied throughout the remaining chapters. The next chapter will focus on the internal organization and resource management.

REVIEW QUESTIONS

1. Why is analysis of the broad environment important for effective strategic management?

2. What are the major components of the broad environment? Give an example of a trend in each area that could affect the welfare of a business organization.

3. What is the difference between a trend and a fad? Give an example of a fad.

4. Why should sociocultural influences be monitored? What are some of the current sociocultural forces in Europe?

5. What are some of the most important factors to track in the global economy? Why are these factors important to organizations?

6. Explain the three characteristics of technological innovation and how an understanding of those characteristics can be used to develop a technological forecasting process.

7. What are the major differences between the operating and broad environments? Can an organization effectively influence its broad environment? Its operating environment?

8. What are the five forces of competition? Describe their potential influence on competition in an industry with which you are familiar (except airlines).

9. What are the primary factors that make some stakeholders more important than others? How do management techniques for high-priority stakeholders differ from those of low-priority stakeholders? Give examples.

10. Describe the major forms of interorganizational relationships, and provide one possible advantage of each form.

CRITICAL THINKING AND APPLICATION QUESTIONS

1. Identify recent sociocultural, economic, political, and technological trends that significantly affect hospitality organizations. List the key trends. Now, briefly explain the two most critical trends affecting the hospitality industry and why. What fads

do you currently see in the industry? You may find the trendwatcher.com web site useful in your search for trends.

2. Select a company. Now complete Table 2.3 for the company you selected. Based on what the table assessment suggests, which opportunities and threats should the company monitor carefully, and which should it just scan from time to time? Why?

3. Conduct a five forces model for the industry of your choice (except airlines). Clearly define your industry before you begin (in other words, how broadly are you defining your industry?). To guide your analysis, begin with the bargaining power of buyers and suppliers. Who are the buyers and suppliers? Discuss whether they have bargaining power. Who are your competitors? What are the barriers to entry into this industry? What other substitutes limit the sales and profits for firms in this industry? When discussing the implications of your five forces model, ask yourself the following questions:

   a. Which forces of competition are most threatening now? Which do you expect will change over the next five years?

   b. What are the implications in terms of profit margins in the industry today? Over the next five years?

   c. What actions does this analysis suggest a current industry player should implement in order to strengthen their competitive strategy?

CHAPTER 3

STRATEGIC DIRECTION

YOU SHOULD BE ABLE TO DO THE FOLLOWING
AFTER READING THIS CHAPTER:

1. Know the key questions managers must ask and answer to create a strategic direction.

2. Understand the challenge of structural inertia and how it limits organizations.

3. Explain the difference between a vision and mission statement, and why values are important to organizational decision makers.

4. List the five different components of social responsibility.

5. Define enterprise strategy and give examples of firms that link ethics and strategy.

6. Explain the five ethical frames of reference and how they shape values.

FEATURE STORY

DIRECTION SETTING WITH DELIGHT

The Mandarin Oriental Hotel Group is an international luxury hotel investment and management group with 34 hotels and resorts worldwide, including 14 under development. The group has an inventory of 9,500 rooms in 20 countries.

OUR AIM

The Mandarin Oriental's aim is to be recognized as one of the best global luxury hotel groups, providing exceptional customer satisfaction in each of its hotels.

OUR MISSION

Our mission is to completely delight and satisfy our guests. We are committed to making a difference every day, continually getting better to keep us the best.

The word DELIGHT is the perfect acronym for everything that Mandarin Oriental represents:

D Distinctive

E Exotic

L Lively

I Imaginative

G Guest-centered

H Harmonious

T Time-giving

OUR GUIDING PRINCIPLES

Delighting our guests: We will strive to understand our client and guest needs by listening to their requirements and responding in a competent, accurate, and timely fashion. We will design and deliver our services and products to address their needs. In fact, we are committed to exceeding their expectations by surprising them with our ability to anticipate and fulfill their wishes.

Working together as colleagues: We will emphasize the sharing of responsibility, accountability, and recognition through a climate of teamwork. By working together as colleagues and by treating each other with mutual respect and trust, we will all contribute to the Group's overall success more productively than if we worked alone.

Promoting a climate of enthusiasm: We are committed to everyone at Mandarin Oriental by providing a caring, motivating, and rewarding environment. As an industry leader, we are committed to bringing out the best in our people through effective training and meaningful career and personal development, and by encouraging individuality and initiative.

Being the best: We will be an innovative leader in the hotel industry and will continually improve our products and services. We will seek from our suppliers the highest-quality products and services at the best value.

Delivering shareholder value: We are committed to being a growing company. Our successes will result in investment returns, which are consistently among the best in the hotel industry.

Playing by the rules: We will maintain integrity, fairness, and honesty in both our internal and external relationships and will consistently live up to our commitments.

Acting with responsibility: We will actively participate in the improvement of the environment, just as we will be responsible members of our communities and industry organizations.

THE FAN

The Mandarin Oriental selected a fan as a symbol to embody the hotel group's luxurious and elegant image yet still reflect each hotel's local charm. Each hotel has a specially designed and unique fan. The group sees the fan as a symbol of its Oriental culture without being overly ethnic. The fan logo symbolizes luxury, elegance, and comfort.[1]

DISCUSSION QUESTIONS:

1. What do the Mandarin Oriental's aim and mission statements reveal about this company?

2. What do the guiding principles reveal about who are the key stakeholders to this hotel group?

INTRODUCTION

The Mandarin Oriental statements of aim, mission, and principles are excellent examples of the major components of strategic direction. We see that Mandarin Oriental has a mission that is centered on completely delighting and satisfying its customers, a set of guiding principles that include the way the company and its colleagues will act, and a logo that symbolizes a shared cultural identity. The group's vision, another element of strategic direction, is made clear in its major aim to be one of the best luxury hotel groups worldwide. *Strategic direction* is established and communicated through tools such as visions, missions, and values, all of which will be discussed in this chapter.

There are no widely accepted guidelines managers use to provide strategic direction. In some companies, little is written down, as is the case for the Hongkong and Shanghai Hotels Limited, parent company of the Peninsula Hotel Group and a competitor of Mandarin Oriental. In contrast to the Mandarin's detailed statements of values and mission, their competitor considers its objective as increasing shareholder value while preserving and enhancing the quality of service and the Peninsula brand name. While some companies adopt formal statements of vision, mission, and values, others may mix and match labels and even confuse the terms, calling a vision a mission and vice versa.

Regardless of the labels and the medium of communication, high-performing companies tend to create an organizational identity that is understood by both internal and external stakeholders. On the inside, a well-established organizational identity can provide guidance to managers at all levels as they make strategic decisions.[2] In addition, communicating strategic direction to external stakeholders can increase their understanding of the motives of the organization, and it may also facilitate the creation of interorganizational relationships, because potential partners have a greater ability to judge the existence of common goals. One corporate president stated that "his company's mission statement has helped create a 'partnering attitude' instead of an adversarial relationship" between his company and its customers.[3]

CREATING A STRATEGIC DIRECTION

Top managers are charged with the responsibility of providing long-term direction for their organizations, while balancing the competing interests of key stakeholders. One of the most vital questions management can ask is "Who are we?"[4] A clear understanding of the business is the starting point of all strategic planning and management.[5]

It provides a framework for evaluating the effects of planned change and for planning the steps needed to move the organization forward. When defining the current state of the business, the question "What is our business?" should be answered from three perspectives: (1) Who is being satisfied? (2) What is being satisfied?, and (3) How are customer needs satisfied?[6] The first question refers to the markets that an organization serves; the second question deals with the specific services

HOTEL INDIGO DEFINES ITS BUSINESS

Hotel Indigo is the industry's first branded lifestyle boutique hotel experience. It is uniquely designed to appeal to style-savvy guests who desire affordable luxury, genuine service, and an alternative to traditional "beige" hotels without sacrificing any of the business amenities they have come to expect. Renewal is the soul of Hotel Indigo's retail-inspired design concept—thoughtful changes are made throughout the year to keep the hotel fresh, similar to the way retailers change their window displays. Guest rooms feature signature murals, area rugs, fluffy duvets, and slip covers that will change periodically, while public spaces will be transformed seasonally through changing aromas, music, artwork, murals, and directional signage. From relaxed café dining to high-style rooms, Hotel Indigo creates an intriguing, warm, and inviting environment for guests.[7]

and products provided to the customers identified in question 1; and the third question refers to the capabilities and technologies the firm uses to provide the services identified in question 2. This approach is, admittedly, marketing oriented. Its greatest strength is that it focuses on the customer, an important external stakeholder for most firms. Hotel Indigo, a brand of InterContinental Hotel Group, defines its business in the "Hospitality Focus" boxed section at the top of the page.

In defining who they are, Hotel Indigo's top management answered the three questions posed in direction setting as follows: Who is being satisfied? The hotel is for the middle-market consumer who is trading up to higher levels of quality and taste, but still seeking value.[8] What is being satisfied is the traveler's desire to experience affordable luxury and style instead of a "beige" hotel. The brand is positioned as "an oasis where you can escape the hectic pace of travel and think more clearly, work more productively, rest more refreshingly. An environment that doesn't just shelter you, but inspires and reenergizes you."[9] The final question, "How are customer needs satisfied?", is revealed in the use of a retail service model that allows the hotel décor to be continually refreshed and flexible.

Finally, the brand replies on the parent company. It is supported by the strength of the InterContinental Hotels Group portfolio, and its infrastructure, consisting of global reservations, global sales, technology, and their Priority Club Rewards program. While defining a business is helpful in communicating to internal and external stakeholders what the organization is all about, the business definition should not constrain strategic choice. In other words, it is an excellent tool for identifying where a company is, but it should not be used to determine where the company should go in the future.[10]

Peter Drucker suggested that direction setting is not just answering the question "What is our business?" but also requires asking future-based questions like "What will it be?" and "What should it be?"[11] The "What will it be?" question refers to the direction that the firm is heading at the current time. In other words, where will the business end up if it continues in its current course? The question, "What should it be?" allows for modifications to the existing strategy to move the company in an appropriate direction. Organizations that come to grips

J.W. MARRIOTT: THE FUTURE OF MARRIOTT

"By managing and franchising rather than owning hotels, we can grow much faster, leveraging our management and brand-building capability. Faster unit growth, in turn, drives greater market share and brand equity, which encourages owners and franchisees to develop yet more hotels flying our flags. Across all our brands we remain focused on finding innovative ways for technology to enhance the guest experience. Selling to customers the way they want to buy is as important as catering to them upon arrival, and we enjoy a tremendous strength in our distribution."[12]

with those two questions force themselves to look forward in time and to think about a vision for the future.

Gary Hamel suggests that rather than determine the future direction of an organization based on what it does, the organization should think in terms of what it knows and the resources it owns.[13] In other words, a company should determine future direction based on its resources and capabilities. Marriott, for example, has 13 different brands in 68 countries, and continues to create value by growing its existing businesses and leveraging its core skills. (See the "Hospitality Focus" boxed section above to read a quote from J.W. Marriott.)

As organizations become involved in businesses outside of their current operations, they are increasing what is referred to as their *scope*. In other words, the scope of an organization is the breadth of its activities both within a market and across markets. Delta Air Lines, like many airlines, has adhered to a narrow business definition. Instead of venturing into new areas, Delta has relied on acquisitions and expansion activities to greatly increase its route coverage and establish an international presence, thus expanding the geographic size of its markets.[14] However, the type of customer served, function, service, and technologies have mostly remained the same. Delta and many other airlines are almost entirely dependent on one business. When the industry experiences downturns and shocks, they have no other businesses to offset losses. This became evident when the downturn in demand for air travel in the early 21st century led to losses that the airlines could not sustain. When it looked as if many U.S. airlines would go out of business, the federal government provided a multibillion-dollar bailout, but restructuring of the company and aggressive changes to the fare structure could not prevent the airline from bankruptcy. After a failed takeover attempt by US Airways, Delta emerged from bankruptcy with a new CEO and an expansion plan.[15] On the other hand, Virgin Atlantic Airways is a part of a highly diversified group. (See the "Hospitality Focus" boxed section on page 86.)

Virgin's business definition is at the opposite extreme from many airline companies that tend to focus on only one type of business. While such high levels of diversity typically are difficult to manage, they do provide a cushion against shocks in particular businesses. Choices regarding appropriate levels of diversification will be discussed in depth in Chapter 6. For now, it is sufficient to say that the execution of a corporate-level strategy results in a particular business definition. For example, if a corporate-level strategy includes increased involvement in particular businesses or business segments, the business definition will be changed to reflect these changes.

DIVERSITY: THE VIRGIN GROUP

Led by adventurous founder, chairman, and owner Sir Richard Branson, Virgin Group has created more than 200 branded companies in businesses ranging from mobile telephones to transportation, travel, financial services, leisure, music, holidays, publishing, and retailing. Revenues around the world exceed $20 billion. This holding company has each of the companies under the Virgin brand operating as separate entities, with some being wholly owned by Branson, while he holds minority or majority stakes in others. The group has 14 businesses alone in the travel and tourism category. Virgin Atlantic Airways is among the group's biggest breadwinners. Virgin Atlantic is complemented by its pan-European and Australian low-fare cousins, Virgin Express and Virgin Blue. Virgin Group also operates two UK rail franchises and sells tour packages. Virgin Trains, Blue Holidays, Virgin Limobike, Virgin Limited Edition, Virgin Vacations, Virgin Balloon Flights, Virgin Limousines, Virgin America, Virgin Charter, Virgin Galactic, and Virgin Nigeria are other tourism businesses. Besides travel and leisure, the group's major operating areas include beverages, retail sales, and telecommunications. The group's Virgin Megastores sell music, videos, and computer games. Other Virgin Group operations include beverages, bridal stores, cosmetics, health clubs, and Internet services.[16]

Key Influences on Direction

Both internal and external stakeholders influence strategic direction, as Figure 3.1 illustrates. The amount of influence stakeholders have is proportional to their economic, political, and formal (legal or contractual) power. The broad environment is also influential. For example, an organization usually tries to establish a value system that is consistent with what society expects, or at least appears to be consistent. Also, economic, technical, and political/legal realities influence the selection of business areas in which to compete. The oceans of the world are Royal Caribbean International's communities, and as such the company is committed to keeping them clean and protected. (See the "Hospitality Focus" boxed section on page 88.)

Strategic direction, including corporate values, forms the foundation on which plans of action are developed. As Royal Caribbean puts it, "Wherever we go, whatever we do, we take our values with us. We know that our acceptance in the communities we call home and the ports we visit depends on our living up to high standards of corporate citizenship. For that reason, Royal Caribbean invests in community organizations and initiatives to enhance the quality of life in communities all over the world."[17] Actions include the firm's competitive strategies, implementation strategies, control systems, and the way internal and external stakeholders and stakeholder relationships are managed. Organizational actions lead to particular outcomes, such as market successes or failures, and to financial performance, which includes sales growth. Also, stakeholders will respond to the actions of organizations in a variety of

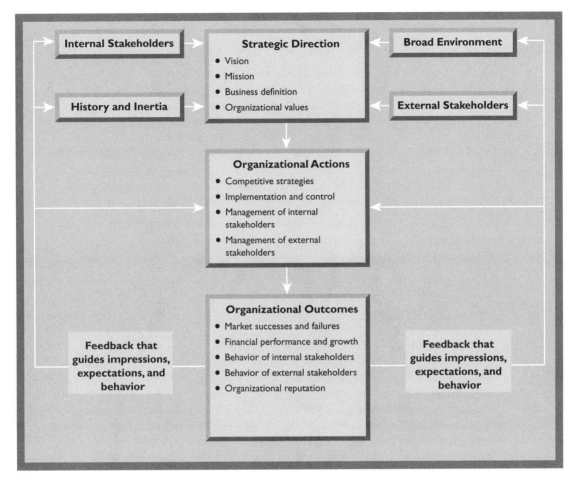

FIGURE 3.1 **Influences on strategic direction**

ways. For instance, customers could be pleased with the services of an organization, or they could be angry and file a lawsuit against the company. Employees could be happy, or they could strike. Government regulators could be cooperative, or they could interfere with operations through fines and penalties. These outcomes translate into feedback that the organization can use to adjust strategic direction, actions, or both direction and actions.

Feedback becomes a part of the organization's history. History can potentially assist strategic planning processes, because organizations can learn from past successes and failures. Unfortunately, history can also be a weakness that stands in the way of forward progress. Past successes sometimes create strong structural inertia, the term for forces at work to maintain the status quo.[18] These forces can include systems, structures, processes, culture, sunk costs, internal politics, and barriers to entry and exit. Anything that favors the status quo has the potential to cause inertia. Inertia is stronger when an organization has been successful in the past, because managers believe that past success will translate into future success, regardless of early warning signals to the contrary. Inertia, then, is another potential threat to the survival and prosperity of an organization.

ENVIRONMENTAL PROTECTION AND ROYAL CARIBBEAN

W̲e at Royal Caribbean International know we have a special responsibility to protect our marine ecosystems. Clean oceans are good for the environment, good for our guests, and good for our business. Because we depend on the sea for our livelihood, and because it's the right thing to do, we have heavily invested in state-of-the-art treatment technologies, such as Advanced Wastewater Purification (AWP) systems, to reduce our impact on the environment. In addition to meeting or often exceeding environmental laws and regulations through our "Above and Beyond Compliance" policies, we closely monitor our activities at sea and on land to ensure standards are strictly maintained.

Royal Caribbean manages its business with a talented, competent team of professionals, who operate with a philosophy of social responsibility, environmental protection, and good corporate citizenship. We are committed to timely, honest, and forthright communications with our employees, guests, shareholders, suppliers, and travel partners. And we will continue to seek the counsel of experts in the environmental field. By maintaining a productive, ongoing dialogue with all of these stakeholders, we will continue to do the best we can to preserve and protect the environment.

We believe companies can be financially successful while serving as stewards of the environment and good corporate citizens. We take our responsibility to the environment very seriously, and we feel it's inextricably linked with our continued success as an industry-leading cruise line.[19]

Structural inertia is the force at work to maintain the status quo, and can be the kiss of death for a restaurant that works to attract that elusive buzz that moves from restaurant to restaurant. Most humans desire a certain amount of predictability in their work. In other words, they have learned to cope with their organizational environment—they are comfortable. They may also fear that changes will reduce their own power or position in the organization or that they will no longer be considered competent. If the forces favoring inertia are strong, and if the organization has been successful in the past, people will be highly resistant to any major shift in missions or strategies.

Take Lutèce, a famous French restaurant in Manhattan for more than 30 years before it closed in 2004. Inertia based on past successes was perhaps one of the reasons for the decline of this restaurant based on white linens, servers in tuxedos, and diners in ties.[20] The owners continued to pursue the same strategies until it was simply too late, and so were replaced with a new guard of fine-dining owner/operators. In order to stay competitive in the restaurant industry, operators are often remodeling interiors, redesigning menus, and sometimes creating entirely new concepts in the process. As one executive of Bennigan's Grill & Tavern noted, "In today's competitive landscape, there are so many choices and so many new concepts, especially with the advent of fast-casual. For brands such as ours, you have to *change* to adapt. Who wants to eat in a place with 25-year-old relics?"[21] (See the "Hospitality Focus" boxed section on page 89.)

NEW YORK CITY RESTAURANT FINDS NEW
STRATEGIC DIRECTION

Breaking from structural inertia motivated chef-partner Wayne Nish to rethink March, a well-respected 16-year-old restaurant on New York City's Upper East Side. Opened in 1990, Mr. Nish and his business partner, Joseph Scalice, over the years helped March develop a reputation as one of the city's premier fancy restaurants, a spot for truffles and tasting menus, earning three stars from Ruth Reichl of the *New York Times*. "Because of our tasting menus and our price point, we were known as a special-occasion restaurant," Nish says. "We saw some of our customers exactly 16 times: once a year." With an average check of $140 per person and an influx of new restaurants, March found its business had evaporated.

The need for a new strategic direction motivated Nish to approach his business partner about lowering prices, moving away from the tasting-menu format, and making the restaurant more casual. The space, now bearing the name Nish, reopened in January 2007 with an à la carte menu. Gone are the servers in black tuxedos, who now wear black slacks and black buttoned shirts. The floral prints have been replaced with contemporary artwork on loan and changed regularly. Checks average $85 per person, and "I'm seeing most people coming in with smiles on their faces, saying that they can come back more often," Nish says. "There are definitely more neighborhood people coming in. It's great."[22]

One of the most common means of communicating strategic direction is in a written mission statement. The next section is a general discussion of organizational mission statements and how they develop over time.

MISSION STATEMENTS

An organization's mission statement is a brief statement of the purpose of the organization that helps answer the question "What are we here to do?" It distinguishes an organization from others by stating the basic scope and operations of the firm, primarily by defining markets, customers, products, locations, or strategic features. For example, Choice Hotels International says its mission is to deliver a franchise success system of strong brands, exceptional services, vast consumer reach, and size, scale, and distribution that delivers guests, satisfies guests, and reduces cost for hotels owners.[23] The clear customer for this mission statement is the franchisee, and the needs they promise to fulfill are a strong brand, services, a large system infrastructure, and good distribution.

For Sunland Park Racetrack and Casino, the mission is to be a premier, total entertainment attraction recognized throughout the region for superior customer service. The company

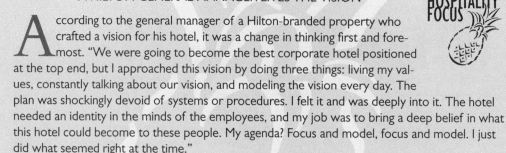

A HILTON GENERAL MANAGER LIVES THE VISION

According to the general manager of a Hilton-branded property who crafted a vision for his hotel, it was a change in thinking first and foremost. "We were going to become the best corporate hotel positioned at the top end, but I approached this vision by doing three things: living my values, constantly talking about our vision, and modeling the vision every day. The plan was shockingly devoid of systems or procedures. I felt it and was deeply into it. The hotel needed an identity in the minds of the employees, and my job was to bring a deep belief in what this hotel could become to these people. My agenda? Focus and model, focus and model. I just did what seemed right at the time."

It was not until almost six years later when the general manager was executive vice president of the hotel group—a company that owned and managed hotels branded with a variety of different midpriced and upper-priced hotel franchisers—that he created a formal vision of what the hotel aspired to become. After considerable thought, he arrived at the simple statement, "the friendliest place to visit."[24]

describes how it will accomplish this purpose by noting that it will, "provide a clean, modern, well-regulated facility that offers the best of horse racing and gaming experiences."[25] The focus is on modern and clean gaming entertainment on a regional scale.

A mission statement provides an important vehicle for communicating ideals and a sense of direction to internal and external stakeholders. It can inspire employees and managers. It can also help guide organizational managers in resource-allocation decisions. A mission statement should help convey what the organization does, how it does it, and for whom. Clearly, not all opportunities that organizations face will be compatible with their missions. If used properly, an organization's mission should provide a screen for evaluating opportunities and threats. Table 3.1 outlines the various uses of mission statements and considerations for writing them.

Sometimes students of strategic management confuse the terms *mission* and *vision*. In general, a mission is what the organization is, its reason for existing, and how it intends to make a profit, whereas a vision is a forward-looking view of what the organization wants to become or what it can become in time. However, when mission statements are written, they often include a vision statement, or statements about the values of an organization. As long as an organization understands what it is, what it values, and where it is going, then it has a well-defined strategic direction. The particular labels are not as important as making sure that all aspects of strategic direction are included. One hotel general manager's direction-setting experience shows that sometimes the vision emerges in discussions with the senior management staff but is not written down initially. (See the "Hospitality Focus" boxed section above.)

As organizations are first established, their mission may be as simple as "Provide low-cost lodging to highway travelers while generating a profit for the owner." The mission is often informal and is seldom written down. But notice that even in its simplest form, this mission encompasses a purpose, a brief definition of the business, and two important stakeholders, the owner and the customer. Most businesses begin with a mission that is just as simple as the

TABLE 3.1 **Multiple Uses of Mission Statements**

Use	Primary Stakeholders Targeted	Considerations
Direct decision making and resource allocations	Managers and employees	Mission statements should use terms that are understandable to internal stakeholders. For example, a clear business definition provides guidance with regard to where an organization should pursue business opportunities. Also, a statement like, "We use state-of-the-art technology" has clear implications for how resources should be allocated. To be effective, missions should be communicated to internal stakeholders on a regular basis.
Inspire higher levels of performance and pride in association	Managers and employees	Mission statements should be worded in such a way that they inspire the human spirit. A person should read the statement and feel good about working for the company. On the other hand, this can be a two-edged sword if the organization does not act accordingly. This can cause a sense of betrayal and hypocrisy.
Communicate organizational purpose and values	Managers, employees, shareholders, and potential investors	Organizational purpose and values help managers and employees resolve dilemmas when faced with trade-offs. They also help external stakeholders know what to expect from the organization in particular situations.
Enhance organizational reputation	Society and most external stakeholder groups, especially customers and potential venture partners	Mission statements should be carefully articulated so that they enhance reputation. Catchy (but not cliché) slogans are helpful so that stakeholders will remember them. They should be short enough so that external stakeholders will attempt to read them and remember them. They should be widely dispersed to media sources and apparent in public settings such as the foyers of office buildings and factories.

example given. The mission is an extension of the entrepreneur or entrepreneurs who form the organization. When Dave Thomas began Wendy's Hamburger Restaurants in the 1960s, his mission was simply to serve great-tasting food, hire and train the best people, provide outstanding customer service, and make a buck along the way. Today the company is a major restaurant operating and franchising company, with 6,300 restaurants in North America.[26]

THE MARRIOTT SPIRIT TO SERVE

The Spirit to Serve Our Associates

- The unshakeable conviction that our people are our most important asset
- An environment that supports associate growth and personal development
- A reputation for employing caring, dependable associates who are ethical and trustworthy
- A home-like atmosphere and friendly workplace relationships
- A performance-reward system that recognizes the important contributions of both hourly and management associates
- Pride in the Marriott name, accomplishments, and record of success
- A focus on growth-managed and franchised properties, owners, and investors

The Spirit to Serve Our Guests

- Evident in the adage, "the customer is always right"
- A hands-on management style, i.e., "management by walking around"
- Attention to detail
- Openness to innovation and creativity in serving guests
- Pride in the knowledge that our guests can count on Marriott's unique blend of quality, consistency, personalized service, and recognition almost anywhere they travel in the world or whichever Marriott brand they choose

The Spirit to Serve Our Community

- Demonstrated every day by associate and corporate support of local, national and international initiatives, and programs
- An important part of doing business the "Marriott Way"[27]

As companies succeed in their business environments, opportunities arise that allow the firm to grow in revenues and number of employees, and encourage it to expand into new product and market areas. The original mission may seem too restrictive. At this point, the organization will probably begin to pay more attention to previously overlooked or neglected stakeholders. For example, the company may increase employee benefits (employees), hire additional tax specialists (government), designate a public–relations officer (society), attempt to negotiate better discounts with suppliers (suppliers), or increase borrowing to help sustain growth (financial intermediaries). In addition, the firm will certainly pay more attention to the

JOHNSON & JOHNSON—OUR CREDO

HOSPITALITY FOCUS

We believe our first responsibility is to the doctors, nurses and patients, to mothers and fathers and all others who use our products and services. In meeting their needs, everything we do must be of high quality. We must constantly strive to reduce our costs in order to maintain reasonable prices. Customers' orders must be serviced promptly and accurately. Our suppliers and distributors must have an opportunity to make a fair profit.

We are responsible to our employees, the men and women who work with us throughout the world. Everyone must be considered as an individual. We must respect their dignity and recognize their merit. They must have a sense of security in their jobs. Compensation must be fair and adequate, and working conditions clean, orderly, and safe. We must be mindful of ways to help our employees fulfill their family responsibilities. Employees must feel free to make suggestions and complaints. There must be equal opportunity for employment, development, and advancement for those qualified. We must provide competent management, and their actions must be just and ethical.

We are responsible to the communities in which we live and work and to the world community as well. We must be good citizens—support good works and charities and bear our fair share of taxes. We must encourage civic improvements and better health and education. We must maintain in good order the property we are privileged to use, protecting the environment and natural resources.

Our final responsibility is to our stockholders. Business must make a sound profit. We must experiment with new ideas. Research must be carried on, innovative programs developed, and mistakes paid for. New equipment must be purchased, new facilities provided, and new products launched. Reserves must be created to provide for adverse times. When we operate according to these principles, the stockholders should realize a fair return.[28]

actions and reactions of competitors. These stakeholders and forces in the broad environment then become forces that are considered as the organization adjusts or enlarges its mission.

On page 92 in the "Hospitality Focus" boxed section, Marriott's fundamental ideals of service to associates, customers, and the community are listed. The "Marriott Way" is built on a set of beliefs that have served as a cornerstone for guiding the enterprise. They attribute their continued growth and employee satisfaction to these ideals.

At some point in the growth of an organization, planning processes are formalized. This may be the first time that a mission statement is put into words. Articulating a mission forces top managers to come to terms with some key issues regarding the current direction of the firm and its future. A well-written mission statement can be an excellent tool for conveying the meaning and intent of an organization to its internal and external stakeholders.

A mission statement can also be an effective way to communicate to important stakeholders. In times of crisis, a mission statement also serves as a guide to direct actions. Johnson & Johnson's adherence to its purpose of first responsibility to doctors, nurses, patients, parents, and all others who use their products helped guide managers in the now-famous recall of Tylenol. Prompt actions, informed by the "credo," saved the firm's reputation.[29] The Johnson & Johnson credo was written over 60 years ago by General Robert Wood Johnson, when the family-owned business was small. Putting customers first and stockholders last was a new idea then and has continued to serve the company well. (See the "Hospitality Focus" boxed section on page 93.)

Unfortunately, in many organizations, the process of developing a written mission statement has deteriorated into an exercise in slogan writing. Managers often worry more about writing a catchy, short phrase that can be printed on a business card than about managing with purpose. For an organization's mission to be a management tool, it must be grounded in the realities of the business.

ORGANIZATIONAL VISION

A *vision* is an ideal and unique image of the future. It is a forward-looking statement that conveys a sense of the possible. For this reason, we often see visions that use the terms "best" or "leader." The vision for Royal Caribbean is, "To empower and enable our employees to deliver the best vacation experience to our guests, thereby generating superior returns to our stakeholders and enhancing the well-being of our communities."[30]

An organization with a vision has a definite sense of what it wants to be in the future. Starbucks' vision is to "be the premier purveyor of the finest coffee in the world while maintaining our uncompromising principles as we grow."[31] The CEO and other key executives have primary responsibility for creating the organizational vision. Howard Schultz, the visionary behind Starbucks, clearly embodies the essential role that leaders play in shaping a unique future for a firm. (See the Hospitality Focus" boxed section on page 95.)

The vision of Marriott is "to be the world's leading provider of hospitality services."[32] With nearly 2,600 properties and 144,000 associates in 67 countries and territories, Marriott is arguably fulfilling that vision. Once it is stated, a vision may be used to focus the efforts of the entire organization.[33] For example, plans, policies, or programs that are inconsistent with the corporate vision may need to be altered or replaced.

A well-understood vision can help managers and employees believe that their actions have meaning. Unfortunately, sometimes firms have a vision but it produces no positive results, because it is not well understood by members of the organization. Managers who wish to enhance their ability to communicate a vision should ask, "How do I passionately convey our dramatic difference to our customers?" They should be sure that the housekeepers, servers, desk clerks, reservationists, and others buy into it.

A study conducted using students at Cornell University asked them to call the free reservation number of various hotel chains. Students asked their contacts if they knew the company's vision. Many of these employees were reservation agents, the point of first contact with the company for many guests. For the majority of the companies, phone calls were made on multiple dates and at varied times to get a better indication of actual knowledge possessed by several employees. Without embarrassing any one lodging company, we will just say that the overall results were not impressive. Of those contacted, 28 percent knew the vision, 3 percent looked it up, 68 percent did not know the vision, and 1 percent provided a rude response.[34]

A COMMON VISION FOR STARBUCKS

Starbucks Coffee, Tea and Spice opened its first store in April 1971 in the Pike Place Market in Seattle, Washington. Its original owners, Jerry Baldwin and Gordon Bowker, had a passion for dark roasted coffee. They loved coffee and tea and wanted Seattle to have access to the best. Howard Schultz joined the company in 1982 as director of retail operations and marketing after visiting the company and meeting its owners.

Schultz also had a passion for the business and tried to convince the owners to test the idea of an Italian espresso bar concept. While the test was a great success, the owners decided not to expand the concept. This disagreement caused Schultz to leave the company in 1985 and start his own coffee-bar company with Dave Olsen. Two years later, the owners of Starbucks, Schultz's previous bosses, sold their business to Schultz and Olsen.

Schultz's return to the Starbucks offices at the roasting plant was an opportunity for him to share the new vision and help set a direction for the small company's future. He called the staff together for his first meeting as the new owner and began by saying:

> All my life I have wanted to be part of a company and a group of people who share a common vision. . . . I'm here today because I love this company. I love what it represents. . . . I know you're concerned. . . . I promise you I will not let you down. I promise you I will not leave anyone behind. . . . . In five years, I want you to look back at this day and say, "I was there when it started. I helped build this company into something great."

During the next five years, Starbucks remained a privately held company and expanded its stores at a faster pace than planned. By 1992, it had 165 stores. Today Starbucks has 12,440 stores in 37 countries.[35]

While this study was not rigorous from a scientific perspective, it is still possible to draw a few simple, though tentative, conclusions. First, it is possible that many of these firms did not have a vision. Second, those firms that had one were not communicating it very well. Either of these situations results in the same problem. The people who are making contact with guests and other stakeholders don't really understand what their companies are trying to become.

ORGANIZATIONAL VALUES

A final but equally important aspect of strategic direction is the establishment of *organizational values*. Values guide organizational decisions and behavior. Take Salty's Seafood Grills, a small company with three restaurants that believes it exceeds guests' expectations through empowered people guided by shared values. For this company, the voice of the guests drives people's actions in this company. Through the values, it is understood that everyone listens to the guests,

THE VALUES AT SALTY'S SEAFOOD GRILLS

Diversity—We respect the individual and seek value and promote differences of race, nationality, gender, age, background, experience, and style.

Communication—We listen and speak clearly, consistently, and respectfully. Clear communication and understanding is the root of our strength and our success.

Integrity—We do what we say.

Honesty—We speak openly and directly, with care and compassion, and work hard to understand and resolve issues.

Attitude—We have a positive, can-do attitude about ourselves, our guests, our fellow associates, and our company.

Accountability—We all understand what is expected of us and are fully committed to meeting those expectations.

Teamwork—Working on real guest needs, we combine functional excellence and cross-functional teamwork to produce exceptional results.

Balance—We respect the decisions individuals make to achieve professional and personal balance in their life.[36]

understands what the guests' needs are, and delivers to exceed those needs. In addition, senior management believes that the associates closest to the guests are at the top of the organization. The rest of the organization's role is to help those closest to the guests by providing resources and removing obstacles. The essence of Salty's values is a belief that what is good for the guests is good for the company and good for them as individuals. Read about Salty's shared values in the "Hospitality Focus" boxed section at the top of this page.

Values statements are common throughout the hospitality industry. The value statement of Starwood Hotels and Resorts Worldwide Inc. is found in the "Hospitality Focus" boxed section on page 98. Notice that there are some similarities between these value statements, but there are also important differences. These differences are a reflection of the culture and ethics of the company.

High-level managers, especially the CEO, have a great deal of influence on the values of the company. For example, Darden Restaurants' values are articulated in communications with shareholders and other key stakeholders (see Table 3.2). When a new top manager takes charge, his or her personal values help shape the entire company, while founders can serve as a guide. Bill Darden and Joe Lee, who founded this large casual-dining restaurant company, provide a uniting value-based culture for CEOs who follow through the establishment of their original core values.

Managers who work with the CEO quickly identify his or her value system and communicate it to lower-level managers and employees. The CEO may also discuss organizational values in speeches, news releases, and memos. To the extent that the CEO controls the reward

TABLE 3.2 The Values of Darden Restaurants, Inc.

Our Core Values

While Darden benefits from an industry that has strong long-term prospects and we employ terrific people, operate outstanding restaurant companies, follow a clear strategy, and enjoy excellent financial strength, we know we cannot be successful without an unmistakable sense of who we are. That's why we understand and appreciate our Core Values that have been forged over our more than 60-year history started by our founder, Bill Darden. As we continue the journey to become the best casual dining company, we will look to these values for guidance and know they will be especially critical when we're faced with unexpected opportunities or challenges.

As an Organization, We Value:

- *Integrity and fairness*. It all starts with integrity. We trust in the integrity and fairness of each other to always do the right thing, to be open, honest, and forthright with others, to demonstrate courage, to solve without blame, and to follow through on all our commitments and ourselves.
- *Respect and caring*. We reach out with respect and caring. We have a genuine interest in the well-being of others. We know the importance of listening, the power of understanding, and the immeasurable value of support.
- *Diversity*. Even though we have a common vision, we embrace and celebrate our individual differences. We are strengthened by a diversity of cultures, perspectives, attitudes, and ideas. We honor each other's heritage and uniqueness. Our power of diversity makes a world of difference.
- *Always learning—always teaching*. We learn from others as they learn from us. We learn. We teach. We grow.
- *Being "of service."* Being of service is our pleasure. We treat people as special and appreciated by giving of ourselves, doing more than expected, anticipating needs, and making a difference.
- *Teamwork*. Teamwork works. By trusting one another, we bring together the best in all of us and go beyond the boundaries of ordinary success.
- *Excellence*. We have a passion to set and to pursue, with innovation, courage, and humility, ever-higher standards.

Our Core Values communicate the behaviors and attitudes we cherish as we strive to deliver on Darden's Core Purpose, which is "To nourish and delight everyone we serve."

"Darden is the Company it is today because we place no limits on what we believe we can achieve. Like Bill Darden, Joe Lee, and the others who founded our Company, we are willing to dream big dreams, and we are united by a strong, values-based culture."

Clarence Otis, Jr.

Chairman & Chief Executive Officer

Source: Darden Restaurants Inc., 2007, Overview, *www.dardenrestaurants.com/abt_overview.asp.*

THE VALUES AT STARWOOD HOTELS AND RESORTS
WORLDWIDE, INC.

HOSPITALITY
FOCUS

Our values serve as the guide for how we treat our customers, our owners, our shareholders, and our associates. We aspire to these values to make Starwood a great place to work and do business. We succeed only when we meet and exceed the expectations of our customers, owners, and shareholders. We have a passion for excellence and will deliver the highest standards of integrity and fairness. We celebrate the diversity of people, ideas, and cultures. We honor the dignity and value of individuals working as a team. We improve the communities in which we work. We encourage innovation, accept accountability, and embrace change. We seek knowledge and growth through learning. We share a sense of urgency, nimbleness, and endeavor to have fun too.[37]

system subjectively, managers who make decisions that are consistent with the values of the CEO are likely to be rewarded, thus reinforcing what is expected. Many of the people who strongly disagree with the new values will voluntarily leave the firm. Or, if their own behavior pattern is inconsistent with the new rules of the game, they will be forced out through poor performance evaluations, missed promotions, or low salary increases. Thus, over a period of time, the example and actions of the CEO are reflected in most of the major decisions that are made by the organization.[38].

Despite the CEO's power, he or she is not the only determinant of organizational values. The values of an organization are also a reflection of the social groups from which managers and other employees are drawn (which makes global management even more challenging). These individuals bring a personal value system with them when they are hired.

In the hospitality industry, the values of a social group are often part of the service experience. Disney's Polynesian resort, for example, offers an entire training program, "Magic of Polynesia," which is designed to facilitate employee understanding and commitment to the authentic vision of Polynesia. (See the "Hospitality Focus" boxed section on page 99.)

If value changes in society are not voluntarily incorporated into a firm, then an employee or manager may become a *whistle blower* in an attempt to force the organization to cease a behavior that society finds unacceptable or to incorporate a practice that is in keeping with the new social value. For example, antidiscrimination lawsuits have prompted many organizations to adopt more stringent equal employment opportunity policies and even affirmative action programs. The values of various social groups are constantly changing. Hiring legal or illegal immigrants in the restaurant industry is another example of a complex issue influenced by changing political and social values. Therefore, strategic managers need to keep abreast of these changes in order to successfully position their firms.

Stakeholder theory is closely aligned with discussions of values and social responsibility, because one of the principles underlying the theory is that organizations should behave appropriately with regard to a wide range of stakeholder concerns and interests.[39] The increasing incidence of lawsuits against top managers and their companies in recent years provides evidence that many organizations are not satisfying all of their stakeholders' expectations very well.[40] (See the "Hospitality Focus" boxed section on page 100.)

THE VALUES AT DISNEY'S POLYNESIAN RESORT

The cast members and management identified four theme values as part of their discussion of "what makes us Polynesian." The values identified as reflecting Polynesian hospitality included (1) a sense of *Ohano*, or sense of family, which describes the way they would like their working relationships to be; (2) a spirit of *Aloha*, which means that the basis of their interactions is their desire to be caring and mindful of others; (3) a sense of *Kina'olea*, the desire to perform all interactions and services in a high-quality way; and (4) a sense of *Mea Ho'okipa*, the desire to be the perfect host by "welcoming and entertaining guests and strangers with unconditional warmth and generosity."[41]

Social Responsibility

Embedded within the concept of organizational values is the notion of social responsibility. Social responsibility contains four major components:

1. *Economic responsibilities*, such as the obligation to be productive and profitable and meet the consumer needs of society

2. *Legal responsibilities* to achieve economic goals within the confines of written law

3. *Moral obligations* to abide by unwritten codes, norms, and values implicitly derived from society

4. *Discretionary responsibilities* that are volitional or philanthropic in nature[42]

In the restaurant industry, wide arrays of large and small organizations work in their communities as responsible corporate citizens. Take, for example, the work of Souza's Brazilian Restaurant, a small restaurant in Burlington, Vermont, that has devised a program offering free and subsidized cab rides to restaurant patrons who have had too much to drink.[43] While the owners of the restaurant believe it is the "right thing to do," which speaks to the third major component of social responsibility noted previously, Souza's also believes that the industry needs to support the existing state laws on zero tolerance concerning impaired driving.

Danny Murphy—a franchisee of Tim Horton restaurants, Wendy's restaurants, and a Holiday Inn—believes helping his community involves a different sort of bottom line. "We're able to do charitable things, so we do them," Murphy says. "It's that simple."[44] Some of the things he does for his community in Canada includes ski trips for underprivileged children, food drives, highway cleanups, and the Easter Seals poster-child campaign. Other programs include a soup campaign each February (for the Heart & Stroke Foundation) and Alzheimer's Day (proceeds from every large coffee sold at Tim Horton's locations benefit the Alzheimer's Society).

SOCIAL RESPONSIBILITY: THE RONALD McDONALD
HOUSE CHARITIES

HOSPITALITY
FOCUS

Large players like McDonald's devote substantial resources to their community efforts. The company now issues social responsibility reports that
highlight what the company is doing in the international communities it
serves. For example, the company conducts approximately 500 animal welfare
audits throughout the world each year and publishes an animal welfare report. It established the Ronald McDonald House Charities, which are dedicated to improving the health
and welfare of children. More than 245 Ronald McDonald houses in 28 countries provide
families with a homelike atmosphere while their children receive care at a nearby hospital.
Ronald McDonald Care Mobiles take medical and dental care directly to underprivileged
children. A large grant will provide immunizations to 1 million children and mothers in Africa.
McDonald's has also provided disaster relief in many countries, including Greece, Turkey,
India, Chile, and the United States. In addition, the corporation has purchased more than $4
billion of recycled materials. These are just a few examples of the many things McDonald's is
doing to be a good citizen.[45]

GREEN INITIATIVES

Hotel companies are beginning to recognize that the choices they make affect the impact their
guests have on the environment. Environmental responsibility is emerging as the hospitality industry recognizes and acts on the notion that it has significantly more responsibility to
the environment and to the world around it than do individuals. In the first quarter of 2007,
more than 70 press releases were sent out about how hotel companies were deploying green
initiatives.[46] Worldwide, the hotel industry has accelerated its focus on green initiatives, with
an eye to profit, people, and preserving the planet.

The importance of sustainable hotelkeeping appears to have captured the attention of
all the major brands, with InterContinental Hotel Group, Starwood Capital Group, Hilton
International, and Fairmont Hotels and Resorts all establishing unique initiatives. Starwood
has devised a new concept called "1" Hotel and Residences, as the first luxury, eco-friendly
global hotel brand.[47] The concept will combine the best of environmentally sustainable architecture and interior design with impeccable service and luxurious comfort. The new brand
will adhere to green construction and operating principles and commit to environmentally
sensitive consumption of natural resources. What remains to be determined is whether these
initiatives are primarily devised to obtain positive publicity or motivated by values. Harve'
Houdre, general manager of the Willard InterContinental, a champion in creating extensive
sustainable development strategies for his hotel, notes, "The hotel industry should not use this
concept as an opportunity, but consider it a responsibility."[48]

PROFITS VERSUS RESPONSIBLE BEHAVIOR

Research evidence does not unequivocally support the idea that firms that rank high on social
responsibility, based on the four components described earlier, are necessarily any more or less

SUSTAINABLE AGRICULTURE PLUS PROFIT AT WHOLE FOODS MARKET

HOSPITALITY FOCUS

Whole Foods Market believes that its success comes from contributing to a higher quality of life. Our motto—Whole Foods, Whole People, Whole Planet—emphasizes that our vision reaches far beyond just being a food retailer. Our success in fulfilling our vision is measured by customer satisfaction, Team Member excellence and happiness, return on capital investment, improvement in the state of the environment, and local and larger community support.

By offering the highest-quality food available, we are helping to transform the diet of America, helping people live longer, healthier, more pleasurable lives while responding positively to the challenge of environmental sustainability.

We earn profits every day through voluntary exchange with our customers. We know that profits are essential to create capital for growth, job security, and overall financial success. Profits are the "savings" every business needs in order to change and evolve to meet the future. They are the "seed corn" for next year's crop. We are the stewards of our shareholder's investments, and we are committed to increasing long-term shareholder value.

As a publicly traded company, Whole Foods Market intends to grow. We will grow at such a pace that our quality of work environment, Team Member productivity and excellence, customer satisfaction, and financial health continue to prosper.

There is a community of self-interest among all of our stakeholders. We share together in our collective vision for the company. To that end, we have a salary cap that limits the maximum cash compensation (wages plus profit incentive bonuses) paid to any Team Member in the calendar year to 19 times the company-wide annual average salary of all full-time Team Members.[49]

profitable than firms that rank low.[50] However, an organization that maintains an untarnished reputation should enjoy greater opportunities to enhance economic performance over the longer term. Studies of hotels in the United States have found that corporate social responsibility will deliver to the bottom line if made part of a marketing and communications strategy.[51] Furthermore, firms that have an overall high rank in the four areas listed in this chapter (one of which is productivity and profitability) have achieved an end in itself.

The classical belief, espoused primarily by economists such as Milton Friedman, is that the only valid objective of a corporation is to maximize profits, within the rules of the game (legal restrictions). He suggests that when businesses engage in efforts to increase profits, they often do what is good for society. If a business can gain goodwill and thereby increase profit, Friedman argues that it is in the self-interest of a business to do so.

Whole Foods Market, the world's leading retailer of natural and organic foods is a notable example of a company that is committed to sustainable agriculture while making a healthy profit for investors. (See the "Hospitality Focus" boxed section above.)

A corporation that becomes too focused on profits is likely to lose the support and cooperation of key stakeholders, such as suppliers, activist groups, competitors, society, and the government. In the long run, this sort of strategy may result in problems such as lawsuits, loss of goodwill, and, ultimately, a loss of profits. One business-ethics expert argued that:

> There is a long-term cost to unethical behavior that tends to be neglected. That cost is to the trust of the people involved. Companies today—due to increasing global competition and advancing technological complexity—are much more dependent than ever upon the trust of workers, specialists, managers, suppliers, distributors, customers, creditors, owners, local institutions, national governments, venture partners, and international agencies. People in any of those groups who believe that they have been misgoverned by bribes, sickened by emissions, or cheated by products tend, over time, to lose trust in the firm responsible for those actions.[52]

Concerning ethical decision making, the approach of many business organizations seems to be to wait until someone complains before actions are taken. This is the type of attitude that can result in food and product safety issues. History has taught us that many human-induced disasters and crises could be avoided if organizations were sensitive to what one or another of their stakeholders is saying. The Sustainable Seafood Forum, a nonpartisan organization that advises restaurateurs and the public about seafood choices that are sustainable and affordable, is one organization launched by a restaurant owner and seafood distributor with a commitment to health and food safety. (See the "Hospitality Focus" boxed section on page 105.)

Enterprise Strategy

One fundamental question an organization should ask in determining its purpose is "What do we stand for?" This question is the critical link between ethics and strategy. *Enterprise strategy* is the term used to denote the joining of ethical and strategic thinking about the organization.[53] It is the organization's best possible reason for the actions it takes. Consequently, an enterprise strategy is almost always focused on serving particular stakeholder needs. For example, an enterprise strategy can contain statements concerning a desire to maximize stockholder value, satisfy the interests of all or a subset of other stakeholders, or increase social harmony or the common good of society.[54] Some organizations get very specific about how they will deal with stakeholder interests. For example, the values of Whole Food Markets can be found in Table 3.3..

Organizational mission statements containing the elements of an enterprise strategy are more likely to be found in high-performing than in low-performing corporations.[55] Enterprise strategy is a natural extension of the ethics of the organization, which are an extension of the values of key managers within the organization. The ethics of a firm are not just a matter of public statements. Ethical decision making is a way of doing business. A company that specifically works to build ethics into its business practice, to develop and implement an enterprise strategy, will have a frame of reference for handling potential ethical problems. For this reason, it is not surprising that a study of hospitality executives revealed that ethics and integrity were considered the most important competencies for the success of future leaders in the industry.[56]

TABLE 3.3 Whole Foods Market Core Values

Our Core Values

The following list of core values reflects what is truly important to us as an organization. These are not values that change from time to time, situation-to-situation, or person to person, but rather they are the underpinning of our company culture. Many people feel Whole Foods is an exciting company of which to be a part and a very special place to work. These core values are the primary reasons for this feeling, and they transcend our size and our growth rate. By maintaining these core values, regardless of how large a company Whole Foods becomes, we can preserve what has always been special about our company. These core values are the soul of our company.

Selling the Highest-Quality Natural and Organic Products Available

Passion for Food: We appreciate and celebrate the difference natural and organic products can make in the quality of one's life.

Quality Standards: We have high standards, and our goal is to sell the highest-quality products we possibly can. We define quality by evaluating the ingredients, freshness, safety, taste, nutritive value, and appearance of all of the products we carry. We are buying agents for our customers and not the selling agents for the manufacturers.

Satisfying and Delighting Our Customers

Our Customers: They are our most important stakeholders in our business and the lifeblood of our business. Only by satisfying our customers first do we have the opportunity to satisfy the needs of our other stakeholders.

Extraordinary Customer Service: We go to extraordinary lengths to satisfy and delight our customers. We want to meet or exceed their expectations on every shopping trip. We know that by doing so we turn customers into advocates for our business. Advocates do more than shop with us, they talk about Whole Foods to their friends and others. We want to serve our customers competently, efficiently, knowledgeably, and with flair.

Education: We can generate greater appreciation and loyalty from all of our stakeholders by educating them about natural and organic foods, health, nutrition, and the environment.

Meaningful Value: We offer value to our customers by providing them with high-quality products, extraordinary service, and a competitive price. We are constantly challenged to improve the value proposition to our customers.

Retail Innovation: We value retail experiments. Friendly competition within the company helps us to continually improve our stores. We constantly innovate and raise our retail standards and are not afraid to try new ideas and concepts.

Inviting Store Environments: We create store environments that are inviting and fun, and reflect the communities they serve. We want our stores to become community meeting places where our customers meet their friends and make new ones.

TABLE 3.3 (*Continued*)

Supporting Team Member Excellence and Happiness

Empowering Work Environments: Our success is dependent upon the collective energy and intelligence of all of our Team Members. We strive to create a work environment where motivated Team Members can flourish and succeed to their highest potential. We appreciate effort and reward results.

Self-Responsibility: We take responsibility for our own success and failures. We celebrate success and see failures as opportunities for growth. We recognize that we are responsible for our own happiness and success.

Self-Directed Teams: The fundamental work unit of the company is the self-directed Team. Teams meet regularly to discuss issues, solve problems, and appreciate each others' contributions. Every Team Member belongs to a Team.

Open & Timely Information: We believe knowledge is power, and we support our Team Members' right to access information that impacts their jobs. Our books are open to our Team Members, including our annual individual compensation report. We also recognize everyone's right to be listened to and heard regardless of their point of view.

Incremental Progress: Our company continually improves through unleashing the collective creativity and intelligence of all of our Team Members. We recognize that everyone has a contribution to make. We keep getting better at what we do.

Shared Fate: We recognize there is a community of interest among all of our stakeholders. There are no entitlements; we share together in our collective fate. To that end, we have a salary cap that limits the compensation (wages plus profit incentive bonuses) of any Team Member to 19 times the average total compensation of all full-time Team Members in the company.

Creating Wealth Through Profits & Growth

Stewardship: We are stewards of our shareholders' investments, and we take that responsibility very seriously. We are committed to increasing long-term shareholder value.

Profits: We earn our profits every day through voluntary exchange with our customers. We recognize that profits are essential to creating capital for growth, prosperity, opportunity, job satisfaction, and job security.

Caring About Our Communities & Our Environment

Sustainable Agriculture: We support organic farmers, growers, and the environment through our commitment to sustainable agriculture and by expanding the market for organic products.

Wise Environmental Practices: We respect our environment and recycle, reuse, and reduce our waste wherever and whenever we can.

Community Citizenship: We recognize our responsibility to be active participants in our local communities. We give a minimum of 5 percent of our profits every year to a wide variety of community and nonprofit organizations.

Integrity in All Business Dealings: Our trade partners are our allies in serving our stakeholders. We treat them with respect, fairness, and integrity at all times and expect the same in return.

Source: Whole Foods web site, *www.wholefoodsmarket.com/company/corevalues.html,* 2007.

KINGS SEAFOOD COMPANY ESTABLISHES THE SUSTAINABLE SEAFOOD FORUM

Sourcing sustainable seafood is often expensive. The CEO of King's Seafood Company, Sam King—faced with the challenge of finding a constant supply of fish for his southern California chain of casual King's Fish Houses and upscale eateries as wild stocks dwindle—joined a partnership with leading seafood restaurants, suppliers, and the Aquarium of the Pacific. Mr. King helped establish the Sustainable Seafood Forum to advise the industry. The partnership is committed to providing its customers with healthy seafood choices that are clearly identified and documented as coming from both sustainable wild stocks and sustainable aquaculture operations. The recommendations of the forum are based on three key criteria:

1. *Healthfulness*. The fish must be free of mercury or toxins.

2. *Environmental sustainability*. The fish must be environmentally sound.

3. *Sociocultural integrity*. The fish must be socioeconomically sound (the industry contributes to the community).[57]

Ethical Frames of Reference

The pattern of decisions made by organizational managers establishes strategy and creates expectations among other organizational members and external stakeholders. For example, a firm that has specialized in the highest-quality services creates an expectation among customers that all services will be high quality. If the firm chooses to change its strategy to include lower-quality services, it runs the risk that customers will perceive the change as a breach of faith. Similarly, if a company has an established relationship with a customer as its sole source of supply of a particular product, then the customer comes to depend on that company. If the supplier then chooses to drop that product from its product line, what might seem to be a clear-cut business decision takes on an ethical dimension: Can the customer's business survive if the product is dropped? Should other alternatives be considered? What obligation does the supplier have to that customer?

These types of decisions carry an ethical dimension, because they go against what some important stakeholders think is right. An *ethical dilemma* exists when the values of different stakeholders of the organization are in conflict. Although there is no real legal dimension, an issue of trust or good faith is apparent. In addition to decisions that violate stakeholder expectations, there are also ethical dilemmas related to the gray area surrounding legal behavior: the definitions of what society views as right and wrong. The values that organizational members bring to their work—the shared values that make up the organizational culture—determine whether the issues of trust, good faith, and obligation are raised when decisions are being deliberated, as well as the degree to which these issues influence the final outcome.

In making decisions that deal with ethical issues, it is important to have a frame of reference. Few ethical dilemmas have simple right-or-wrong answers. Instead, they are complex and require balancing the economic and social interests of the organization.[58] The following are five theoretical models that often influence organizational decisions:[59]

> *Economic Theory.* Under economic theory, the purpose of a business organization is to maximize profits. Profit maximization will lead to the greatest benefit for the most people. Other than profit maximization, there are no ethical issues in business.

>> *Limitations of Economic Theory:* Assumptions of profits being evenly distributed is naive. Not all business decisions relate to profit making, and some ways of increasing profits hurt society.

> *Legal Theory.* Laws are a reflection of what society has determined is right and wrong. Compliance with the law ensures ethical behavior.

>> *Limitations of Legal Theory:* The social and political processes used to formulate laws are complex and time consuming. Because the processes are subject to manipulation, the laws may not truly reflect the interests of society.

> *Religion.* Everyone should act in accordance with religious teachings.

>> *Limitations of Religion:* As a model for business decision making, religious values are difficult to apply. There are many different religious beliefs, and there is no consensus on the behaviors that are consistent with the beliefs.

> *Utilitarian Theory.* Utilitarian theory says to focus on the outcome of a decision. Everyone should act in a way that generates the greatest benefits for the largest number of people.

>> *Limitations of Utilitarian Theory:* Under this model, immoral acts that hurt society or a minority group can be justified if they benefit the majority.

> *Universalist Theory.* Universalist theory says to focus on the intent of the decision. Every person is subject to the same standards. Weigh each decision against the screen: Would I be willing for everyone else in the world to make the same decision?

>> *Limitations of Universalist Theory:* This model provides no absolutes. What one person believes is acceptable for all in society may be offensive to others.

CHICK-FIL-A: EMBRACING CHRISTIAN PRINCIPLES

HOSPITALITY FOCUS

Chick-fil-A is a privately held fast-food chicken restaurant chain with $2.3 billion in systemwide sales and more than 1,300 franchised stores in the United States. Known for its chicken-breast sandwiches, this 60-plus-year-old company has as its corporate purpose, "to glorify God by being a faithful steward of all that is entrusted to us and to have a positive influence on all who come in contact with Chick-fil-A." The founder and CEO S. Truett Cathy believes, "No amount of business school training or work experience can teach what is ultimately a matter of personal character. Businesses are not dishonest or greedy, people are. Thus, a business, successful or not, is merely a reflection of the character of its leadership." As Cathy puts it, "You don't have to be a Christian to work at Chick-fil-A, but we ask you to base your business on biblical principles because they work."

The founder's beliefs are reflected in a host of practices. It is the only national fast-food chain that closes on Sundays so operators can go to church and spend time with their families. This rule is referred to as a "biblical business principle," held so dear that if franchisees don't adhere to this practice, they risk having their contracts terminated. Company meetings and retreats include prayers, and franchisees are encouraged to market their restaurants through church groups.

Cathy, now in his eighties, prefers to hire married workers, believing they are more industrious and productive. Thirty-three percent of the company's operators have attended a Christian-based relationship-building retreat, and many grew up in Christian foster homes funded by Chick-fil-A. The families of prospective operators are often interviewed so Cathy can learn more about their home life. He notes, "If a man can't manage his own life, he can't manage a business."

While this business is belief-focused, it has also provoked legal challenges to the inclusion of religion in the workplace. The company has been sued several times on charges of employment discrimination. One notable case was that of Aziz Latif, a former Chick-fil-A restaurant manager who claimed he was fired a day after he didn't participate in a Christian group prayer. That suit was settled out of court.[60]

It is obvious that the five models do not provide absolute guidance on how to handle an ethical dilemma. Instead, they provide a departure point for discussing the implications of decisions. In addition, conflicts sometimes are easier to resolve if the two parties to the conflict understand each other's perspectives. An awareness of different frames of reference is especially important for hospitality firms that participate in foreign environments. For example, Eastern countries tend to be much more utilitarian in their approach to decisions, whereas larger industrialized Western countries tend to give economics a lot of weight. The influence of religion is strong in some Latin countries. These are obviously overgeneralizations that do not always hold true, but the key is not so much to pinpoint exactly what perspective a decision maker favors, but rather to look at decisions and conflicts from a variety of perspectives and to be aware that the other party to a transaction may not share your frame of reference. Companies often find themselves juggling competing rights such as freedom of religious expression and freedom from religious harassment in the workplace.

The challenge of handling conflicts is clearly illustrated by Chick-fil-A, a restaurant company that includes Christian religious principles and practices in its business. (See the "Hospitality Focus" boxed section on page 107.)

Codes of Ethics

Many organizations create a code of ethics in a further effort to communicate the values of the corporation to employees and other stakeholders. Another benefit of a code of ethics is that it allows the firm to clarify to employees what behavior is considered appropriate. Some codes of ethics set a minimum standard of behavior by stating that employees are expected to obey all laws. Other organizations make specific statements about values, duties, and obligations to customers, employees, and societies. Clearly, in those cases, the organization expects members to maintain standards of ethical behavior that transcend minimum legal standards.

The Seneca Gaming Corporation, a wholly owned, tribally chartered corporation of the Seneca Nation of Indians, has a 22-page code of business conduct and ethics. The introduction to the code of conduct and ethics is stated in the "Hospitality Focus" boxed section on page 109.

ETHICS SYSTEMS

To ensure that employees abide by the corporate code of ethics, some companies establish an ethics system, including an audit process to monitor compliance. Employees are encouraged to report violations to their supervisors or a designated corporate ethics officer. Some companies allow these reports to be anonymous through use of toll-free numbers to reduce the possibility of retribution against employees for making reports of violations. According to the Seneca Gaming Corporation, all of their employees are obliged to report violations of their code or the law and to cooperate in any investigations into such violations. While they prefer that employees give their identity when reporting violations, to allow the company to contact them for further information to pursue an investigation, they permit anonymous reporting of violations.[61]

Sometimes formal systems are not enough to ensure ethical behavior.[62] In an award-winning article, "The Parable of the Sadhu," Bowen McCoy, an investment banker with Morgan Stanley, discussed what he thought was the core, underlying problem when an organization handles ethical dilemmas poorly.[63] In his view, people who are part of an organization often do not personalize ethical issues. It is as if the organization is responsible, and the individuals are not. Even individuals who see themselves as very ethical will tend to pass through an ethical dilemma without recognizing it as one, or they will view the dilemma as ultimately someone else's problem. For many ethical dilemmas, one person is not physically capable of correcting the problem alone.

When faced with a major crisis, such as finding that a service is dangerous to the customers who purchase it, many organizations do not know what to do. There is no guiding

SENECA GAMING CORP.: CODE OF CONDUCT

All of our employees, officers, and directors must read and use this code of conduct to ensure that each business decision follows our commitment to the highest ethical standards and the law. Adherence to this code and to our other official policies is essential to maintaining and furthering our reputation for fair and ethical practices among our customers, shareholders, employees, and communities.

It is the responsibility of every one of us to comply with all applicable laws and regulations and all provisions of this code and the related policies and procedures. Each of us must report any violations of the law or this code. Failure to report such violations, and failure to follow the provisions of this code, may have serious legal consequences and will be disciplined by the company. Discipline may include termination of your employment.

This code summarizes certain laws and the ethical policies that apply to all of our employees, officers, and directors. Several provisions in this code refer to more detailed policies that either (1) concern more complex company policies or legal provisions or (2) apply to select groups of individuals within our company. If these detailed policies are applicable to you, it is important that you read, understand, and be able to comply with them. If you have questions as to whether any detailed policies apply to you, contact your supervisor or our Senior Vice President & General Counsel.

Situations that involve ethics, values, and violations of certain laws are often very complex. No single code of conduct can cover every business situation that you will encounter. Consequently, we have implemented the compliance procedures outlined in the sections of this code entitled "Administration of the Code" and "Asking for Help and Reporting Concerns." The thrust of our procedures is *when in doubt, ask.* If you do not understand a provision of this code, are confused as to what actions you should take in a given situation, or wish to report a violation of the law or this code, you should follow those compliance procedures. Those procedures will generally direct you to talk to either your immediate supervisor or our Senior Vice President & General Counsel. There are few situations that cannot be resolved if you discuss them with your supervisor or our Senior Vice President & General Counsel in an open and honest manner.[64]

precept, no system of shared values, to unite the company behind a clear understanding of correct behavior. Although some company members may feel discomfort with the course of action being pursued by the firm, a change in action requires a structured, systematic effort by the entire organization. According to McCoy, "Some organizations have a value system that transcends the personal values of the managers. Such values, which go beyond profitability, are usually revealed when the organization is under stress.... Members need to share a preconceived notion of what is correct behavior, a 'business ethic,' and think of it as a positive force, not a constraint."[65]

CORPORATE CITIZENSHIP: ALGAR S.A. EMPREENDIMENTOS E PARTICIPACOES

Algar S.A. Empreendimentos e Participacoes is known today as being one of the most active companies in Brazil in terms of corporate citizenship, as well as one of the best companies in which to work. We take great pride in such recognition. But above all, these are things that are part of our core values and beliefs. We have conducted training programs for our associates for many years now, and our companies believe in—and invest in—actions of social responsibility. We know that these projects go hand in hand with the respect we give our human talents, our partners and, of course, our customers. All of these relationships merge into an overall chain of action involving ethics, quality, commitment, and attitude. And believing in a better Brazil is also a business investment.[66]

The individual has a critical role in the development of shared values. McCoy writes: "What is the nature of our responsibility if we consider ourselves to be ethical persons? Perhaps it is to change the values of the group so that it can, with all its resources, take the other road."[67]

Ethics in Global Environments

Dealing with the ethics of employees, customers, and other stakeholders and the society from which they are drawn is a difficult task even in organizations that compete within a single domestic economy. However, the difficulty level increases for global organizations, because value systems are highly divergent across international boundaries. For example, a survey of 3,783 female seniors attending 561 universities and colleges in Tokyo revealed that they not only expected sexism in the workplace, but also didn't seem to mind it. "More than 91 percent said they would not mind being treated as 'office flowers.' Nearly 25 percent considered that to be a woman's role. Over 66 percent said acting like an office flower would make the atmosphere more pleasant."[68] This attitude concerning the role of women, which is still widely held in Japan, would be considered unacceptable in many other countries, including the United States.

As modern Japanese women and their roles in society continue to evolve, we are seeing more women entrepreneurs. They're exploring new paths to economic and personal fulfillment—like Makiko Fujino, who ran for office after years of being a television chef and won a seat in the Diet (Japan's legislature), and Junko Asazuma, who became an international snowboarder after spending years as a "freeter," or part-time worker. However, according to Veronica Chambers, author of *Kickboxing Geishas: How Modern Japanese Women are Changing their Nation,* Japanese women are more comfortable than their American counterparts in taking from the old and new without feeling bad about either.[69]

Value differences regarding the role of women across national cultures help illustrate the types of problems that exist across many international relationships. U.S. companies often experience cultural clashes when doing business with companies in China, Latin America, Russia, and many other countries, and firms from other countries often have difficulty understanding the values of Americans, Europeans, Australians, and so forth. The problem is a common one. The key to overcoming cultural clashes is working to understand the host-country culture and developing strategies that are consistent with that culture instead of fighting it. The discussion of ethical frames of reference found earlier in this chapter is helpful in doing this, because people in many countries tend to favor one or another of the ethical frames.

Although there are dissimilarities among international cultures, it would be an overstatement to say that everything is different. In fact, as organizations grow, develop, and internationalize, they tend to adopt values that are friendlier to a wider group of international constituents. This is certainly true of hospitality companies. The chapter will close with a statement from Luiz Alberto Garcia, chairman of the board of directors of Algar S.A. Empreendimentos e Participacoes, a large and successful Brazilian holding company with investments in a wide variety of businesses, including hotels and theme parks. Many of the elements of values, social responsibility, and enterprise strategy are included in the chairperson's message. In fact, it could just as well have been the opening statement in the annual report of a U.S., European, or Asian company. (See the "Hospitality Focus" boxed section on page 110.)

KEY POINTS SUMMARY

- Strategic managers are charged with the responsibility of providing long-term direction for their organizations, while balancing the competing interests of key stakeholders.

- Strategic direction should be established based, in part, on an analysis of the internal and external environments and the history of success or failure of the business. However, managers need to be careful that past success does not lead to failure due to resistance to change. Structural inertia is the term used to describe the forces that cause a company to resist change.

- A clear direction is the starting point of all strategic planning and management. It provides a framework for evaluating the effects of planned change and for planning the steps needed to move the organization forward.

- Businesses are defined with answers to three questions: (1) Who is being satisfied? (2) What is being satisfied? and (3) How are customer needs satisfied? While defining a business is helpful in communicating to internal and external stakeholders what the organization is all about, the business direction should not be used to limit where the company should go in the future.

- The business definition question should be stated not only as "What is our business?" but also as "What will it be?" and "What should it be?" In answering these questions, the organization should think in terms of what it knows and the assets it owns, its resources, and capabilities.

- Vision statements focus on what an organization wants to be in the future. Sometimes the terms mission and vision are confused. A mission is what the company is, whereas a vision is a forward-looking view of what the company aspires to become. However, when mission statements are written, they often include a vision statement. Many times, mission statements also include statements about the values of an organization.

- The final aspect of strategic direction discussed in this chapter was the establishment of organizational values. Values guide organizational decisions and behavior. Values help determine a firm's attitude toward social responsibility and treatment of various stakeholder groups.

- Enterprise strategies define how a company will serve particular stakeholder needs. Many organizations create a code of ethics to communicate the values of the corporation to employees and other stakeholders.

- Viewing problems from multiple frames of reference is an important tool for understanding the values of other cultures, because very few ethical dilemmas have simple right-or-wrong answers. Common frames of reference include economic, legal, religious, utilitarian, and universalist.

- Dealing with the ethics of employees, customers, and other stakeholders and the society from which they are drawn is considerably more difficult as organizations become global. Value conflicts are common across international boundaries. The key to overcoming cultural clashes is working to understand the host-country culture and developing strategies that are consistent with that culture instead of fighting it.

REVIEW QUESTIONS

1. What are some of the key forces influencing strategic direction in an organization? What is structural inertia, and how can it lead a successful firm to failure?

2. Describe the three elements that are critical in defining the business or businesses of an organization.

3. Define the business of a large, diversified organization with which you are familiar. Do not use a company that was described in this chapter.

4. What is an organizational mission? What can a mission include? Does a mission have to be formally written down to be effective?

5. What is a vision? What should a vision include? What is the difference between a mission and a vision?

6. How does the establishment of organization values help guide decision making?

7. How important is environmental sustainability and community involvement to the hospitality industry? Is it more important in hospitality than in other industries? Why or why not?

8. What are five common ethical frames of reference? What are their limitations?

9. What is an enterprise strategy? Why is an enterprise strategy important to an organization? Write an enterprise strategy for a firm with which you are familiar.

CRITICAL THINKING AND APPLICATION QUESTIONS

1. Create a strategic direction for the university or college you are attending. Make any logical assumptions that are necessary to complete the task. Include all of the elements of strategic direction, including a vision, a mission statement, and a list of organizational values.

2. Is the hospitality industry just giving lip service to concerns for the environment? Make the case for why green hotelkeeping is a real and important movement, and then prepare a counterargument for why it is a public-relations and marketing ploy. Provide evidence for both arguments.

3. Select several hotel companies and call the corporate reservations number, or a specific property directly, or both. Ask the simple question, "Could you please tell me the vision of your company?" Then record the reactions to the question. Summarize the results of your phone call.

   What did they say or do?

   Did the receptionist know the vision?

   Did you have to explain what a vision was?

   How long did it take?

   Did they understand your question?

   Did they refer you to someone else?

   What did you learn from this exercise?

4. Research any company you like, and find the organization's vision, mission statement, and values. Prepare a one-minute speech that captures this company's vision of the future. To help craft your brief speech, here are some suggestions:

   What does this company believe in?

   What does it do?

   How does it do it?

   For whom does it do it?

   What is its unique selling proposition?

   What makes it different from the competition?

   What benefits do the customers derive from its products and services?

CHAPTER 4

ORGANIZATIONAL RESOURCES AND COMPETITIVE ADVANTAGE

YOU SHOULD BE ABLE TO DO THE FOLLOWING AFTER READING THIS CHAPTER:

1. Ask six key questions to determine whether an organizational resource or capability will lead to a sustainable competitive advantage.

2. Understand the value chain and know how to create an industry or subindustry value chain.

3. Know the difference between tangible and intangible resources.

4. Determine which of five key resource areas is likely to lead to a sustainable competitive advantage.

5. Understand what types of knowledge are more likely to be associated with a sustainable competitive advantage.

6. Appreciate the importance of patents, copyrights, trademarks, brands, and reputations in determining the competitiveness of a firm.

FEATURE STORY

BUILDING COST-SAVING CAPABILITIES

Ryanair is one of Europe's largest low-cost carriers and one of the world's most profitable airlines. Founded in 1985 by Christy Ryan, Liam Lonergan, and Tony Ryan, the original airline offered service from Waterford in southeastern Ireland to Gatwick in London. In its first full year of operation under partial European Union (EU) deregulation, the small airline obtained permission to challenge the duopoly of Air Lingus and British Airways on the Dublin–London route. With two routes and two planes, this small Irish airline was off and running. By 1991, the airline had been running continuous losses; it abandoned its business-class product and discontinued its frequent flyer club.

To save the company from ruin and make the airline profitable, Michael O'Leary, the CEO, visited America to borrow ideas from Southwest Airlines, a well-established low-cost carrier. He returned with several key elements for a no-frills model, including the importance of quick turnaround times, no extras, and a single aircraft for operating efficiency. With an additional Ryan family investment of €20 million, the firm emerged from restructuring as Europe's first low-fare airline, making a profit for the first time. Deregulation of the European airline industry in 1992 gave carriers from any EU country the right to operate a schedule between other EU states, paving the way for Ryanair to begin launching new routes throughout Europe.

Today the airline serves more than 42 million passengers, with 2007 profits of €401.4 million. A comparison of 2007 to 2006 performance shows profit growth of 33 percent, traffic growth of 22 percent, revenue growth of 32 percent, and yield increases of 7 percent. Ryanair's passenger numbers have grown by up to 25 percent per year for most of the last decade. With plans to double traffic and profits by 2012, Ryanair continues to execute on its low-cost strategy by offering low fares that generate increased passenger traffic while maintaining a dedication to cost containment and operating efficiencies.

The key elements of Ryanair's strategy are low fares to stimulate demand, and customer service in the form of punctuality, fewer lost bags, and fewer cancellations than its primary competitors had. To accomplish these activities, Ryanair stresses quick turnaround times for aircraft, and chooses point-to-point short-haul routes to secondary and regional airports versus hub-and-spoke service. Short-haul and point-to-point service allows for direct nonstop service and avoids the cost of service for connecting passengers, including baggage transfer and passenger assistance. These regional airports offer lower landing and handling charges, faster turnaround times, less congestion, and fewer terminal delays. Ryanair negotiates extremely aggressive contracts with its airports, demanding low fees as well as financial assistance with marketing and promotional campaigns. In subsequent contract renewal negotiations, the airline plays airports off against each other, threatening to withdraw services and deploy the aircraft elsewhere if the airport does not make further concessions.

Lower operating costs also come from aircraft equipment costs and personnel productivity. Operating a fleet of aircraft with a single model, the Boeing 737-800 series provides operating efficiencies in maintenance and pilot scheduling. Taking advantage of the slump in airplane sales, the company ordered Boeing 737-800 series aircraft in 2001 at a substantial discount. Additional savings have come from more recent orders of aircraft without window shades, seat-back recline, or seat-back pockets. Reduced cleaning and repair costs for these planes have accompanied the savings of several hundred thousand dollars per aircraft when purchasing these bare-bones planes. Third parties are used at certain airports for passenger and aircraft handling, further lowering costs. Taking advantage of the Internet, direct selling to passengers through online bookings cuts out the cost of using travel agents, with the web site now handling 96 percent of all reservations. Ryanair does not employ an advertising agency, instead producing all of its advertising material in-house.

With a clear and focused strategy as a low-cost carrier, future plans include manageable growth, continuing efforts to appeal the EU commission decision to prevent acquisition of Aer Lingus, and the possibility of entering into the long-haul market with a transatlantic low-cost airline.[1]

DISCUSSION QUESTIONS:

1. What are the major contributors to Ryanair's profitability?

2. Would the acquisition of Aer Lingus complement Ryanair's key capabilities?

INTRODUCTION

Resources and capabilities are the bread and butter of organizational success. Better resources and capabilities lead to higher levels of success. Poor resources and capabilities lead to failure. However, not all resources and capabilities are equal in their ability to help an organization achieve sustainable performance. Because of its relentless focus on cost containment, Ryanair has been able to sustain a consistently high level of profitability compared to its competitors. However, a single resource does not create a competitive advantage; instead, resources must work together to create a firm's capabilities. Capabilities taken together are the source of a firm's core competencies. These core competencies form the basis of a competitive advantage. For Ryanair, building a core competency as a low-cost carrier came from assembling a bundle of complementary resources, including a fleet of easy-to-maintain aircraft, flying into regional airports, managing customer service costs, and selling primarily through an online distribution channel. Ryanair's enviable profits are the result of a dedication to ensuring that all resources and capabilities reduce costs and increase capacity. This chapter will provide tools to evaluate internal firm resources. It will help you understand how managers may identify and/or develop those resources and capabilities that are most likely to lead the firm to obtain a sustainable competitive advantage.

INTERNAL ANALYSIS AND COMPETITIVE ADVANTAGE

Matching a firm's resources and capabilities to emerging opportunities in the broad environment is the basis of strategy formulation. In Chapter 2, we explored how to examine external and market forces; we now turn to the role that internal resources play in securing a firm's strategy. When a firm earns a persistently higher level of profit than its competitors, it is believed to possess a competitive advantage.[2] Ryanair, for example, reports net margins of 18 percent compared to margins of 6 percent for Aer Lingus and EasyJet, 4 percent for Lufthansa, and 3 percent for British Airways.[3]

Sustainable Competitive Advantage

A *competitive advantage* exists when a firm has a long-lasting business advantage compared to rival firms that is a significant edge over the competition. Usually this means that the firm can do something competitors can't do, or has something competitors lack. While it is extremely difficult to sustain a competitive advantage, firms work to create advantages through the development of resources and capabilities. The ability of resources or capabilities to lead to a sustainable competitive advantage depends on the answers to the following six questions:

1. *Does the resource or capability have value in the market?* These types of resources allow a firm to exploit opportunities and/or neutralize threats.

2. *Is the resource or capability unique?* If an organization is the only one with a particular resource or capability, then it may be a source of competitive advantage. If numerous organizations possess a particular resource or

capability, then the situation is described as *competitive parity*—no company has the advantage. Note that uniqueness does not mean that only one organization possesses a capability or resource—only that few firms do. The uniqueness dimension also implies that a resource or capability is not easily transferable. That is, it is not readily available in the market for purchase.

3. *Is there a readily available substitute for the resource or capability?* Sometimes, competing organizations may not have the exact resource or capability, but they have easy access to another resource or capability that will help them accomplish the same results. For example, some car rental companies have arrangements with airports that allow them to lease space on the airport premises. This provides a location benefit. However, the benefit is not as large as it could be because competitors offer frequent and convenient shuttle service to car rental lots just outside these airports.

Positive answers to the first two questions and a negative answer to the third question mean that a resource or capability has the potential to lead to a competitive advantage for the firm. However, that potential is not realized unless two other questions are also answered in the affirmative:

4. *Do organizational systems exist that allow the realization of potential?* For potential to be realized, the firm must also be organized to take advantage of it. Disney is a master of exploiting profit potential from its animated features. Even before a movie is released, toys featuring the major characters and a soundtrack are available for purchase. Characters quickly become part of parades and shows at Disney's theme parks, and sometimes a major attraction or ride is developed.

5. *Is the organization aware of and realizing the advantages?* One of the great differentiators between successful and unsuccessful companies is the ability of managers to recognize and tap into resource advantages. An organization may have employees who have great potential in an area, but the organization does not know it. The company may have the ability to deliver a service that is highly unique and valuable to a particular market segment, but the firm does not realize it. In fact, an organization may even have systems in place that would allow realization of potential. Nevertheless, managers have to be able to identify sources of competitive advantage and take positive actions for potential to be realized.

At this point, an organization is using its systems and knowledge to take advantage of a unique and valuable resource or capability. However, resource advantages may not be sustainable. A final question determines the long-term value of a resource or capability:

6. *Is the resource or capability difficult or costly to imitate?* Competing firms should face a cost disadvantage in imitating a resource or capability. The more difficult or costly a resource or capability is, the more valuable it is in

producing a sustainable competitive advantage.[4] Investing in people is one powerful way of building capability that is difficult to imitate.

Figure 4.1 demonstrates how resources and capabilities become sustainable competitive advantages. If a resource or capability is valuable, unique, nonsubstitutable, or difficult to imitate, and if it also can be applied to more than one business area, it is called a *core competency* or *capability*. For example, Marriott has applied its skill in managing financial assets across a broad range of business segments, and Four Seasons has focused on building a culture of customer care. Successful companies pay critical attention to developing and applying their core competencies. Starwood has identified several capabilities that it sees as contributing to its competitive advantage as detailed in the "Hospitality Focus" boxed section on page 120.

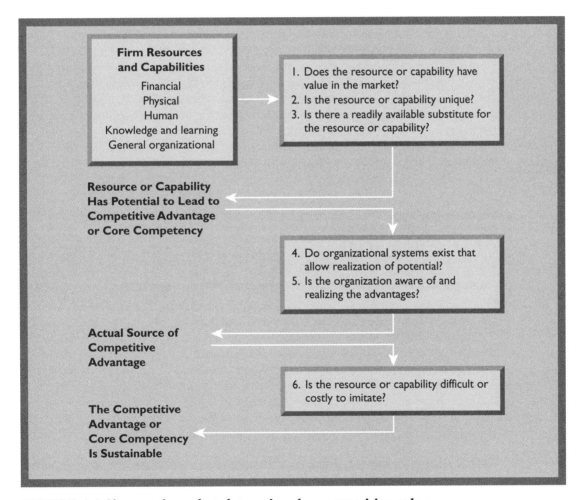

FIGURE 4.1 Six questions that determine the competitive value of resources and capabilities

HOSPITALITY FOCUS

STARWOOD'S CAPABILITIES

The foundation of Starwood's business strategy includes six capabilities:

1. Strong Brands
2. Extensive loyalty program
3. Location in major cities
4. Diversified property types
5. Economies of scale
6. Diversified assets and cash flow

Starwood considers its brand capability to be the result of strong brand recognition and worldwide global distribution. The Starwood Preferred Guest® (SPG) program has over 33 million members, and is recognized for its outstanding customer service, hassle-free award redemption, and member promotions. A significant presence in key markets has allowed Starwood to have entry into premier locations that are now expensive to access and develop. Size, as one of the largest hotel and leisure companies, gives Starwood economies of scale that help support at lower costs such activities as marketing, reservations, insurance, energy, telecommunications, technology, employee benefits, and operating supplies. The final capability rests in managing cash flow and assets by having a diversity of brands, market segments, and geographic locations served.[5]

VALUE-ADDING ACTIVITIES

One way to think about organizational resources and capabilities is to visualize the activities and processes of an organization and determine how they add value to the services that the organization provides in the marketplace.[6] Michael Porter developed a framework, called the value chain, that is a useful tool in identifying potential sources of competitive advantage. The *value chain* divides organizational processes into distinct activities that create value for the customer. In the wine industry, for example, key activities might include grape growing, wine making, distribution, marketing, and retail, as shown in Figure 4.2. Value-adding activities are a source of strength or competitive advantage if they meet the requirements identified in the previous section, such as value, uniqueness, nonsubstitutability, and inimitability.

The Value Chains of Winemakers

Firms in the same industry may have similar value chains, but they often differ. New World winemakers, for example, do not engage in the same activities as Old World producers, which

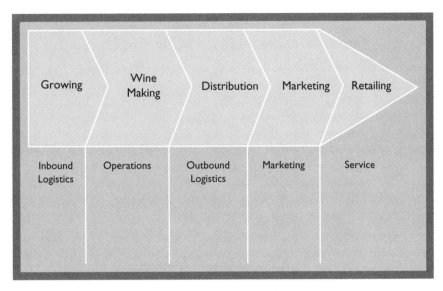

FIGURE 4.2 **Value chain for the wine industry**

may give them a competitive advantage over these European competitors.[7] Australian growers for years have innovated in growing and grape-making activities using drip irrigation, new trellis systems and techniques, and other developments in viticulture. These winemakers have crafted a competitive advantage on product consistency and quality to reduce the Old World benefits of terroir (i.e., soil) and history. In addition, clear and flexible labeling and a critical mass of supply may give these firms a competitive advantage in distribution and marketing.

New World vineyards tend to be larger than those in, say, Burgundy, which enables economies of scale and a better ability to negotiate with mass-market retailers. With supermarkets selling an increasing proportion of wine in many markets, New World producers are also better positioned to take advantage of this retail trend toward high volumes and low margins. A notable South African academic in wine marketing noted, "You shouldn't grow grapes without understanding marketing and business—it's about the whole wine value chain. It beats me how people can spend on equipment and build fancy cellars, and only then look for a market without having a business plan. One of the key factors to Australia's collective wine success is market research."[8] (See the "Hospitality Focus" boxed section on page 122.)

Value-Chain Activities

The operations of a hotel or a restaurant can be envisioned as a complicated assembly operation. Like manufacturing firms that divide their activities based on whether they are a primary part of the production chain or an activity that supports those production activities, a similar thought process takes place when a service firm such as a hotel or restaurant divides its activities

HOSPITALITY FOCUS

"CRITTER" LABELS MAKE AUSTRALIAN WINES FUN

Welcome to critter wines, with wallabies, crocodiles, goats, emus, and other animals featured on the labels, these new and playful wines are attracting attention. Take, for example, R. H. Phillips Toasted Head Chardonnay with a picture of a bear on the label, a $12.91 price tag, and lively apple pie à la mode notes mingled with citrus and pear aromas. Sales of critter wines have reached $600 million and appear to outperform other new table wines by two to one. Of the 438 table-wine brands introduced in the past three years, 18 percent featured an animal on the label, according to a recent survey by ACNielsen, a national marketing information company. While placing a critter on a label doesn't guarantee success, it does appeal to a group of consumers who don't take their wine too seriously.

Not everyone is amused by various wine marketers' efforts to make wines look fun and dynamic. One online review of wines has a policy that it will not review any wine with a label that, as they put it, "prominently features an animal—no ducks, no rabbits, no swans and penguins, and absolutely, positively, no 'f------ kangaroos'. For some, critter wines are viewed as the commoditization of wine by large conglomerate wine companies whose market research tells them that a given percentage of supermarket consumers want a wine with a cute raccoon on the label.

This criticism may be true, but it simply means that some in the wine industry are experimenting with one key aspect of the wine industry value chain—marketing—and are striving to create something new and valued. Unfortunately, these colorful and intriguing labels lining the shelves may not ensure sustainability, as more and more producers are introducing wines with an animal on the label.[9]

into what we will call core and support activities.[10] In a hotel, these *core activities* include site development and construction (by local owner), marketing and sales (by brand, regional office, and property), service delivery and operations (i.e., check-in, checkout, and in-room services at property level and by management company), service monitoring, and post-stay service enhancement. *Support activities* allow the hotel to function and to provide the core activities. Examples include human resources, maintenance, information technology, accounting, and purchasing.

One of the reasons the breakdown between core and support activities is useful is that it can help focus attention on areas in which the experience of guests or key stakeholders are most strongly influenced. Of course, the distinction between these two types of activities is not critical enough to argue. If you feel better about putting reservations as a support activity or reclassifying any of the other activities, it is perfectly acceptable, and may even be better, as long as it works for the firm. The key is to list all of the major activities of the firm that add value to the overall process and thus influence performance.

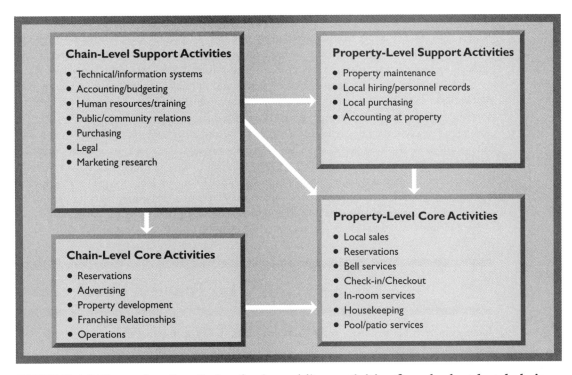

Chain-Level Support Activities

- Technical/information systems
- Accounting/budgeting
- Human resources/training
- Public/community relations
- Purchasing
- Legal
- Marketing research

Property-Level Support Activities

- Property maintenance
- Local hiring/personnel records
- Local purchasing
- Accounting at property

Chain-Level Core Activities

- Reservations
- Advertising
- Property development
- Franchise Relationships
- Operations

Property-Level Core Activities

- Local sales
- Reservations
- Bell services
- Check-in/Checkout
- In-room services
- Housekeeping
- Pool/patio services

FIGURE 4.3 **Example of analysis of value-adding activities for a budget hotel chain**

Figure 4.3 provides a starting point for analysis of value-adding activities for a budget hotel chain that owns and operates its own hotels. The list is not comprehensive, nor is the breakdown into boxes reflective of all budget hotel chains, but the example provides an illustration of how a value analysis of firm activities can be conducted. It also demonstrates that value nalysis can be conducted at the chain or property levels in a multiunit firm. In this example, many of the activities that lend themselves to economies of scale are centralized at the chain level. For example, the chain provides legal services, marketing research, and purchasing support. The chain also creates a standardized information system that all of the properties use. If an individual property manager has a problem with the system, assistance is provided by the central office. Its core activities are reservations, property development, operating standards, and advertising. Human resources services such as training are provided mostly at the chain level; however, a local manager is responsible for local hiring and maintenance of personnel records. Most of the accounting is provided centrally, but a certain amount of bookkeeping is required at the property.

Once the core and support activities are described, the firm should compare how well it conducts those activities relative to close competitors. A close competitor competes directly for the same sales dollars. For a chain, close competitors include other chains in the same approximate pricing segments and geographic markets. For an individual property, close competitors are typically defined as those in the same general proximity and price range. However, a hotel that aspires to be better may find it useful to expand comparisons to hotels in higher price ranges. Also, a large resort may consider its competitors to include large resorts in other cities that could potentially lure away its business or leisure travelers. The key is to be flexible enough to conduct an analysis at the level at which it is most relevant to the organization.

The cumulative effect of value-chain activities and the way they are linked inside the firm and with the external environment determine organizational performance relative to competitors. An organization can develop a competitive advantage in any of the primary or support activities. For each area, the relevant question is, "How much value is produced by this area versus our cost of producing that value?" This analysis of value and costs is then compared with competing firms. For example, one firm may have superior human resources training, accompanied by higher training costs, whereas another firm may have a superior reservations systems, accompanied by higher reservation costs. These two firms may actually provide an overall service quality that is similar in the market (as indicated by price and demand).

The Tourism Value Chain

Recent research has begun to apply the value-chain model to the overall tourism industry and highlights the fact that an industry value chain or value system is often composed of many different companies, such as airlines, rental cars, tour operators, hotels, and travel agents.[11] Figure 4.4 provides

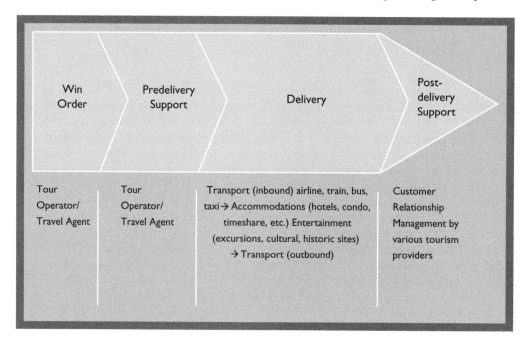

FIGURE 4.4 Value chain for the tourism industry
Source: Adapted from Y. Yilmaz and U. Bititci, "Performance Measurement In Tourism: A Value Chain Model," *International Journal of Contemporary Hospitality Management,* 18, 4, 2006, 341–349.

a value chain that starts with winning the order, predelivery support, delivery, and post-delivery support. As this figure shows, different tourism businesses may win the order and provide pre-delivery, including travel agents and tour operators. Delivery of the tourism product involves inbound transportation, accommodation, entertainment operations, and outbound transportation. Finally, post-delivery support can involve ongoing customer relationship management by several tourism providers. Key to a value-chain analysis is isolating and separating activities to determine the activities that will produce competitive advantage and those that are unimportant.

TANGIBLE AND INTANGIBLE RESOURCES

Chapter 1 described internal resources and capabilities as a bundle that fall into the general categories of financial, physical, human-based, knowledge-based, and general organizational. Figure 4.5 provides examples of the types of resources and capabilities that fall into each of these five areas.

Tangible resources can be seen, touched, and/or quantified.[12] Examples include land, buildings, materials, and money. These resources tend to be easy to imitate. Conversely, some of the most important resources and capabilities are *intangible*, such as the brand, employee trust, knowledge, and reputation of the firm. These intangibles are more difficult to quantify and the most difficult resources and capabilities to imitate. For example, knowledge about how to innovate is much more difficult to imitate than any particular architectural design or building material innovation. Organizational reputations cannot be fully imitated, even in the long term.

Other intangibles include good relationships with external stakeholders, a high-performing culture, and a well-known corporate brand. One of the reasons that intangible capabilities are difficult for competitors to imitate is that it is difficult to determine exactly how the source of capability was created (sometimes called *causal ambiguity*). Whereas a new product can be imitated, the processes used over time to hire, develop, retain, and build loyalty and shared values within the workforce are difficult to observe and even more difficult to imitate. Consequently, intangible resources and capabilities are often the ones most likely to lead to competitive advantage.

The resources and capabilities that lead to competitive advantage are different in each industry and can change over time. For example, high-performing film studios during the period from 1936 to 1950 built capability by having exclusive long-term contracts with actors and theaters. However, during the period from 1951 to 1965, managing the costs and production budgets were associated with high performance. These findings can be traced to the capabilities needed to deal with increasing uncertainty in the film industry and rising costs. While a strong service orientation from employees has long been a critical capability for the hospitality industry, the importance of interior design, financial resources, and value of brand has evolved.

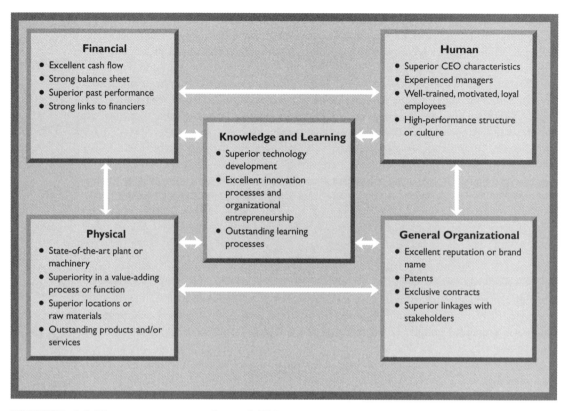

FIGURE 4.5 Firm resources and capabilities

In a recent study of the impact of tangible versus intangible assets on hotel operating performance, researchers at Cornell University found that greater investments in tangible resources such as the physical asset led to performance for full-service but not limited-service hotels. In contrast, investments in intangible resources such as brand and service employees enhanced future performance for all types of hotels.[13]

Resources and Capabilities

The rest of this chapter will discuss resources and capabilities in five sections. For the sake of simplicity, the term *resources* will sometimes be used to mean both resources and capabilities, unless a specific capability is being described. The five sections are financial resources, physical resources, human-based resources, knowledge-based resources, and general organizational resources. Although these resources will be discussed separately, it is important to note that in reality, they are all tied together. This point is demonstrated in Figure 4.5.

An organization can enter Figure 4.5 at any point, but we will start at financial resources. An organization with very strong financial resources can hire better managers and employees and train them better. A strong financial position can also lead to investments in superior physical assets, such as a hotel with distinctive architectural features or a restaurant in an excellent location. In addition, if an organization uses strong financial resources to hire the most-talented people and train them well, those employees are more likely to learn better and innovate. This innovation and learning will result in better operational processes, which reinforce investments in superior physical assets. The result should be better products and services, which lead to a strong brand, an excellent organizational reputation, and excellent relationships with stakeholders. Strong brands and superior products and services are likely to lead to financial success. Thus, the cycle continues.

To be successful over the longer term, companies need to pay attention to all five resource areas. Lack of attention to any of the five areas can remove a firm from the loop. A solid investment strategy should focus on human-resource development and superior physical assets and processes. If financial resources are misused, they will not result in better human resources or superior physical assets and processes. Eventually, the organization will no longer be competitive. Human resources need to be managed effectively so that learning and innovation are the result. If human-resource development is neglected or misguided, learning and innovation will cease, and the organization will eventually wear down, thus breaking out of the loop. Knowledge creation and innovative activities should be channeled so as to produce better processes and more innovative services. If this does not happen, the value of a company's brand will be eroded, and its reputation may suffer. Finally, brand names, organizational reputation, and stakeholder relationships should be carefully guarded and developed in order to produce strong financial results. The point here is that all of the resource areas are interdependent, and an organization can't afford to neglect any of them.

Entrepreneurs enter the cycle at any of several stages, but most often an entrepreneur will begin with an idea. He or she will then seek to build an organization around the idea. Financing will need to be arranged. Human resources will need to be acquired. Once a venture is formed, the innovation may lead to superior processes or services. If not, then it is unlikely to be successful. However, if superior processes or services result, financial success may be obtained. The entrepreneur then uses financial success as a platform for building the human resources of the organization. The cycle has begun.

FINANCIAL RESOURCES

Financial resources can be a source of advantage, although they rarely qualify as unique or difficult to imitate. Nevertheless, strong cash flow, low levels of debt, a strong credit rating, access to low-interest capital, and a reputation for creditworthiness are powerful strengths that can serve as a source of strategic *flexibility*, which means that firms can be more responsive to new opportunities and new threats. Essex Partners, an independent management company that specializes in opeaing budget hotels, realized that in order to compete in a very crowded and competitive market, it would have to prove that its operations were more efficient and produced a higher gross operating profit (GOP) than comparable properties. The firm has established a system of budgeting and cost controls that allow it to perform at a level that attracts the attention of both property owners and financial lenders. Part of this success comes because Essex is able to obtain better financing for its owners and to reduce other expenses usually not deemed the management company's responsibility, such as interest rates, insurance, legal, and audit costs.[14] These types of firms are also under less pressure from stakeholders than are their competitors who suffer financial constraints.

Financial Ratios

Financial ratios, such as the ones found in Table 4.1, may be used to determine the financial strength of an organization and its ability to finance new growth strategies. Often companies will track trends of key ratios over several years, assessing changes over time. Also, because ratios are useful for comparisons, firms may compare their numbers against industry averages from a major competitor to assess comparative financial strength.

Profitability ratios are a common measure of overall financial success. They provide a barometer for management with regard to how well strategies are working, and they may also provide warning of downward trends and thus the need for more-dramatic changes. External stakeholders pay critical attention to profitability ratios, as they are a primary determinant of share prices, the ability to repay loans, and future dividends. Also, other types of performance measures are highly relevant, depending on the industry. For example, load factors, which are basically a measure of how full planes are on average, are a key metric in the airline industry. In the hotel industry, revenue per available room (RevPAR) is a widely used measure of performance.

Liquidity ratios help an organization determine its ability to pay short-term obligations. Financiers are especially interested in these ratios, because lack of liquidity can lead to immediate insolvency during downturns. Insufficient liquidity may be a sign that the company is performing poorly. However, it might also be an indication of the need for more long-term financing. For example, an organization may have relatively low levels of liquidity, but also low levels of long-term debt such as bonds. By selling bonds, the organization can increase its cash flow, thus relieving tight liquidity. This often happens when firms are growing. Two common liquidity measures, the current and quick ratios, focus on solvency of a firm if it liquidates.

Unfortunately, these static ratios fail to capture the operating liquidity enjoyed by restaurants. In a recent study comparing restaurants to manufacturing firms, researchers found that when using an integrative measure of liquidity, one that uses both operating and financial liquidity, restaurants were shown to be more liquid.[15] Consequently, dynamic and static liquidity needs to be measured against other ratios and trends to achieve an accurate picture of financial strength.

Leverage is a common measure of financial risk, which often takes the form of a loan or other borrowing (debt) to allow for greater potential gain, but also can lead to greater loss. The

TABLE 4.1 Commonly Used Financial Ratios

Ratio	Calculation	What It Measures
	Profitability Ratios	
Gross profit margin	$\dfrac{\text{Sales} - \text{COGS}}{\text{Sales}} \times 100$	Efficiency of operations and product pricing
Net profit margin	$\dfrac{\text{Net profit after tax}}{\text{Sales}} \times 100$	Efficiency after all expenses are considered
Return on assets (ROA)	$\dfrac{\text{Net profit after tax}}{\text{Total assets}} \times 100$	Productivity of assets
Return on equity (ROE)	$\dfrac{\text{Net profit after tax}}{\text{Stockholders' equity}} \times 100$	Earnings power of equity
	Liquidity Ratios	
Current ratio	$\dfrac{\text{Current assets}}{\text{Current liabilities}}$	Short-run debt-paying ability
Quick ratio	$\dfrac{\text{Current assets} - \text{inventories}}{\text{Current liabilities}}$	Short-term liquidity
	Leverage Ratios	
Debt to equity	$\dfrac{\text{Total liabilities}}{\text{Stockholders' equity}}$	Extent to which stockholders' investments are leveraged (common measure of financial risk)
Total debt to total assets (debt ratio)	$\dfrac{\text{Total liabilities}}{\text{Total assets}}$	Percent of assets financed through borrowing (also financial risk measure)
	Activity Ratios	
Asset turnover	$\dfrac{\text{Sales}}{\text{Total assets}}$	Efficiency of asset utilization
Inventory turnover	$\dfrac{\text{COGS}}{\text{Average inventory}}$	Management's ability to control investment in inventory
Average collection period	$\dfrac{\text{Receivables} \times 365 \text{ days}}{\text{Annual credit sales}}$	Effectiveness of collection and credit policies
Accounts receivable turnover	$\dfrac{\text{Annual credit sales}}{\text{Receivables}}$	Effectiveness of collection and credit policies

potential for loss is greater because if the investment goes bad, money is lost and the loan still requires repayment. For example, the U.S. airlines had so much leverage and such low liquidity before the disaster on September 11, 2001, that the government had to give them billions of dollars within weeks just to help them continue to operate.

Finally, Table 4.1 contains a few ratios that measure the efficiency of organizational activities. These ratios may be difficult for outside observers to measure. For example, annual credit sales, a factor in two of these ratios, may not be reported. Consequently, you might consider average accounts receivable in which you take the beginning-of-the-period plus the end-of-the-period accounts receivable and divide by two. Don't be frustrated if you can't get information to calculate all of these ratios. Instead, focus on information that is available. For example, information on sales and total assets, used to calculate asset turnover, is almost always available.

In addition to general financial health, special arrangements such as *real estate investment trusts* (REITs) can provide financial benefits. A REIT is a financial arrangement in which investors own shares of a holding company that invests in real estate such as hotels and resorts. As long as the REIT pays out at least 95 percent of its income as dividends, it does not have to pay income taxes.[16] Many hotels are owned by REITs but managed by other companies. REITs allow hotel management companies such as Marriott to greatly expand their operations by reducing the capital needed for land and buildings. Franchising offers many of the same benefits because the franchisor typically does not have an ownership interest in the real property associated with a particular franchise.

Strong financial resources are increasingly important in the highly competitive environments that make up the hospitality industry. Deep financial resources are needed to wage battles in markets where other forms of advantage are not sustainable for long. In the hotel industry, innovations are quickly imitated. Also, the ability to invest in unique, valuable, difficult-to-imitate capabilities is often tied completely to the available financial resources. For example, the ability to build a brand name, to create an innovative process, or to compensate fairly and retain a highly creative workforce depends on financial resources. While financial resources may not be unique, they provide the lever for developing those types of resources-elsewhere in the organization.

PHYSICAL RESOURCES

This section is about physical assets and processes. These are the resources people see when they observe the organization. Superior physical resources such as prime locations and outstanding facilities are obvious sources of competitive advantage. The importance of hotel design is reflected in the role physical space plays in delivery of service. Lobbies, for example, are used for entertainment, while bars and restaurants are often integrated into the lobby for evening. In the guest rooms, the boundary between the bedroom and bathroom has become more transparent with the use of materials such as frosted glass instead of a wall.[17]

GRAMERCY PARK: A LIFE STYLE HOTEL

HOSPITALITY FOCUS

The Gramercy Park Hotel in New York City has developed a private roof club and garden in what Ian Schrager envisions as "the lobby as a new kind of gathering place." The club is enclosed by a retractable roof that is intended to combine the look of a private London gentlemen's club, a Viennese coffeehouse, and a rooftop garden. The intimate space uses artist Julian Schnabel's bold colors, custom outdoor furniture, lush greenery, and eye-catching lighting. Schrager explains his focus on the physical assets, noting "I wanted to create a new kind of public space . . . a private lobby in the sky as a counterpoint to the public lobby on the ground floor."[18]

Architectural and Sustainable Design

Ex-nightclub entrepreneur Ian Schrager is often credited for radically changing the mind-set in hotel development from the creation of a banal box to an interesting, sleek, ultra-modern tyle in the late '80s and '90s, with the help of Andrée Putman and Philippe Starck. The French designer Philippe Starck noted, "Twenty-five years ago, we made a revolution in the hotel business with what people call now the boutique hotel."[19] Starck is currently designing the space station for Virgin Galactic, the space-tourism company founded by Richard Branson of the Virgin Group, while Schrager is busy taking boutique hotels to the next level with a possible partnership with Marriott.

Boutique hotels, sometimes called design hotels or lifestyle hotels, differentiate themselves from larger chain or branded hotels by their intense focus on the physical space through the design of their facilities. Furnished in a themed, stylish, or aspirational manner, these hotels are usually small and attentive to imaginative and innovative building solutions. The first boutique hotels were opened in the early 1980s: The Blakes Hotel in South Kensington, London (designed by celebrity stylist Anouska Hempel) and the Bedford in Union Square, San Francisco (the first of many boutique hotels currently operated under the Kimpton Group). In 1984, Ian Schrager opened his first boutique hotel in Murray Hill in New York City: the Morgans Hotel.[20] Since then, chains such as Starwood with its W brand and Le Meridien's Art + Tech group (now a Starwood brand) produced architecturally interesting hotels on a larger scale. (See the "Hospitality Focus" boxed section above.)

While the movement toward boutique hotels is a clear example of using physical resources to build competitive advantage, Europe and Asia continue to lead the way in producing architecturally interesting hotels. Another element of resource capability through physical resources is the construction and location of hospitality products. One emerging area for future competitive positioning is the movement toward green or sustainable design. *Sustainability* is

TABLE 4.2 Sustainable Hotel Design

Green Materials and Physical Asset Utilization
Lighting, air conditioning, and heating intelligent control systems that monitor guests in room
Less furniture pieces and Green Guard–certified furniture when possible
Carpet rental and carpet tile: Green Label Plus carpets
Green products: Companies with a low carbon footprint
Materials that are recyclable or renewable, including cork, bamboo, agrifiber, and substrates for millwork
Materials and finishes that do not offgas
Local and regional materials
Green Operating System and Procedures
Reuse water for washing dishes and laundry
Operational coordination with guest: Reuse towels and bedding for a multinight stay
Capture energy from washing wastewater, preheated water
Proper selection of light lamps for low energy and long life cycle
More efficient HVAC (heating, ventilation, and air-conditioning) systems
Renewable energy sources

Source: Lodging Hospitality, 2007.

based on the idea of providing for current needs without sacrificing the needs of future generations. Environmental concerns have motivated designers to use natural ventilation and grey water in toilets when possible, while biodegradable materials are replacing aluminum and alucobond in construction. New materials such as low-VOC (volatile organic compounds) paints and formaldehyde-free wood substrates can enhance sustainable design.[21]

Table 4.2 provides a brief summary of several environmentally sensitive ideas for hotel design and development. The green movement may attract even more hotel developers as the cost savings become more compelling. A study conducted in conjunction with the U.S. Green Building Council found that the current cost premium for building sustainable buildings has come down to only 1 to 2 percent of total project cost and is recoverable in one to two years.[22] What may make the green movement more important for physical resource development is the cost savings that can accrue over the life of the building. Buildings that meet *LEED-certified* (Leadership in Energy and Environmental Design) sustainability standards can obtain energy savings ranging from 30 to 50 percent, water savings of up to 40 percent, and solid waste reduction of 70 percent. As one expert notes, "as shortages of energy, water, and waste disposal sites loom bigger, the cost of these resources is bound to go up significantly. This will only make the long-term economics of green building even more compelling than they already are."[23]

FAIRMONT RESORTS AND HOTELS ENVIRONMENTAL PROGRAM

HOSPITALITY FOCUS

Fairmont Resorts and Hotels Green Partnership Program is considered to be the "most comprehensive environmental program in the North American hotel industry," according to *National Geographic Traveler*. The program focuses on improvements in the areas of waste management, energy, and water conservation, as well as a strong element of community outreach through local groups and partnerships. Some of the initiatives that incorporate clean energy use into daily operations include:

Wind power. Currently, 40 percent of the electricity needs of the Fairmont Chateau Lake Louise in Alberta, Canada, are met by a blend of wind and run-of-river electricity generation. The Fairmont in Washington, D.C., has partnered with Pepco Energy Services to supply the hotel with more than 3 million kilowatt hours (kWh) of electricity generated from renewable resources, 10 percent of which will be derived from wind farms located in the mid-Atlantic region.

Solar power. Solar systems have now been installed in nine chalets at the Fairmont Kenuak at Chateau Montebello in Canada. These chalets draw 50 percent of their power from solar means. This energy is used to power well water pumps, some kitchen and furnace fans, dishwashers, supplementary lighting, and emergency radios.

Heat recovery. The Fairmont Waterfront, in Vancouver, British Columbia, installed a heat-recovery system that captures steam that has been condensed back into water from domestic hot-water tanks, and then uses it to preheat incoming city water. This process saves an estimated 305,380 kWh (1,100 GJ) per year.

Lighting. The Fairmont Sonoma Mission Inn & Spa in California replaced 4,440 incandescent bulbs with energy-efficient fluorescent lighting. As a result, the hotel now saves more than 203,000 kWh of energy annually, representing a cost savings of $61,000.[24]

Equally important to a service setting are the ways in which a firm uses its physical resources to generate customer value. McDonald's was able to turn a filthy restaurant in a terrible location into a model of efficiency and quality through its standard operating procedures:

McDonald's has a restaurant on the eastbound side of the Connecticut Turnpike Interstate 95 in Darien. For years, the place had been an almost unimaginably filthy highway eatery before being converted into a McDonald's. Three years later, it was one of the busiest McDonald's locations in America.[25]

Competitive advantages can also be created through superior linkages with stakeholders in the external environment. For example, building alliances with green suppliers and obtaining

LEED certification from the U.S. Green Building Council (USGBC), a nonprofit organization composed of leaders from every sector of the building industry, can enhance physical resources. Fairmont Hotels and Resorts, for example, works with the Pembina Institute, a nonprofit environmentl organization, to purchase Eco-Logo–certified wind power to offset the greenhouse gas emissions generated by all of its front-desk check-in computers. (See the "Hospitality Focus" boxed section on 133.)

The design and style of hospitality products is a key competitive resource, and location, location, location has always been a factor in establishing a unique position. Nevertheless, the enduring success of service organizations often rests on the daily encounters between employees and guests. We now turn to a key resource in the hospitality industry—people.

HUMAN-BASED RESOURCES

The humans that make up an organization are its lifeblood—its unique and most valuable asset. Most of the other factors of production—such as properties and even special knowledge—may be duplicated over the long term, but every human being is totally unique. This section deals with the internal stakeholders of the firm, which include managers, employees, and owners. It begins by highlighting the importance of the CEO in creating organizational success, followed by a general discussion of effective strategic leadership. Employees, structure, and culture will also be discussed. Analysis of the human-based resources of a firm can provide an indication of future competitiveness, as well as highlighting areas that need attention.

Strategic Leadership

The highest-ranking officer in a large organization can be called by many titles, but the most common is chief executive officer, or CEO. Most of the research evidence indicates that CEOs have a significant impact on the strategies and performance of their organizations.[26] In fact, in some cases, a CEO can be a source of sustainable competitive advantage. A CEO such as Isadore Sharp of Four Seasons Hotels and Resorts or Joseph Neubauer of Aramark can leave little doubt that much of the success or failure of an organization depends on the person at the top. Neubauer, who presides over one of the most successful managed-services firms in the world, has experienced an array of leadership challenges, including corporate raiders. (See the "Hospitality Focus" boxed section on page 135.)

Neubauer, who emigrated from Israel at age 14 and worked his way to the top of a highly successful company, epitomizes effective leadership. However, just as excellent leadership can have an enormous positive influence on a firm, poor leadership can have a powerful negative influence. Coca-Cola enjoyed many years of double-digit growth under the leadership of Roberto Goizueta. However, some analysts have argued that since his death in 1997, the company has felt a leadership void and struggled as a result.[27]

In the traditional model of leadership, the CEO decides where to go, and then, through a combination of persuasion and edict, directs others in the process of implementation.[28]

STRATEGIC LEADERSHIP AT ARAMARK

When corporate raiders tried to take over Aramark and get CEO Joseph Neubauer to join them, he mortgaged his house, took out a personal loan, and helped lead a management buyout with 70 other execs to fend off the raiders. "I felt an obligation to the people who worked with me," he says. "We wanted to control our destiny." It was a winning bet. In 2001, he took a larger, more successful Aramark public again to finance overseas growth. "We made 250 people millionaires from hot dogs and dirty laundry. Only in America," he quips. His latest move was to join with a private investor group and acquire the company in a transaction valued at $8.3 billion.[29]

However, the traditional view of CEOs as brilliant, charismatic leaders with employees who are good soldiers is no longer valid in many organizational settings. Turbulent global competitive environments and multibusiness organizations are far too complex for one person to stay on top of all the important issues. Shared leadership is needed because a leader cannot be everywhere at once. It would be naive to assume that a leader can, at any given time, control all the actions of members of an entire business. Also, companies are influenced by multiple stakeholders with competing demands. Consequently, while the CEO is the most important leader in a firm, other leaders are also vital to organizational success. While the smallest organizations may have a single owner/manager who makes all important strategic and operating decisions, in large organizations, strategic leadership is distributed among a wide variety of individuals.[30]

The CEO has primary responsibility for setting the strategic direction of the firm, but other executives and managers are expected to show leadership qualities and participate in strategic management activities. Many effective CEOs assemble a heterogeneous group of three to ten top executives that make up the top management team (TMT).[31] Each member of the TMT brings a unique set of skills and a unique perspective of how the organization should respond to demands from a diverse set of stakeholders. CEOs work with TMT members to tap their skills, knowledge, and insights. Consequently, while this section will focus primarily on CEOs as the primary source of leadership in organizations, it is assumed that strategic leadership is distributed among the TMT and other influential managers and organizational members.

The literature on strategic leadership is vast, and there is no consensus on the characteristics that distinguish excellent leaders. However, most scholars would agree on five important responsibilities of strategic leadership that seem to be evident in most successful organizations. They are:

1. Creating organizational vision
2. Establishing core values for the organization
3. Developing strategies and a management structure
4. Fostering an environment that is conducive to organizational learning and development
5. Serving as a steward for the organization

HOSPITALITY FOCUS

ACCOR: SENIOR LEADER REFOCUSES STRATEGY

In January 2006, a new Board of Directors was elected at Accor, which in turn chose a new CEO, Gilles Pélisson. One of Pélisson's first initiatives was to change his senior management team and develop a clearer strategy to enable the group to identify development priorities and focus its managerial and financial resources. Quickly, Accor sold its equity stake in Club Mediterranee and Carlson Wagonlit Travel. Senior management under the leadership of Pélisson developed an expansion strategy that focuses on key acquisitions in their service vouchers business and organic growth in hotels, especially in China and India. In addition, the upper upscale Sofitel brand was repositioned. Rounding out his first year as CEO, Pélisson devised and communicated an "asset right" real estate strategy of adapting operating structures to unique country and market segments.[32]

CREATING ORGANIZATIONAL VISION

The traditional view of leaders in organizations is that they set the direction, make the important decisions, and rally the followers (usually employees).[33] Many CEOs have been described as visionaries. They have a vision of what the organization should become, and they communicate that vision to other managers and employees. They *make* their vision a reality. The French entrepreneurs Paul Dubrule and Gerard Pelisson have presided over one of the great success stories in the hotel industry. Beginning with a roadside hotel in Lille, France, Accor is now the third-largest hotel group in the world, with nearly half a million rooms in almost 100 countries. Unlike many hotel groups that focus on higher-quality segments, Accor's vision is to appeal to the masses, with around 90 percent of its revenues in the economy and midpriced segments. Brands include Novotel, Etap, Ibis, Formule 1, and Motel 6, among others.[34] While Dubrule and Pelisson, as founding cochairs attend board meetings in an advisory capacity, the direction of the firm is under the guidance of CEO Gilles Pélisson. (See the "Hospitality Focus" boxed section above.)

Visionary leadership can be divided into three stages:

1. Envisioning what the organization should be like in the future
2. Communicating this vision to followers
3. Empowering these followers to enact the vision[35]

Paul Dubrule and Gerard Pélisson developed a vision of making their companies one of the largest hoteliers in the world. Then they tirelessly communicated this vision in word and deed to managers and associates. When a new CEO was selected, they and the Board of Directors made sure that he shared their vision.

ESTABLISHING CORE VALUES

It would be naive to assume that a leader can, at any given time, control all the actions of members of an entire business. Effective leadership is much more subtle. Leaders basically

INTERCONTINENTAL HOTELS GROUP (IHG): CEO RESIGNS

HOSPITALITY FOCUS

An award-winning and highly respected senior leader at InterContinental Hotels Group (IHG) resigned from his position as CEO of the Asia-Pacific Region after a routine internal investigation revealed he had falsified his academic qualifications. Mr. Patrick Imbardelli, named "Hotelier of the Year 2006," had been scheduled to join IHG's Board when an internal review of his academic qualifications from Australia's Victoria University and Cornell University revealed that he had falsified his degrees and had not graduated from these universities. He promptly resigned and an acting CEO for Asia-Pacific was put in place.[36]

DAY HOSPITALITY GROUP: SABBATICAL PROGRAM

HOSPITALITY FOCUS

Frederick Cerrone, president of Day Hospitality Group, believes there is more to life than just work. After a trip to India, he recognized that he was finally taking the time to do something that he had always wanted to do. This realization inspired him to develop a sabbatical program for his relatively young general managers. He instituted a mandatory 90-day paid sabbatical leave program for every general manager with five years' tenure in his company. The sabbatical concept ties into one of the company's 17 value statements: "Believe in balanced living in all areas of life—career, family, spiritual, physical, financial, social, and educational."[37]

establish a social system that defines and reinforces desired behaviors. Consequently, when members of a company face an unexpected situation, they are guided by the social system.[38]

One important way that leaders influence the social system in their organizations is through the values they bring to the organization. These values can be conveyed in several ways. For instance, they can be communicated directly through public statements, memoranda, and e-mails. Highly visible decisions are also an effective way to communicate a value. For example, the head of Asia-Pacific operations at InterContinental Hotels Group resigned after it was confirmed that he had misrepresented his academic qualifications. (See the first "Hospitality Focus" boxed section above.)

Small talk is also vital to effectively establishing organizational values. Small talk refers to private discussions that take place in offices or in lunchrooms. Conversations of this kind are a forum for discussing issues, problems, situations, incidents, processes, and individuals.[39]

Leaders can also influence value systems through the way they administer rewards. The organization's individuals who demonstrate the desired attitudes and behavior can be rewarded with salary increases, promotions, attention (i.e., awards), or special privileges. (See the second "Hospitality Focus" boxed section above.)

In addition, core values can provide a basis for determining which alternative strategies to select, how they are to be selected, how strategic decisions will be communicated, and to whom. If leaders are responsive to the values of key stakeholders when making and communicating decisions, the decisions are more likely to be perceived as ethical by those stakeholders.

One example of communicating values is set in Arizona's desert: "Sara Bird-in-Ground sees her mission as telling the world about the rich culture of her community—the Pima and Maricopa tribes of Arizona who for centuries farmed the area, sharing their bounty with travelers."[40] Sheraton Wild Horse Pass resort, a 500-room luxury inn in the desert, has crafted its strategy around providing employees and guests with the Indian tribes' history and culture. Culturally themed programs and events, such as the Kid Club, which includes nature walks, pottery making, and basket weaving, are designed to persuade vacation decision makers to select Arizona hotels over other destinations with sun and great golf.

DEVELOPING STRATEGIES AND STRUCTURE

Strategic leaders are directly responsible for overseeing the development of strategies the organization should follow. When CEOs fail to deliver on these expectations, powerful stakeholders often step in. For example, Jack Schuessler, CEO of Wendy's International, retired after 30 years with the company and in the wake of franchisee complaints. The move to replace the CEO came after more than a year of weak sales and one week after the 700 franchisees formed a breakaway group, complaining that the company needed to devote more attention to franchisee needs and operational issues.[41] Effective strategy development implies a strong awareness of the resources and capabilities that an organization has or can develop or acquire that will lead to a sustainable competitive advantage.[42]

In small organizations, the entrepreneur typically serves as the sole strategist. As organizations grow, the top-management team is assembled for the same purpose. Furthermore, as companies grow, they tend to have more managers and more levels of management. The variety and number of these other managers are as varied as the businesses themselves. Strategic leaders have the opportunity to "influence patterns of interaction and to assign responsibility to particular individuals."[43] They do this by creating a management reporting structure. As organizations continue to grow, they often become involved in more than one business area. As this happens, typically the CEO will delegate responsibility for developing competitive strategies to the managers who are responsible for each business. The reporting structure is then altered accordingly. Specific strategies will be discussed in Chapters 5, 6, and 9, and organization structures will be treated at length in Chapter 8.

FOSTERING ORGANIZATIONAL LEARNING

Many organizational scholars believe that the true role of a leader is to harness the creative energy of the individual, so that the organization as a whole learns over time.[44] Leaders should create an environment for organizational learning by serving as a coach, teacher, and facilitator.[45] A learning environment is created by helping organizational members question their assumptions about the business and its environment: what customers want, what competitors are likely to do, which technology choices work best, and how to solve a problem. For learning to take place, members must understand that the organization is an interdependent network of people and activities. Furthermore, learning requires that members keep their work focused on creating patterns of behavior that are consistent with strategy rather than reacting haphazardly to problems. Leaders play the essential role in creating an environment where employees question assumptions, understand interdependency, see the strategic significance of their actions, and are empowered to lead themselves.[46] Organizational learning will be treated further later in this chapter.

SERVING AS A STEWARD

Finally, effective leaders are stewards for their firms: they care about the company and the society in which it operates, both voluntary and involuntary stakeholders.[47] Leaders must feel and convey a passion for the organization, its contribution to society, and its purpose. They should feel that "they are part of changing the way businesses operate, not from a vague philanthropic urge, but from a conviction that their efforts will produce more productive organizations, capable of achieving higher levels of organization success and personal satisfaction than more traditional organizations."[48]

LEADERSHIP APPROACHES AND ORGANIZATIONAL FIT

There are many ways to lead, depending on the circumstances and the personality of the individual. Bourgeois and Brodwin identified five distinct leadership approaches or styles.[49] The styles differ in the degree to which CEOs involve other managers and lower-level employees in the strategy formulation and implementation process. The first two styles correspond to the traditional model of leader as director and decision maker; the latter three styles represent more participative styles of leadership that are probably more relevant in today's global economy.

- *Commander.* The CEO formulates strategy and then directs top managers to implement it.

- *Change.* The CEO formulates strategy, then plans the changes in structure, personnel, information systems, and administration required to implement it.

- *Collaborative.* The CEO initiates a planning session with executive and division managers. After each participant presents ideas, the group discusses and agrees to a strategy. Participants are then responsible for implementing strategy in their areas.

- *Cultural.* After formulating a vision and strategy for the company, the CEO and other top-level managers mold the organization's culture so that all organizational members make decisions that are consistent with the vision. In this approach, the culture inculcates organizational members into unity of purpose and action.

- *Crescive.* Under this leadership model, lower-level managers are encouraged to formulate and implement their own strategic plans. The CEO's role is to encourage innovation while filtering out inappropriate programs. Unlike the other models, the crescive (meaning "gradual, spontaneous development") model of leadership uses the creative energies of all members of the organization, which is consistent with the philosophy of Total Quality Management (TQM).

Not only do different executives have different leadership styles, but they also have varying capabilities and experiences that prepare them for different strategic environments. While managers are capable of adapting to changing environments and strategies, it is not likely that they are equally effective in all situations. A manager who was part of the turbulent growth years of a start-up company may have serious difficulty adjusting to the inevitable shifts in scale and scope of a growing business. Take Papa John's Pizza president and CEO Nigel Travis, who took over from the passionate founder John Schattner. The new CEO plans to move the company forward by using a strategy that served him well as president and COO (Chief Operating Officer) at Blockbuster Inc.[50] Leaders often bring experiences and capabilities they refined in different industries with them to new positions.

The debate continues regarding whether it is appropriate to try to fit a manager to a particular organization's strategy.[51] Some research suggests that low-cost strategies are best implemented by managers with production/operations backgrounds because of the internal focus on efficiency and engineering. The research also suggests that differentiation strategies need to be managed by executives who are trained in marketing and research and development because of the innovation and market awareness that are needed.[52] There is also some tentative evidence that strategic change or innovation in companies is more likely to occur with managers who are younger (both in age and in time in the company) but well-educated.[53] Growth strategies may be best implemented by managers with greater sales and marketing experience, willingness to take risks, and tolerance for ambiguity. However, those same characteristics may be undesirable in an executive managing the activities of a retrenchment or some other strategy.[54] For example, Stephen Bollenbach, currently of Hilton, spent time at Trump, Marriott, and Disney/ABC/Capitol Records prior to Hilton. During those years, the companies he was working for were pursuing aggressive growth via mergers and acquisitions; however, Bollenbach did not remain once those phases changed.

When radical restructuring is required, an outsider may be needed. The person who helped create problems in the organization is likely to resist selling cherished assets, closing plants, or firing thousands of people. "In many cases, the emotional ties of the career CEO are just too strong," says Ferdinand Nadherny, vice chair of Russell Reynolds Associates, the nation's largest executive-recruiting firm. "The guy would be firing close friends."[55]

Ownership and Management

In sole proprietorships, the owner and top manager is the same individual. Therefore, no owner–manager conflicts of interest exist. This is also the case in privately held or closely held companies in which all of the stock is owned by a few individuals, often within the same family. In these cases, the owners have direct control over their firms. However, as soon as ownership and management are separated, the potential for conflicts of interest exists. In this case, top managers become agents for the owners of the firm—they have a fiduciary duty to act in the owners' best interests.

Theoretically, in a publicly held corporation, both shareholders and managers have an interest in maximizing organizational profits. Shareholders want maximum organizational profits so they can receive high returns from dividends and stock appreciation. Managers should also be interested in high profits to the extent that their own rewards, such as salary and bonuses, depend on profitability. However, top managers, as human beings, may attempt to maximize their own self-interests at the expense of shareholders. This is called an *agency problem*. Entrenchment occurs when "managers gain so much power that they are able to use the firm to further their own interests rather than the interests of shareholders."[56] Chief executives can become entrenched by recommending their friends and internal stakeholders such as other managers for board membership. Often the recommendations of the CEO are taken without much resistance.

Agency problems are manifest in several ways. Some power-hungry or status-conscious top managers may expand the size of their empires at the expense of organizational shareholders. For example, two decades ago, Harding Lawrence led Braniff Airways to financial ruin through overzealous growth.[57] The highly unsuccessful unrelated acquisitions of the 1960s may have resulted, in part, from managers who were more interested in short-term growth than in long-term performance. This agency problem can be precipitated by compensation systems that link organizational size to pay.

EXECUTIVE COMPENSATION

Agency problems often arise because of the way executives are compensated. For example, an executive who is compensated according to year-end profitability may use his or her power to maximize year-end profits at the expense of long-range investments such as research and development.[58] Some business writers argue that the extremely high salaries of some CEOs, which often reach millions of dollars, are evidence that agency problems exist.[59] David Michels, former CEO of the Hilton Group and one of the highest-paid executives in the hotel industry, saw his total income soar by 201 percent from a reported £826,000 (approximately $1.6 million) in 2002 to £2.5million (around $5 million) in 2005.[60] During this same time, company profits grew by 152 percent.

Because shareholders are numerous and often not very well organized, their influence on decisions such as CEO compensation is nominal. Consequently, self-serving forces within the organization can sometimes prevail. For example, Roberto Goizueta of Coke once received an $81 million restricted stock award. The award was initiated by an old associate whose firm had received $24 million in fees from Coke over the previous six years.[61] Unfortunately, conflicts of interest of this type are common.[62]

The real issue concerning salary is whether CEOs are worth what they receive. For example, in *Business Week*'s annual report on executive pay, compensation is compared to the performance of the organizations for which these executives work. This analysis is revealing, and it often demonstrates that some CEOs are a real bargain. CEOs who have more-demanding jobs, as indicated by the amount of information they have to process and the firm's strategy, tend to be more highly paid.[63] Because of all of the ramifications associated with executive pay, the decision is as much ethical as it is financial.

To help overcome problems with excessive compensation of some CEOs, top management compensation should probably be linked to corporate performance.[64] One risk in relating compensation to performance is that a lot of these schemes tie annual compensation to annual, as opposed to long-term, performance. The impact of this approach was evident in 2001 when foodservice CEOs saw their total compensation decline for the first time in a decade as company profitability dropped in that year.[65] Whenever possible, compensation packages should be developed that encourage, instead of discourage, actions that will lead to high long-term performance.

For example, if CEO bonuses depend on profit, board members in charge of compensation should add back research-and-development expenditures before calculating profits for the year. This helps ensure that CEOs will not hesitate to allocate resources to potentially profitable long-term research-and-development projects. In the restaurant industry, goals that focus on brand-awareness levels or franchise strategies are suggested as complements to the hard number metrics of EPS (earnings per share) or *EBITDA* (earnings before interest, tax, depreciation, and amortization). Another trend in CEO compensation is rewarding with stock instead of cash. When managers receive stock and stock options, they become owners, and their interests should converge with those of other shareholders.[66] Here is an example of how stock options can figure into pay:

Stock options are a creative way to align CEO interests with the long-term interests of the organization. If a stock is currently selling at $50, a CEO might receive options to buy 100,000 shares of stock at $50, which is called the strike price. However, the options may not be exercisable for some specified time, such as three years. If, over the next three years, the stock price rises to $100, the options are now worth $5 million, since the CEO can buy 100,000 shares at $50 and sell them at $100. In this situation, if the stock price declines or remains the same, the options are worthless. Thus, it is in the best interests of the CEO to maximize the share price of the company, which is also in the best interests of the shareholders.

BOARDS OF DIRECTORS

Perhaps the greatest agency problems occur when top managers serve on the board of directors, which is often the case in U.S. corporations. In fact, it is not uncommon to find the CEO in the position of chairperson of the board. This condition is known as *CEO duality*. As chairperson of the board of directors, the CEO is in a strong position to ensure that personal interests are served even if the other stakeholders' interests are not. For example, a CEO/chairperson may influence other board members to provide a generous compensation package. Also, a CEO/chairperson is instrumental in nominating future board members, and therefore has the opportunity to nominate friends and colleagues who are likely to rubber-stamp his or her future actions and decisions.

The fiduciary responsibility for preventing agency problems lies with boards of directors. Some business experts believe that many boards of directors have not lived up to their fiduciary duties. These experts argue that, for the most part, boards have not reprimanded or replaced top managers who acted against the best interests of shareholders. However, the incidence of shareholder suits against boards of directors has increased.[67] In addition, large-block shareholders such as mutual-fund and pension-fund managers put lots of pressure on board members and directly on CEOs to initiate sweeping organizational changes that will lead to more accountability and higher performance.[68]

HOSPITALITY FOCUS

CANADIAN PACIFIC HOTELS: HUMAN RESOURCE STRATEGY

It was 1988, and Canadian Pacific Hotels had just invested $750 million in the bricks-and-mortar side of the business, updating its hotels nationwide. Management was confident that the newly renovated hotels would attract guests for a first stay, but bringing them back again would be the real return on investment (ROI) challenge. To meet that challenge, Canadian Pacific management looked to its human capital and Carolyn Clark, the newly appointed vice president of human resources. Human resources had become a strategic player at the boardroom level, and now it was time to help the company achieve its overall goals. Clark knew that in the service-intensive hotel industry, people can provide a critical competitive advantage, so her strategic HR plan focused on the development of human capital.[69]

EMPLOYEES

Labor is the single greatest cost item in most hospitality businesses, which is why employees and the way they are managed can be important sources of competitive advantage. Unfortunately, many hospitality firms fail to realize the strategic importance of the human resource area. Research has shown that more-sophisticated human-resource planning, recruitment, and selection strategies are associated with higher labor productivity, especially in capital-intensive organizations.[70] Also, a large-sample study of nearly 1,000 firms indicated that "high performance work practices" are associated with lower turnover, higher productivity, and higher long- and short-term financial performance.[71] Chapter 7 will describe human-resources strategies hospitality firms can use to maximize competitiveness. For now, the objective is to highlight the importance of this area and to provide guidelines regarding what should be evaluated during an internal analysis of the firm. (See the "Hospitality Focus" boxed section above.)

Canadian Pacific Hotels is now known as Fairmont Hotels and Resorts, North America's largest luxury hotel chain. Because of their importance to competitiveness, employees are being given increasing amounts of managerial attention in the organizational planning of a lot of large organizations. In fact, human capital considerations, such as the ability to attract qualified workers, top the list of factors that concern managers in the hospitality industry.[72]

Labor productivity and employee turnover are important outcomes that are worthy of assessment. Labor productivity is a good indication of how well managed employees are and their levels of experience and training. For example, hotels often track how many rooms a housekeeper can clean in an hour. Restaurants look at how many meals can be served at various times and with various personnel configurations. Turnover is at least partially an indication of how employees feel about their jobs and the organization, including their satisfaction with compensation and the way they are managed. These are only examples of possible indicators.

Human-resources systems and processes should also be examined. These include reporting systems, hiring programs, compensation systems, training programs, and supervisory systems. Finally, the overall quality of the laborers in a hotel or restaurant can be assessed by their motivation levels, attitudes, experience, and the amount of training they have received. If a union is present, relationships with union officials should also be assessed.

STRUCTURE AND CULTURE

Leaders, managers, directors, and employees can all be sources of competitive advantage. However, the way they are organized also leads to competitiveness. Organization structure has a lot to do with how successful a firm will be. For example, in a world where innovations are widely understood by competitors within a year, a flexible structure is a key to success in many companies.[73] Big companies are trying to increase speed and flexibility by altering their organization structures and management systems so that they focus on one core business and allow other firms to fill in the gaps.[74] Accor, highlighted earlier in this chapter, is one such company. Another way large organizations can improve flexibility is by decentralizing responsibility and rewarding employees for innovations and flexibility.[75] Chapter 8 will explore in great detail various organizational structures that are used to support strategic objectives. It is sufficient to say at this point that structure is another potential source of sustainable competitive advantage.

Closely related to structure is an organization's culture, the shared experiences, attitudes, values, and beliefs of its members. *Organization culture* often reflects the values and leadership styles of executives and managers, and is greatly a result of past practices in human resource management, such as recruitment, training, and rewards. Many hospitality companies realize the benefits of a shared set of values as a potential source of competitive advantage because customers and employees interact so frequently that supervision alone cannot sufficiently direct employees. Culture becomes a key management tool to influence employee thoughts, feelings, and behaviors.

According to Barbara Talbott, former executive vice president of marketing for Four Seasons Hotels and Resorts, "Competing on service is an investment in the quality of staff and guest experiences, which over the history of the company has been the source of superior profitability, reputation, and growth."[76] Part of the Four Seasons service culture rests on the idea that receiving personal service powerfully encourages the ability to pass the service on to others, and the general managers of these luxury hotels are key to building this culture, as the example in the "Hospitality Focus" boxed section on page 145 illustrates.

Stakeholders look for an intangible quality when making decisions about the products and services they purchase or in selecting alliance partners. They want to be able to rely on the company. They want promises and commitments to be fulfilled. There are many pragmatic benefits to a high-profile organizational culture that can help an organization in its recruiting, employee development, and relationships with customers.[77]

An organization's culture can be its greatest strength or its greatest weakness. Some firms have created cultures that are completely consistent with what the company is trying

FOUR SEASONS: POSITIVE SERVICE CULTURE

HOSPITALITY FOCUS

At the Four Seasons, general managers are largely promoted from within and work to create a positive culture for the staff. When the Four Seasons began to manage a hotel in Atlanta as the third management entity in the hotel's brief history, the leadership expected some apprehension and concern from the staff. As the official handover occurred at midnight, the first shift of employees the next morning were greeted by a new leadership team that had arranged to have the staff areas painted and cleaned. Mannequins dressed in new employee uniforms were set up in the locker rooms. Hot coffee and donuts were ready and waiting. Along with handshakes, the management conveyed the key role employees would play in making the hotel great. In this hotel, the managers acknowledged the staff through empathy and respect; led through actions as well as words; and set high but achievable aspirations in which every employee could take pride. The Four Seasons Hotel Atlanta became the city's first AAA Five Diamond and Mobile Five Star Hotel, a distinction it still holds today.

The creation of a service culture is evident in other hotels in the company:

- In Singapore, the management team used a modest renovation budget to make the new staff cafeteria look and feel like a freestanding restaurant, called Kutulu.

- Staff in Maui are encouraged to recognize one another's outstanding service to guests and colleagues, on a "Maui Mahalo" board.

- In Atlanta, the human resources team created a "benefits concierge" to help employees choose the best options for them and their families.[78]

to accomplish. These are called high-performance cultures. For example, JetBlue airlines has a culture that stresses a warm and friendly atmosphere, high-quality service, and efficiency. Table 4.3 provides guidelines for identifying the culture of an organization based on factors such as attitude toward customers and competitors, risk tolerance, and moral integrity. For each of these factors, an organization should ask:

1. Which characteristics support the vision and strategies of the organization and should be sustained in the future?

2. Which characteristics do not support the vision and strategies and should be modified?

3. What efforts will be necessary to make the required changes happen?

A strong culture can be a two-edged sword. Sometimes very successful corporations so firmly attach themselves to their successful business practices that they exaggerate the features of the successful culture and strategy, and fail to adapt them to changing industry conditions.

TABLE 4.3 Defining an Organization's Culture

Dimensions	Description
Attitude toward customers	Respect vs. indifference
Attitude toward competitors	Compliance, cooperation, or competitiveness
Achievement orientation	Industry leader or follower
Risk tolerance	Degree to which individuals are encouraged to take risks
Conflict tolerance	Degree to which individuals are encouraged to express differences
Individual autonomy	The amount of independence and responsibility given to individuals in decision making
Employee relations	Cooperative vs. adversarial relationships among employees
Management relations	Cooperative vs. adversarial relationships between managers and employees
Goal ownership	Identification with goals and concerns of organization as a whole vs. identification with goals and concerns of a work group or department
Perceived compensation equity	Perceived relationship between performance and rewards
Decision-making style	Rational and structured vs. creative and intuitive
Work standards	Diligent, high-performing vs. mediocre
Moral integrity	Degree to which employees are expected to exhibit truthfulness
Ethical integrity	Degree to which decisions are expected to be balanced with regard to stakeholder interests vs. focused exclusively on a key objective such as profitability

Source: Adapted from P. McDonald and J. Gandz, "Getting Value from Shared Values," *Organization Dynamics* (Winter 1992), 68; E. H. Schein, *Organization Culture and Leadership* (San Francisco: Jossey–Bass, 1985).

Four very common organization orientations associated with excellent performance can lead to four extreme orientations, which can lead to poor performance:

Craftspeople. In craftspeople organizations, employees are passionate about quality. Quality is the primary driver of the corporate culture and a source of organizational pride. However, a culture that is focused on quality and detail can evolve to an extreme where craftspeople become *tinkerers*. Obscure technical details and obsessive perfection result in products that are overengineered and service managers who are overly autocratic. Another version of the obsessive concern for quality is a passion for low costs, which paralyzes an organization's ability to make timely, necessary investments.

Builders. In builder organizations, growth is the primary goal. Managers are rewarded for taking risks that result in growth, new acquisitions, and new market niches. When efforts to grow and expand become careless, builders become *imperialists*, with high debt, too many unrelated businesses, and neglected core businesses.

Pioneers. Pioneers build their businesses through leadership positions in new product and service development. The strengths of these organizations lie in their entrepreneurial teams and flexible structures, which promote idea sharing. Pioneers begin to decline when they evolve into *escapists*, who invent impractical products and pursue service ideas with limited customer value.

Salespeople. Salespeople are excellent marketers who create successful brand names and distribution channels, and pursue aggressive advertising and innovative bundling of services. They become so confident in their marketing abilities that they ignore product needs and quality, and begin to market imitative services that customers do not value. They evolve into *drifters*.[79]

In all of the orientations described, the organization becomes too focused on its own capabilities and loses sight of its customers and evolving industry conditions. One stakeholder group becomes too dominant at the expense of others and resists change. Several contributing factors can drive a successful organization to an unsuccessful extreme:

Overconfidence. Leadership may get overconfident from its past successes, thinking that what has worked in the past will continue to work in the future.

Dominant managers and subunits. One manager or unit may become overly dominant, attracting the best managerial talent and exercising unbalanced influence over the decisions made within other departments. The dominant managers and areas may keep the organization focused on strategies and policies that may no longer be relevant. An acknowledgment that change is needed would erode their base of power and influence.

Complacency. The successful strategies of the past may have become embedded in the routine policies and procedures of the organization. Those policies and procedures create an air of continuity that is very resistant to change.[80]

In summary, structure and culture can be added to an already impressive list of human-based sources of competitive advantage. Just as these factors can be sources of advantage, they can also be sources of weakness when they are neglected or poorly managed. Attention will now be drawn to knowledge-based and general organizational resources.

KNOWLEDGE-BASED RESOURCES

We live in what is sometimes called a *knowledge economy*, meaning that knowledge is used to produce economic value. A knowledge economy is driven by the importance of intangible people skills and intellectual assets. More than 50 percent of the gross domestic product (GDP) in developed economies is knowledge-based, which means that the GDP is based on intangible people skills and intellectual assets.[81] Consequently, wealth is increasingly being created through the management of knowledge workers instead of physical assets. According to David Teece:

> *Fundamental changes have been wrought in the global economy, which are changing the basis of firm level competitive advantage, and with it the functions of management. The decreased cost of information flow, increases in the number of markets ..., the liberalization of product and labour markets in many parts of the world, and the deregulation of international financial flows is stripping away many traditional sources of competitive differentiation and exposing a new fundamental core as the basis for wealth creation. The fundamental core is the development and astute deployment and utilization of intangible assets, of which knowledge, competence, and intellectual property are the most significant.*[82]

Knowledge is an intangible asset. Intangible assets differ from physical assets in fundamental ways. First, physical assets can be used only by one party at a time, whereas knowledge can be used by several parties simultaneously. Second, physical assets wear out over time and are depreciated accordingly. While knowledge does not wear out, its value depreciates rapidly as new knowledge is created. Third, it is relatively easy to set a price based on how much of a physical asset is sold or transferred, but it is difficult to measure the amount of knowledge transferred or its value. Finally, rights to tangible property are fairly clear and easy to enforce, whereas it is difficult to protect and enforce protection of intellectual property.[83]

In recent years, chefs and restaurateurs have invoked intellectual property rights concerns regarding trademarks, patents, and *trade dress*—the distinctive look and feel of a business—in an effort to defend their restaurants, their techniques, and their recipes from those who would steal their knowledge assets. (See the "Hospitality Focus" boxed section on page 149.)

Knowledge can be divided into two general types: core knowledge and integrative knowledge.[84] *Core knowledge* is scientific or technological knowledge that is associated with actual creation of a product or service. For example, knowledge about integrated circuitry formed

PEARL OYSTER BAR OWNER FILES AN INTELLECTUAL
PROPERTY LAWSUIT

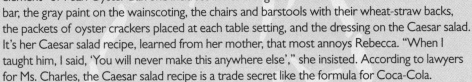

HOSPITALITY
FOCUS

Rebecca Charles, the owner of Pearl Oyster Bar in New York City, is one of the first small chef-proprietors to file a lawsuit claiming theft of her intellectual property. The suit against her former sous chef of six years, Ed McFarland, now the proprietor of Ed's Lobster Bar, is based on her claims that he copied "each and every element" of Pearl Oyster Bar. She includes in her charges the white marble bar, the gray paint on the wainscoting, the chairs and barstools with their wheat-straw backs, the packets of oyster crackers placed at each table setting, and the dressing on the Caesar salad. It's her Caesar salad recipe, learned from her mother, that most annoys Rebecca. "When I taught him, I said, 'You will never make this anywhere else'," she insisted. According to lawyers for Ms. Charles, the Caesar salad recipe is a trade secret like the formula for Coca-Cola.

Ed McFarland argues that Ed's Lobster Bar is not an imitator. "I would say it's a similar restaurant," he said. "I would not say it's a copy." While some believe that restaurants' and chefs' discovery of intellectual property rights is long overdue given the level of competition and the high cost of opening a restaurant, others argue that the sous chef dedicated six years of his life to that restaurant and has the right to take with him what he learned. Top British chef, restaurant owner, and food consultant Paul Heathcote notes that most chefs find inspiration in other chefs' work, particularly their mentors. "All chefs are magpies and take ideas from one another. I don't think Charles stands a chance in court."[85]

the foundation for creation of semiconductors. *Integrative knowledge* helps integrate various activities, capabilities, and products. For example, an organization that wants to be involved in selling personal computers has to understand how they are assembled and manufactured (core knowledge), but also has to understand how computer manufacturing fits into an entire system, which includes suppliers of component parts, marketing, financing, and even linkages between personal computers and other types of products (integrative knowledge).

Core knowledge is comparatively easier to acquire than integrative knowledge because integrative knowledge deals with a complex system. Consequently, integrative knowledge is probably more likely to lead to a sustainable competitive advantage. Wal–Mart, for instance, developed a complete and unique retailing system that involves complex coordination of codified information across suppliers, distribution centers, and stores; feedback from customers in the form of daily sales information; information about the products; and forecasts of needs. Innovations have included cross-docking, which occurs when merchandise is unloaded from suppliers' trucks directly onto Wal-Mart's trucks for distribution to stores.[86]

Another way to differentiate knowledge is based on whether it is codified or tacit. *Codified knowledge* can be communicated completely through written means. For example, blueprints, recipes, formulas, and computer code are codified. "*Tacit knowledge* is that which is difficult to articulate in a way that is meaningful and complete."[87] Creation of an artwork such as a sculpture or a modern dance, for instance, would be very difficult to describe in words that would have real meaning. You have to experience it. In general, the easier it is to codify knowledge, the easier it is to transfer. Tacit knowledge can be very valuable to organizations in creating a sustainable competitive advantage.

Internal Knowledge Creation and Organizational Learning

Some organizations are clearly more innovative than others. They consistently create greater numbers of successful products or services. Other organizations may not develop a lot of products or services, but they are adept at creating more-efficient ways of creating or delivering them. The distinction here is between *product or service development* and *process development*. Still other organizations seem better at both types of innovation. Knowledge creation is at the center of both product or service development and process development.

One of the most important managerial tasks is facilitating knowledge (1) creation, (2) retention, (3) sharing, and (4) utilization. Each of the four knowledge facilitation tasks requires different management skills and organizational arrangements. Outstanding execution of these tasks can lead to superior performance.[88] The 24-hour check-in and checkout process at the Peninsula Hotel in Beverly Hills is an example of a hotel innovation that was created by the general manager (GM), refined in conversation with guests, shared with staff, and is still in use even though the GM is no longer at the hotel. (See the "Hospitality Focus" boxed section on page 151.)

Knowledge Creation

Knowledge creation requires systems that encourage innovative thinking throughout the firm. Most organizations tap only a fraction of the creative potential of employees and managers. An organization that wants to create knowledge will select employees and managers who contribute innovative ideas and will reward those employees and managers through salary increases, recognition, bonuses, and promotions. Some organizations even allow managers or employees the opportunities to lead in the execution of their ideas. Organizations also need to establish forums through which ideas can be conveyed to managers. A suggestion box is a rudimentary system to encourage ideas. Work meetings and interviews are other means of sharing knowledge. To create knowledge, organizations should also allocate human and financial capital to research and development.

KNOWLEDGE RETENTION

A lot of knowledge exists in an organization. Only part of that knowledge is shared, but very little of that sharing gets recorded unless it is associated with an actual research or development project. Low-cost information systems have made it possible to record and store vast amounts

THE PENINSULA BEVERLY HILLS INNOVATES WITH 24-HOUR CHECK-IN CHECK-OUT

HOSPITALITY FOCUS

"If the day is 24 hours long, guests should be able to check in and check out at any time they like," reasoned Ali Kasikci, the charismatic and innovative GM of the Peninsula Hotel in Beverly Hills for over a decade. The implementation of 24-hour check-in and checkout with no surcharge to guests began as an idea Kasikci obtained during an executive education program at Cornell's Hotel School. The practice was tested in the summer and fully implemented by the staff of the Peninsula Hotel a year later. Kasikci began by discussing the idea with the marketing director, sales managers, and front-office manager. Each of these managers informally collected feedback from customers about the concept and talked it up to other managers in the hotel. Customers were very responsive to the idea, especially those from Australia and New Zealand whose 14- to 17-hour flights generally arrived in the early morning hours and departed late in the evening.

Armed with the support of guests and various managers, the next step was to determine whether it was operationally feasible. With the help of the executive housekeeper, data on departures was gathered, and once the idea appeared feasible to implement, special equipment was purchased to clean rooms quietly in the dark. Before the practice was put in place, Kasikci also discussed the idea with competitor hotels in his market. These competitors were the biggest critics; they said the idea would never work and that the Peninsula would be quickly forced to give up the practice. The housekeeping staff was also hesitant, but their attitudes changed after extensive discussions and efforts to focus on the positive implications for the hotel.

While Kasikci is no longer the GM of this hotel, the practice, conceived in the 1990s, is still in use. A lot of ideas are never put into practice because, as Kasikci notes, "we always make excuses that operationally it is not possible." This practice was easy, and it astonished the guest, ultimately leading to both customer loyalty and repeat business, according to the hotel's managers. As this innovation illustrates, facilitating knowledge can lead to high performance.[89]

of information very affordably. An important part of documentation is recording not only the new knowledge, but also how a manager or the organization responded to it. Also, an organization should record information on whether such actions were a success or a failure.

KNOWLEDGE SHARING

Sharing of knowledge is as important as creating it. For example, Marriott has used knowledge gained in the lodging industry in its time-share business. Disney applied its knowledge in staging dramatic presentations (developed in its theme parks and moviemaking) to Broadway musicals. Many companies have newsletters and intranets in which new ideas are shared. Creating an information system for the sharing of ideas is, by itself, a possible source of competitive advantage.

KNOWLEDGE UTILIZATION

An organization has to clear the way for knowledge to be translated into new processes and programs. This sometimes means eliminating barriers to innovation. For example, some companies require many signatures and approvals on even the smallest projects before they will be funded. An organization should also encourage taking risks by not harshly penalizing managers whose projects or ideas fail and richly rewarding managers whose projects or ideas succeed. Table 4.4 reviews the four tasks associated with knowledge creation and utilization. Attention will now be drawn to generating knowledge through partnerships with external stakeholders.

Knowledge Creation and Interorganizational Relationships

If firms perform the tasks associated with internal knowledge creation, they will still be limited in how much knowledge they acquire unless they also have a productive program for acquiring knowledge from outside of their organizations. As discussed in Chapter 2, a part of obtaining knowledge from the outside is studying the innovations of others in the industry, other industries, and the technological environment in general. In fact, most of the knowledge that will revolutionize an industry actually comes from outside the industry. For example, semiconductors were developed in the computer industry, but had far-reaching implications for most other industries, including the hospitality industry. Knowledge about innovations in other industries comes into an organization through hiring people with varied backgrounds, hiring consultants and trainers, providing educational programs and opportunities to employees, and assigning researchers to specifically follow various scientific streams through journals, newsletters, books, and seminars.

Another important source of external knowledge comes from interorganizational relationships.[90] Organizations can learn from each other. In fact, knowledge is not always created within a single firm, but rather in a network of firms working together. An example of this phenomenon is found in the biotechnology industry, where there is a large-scale reliance on collaborations to produce innovation.[91]

Several factors can lead an organization to enhance organizational learning from interorganizational relationships, including its relational ability, its location in a network, and its capacity to absorb new knowledge.

RELATIONAL ABILITY

Relational ability, defined as the ability to interact with other companies, can increase a firm's ability to obtain and transfer knowledge.[92] Firms can enhance their relational ability through practice (e.g., increasing the use of interorganizational relationships) or through hiring managers who have already developed relational skills.[93] Often CEOs develop excellent relational skills.

TABLE 4.4 Tasks Associated with Internal Knowledge Creation
and Utilization

Task	Description
Knowledge creation	Develop reward systems that encourage innovative thinking. Create a forum whereby creative ideas are shared. Invest in research-and-development programs.
Knowledge retention	Document findings from research-and-development programs. Create information systems that record and organize innovative ideas. Document both the ideas and managerial responses or organizational responses to them. Document successes and failures.
Knowledge sharing	Create an information system that shares results from research-and-development projects with other parts of the organization. Routinely pass new ideas on to managers who can act on them. Create a database-management system to organize ideas generated from employees and managers so that they can be retrieved systematically at a later date.
Knowledge utilization	Reduce bureaucratic barriers that prevent knowledge from resulting in new programs and projects. Encourage risk taking. Reward success.

CENTRAL IN A NETWORK

The more embedded into a network of interorganizational relationships an organization becomes, the more it is able to acquire competitive capabilities.[94] Consequently, increasing the use of joint ventures, alliances, and other interorganizational relationships can position a firm in a more central location to what is happening in its industry and across relevant industries. Proximity can lead to enhanced learning.[95] The lodging industry is a good example of this, because hotels often cluster in one geographic area.

ABSORPTIVE CAPACITY

An organization needs to be deliberate about taking steps to increase its *absorptive capacity*, which refers to the ability of a firm to absorb knowledge. Just like internally generated knowledge, if knowledge gained through interorganizational relationships is not retained, shared, and used, it is of no worth to the organization.

TABLE 4.5 Facilitating Knowledge Transfer in Joint Ventures

FACILITATION MECHANISM	DESCRIPTION
Flexible learning objectives	Organizations should enter into a venture with objectives regarding what the organization would like to learn from the venture. However, conditions often change, and managers should be willing to adjust those objectives if needed.
Leadership commitment	At least one strong, higher-level manager must champion the learning objective. This person acts as a catalyst for knowledge transfer. For example, in one case, an American president had a long-standing relationship with the chairperson of the Japanese partner. They worked together to facilitate transfer of both technical and management ideas.
A climate of trust	Trust is critical to the free exchange of knowledge. One of the greatest disadvantages of a joint venture is the risk of opportunistic behavior. This is the risk that one of the partners will use information gained in the venture to the disadvantage of the other partner. Consequently, trust must be carefully guarded or information transfer will be stifled.
Tolerance for redundancy	This means that there is deliberate overlapping of company information, processes, and management activities. Redundancy leads to more interaction among participants, and interaction leads to more sharing of information.
Creative chaos	Disruptive or high-stress events can enhance transfer of knowledge by focusing partners on solving problems and resolving difficulties.
Focus on learning despite performance	Some ventures perform poorly, at least on financial measures, but organizations can still learn from them. The American firms tended to let poor performance reduce or eliminate learning, whereas the Japanese firms took a longer-term view and were less distracted by short-term performance.

Source: Based on A. C. Inkpen, "Creating Knowledge through Collaboration," *California Management Review* 39, 1 (Fall 1996): 123–140.

Andrew Inkpen, an expert on interorganizational relationships, studied 40 American–Japanese joint ventures with the intention of finding out what organizational conditions facilitate effective transfer of knowledge. His conclusions, contained in Table 4.5, are a fitting summary to this section on the important role of knowledge in creating a sustainable competitive advantage.

GENERAL ORGANIZATIONAL RESOURCES

The final category of organizational resources is a varied collection of organizational possessions that can have a tremendous impact on financial success and survival. In this section, only a few of many such resources will be discussed. However, the ones that are discussed have been found to be powerful sources of competitive advantage in some instances. First, we look at patents, copyrights, trademarks, and servicemarks. Brands, organizational reputation, and superior relationships with external stakeholders are also critical intangible resources that can produce strategic benefit.

Patents, Copyrights, Trademarks, and Servicemarks

Patents, copyrights, trademarks, and servicemarks are used to protect knowledge creation from competitive imitation. *Patents* protect an invention, while copyrights protect "original works of authorship."[96] Trademarks and servicemarks protect words, names, and symbols used to distinguish a good or service, respectively. The term *mark* or *trademark* is often used to refer to both trademarks and servicemarks.

Organizations file for patent protection to prevent other companies from using, selling, or importing their innovations for the term of the patent. In exchange, the patent holder agrees to share the details of the invention. Patents can sometimes be a source of competitive advantage for a period of time. However, they do not really offer much protection and, eventually, they run out.

In 1936, Tom Carvel, the founder of Carvel Ice Cream, patented the "no air pump" super-low-temperature ice cream machine, developed a secret soft-serve ice cream formula, and invented the marketing concept of "buy one, get one free." Three years later, he patented the first soft-serve ice cream machine.[97] In 1947, he patented the all-glass-front building with pitched roof, which was later copied by McDonald's. Like other property rights, a patent may be sold, licensed, mortgaged, assigned or transferred, given away, or simply abandoned.

While culinary inventions have long been patented, copyrighting a chef's dish or cooking method has only recently become important. A *copyright* is literally "the right to copy" an original creation and constitutes a set of exclusive rights to the use of an idea or information.

CHEF AT MOTO'S PATENTS UNIQUE FOOD CREATIONS

One chef who has been proactive in protecting his foodie inventions is Homaro Cantu, Executive Chef at Moto's and the inventor of an edible paper on which he prints his menus using organic inks and a Canon printer. The edible paper—a soybean and cornstarch concoction—can be imprinted with virtually any image and any flavor. The chef has also developed a spiral-handled fork, which is designed to hold a sprig of basil, adding an aromatic element to his dishes. A useful business management tool he created involves a camera set unobtrusively into an upper wall of Moto's linked to a computer. The system allows Cantu to track important aspects of kitchen operation. For example, the system can warn him when usage rates threaten to deplete supplies and can notify the kitchen when a diner leaves for the restroom so the chefs can adjust the spacing of preparations.

What makes Cantu's paper, and many of his other creations, different is the fact that he is applying to have them patented. He even goes so far as to print the following legal jargon on his tasty paper: "Confidential Property of and © H. Cantu. Patent Pending. No further use or disclosure is permitted without prior approval of H. Cantu." This prolific chef says he worries about corporations, not individual diners, capitalizing on his inventions and management systems. The value of patenting he believes will come from the profits he will get from these ideas rather than having to build more restaurants. In the meantime, no one can visit the kitchen at Moto's without first signing a multipage nondisclosure agreement.[98]

We are familiar with the copyright protections that exist for, say, a Mickey Mouse cartoon, that prohibits unauthorized parties from distributing copies of the cartoon or creating derivative works, but you are probably less aware of the growing trend toward protecting culinary works. (See the "Hospitality Focus" boxed section above.)

Brands and their associated trademarks offer a higher level of protection. A *trademark* protects a name, logo, design, word, phrase, image, or a combination of these elements that are associated with a business or good. Coca-Cola's hourglass-shaped bottle and Absolut Vodka's widebodied, slim-necked vessel are distinctive symbols of their brands that are protected by registered trademarks. A *servicemark* is the same as a trademark but distinguishes services versus products. In a global world, it is a challenge to protect trademarks, copyrights, and patents, because various countries have their own laws governing protection. Treaties among member countries are often used to protect these intangible assets across boarders.

Brands and Organizational Reputation

The identity of a good or service is often captured in the *brand*, defined as the name, term, symbol, and/or design associated with the product. Brands are viewed as a key value-creating resource, because they are firm specific and difficult to imitate.[99] A key question for developers of hotels is whether a brand actually contributes to market value (i.e., hotel sale price). In a study of 2,000 recent hotel sales transactions, researchers found support for the impact of brand on value, particularly for hotels in the midscale and upscale segments.[100] If managed well, strong brands can be powerful sources of sustainable competitive advantage.[101] Disney takes full advantage of its brand, which is one of its core competencies.

> *We are fundamentally an operating company, operating the Disney Brand all over the world, maintaining it, improving it, promoting and advertising it with taste. Our time must be spent insuring that the Brand never slides, that we innovate the Brand, nurture the Brand, experiment and play with it, but never diminish it. Others will try to change it, from outside and from within. We must resist. We are not a fad! The Disney name and products survive fads.[102]*

Global brands have an even greater challenge to maintain a single-minded consistency while also adapting to different geographies, cultures, and customer needs. Table 4.6 summarizes the *Interbrand/Business Week* ranking of the top 25 global brands, based on a series of criteria that evaluate brand value. McDonald's and Disney are hospitality firms in the top 25 global brands.[103] Others include KFC ranked 60th, Pizza Hut ranked 74th, Starbuck's ranked 88th, and Hertz ranked 100th. The study does not include airlines, and it is interesting to note that no hotel company brand appears in the rankings. The proliferation of hotel brands may be one of the reasons why no single hotel brand is a top-ranked global brand. Hotel companies have used their brand names to expand into different segments of the market so as to retain customers, a strategy that has met with brand proliferation and some success.[104] Hyatt, for example, introduced three new brands in a single year—Hyatt Place, Hyatt Summerfield Suites, and Andaz—across three different hotel segments.[105]

TABLE 4.6 Top 25 Global Brands

BRAND RANK	BRAND NAME	PARENT COMPANY	COUNTRY	BRAND VALUE ($MIL)
1	Coca-Cola	Coca-Cola	U.S.	67,525
2	Microsoft	Microsoft	U.S.	59,941
3	IBM	International Business Machines Corporation	U.S.	53,376
4	GE	GE	U.S.	46,996
5	Intel	Intel	U.S.	35,586
6	Nokia	Nokia	Finland	26,452
7	Disney	Walt Disney Company	U.S.	26,441

TABLE 4.6 (Continued)

8	McDonald's	McDonald's Corporation	U.S.	26,014
9	Toyota	Toyota Motor Corporation	Japan	24,837
10	Marlboro	Altria Group	U.S.	21,189
11	Mercedes-Benz	DaimlerChrysler AG	Germany	20,006
12	Citi	Citigroup	U.S.	19,967
13	Hewlett-Packard	Hewlett-Packard	U.S.	18,866
14	American Express	American Express	U.S.	18,559
15	Gillette	Gillette	U.S.	17,534
16	BMW	Bayerische Motoren Werke AG	Germany	17,126
17	Cisco	Cisco	U.S.	16,592
18	Louis Vuitton	LVMH Moët Hennessy Louis Vuitton	France	16,077
19	Honda	Honda	Japan	15,788
20	Samsung	Samsung	S. Korea	14,956
21	Dell	Dell	U.S.	13,231
22	Ford	Ford	U.S.	13,159
23	Pepsi	Pepsi	U.S.	12,399
24	Nescafé	Nestlé	Switzerland	12,241
25	Merrill Lynch	Merrill Lynch	U.S.	12,018

Source: Interbrand and *Business Week*, 2007.

A reputation can be thought of as an economic asset that signals observers about the attractiveness of a company's offerings. A reputation is also an assessment of past performance by various evaluators. It is a part of a social system and is based more on interpretation than fact.[106] Like a brand, an organization's reputation is difficult to imitate. A good reputation may be associated with excellent quality or highly innovative products or services, excellent human-resource management, or other factors. Reputation, which can transcend international borders, is thus a potential source of global competitive advantage.[107] Of course, an organization's reputation is often linked to a well-known brand name. Destinations can also develop reputations that help build strong customer perceptions and increased tourism expenditures. A tourism destination that increasingly attracts visitors may do so in part on the reputation conveyed by past visitors.

Much has been said in this book about how to develop a good reputation through socially responsible actions and stakeholder satisfaction. Some of the potential benefits of a good reputation include the ability to attract talented workers, charge premium prices, keep loyal customers, raise capital with less difficulty by attracting investors, avoid constant scrutiny by regulators and activists, or enter international markets with less difficulty.[108] Some business writers have argued that a corporate reputation may be the only source of truly sustainable competitive advantage.[109] They argue that it is the only component of competitive advantage that can't ever be duplicated in its entirety. Therefore, organizations should devote considerable time and effort to safeguarding a good reputation. Organizations with the best reputations in the *Fortune* survey had strong financial performance, but it was combined with strong performance in nonfinancial areas as well.[110]

Superior Relationships with Stakeholders

Stakeholder relationships were described in detail in the previous chapter. Furthermore, the chapter demonstrated how strong relationships with stakeholders can lead to sustainable competitive advantage. This section will not be redundant with Chapter 2, but it is included to demonstrate an important point. Stakeholder theory and the resource-based view are closely linked.

Relationships with external stakeholders can also be described as an organizational resource. The fact is that all five areas of resources and capabilities described in this chapter are closely linked to external stakeholders. For example, financial resources are based, in part, on relationships with financial intermediaries. The strength of human resources may depend on linkages with unions, trainers, human resources associations, communities, or educational institutions from which an organization recruits. Valuable knowledge comes from interorganizational relationships with competitors, customers, suppliers, or other stakeholders. Inputs necessary to develop physical resources are provided by suppliers. In managing a destination, a local government, hotel operators, and destination marketing firms often work in cooperation, bringing unique and complementary resources together to build the competitive advantage for a location. Finally, contracts with many types of stakeholders are a general organizational resource.

Internal resource analysis may be combined with stakeholder analysis to identify strengths and weaknesses, and for uncovering opportunities for cost savings or ways to add value for customers. For instance, the intersection between activist groups and technology development could result in low-cost solutions to problems with pollution and other externalities. Also, customers may be able to help a firm increase the effectiveness of its marketing, sales, or service activities. The combination of stakeholder analysis with resource analysis holds great potential for developing strategies that are both efficient and effective.

The conceptual link between stakeholder theory and the resource-based view has important implications. Basically, an organization that is incapable of successful stakeholder management will have a difficult time developing resources and capabilities that will lead to a sustainable competitive advantage. Also, an organization with weak resources and few capabilities will find it difficult to develop strong stakeholder relationships, because stakeholders will find the firm unattractive for partnerships and contracts.

KEY POINTS SUMMARY

- This chapter evaluated organizational resources and capabilities and their ability to lead to competitive advantage.
- The value of a resource or capability in leading to a competitive advantage depends on the answers to six questions:
    1. Does the resource or capability have value in the market?
    2. Is the resource or capability unique?
    3. Is there a readily available substitute for the resource or capability?
    4. Do organizational systems exist that allow realization of potential?
    5. Is the organization aware of and realizing the advantages?
    6. Is the resource or capability difficult or costly to imitate?
- If a capability or resource is valuable, unique, and not easily substitutable, it has potential to lead to a competitive advantage. If the firm has systems to support the resource or capability and is using them, a competitive advantage is created. If the resource or capability is difficult to imitate, then the competitive advantage will be sustainable.
- Value-chain analysis permits a firm to identify and evaluate the competitive potential of resources and capabilities. By studying their skills in comparison to those associated with primary and support activities, firms can understand their cost structure and identify the activities through which they can create value.
- Core activities are directly concerned with creating a product or service, whereas support activities help the firm in its administrative processes. After these activities are described, they are then compared with the same activities for close competitors.
- An organization can develop a competitive advantage by excelling at any of the core or support activities, relative to competitors or by linking internal activities to external stakeholders in unique and productive ways.

- The cumulative effect of value-adding activities and the way they are linked inside the firm and with the external environment determine firm performance relative to competitors.

- Tangible resources such as money and land can be seen and touched, whereas intangibles like brand and culture are more difficult to quantify.

- An organization must pay close attention to each of the following tangible and intangible resource areas to remain competitive over the long term: financial, physical, human-based, knowledge-based, and general organizational resources. Although these resources were discussed separately, in reality they are all tied together.

    1. Financial resources can be a source of advantage, although they rarely qualify as unique or difficult to imitate. Nevertheless, strong cash flow, low levels of debt, a strong credit rating, access to low-interest capital, and a reputation for credit worthiness are powerful strengths that can serve as a source of strategic flexibility.

    2. Physical resources were discussed in the context of the emerging importance of architectural design and environmentally sound materials and processes. The movement toward boutique hotels is a clear example of using the building as a source of competitive advantage. Environmentally sound hotel construction also offers growing cost savings, as well as preserving scarce natural resources for future generations.

    3. Human-based resources and capabilities are an organization's most valuable and unique asset. An organization's structure and culture are also potential sources of competitive advantage.

        Culture often reflects the values of management, the human-resource management practices that create the working conditions, and the experiences of employees. Culture can be a tremendous source of advantage for a firm, or a millstone.

        Owners and managers in a for-profit, publicly held corporation may experience agency problems if the managers' self-interests are in conflict with those of the shareholders.

    4. We live in a knowledge-based economy, so knowledge management is very important to organizational success. Internal knowledge management focuses on knowledge (1) creation, (2) retention, (3) sharing, and (4) utilization. Also important is acquiring knowledge through interorganizational relationships.

    5. General organizational resources include superior brands, patents, trademarks, copyrights, and reputations.

- An organization that is incapable of successful stakeholder management will have a difficult time developing outstanding resources and capabilities, and an organization with weak resources and few capabilities will find it difficult to develop strong stakeholder relationships.

REVIEW QUESTIONS

1. What six questions must be asked to determine whether a resource or capability will lead to a sustainable competitive advantage?

2. Describe the value-adding activities of a typical restaurant (not a chain). Determine which of these activities are core and support. How can the restaurant use this information to help determine ways to create competitive advantage?

3. What is the difference between tangible and intangible assets? What five resource areas should an organization analyze to determine internal sources of competitive advantage? Why must a firm pay attention to all five areas?

4. Describe the five distinct leadership approaches or styles CEOs use. Which of these styles is more authoritarian? Which is more participative? Is any one style the best? Why?

5. What is an agency problem? How can agency problems be avoided?

6. Why is human resource management becoming an even more important part of strategic management in many organizations?

7. Name four common cultural orientations that are often associated with excellent performance. How can these orientations lead to extremes that ultimately lead to poor performance?

8. What is the difference between core knowledge and integrative knowledge? Which type of knowledge is more likely to be associated with a sustainable competitive advantage? Why? What is the difference between tacit knowledge and codified knowledge? Which type of knowledge is more likely to be associated with a sustainable competitive advantage? Why?

9. Name several factors and organizational conditions that can lead an organization to enhance organizational learning from interorganizational relationships.

10. Which sources of competitive advantage are usually more sustainable: a patent or a brand? Why?

11. What is an organizational or destination reputation? What are the benefits of having an excellent reputation? Are those benefits typically sustainable?

CRITICAL THINKING AND APPLICATION QUESTIONS

1. Develop a value chain for a hotel company and search for sources of added value. Identify the primary and support activities. Primary activities are involved with a hotel's primary service delivery or operations. Support activities provide the assistance

necessary for the primary activities to take place. The chain shows how a product or service is developed and delivered from the input stage to the final customer. Where in the company are various resources and capabilities adding value? What are the key factors for success in each activity? Now identify ways to create additional value without incurring significant costs while doing so and to capture the value that has been created.

2. Pick any pair of rivals in the industry. Explain why one company outperforms another. Focus on the competitive advantage that the one firm has over the other. That is, examine the things one organization can do that its competitor can't or something an organization has that its competitor lacks. List the resource base of each firm. Include both tangible (e.g., land, building, material, money) and intangible resources (e.g., human, innovation, and reputation resources). What resources and capabilities must the nonleading firm acquire to outcompete the leading firm?

3. Do a strengths and weaknesses analysis of any company you wish. Identify and list factors you consider to be the strengths and weaknesses of the company.

To identify the strengths, ask yourself the following questions about the company:

- What does this company do exceptionally well?
- What advantages does it have?
- What valuable assets and resources does it have?
- What do customers identify as the company's strengths?

To identify the weaknesses, ask yourself:

- What could this company do better?
- What is the company criticized for or does it receive complaints about?
- Where is the company vulnerable?

CHAPTER 5

STRATEGY FORMULATION AT THE BUSINESS-UNIT LEVEL

YOU SHOULD BE ABLE TO DO THE FOLLOWING AFTER READING THIS CHAPTER:

1. Distinguish the business-level strategy of any hospitality organization by determining if it is a cost leader, differentiator, or best value and whether it addresses a broad or narrow market focus.

2. Identify the risk factors associated with pursuing various business strategies.

3. Explain the key factors firms use to create a low-cost or differentiation strategy.

4. Know the definition of *creative destruction* and why it is important for making sense of competitive dynamics.

5. List the offensive and defensive strategies firms can use to compete effectively.

6. Create a strategic group map to help you understand the strategies of competitors in an industry.

FEATURE STORY

BETTING ON LUXURY

Picture a famous casino real estate developer and idea maker atop the 50th floor of a $2.7 billion dollar Las Vegas casino in a television advertisement proclaiming, "I'm Steve Wynn, and this is my hotel—the only one I've ever signed my name to." Steve Wynn, formerly the Chairman of the Board, President, and CEO of Mirage Resorts, Inc., and credited with development of the Bellagio, the Mirage, Treasure Island, and the Golden Nugget, has now changed all the rules in his own company.

In contrast to luring guests with visible outdoor attractions like his dancing waters at the Bellagio, pirate ship at Treasure Island, and volcano at the Mirage, Wynn's newest high-end creation was designed from the inside out. Wynn Las Vegas has put its waterfalls and giant screens behind human-made mountains, reserving them for diners, gamblers, and guests. It's buzz, not glitz, that's intended to draw them to the place. Dropping the theme-hotel motif, this new luxury casino hotel has low hallways and intimate spaces.

Picture a beautiful and opulent property with flowers, mosaic tiles inlaid inside the floors, and a 150-foot-tall artificial pine-covered mountain and a waterfall that cascades into a human-made lake. While maintaining the Vegas focus on entertainment, Wynn has again broken the most basic rules of casinos by flooding the new hotel with natural light and focusing on small, calm spaces.

Wynn Resorts, Ltd. owns and operates two luxury hotels and destination casino resorts, one in Las Vegas and a second in Macau, China. The Wynn Las Vegas, LLC is the flagship of the company, opening in 2005 at one of the best locations on the strip. The previous home of the historic Desert Inn Hotel was imploded to make room for this new highly differentiated casino hotel and golf course project.

The Wynn Las Vegas features 2,716 guest rooms and suites; a 111,000-square-foot casino; 22 food and beverage outlets; an on-site 18-hole golf course; approximately 223,000 square feet of meeting space; an on-site Ferrari and Maserati dealership; and approximately 76,000 square feet of retail space. This luxury resort offers up food from some of the most famous chefs in the world, including Alex Stratta (Alex), Paul Bartolotta (Bartolotta Ristorante di Mare), Takashi Yagihashi (Okada), and Daniel Boulud, whose New York restaurants (Daniel, DB Bistro Moderne, and Café Boulud) have dazzled diners. The Daniel Boulud Brasserie overlooks the Lake of Dreams. When the sun goes down, both the waterfall wall and lake become projection screens for a light show that is visible from the Brasserie and SW Steakhouse.

Quality entertainment includes shows, such as the Tony Award–winning Spamalot, and nightclubs. Wynn has expanded his theater's balcony so he can sell 1,500 tickets to each show, and his deal with Spamalot bars the show from playing in Southern California and Arizona, two states that provide one-third of Vegas' visitors. To enable the show to run twice a night, Wynn has also hired the co-writer of the musical to trim 20 minutes from the original version. This not only lets him run two shows a night, but also gets guests out and into the shopping, dining, and gambling areas in less time.

The Tower Suites at Wynn Las Vegas feature a private drive, check-in area, pool, and elevators. These rooms and suites were evaluated independently from the rest of the property by both the Mobil Five Star and the AAA Five Diamond ratings, becoming the only casino resort in the world to gain both accolades. In addition, the resort is the first Las Vegas property in Mobil's 49-year rating history to earn the Five Star recognition. Mobil Five Star destinations are exceptionally distinctive luxury environments, offering expanded amenities and consistently superlative service, with attention to detail and the anticipation of every need.

Technological innovations were created to offer unique features valued by customers and perceived to be different from those of competitors. Among its many distinguishing characteristics, the Wynn Las Vegas is the first casino to combine the room key and the casino frequent-player card in one card, keeping track of each guest's every purchase. It is the first casino resort to include a luxury car dealership (Ferrari-Maserati). Each of the rooms is connected to one another and the outside world via the largest installation of Voice over IP technology. High-speed Cat-6 Ethernet cables help make Internet access extremely fast. It is also the first hotel to install radio frequency identification (RFID) tags inside chips to better discover counterfeiting.

What could possibly be more luxurious than this upscale resort? Try the Encore, a $1.4 billion project next door that is planned to be an even more upscale version of its sister property. Encore features approximately 2,000 guest rooms, an intimate casino, 45,000 square feet of meeting space, and design details like an entrance area that is entirely separate from the casino experience and guest rooms that are each about 100 square feet larger than those at Wynn Las Vegas. In Las Vegas, creating a new over-the-top casino is harder than beating the house, but Wynn Resorts Limited is giving it a go.[1]

DISCUSSION QUESTIONS:

1. What, if anything, makes the Wynn Las Vegas different from other casinos on the strip?

2. Why do you think Steve Wynn plans to put a second mega resort, the Encore, next to the Wynn Las Vegas?

I N T R O D U C T I O N

*B*usiness-level strategy defines an organization's approach to competing in its chosen markets. Sometimes this type of strategy is referred to as competitive strategy. However, all strategies are competitive strategies, so, to avoid confusion, this book uses the term "business level" to describe strategies within particular businesses. The strategy of Wynn Las Vegas can be described as differentiation, which is a popular approach to creating value in the hospitality industry. Wynn Las Vegas achieves differentiation by creating a distinctive luxury experience in gaming, rooms, entertainment, and food and beverage. Offering unique spa and golf amenities, superlative service with attention to detail and guest needs, all in a prime location are other differentiating features of this casino resort. A differentiation strategy requires creating something that is perceived as unique and provides superior value for customers, not an easy feat in the extravaganza-focused gaming business of Las Vegas.

The golf course, for example, is the only one on the Las Vegas Strip that is restricted to hotel guests and costs more than $500 per round, illustrating one way in which Steve Wynn has sought to develop a value-added unique feature to his operation.[2] More than 800,000 cubic yards of earth were moved to create the dramatic elevation changes designed into the 18-hole course developed by Tom Fazio and considered impossible on the Las Vegas Strip.[3] The success of Wynn's differentiation strategy will depend on his being able to charge a premium price to cover the additional costs.

This chapter will begin with a discussion of the basis for competing in particular markets through specific business-level strategies. Attention will then turn to competitive dynamics—the moves and countermoves of firms and their competitors. Some of the major strategic management responsibilities of business-level managers are listed in Table 5.1. They include establishing the overall direction of the business unit, conducting ongoing analysis of the changing business situation, selecting a generic strategy and the specific strategies needed to carry it out (*strategic posture*), and managing resources to produce a sustainable competitive advantage. These responsibilities and the methods for carrying them out are similar in for-profit and nonprofit organizations.[4] They are also similar in both manufacturing and service settings.

GENERIC BUSINESS STRATEGIES

Business strategies are as different as the organizations that create them. That is, no two business strategies are exactly alike. However, classifying strategies into generic types helps firms identify common strategic characteristics. For example, a firm that is trying to achieve a competitive advantage by producing at lowest cost should seek some combination of efficiency, low levels of overhead, and high volume. Also, because generic strategies are widely understood, they provide a means of meaningful communication. Instead of having to explain the strategy each time, managers can simply use the generic label.

The generic strategy types proposed by Michael Porter are perhaps the most widely used and understood. Porter advanced the idea that a sustainable competitive advantage is related to

TABLE 5.1 Major Business-Level Strategic Management Responsibilities

MAJOR RESPONSIBILITIES	KEY ISSUES
DIRECTION SETTING	Establishment and communication of mission, vision, ethics, and long-term goals of a single business unit Creation and communication of shorter-term goals and objectives
ANALYSIS OF BUSINESS SITUATION	Compilation and assessment of information from stakeholders, broad environmental analysis, and other sources Internal resource analysis Identification of strengths, weaknesses, opportunities, threats, sources of sustainable competitive advantage
SELECTION OF STRATEGY	Selection of a generic approach to competition—cost leadership, differentiation, focus, or best value Selection of a strategic posture—specific strategies needed to carry out the generic strategy
MANAGEMENT OF RESOURCES	Acquisition of resources and/or development of competencies leading to a sustainable competitive advantage Ensuring development of functional strategies and an appropriate organizational design (management structure) to support business strategy Development of control systems to ensure that strategies remain relevant and that the business unit continues to progress toward its goals

the amount of value a firm creates for its most important stakeholder, the customer.[5] According to Porter, firms create superior value for customers by offering them either a basic product or service that is produced at the lowest possible cost or a preferred product or service at a somewhat higher price, where the additional value received exceeds the additional cost of obtaining it.

The first option, called *low-cost leadership*, is based on efficient cost production. In this book, as in practice, the terms *low-cost leadership* and *cost leadership* are used interchangeably. The second option, referred to as *differentiation*, requires the company to distinguish its products or services on the basis of an attribute such as higher-quality product features, location, the skill and experience of employees, technology embodied in design, better service, or intense marketing activities. Both of these strategies assume that an organization is marketing its products or services to a very broad segment of the market.

Porter identified a third strategic option, called *focus*, in which companies target a narrow segment of the market. According to Porter, a firm can focus on a particular segment of the market through either low-cost leadership or differentiation. Consequently, Porter's original generic strategies were low-cost leadership, differentiation, and focus through either low cost or differentiation (for a total of four strategic approaches). JetBlue Airlines, for example, pursues a strategy of low-cost leadership for a broad market, whereas Four Seasons Hotels and Resorts

HOSPITALITY FOCUS

CASA CUPULA: FOCUSES ON GAY/LESBIAN CLIENTELLE

"It's just like a mini–Four Seasons for gay people!" says Don Pickens, founder of Milagro Properties Development. Don opened Casa Cupula in Puerto Vallarta in 2002 to cater to gay travelers. A member hotel of the World's Foremost Gay and Lesbian Hotels—an international alliance of upscale gay and/or lesbian hotels, resorts, guesthouses, and inns—Don recognized the need for upscale accommodations as Vallarta's reputation as a gay destination became more well known. Combining the elegance of an upscale boutique hotel (a differentiation strategy) with the friendliness and comfort of a gay-friendly guesthouse (focused market segment) led to the establishment of Casa Cupula. The hotel has become incredibly popular, with more than 50 percent of guests now being return guests or referrals.

Casa Cupula provides the kind of romantic environment his guests appreciate. As the hotel tells its guest, "no kids, no package-deal cruise ship patrons to look at you funny because you're with your boyfriend. Go ahead: hold hands, kiss, and swim naked!" The hotel believes it is small enough to feel comfortable, but large enough to find a private spot to snuggle.

Don notes that it has been extremely rewarding to have made a difference in the lives of hundreds of guests. For some, it's their first time at a gay hotel. Others have returned half a dozen times and have made Casa Cupula their vacation home. The hotel offers a welcoming and warm embrace to people from every walk of life: men, women, bisexuals, straight friends, singles, couples, threesomes, circuit boys, bears, nerds, politicos, older, younger, people of every color and nationality. This focused hotel was named one of the "Top 5 Most Luxurious Gay Guesthouses" and one of the "Top 10 North American Gay and Lesbian Guesthouses" by the editors of Out & About and Gay.com.[6]

relies on a strategy of differentiation. An example of a differentiation focus strategy would be the hotels catering to gay and lesbian travelers developed by Milagro Properties. (See the "Hospitality Focus" boxed section above.)

Porter referred to companies that were not pursuing a distinct generic strategy as "*stuck-in-the-middle*."[7] According to Porter, these uncommitted firms should have lower performance than committed firms because they lack a consistent basis for creating superior value. He argued that companies that exclusively pursue one of the generic strategies center all of their resources on becoming good at that strategy. More recently, many firms have succeeded at pursuing elements associated with cost leadership and differentiation simultaneously. In this book, we refer to this hybrid as *best value*. Increasing global competition has made a best-value strategy increasingly popular.

Combining low cost, differentiation, and best-value approaches with a broad-versus-narrow market focus results in six generic-strategy types, outlined in Table 5.2. Notice that for each strategy, the phrase "firms attempt" is used. These describe strategies that businesses are pursuing and do not depend on whether a company is successful in pursuing their strategy. For example, five firms can pursue a cost-leadership strategy, while only one of them will be the cost leader.

It is important to understand that one corporation can be pursuing several business-level strategies simultaneously through its different business units. For example, InterContinental Hotels Group owns many brands with a wide variety of strategies, as shown in Figure 5.1.

TABLE 5.2 Generic Business-Level Strategies

Business-Level Strategy	Broad or Narrow Market	Source of Advantage	Description
Low-cost leadership	Broad	Lowest-cost production or service delivery	Firms attempt to provide product or service at the lowest cost to the customer. The product or service is targeted at a very broad segment of the market.
Differentiation	Broad	Preferred product or service	Firms attempt to provide a product or service that is preferred above the products or services of competing firms. The product or service is targeted at a very broad segment of the market.
Best value	Broad	Low-cost and highly desirable product or service	Firms attempt to provide a product or service that is very attractive to customers, but also delivered at a reasonably low cost, thus providing the best service value for the cost. The product or service is targeted at a very broad segment of the market.
Focus through low-cost leadership	Narrow	Lowest-cost production or service delivery	Firms attempt to provide a product or service at the lowest cost to the customer within a specific segment (niche) of the market.
Focus through a differentiation	Narrow	Preferred product or service	Firms attempt to provide a differentiated product or service that is preferred above the products or services of competing firms within a specific segment (niche) of the market.
Focus through best value	Narrow	Low-cost and highly desirable	Firms attempt to provide a product or service that is very attractive to customers, but also produced at a reasonably low cost, thus providing the best value for cost in a particular segment (niche) of the market.

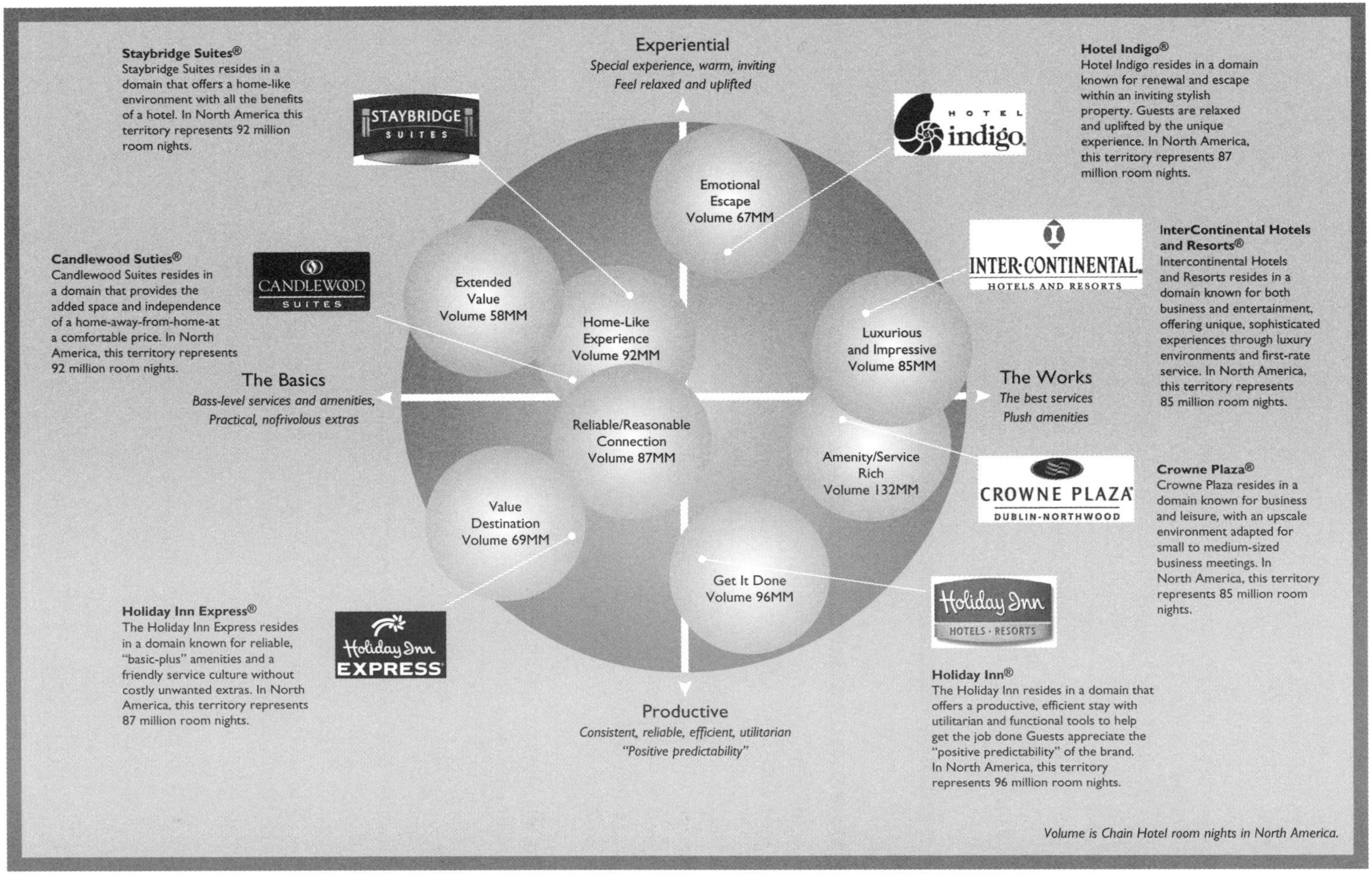

Staybridge Suites®
Staybridge Suites resides in a domain that offers a home-like environment with all the benefits of a hotel. In North America this territory represents 92 million room nights.
Experiential
Special experience, warm, inviting
Feel relaxed and uplifted
Hotel Indigo®
Hotel Indigo resides in a domain known for renewal and escape within an inviting stylish property. Guests are relaxed and uplifted by the unique experience. In North America, this territory represents 87 million room nights.
STAYBRIDGE SUITES
HOTEL indigo
Emotional Escape Volume 67MM
Candlewood Suties®
Candlewood Suites resides in a domain that provides the added space and independence of a home-away-from-home-at a comfortable price. In North America, this territory represents 92 million room nights.
CANDLEWOOD SUITES
Extended Value Volume 58MM
Home-Like Experience Volume 92MM
INTER·CONTINENTAL HOTELS AND RESORTS
InterContinental Hotels and Resorts®
Intercontinental Hotels and Resorts resides in a domain known for both business and entertainment, offering unique, sophisticated experiences through luxury environments and first-rate service. In North America, this territory represents 85 million room nights.
Luxurious and Impressive Volume 85MM
The Basics
Bass-level services and amenities,
Practical, nofrivolous extras
The Works
The best services
Plush amenities
Reliable/Reasonable Connection Volume 87MM
Amenity/Service Rich Volume 132MM
Value Destination Volume 69MM
CROWNE PLAZA DUBLIN-NORTHWOOD
Crowne Plaza®
Crowne Plaza resides in a domain known for business and leisure, with an upscale environment adapted for small to medium-sized business meetings. In North America, this territory represents 85 million room nights.
Get It Done Volume 96MM
Holiday Inn HOTELS · RESORTS
Holiday Inn Express®
The Holiday Inn Express resides in a domain known for reliable, "basic-plus" amenities and a friendly service culture without costly unwanted extras. In North America, this territory represents 87 million room nights.
Holiday Inn EXPRESS
Holiday Inn®
The Holiday Inn resides in a domain that offers a productive, efficient stay with utilitarian and functional tools to help get the job done Guests appreciate the "positive predictability" of the brand. In North America, this territory represents 96 million room nights.
Productive
Consistent, reliable, efficient, utilitarian
"Positive predictability"
Volume is Chain Hotel room nights in North America.

FIGURE 5.1 A portfolio of brands at InterContinental Hotel Group

Source: Development Opportunities World Wide, InterContinental Hotel Group.

The strategy of Holiday Inn Express is probably best described as low-cost leadership because of its broad appeal to the mass market and emphasis on limited service, cleanliness, timelessness, and cost efficiency—to ensure optimal use of space, ease of maintenance, and a higher return on investment for owners. This is not to say that Holiday Inn Express is a low-quality lodging brand. In contrast, the prestige brand of the company, InterContinental Hotels and Resorts, is focused on outstanding facilities and superior service within unique local contexts and cultures. The Holiday Inn brand offers full-service comfort and value to a broad market, while Candlewood Suites offers a hotel experience created for stays of a week or longer. Hotel Indigo (featured in Chapter 4) is a boutique hotel, while Crowne Plaza focuses on the convention and meetings business. Because a single corporation can pursue multiple strategies, this chapter will discuss specific brands instead of their corporate parents. Each of the strategy types will now be discussed in detail.

Cost Leadership

Firms pursuing cost leadership set out to become the lowest-cost providers of a good or service. The broad scope of cost leaders means that they attempt to serve a large percentage of the total market. For instance, Etap and Motel 6 are both pursuing cost leadership. (See the "Hospitality Focus" boxed section on page 173.)

Some hoteliers would bristle at the thought that they are pursuing a low-cost leadership strategy. Rather, they envision their firms as pursuing some sort of balance between low costs and differentiation. While a clean room and linens and some level of comfort (i.e., telephone and television) is expected at every lodging property, efforts to differentiate may result in increased cost but not added value, making a firm more stuck-in-the middle than competitive. Once the basic quality standards have been met, differentiation occurs as companies offer significantly more than just a clean, comfortable room. Brands like Etap and Motel 6 do not offer significantly more than the basics—simply furnished rooms with a bed, shower, and toilet.

Ryanair and JetBlue provide no-frills flights at the lowest prices possible. Burger King and Taco Bell work on value pricing to deliver food fast to those who want convenience and low price. Management in these companies is very good at keeping costs at a minimum. Consequently, they can keep prices low and attract a wide segment of the market that is interested in an inexpensive product or service offering.

To appreciate the significance of the cost-leadership strategy, it is important to understand the factors that underlie cost structures in firms. Companies pursuing a low-cost strategy will typically employ one or more of the following factors to create their low-cost positions:

1. Accurate demand forecasting combined with high-capacity utilization

2. Economies of scale

3. Technological advances

4. Outsourcing

5. Learning/experience effects[8]

MOTEL 6: COST LEADERSHIP

"We'll leave the light on for you," says the folksy voice of Tom Bodett, in a well-known television advertisement for Motel 6, the economy hotel brand with more than 850 properties in the United States and Canada. Owned by French hotel giant Accor, Motel 6 had its beginnings in 1962, when two California building contractors, William Becker and Paul Greene, developed a plan to build motels with rooms at bargain rates. They decided on a $6 room rate per night that would cover building costs, land leases, mortgages, managers' salaries, and maid service, hence the company name.

Becker and Greene specialized in building low-cost housing developments, and spent two years formulating a business model for Motel 6 based on cutting costs as much as possible to offer an alternative to other major hotel chains, such as Holiday Inn, whose locations were becoming increasingly upscale in quality and price. Motel 6 emphasized no-frills lodging with rooms featuring coin-operated black-and-white TVs instead of the free color TVs found in the more expensive motels, along with shower-only bathrooms and functional interior décor (to reduce the time it took to clean the rooms). The first location in Santa Barbara had no restaurant on-site, a notable difference from other hotels of the era. Unlike most hotel chains, Motel 6 allows pets and directly owns and operates most of its locations. In 1990, the company was bought by Accor and began franchising in 1994. Accor is the largest owner-operator of economy lodging in the world. In Europe, Accor has the Etap brand. Etap hotels are located in city centers and near airports, with more than 370 hotels across Europe, primarily in France.

Today, both of these brands cater to a large segment of the population that is interested in economical lodging. They are both large enough to enjoy economies of scale and provide travelers with the opportunity to stay within the chain on longer trips. They both have huge information and reservation networks. And they both strive to keep costs at absolute minimums while providing clean, functional, and modestly comfortable rooms. Motel 6 claims to be the lowest-priced budget hotel in the United States.[9]

HIGH-CAPACITY UTILIZATION

When demand is high and capacity is fully used, a firm's fixed costs are spread over more units, which lowers average unit costs. However, when demand falls off, the fixed costs are spread over fewer units, so unit costs increase. This basic concept suggests that a firm that is able to maintain higher levels of capacity utilization, through better demand forecasting, conservative capacity-expansion policies, or aggressive pricing, will be better able to maintain a lower-cost structure than a competitor of equal size and capability. Consequently, the lodging industry puts high importance on occupancy rates, and restaurants pay close attention to meals served per hour and day parts. In the airline industry, the metrics of interest are load and yield per passenger mile. (See the "Hospitality Focus" boxed section on page 174.)

High-capacity utilization is particularly important in industries like hotels, rental cars, and airlines, in which fixed costs represent a large percentage of total costs. In these situations, entry barriers make industry participants extremely sensitive to even small fluctuations in demand.

HOSPITALITY
FOCUS

JETBLUE'S CAPACITY MANAGEMENT

"Our customers love to fly JetBlue, and our load factors have historically been industry leading," says the CEO of the airline. A *load factor* is the ratio of revenue passenger miles to available seat miles of a particular flight. In 2006, JetBlue made the strategic decision to price their product to achieve a higher yield, at the expense of load factor. This decision means that the airline monitored how seats were being reserved and reacted accordingly, by offering discounts when it appeared as if seats would otherwise be vacant. By year end, the load factor was 81.6 percent, and yield per passenger mile climbed to 9.53 cents—nearly a 19 percent increase year over year. Despite additional capacity in many of their markets, the revenue management strategies resulted in higher passenger yields. Distribution costs were minimized by using online systems, with nearly 80 percent of total ticket sales booked via the web site.[10]

For example, small variations in demand can cause wide fluctuations in profitability. In these types of businesses, where capacity utilization is so important, companies that are faced with falling demand typically attempt to stimulate sales by employing massive price-cutting.

Despite industry efforts to price discount when demand flattens, research on hotels has revealed that customer demand does not appear to be easily stimulated by price reductions.[11] Figure 5.2 shows how customer demand (occupancy levels) remains constant (flat) for hotels in both the United States and Asia, even when the hotels price below their competitors. The figure also shows that revenue per available room (RevPAR) rises when hotels price higher than their competitors do and falls when hotels price below their direct competition. Nevertheless, careful revenue management can help firms maximize revenue by knowing when to raise or lower prices according to occupancy levels. In short, while hotel demand (occupancy levels) cannot easily be stimulated, a hotel can engage in dynamic pricing to effectively manage inventory.[12]

ECONOMIES OF SCALE

The second major factor with the potential to lead to cost advantages is economies of scale. *Economies of scale* are often confused with increases in volume. As described previously, increases in capacity utilization that spread fixed expenses can lead to lower unit costs. However, true economies of scale are associated with size rather than capacity utilization. The central principle of economies of scale is that costs per unit are less when a firm expands its scale or size of operation. For example, the cost of constructing a 200-room hotel will not necessarily be twice the cost of building a 100-room hotel, so the initial fixed cost per unit of capacity will be lower. Also, the manager of the larger facility will not generally receive double the salary of the manager of the smaller facility. In addition, activities such as quality control, purchasing, and reservations typically do not require twice as much time or twice as many laborers.

Large hotel brands with growing portfolios create economies of scale through frequent traveler programs, reservation systems, and global sales and marketing programs that take advantage of their size. Owners and developers who select a well-regarded brand may find they can obtain

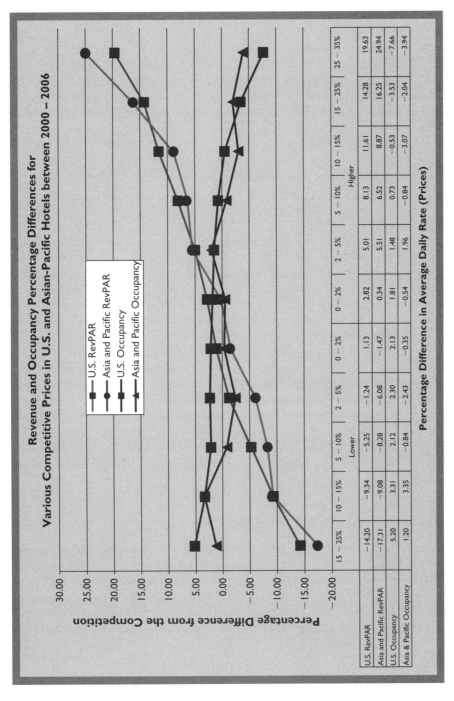

FIGURE 5.2 Hotel revenue and demand under various pricing strategies

Source: L. Canina and C. Enz, "Pricing for Revenue Enhancements in Asian and Pacific Region Hotels: A Study of Discounting from 2001–2006," 8 (*CHR Report*), Cornell University, 2008.

Revenue and Occupancy Percentage Differences for
Various Competitive Prices in U.S. and Asian-Pacific Hotels between 2000 – 2006

	15 – 25%	10 – 15%	5 – 10%	2 – 5%	0 – 2%	0 – 2%	2 – 5%	5 – 10%	10 – 15%	15 – 25%	25 – 35%
	Lower					Higher					
U.S. RevPAR	−14.20	−9.34	−5.25	−1.24	1.13	2.82	5.01	8.13	11.61	14.28	19.63
Asia and Pacific RevPAR	−17.31	−9.08	−8.28	−6.08	−1.47	0.34	5.51	6.52	8.87	16.25	24.94
U.S. Occupancy	5.20	3.31	2.12	2.30	2.13	1.81	1.48	0.73	−0.53	−3.53	−7.66
Asia & Pacific Occupancy	1.20	3.35	−0.84	−2.43	−0.35	−0.54	1.96	−0.84	−3.07	−2.04	−3.94

Percentage Difference in Average Daily Rate (Prices)

Legend: U.S. RevPAR; Asia and Pacific RevPAR; U.S. Occupancy; Asia and Pacific Occupancy

Y-axis: Percentage Difference from the Competition (30.00, 25.00, 20.00, 15.00, 10.00, 5.00, 0.00, −5.00, −10.00, −15.00, −20.00)

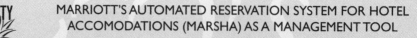

Marriott's Automated Reservation System for Hotel Accommodations (MARSHA) is a reservation network and demand management tool. MARSHA is linked directly with the global distribution systems (GDS) operated by major airlines and travel organizations, and leads the industry in GDS productivity. With 3 percent of the worldwide supply of hotel rooms, Marriott International realizes 20 percent of all reservations made via the GDS. MARSHA generated nearly one out of every five room nights booked through GDS. In 2005, MARSHA handled 70 million reservations, 168 million gross room nights, and US $22 billion in gross room revenue, including US $280 million in cross-sales among Marriott brands.[13]

lower interest charges when borrowing from banks and have access to a greater range of financial instruments because of the size of the brand. For the brand, its marketing costs can be spread over a greater range of properties as it grows in size. Finally, owners and franchisees of large hotel companies can enjoy the managerial specialization of the brand company in hotel development and renovation projects. Support in the areas of architectural and interior design, project and construction management, and procurement-related services can reduce the long-run average cost of running an individual hotel.

In summary, the larger hotel firm may be able to provide an owner and operator with per-unit savings in fixed costs and indirect labor costs. *Diseconomies of scale* occur when a firm builds facilities that are so large that the sheer administrative costs and confusion associated with the added bureaucracy overwhelm any potential cost savings. Many of the largest hotel companies view their scale of operations as a key competitive strength. Starwood Hotels and Resorts Worldwide believes that its scale is one of the foundations of its business strategy, as noted in Chapter 4. In addition to having the scale to support their marketing and reservation functions, the company relies on their large portfolio of luxury and upscale hotels to lower the cost of operations through purchasing synergies.[14]

TECHNOLOGICAL ADVANCES

Companies that make investments in cost-saving technologies are often trading an increase in fixed costs for a reduction in variable costs. If technological improvements result in lower total-unit costs, then firms have achieved a cost advantage from their investments referred to as economies of technology.[15] The reservation systems maintained by the major airlines and lodging companies represent investments in technology that reduce overall costs and provide a degree of information control that was previously impossible. (See the "Hospitality Focus" boxed section above.)

OUTSOURCING—MAKE VERSUS BUY

Traditional thinking in management was that organizations should perform as many value-adding functions as possible in-house in order to retain control of the production process and

HOSPITALITY FOCUS

LE COLONIAL: OUTSOURCING HOME DELIVERY

Le Colonial, a premier upscale French-Vietnamese restaurant in Chicago's Gold Coast neighborhood, offers fine food in a beautiful environment. The first-floor dining room uses a tasteful décor to transport guests to tropical Southeast Asia of the 1920s. The main-floor dining room, seasonal café, bar, lounge, and all-season terrace of this charming two-story vintage rowhouse offer customers excellent cuisine in a romantic setting. What would you outsource in this restaurant?

The answer is home delivery. Only three years ago, customers who lived within walking distance of this 120-seat restaurant could phone in orders and busboys would walk to customers' homes (or go by cab in bad weather) with meals. To expand its delivery business without additional payroll or overhead costs, the restaurant decided to outsource its delivery operation.

Joe King, a partner at Le Colonial, chose a contractor who delivers to most Chicago neighborhoods and uses an online web site. With a menu posted online, the contractor receives an order, routes it to the restaurant, and then picks it up for delivery. If a customer complains about cold or messy food or a late-arriving order, the delivery company absorbs the cost of the order. The service fee to the contractor is 30 percent of each delivery.

Using the service has increased delivery orders from about 1 percent of business to 4 percent of sales and is cost-effective because the restaurant is no longer using restaurant staff to perform these tasks and is able to expand its operation.[16]

gain technological efficiencies through creating synergies among processes. However, competitive reality has set in, and corporations realize that sometimes another company can perform a process better or more efficiently than they can. This has led to *outsourcing*, which means contracting with another firm to provide services that were previously supplied from within the company. For example, a hospitality firm could subcontract its accounting, reservations, information systems, or even hotel management. A real estate investment trust is, in essence, subcontracting management of the properties it owns to other firms. An individual hotel might outsource food and beverage, janitorial, airport shuttle, valet, human resources, or even housekeeping services. A restaurant could outsource cleaning, marketing, and many other activities, perhaps even the chef. SoulFire, a 75-seat casual barbecue restaurant, used a consulting chef to help with the initial design of the kitchen and menu.[17] Now the outsourced chef meets with the owner regularly to discuss the menu as well as operational procedures.

Purchasing value-creating activities through outsourcing can increase a firm's flexibility, while reducing risk and costs. However, it does require effective coordination and selection of the right activities to outsource. In addition, recent studies have revealed that unforeseen complexity and conflicts with outsourcing have led to higher total costs than anticipated.[18] Outsourcing allows a firm to concentrate resources on the core business activities, but too much outsourcing may lead to a loss of innovative activity. When costs begin to rise, which is in direct contrast to the primary motive of outsourcing, firms bring the outsourced service or good back in-house, a practice called *backsourcing*. (See the "Hospitality Focus" boxed section above.)

Local outsourcing, like that used by Le Colonial to respond to home delivery, is in contrast to offshoring. *Offshoring* is when a company outsources to a supplier in a foreign country. Foreign labor costs and supportive regulatory environments are the primary reasons why firms select to outsource abroad. Whether local or offshore, outsourcing can be a source of efficiency and cost reduction. However, it is important that a firm continue to control delivery of the unique features that provide competitive advantage to the company. In other words, it should nurture a few core competencies and focus on them while outsourcing noncore activities.

LEARNING EFFECTS

A final factor that influences cost structures is learning effects.[19] If you are a student, you probably spent a long time the first time you registered for classes. Now, as a veteran of several registrations, you know how to get through the process much faster. When an employee learns to do a job more efficiently with repetition, then learning is taking place. The *learning-curve* effect says that the time required to complete a task will decrease as a predictable function of the number of times the task is repeated. Dramatic time savings are achieved early in the life of a company. However, as the company matures, tangible cost savings from labor learning are more difficult to achieve, because it takes longer to see a true doubling of cumulative volume, and because most of the opportunities for learning have already been exploited. Also, learning effects do not just happen. They occur only when management creates an environment that is favorable to both learning and change and then rewards employees for their productivity improvements.

Learning effects can be described by a curve such as the one found in Figure 5.3.[20] Following from the logic of this curve, a market-share leader should enjoy a cost advantage relative to competitors because of the extra learning and experience that has occurred by producing the additional output. This concept has led many firms to fight aggressively on price in order to obtain the highest market share and thus move to the right on the curve as far as possible. As the curve flattens, it becomes increasingly difficult to gain cost advantages from learning effects. The same sort of phenomenon exists with respect to economies of scale.

Companies that are able to achieve the lowest cost do not have to charge the lowest price. In other words, a cost leader does not have to be a price leader. If an organization is able to achieve the lowest cost but charge a price that is the same as competitors charge, then it will enjoy higher profits. However, if the low-cost leader's price is the same as or higher than the

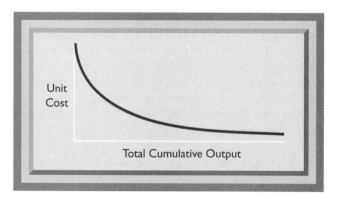

FIGURE 5.3 A typical learning curve

price others charge, then customers may switch to a competitor, undermining the low-cost producer's efforts to benefit from capacity utilization, learning effects, or other sources of low cost. Consequently, many low-cost leaders try to underprice competitors slightly in order to give customers an incentive to buy from them and to keep their volumes high enough to support their low-cost strategy.

RISKS ASSOCIATED WITH A COST-LEADERSHIP STRATEGY

There are some risks associated with a cost-leadership strategy. Firms pursuing cost leadership may not detect changes in services that are becoming expected because of a preoccupation with cost. They run the risk of making large investments in new properties or businesses only to see them become obsolete because of changing trends. Their large investments make them reluctant to keep up with changes that are not compatible with their existing facilities. Another risk is that competitors will quickly imitate the technologies that are resulting in lower costs. As Michael Porter observed, "A company can outperform rivals only if it can establish a difference it can preserve."[21]

Another risk associated with a cost-leadership strategy is that the company will go too far and perhaps even endanger customers or employees in the process. ValuJet's penny-pinching allowed it to achieve a very low-cost position in the airline industry. ValuJet passed the savings on to consumers and experienced unprecedented growth. However, their stinginess came under close scrutiny after the crash of ValuJet flight 592 into the Florida Everglades. Federal investigators found that some of ValuJet's procedures, especially maintenance procedures, were unsafe, and they ultimately shut down the airline until safety concerns could be worked out.[22]

Differentiation

In differentiation strategies, the emphasis is on creating value through uniqueness, as opposed to lowest cost. Hospitality services are often complex and satisfy self-identity and social affiliation needs, creating tremendous opportunities for differentiation, which explains why this business-level strategy is so popular. Unlike products that are often simple and require performance to a technical standard, tourism products, such as a vacation, do not conform to detailed technical standards and offer limitless opportunities for differentiation. Service experiences that complement consumers' lifestyles and brands that communicate their aspirations may allow the firm that creates these products and services to charge a premium price. The higher price is necessary to cover the extra costs incurred in offering the unique experience. To understand and profit from a differentiation strategy, it is important to understand customer lifestyles and aspirations so that the unique offerings are valued by customers.

LIFESTYLE AND EXPERIENCE

The customer of the future is expected to be more demanding, self-indulgent, and hedonistic.[23] As markets mature, and consumers become increasingly cynical and distrusting, hospitality firms will be

HOSPITALITY FOCUS

PRICE WATERHOUSE COOPERS EUROPEAN LIFESTYLE SURVEY: READING CONSUMER PATTERNS

"Research shows that we will pay more for food that we perceive to be better for us. Similarly with hotels, we are more likely to pay for attributes and experiences we value, such as location, safety, experience, ambience, and 'ego-fit'. It is not just about money and 'premiumisation' of the offer that endorses the value shift. Value has emotional as well as financial attributes; for example, Malmaison-branded iPods connected to a play list are already offered to hotel guests, but now the group plans to create compilation CDs and single-artist albums that reflect the 'Malmaison experience' and encourage an emotional link with the brand. Hotels will need to ensure this means they know what consumers really value and what they will pay for; it's no good adding amenities consumers don't value and could lose operators an operating advantage."[24]

expected to provide higher-quality services tailored to meet evolving lifestyles. In Chapter 2, we discussed consumer trends, and we return to this topic now to highlight the importance of understanding and identifying what customers are willing to pay for in hospitality and travel services. "Lifestyle really applies to customers' growing desires to take the lifestyle they either have at home or the lifestyle that they imagine themselves having at home and take it on the road," according to Mike Depatie, president of San Francisco–based Kimpton Hotels & Restaurants.[25] Key questions should include, "What motivates the customer?" and "By what criteria do they select a hospitality product?"[26] In a recent Pricewaterhouse Coopers European lifestyle survey, the challenge of reading consumer patterns and the importance of creating value were noted. (See the "Hospitality Focus" boxed section above.)

A customer lifestyle approach to hospitality is based on customer aspirations, meaning that as customers become more affluent and sophisticated, they want travel and leisure offerings that are as nice, if not nicer, than what they have at home. Operators report that people's bathrooms and bedrooms are now nicer than those of traditional hotels. This shift in consumer wants creates new opportunities for differentiation. However, building unique value-enhancing service experiences is not easy.

In the book *The Experience Economy*, Joseph Pine and James Gilmore argue that experiences are as distinct from services as services are from goods. They go on to suggest that staging experiences is not about entertaining customers, but engaging them.[27] New lifestyle hotels, such as aloft by Starwood, NYLO, and Cambria Suites by Choice, are in different ways hoping to provide travelers with alternatives to the traditional unemotional hotel experience. Figure 5.3 provides a summary of the top European hotels that are carving out what is now called the lifestyle hotel.

Uniqueness can be achieved in an almost unlimited number of ways, including:

- Product features
- Complimentary services
- Technology embodied in design
- Location
- Service innovations

TABLE 5.3 Top 25 European Lifestyle Hotel Companies

HOTELS (OWNER/OPERATOR)	NUMBER OF HOTELS 2006	NUMBER OF ROOMS 2006
1. Sorat Hotels	16	1,376
2. Innside Premium Hotels	8	1,072
3. Malmaison Hotels (MWB)	10	1,031
4. Derby Hotels Collection	9	850
5. Melia Boutique (Sol Melia)	13	838
6. Silken Group	3	715
7. Artotels (Park Plaza)	5	653
8. Red Carnation Collection	7	543
9. Stein Hotels	14	518
10. Habitat Hotels	5	489
11. Morgans Hotel Group (formerly Lan Schrager)	2	354
12. Hotel du Vin (MWB)	8	338
13. Firmdale Hotels (Kemps)	7	404
14. Eton Hotels Group	5	272
15. JJW Luxury Hotels & Resorts	3	203
16. Quest	1	200
17. Como Group	2	196
18. Dakota	2	184
19. Columbus	1	181

TABLE 5.3 (Continued)

20. ABode	3	180
21. Lungarno Hotels (Ferragarno)	5	180
22. Loock	3	175
23. Alias Hotels	3	149
24. Big Sleep (Bedfactory Hotels)	2	144
25. Town House Company	4	141
Total	141	11,386

Based on the best of our knowledge at August 2006 - some may not open or they may add more rooms.
Alas: The Rosetti will be re-branded ABode in 2007.
JJW Luxury Hotels & Resorts is part of MBI which acquired the former Bootsman Group.
Note: We have excluded the Guoman brand this year as despite some great design, it is just too large for the survey.
Tristie have added the Tower Hotel in London to this brand and these two hotels would, had we included them,
have accounted for around 1,700 rooms.
Source: Pricewaterhouse Coopers Lifestyle Hotels Survey, 2006.

- Superior service
- Creative advertising
- Better supplier relationships leading to better services

The key to success is that customers must be willing to pay more for the uniqueness of a service than the firm paid to create it. As in the cost-leadership strategy, an organization pursuing a differentiation strategy is targeting a broad market; consequently, the differentiated product or service should be designed so that it has wide appeal to many market sectors. Returning to Starwood Hotels, another factor they have identified as contributing to their position in the industry is their high-quality guest experiences that appeal to both business and personal travelers. (See the first "Hospitality Focus" boxed section on page 183.)

Companies like Starwood cannot ignore their cost positions, as we saw in their emphasis on scale as well and distinctiveness. When its costs are too high relative to competitors' costs, a firm may not be able to recover enough of the additional costs through higher prices. Therefore, differentiators have to keep costs low in the areas that are not directly related to the sources of differentiation. Many large hotel companies reduce their investments in owning properties so that they can focus on brand and franchise versus real estate. (See the second "Hospitality Focus" boxed section on page 183.)

DIFFERENTIATION VERSUS SEGMENTATION

It is easy to confuse differentiation with segmentation, but they are not the same. Differentiation focuses on offering unique products or services that customers perceive to be different and

STARWOOD HOTELS: QUALITY STRATEGY THROUGH DISTINCTIVE PROPERTIES

The St. Regis in New York, New York; The Phoenician in Scottsdale, Arizona; the Hotel Gritti Palace in Venice, Italy; and the St. Regis in Beijing, China, are a few examples of the distinctive properties in the Starwood portfolio. Many of the brand's hotels are consistently recognized as the best of the best by readers of *Condé Nast Traveler* magazine, providing the highest quality and service. Recent issues of *Condé Nast Traveler* have included over 35 Starwood properties among its prestigious Gold List.[28]

STARWOOD HOTELS: COST STRATEGY THROUGH REDUCED INVESTMENT IN REAL ESTATE

At Starwood, we have implemented a strategy of reducing our investment in owned real estate and increasing our focus on the management and franchise business. In furtherance of this strategy, during 2006 we sold a total of 43 hotels for approximately $4.5 billion, including 33 properties to Host for approximately $4.1 billion in stock, cash, and debt assumption.

As a result, our primary business objective is to maximize earnings and cash flow by increasing the number of our hotel management contracts and franchise agreements; acquiring and developing vacation ownership resorts and selling VOIs (vacation ownership interests); and investing in real estate assets where there is a strategic rationale for doing so, which may include selectively acquiring interests in additional assets and disposing of noncore hotels (including hotels where the return on invested capital is not adequate) and trophy assets that may be sold at significant premiums. We plan to meet these objectives by leveraging our global assets, broad customer base, and other resources and by taking advantage of our scale to reduce costs.[29]

better than the offerings of the competition. Segmentation is the grouping together of customers and their demand based on their behaving in the same way or having similar needs. For example, just because a hotel is located within the same upscale segment of the market as its competitors does not mean it has differentiated itself from them. *Competitive convergence* exists when companies are indistinguishable from each other.[30] While the potential for differentiation is great in service businesses, the ease of imitation can make it difficult to avoid competitive convergence. Some might even argue the following:

The hotel industry has a surplus of similar companies, employing similar people, with similar educational backgrounds, working in similar jobs, coming up with similar ideas, producing similar things, with similar prices and similar quality.[31]

Differentiation is a strategic choice, not a feature of the market, and as such needs to be based on creating a bundle of resource capabilities. Chapter 3 contained a detailed discussion of resource-based sources of competitive advantage. No attempt will be made to repeat that discussion here, but it is worth mentioning that some resources are more likely to lead to a source of sustainable differentiation. For example, reputations and brands are difficult to imitate, whereas particular service features may be easy to imitate.

In general, intangible resources, such as a high-performance organizational culture, are difficult to imitate, whereas tangible resources, such as the fixtures and furnishings in a hotel, are easy to imitate. Difficult-to-imitate resources are more likely to lead to a sustainable advantage. So, creating value extends beyond just the product, as Starbucks has illustrated with its fostering of an overall "Starbucks Experience." The ability of Starbucks to get a price premium for a cup of coffee rests in part on the overall experience it has created. However, sustaining the differentiation advantage of a firm is not easy, as the chairman of Starbucks, Howard Schultz warns in a leaked internal memo sent to the CEO. Schultz fears that rapid expansion has led to the dilution of the customer experience and the commoditization of the brand. He notes in the memo, "I have said for 20 years that our success is not an entitlement and now it's proving to be a reality. Let's be smarter about how we are spending our time, money, and resources. Let's get back to the core. Push for innovation and do the things necessary to once again differentiate Starbucks from all others."[32]

RISKS ASSOCIATED WITH A DIFFERENTIATION STRATEGY

It is important to recognize that differences in value may be a result of buyer perceptions rather than actual service attributes. Furthermore, it is not always easy to recognize the value added from a hospitality service, because production and consumption occur at the same time. Economists distinguish *experience goods*, in which it is difficult to determine product characteristics in advance of consumption, from *search goods*, which a consumer can inspect in advance of purchase.[33] Before you buy an MP3 player, you can go to several stores, touch and listen to various products, and compare prices. In contrast, a dinner or hotel stay cannot be assessed by the potential buyer beforehand. To resolve this problem, branding and advertising are used to signal quality and credibility. Effective advertising may result in a strong brand preference, even though the services in a particular segment of the industry are essentially the same.

Consequently, the major risks associated with a differentiation strategy center on the difference between added costs and incremental price. One risk is that customers will sacrifice some of the features, services, or image possessed by a unique service because it costs too much. Another risk is that customers will no longer perceive an attribute as differentiating. They may come to a point at which they are so familiar with a service that brand image is no longer important. If a source of differentiation is easy to imitate, then imitation by competitors can also eliminate perceived differentiation among products or services.

For example, as Wi-Fi becomes a standard feature on planes or in hotel rooms, it will no longer be a source of differentiation. Consequently, staying ahead of the competition in service development requires constant innovation.[34] As one business writer put it: "For outstanding performance, a company has to beat the competition. The trouble is the competition has heard the same message."[35]

Best Value

Some strategy scholars argue that a combination of strategic elements from both differentiation and low cost may be necessary to create a sustainable competitive advantage: "The immediate effect of differentiation will be to increase unit costs. However, if costs fall with increasing volume, the long-run effect may be to reduce unit costs."[36] Volume is expected to increase because differentiation makes the product or service more attractive to the market. Then, as volume increases, costs will decrease. For example, Anheuser-Busch has created brewing products that have a good image and high quality, yet the company is a cost leader because of efficiencies created by high-volume production and sales.

The key to a best-value strategy is simple supply-and-demand economics. For example, assume that three vendors sell hot dogs on the street corners of a major city. The first vendor pursues a low-cost strategy. She is able to buy hot dogs at 20 cents each and buns at 8 cents each. Her hot dogs are known by locals to be of low quality, but some of them buy from her anyway, and she gets almost all of the drive-by business at a price of $1. Her average daily sales are $100, for a gross profit of $72. Her cart costs are $30 per day, so she nets $42.

Another vendor specializes in the highest-quality imported sausages. They cost him $2 each, and he buys a little better bun at 10 cents each. He sells an average of 40 sausages for $4 each. His nicer cart costs him $40 per day. After making the calculations, you will see that his gross is $76 and his net is $36.

However, assume that a third vendor can buy a domestic sausage that is almost as good as the imported sausage and sell 80 per day at $3. She buys the sausages locally for $1 each, which is five times as much as the first vendor pays for cheap hot dogs but half the cost of the imported sausages. The better buns are 10 cents each, and the nicer cart is $40 per day. Gross profit is $152 and net is $112. Obviously, this third vendor has found a better strategy.

Hospitality is often a lot like the hot dog vendors. A little extra service in a room, better technology, or a fun and engaging service provider are not very expensive. Taken together, however, they can enhance the guest experience and thus make the service more valuable in the eyes of consumers. Best value is about making sure that the things that provide the most perceived value to a customer are done very well, while looking for ways to keep costs low through technology, economies of scale, learning, or reducing waste.

QUALITY AND BEST VALUE

An emphasis on quality may help hospitality firms that want to pursue a best-value strategy. Much has been said and written on the topic of quality. According to the American Assembly, which consists of 65 leaders of business, labor, government, and academia: "This does not mean quality merely to specifications but that improves constantly, quality that is characterized by constant innovations that create a loyal customer. It means achieving this attitude from top to bottom, from the board room to the factory floor."[37] W. Edwards Deming, an expert on quality, argued that producing higher-quality products through superior designs also reduces costs.[38] It is less expensive to produce 10 products right the first time than to build 11 products and have to throw one away because of quality defects.

IMPLEMENTING SIX SIGMA

Since 2001, Starwood has found Six Sigma to be a powerful way to combine creativity and efficiency. Hundreds of projects have been completed using the process, including a menu engineering program that reworks the contents of an in-room refrigerator based on their popularity to drive higher profits, and the development of a pool concierge who helps guests in Latin American resorts book spa appointments and restaurant reservations.

Since the program launch, the vice president of Six Sigma and his group have trained 150 employees as "black belts" and more than 2,700 as "green belts" in the arts of Six Sigma. Based mostly at the hotels, the specialists are change agents who help dream up and oversee the development of projects. The key to their success is that the Six Sigma specialists operate like partners to help the hotels meet their own objectives.

One project devised by the Westin group is called "Unwind," the purpose of which is to imagine a set of nightly activities that would draw guests out of their rooms and into the lobby where they could meet and mingle, in the hopes of developing greater loyalty to the hotel. One local hotel, the Westin Chicago River North, came up with the idea of offering a massage.

After figuring out the logistics and pilot-testing the concept, the project was turned over to the hotel sponsor. After rolling out the prototype, the Six Sigma team shifts to analysis. A web-based system allows Starwood to monitor performance metrics to gauge the success or failure of a new project. In the case of Unwind, the hotel kept close tabs on the massage revenue produced by each room, revealing that revenues from massages in the hotel spa jumped 30 percent after the hotel launched the lobby chair massage program.[42]

Although these concepts were developed in a manufacturing setting, there is little reason to believe that they cannot apply equally well in services. Many organizations have implemented in the past, and some are still pursuing, Total Quality Management (TQM) programs in an effort to improve quality. TQM is so comprehensive in its scope that virtually all parts of an organization are affected. However, implementation of TQM has been found to be particularly difficult in small and medium-sized hotels in developing regions of the world, such as Cyprus, because of high employee turnover and seasonality.[39]

SIX SIGMA

Six Sigma, a quality-control process, has also had a pervasive effect on organizations in the United States and elsewhere. It is a philosophy based on minimizing the number of defects found in a manufacturing operation or service function. Originally developed by Motorola in the 1980s, the term comes from Sigma, the Greek letter that statisticians use to define one standard deviation from the center of the normal bell-shaped curve. At one Sigma, about one-third of whatever is being observed falls outside the range. Two Sigmas means that about 5 percent falls outside the range. Six Sigmas is so far out that virtually nothing is out there. This is the goal with regard to the number of defects that are considered acceptable. According to C. H. Deutsch:

> *In consultant-speak, it denotes the path to a corporate nirvana where everything—from product design to manufacturing to billing—proceeds without a hitch. In engineer-speak, it means no more than 3.4 defects per million widgets or procedures. In practice, Six Sigma is a statistical quality control method that combines the art of the efficiency expert with the science of the computer geek.*[40]

Starwood was one of the first hospitality companies to implement a Six Sigma program, and it claims to have delivered more than $100 million in profit to its bottom line annually through the use of the techniques.[41] (See the "Hospitality Focus" boxed section on page 186.)

RISKS ASSOCIATED WITH A BEST-VALUE STRATEGY

To review, cost leadership is associated with risks that:

1. A firm will become preoccupied with cost and lose sight of the market.
2. Technological breakthroughs will make process-cost savings obsolete.
3. Competitors will quickly imitate any sources of cost advantage.
4. The company will take the cost-reduction emphasis too far, thus endangering stakeholders.

The risks associated with differentiation are that:

1. The company will spend more to differentiate its service than it can recover in the selling price.
2. Competitors will quickly imitate the source of differentiation.
3. The source of differentiation will no longer be considered valid by customers.

A best-value strategy represents somewhat of a trade-off between the risks of a cost-leadership strategy and the risks of a differentiation strategy. The risk that technological breakthroughs will make the strategy obsolete is as much a problem with best value as it is with cost leadership. Also, the risk of imitation, found in both of the other two strategies, is evident in a best-value strategy as well. Conversely, a firm pursuing best value is unlikely to become preoccupied with either cost or differentiation; instead, it should try to balance these two factors. Also, the company probably would not be prone to take the cost-saving strategy too far, thus endangering employees or customers. Finally, because of the balance between cost and differentiation, a hospitality firm pursuing a best-value strategy is less likely than a pure differentiator to put so much into differentiating a service that the company will be unable to recover the additional costs through the selling price.

Focus

Focus strategies can be based on differentiation, lowest cost, or best value, but a focus strategy emphasizing lowest cost would be difficult in the hospitality industry because it is difficult to please a particular guest segment without some form of differentiation. The key to a focus strategy is providing a product or service that caters to a particular segment in the market. For example, Bedandbreakfast.com is an online travel service that has targeted a niche market of users who can bypass navigating through sites designed for a broad array of travel services. Cereality Cereal Bar and Café offers 40 varieties of breakfast cereals with 30 choices of toppings and nine varieties of milk.

Firms pursuing focus strategies have to be able to identify their target market segment and both assess and meet the needs and desires of buyers in that segment better than any other competitor. Hotels that provide services exclusively for guests with pets might be pursuing a focus strategy, as would those who specialize in gay and lesbian customers. Four Seasons focuses on the luxury consumer. In articulating their focus, this company notes:

> *We have chosen to specialize within the hospitality industry, by offering only experiences of exceptional quality. Our objective is to be recognized as the company that manages the finest hotels, resorts, residence clubs and other residential projects wherever we locate. We create properties of enduring value using superior design and finishes, and support them with a deeply instilled ethic of personal service. Doing so allows Four Seasons to satisfy the needs and tastes of our discriminating customers, and to maintain our position as the world's premier luxury hospitality company.*[43]

The Jumeirah Group's Burj Al Arab hotel, a sail-shaped hotel built on a human-made island, is an extreme example of catering to a focused elite. (See the "Hospitality Focus" boxed section on page 189.)

Another group of lodging companies is focusing on young and affluent travelers who have different ideas than their parents about what makes a good hotel. These trendy boutique, or designer, hotels "typically emphasize provocative modern design, encourage 'lobby socializing,' and are often anchored by bars or restaurants favored by locals, not just standard travelers. They are also celebrity magnets, if one is to believe gossip columnists."[44] W Hotels, owned by Starwood, were born of the frustration of its then CEO, Barry Sternlicht (now Executive Chair of the Board), over hotel monotony. They have striking interiors and run wild promotions.[45] Many of the lifestyle hotels noted in discussing differentiation may be considered as focused differentiators if they are targeting a narrow segment of the market.

The risks of pursuing a focus strategy depend on whether the strategy is pursued through differentiation, cost leadership, or best value. The risks of each of these strategies are similar to the risks faced by adopters of the pure strategies. However, the focus strategy has two risks that are not associated with any of the three pure strategies. First, the desires of the narrow target market may become similar to the desires of the market as a whole, thus eliminating the advantage associated with focusing. Second, a competitor may be able to focus on an even more narrowly defined target and essentially outfocus the focuser. Take Four Seasons Hotels, for example: they focus on a high-end discriminating customer, but it is possible that new luxury boutique and lifestyle hotels have outfocused this focuser.

Business-level strategies should be formulated on the basis of the existing or potential resources and abilities of the organization. However, they should also be selected on the basis

HOSPITALITY FOCUS

BURJ AL ARAB HOTEL: CATERING TO THE ELITE

The Burj Al Arab stands 321 meters above sea level in the gulf waters of Dubai in the United Arab Emirates. The hotel has 202 suites ranging from about US $1,000 to $6,000. The hotel is targeted at members of royal families who visit from Europe, Asia, and the Middle East, as well as celebrities and wealthy industrialists and visitors. Regarded as one of the most luxurious and innovative hotels in the world, the mission of the hotel is "to be the world's most luxurious hotel with a team dedicated to outstanding personalized service, surpassing guest expectations, by providing the ultimate Arabian hospitality experience." Those who stay at this sail-shaped hotel can enjoy a chauffeur-driven Rolls Royce, discreet in-suite check-in, a private reception desk on every floor, and highly trained butlers who provide around-the-clock personalized service.

The Jumeirah Group is a fast-growing, Dubai-based hospitality group, with hotels such as the Jumeirah Beach Hotel, Jumeirah Emirates Towers, Madinat Jumeirah and Jumeirah Bab Al Shams Desert Resort and Spa in Dubai, the Jumeirah Carlton Tower and Jumeirah Lowndes Hotel in London, and the Jumeirah Essex House on Central Park South in New York. The group's portfolio also includes Wild Wadi, regarded as one of the premier water parks outside of North America, and The Emirates Academy of Hospitality Management, the region's only third-level academic institution specializing in the hospitality and tourism sectors. Jumeirah plans to grow its portfolio of luxury hotels and resorts worldwide to 57 by 2011.[46]

of how well the resulting products and services are expected to be received in the market. Otherwise, an organization might develop a wonderful product or service that is largely unsuccessful. "It would be a little like having a concert pianist in a street gang who has a skill that is unique in that environment, but that hardly helps to attain the gang's goals."[47]

COMPETITIVE DYNAMICS

Even well-designed strategies may not be as successful as anticipated due to the reactions of competitors. For instance, suppose a large independent hotel decides to pursue a low–cost leadership strategy through cutting the price of rooms to increase sales volume. To meet anticipated demand, the company expands its inventory by building a new addition. However, when the firm cuts prices, competitors do likewise. So the organization launches a major advertising campaign. Competitors also increase advertising. These actions may increase demand in the area as a whole, but the increased demand probably is not enough to cover the increased expenses and loss of profit margins. The result is that the organization still has approximately the same market share as before, with an expensive new addition that is not being fully used.

TRAVELOCITY TERMINATOR: FIVE AIRLINES RESPOND TO ONLINE TRAVEL SERVICES

Five leading airlines in response to the online travel services of Expedia and Travelocity pooled their efforts in the early 21st century to sell discounted tickets. With a combined investment of $145 million, Delta Air Lines, United Airlines, Northwest Airlines, and Continental Airlines started a project code named T2—some claimed to mean "Travelocity Terminator." The brand name Orbitz was attached to the business, with a corporate identity as DUNC, LLC (the initials of its first four founding airlines). Travelocity, Sabre, and others objected to the business, stating that not making these tickets available on other sites would create a de facto monopoly for the five major airlines. After years of intense antitrust claims and battles, the Department of Justice ruled that Orbitz was not a cartel and did not pose a threat to competition. Orbitz was later acquired by Cendant Corporation. Even more recently, Cendant sold its travel distribution subsidiary, which includes the Orbitz travel reservation web site, the Galileo computer reservations system used by airlines and travel agents, Gulliver's Travels and Associates—a wholesale travel business, and other travel-related software brands to a subsidiary of the Blackstone Group, a private equity firm.[48]

Competitive dynamics are particularly important because of what a well-known economist, Joseph Schumpeter, called "creative destruction."[49] *Creative destruction* describes the inevitable decline of leading firms due to competitive moves and countermoves. Competitors pursue creative opportunities in an attempt to eliminate the competitive advantages of market leaders. As long as the playing field is level, which means that the government enforces rules of fair competition, eventually competitors will succeed.

In the past few decades, increasing globalization of markets has made competitive dynamics even more important, as firms now have to contend with a larger group of competitors. Most recently, the Internet has dramatically increased the amount of information available to consumers and hotel competitors around the world. For example, if you want to book a room in Spain from Japan, it is easy to go on the Internet to read blogs and consumer reviews, and then book the trip on any one of several websites including the hotel's site or numerous intermediaries.

Innovations are also being adopted at a higher rate. Consequently, the actions of a hospitality company anywhere in the world now have a ripple effect on all other industry participants. For example, if Hyatt develops a more efficient process for maintaining its customer databases, the technology is likely to be communicated and adopted at other lodging companies in a relatively short amount of time.

Markets are always in a state of flux: in Asia, we have seen currency devaluations, devastating bombings, the tsunami, SARS, bird flu, and earthquakes, to name a few regional factors. The actions of one competitor result in countermoves from other industry participants.[50] Countermoves set off another series of actions, and then reactions to those actions. (See the "Hospitality Focus" boxed section above.)

Across all industries, the number of competitive moves and countermoves has been increasing.[51] In addition, the number of new products introduced and the number of patents issued have both increased. Along with these trends, brand loyalty has been dropping, and the popularity of foreign brands has been steadily increasing. Consequently, increasingly disloyal consumers now have more to choose from, and it comes from a lot more places. It is not surprising, then, that the number of new-business failures is also increasing.[52]

Strategies That Reflect Competitive Dynamics

Given these trends, it is clear that competitive dynamics plays an important role in strategy formulation. An organization can respond in many ways to the dynamics in its industry. Offensive strategies such as aggressive competition or seeking first-mover advantages are intended to increase market share and diminish the ability of competitors to compete. Defensive strategies such as threatening retaliation, seeking government intervention, or erecting barriers to imitation are intended to deter or slow down rivals from taking actions that would reduce the effectiveness of a firm's own strategies. Collaboration with stakeholders can be used offensively or defensively. Finally, a firm may avoid direct competition (avoidance) or be so flexible that it can easily leave an industry segment if the battle becomes too intense.

AGGRESSIVE COMPETITION

Aggressive competitors use every available resource in an effort to overwhelm rivals, thus reducing the chance that any countermove will be effective. The opening of the Borgata Casino in Atlantic City is an example of overwhelming the competition. (See the "Hospitality Focus" boxed section on page 192.)

Walt Disney Company is another example. Disney uses the most-advanced technologies and the most-talented workers in producing its animated feature films. Then the company floods the market with advertising and promotion. A similar offensive strategy is pursued in its theme parks. High-tech, innovative rides and world-class entertainment based on Disney characters and feature films create a "magical" place that is especially appealing to young people and families.

To be successful, aggressive competition requires significant resources that have high value and are at least somewhat rare. In addition, if those resources are difficult or costly to imitate, the attack may be effective over a longer time frame. Disney has been effective for many years at overwhelming competitors in theme parks and animated feature films due largely to its incredible brand name and its ability to attract the most-talented people for feature films and to attract and train low-cost laborers for its theme parks. Resources that tend to provide a strong base for aggressive competition include:

- Superior market position
- Strong financial position
- Possession of patents or trade secrets
- Exclusive contracts
- Involvement in a well-organized network of external stakeholders that includes major suppliers, financial institutions, government leaders, and other competitors

**THE BORGATA CASINO OVERWHELMS
THE COMPETITION**

The debut of the $1.1 billion Borgata Hotel, Casino and Spa was heralded by an enthusiastic critique of current competitors. "There is, to a large degree, a generation gap between Borgata and existing properties in Atlantic City," said Robert L. Boughner, CEO of the casino that rises like a 40-story gold ingot at the north end of this island city. "Many of the other places are just reincarnated old hotels, and they just don't have the technology and the amenities to keep up with us."

Dressed in gunfighter black, Mr. Boughner took a few more shots at his competitors. The other casinos are "slots warehouses," he said in an interview just as the casino opened, and because they have inadequate ventilation, they smell. "They do—they can't help it," he said. The Borgata, a joint venture between MGM Mirage Inc. and the Boyd Gaming Corporation, entered the market with all the latest casino technology. Instead of opening new restaurants, it featured well-known establishments such as the Old Homestead Steakhouse in New York. In addition, the casino featured a 35,000-square-foot spa and Borgata Babes, reminiscent of the extinct Playboy Bunnys.[53]

RISKS OF AGGRESSIVE COMPETITION

One of the greatest risks of aggressive competition is that a rival will try to match the attack or even top it. Another risk is that the basis for competition may lose power over time. Disney, for instance, enjoyed many decades of almost unchallenged domination in the theme-park industry. The company built its dominant position through a strategy that focused on children and the families that bring them to the parks, with little that appealed directly to teenagers and young adults with no children. Now Americans are having fewer children and having them later in life. Furthermore, several major competitors have entered the scene with products that have specific appeal to teenagers and young adults. For example, in Orlando, Universal Studios was expanded to become Universal Escape, a complete vacation destination featuring themed resorts and Islands of Adventure, a state-of-the-art, high-tech adventure park that appeals to almost everyone under age 40. Universal Studios Japan competes directly with Disneyland Tokyo. Disney is still "top dog" in the theme-park market, but its position is weakening, and its original strategy in this segment is losing some of its power. In response, Disney expanded the resort to include Tokyo DisneySea in 2001 and built Hong Kong Disneyland several years later.

Despite these hazards, aggressive firms tend to have higher performance than do laggards. For example, software firms that engage rivals with a greater number of competitive moves have the highest performance.[54] Also, these sorts of companies tend to elicit slower responses to their moves by competitors, an indication that intimidation is working.[55]

FIRST-MOVER ADVANTAGE

First-movers also tend to enjoy a competitive advantage. These are firms that stay at the forefront of advances in their industries. Domino's Pizza is an example of a company that has benefited by being a first-mover. (See the "Hospitality Focus" boxed section on page 193.)

DOMINO'S PIZZA AS A FIRST-MOVER

Domino's Pizza built an initial advantage over rivals by being the first to offer home delivery in a half hour or less with a free product guarantee. Rivals at first scorned that tactic, but they eventually imitated it. Once most pizza retailers offered home delivery, Domino's initial advantage was gone. Domino's second action was to offer a giant pizza, the "Big Foot." Later it distributed direct-mail coupons and gave its customers handy magnets for easy access to Domino's phone number. Only through a string of actions could Domino's maintain its advantage and keep rivals off guard.[56]

Consistent with the principle of creative destruction, industry leaders are often dethroned by aggressive moves by number-two competitors.[57] Consequently, to remain the first-mover in an industry, significant investments in research and development typically are required. Organizational learning ability is also important to this strategy. Not only first-movers, but early imitators as well, or *second-movers* may enjoy higher performance.[58] Some firms have a deliberate strategy of rapidly imitating the innovations of competitors. They enjoy many of the same benefits without all of the research-and-development costs.

COLLABORATION

Organizations often combine resources in an effort to gain a stronger resource position, as the airlines did to compete with online travel services. In some cases, a leading firm will collaborate with a handpicked group of firms and deliberately exclude others in an effort to weaken them or put them out of business. Or weaker rivals may join forces to gain position relative to a market leader. Many small travel agencies have joined travel consortiums to protect the industry from complete consolidation by mega-agencies.

Collaborative relationships can be difficult to duplicate, thus increasing their value as a competitive tool. The joint venture described in Chapter 2 among major competitors Hilton, Hyatt, Marriott, Six Continents, and Starwood to sell discounted hotel rooms over the Internet is an excellent example of this type of collaboration.[59] Rivals should have a difficult time duplicating the collective clout of these industry giants. In the airline industry, code-sharing agreements allow airlines to sell one another's seats. These types of agreements put airlines without such arrangements at a competitive disadvantage.

THREAT OF RETALIATION

Sometimes organizations will threaten severe retaliation in an effort to discourage competitors from taking actions. For a threat to be believable, an organization should be perceived as having enough resources to carry out an effective battle if one ensues. High liquidity, excess capacity, and new-product designs that are being held back for a rainy day can be significant in convincing competitors that they would lose more than gain from the conflict.[60]

HOSPITALITY FOCUS

RETALIATION: EUROPEAN CHARTER CARRIERS vs. REGULAR AIRLINES

Historically, Europe's charter carriers did not compete directly with regular airlines. In addition, low-cost carriers were not particularly interested in holiday destinations served by the charter airlines. However, the UK's low-cost carriers are now encroaching on holiday business in areas such as Malaga, Alicante, and Palma de Mallorca. Also, a sluggish packaged holiday business has led the major charter travel groups to compete more directly with low-cost carriers. For example, the UK company MyTravel (formerly Airtours) has started the budget airline MyTravelLite, and in Germany TUI formed a venture with Germania to launch Hapag-Lloyd Express.[61]

Multimarket competition means that firms compete in multiple markets simultaneously. When this is the case, a company may fear that its actions in one market could lead to retaliation in another market. (See the "Hospitality Focus" boxed section above.)

These developments mean that two previously separate transportation segments will be competing against each other in multipoint competition, which is likely to change the dynamics of competition in both industry segments over time. Industries consisting of competitors with a lot of multimarket competition are expected to demonstrate a lot of mutual forbearance, which limits rivalry.[62] Because rivalry is limited, profit margins are expected to be higher in these situations.[63] However, lack of multimarket contact can lead to more-intense rivalry and lower profit margins.[64]

GOVERNMENT INTERVENTION

Political and legal strategies can be used in an attempt to help shape the rules of competition or change the competitive landscape altogether. Online gaming is one area in which legal issues are particularly complex. Various countries have approached the legality of Internet gambling differently. Many Caribbean nations have chosen to permit and license Internet gambling operations. For example, Antigua has registered more than 31 Internet gambling operations.[65] Other Caribbean states, such as Curacao, Grenada, Netherland Antilles, Trinidad, St. Vincent, the Cayman Islands, and the Dominican Republic, have issued Internet gambling licenses. In contrast, the Bahamian government plans to completely prohibit all Internet gambling in the Bahamas. In Australia, the Queensland government and the Government of the Northern territory have developed legislation designed to permit and regulate Internet gaming operations. (See the "Hospitality Focus" boxed section on page 195.)

BARRIERS TO IMITATION

One of the most common competitive countermoves is imitation. A follower organization can simply imitate the leader's strategy point by point. In fact, most innovations in hospitality are very easy to imitate. Consequently, some leading companies attempt to thwart imitation by erecting a variety of barriers. Some barriers to imitation are similar to the barriers to entry

AUSTRALIAN GOVERNMENT INTERVENTION IN INTERNET GAMING OPERATIONS

Online gaming is illegal in the United States under the Wire Act of 1961, which prohibits "knowingly using a wire communication facility for the transmission in interstate or foreign commerce of bets or wagers, or information assisting in the placing of bets or wagers, on any sporting event or contest," although three states—North Dakota, Georgia, and Illinois—are considering making the practice legal, a move that would likely lead to court battles between the federal and state governments. American law is glaringly inconsistent as it has strengthened rules against some forms of online gambling while allowing bets on horse races and state lotteries. The World Trade Organization ruled that America's practice of allowing state-authorized firms to take online bets on horse races was inconsistent and discriminated against foreign operators.

The overall market for online gambling is estimated to be approximately $49 billion worldwide, making it a large and profitable business. With online gambling illegal in the United States, it is likely to put American firms at a competitive disadvantage. As one expert notes, "In the long run, America's prohibition is unsustainable because regulating, taxing and letting American firms compete against offshore rivals makes far more sense. Australia allows online gambling, but regulates it and collects tax revenues." New laws in Britain permitting online casino operations have helped to bring betting firms that were moving rapidly offshore back to the country. The British government has seen these online operators willingly accepting regulation in exchange for more legitimacy with their customers.[66]

discussed in Chapter 2. The primary difference is that *barriers to imitation* are intended to prevent existing competitors from imitating sources of cost savings or differentiation, whereas *barriers to entry* are created to discourage other companies from entering the industry. Also, many barriers to entry are possessed by most existing firms; therefore, they affect new entrants rather than incumbent firms. As a practical matter, many of the entry barriers are the same as imitation barriers.

Organizations may discourage imitation in several ways. A company may build a significantly larger portfolio of hotels or stores, thus achieving economies of scale that are difficult to duplicate. A firm may develop a highly valuable and difficult-to-imitate brand name or trademark. In addition, special relationships with external stakeholders can be difficult to copy. For example, an organization may have special arrangements with a financial institution, an excellent relationship with its union, or an exclusive-supply agreement with one of its suppliers. In addition, an organization may deter entry through new service proliferation, significant investments in advertising, cutting prices, or withholding information about the profitability of a service so that potential competitors will not be eager to duplicate it.[67]

As discussed in Chapter 3, intangible assets are among the most difficult to imitate. For example, a particular service is fairly easy to imitate, but the research-and-development processes that went into creating the service are more difficult to reproduce. Consequently, an organization with an excellent ability to innovate may be able to create a barrier to imitation. By the time competitors have imitated a service, the company has moved on to other new

HOSPITALITY FOCUS

HVS INTERNATIONAL FINDS A NICHE

Steve Rushmore, founder and president of hotel consulting company HVS International, got his start by performing hotel feasibility studies and appraisals. "Back then [the early 1980s], you had companies such as Laventhol and PKF, both of which could do feasibility studies, but not appraisals," Rushmore recalls. "Then there were the appraisers, and they were regionally oriented generalists. All of the appraisers were economic majors and some were engineers, but none were from hotel schools."[68]

services. Organizational-learning ability is similarly difficult to imitate. Organizational learning can lead to private information (secrets) that results in higher performance. Consequently, an organization can build a barrier to imitation by fostering learning processes (Chapter 9 will cover this topic in detail). Finally, a high-performance organizational culture is difficult to copy.

STRATEGIC FLEXIBILITY

Strategic flexibility allows a firm to earn high returns while managing the amount of risk it faces.[69] Flexibility means that a company can move its resources out of declining markets and into more-prosperous ones in a minimum amount of time. *Exit barriers* influence a firm to remain in a market or industry after it is no longer attractive for investment. For example, an organization may have a significant investment in a large resort. Selling the resort would result in a major loss, and closing it is not a reasonable option. Strategic exit barriers can also reduce flexibility. These barriers are a result of reluctance to sacrifice the benefits of intangible assets that have accumulated through previous investments. Some of these may include loss of synergies created through linkages with other businesses, loss of customers, or loss of a market position.

Organizations can retain strategic flexibility by reducing investments in assets that are likely to create large exit barriers. For example, lodging companies greatly enhance their strategic flexibility when they manage properties that are owned by others. Similarly, restaurants often lease space, and many airlines lease their planes. Keeping large capital assets off the balance sheet frees up capital for expansion and reduces potential losses if the assets become unproductive. However, companies forego the additional revenue potential from owning the assets. The important thing to remember at this point is that the level of strategic flexibility is a decision.

AVOIDANCE

Each of these strategies can require a great deal of managerial attention and, in some cases, significant other resources. However, some firms simply avoid confrontation completely by focusing on a particular niche in the market in which other firms have little interest (Porter's focus strategy). In hospitality, a niche can be a small segment of the market or a small geographic area. A restaurant company, for instance, might specialize in a particular nationality of food that does not draw a lot of customers. Or a company could locate its hotels in out-of-the-way areas. A small travel agency might rely on a key corporate account from one of the smaller businesses (those with fewer than 100 employees) that gets better served by a small agency. Or, as in the case of Steve Rushmore, a company can offer services that nobody else is offering. (See the "Hospitality Focus" boxed section on page 196.)

Resources, Industry Structure, and Firm Actions

Many of the strategies contained in this section require a strong resource position or excellent stakeholder relationships.[70] For example, for aggressive competition to succeed, a firm must have better or more resources than competitors do. First-movers need significant resources associated with innovation and learning. Collaboration requires a network of excellent relationships with external stakeholders. Successful government intervention comes from excellent relationships with government leaders or parties. Firms with strong or unused (slack) resources are in a strong position to pursue most of the strategic options, but firms with poor resources are limited in their abilities to pursue aggressive strategies. They may need to avoid direct competition or to develop strategic flexibility until their resource positions are stronger.

The characteristics of an industry determine, in part, the tactics an organization will pursue. Rapid industry growth typically is associated with lower levels of rivalry because firms do not have to steal market share to increase sales.[71] Also, a high level of concentration

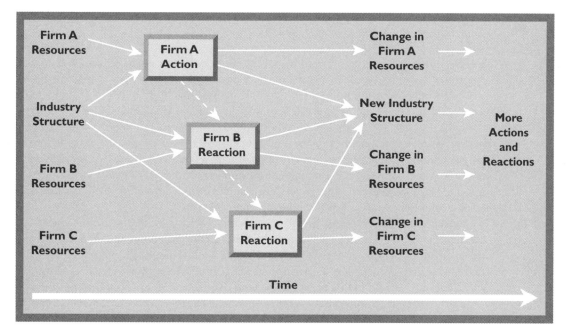

FIGURE 5.4 The relationship among resources, industry structure, and actions over time

Source: This model was inspired by K. G. Smith, W. J. Ferrier, and H. Ndofor, "Competitive Dynamics Research: Critique and Future Directions," in *The Blackwell Handbook of Strategic Management,* ed. M. A. Hitt, R. E. Freeman, and J. S. Harrison (Oxford: Blackwell Publishers, 2001), 315–368.

BOEING'S COUNTERMOVE AGAINST AIRBUS

Boeing has historically dominated the Japanese market for commercial aircraft. In fact, Boeing's planes account for 84 percent of the nation's commercial fleets. Recently, the European rival Airbus Industrie began an attack on Boeing's dominance through expanding its Japanese office and making allies of Japanese businesses. Airbus recently targeted Japan with its new A380 super jumbo jet, which holds up to 800 people. Large jets are important in Japan because its airports are so congested. Airbus should have expected a strong reaction. It came in the form of a newly designed Boeing 747X, a stretch model that will accommodate up to 520 passengers and will cost $20 million less than the Airbus A380.[72]

(a few firms hold most of the market share) should reduce the motivation of rivals to compete aggressively. If entry or imitation barriers are high, there is less competitive pressure from potential entrants.[73] Figure 5.4 illustrates the effect firm resources and industry structure have on firm actions and competitor reactions over time. After an organization acts, competitors will respond in turn, thus changing the resource positions of each company, as well as industry structure. The cycle then continues with moves, countermoves, and resulting changes.

COUNTERMOVES OF RIVALS

Thus far, this discussion has centered on specific strategies firms might pursue to deal with competitive dynamics. Another important aspect of competitive dynamics is anticipating the countermoves of rivals. The question is, "How are competitors likely to respond to a strategic move?" Anticipation of competitor reactions is vital to understanding how effective a strategy may be. The two factors already identified in this section—resource position and industry characteristics—are very important to predicting countermoves. For example, a rival with a strong resource position is much more likely to respond with a countermove. Also, a slow-growing industry is more likely to elicit a response from competitors than is an industry that is growing rapidly. However, several other factors can play a role in determining whether a firm will deploy a countermove and what form the response will take.

Predicting the potential response of a competitor also has a lot to do with the goals of its managers.[74] If a planned strategy is likely to interfere with the goals found in a competitor organization, that organization is likely to respond with a countermove. For example, a company may launch a strategy to grow in a particular market. If another company's goals depend on that market, a strong reaction can be expected. (See the "Hospitality Focus" boxed section above.)

On the other hand, sometimes companies pursue different segments of the market (avoidance strategy), allowing a less aggressive atmosphere to develop. An organization should also try to understand the assumptions of competing firm managers about their organization and the industry. For example, managers may assume that a countermove will be detrimental because such moves have been harmful in the past. Or firm managers may see their organization as a follower.

Of course, a competitor is not likely to respond if it is unaware that a firm has pursued a strategic action. Consequently, the strength of a firm's environmental-scanning and -analysis abilities and the awareness of its top managers about significant events in the industry also play a role in whether a countermove will be pursued.[75] Newer or smaller organizations are less likely to be aware of precisely what larger, older competitors are doing.

In summary, some of the characteristics that help an organization anticipate the response of a competitor to a particular strategic move include strength of its resource position, characteristics of the industry, goals and assumptions of competing-firm managers, and awareness of competitive actions. When a strategy is formulated, managers should try to anticipate the reactions of competitors in order to more accurately assess the potential outcomes.

STRATEGIC GROUP MAPPING

One way to keep track of the strategies of competing firms is with a strategic-group map such as the one in Figure 5.5. A *strategic-group map* categorizes existing industry competitors into groups that follow similar strategies. Rather than look at the industry as a whole or individual

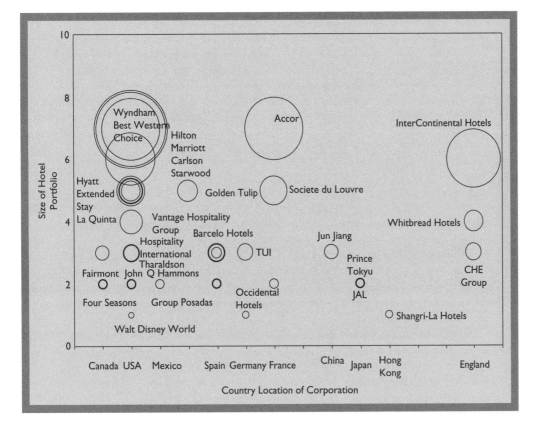

FIGURE 5.5 **Strategic-group map of hotel size by country of origin**

firms, this technique helps to understand clusters of competitors. Paying attention to what other competitors are doing is critical to making appropriate competitive moves and counter-moves. The hotel strategic-group map in the figure shows that most of the large hotel companies are located in key countries, primarily the United States, France, and England.

Developing a Strategic-Group Map

To construct a strategic-group map, a series of steps can be followed:

Step 1: First identify strategic dimensions that are important in the industry, such as breadth of services (limited or full service), quality/price level (high, medium, low), geographic coverage (local, regional, national, or international), or use of distribution channels (one, some, many). See Table 5.4 for a list of possible dimensions to use in creating a strategic map.

Step 2: Map the firms on a two-variable grid using different strategic dimensions. The axes of a strategic-group map should describe strategy and not performance. Therefore, variables such as pricing strategy, customer-service approach, level of advertising, and service mix are appropriate, whereas return on assets and earnings per share are not. Furthermore, to reveal more about the industry, the dimensions should not be highly correlated with one another. Once the variables are selected, a map may be constructed by plotting industry rivals on the relevant dimensions.

Step 3: Put firms that fall in about the same space in the same strategic group. You can draw circles around each strategic group. The circles should be proportional to the size of the group's share of total industry sales revenues.

Organizations that end up in the same general location on a map are called strategic groups. Consequently, they have similar strategies based on the dimensions found in the map. Strategic-group maps can help an organization understand the strategies of competitors. For example, competitors within the same strategic group, such as Applebee's and Chili's, are in direct competition for customers, whereas competitors in different strategic groups, such as McDonald's and Sodexho, do not compete directly. Strategic-group maps sometimes highlight an area in the industry in which no firms are currently competing (a strategic opportunity). For instance, short-haul, no-frills airlines occupy a competitive arena that was almost empty before airline deregulation.

Strategic-group maps may also be used to track the evolution of an industry over time. In the past few years, traditional low-end fast-food restaurants have moved closer to fast-casual restaurants with upgrades to products and décor. In addition, lower-end family restaurants like Denny's have given up market share to more upscale family restaurants such as Applebee's and Cracker Barrel. As casual-dining sales have slumped, operators like Olive Garden and Red Lobster have retooled menus and marketing efforts. These moves may reveal shifting strategic-group membership.

TABLE 5.4 Possible Dimensions for Strategic-Group Maps

DIMENSION	EXPLANATION
1. Specialization	1. Narrow or broad range of services
2. Quality	2. Level of quality, consistency of quality
3. Distribution channels	3. Use of channels (few, some, many)
4. Vertical integration	4. Extent of backward or forward integration into sources of supply or customer markets (none, partial, full)
5. Cost position	5. High cost vs. low cost
6. Service	6. Degree of service (no-frills, limited, full-service)
7. Pricing policy	7. High price vs. low price, aggressive pricing vs. reactive pricing, inclusive or àla carte
8. Geographic coverage	8. Local, regional, national, global

One of the weaknesses associated with strategic-group maps is that organizations can belong to several strategic groups, depending on the dimensions that are used to form the groups. Because the choice of dimensions is somewhat subjective and dependent entirely on the industry under study, strategic-group maps do not provide answers, but they help raise relevant questions about the current state and direction of competitive rivalry. As noted, they may also help firms discover untapped market opportunities.

KEY POINTS SUMMARY

- The responsibilities of business-level managers include establishing the overall direction of a business unit, conducting ongoing analysis of the changing business situation, selecting a generic strategy and a strategic posture through which to implement it, and acquiring and managing resources.
- The generic business-level strategies described in this chapter are cost leadership, differentiation, best value, and focus.

- Firms may focus through cost leadership, differentiation, or best value. The distinguishing feature of a focus strategy is that energy is focused on a narrow, as opposed to a broad, segment of the market.

- Companies that pursue cost leadership actively seek resources that will allow them to produce services at the lowest possible cost.

- Hospitality firms that pursue differentiation attempt to distinguish services in such a way that they have greater value to their consumers.

- Best-value strategies combine elements of both differentiation and low cost. Many organizations have implemented programs that enhance speed or quality in an effort to produce a service that is the best value.

- Organizational dynamics is defined as the moves and countermoves of industry competitors. Organizations can pursue a variety of strategies in response to competitive dynamics, sometimes combining these approaches.

- Competitive moves include aggressive competition, seeking a first-mover advantage, collaborative agreements with stakeholders, threats of retaliation, seeking government intervention, erecting barriers to imitation, remaining flexible enough to move in and out of markets with relative ease, and avoiding direct competition completely. Groups of firms that pursue similar types of strategies within the same industry can be clustered using a mapping technique discussed in the chapter. Competitive pressures often favor some strategic groups over others.

- Strategic-group maps help identify strategic opportunities by revealing areas in the industry in which no or very few firms currently compete.

REVIEW QUESTIONS

1. What are the strategic management responsibilities of a business-unit manager? Explain what each of these responsibilities entails.

2. Describe the generic business-level strategies found in this chapter. Provide an example of hospitality brands that you think are pursuing each of these strategies.

3. How can an organization pursue the business-level strategy of low-cost leadership?

4. How can an organization pursue a differentiation strategy?

5. What are some of the risks associated with a cost leadership, differentiation, best value, and focus strategy?

6. How can an emphasis on quality help a firm that is pursuing a best-value strategy?

7. What are competitive dynamics? Why has competition become more dynamic in the past few decades?

8. Describe the eight strategies that reflect competitive dynamics.

9. Of the strategies that reflect competitive dynamics, which one seems to be the highest risk? Why? Which one seems to be the lowest risk? Why?

10. If you were a market leader in a segment of the hotel industry, which of the strategies that reflect competitive dynamics would probably be the most attractive to you? If you were a weak competitor with few resources, which strategy would you likely find attractive?

CRITICAL THINKING AND APPLICATION QUESTIONS

1. You have been asked to develop two contrasting brand concepts for presentation to the senior management of a major chain. Begin by deciding what business-level strategies your two concepts will be based on (i.e., low cost, differentiation, best value, either narrow or broad). Using the following table, prepare your strategic analysis for each concept.

	CONCEPT A	CONCEPT B
What business strategy did you select?		
What factors will you take into consideration in creating your strategy?		
Describe the main features of your concept.		
Identify three specific skills or resources you will use to create your concept.		
What risks are associated with your concept and our strategy for making it a reality?		

2. Select any two hospitality firms that compete on the basis of differentiation. Compare and contrast these two players. Which one is more successful and why? If a firm were to enter the market and pursue a focused differentiation strategy, how might it outfocus the two firms you examined.

3. Develop a strategic-group map. First, identify characteristics that differentiate firms in the industry. Plot the firms on a two-variable map. Assign firms that fall in about the same space to the same strategic group. Draw circles around each group, making the circles proportional to the size of the group's respective share of the total industry sales revenues. What does this group map tell you about the current state of the industry? What does it reveal about future opportunities?

CHAPTER 6

CORPORATE-LEVEL STRATEGY AND RESTRUCTURING

YOU SHOULD BE ABLE TO DO THE FOLLOWING
AFTER READING THIS CHAPTER:

1. Define corporate-level strategy and explain the major responsibilities for a corporate-level manager.

2. Distinguish among concentration, vertical integration, and diversification strategies.

3. Describe the advantages and disadvantages of a concentration strategy.

4. Know the meaning of forward and backward integration.

5. Explain the reasons why firms diversify.

6. Understand the sources of synergy that can be obtained from diversification and what undermines its use.

7. Know the reasons for mergers and acquisitions and some of the problems attached to this strategy.

8. List and explain the most common restructuring approaches, including turnaround, down-sizing, refocusing, bankruptcy, and leveraged buyouts.

9. Create a BCG Portfolio Matrix.

FEATURED STORY

DIVERSIFICATION AT WHITBREAD

Whitbread PLC is a leading food and leisure company in the United Kingdom with a focus on restaurants, meeting services, and a budget hotel brand. This company began in 1742, when Samuel Whitbread established a brewery in Britain. The company's brewing tradition came to a close at the start of the 21st century, when Whitbread sold its breweries and exited from the pubs and bars business.

After several decades of diversification, during which the beer and pubs giant branched out into new markets (including brief flirtations with wines, spirits, and nightclubs), the company refocused its business on the growth areas of hotels and restaurants. It began this process by offloading brands and licensed franchises, including Britvic, a large UK manufacturer of soft drinks; Whitbread Inns; Marriott hotels (sold to brand owner Marriott Corporation); TGI Friday's (sold to brand owner Carlson); Pizza Hut UK (sold to brand owner Yum!); David Lloyd Leisure health clubs (sold to Versailles Bidco Ltd.); Hogshead Pubs; and Threshers (a retail chain of shops that sell alcoholic beverages for off-premise use).

The strategy of Whitbread is to manage market-leading hospitality businesses. The portfolio currently consists of Premier Inn, Brewers Fayre, Beefeater, Costa, and Touchbase. Premier Inn, rebranded from Premier Travel Inns in 2004, is the United Kingdom's biggest budget hotel brand, considered the market leader with 480 locations. The hotel chain was created through the merger of the number-one and number-three brands in the UK branded budget hotel sector: Whitbread's homegrown Travel Inn and Premier Lodge, acquired from Spirit Group, the pub operator.

Most Premier Inn properties are located alongside Whitbread's popular restaurants, Brewers Fayre and Beefeater. Beefeater provides grilled food and steaks, while Brewers Fayre—the United Kingdom's largest pub restaurant brand—presents a unique identity in each restaurant. More than 270 restaurant sites are located next to Premier Inns, and plans exist to build more hotels on a further 100 restaurant sites over the next few years. Whitbread has also begun to dispose of several stand-alone Brewers Fayre and Beefeater sites because of their lower revenues.

The third foodservice business, Costa, provides coffee for millions of customers at more than 500 stores across the United Kingdom every year. Costa is the United Kingdom's leading coffee company, and it is growing fast, with a target of 2,000 stores worldwide by 2011. The Costa chain also operates in the Middle East and India through franchise partners, and in China through a joint-venture agreement. Costa's success is built on the genuine Italian expertise of the Costa brothers, who imported not only their knowledge of roasting coffee beans but also the passion of their native Italy for coffee excellence.

Touchbase, a division of Whitbread, operates purpose-built business centers situated adjacent to some of Whitbread's busiest Premier Inns throughout the United Kingdom. The conferencing and meeting rooms brand provides a desk space for hourly rent, meeting rooms, or a business lounge equipped with tea or Costa coffee. The business model stresses high-quality, fully equipped facilities at affordable, inclusive prices for the business market.

The next stage in Whitbread's history is to focus on growth in Premier Inns and the Costa coffee chain. After divesting of various brands and eliminating debt, the company is now positioned to be a focused international hospitality firm.[1]

DISCUSSION QUESTIONS:

1. Why do you think Whitbread divested the wine, spirits, beer, pub, and nightclub businesses? Was this a wise strategy?

2. Does the business portfolio of Premier Inn, Brewers Fayre, Beefeater, Costa, and Touchbase lead to synergy for Whitbread?

3. What advice would you offer Whitbread to help achieve its desire for growth?

INTRODUCTION

Like many hospitality companies, Whitbread is pursuing a strategy called related diversification. The primary operations of the company focus on the Costa coffee chain and the budget hotel chain Premier Inn. The Touchbase operations represent a business that enhances the hotel business, as do the Brewers Fayre and Beefeater restaurants. As noted, Whitbread actively reduced its diversification in the early 21st century through the selling of various brands and licensed franchises, freeing the company up to focus on a few market-leading businesses. The company has also relied on acquisitions and joint ventures to carry out its current related diversification strategy.

This chapter begins with a discussion of concentration, vertical integration, and diversification, the three basic corporate-level strategies. A comparison of these three strategies is followed by a detailed analysis of acquisition strategies, an important tactic firms use to diversify. Note that vertical integration, diversification, and mergers are corporate-level strategies and tactics, but they can also be applied within the business units of larger companies. For example, the president of a single division could decide to diversify the business through an acquisition of a firm in a related industry. The acquisition might have to be approved at the corporate level, but it could still be executed at the business level. Nevertheless, the focus of this chapter will be on the corporate level, while recognizing that much of this discussion can sometimes apply to individual business units as well.

Corporate-level strategy is formulated by the CEO and other top managers. An organization may have several business units or divisions that are run by individual managers. Those managers establish strategy for their own units, such as the Premier Inn chain, but not for the corporation (i.e., Whitbread PLC) as a whole. At the corporate level, primary strategy-formulation responsibilities include setting the direction of the entire organization, formulating a corporate strategy, selecting businesses in which to compete, selecting tactics for diversification and growth, and managing corporate resources and capabilities. An example of a corporate-level decision was Whitbread's divesting 45 TGI Friday's in a sale of $137.8 million to Carlson Restaurants Worldwide and ABN AMRO capital.[2]

Corporate-level responsibilities such as selling a business, and the key issues associated with each responsibility, are listed in Table 6.1.

Hospitality organizations typically begin as entrepreneurial ventures providing a single hotel, restaurant, casino, or service, or, in the case of an airline, one or a few flights in a limited market. This type of corporate-level strategy, called *concentration,* is associated with a narrow business definition. As long as an organization has virtually all of its resource investments in one business area, it is still concentrating. With this strategy, a firm may pursue growth through internal business ventures, mergers and acquisitions, or joint ventures. Some organizations never stop concentrating, despite their size. For instance, Delta Air Lines is still pursuing a concentration strategy.

As they grow, successful organizations often abandon their concentration strategies because of market saturation, excess resources that they need to find a use for, or some other reason. Through internal ventures, mergers and acquisitions, or joint ventures, they pursue businesses outside of their core business areas. Corporate strategy typically evolves from concentration to some form of vertical integration or diversification of products, markets, functions served, or technologies (see Figure 6.1).[3] *Diversification* that stems from common markets, functions served, technologies, or services is referred to as *related diversification.* *Unrelated diversification* is not based on commonality among the activities of the corporation. Organizations may continue to pursue vertical integration and/or diversification successfully for many years, each time expanding their business definitions.

Many organizations eventually come to a point at which slow growth, declining profits, or some other situation forces corporate-level managers to rethink their entire organizations. Disgruntled stakeholders—including stockholders, employees, and managers—often drive this process. The result is usually some form of restructuring. *Restructuring* often involves reducing the business definition, combined with refocusing efforts on the things the

TABLE 6.1 **Major Corporate-Level Strategic Management Responsibilities**

MAJOR RESPONSIBILITIES	KEY ISSUES
Direction setting	Establishing and communicating organizational mission, vision, enterprise strategy, and long-term goals
Development of corporate-level strategy	Selecting a broad approach to corporate-level strategy concentration, vertical integration, **and** diversification Selecting resources and capabilities in which to build corporate-wide distinctive competencies
Selection of businesses and portfolio management	Managing the corporate portfolio of businesses—buying businesses, selling businesses Allocating resources to business units for capital equipment, R&D, etc.
Selection of tactics for diversification and growth	Choosing among methods of diversification—internal venturing, acquisitions, joint ventures
Management of resources	Acquiring resources and/or development of competencies leading to a sustainable competitive advantage for the entire corporation Hiring, firing, and rewarding business-unit managers Ensuring that the business units (divisions) within the corporation are well managed, and provide training where appropriate including the area of strategic management Developing a high-performance corporate management structure Developing control systems to ensure that strategies remain relevant and that the corporation continues to progress toward its goals

organization does well. It is interesting to note that before restructuring, Whitbread was significantly more diversified, but the company has now reduced the scope of its activities. This type of restructuring strategy is called *downscoping*. Most successful restructuring efforts result in a leaner (i.e., fewer employees, less capital equipment), less-diversified organization. The organization may then cycle back and begin a cautious, better-educated, and more focused program of diversification or vertical integration. Restructuring is discussed at the end of this chapter.

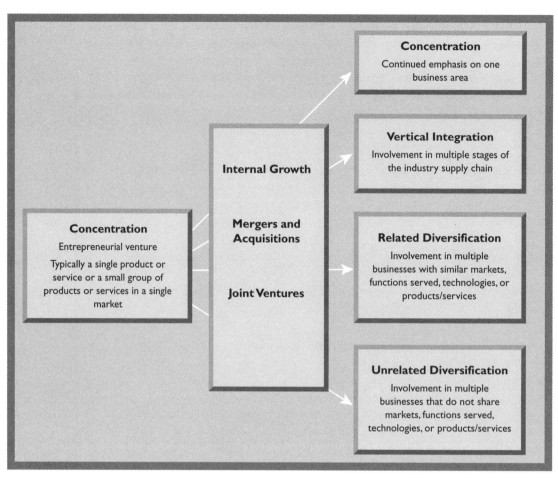

FIGURE 6.1 **Corporate-level strategies**

CONCENTRATION STRATEGIES

Concentration is the least complicated of the corporate-level strategies, but it is still pursued by many large and successful companies. Domino's Pizza, for example, started out small, with just one store in 1960. By 1983, there were 1,000 Domino's stores, and 5,000 in 1989. Today, there are more than 8,000 stores—located in 55 countries. As the largest pizza delivery company in the United States, with a 20 percent market share, and the second-largest pizza chain worldwide, it has an operating network of company-owned and franchise-owned stores, but it continues to be a single-business enterprise.[4] (See the "Hospitality Focus" boxed section on page 211.)

Many regional casinos, airlines, and hotel and restaurant chains also operate with a concentration strategy. Diversification is sometimes a necessity, because too much dependence on

DOMINO'S CONCENTRATION STRATEGY

Domino's Pizza was founded in 1960 by Thomas Monaghan, who borrowed $500 and bought DomiNick's, a failed pizza parlor in Ypsilanti, Michigan. Domino's expansion was phenomenal in the 1980s, helped by national advertising. In the late 1990s, Monaghan sold most of his stake in the company to Bain Capital for $1 billion. In 2004, the company went public using the capital raised from its initial public offering (IPO) to reduce its debt load. Domino's defines its success in the following way:

- Domino's is a powerful global brand.
- We are the number-one pizza delivery company in the United States.
- We have a large and growing international presence.
- We have a strong and proven business model with superior returns.
- We operate a profitable, value-added distribution system.
- Our leadership team has a track record of success.[5]

one business area provides a substantial business risk. Consequently, a concentration strategy is associated with both strengths and weaknesses (see Table 6.2).

Advantages and Disadvantages of a Concentration Strategy

The strengths of a concentration strategy are readily apparent. First, concentration allows an organization to master one business. This specialization allows top executives to obtain in-depth knowledge of the business, which should reduce strategic mistakes. Also, because all resources are directed at doing one thing well, the organization may be in a better position to develop the resources and capabilities necessary to establish a sustainable competitive advantage. Domino's, for example, was the innovator behind the sturdy, corrugated pizza box and the "spoodle," a saucing tool that combines the features of a spoon and a ladle, which cuts the time spent saucing a pizza.

Furthermore, organizational resources are under less strain. Lack of ambiguity concerning strategic direction may also allow consensus to form among top managers. High levels of consensus are sometimes associated with superior organizational performance. In fact, a concentration strategy has sometimes been found to be more profitable than other corporate-level strategies.[6] Of course, the profitability of a concentration strategy depends largely on the industry in which a firm is involved.

TABLE 6.2 Advantages and Disadvantages of a Concentration Strategy

ADVANTAGES	DISADVANTAGES
• Allows an organization to master one business • Less strain on resources, allowing more of an opportunity to develop a sustainable competitive advantage • Lack of ambiguity concerning strategic direction • Often found to be a profitable strategy, depending on the industry	• Dependence on one area is problematic if the industry is unstable • Primary service or product may become obsolete • Difficult to grow when the industry matures • Significant changes in the industry can be difficult to deal with • Cash flow can be a serious problem

On the other hand, concentration strategies entail several risks, especially when environments are unstable. Because the organization depends on one product or business area to sustain itself, change can dramatically reduce organizational performance. The airline industry is a good example of the effects of uncertainty on organizational performance. Before deregulation, most of the major carriers were profitable. They had protected routes and fixed prices. However, deregulation and the ensuing increase in competition hurt the profitability of all domestic carriers. Because most of the major carriers were pursuing concentration strategies, they did not have other business areas to offset their losses. Consequently, several airlines were acquired or went bankrupt. Continental went bankrupt in 1983 and again in 1990, and TWA filed for bankruptcy three times before disappearing for good.[7] However, the industry did not seem to learn its lesson. Delta Airlines, Northwest Airlines, USAirways, and United have all declared bankruptcy in the early 21st century. Once again, inadequate diversification reduced their ability to deal with the shock. (See the "Hospitality Focus" boxed section on page 213.)

Product obsolescence and industry maturity create additional risks for organizations pursuing a concentration strategy. If the principal product or service of an organization becomes obsolete or matures, organizational performance can suffer until the company develops another product that appeals to the market. Consumer demand for healthy food, for example, spurred McDonald's Corporation to offer new menu items such as McDonald's "Salads Plus" and to sell burgers free of antibiotics.[8] Some firms are never able to duplicate earlier successes.

Furthermore, because they have experience in only one line of business, they have limited ability to switch to other areas when times get tough; consequently, many are eventually acquired by another company or go bankrupt. Fortunately, obsolescence is not a particularly strong influence in the hospitality industry. Services such as lodging, gaming, restaurants, and vacations are not likely to disappear. However, a particular format can become obsolete. For example, many low-tech basic casino hotels in Las Vegas have been torn down to make room for more trendy themed casino hotels.

Concentration strategies are also susceptible to problems when the chosen industry is undergoing significant evolution and is converging with other industries, as is the case in the telecommunications industry. In hospitality, technological advancements are also causing a lot of convergence, especially in reservations and the level of technology-based services offered to guests.

DIVERSIFICATION AND CONCENTRATION IN THE AIRLINE INDUSTRY

HOSPITALITY FOCUS

Airlines have not always followed concentration strategies; in fact, they have often been in the hotel business. Early on, Pan Am created the InterContinental chain, with locations at "every way stop where the company might touch down." Air France started its hotel operations in 1948 with the subsidiary Relais Aeriens FrancaisBack, to provide hotel facilities in African destinations served by the airline. Whether we look at Japan Airlines' (JAL's) and Nikko hotels, or KLM's affiliation with Golden Tulip Hotels, the two businesses have often been linked. Golden Tulip Hotels relied on KLM to help it internationalize the brand before demerging in the late 1990s.

American Airlines entered the hotel business in the early 1970s, with American Hotels Chain, but exited later in that decade. United Airlines owned the Westin chain. Trans World Airlines (TWA) purchased Hilton International as part of its diversification strategy in the late1960s, but later sold the hotel company to corporate raider Carl Icahn. Today, U.S. airlines have gotten out of the hotel business, admitting that it required too much time and effort following deregulation. In addition, the hotel/airline relationships have not provided the necessary offsets in bad times; when one industry is doing poorly, typically the other one is also taking losses.[9]

As the quick-service segment of the restaurant industry matures and evolves, even McDonald's, an organization that has been extremely successful with a concentration strategy, made moves toward diversification, but has now refocused on the core McDonald's brand. Companies that fail to diversify in ways that are consistent with industry evolution and convergence can often find themselves short of the next generation of products and services. However, in the quick-service segment of the restaurant industry, McDonald's has led the way with a strategy of staying focused on the core brand and upgrading the employee and customer experience, building brand transparency, and preserving local relevance.[10] (See the "Hospitality Focus" boxed section on page 214.)

Concentration strategies can also lead to cash flow problems. While a business is growing, the organization may find itself in a cash-poor situation, since growth often entails additional investments in capital equipment and marketing. On the other hand, once growth levels off, the organization is likely to find itself in a cash-rich situation, with limited opportunities for profitable investment in the business itself. In fact, this may be one of the most popular reasons that organizations in mature markets begin to diversify.[11] Having exhausted all reasonable opportunities to reinvest cash in innovation, renewal, or revitalization, organizational managers may look to other areas for growth. Of course, the company might also consider increasing dividends, but at some point managers feel a responsibility to profitably invest cash rather than simply returning it to shareholders.

Finally, a concentration strategy may not provide enough challenge or stimulation to managers. In other words, they may begin to get tired of doing the same things year after year. This is less true in organizations that are growing rapidly, because growth typically provides excitement and promotion opportunities. In multiunit restaurant chains, the opportunities for

McDONALD'S STAYS FOCUSED

Outside of Munich, McDonald's franchisee Michael Heinritze's sales are up by 22 percent since he reimaged his 125-seat restaurant. Upgrades to the McCafé portion of his restaurant have included wooden floors, leather chairs, a fireplace, and fresh flowers. All of his German units are expected to offer Wi-Fi, and in some locations customers can download cell phone ring tones and burn photos from their digital cameras onto CDs. Coffee sales have risen 25 percent in Europe, and McDonald's recently switched to organic milk. Premium items and extra-value meals have also helped to drive sales and reduce the need to diversify.[12]

growth in new regions of the world may be one reason why concentration strategies continue to exist, even as the industry matures.

VERTICAL INTEGRATION STRATEGIES

Vertical integration is determined by the degree to which a firm owns its upstream suppliers and its downstream buyers. A company that is fully *vertically integrated* would handle all of the activities from obtaining raw materials through delivery of the finished product. One of the best examples of vertical integration in the hospitality industry is TUI AG, the world's largest tourism firm. By owning travel agents, hotels, airlines, and cruise ships, this European-based company has positioned itself to be its own supplier and buyer of travel services.[13] A traveler could make a reservation at one of TUI's travel agencies, fly on one of its charter airlines, stay in its hotels or onboard one of its cruise ships, and enjoy various tours, flying home using businesses owned and integrated by TUI. (See the "Hospitality Focus" boxed section on page 215.)

As noted earlier, numerous attempts have been made to integrate hotels and airlines, although most of these efforts have proved to be unsuccessful. Some industries, such as steel and wood products, contain firms that are predominantly vertically integrated. In hospitality, vertical integration strategies have been frequently tried in the airline industry but often failed to provide the anticipated synergies. Often hotel companies like Hyatt exit from the airline sector, as it did five years after buying Braniff Airlines. However, because research has not generally found vertical integration to be a highly profitable strategy relative to other corporate-level strategies, this may not be a serious issue.[14]

Vertical growth can be accomplished by either *backward integration* (upstream), when a company produces its own inputs, or *forward integration* (downstream), when it provides its own distribution. Importing and roasting coffee beans, acquiring a bakery, or growing its own vegetables are examples of backward integration, because the restaurant company assumes

VERTICAL INTEGRATION AT TUI AG

HOSPITALITY FOCUS

TUI AG (whose name was changed from Preussag AG in 2002) did not always operate in the tourism business. Back in the 1920s, the company was called Preussische Bergwerks-und Hutten-Aktiengesellschaft (Prussian Mine and Foundry Company), and operated as a state-owned company in the mining, saltworks, and smelter businesses. The transformation of Preussag AG from an industrial conglomerate to a tourism and shipping powerhouse began in the 1990s, when the CEO and senior management of the company made the bold strategic choice to move the company away from its rusting steel production history. Through a process of divestiture, acquisition, and restructuring, the firm shifted its focus to two sectors, tourism and shipping.

For the tourism sector of the business, the first but far-reaching investment was the acquisition of a 30 percent interest in the travel firm Hapag-Lloyd. By the end of the 1990s, the company had become Europe's top tourism group, buying Touristik Union International (TUI), First Reisebuero Management, and a 50.1 percent stake in the United Kingdom's Thomas Cook. Acquisition of a stake in French package tour leader Nouvelles Frontières also helped to round out its portfolio of businesses, while it continued to sell its nontourism operations.

TUI Hotels & Resorts includes an inventory of 300 hotels and is one of Europe's largest holiday hoteliers. The brands cover a wide range of hotel concepts, including Riu, Grecotel, Grupotel, Iberotel, DORFHOTEL, ROBINSON; MAGIC LIFE, Paladien, and Nordotel. With a fleet of more than 150 aircraft, plans are underway to merge the Hapagfly and Hapag-Lloyd Express airline units with the TUIfly brand. Its other five airlines (Thomsonfly, TUIfly Nordic, Arkefly, Corsair, and Jetair) are expected to be integrated. On a smaller scale, TUI AG recently acquired the hotel portal Asiarooms.com, the ski holiday supplier Ski Alpine, and the sporting event organizer Australian Sports Tours. Fifteen travel agencies were also recently purchased, with plans to purchase an additional 80 agencies in new regions of the world within the next three years. TUI AG continues to expand its travel business by buying First Choice Holidays in 2007 and combining the UK-based company with its existing tourism operations to form TUI Travel, a publicly traded company in which TUI holds a controlling interest.[15]

functions previously provided by a supplier. Site selection, design, and construction of hotel projects through the late 1980s made Marriott Corporation a backward–integrated hotel developer with skill in constructing large numbers of hotels. Cendant Corporation characterized itself as "one of the most geographically diverse and vertically integrated travel distribution companies in the global travel industry" before its break–up and sale of various businesses.[16] Its use of forward integration was reflected in its travel distribution services, such as Galileo International, Travelport, Travelwire, Cheap Tickets, and Lodging.com. Until the corporation began to restructure in 2005, customers could book through Cendant travel agents, stay in Cendant hotels, and rent a car from Cendant-owned Avis or Budget rental car companies. Cendant spun off its hotel (Wyndham Worldwide) and real estate (Realogy) businesses in 2006, sold its travel business (Travelport), and renamed its rental car group, Avis Budget Group Inc., to include both Avis Rental and Budget Rental operations.[17]

Advantages and Disadvantages of a Vertical Integration Strategy

As one vertical integration expert explained, vertical integration can "lock firms in" to unprofitable adjacent businesses.[18] Also, just because a firm excels in one part of the vertical supply chain, it is not guaranteed to excel in others. For example, let's assume a growing restaurant chain decides that it is not satisfied with the price or quality of the meats it is able to obtain. This firm could take some of its growing cash flows and purchase a meat-processing facility. After a short time, the chain might realize that it does not have the expertise to manage the processing of meats in an efficient manner, and it might sell the facility. Examples such as these are common in all industries. However, this does not mean that all vertical integration is unsuccessful. In fact, one study suggested that vertical integration may be associated with reduced administrative, selling, and R&D costs, but higher production costs. The researchers believe that the higher production costs may be a result of a lack of incentive on the part of internal suppliers to keep their costs down. Because internal suppliers have a guaranteed customer, they do not have to be as competitive.[19] An important point to remember with regard to all of the strategies is that some companies are pursuing them successfully.

From a strategic perspective, vertical integration contains an element of risk that is similar to concentration. If a firm is vertically integrated and the principal activity experiences a recession, then the whole organization can suffer unless its value-chain activities are sufficiently flexible to be used for other products and services. Researchers have found that both high levels of technical change and high levels of competition reduce the expected profits from vertical integration.[20] Among the most significant advantages are internal benefits, such as the potential for efficiency through synergy from coordinating and integrating vertical activities. *Synergy* occurs when the whole is greater than the sum of its parts.

Thomas Cook Group, like TUI AG, relies on a strategy of vertical integration in the selection of its travel services companies. With a focus on the European market, the group operates Thomas Cook Airlines (with a fleet of almost 100 aircraft) and maintains a network of more than 3,000 owned or franchised travel agencies. The group also operates the businesses of Airtours, Direct Holidays, Going Places, Manos, Panorma, and Sunset.[21]

Vertical integration can also help an organization improve its access to customers, differentiate its products, or gain greater control over its market. Some of the cost advantages that might be possible are those derived by reducing the profit margins of intermediaries, simplifying the activity chain, reducing coordinating costs, or gaining economies of scale. On the other hand, activities associated with vertical integration can increase overhead, reduce flexibility, produce different business conflicts, link firms to unprofitable adjacent firms, or cause firms to lose access to important information from suppliers or customers. Other advantages and disadvantages of vertical integration are listed in Table 6.3.

TABLE 6.3 Advantages and Disadvantages of Vertical Integration

ADVANTAGES	DISADVANTAGES
Can eliminate steps, reduce duplication, and cut costs	Need for overhead to coordinate vertical integration
Avoids time-consuming tasks, such as price shopping, communicating design details, and negotiating contracts	Burden of excess capacity if not all output is used
Avoids getting shut out of the market for rare inputs	Poorly organized firms do not enjoy enough synergy to compensate for the higher costs
Improves marketing or technological intelligence	Obsolete processes may be perpetuated
Can create differentiation through coordinated effort	Reduces strategic flexibility due to being locked in to a business
Provides superior control of firm's market environment	May link to unprofitable adjacent businesses
Offers an increased ability to create credibility for new products	Lose access to information from suppliers or customers
Can create synergies through careful coordination of vertical activities	May not be potential for synergy because vertically integrated businesses are so different
	May use the wrong method of vertical integration (i.e., full integration instead of contracting)

Vertical Integration and Transaction Costs

Transaction-cost economics, which is the study of economic transactions and their costs, helps explain when vertical integration may be appropriate.[22] From this perspective, firms can negotiate either with organizations or with individuals on the open market for the products and services they need, or they can provide these products and services themselves. According to Oliver Williamson, an influential transaction-cost economist, "Whether a set of transactions ought to be executed across markets or within a firm depends on the relative efficiency of each mode."[23] If required resources can be obtained from a competitive open market without allocating an undue amount of time or other resources to the contracting process or contract enforcement, it is probably in the best interests of an organization to buy from the market instead of vertically integrating. For example, a hotel may find it in their best interests to lease their restaurant to an operator than to run it themselves. However, when transactions costs are high enough to encourage an organization to provide a good or service in-house instead of buying it from the open market, a market failure is said to exist. The market is likely to fail, which means that transaction costs are prohibitively high, under a variety of conditions.[24]

The following four situations provide examples of conditions when it is better to use vertical integration than to obtain suppliers or distributors in the open market.

It is better to use vertical integration:

- If the future is highly uncertain, it may be too costly or impossible to identify all of the possible situations that may occur and to incorporate these
possibilities into the contract. As a result, the supplier or distributor of the
good or service will increase the price during negotiations in order to
offset the risks (or demand other unusual contract terms). At some point,
the price is going to get so high that it will actually be in the buyer's best
interest to provide the good or service rather than contract it out.

- If there is only one or a small number of suppliers or distributors of a good
or service and these companies are opportunistic, which means that they
take advantage of the situation, a market failure may occur. In this case,
the market failure could take place in the form of a lack of candor or honesty and/or in a high price. Limited supplies of a needed good or service
or few distributors are primary reasons why a firm might consider providing it in-house or handling its own distribution.

- When one party to a transaction has more knowledge about the transaction or a series of transactions than does another party, once again opportunism can result. This may happen when, for example, a private company
is selling to a publicly held corporation, because a lot of information is
readily available on the public corporation but not on the privately held
corporation. The supplier can use this additional information to its advantage during the bargaining process.

- If a supplier has to invest in an asset that can be used only to provide a specific
good or service for the other party to the transaction (called asset specificity),
the other party can take advantage of the provider after the asset is in place.
To offset this risk, the supplier will establish a higher price or difficult contract
terms. At some point, it is no longer worth it for the buyer to deal with the
supplier. Instead, the buyer provides the product or service in-house.

Where transaction costs are low, an organization would usually be better off contracting for the required goods and services instead of vertically integrating. Remember that transactions costs are assumed to be low only if there are a large number of potential suppliers. Under these circumstances, there is probably no profit incentive to vertically integrate, because competition would eliminate abnormally high profits. For example, a hotel company with resorts in remote locations might rely on tour wholesalers to fill rooms. However, if the company had only one tour wholesaler that sells 95 percent of its inventory, the transaction costs would likely be high, and the wholesaler would have more power in the transaction. If no other wholesalers were available, this company might be better off trying to do its own sales and marketing.

Vertical integration often requires substantially different skills than those possessed by the firm. In this regard, vertical integration is similar to unrelated diversification.[25] As mentioned previously, a firm that can master one stage of the industry supply chain will not necessarily excel at other stages. Tour wholesalers who book hotels at an agreed-upon rate must sell the rooms or incur the costs, so they prepare and distribute marketing materials to a worldwide distribution network including a wide array of travel agencies. Unlike the hotel company, the wholesaler has invested in building this sales and marketing infrastructure. The hotels located on Caribbean islands or in the jungles of Africa that are not affiliated with chains or large reservation networks may simply not have the resources to reach their European or American guests.

Substitutes for Full Vertical Integration

Much of this discussion assumes that when a firm vertically integrates, it will do so at full scale. In other words, the firm will become fully involved in becoming its own supplier or distributor. However, in most cases, it is impractical for a hospitality firm to become its own supplier, because the skills and other assets needed to produce something like a gaming machine, ground beef, or towels are so different from the skills and assets needed to provide hospitality services. Similarly, being the sole distributor of its services can limit the hospitality firm's ability to access important customers. Few hotel chains can afford to rely on just their own reservation systems and ignore Expedia or Travelocity. However, sometimes the forces that might lead to vertical integration are strong. For example, there may only be one supplier of a good in a given market, or the quality or quantity of what is supplied may not be adequate. Resort operators in some remote locations, for example, have sought to reduce their dependence on one or a few large tour operators who control the flow of guests to their destinations. In these situations, a hospitality firm may pursue partial vertical integration to overcome some of the disadvantages of full integration.[26]

Partial vertical integration strategies include taper integration, quasi-integration, and long-term contracting. Taper integration means that an organization produces part of its requirements in-house and buys the rest of what it needs on the open market. A restaurant chain may grow some of its own herbs and vegetables but rely on vendors for the rest.

Quasi-integration involves purchasing most of what is needed of a particular product or service from a firm in which the purchasing organization holds an ownership stake. For example, by purchasing a 12 percent stake in Grill Concepts, Starwood helps guarantee its access to the full-service Daily Grill and The Grill on the Alley concepts in Sheraton and Westin properties.[27] An example of forward quasi-integration is when a large manufacturer of ice cream acquires part interest in a chain of ice cream stores to guarantee access to the distribution channel.

Some hospitality firms use long-term contracts to achieve many of the benefits of vertical integration. Long-term agreements are considered to be vertical integration only when the two firms that provide the agreed-upon goods and services to each other do not have contracts with competitor firms. In the hotel business, many firms have long-term contracts that would not be considered a vertical integration strategy, because the supplier or distributor is not a "captive company" that although independent does most of its business with the contracting firm. Each of the alternatives to complete integration contains trade-offs. That is, while they each reduce the level of exposure to the ill effects of vertical integration, they also reduce the potential for benefits arising from vertical integration. For example, taper integration, quasi-integration, and long-term contracting all yield less control over resources than does full integration.

Because of the potential disadvantages of vertical integration and the limited potential for profitability that may exist at other stages in the industry supply chain, many organizations don't ever pursue vertical integration. As they feel the need to expand beyond the scope of the existing business, they pursue diversification directly. Other organizations may vertically integrate for a while but eventually pursue diversification. Diversification is the topic of the next section.

DIVERSIFICATION STRATEGIES

Diversification, sometimes called horizontal integration, is one of the most studied topics in all of strategic management and can be divided into two broad categories.[28] Related diversification implies organizational involvement in activities that are somehow related to the dominant or core business of the organization, often building on key capabilities or competencies through common or complementary markets or technologies. Unrelated diversification does not depend on any pattern of relatedness and often seeks to reduce risk.

Some of the most common reasons for diversification are listed in Table 6.4, with risk reduction, growth, and improved profitability being key.[29] The table divides the reasons for diversification into strategic reasons, which are frequently cited by executives in the popular business press, and personal motives that CEOs may have for pursuing diversification. In addition to these strategic and personal reasons, some diversification may be simply a result of less familiarity with the diversified business areas than with the core business areas of the organization. In other words, diversification opportunities may look good because organizational managers do not possess enough information about problems and weaknesses associated with the diversified areas—they "leap before they look."[30]

Related Diversification

Related diversification is based on similarities or linkages among the products, services, markets, or resource-conversion processes of different parts of the organization. These similarities

DARDEN RESTAURANTS: A SYNERGISTIC APPROACH

HOSPITALITY FOCUS

Darden Restaurants Inc., the world's largest casual-dining restaurant company, sees itself as well positioned to capture long-term growth in full-service restaurants because of the synergies from increased efficiency and effectiveness in purchasing, distribution, and other corporate support services provided to its various restaurant businesses. With more than 1,700 restaurants, primarily company owned and operated, Darden also brings expertise in operations, brand management, national advertising, and real estate development to its various restaurant concepts. Its flagship restaurants include seafood segment leader Red Lobster and the top Italian-themed Olive Garden concept. Other restaurant chains include upscale Capital Grille, Caribbean-inspired Bahama Breeze, and a casual grill and wine bar Seasons 52 chains, all a part of a new division called the Specialty Restaurant Group. The company closed its troubled Smokey Bones Barbeque and Grill restaurants in 2007, while acquiring RARE Hospitality, operator of the LongHorn Steakhouse chain.[31]

TABLE 6.4 Commonly Stated Reasons for Diversification

STRATEGIC REASONS	MOTIVES OF THE CEO
• Risk reduction through investments in dissimilar businesses or less dynamic environments • Stabilization or improvement in earnings • Improvement in growth • Use of excess cash from slower-growing businesses • Application of resources, capabilities, or core competencies to related areas • Generation of synergy through economies of scope • Use of excess debt capacity • Ability to learn new technologies • Increase in market power	• Desire to increase the value of the firm • Desire to increase personal power and status • Desire to increase personal rewards such as salary and bonuses • Craving for a more interesting and challenging management

are supposed to lead to synergy, which means that the whole is supposed to be greater than the sum of its parts. In other words, one corporation should be able to operate two related businesses more efficiently than can two organizations each producing one of the products or services on its own. (See the "Hospitality Focus" boxed section above.)

Many large hotel companies deploy related diversification strategies to achieve a greater degree of concentration in the lodging industry while leveraging shared distribution and marketing capabilities. Examples would include several of the largest hotel companies worldwide, including Intercontinental Hotels Group, Marriott International, Choice Hotels, Starwood Hotels and Resorts Worldwide, and Sol Melia SA. Most of the research on diversification strategies indicates that some form or other of relatedness among diversified businesses leads to higher financial performance.[32] Related diversification can also reduce risk.[33]

TANGIBLE RELATEDNESS

Relatedness comes in two forms: tangible and intangible.[34] *Tangible relatedness* means that the organization has the opportunity to use the same physical resources for multiple purposes. Tangible relatedness can lead to synergy through resource sharing. For example, if two services are provided in the same facility, operating synergy is said to exist. This phenomenon is referred to as *economies of scope*. Economies of scope occur anytime slack resources that would not have been otherwise used are being put to good use. These economies primarily focus on demand efficiencies, such as those that can be obtained through various marketing efforts, including product bundling and family branding.[35] Sharing facilities can also lead to economies of scale through producing services in an optimally sized (typically larger) facility.[36] Other examples of synergy resulting from tangible relatedness include:

- Using the same marketing or distribution channels for multiple related services
- Buying similar supplies for related services through a centralized purchasing office to gain purchasing economies
- Providing corporate training programs to employees from different divisions that are all engaged in the same type of work
- Advertising multiple services simultaneously

(See the "Hospitality Focus" boxed section on page 223.)

INTANGIBLE RELATEDNESS

Intangible relatedness occurs anytime capabilities developed in one area can be applied to another area. It results in managerial synergy.[37] For example, Four Seasons used capabilities from its lodging businesses to help develop Four Seasons Residence Clubs, its vacation ownership business.[38] This example demonstrates effective use of another intangible resource, image or goodwill. Goodwill means that a company that has an established trade name can draw on this name to market new products. Synergy based on intangible resources such as brand name or management skills and knowledge may be more conducive to the creation of a sustainable competitive advantage, since intangible resources are difficult to imitate and are never used up.[39]

The Creation of Synergy

The potential for synergy based on relatedness in diversified firms is limited only by the imagination. However, even if relatedness is evident, synergy has to be created.[40] McDonald's,

MULTIBRANDING AT YUM! BRANDS

HOSPITALITY FOCUS

"The biggest thing that multibranding offers is the chance to leverage our existing assets that have lower volumes than, say a McDonald's, for instance," notes David Deno, Yum! Brands CFO.[41] Yum! Brands Inc., with such well-known quick-service restaurant brands as Pizza Hut, Taco Bell, KFC, A&W All-American Food, and Long John Silver, is the worldwide leader in multibranding, offering consumers a combination of two of the company's brands in one restaurant location. Starting with combinations of KFC–Taco Bell and Taco Bell–Pizza Hut, it has added $100,000 to $400,000 per unit in average sales, dramatically improving unit economics. The company and its franchisees operate more than 3,600 multibrand restaurants.

Allied Domecq Quick Service Restaurants, a unit of Britain's Allied Domecq PLC, combined its Dunkin' Donuts and Baskin Robbins brands under one roof, sometimes with the Togo's sandwich shop added in to provide a lunch option. The use of a common facility to gain operations synergies is a major benefit of multibranding, although this firm's motivation was different than that of Yum!. Allied Domecq kept customers moving through the store at all hours by offering choices tailored for breakfast, lunch, and snacks. In recent developments, competitor Pernod Ricard purchased Allied Domecq and then sold the restaurant businesses including Dunkin' Brands to a consortium of private equity firms who plan to divest the Togo brand, leaving the future of multibranding less certain for this company.[42]

the number-one fast-food chain, is a strong brand and would most likely overshadow any other brands added to its stores. Besides, these units operate at volume capacity in most stores, diminishing the capacity-enhancing benefits. The potential management synergies from multibranding might be limited because this strategy requires a high level of cooperation—for instance, sharing marketing, labor, or engineering costs—and some brands guard their autonomy too closely to allow for such cross-fertilization. Finally, companies need to preserve the intangible asset of brand equity even as they compress multiple restaurants into a single outlet.[43] The requirements for synergy creation are outlined in Figure 6.2. Some examples of potential sources of synergy from related diversification are shown in Table 6.5.

Some managers seem to believe that if business units are somehow related to each other, synergy will occur automatically. Unfortunately, this is not the case. One factor that can block the ability of organizational managers to create synergistic gains from relatedness is a lack of strategic fit. *Strategic fit* refers to the effective matching of strategic organizational capabilities. For example, if two organizations in two related businesses combine their resources, but they are both strong in the same areas and weak in the same areas, then the potential for synergy is diminished. Once combined, they will continue to exhibit the same capabilities. However, if one of the organizations is strong in operations but lacks marketing power, while the other organization is weak in operations but strong in marketing, then there is real potential for both organizations to be better off—if managed properly.

Another factor that can block managers from achieving synergistic gains is a lack of organizational fit. *Organizational fit* occurs when two organizations or business units have

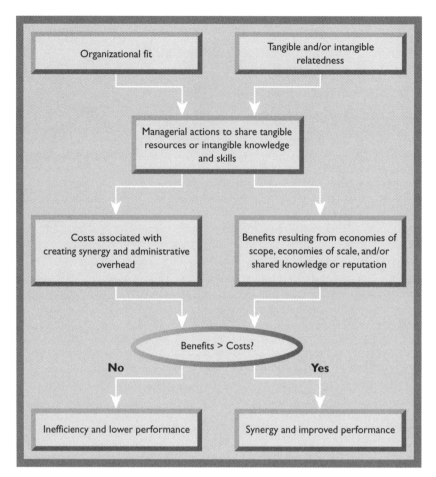

FIGURE 6.2 **Requirements for the creation of synergy**

similar management processes, cultures, systems, and structures.[44] This makes them compatible, which facilitates resource sharing, communication, and transference of knowledge and skills. Unfortunately, relatedness on a dimension such as common markets or similar resource-conversion processes does not guarantee that business units within a firm will enjoy an organizational fit. Lack of fit is especially evident in mergers and acquisitions. For instance, two related companies may merge in an effort to create synergy but find that they are organizationally incompatible. (See the "Hospitality Focus" boxed section on page 226.)

Synergy creation requires a great deal of work on the part of managers at the corporate and business levels. The activities that create synergy include combining similar processes, coordinating business units that share common resources, centralizing support activities that apply to multiple units, and resolving conflicts among business units. Many organizations do not engage in these activities to any degree. Synergy, which is supposed to result in 2 + 2 = 5, often ends up being 2 + 2 = 3. Not only are the coordinating and integrating activities expensive, but corporate-level management also creates an administrative overhead burden that must be shared by all of the operating units.[45]

TABLE 6.5 Potential Sources of Synergy from Related Diversification

Synergies are created by linking value activities between two separate businesses. Here are some examples:

Potential Marketing-Based Synergies

- Shared brand names: Build market influence faster and at lower cost through a common name
- Shared advertising and promotion: Lower unit costs and tie-in purchases
- Shared distribution channels: Bargaining power to improve access and lower costs
- Cross-selling and bundling: Lower costs and more integrated view of the marketplace

Potential Operations Synergies

- Common new facilities: Larger facilities may allow economies of scale
- Shared facilities and capacity: Improved capacity utilization allows lower per-unit overhead costs
- Combined purchasing activities: Increased influence leading to lower costs
- Shared computer systems: Lower per-unit overhead costs and ability to spread the risk of investing in higher-priced systems
- Combined training programs: Lower training costs per employee

Potential R&D/Technology Synergies

- Technology transfer: Faster, lower-cost adoption of technology at the second business
- Development of new core businesses: Access to capabilities and innovation not available in the market
- Multiple use of creative professionals: Opportunities for innovation across business via individual experience and business analogy

Potential Management Synergies

- Similar industry experience: Faster response to industry trends
- Transferable core skills: Experience with previously tested, innovative strategies and skills in strategy and program development

Consequently, organizational performance is increased only if the benefits associated with synergy are greater than the costs related to corporate-level administration, combining activities, or sharing knowledge and resources. When the economic benefits associated with synergy are highest, the administrative costs are also highest, because a lot more information and coordination are required to create the synergy.[46] For example, if two business units are

HOSPITALITY FOCUS

FORTE AND GRANADA: A LACK OF FIT

A little more than a year after acquiring Le Meridien Hotels and Resort, Forte PLC found itself the object of a hostile takeover bid from leisure and media titan Granada PLC. A tumultuous two months later, the CEO of Forte left behind a splintered culture comprised of not-nearly-assimilated Le Meridien executives and Forte's old guard, many of whom were destined to be replaced by new appointees from the new owner Granada. Four years later, Granada merged with Compass Group, and again Le Meridien was sold, this time to Nomura International Plc. In late 2005, Starwood Hotels and Resorts acquired the brand.[47]

unrelated to each other, they do not ever have to communicate or coordinate. But if they are related and want to share knowledge or skills, they will have to engage in meetings, joint training programs, and other coordination efforts. If two related businesses are using the same facility or store, they will have to work out operations (e.g., kitchen design and purchasing). Coordination is also required when using the same sales force for related products, combining promotional efforts, and transferring products between divisions. Coordination processes can be costly in time and other resources. Consequently, the benefits of synergy may be offset, in part, by higher administrative costs. The various costs and forces that can undermine the creation of synergies are listed in Table 6.6.

In summary, organizations may pursue related diversification by acquiring or developing businesses in areas that are related on some basic variable, such as a similar production technology, a common customer, a complementary brand, or other dimensions. However, synergy is not instantaneously created if businesses are related. The creation of synergy requires related businesses to fit together common processes. This can be a difficult managerial challenge. The level of difficulty depends on the amount of strategic and organizational fit that exists among related businesses. In addition to the synergy that can be created through related diversification, corporate-level managers sometimes try to add value to their organizations through the development of corporate-level distinctive competencies that may or may not be associated with a relatedness strategy.

Unrelated Diversification

Large, unrelated diversified firms are often called *conglomerates*, because they are involved in a conglomeration of unrelated businesses.[48] Cash-flow management and risk reduction are two reasons why corporate strategists adopt strategies of unrelated diversification. For example, if a gaming company has excess cash and wants to spread its risk, it might consider a company with stable and constant cash flows in an industry unrelated to hospitality.

Richard Rumelt documented the rise of unrelated diversification in the United States from the 1950s to the early 1970s.[49] Despite the popularity of this strategy during the period,

TABLE 6.6 Forces That Undermine Synergies

Management Ineffectiveness

- Too little effort to coordinate between businesses means synergies will not be created
- Too much effort to coordinate between businesses can stifle creativity

Administrative Costs of Coordination

- Additional layers of management and staff add costs
- Executives in larger organizations are often paid higher salaries
- Delays from and expense of meetings and planning sessions necessary for coordination
- Extra travel and communications costs to achieve coordination

Poor Strategic Fit

- Relatedness without strategic fit decreases the opportunity for synergy
- Overstated (or imaginary) opportunities for synergies
- Industry evolution that undermines strategic fit
- Overvaluing potential synergies often results in paying too much for a target firm or in promising too much improvement to stakeholders

Poor Organizational Fit

- Incompatible cultures and management styles
- Incompatible strategies, priorities, and reward systems
- Incompatible production processes and technologies
- Incompatible computer and budgeting systems

---

he concluded that unrelated firms experience lower profitability than firms pursuing other corporate-level strategies. His findings have been generally, although not unequivocally, supported by other researchers.[50] Perhaps of greater concern, some evidence suggests that unrelated diversification is associated with higher levels of risk than other strategies.[51] This is particularly distressing because one of the most frequently cited arguments for unrelated diversification is that it leads to reduced risk.

Unrelated diversification places significant demands on corporate-level executives as a result of increased complexity and technological changes across industries. In fact, it is very difficult for a manager to understand each of the core technologies and appreciate the special requirements of each of the individual units in an unrelated diversified firm. Consequently, the effectiveness of management may be reduced. By the late 1960s, conglomerates began suffering performance problems. In early 1969, the stock prices of many conglomerates fell by as much as 50 percent from their highs of the previous year, while the Dow Jones Industrial Average fell less than 10 percent during the same period.[52]

THE ACQUISITION HISTORY OF OMNI HOTELS

Omni Hotels is a privately owned, midsize company operating 39 luxury hotels in top business gateways and leisure destinations in the United States, Mexico, and Canada. It was founded in 1958 by the Dunfey family of New England. The business, originally known as Dunfey Hotels, grew to more than 8,000 rooms in the 1960s and 1970s, changing owners twice—first to Aetna Insurance and then to Aer Lingus, the Irish national airline. In 1983, Dunfey Hotels acquired Omni International Hotels, and soon after changed its name to Omni Hotels.

The third firm to acquire Omni Hotels was World International Holdings Ltd. and Wharf Holdings Ltd. of Hong Kong, a diversified trading company representing some 10 percent of the Hong Kong stock market. In February 1996, TRT Holdings, Inc., a private firm that specialized in oil, gas, and pipelines and had expanded into banking, purchased the Omni Hotel chain. TRT Holdings sold its Teco Pipeline subsidiary company in 1997 and dedicated $400 million to improving and expanding Omni Hotel properties. Today, Omni Hotels remains one of several companies owned by TRT Holdings, a holding company for Texas billionaire Robert Rowlling. In addition to owning the Omni Hotel chain and oil and gas exploration businesses, this conglomerate owns Gold's Gym International.[53]

THE TATA GROUP: SUCCESS THROUGH UNRELATED DIVERSIFICATION

India's largest conglomerate is The Tata Group, with 98 companies in seven business sectors spread over six continents. The business sectors include engineering, materials, chemicals, services, consumer products, energy, communications, and information systems. Two of its largest operations are steelmaking (Tata Steel) and vehicle manufacturing (Tata Motors). The second largest tea producer in the world, Tata Tea owns the Tetley brand. Within the services sector, The Indian Hotels Company and its subsidiaries are collectively known as Taj Hotels Resorts and Palaces. Taj Hotels are organized into luxury, leisure, and business hotels, with more than 50 hotels in their portfolio. The following pie chart shows the contribution of each business sector to the overall financial makeup of the Tata Group.[54]

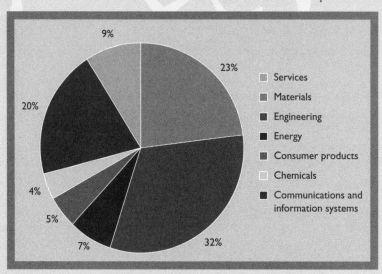

Over the years, many conglomerates have acquired hotel chains, often to sell them after a short period. For instance, Granada PLC, the media conglomerate that bought Forte, merged with Compass Group PLC, one of the world's leading foodservice and hotel groups, and a year later demerged. The Compass Group then began to sell Le Meridien Hotels, Posthouse Hotels, London Signature, and Heritage Hotels, all previously part of Forte Hotels.[55] These mergers, acquisitions, and demergers all occurred in a five-year period. Omni Hotels is not unlike others, having been owned by four large corporations, as revealed in the first "Hospitality Focus" boxed section on page 228.

Now managers and researchers alike believe that unrelated diversification typically is not a high-performing strategy. Between 1950 and 1980, diversification was a popular growth strategy for many organizations. The 1980s were marked with a dramatic decrease in unrelated diversification, accompanied by an increase in related diversification.[56] Related diversification, accompanied by sell-offs of unrelated businesses, is a continuing trend among U.S. firms.[57] Cendant Corporation, for example, separated itself into four separate companies, and after spinning off and selling businesses consists of just the Avis Budget Group business.[58] Refocusing is also becoming increasingly popular, as McDonald's strategy illustrates. However, some firms have had great success with unrelated diversification, such as the Tata Group. (See the "Hospitality Focus" boxed section on page 228.)

MERGERS AND ACQUISITIONS

Some companies rely on internal venturing for most of their growth and diversification. However, managers sometimes feel that their own firm's resources are inadequate to achieve a high level of growth and diversification. Consequently, they seek to acquire skills and resources through purchase of or merger with another firm. Many firms in the hotel and restaurant industries focus on acquisitions and mergers as their primary method for growth, such as the acquisition of Applebee's International by IHOP Corporation. Compared to internal venturing, mergers and acquisitions are a relatively rapid way to pursue growth or diversification, which may partially account for the dramatic increase in their popularity over the past few decades.[59] (See the "Hospitality Focus" boxed section on page 230.)

Mergers occur when two organizations combine into one. *Acquisitions*, in which one organization buys a controlling interest in the stock of another organization or buys it outright from its owners, are the most common type of merger. Acquisitions are a relatively quick way to:[60]

- Enter new markets
- Acquire new products or services

CONSOLIDATION VIA MERGERS

Over the last several years, we have seen numerous mergers of hotel organizations in what was widely touted as a period of significant consolidation in the U.S. hotel industry. Driven by inexpensive acquisition capital—frequently the result of the frothy pricing of hotel stocks on Wall Street—the "urge to merge" was close to a fever pitch in late 1997 and early 1998. Both new brand rollouts and acquisitions aimed at diversification continue to be strategies of the largest hotel companies. A total of 24 new hotel brands were launched in the United States in 2005 and 2006. Industry consolidation is expected to continue as single-brand firms use acquisitions to build themselves into segment-spanning companies. Global Hyatt is one example of this effort when it acquired U.S. Franchise Systems and AmeriSuites.

Private equity firms have also entered the fray, with Blackstone acquiring Prime Hospitality, Wyndham International, La Quinta, and Hilton Hotels Inc. In the fast-casual segment, firms like IHOP are using acquisition to become larger, more diversified businesses, with "more opportunities to create value," according to Julia Steward, CEO of IHOP.[61]

- Learn new resource-conversion processes
- Acquire knowledge and skills
- Vertically integrate
- Broaden markets geographically
- Fill needs in the corporate portfolio

As a portfolio-management tool, managers often seek acquisition targets that are faster growing, more profitable, less cyclical, or less dependent on a particular set of environmental variables. In the case of restaurants and hotels, underperforming multiunit operators like Applebee's are also targeted for acquisition. (See the first "Hospitality Focus" section on page 231.)

Consolidation

Industry consolidation, which occurs as competitors merge, is a major trend. For example, significant consolidation has occurred in the hotel, airline, restaurant, healthcare, and many other industries. In China, nine airlines were merged into three companies as part of a state-ordered consolidation that gives these firms together 80 percent of the Chinese market.[62] Mergers and acquisitions are on the rise in restaurants as well. Much of the consolidation is due to conversion, such as when Lone Star Steakhouse Inc. acquired Ground Round units or Wendy's purchased

RESTAURANT CONSOLIDATION

HOSPITALITY FOCUS

With so many seats in the marketplace, a trend toward a shakeout-based consolidation is inevitable, according to many foodservice observers and participants. "It's going to happen," said Lone Star founder Jamie Coulter, speaking about the move toward consolidation. "The efficient operators are going to recycle the inefficient ones," he notes. After the churning of the merger and acquisition waters calms down again, the experts expect the restaurant industry to emerge stronger than ever before, as the best operators rise to the top, able to take advantage of sites and operations that could no longer be profitably maintained by previous owners. Lone Star acquired the Texas Land & Cattle Steak House chain, saving it from bankruptcy. More recently, the company went private after a $586 million buyout from a private equity firm.[63]

DIVESTING POOR PERFORMING RESTAURANTS

HOSPITALITY FOCUS

Macaroni Grill, the second largest of Brinker International's four-chain portfolio of casual-dining concepts, is up for sale, having posted negative traffic growth for more than five years. This well-known but underperforming brand is not the only one to be sold. The entire casual-dining segment of the restaurant industry has struggled with underperforming brands. With quick-service and fast-casual competitors offering more premium menu items, a weakening consumer environment from lower-income customers, and the popularity of upscale-casual steakhouses, many casual-dining operators are suffering.

Landry's Restaurants Inc. divested its Joe's Crab Shack to help it focus on higher-end, more successful brands like Saltgrass Steak House and Landry's Seafood House. Outback Steakhouse is also considering shedding its secondary brands to focus on a turnaround at Outback. Some industry experts contend that it is a sign of the times that the giants in the industry—especially the public companies that need to answer to hasty and demanding shareholders—no longer are afforded the time to develop a growth concept.[64]

Rax Restaurants. Many other acquisitions can be attributed to financial problems being experienced by the sellers, as shown in the second "Hospitality Focus" boxed section above.

Corporate raiding is another interesting phenomenon associated with mergers and acquisitions. *Corporate raiders* are organizations and individuals who engage in acquisitions, often against the wishes of the managers of the target companies. This type of acquisition is called hostile, and it tends to be more expensive than a friendly acquisition, because the premium paid to acquire the firm is higher.[65] From a social perspective, some corporate raiders have argued that

HOSPITALITY FOCUS

TWO MALL EMPIRE GIANTS LOCKED IN HOSTILE TAKEOVER BATTLE

On one side is David Simon, CEO of the country's largest mall empire, who has launched a hostile bid for the 30 upscale regional centers controlled by Robert Taubman and his family. On the other is the Michigan-based Taubman, who accuses Simon of opportunism and "belligerent badgering." "He said that it was a wonderful opportunity for his company to take over our company and that he really didn't care what we thought," Taubman recounted.[66]

they are doing society a favor, because the threat of takeover motivates managers to act in the best interests of the organization's stockholders.[67] They believe that they are keeping managers from becoming entrenched. However, this argument remains to be proven. Hostile takeovers have come to the shopping-center industry, as two of the most powerful families in this industry were locked in a bitter takeover battle. (See the "Hospitality Focus" boxed section above.)

Merger Performance

The shareholders of an acquired firm typically enjoy a huge payoff because they receive an enormous premium over market value for the shares of stock they hold before the acquisition announcement.[68] However, most of the research evidence seems to indicate that mergers and acquisitions are not, on average, financially beneficial to the shareholders of the acquiring firm.[69] In one study of 191 acquisitions in 29 industries, researchers found that acquisitions were associated with declining profitability, reduced research-and-development expenditures, fewer patents produced, and increases in financial leverage.[70] John Chambers, CEO of Cisco Systems, made 71 acquisitions between 1993 and 2000. Reflecting on that activity, he said, "I don't know how to make large mergers work."[71] In the IHOP acquisition of Applebee's, some analysts predict that the most dissatisfied are likely to be IHOP shareholders.[72]

Table 6.7 provides several explanations for why acquisitions, on average, tend to depress profitability (at least in the short term). High premiums, increased interest costs, high advisory fees and other transaction costs, and poison pills (actions that make a target company less attractive) can cause acquisitions to be prohibitively expensive and thus reduce any potential gains from synergy. In addition, strategic problems such as high turnover among target-firm managers, managerial distraction, lower innovation, lack of organizational fit, and increased leverage and risk can reduce any strategic benefits the organization was hoping to achieve.

The president and COO of Radisson Hotels and Resorts Worldwide has observed: "Most big-company acquisitions have not been lucrative. Deals are easy on paper, but hard to execute day to day. With that in analysts' minds, public companies will be under incredible scrutiny when it comes to acquisitions."[73] Also, if there are several suitors for a company, bids can get so high that the additional premium is hard to offset through any efficiencies created. For example, a fierce bidding war between Hilton and Starwood Hotels and Resorts existed

TABLE 6.7 A Few of Many Potential Problems with Mergers and Acquisitions

High Costs

- High premiums typically paid by acquiring firms: If a company was worth $50 per share in a relatively efficient financial market prior to an acquisition, why should an acquiring firm pay $75 (a typical premium) or more to buy it?
- Increased interest costs: Many acquisitions are financed by borrowing money at high interest rates. Leverage typically increases during an acquisition.
- High advisory fees and other transaction costs: The fees charged by the brokers, lawyers, financiers, consultants, and advisors who orchestrate the deal often range in the millions of dollars. In addition, filing fees, document preparation, and legal fees in the event of contestation can be very high.
- Poison pills: These anti-takeover devices make companies very unattractive to a potential buyer. Top managers of target companies have been very creative in designing a variety of poison pills. One example of a poison pill is the "golden parachute," in which target-firm executives receive large amounts of severance pay (often millions of dollars) if they lose their jobs due to a hostile takeover.

Strategic Problems

- High turnover among the managers of the acquired firm: The most valuable asset in most organizations is the people, their knowledge, and their skills. If most managers leave, what has the acquiring firm purchased?
- Short-term managerial distraction: "Doing a deal" typically takes managers away from the critical tasks of the core businesses for long durations. During this time period, who is steering the ship?
- Long-term managerial distraction: Because they are too distracted running diversified businesses, organizations sometimes lose sight of the factors that led to success in their core businesses.
- Less innovation: Acquisitions have been shown to lead to reduced innovative activity, which can hurt long-term performance.
- No organizational fit: If the cultures, dominant logics, systems, structures, and processes of the acquiring and target firms do not "fit," synergy is unlikely.
- Increased risk: Increased leverage often associated with mergers and acquisitions leads to greater financial risk. Acquiring firms also take the risk that they will be unable to successfully manage the newly acquired organization.

Source: M. A. Hitt, J. S. Harrison, and R. D. Ireland, *Mergers and Acquisitions: A Guide to Creating Value for Stakeholders* (New York: Oxford University Press, 2001); S. Chatterjee, et al., "Cultural Differences and Shareholder Value in Related Mergers: Linking Equity and Human Capital," *Strategic Management Journal* 13 (1992): 319–334; J. S. Harrison, "Alternatives to Merger—Joint Ventures and Other Strategies," *Long Range Planning* (December 1987): 78–83; J. P. Walsh and J. W. Ellwood, "Mergers, Acquisitions, and the Pruning of Managerial Deadwood," *Strategic Management Journal* 12 (1991): 201–207.

when the multinational conglomerate ITT, a one-time owner of Sheraton Hotels and Caesars World, spun-off its nonmanufacturing businesses.

Perhaps the most condemning evidence concerning mergers and acquisitions was presented by Michael Porter. He studied the diversification records of 33 large, prestigious U.S. companies over a period of 37 years. He discovered that most of these companies divested many more of their acquisitions than they kept. For example, CBS, in an effort to create an entertainment company, bought organizations involved in toys, crafts, sports teams, and musical instruments. All of these businesses were eventually sold due to lack of fit with the traditional broadcasting business of CBS. CBS also bought Ziff-Davis publishers, which they unloaded a few years later for much less than they paid after having run all its magazines into the ground. Porter's general conclusion was that the corporate-level strategies of most of the companies he studied had reduced, rather than enhanced, shareholder value.[74]

Successful and Unsuccessful Mergers and Acquisitions

Does the discouraging evidence about merger performance mean that all mergers are doomed to failure? An examination of the market's reaction to merger and tender-offer announcements in the lodging industry found that the equity markets view lodging mergers and acquisitions favorably. In contrast to the results for the overall market, a study of 41 lodging acquisitions from 1982 to 1999 revealed a positive stock-price reaction for both the acquiring firms and their targets.[75] While mergers in lodging may be viewed more favorably, their post-merger success is still a challenge for corporate managers. Researchers have identified factors associated with successful and unsuccessful mergers. Unsuccessful mergers are associated with a large amount of debt, overconfident or incompetent managers, poor ethics, changes in top management or organization structure, or diversification away from the core area of the acquiring firm.[76]

Some factors seem to lead to success in mergers. For example, some researchers have found that successful mergers are made by acquiring firms with relatively small amounts of debt. Merger negotiations are friendly (no resistance), which helps keep acquisition premiums to a minimum and helps make post-merger integration of the companies a lot easier.[77] *Acquisition premiums* are the percentage paid for shares of stock above their market value before the acquisition announcement.

Successful mergers also tend to involve companies that share a high level of complementarity among their resources, thus creating the potential for synergy. *Complementarity* occurs when two companies have strengths in different areas that complement each other.[78] Furthermore, researchers have discovered that the largest shareholder gains from mergers occur when the cultures and the top-management styles of the two companies are similar (organizational fit).[79] In addition, sharing resources and activities has been found to be important to post-merger success.[80] However, it is fair to say that "there are no rules that will invariably lead to a successful acquisition."[81] (See the "Hospitality Focus" boxed section on page 235.)

One of the most important factors leading to a successful merger is the due-diligence process. Warren Hellman, former CEO of Lehman Brothers, suggests that because so many

COMPLIMENTARITY IN THE SAB MILLER AND MOLSON COORS MERGER

HOSPITALITY FOCUS

"Our two businesses are very complementary, and our cultures are surprisingly similar. Together we will have a superb brand portfolio, a stronger distribution system, and some very talented people. And these enhanced strengths and capabilities will well position us to compete in the marketplace," noted the CEO of SAB Miller when announcing that SAB Miller and Molson Coors Brewing Company would merge their U.S. operations. SABMiller and Molson Coors are both products of mergers. SAB PLC. acquired Miller Brewing Company in 2002, and Molson Coors was formed by the 2005 merger of Adolph Coors Co. and Canada's Molson Inc. The two firms are hoping to use their combined brand power (roughly 30 percent market share) to launch a direct assault on Anheuser-Bush companies, which lead the United States with 48 percent of the market.[82]

acquisitions fail, organizations should assume that *all* of them will fail. The burden is then on the shoulders of the managers who want the merger to take place to prove why their particular deal will be an exception to the general rule.[83] The due-diligence process is an excellent way to obtain the necessary evidence. *Due diligence* involves a complete examination of the merger, including such areas as management, equity, debt, sale of assets, transfer of shares, environmental issues, financial performance, tax issues, human resources, customers, and markets. Typically, the process is conducted by accountants, investment bankers, lawyers, consultants, and internal specialists.[84] The due-diligence team should be empowered by top managers of both companies with responsibility and authority to obtain all of the necessary data. For those acquisitions that finally occur, information gained during due diligence is invaluable for integration planning.

Many of the major problems with mergers and acquisitions can be avoided through effective due diligence, even if it means avoiding the deal altogether. For example, the president of a billion-dollar division of one of the largest corporations in the United States walked away from an acquisition because of accounting irregularities discovered during due diligence.[85] Joseph Neubauer, CEO of Aramark, provides another example. (See the "Hospitality Focus" boxed section on page 236.)

Chapter 4 discussed organizational learning through interorganizational relationships. Organizations can also learn through acquisitions. In fact, some experts have argued that "acquisitions may broaden a firm's knowledge base and decrease inertia, enhancing the viability of its later ventures."[86] However, mergers and acquisitions represent a paradox with regard to innovative activities. While organizations can learn from the companies they acquire, acquisitions can lead to a reduction in innovative activities. This negative effect may come from a loss of focus on the core business or absorption of new debt that directs cash flow toward interest payments and away from research and development. Regardless of the reasons, acquisitions seem to be a way to "buy" innovation from external sources while damaging internal innovation. Consequently, some experts call acquisitions "a substitute for innovation."[87]

In summary, mergers and acquisitions have a high incidence of failure, but, if carefully executed, may enhance firm performance. Once a firm has created a portfolio of

CEO OF ARAMARK WALKS AWAY FROM ACQUISITION

It was a crucial moment for Aramark Worldwide Corp. After months of nego-tiating and millions spent on due diligence, the $7.8 billion outsourcing service company was close to wrapping up deals for a pair of overseas acquisitions. The target companies fit perfectly with Aramark's goal of expanding internation-ally, and the price—more than $100 million—was right, too. But when CEO Joseph Neubauer finally got a close look at the operations and books, he didn't like what he saw. Despite the huge investment in time and money, he didn't think twice. Neubauer walked away. "It takes a lifetime to build a reputation and only a short time to lose it all," he says matter-of-factly. "We chose to eat the loss on the time and the money because we couldn't live with their business practices."[88]

businesses—through either acquisitions, joint ventures, or internal growth—the emphasis becomes managing those businesses so that high organizational performance is achieved. One of the keys to doing so is creating competencies that span multiple businesses. The "Hospitality Focus" boxed section on page 237 discusses this important topic.

STRATEGIC RESTRUCTURING

Disgruntled stakeholders are often the force that causes corporate-level managers to con-sider restructuring. For example, one of Applebee's largest and most vocal shareholders made numerous suggestions that IHOP's turnaround plan for Applebee's will likely implement including reduced costs, refranchising, and leadership replacements.[89] Stockholders may be dissatisfied with their financial returns, or debt-rating agencies such as Standard & Poor's may devalue firm securities due to high risk. If an organization has spent many years diversifying in various directions, top managers may feel as though the organization is out of control. This feeling of loss of control is also related to organizational size. In the largest organizations, top managers may even be unfamiliar with some of the businesses in their portfolios. Also, many organizations have acquired high levels of debt, often associated with acquisitions. For these companies, even small economic downturns can be a rude awakening to the risks associated with high leverage.[90] For all of these reasons, restructuring has become commonplace in recent years.

Researchers have observed that as organizations evolve, they tend to move through what is called a period of convergence, followed by a period of reorientation or radical adjustment, and then another period of convergence.[91] During convergence stages, the organization makes minor changes to strategies in an effort to adapt, but for the most part follows a consistent approach. During this time, the structure and systems are more or less stable, performance is acceptable, and managers develop mental models, or assumptions, about how the industry and

HOSPITALITY FOCUS

COSI SANDWICH CHAIN: MANAGEMENT SHAKEUPS THREATEN PERFORMANCE

Less than six months after going public, Cosi—the upscale sandwich chain—underwent its second major management shakeup, closing restaurants and seeking financing to fund its greatly diminished growth plans. Cosi's explanation that the change was the result of insufficient financing prompted a flurry of lawsuits by shareholders, who alleged that they were deceived by the firm's growth projections in its IPO prospectus.

Four years since the IPO, this premium convenience restaurant company continues to have financial woes. With 114 company-owned and 23 franchise restaurants, management has decided to close most Macy's store locations since they are not achieving acceptable operating margins.[92]

the organization work.[93] A period of convergence can continue indefinitely, as long as the industry conditions and organization characteristics are not significantly out of alignment.[94] However, when gradual drift results in a substantial misalignment, or an environmental discontinuity does occur, the organization is forced to reorient itself. At this time, the mental models that were developed during the convergence period may prevent executives, managers, and employees from recognizing the need for change. The information that doesn't fit the preconceived mental model is just not seen at all. As one researcher described it: "The writing on the wall cannot be read."[95]

A reorientation is a significant realignment of organization strategies, structure, and processes with the new environmental realities.[96] *Transformation, renewal, reorientation*, and *restructuring* are all words that describe the same general phenomenon: a radical change in how business is conducted. Organizations may use any one or a combination of strategies in restructuring efforts. Some of the most common restructuring approaches include:

- Turnaround strategies and downsizing
- Refocusing corporate assets on distinctive competencies
- Chapter 11 reorganization
- Leveraged buyouts
- Changes to organizational design

Turnaround Strategies and Downsizing

Turnaround strategies (sometimes called *retrenchment*) can involve workforce reductions, selling assets to reduce debt, outsourcing unprofitable activities, implementation of tighter cost or quality controls,

HOSPITALITY FOCUS

EXPERTS AT TURNING AROUND UNDER PERFORMING HOTELS

Some management companies crave properties that need improvement. Turning around underperforming properties is how management companies develop a reputation and how they acquire more business sources. "I love going into an asset where the previous management company has missed the low-hanging fruit," said Robert Dann, Executive VP of Boykin Management Co. "To take a hotel and turn it around, people remember that," said David McCaslin, former president of MeriStar Hotels and Resorts. "About half our business is with turnaround properties," said William Hoffman, founder of Trigild Corp.[97]

or new policies that emphasize quality or efficiency. Turnaround can occur at the corporate level of a company or on a property-by-property basis. (See the "Hospitality Focus" boxed section above.)

Workforce reductions, or downsizing, have become a common part of turnaround strategies in the United States as a response to the burgeoning bureaucracies in the post–World War II era. Even the U.S. military has a new focus on a "lighter fighter" division that can respond faster to combat situations. Staff reductions and office closings were key elements of InterContinental Hotels Group's effort to remove $100 million in costs from its balance sheet. The company closed its London headquarters office, consolidated operations, and reduced its global corporate staff by 800.[98] The great mystery is that some companies lay off employees despite strong profits. For example, Mobil once posted "soaring" first-quarter earnings—and then announced plans to cut 4,700 jobs.[99]

The evidence is mounting that "downsizing does not reduce expenses as much as desired, and that sometimes expenses may actually increase."[100] Companies may experience problems, such as reductions in quality, a loss in productivity, decreased effectiveness, lost trust, increased conflict, and low morale.[101] According to one CEO involved in a major layoff, "The human impact of our decisions is very real and very painful."[102] Many organizations cut muscle, as well as fat, through layoffs. One reason the muscle is cut is that some of the best employees leave, either because of attractive severance packages or fear of future job loss. Because the best employees can usually get new jobs fairly easily, they may decide to leave while all of their options are open to them. Also, studies have shown that the surviving employees experience feelings of guilt and fear that may hurt productivity or organizational loyalty.[103] It is not surprising, then, that the stock market often reacts unfavorably to announcements of major layoffs.[104]

WORKFORCE REDUCTIONS

Sometimes layoffs are critical to survival, as was the case following the events of September 11, 2001. According to the Bureau of Labor Statistics, during the five weeks following the terrorist attacks, more than 88,500 workers were discharged. This job loss occurred across industries and was viewed as either a direct or indirect result of the attacks.[105] Among the workers who were reported laid off, 43 percent belonged to the airline industry and 36 percent to the hotel industry.[106] A Cornell University study in the weeks after the events revealed that seven out of

RESTRUCTURING AT CBRL GROUP

HOSPITALITY FOCUS

After a strategic review, massive restructuring at CBRL Group Inc. has included the sell of Logan's Roadhouse steakhouse chain. The company began in the late 1960s, when Dan Evins opened the first Cracker Barrel Old Country Store in Lebanon, Tennessee. As the company grew, it acquired Carmine's Prime Meats (later Carmine Giardini's Gourmet Market), a chain of gourmet food stores, restructured into a holding company, and acquired the Logan's Roadhouse steakhouse chain. This latest restructuring and divestiture began when CBRL closed 30 money-losing restaurants. In addition, the restructuring may be attributed in part to pressure from Nelson Peltz, a shareholder who owns 4.9 percent of CBRL's outstanding shares, is the Chairman of Triarc Companies Inc., parent of Arby's brand, and was behind the restructuring at Wendy's.[107]

ten hotel general managers surveyed employed some form of staff reduction.[108] "On September 15, Continental announced that it would cut 12,000 jobs. One by one, the other airlines followed suit: United and American announced 20,000 layoffs each; Northwest, 10,000; US Airways, 11,000; Delta forecast eliminating 13,000."[109] Obviously, the airlines could not have been prepared for such events, although occupancies in the hotel industry were beginning to erode in the first quarter of the year. Barry Sternlicht, then-CEO of Starwood Hotels and Resorts (now Chairman and CEO of Starwood Capital Group), stated: "Our focus in this crisis has been to react flexibly and entrepreneurially and to run a lean, mean machine."[110]

A survey by the American Management Association of 1,142 companies that had been involved in workforce reductions indicated that about half of these companies were poorly prepared for these activities.[111] One of the keys to successful downsizing, then, may be sufficient preparation with regard to outplacement, new reporting relationships, and training, when possible. Of course, another important element in all successful restructuring activities, especially workforce reductions, is effective communication with and examination of the needs of key stakeholders.[112] Managers anticipating layoffs should combine caring with cost consciousness and should humanize their approaches to workforce reductions.[113] Many organizations avoid layoffs through hiring freezes, restricting overtime, retraining and redeploying workers, switching workers to part-time, starting job-sharing programs, giving unpaid vacations, shortening the workweek, or reducing pay.[114]

Refocusing Corporate Assets

Most restructuring companies are moving in the direction of reducing their diversification, as opposed to increasing it.[115] For example, Carlson Restaurants sold off its emerging brands division to focus on T.G.I. Fridays and Pick Up Stix.[116] Refocusing activities are generally viewed favorably by external stakeholders such as the financial community.[117] Wyndham International recapitalized in 1999 and held a large portion of its nonstrategic assets.[118] Refocusing entails trimming businesses that are not consistent with the strategic direction of the organization. (See the "Hospitality Focus" boxed section on page 239.)

DOWNSCOPING

This type of refocusing is often called downscoping. *Downscoping* involves selling off nonessential businesses that are not related to the organization's core competencies and capabilities.[119] Furthermore, innovative activities tend to increase in companies involved in this type of restructuring. You may recall that this is opposite of the impact of acquisitions.[120]

On the other hand, sell-offs that do not improve the strategic focus of the organization may signal failure or market retreat, which can cause concern among stakeholders such as owners, debtholders, and the financial community. For instance, the stock market tends to react positively to divestitures linked to corporate-level or business-level strategies and negatively to divestitures that are portrayed as simply getting rid of unwanted assets.[121]

DIVESTITURES

A *divestiture* is a reverse acquisition. In the lodging industry, this type of activity is sometimes referred to as a demerger. One type of divestiture is a sell-off, in which a business unit is sold to another firm or, in the case of a leveraged buyout, to the business unit's managers. Another form of divestiture is the *spin-off*, which means that current shareholders are issued a proportional number of shares in the spun-off business. For example, if a shareholder owns 100 shares of XYZ Company and the company spins off business unit J, the shareholder would then own 100 shares of XYZ Company and 100 shares of an independently operated company called J. The key advantage of a spin-off relative to other divestiture options is that shareholders still have the option of retaining ownership in the spun-off business. InterContinental Hotel Group (previously Six Continents Hotels and Bass Hotels and Resorts), renamed twice in less than two years, spun off its pub operations from its hotel business. The demerger resulted in two separate, publicly traded companies.[122]

Refocusing may also involve new acquisitions or new ventures to round out a corporate portfolio or add more strength in an area that is essential to corporate distinctive competencies.[123] For instance, Grand Metropolitan bought Pillsbury and simultaneously sold Bennigan's and Steak & Ale restaurants in an effort to redefine its domain in the food-processing industry.[124]

Chapter 11 Reorganization

An organization that is in serious financial trouble can voluntarily file for Chapter 11 protection under the Federal Bankruptcy Code:

> Chapter XI *provides a proceeding for an organization to work out a plan or arrangement for solving its financial problems under the supervision of a federal court. It is intended primarily*

BANKRUPTCY AT GEORGETTE KLINGER SPA

Little did Angela Krivulka think that two months after she purchased the 11-unit spa chain Georgette Klinger from TrueYou.com, she would be filing for Chapter 11. Like many firms that file for bankruptcy, the company faced serious financial problems. TrueYou.com informed the Securities and Exchange Commission (SEC) that since its inception, the spas had experienced substantial operating losses and negative cash flow. Faced with declining revenue and cash flow, TrueYou.com stated that it sold its spa business.

According to Krivulka, the current CEO, "The 11 spa facilities had suffered from neglect, there was low employee morale, a lack of retail products, minimal marketing, large outstanding payments due to creditors, and many internal problems that needed to be corrected immediately." The largest creditors include Cigna Healthcare, $370,237; NorthPark Partners, $199,951; Allergan, the makers of Botox, $127,747; luxury haircare brand Krastase Paris, $66,340; and high-end skin care company Innovative Skincare, $65,735. Already the firm has begun to work on its problems. The senior managers have cut costs, including shuttering the chain's unprofitable Boca Raton, Florida spa. Improving on inventory management and product delivery, reducing payroll redundancies, and trimming its employee count to 360 from 410 are just a few of the ways the company hopes to resolve its financial woes.[125]

for debtors who feel they can solve their financial problems on their own if given sufficient time, and if relieved of some pressure.[126]

For example, Kmart became the largest retailer in history to file for Chapter 11, "hoping to buy itself time to repay creditors while it restructures its businesses."[127] Chapter 11 became very common in the hospitality industry in the aftermath of September 11, including companies such as Renaissance Cruises, US Airways, Boston Chicken, United Airlines, and Lodgian. Another example is Georgette Klinger, a chain of spas. (See the "Hospitality Focus" boxed section above.)

While Chapter 11, if executed properly, can provide firms with time and protection as they attempt to reorganize, it is not a panacea for firms with financial problems. Chapter 11 can be expensive. Fees from lawyers, investment bankers, and accountants can total millions of dollars.[128] Another disadvantage is that, after filing, all major restructuring decisions are subject to court approval. Thus, managerial discretion and flexibility are reduced. Researchers do not agree on the potential for successful reorganization. Some researchers have argued that it is in the best interests of organizations that are facing high amounts of adversity to quickly select Chapter 11 (instead of having it imposed on them), unless they have high levels of organizational slack.[129] In a study of firms that had voluntarily filed for Chapter 11 protection, however, only a little more than half of the companies were "nominally successful in reorganizing," and "two-thirds of those retained less than 50 percent of their assets on completion of the reorganization process."[130] For example, American Restaurant Group emerged from bankruptcy with creditors controlling more than 98 percent of the company.[131] While larger firms have a better chance of successfully reorganizing, Chapter 11 should probably still be used as a strategy of last resort.

Leveraged Buyouts

Leveraged buyouts (LBOs) involve the private purchase of a business unit by managers, employees, unions, or private investors. They are called "leveraged" because much of the money that is used to purchase the business unit is often borrowed from financial intermediaries (often at higher than normal interest rates). An LBO made possible the sale by Compass of its Little Chef and Travelodge units following a strategic review that concluded the two businesses did not fit within its core focus of contract food service.[132] Permira, a leading European-based private equity firm, was granted exclusivity in handling the deal, which involved a debt package from five banks and an additional investor. Because of high leverage, LBOs are often accompanied by selling off the company's assets to repay debt. Consequently, organizations typically become smaller and more focused after an LBO. For example, Planet Hollywood is now a much smaller company and is privately owned, having been a publicly traded company before its LBO.

During the late 1970s and early 1980s, LBOs gained a reputation as a means of turning around failing divisions.[133] However, some researchers have discovered that LBOs stifle innovation, similar to what can happen with mergers and acquisitions.[134] Others have found that LBO firms have comparatively slower growth in sales and employees, and that they tend to divest a larger proportion of both noncore and core businesses, compared to firms that remained public.[135] Also, some executives who initiate LBOs seem to receive an excessive return, regardless of the consequences to others. For example, John Kluge made a $3 billion profit in two years through dismantling Metromedia following an LBO.[136] Plant closings, relocations, and workforce reductions are all common outcomes. Consequently, some businesspeople are starting to wonder if LBOs are really in the best interests of all stakeholders. LBOs can certainly do seemingly irreparable damage to organizational resources. (See the "Hospitality Focus" boxed section on page 243.)

It is the responsibility of the board of directors to ensure that stakeholder interests are considered prior to approving an LBO:

> *When considering a leveraged buyout, board members must treat fairly not only shareholders but other stakeholders as well. Corporate groups—employees, creditors, customers, suppliers, and local communities—claim the right to object to leveraged buyouts on the grounds that they have made a larger investment in—and have a more enduring relationship with—the corporation than do persons who trade share certificates daily on the stock exchanges. . . . Similarly, if short-run profit is at the expense of and violates the expectations of employees, customers, communities, or suppliers, companies will find themselves unable to do business. The better employees will leave. Customers will stop buying. Communities will refuse to extend services. Suppliers will minimize their exposure.[137]*

Not surprisingly, reports of failed LBOs are not uncommon. Successful LBOs require buying a company at the right price with the right financing, combined with outstanding management and fair treatment of stakeholders.[138]

LEVERAGED BUYOUT OF HARRAH'S ENTERTAINMENT

HOSPITALITY FOCUS

The leveraged buyout of Harrah's Entertainment by a partnership between Apollo Management and Texas Pacific Group, two private equity firms, represents the largest deal ever for a casino company, and the fifth-largest leveraged buyout on record. Harrah's is the world's largest gaming company by revenue, owning or operates 48 casinos worldwide, including 13 in Nevada. In Las Vegas, the company owns Caesar's Palace, Paris, Bally's, Rio, Bill's, Flamingo, Imperial Palace, and Harrah's, as well as an estimated 350 acres of real estate. Harrah's shareholders voted to approve the $17.1 billion buyout, and upon completion of the sale will receive $90 per share of Harrah's stock. This deal signals the emerging interest in the gambling sector for heavily funded private equity groups.[139]

Changes to Organizational Design

Organizational design can be a potent force in restructuring efforts. For example, as organizations diversify, top managers have a more difficult time processing the vast amounts of diverse information that are needed to appropriately control each business. Their span of control is too large. Consequently, one type of change to organization design may be a move to a more decentralized product/market or divisional structure. The result is more managers with smaller spans of control and a greater capacity to understand each of their respective business areas. On the other hand, a company may desire more consistency and control over operations, thus moving toward centralization rather than decentralization. (See the "Hospitality Focus" boxed section on page 244.)

Because organization structure will be thoroughly covered in Chapter 8, we will not say more about it at this point. However, closely linked to changes in organizational structure are adjustments to the culture of the firm, the unseen glue that holds the structure together. A successful turnaround is often accompanied by a dramatic change in culture. If restructuring activities are precipitated by unusually poor economic or competitive conditions, a strong strategy-supportive culture can be undermined by the actions taken during the restructuring.[140] In other retrenchment situations, the existing culture may be part of the problem: too little focus on quality, too little learning and sharing, a poor attitude toward customers, or a lack of innovation.

If the culture is part of the problem, then the restructuring effort has to address the necessary changes in culture. It is difficult for an organization to throw off its old way of doing business. For instance, many vacation ownership companies have historically been excellent at real estate development, with a depth of knowledge about feasibility, development, and construction design. Once a resort is developed, the sales and marketing know-how then kicks in. Unfortunately, many of these firms are deficient in the financial components of the business and need to undergo significant restructuring in systems. Once acquired, these companies need to transition from an entrepreneurial structure to one with much stronger corporate

HOSPITALITY FOCUS

CHOICE HOTELS INTERNATIONAL MOVES TOWARD CENTRALIZATION

Choice Hotels International wanted to operate more efficiently and wanted to provide more consistent service to franchisees. To accomplish that, the company underwent a reorganization. The restructuring reduced the regional sales offices from five to three, centralized franchise sales in Silver Spring, Maryland, and realigned marketing operations to increase business.[141]

disciplines.[142] Following a hostile takeover, Linda Wachner, CEO of Warnaco, says she had to instill a hardworking, "do-it-now" culture to improve the organization's performance.[143]

Reengineering can also lead to significant changes in the way an organization is designed:

Business Process Reengineering *involves the radical redesign of core business processes to achieve dramatic improvements in productivity cycle times and quality. Companies start with a blank sheet of paper and rethink existing processes, typically placing increased emphasis on customer needs. They reduce organizational layers and unproductive activities in two ways: they redesign functional organizations into cross-functional teams, and they use technology to improve data dissemination and decision making.[144]*

Based on a survey of executives of American firms, more than three-quarters of large firms in the United States were involved in reengineering. However, satisfaction rates were low for reengineering, and use of it has dropped significantly. Some business experts think that reengineering may have been just a fad.

Some authors suggest that restructuring should be a continuous process.[145] Changes in global markets and technology have created a permanent need for firms to focus on what they do best and to divest any parts of their organizations that no longer contribute to their missions or long-term goals. However, most organizations have a difficult time achieving significant changes, and managers' mental models cause them to resist change. Consequently, continuous restructuring is a good idea, and perhaps even essential to remaining competitive, but it is certainly difficult to accomplish.

PORTFOLIO MANAGEMENT

Thus far in this chapter, we have discussed the basic corporate-level strategies and the techniques organizations use to carry them out. For example, we discussed formulation of a related-diversification strategy and also described how acquisitions can be used to implement it. As a firm begins to diversify, it will start to develop a portfolio of businesses. Consequently, the final corporate-level tool discussed in this chapter is portfolio management. Portfolio management refers to managing the mix of businesses in the corporate portfolio. CEOs of large, diversified organizations continually face decisions concerning how to divide organizational resources among diversified units and where to invest new capital, as well as which businesses to divest. Portfolio models are designed to help managers make these types of decisions.

Portfolio planning gained wide acceptance during the 1970s, and, by 1979, approximately 45 percent of *Fortune* 500 companies were using some type of portfolio planning.[146] Despite their adoption in many organizations, portfolio-management techniques are the subject of a considerable amount of criticism from strategic management scholars.[147] But because these techniques are still in wide use, this book would be incomplete without them. Keep in mind that they are not a panacea and should not replace other types of sound strategic analysis.

The Boston Consulting Group (BCG) Matrix

The simplest and first widely used portfolio model was the Boston Consulting Group (BCG) Matrix, displayed in Figure 6.3. The model is simple, but most of the other portfolio techniques

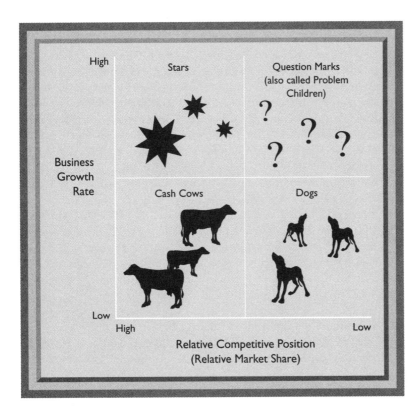

FIGURE 6.3 The Boston Consulting Group (BCG) Portfolio Matrix
Source: Boston Consulting Group, copyright © 1970, used with permission.

are adaptations of it. Consequently, if you understand how to use it, you can develop a variation of it that fits the company you are studying much better. The BCG Matrix is based on two factors: business growth rate and relative market share. Business growth rate is the growth rate of the industry in which a particular business unit is involved. Relative market share is calculated as the ratio of the business unit's size to the size of its largest competitor. The two factors are used to plot all of the businesses in which the organization is involved, represented as Stars, Question Marks (also called Problem Children), Cash Cows, and Dogs.

The BCG Matrix can be useful in planning cash flows. Cash Cows tend to generate more cash than they can effectively reinvest, while Question Marks require additional cash to sustain rapid growth, and Stars generate about as much cash as they use, on average. According to BCG, Stars and Cash Cows, with their superior market-share positions, tend to be the most profitable businesses. Consequently, the optimal BCG portfolio contains a balance of Stars, Cash Cows, and Question Marks. Stars have the greatest potential for growth and tend to be highly profitable. However, as the industries in which Stars are involved mature and their growth slows, they naturally become Cash Cows. Therefore, Question Marks are important because of their potential role as future Stars in the organization. Dogs are the least attractive types of business. The original prescription was to divest them. However, even Dogs can be maintained in the portfolio as long as they do not become a drain on corporate resources. Also, some organizations are successful at positioning their Dogs in an attractive niche in their industries.

One of the central ideas of the BCG Matrix is that high market share leads to high profitability due to learning effects, experience effects, entry barriers, market power, and other influences. In fact, there is evidence, both in the strategic management literature and in the economics literature, that higher market share is associated with higher profitability in some instances. However, some low-share businesses enjoy high profitability.[148] The real relationship between market share and profitability depends on many factors, including the nature of the industry and the strategy of the firm. For example, one researcher found that the market share–profitability relationship is stronger in some industries than in others. He also discovered that beyond a certain market share, profitability tended to trail off.[149]

A lot of the criticism related to the BCG Matrix is due to its simplicity. Only two factors are considered, and only two divisions, high and low, are used for each factor. Also, growth rate is an oversimplification of industry attractiveness, and market share is an inadequate barometer of competitive position. A common criticism that applies to many portfolio models, and especially the BCG Matrix, is that they are based on the past instead of the future. Given the rate of change in the current economic and political environments, and the dynamic nature of hospitality firms, this criticism is probably valid. Finally, another problem inherent in all matrix approaches is that industries are difficult to define.

Numerous organizational managers and business writers have developed portfolio matrices that overcome some of the limitations of the BCG Matrix.[150] Virtually any variables or combination of variables of strategic importance can be plotted along the axes of a portfolio matrix. The selection of variables depends on what the organization considers important. By applying resource analysis and environmental analysis to a portfolio model, it may be possible to tap the potential of a business unit as well as its current competitive standing. For example, based on a thorough resource analysis, a firm's competitive position could be determined based on the strength of its human, physical, financial, knowledge-based, and general organizational resources, especially as they relate to competitive advantage. Industry attractiveness may be assessed by evaluating the power of suppliers and customers, the level of competitive rivalry, the threat of substitutes, the height of entry barriers, the amount and type of regulation, the power of unions, rate of growth, current profitability, and resiliency during downturns. From a portfolio-management perspective, businesses that are in a strong competitive position in attractive industries should be given the highest priority with regard to resource allocations.

Destination Portfolio Analysis

Portfolio analysis can also be adapted to tourism, in which the focus is not on a specific company but the destination itself, such as a country, region, or city. Managing destination tourism is often the responsibility of national and regional nonprofit tourism organizations, which use a series of factors/variables relating to potential tourism markets, the destination, and the competition to create portfolio matrices. While these organizations typically do not have a direct economic interest in tourism products, they do need to diagnose and strategically assess the attractiveness of each current and potential market segment and their competitive position. Portfolio analysis is a useful tool for tourist destination management and can help focus marketing and promotion activities. In a study of Portugal as a tourist destination, examples of the factors used on the attractiveness axis included market size, market growth rate, disposable income per capita, average daily spending, seasonality, distance from destination, benefits sought by tourists when they travel abroad, and accessibility by air. To measure competitiveness, factors such as levels of prices, travel costs to destination, and quality of services, products, and benefits of tourism were included in the matrices. The study indicated that Portugal is most competitive in Spain, followed by France and the United Kingdom, suggesting that it has different levels of competitiveness for various tourism-generating markets.[151]

In conclusion, while portfolio-management models have weaknesses and limitations, they provide an additional tool to assist managers in anticipating cash flows and making resource-allocation decisions. Hotel and restaurant-chain executives may find them especially useful in determining how to allocate resources among a variety of hotel or restaurant brands. Airline and cruise line executives might conduct similar analyses of particular market segments. Finally, not-for-profit tourism organizations can use the analysis for destination management. The key is to apply portfolio techniques in the way that is most useful to the organization in combination with other strategic tools.

KEY POINTS SUMMARY

- Corporate-level strategy focuses on the selection of businesses in which the firm will compete and on the tactics used to enter and manage those businesses and other corporate-level resources.

- At the corporate level, primary strategy-formulation responsibilities include setting the direction of the entire organization, formulating a corporate strategy, selecting businesses in which to compete, selecting tactics for diversification and growth, and managing corporate resources and capabilities.

- The three broad approaches to corporate-level strategy are concentration, vertical integration, and diversification, which is divided into two broad categories, related and unrelated. These strategies, and their strengths and weaknesses, were discussed in depth.

- Concentration is associated with a narrow business definition. As long as a company has virtually all of its resource investments in one business area, it is concentrating.

- Concentration strategies allow a company to focus on doing one business very well; however, a key disadvantage is that the company depends on that one business for survival. Consequently, most successful organizations abandon their concentration strategies at some point due to market saturation, excess resources for which they need to find a use, or some other reason.

- Vertical integration is a strategy that involves an organization becoming its own supplier (backward integration) or customer/distributor (forward integration). Compared to other corporate-level strategies, vertical integration has not been found to be highly profitable because it reduces strategic flexibility.

- According to the theory of transaction-cost economics, if required resources can be obtained from a competitive open market without allocating an undue amount of time or other resources to the contracting process or contract enforcement, it is probably in the best interests of an organization to buy from the market instead of vertically integrating.

- Diversification that stems from common markets, functions served, technologies, or products and services is referred to as related diversification. For a related-diversification strategy to have its full positive impact, synergy must be created. In addition to some form of relatedness, organizational fit is required, as are actions on the part of managers to actually make synergy a reality.

- Unrelated diversification is not based on commonality among the activities of the corporation. It was a very popular strategy during the 1950s, 1960s, and the early 1970s. However, research results seem to indicate that it did not lead to the high performance that many executives had expected.

- Mergers and acquisitions are the quickest way to diversify; however, they are fraught with difficulties, and most of them fail to meet the expectations of the firms involved. Nevertheless, friendly acquisitions between companies that have complementary skills or resources, executed after a thorough due-diligence process, are more likely to succeed.

- Many firms eventually come to a point at which slow growth, declining profits, or some other crisis forces corporate-level managers to rethink their portfolio of organizations. The result of this process is usually some form of restructuring.

- Some of the most common restructuring approaches include turnaround strategies and downsizing, refocusing corporate assets on distinctive competencies, Chapter 11 reorganization, leveraged buyouts, and changes to organizational design.

- Portfolio management tools help top executives manage a portfolio of businesses. They are flexible enough to incorporate a variety of strategic variables, but they should be used with caution and only in combination with other tools of strategic management.

REVIEW QUESTIONS

1. Describe the three basic corporate-level strategies.

2. What are the strengths and weaknesses of a concentration strategy? What are the strengths and weaknesses of a vertical integration strategy?

3. How is a vertical integration strategy like a concentration strategy? How is it like an unrelated diversification strategy?

4. What is the difference between forward and backward integration? Which is likely to be more profitable for hospitality firms? Why?

5. Why is an unrelated diversification strategy generally not a good idea?

6. What is required for a related diversification strategy to produce synergy? Please explain.

7. What are 10 common reasons for mergers and acquisitions? What are some of the major reasons that mergers and acquisitions often produce unsatisfactory results?

8. Which of the major restructuring techniques is most likely to provide rapid results? Defend your answer.

9. Is downsizing or downscoping typically a more appropriate restructuring technique? Why? Also, what are some of the ill effects from layoffs? How can an organization avoid layoffs and still reduce labor costs?

10. Why do you think Chapter 11 doesn't work out for most firms?

11. What are some of the key factors that lead to success in restructuring, regardless of the technique used to restructure?

CRITICAL THINKING AND APPLICATION QUESTIONS

1. Pick 10 hospitality firms and then investigate which corporate strategy they are currently pursuing: concentration, vertical integration, or diversification. A good source for company information is Hoover's, Inc., a business research company that provides information on companies and industries available on its web site: *www.hoovers.com*. The Nestle Library at Cornell University's School of Hotel Administration also maintains a web site that provides links to key players in various hospitality industry segments at *www.hotelschool.cornell.edu/research/library/links*.

   Put your analysis in a chart as follows:

FIRM (LIST 10)	CONCENTRATION	VERTICAL INTEGRATION	DIVERSIFICATION

   Was it easy to identify a strategy, or did some firms pursue several strategies at the same time (i.e., vertical integration and diversification)? What did you discover about the various firms? Is there a more or less popular strategy among the firms you picked? What does this tell you about creating value in hospitality firms?

2. Select a recent industry merger or acquisition. Is this a successful or unsuccessful merger or acquisition? Why? List some of the factors that you believe have led to the success or failure of the merger or acquisition you selected.

3. First read the section of Chapter 6 on portfolio management. Autonomous divisions (or profit centers) of an organization make up what is called a business portfolio. When a firm's divisions compete in different industries, a separate strategy is often developed for each business. The Boston Consulting Group (BCG) Matrix graphically portrays differences among divisions in terms of relative market share position and industry or business growth rate. Select a large, diversified hospitality firm and develop a Boston Consulting Group (BCG) Portfolio Matrix for all of the businesses in which the corporation is involved. Based on your matrix, briefly discuss patterns of profits and cash flow. Also offer strategy recommendations.

   Steps:

   1. Divide the firm into divisions or unique product market segments.

   2. Measure the growth rate of each division.

   $$\text{Growth Rate, year x} = \frac{\{(\text{Market Size, year x}) - (\text{Market Size, year x} - 1)\}}{\text{Market Size, year X} - 1} \times 100$$

3. Measure the relative market share of each division

$$\text{Division Relative Market Share, year x} = \frac{\text{Division Sales} \cdot \text{year x}}{\text{Largest Competitor's sales, year x}}$$

For example, a market share ratio of 2 means the division has a relative market share twice that of its leading competitor. A ratio of .5 means the division has a relative market share half of that of its leading rival.

4. Position each division along the matrix dimensions.

Plot growth rate on the vertical axis and relative market share on the horizontal axis.

It is not uncommon to use 10 percent as the line of demarcation between high and low growth rate. A corporate target or the average market growth rate can also be used as the middle point. For the horizontal axis, a relative market share of 1.0 is often used to demarcate high from low.

5. Plot contribution bubbles.

Plotting the growth rate versus relative market share will only give pinpoint locations on the matrix. A helpful technique is to plot bubbles around these points to indicate the relative size of each division in terms of its contribution to total firm sales or profitability.

$$\text{Relative size of bubble} = \frac{\text{Division sales or profitability}}{\text{Total firm sales or profitability}}$$

6. You should now be able to produce a matrix similar to the one in Figure 6.3.

CHAPTER 7

STRATEGY IMPLEMENTATION THROUGH INTERORGANIZATIONAL RELATIONSHIPS AND MANAGEMENT OF FUNCTIONAL RESOURCES

YOU SHOULD BE ABLE TO DO THE FOLLOWING AFTER READING THIS CHAPTER:

1. Identify the advantages and disadvantages of interorganizational relationships.

2. Understand how firms in a tourism cluster work together.

3. Explain what factors affect the strategic importance of various stakeholders.

4. Know the guidelines for deciding which stakeholders are most attractive for the formation of partnerships.

5. List effective partnering and inclusion strategies for key stakeholder groups.

FEATURE STORY

THE MARRIAGE OF DEVELOPMENT PARTNERS

Lights, camera, action! The W Hollywood Hotel and Residences is a dense, urban, mixed-use project that was more than six years in the planning stage. This urban redevelopment project sits at the famous intersection of Hollywood and Vine in the heart of historic Hollywood, California. Gatehouse Capital and Legacy Partners are the developers; W Hotels of Starwood Hotels and Resorts is the operator; and HEI Hospitality Fund and the California Public Employees' Retirement System (CalPERS) are the project capital partners.

The project utilizes a combination of city assistance, private developer and investor capital, and private and public (both state and federal government) financing. The $600 million project contains a Metro station and includes a W Hotel, retail space (including a health spa, nightclub, pool bar, and high-profile restaurant), apartments, high-rise condominium flats and penthouses with concierge services, and 30,000 square feet of advertising signage attached to the hotel. "We hope to greatly enhance the social design and economic fabric of Hollywood by bridging the glamorous Hollywood past with its hip urban vibe of the future," notes the CEO of Gatehouse Capital. This high-margin, low-volume real estate development firm specializes in upscale hotels and is the largest third-party developer of W hotels. One of its partners, HEI Hospitality, is a leading hospitality investment firm, owning and operating 28 first-class and full-service hotels in the United States. CalPERS is the largest pension fund in the United States and owns more than $250 billion worth of stock, bonds, funds, private equity, and real estate.

Mixed-use developments are complex by their very nature, requiring coordination among an array of different partners. Developers, equity partners, and lenders are interested in integrated projects like the W Hollywood to reduce construction costs and permanent debt as quickly as possible, thus minimizing their risk. As a result, projects with mixed-use components are widespread in the industry's upper upscale and luxury segments. In addition, high-net-worth consumers are willing to pay 24 to 40 percent more for residences when the project includes a premium-brand hotel in the mix.

Synergy in a mixed-use development is often created by having complementary project components that enhance revenue streams. The restaurant and spa at the W complement the hotel and condos. But, planning and coordinating complex development projects when you have integrated ownership, along with operating and management agreements, poses challenges. Many aspects of these complex projects involve shared land and common mechanical systems and facilities, necessitating careful advance planning and substantial agreement on the details.

Given the interdependence of the components of a mixed-use project such as the W Hollywood Hotel and Residences, each of the developers (and each of their lenders and equity partners) needs to build partnerships with other co-developers to ensure that all parties perform their development, construction, and financing roles. Some have likened the relationship between owners and contractors to a marriage, "where both parties have to learn to compromise and get along to accomplish common goals—and like marriages, most disputes are over time and money." Regardless of the complexity and risk, this new development is a once-in-a-lifetime project. "We are creating something entirely different than anything in the market with a world-class team and collection of brands," according to Gatehouse Capital's CEO.[1]

DISCUSSION QUESTIONS:

1. What are some of the advantages and disadvantages of developing mixed-use projects with so many different types of partners?

2. What general advice would you offer developers about when and with whom to partner?

INTRODUCTION

As the W Hollywood's mixed-use development demonstrates, formation of partnerships is one way to take advantage of opportunities that arise in the external environment. Some business projects may even be infeasible unless several different developers, lenders, and equity partners are involved. Productive interorganizational relationships can be sources of competitive advantage. The interdependent nature of tourism, composed of complementary sectors, such as lodging, transportation, food and beverage, attractions, recreation, leisure, travel organizers, government tourist organizations, and wholesale travel agencies, makes the management of alliances and cooperative relationships a critical skill.

Since 1841, when Thomas Cook packaged the first tour, hospitality and tourism enterprises have relied on long-term cooperative alliances with one another.[2] Cooperative interfirm relationships, so common in the industry, involve two firms working together for mutual strategic value. Companies may also develop competitive advantages through superior acquisition, development, and management of internal resources and capabilities, as discussed in Chapter 4. Internal and external approaches to strategy implementation are not mutually exclusive. That is, firms use both approaches simultaneously. Hospitality firms compete energetically but are quick to forge cooperative alliances when necessary.

The focus of this chapter is on *strategy implementation*. It presupposes that the firm has established an appropriate strategic direction and strategies at the corporate and business levels, as well as a growth strategy. The organization then needs to develop specific tactics for executing those strategies. The first section in this chapter emphasizes the collaborative nature of the tourism industry, the role of interorganizational relationships in the successful execution of strategies. The second section deals with the methods of effectively managing relationships with external stakeholders and the selection of partners. The chapter concludes with how companies can manage resources in the functional areas so as to develop competitive advantage. Taken together, these sections provide a wealth of ideas that can help firms achieve competitive success as they implement their strategies.

Chapter 2 introduced common forms of interorganizational relationships, including joint ventures, networks, consortia, alliances, trade groups, and interlocking directorates (see Table 2.4 for a review of these terms). All of these arrangements represent various types of partnerships; therefore, the term *partnership* will be used interchangeably with interorganizational relationship in the remainder of this text. Partnerships can help organizations achieve many of the same objectives that are sought through mergers and acquisitions. Some of the most commonly cited reasons for acquisitions are that they can lead to sales growth, increased earnings, or a balance in a portfolio of businesses.[3] Working in partnership with other firms can also help establish a destination as a desirable travel site.

INTERORGANIZATIONAL RELATIONSHIPS AND THE TOURISM CLUSTER

The travel industry is the world's largest because it is composed of a complex and diverse variety of types of organizations. These firms must work together to provide the overall experience in what is called a *tourism cluster* or overall system, and thus the motivation to partner is particularly great. Tourism clusters are geographic concentrations of competing, complementary, and

HOSPITALITY FOCUS

BARRA HONDA NATIONAL PARK: TOURISM CLUSTER

Visitors to the Barra Honda National Park find services that are typically nonexistent in these locations: a local-food restaurant, lodging, camping facilities within a natural dry forest, a deer nursery, a handicraft shop, a parking area, and local guides. All of these services are the responsibility of a pro-development association, made up of community members, and are offered on the park periphery to leave the natural reserve untouched. Additionally, this cluster of tourism organizations is voluntarily involved in controlling fires within the park and reforesting with pochote (*Bombacopsis quinatum*) trees. Finally, training is provided in such diverse topics as food handling, English-language skills, fire control, and soil conservation.[4]

interdependent firms. The industry can be divided into three types of organizational sectors that work cooperatively:

1. Direct providers of travel services
2. Support services or suppliers to the industry
3. Tourism development organizations, agencies, and institutions that affect provider firms, support services organizations, and the traveler[5]

These organizational sectors can represent an important competitive advantage for a city, region, or country. Figure 7.1 illustrates the cooperative system of a tourism cluster in Costa Rica. At the center of the Costa Rican tourism cluster are the motivations to visit the country. In a circle around motivations are industry sectors with a direct interface with tourists. These are the lodging, transportation, food and beverage, attractions, and promotion sectors. In the peripheral circle are support services, training, support organizations, and transportation infrastructure. These sectors are important to the service ultimately received by tourists, although they do not have a direct interaction with visitors. Development and enhancement of the tourism clusters provide benefits to all businesses as they share information and help establish a destination as desirable for travelers. A detailed illustration of this cooperation can be seen in the Barra Honda National Park of Costa Rica. (See the "Hospitality Focus" boxed section above.)

Advantages and Disadvantages of Interorganizational Relationships

Becoming world class means joining the world class. Success in the global economy derives not just from meeting high standards for competition in world contests, but also from strong relationships—networks that link to global markets and build collective local strength.[6]

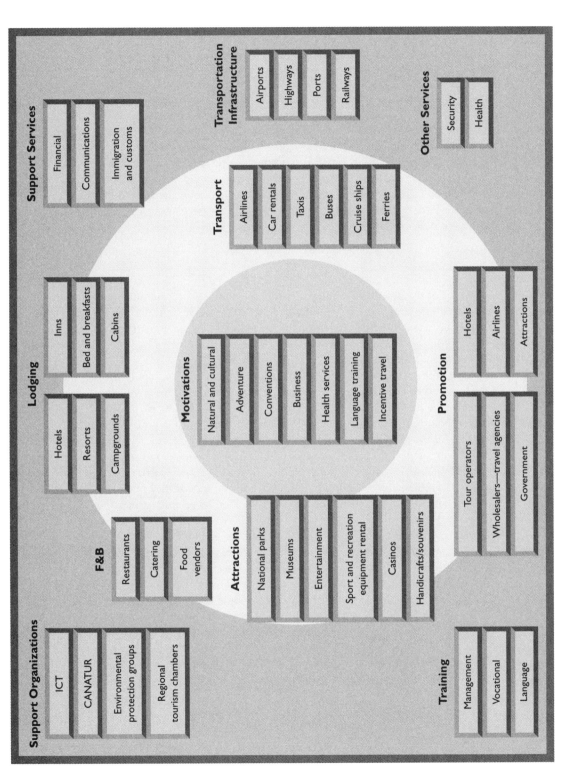

FIGURE 7.1 Tourism cluster in Costa Rica

Source: C. Enz, C. Inman, and M. Lankau, "Strategic Social Partnerships for Change: A Framework For Building Sustainable Growth in Developing Countries," in P. Christopher Earley and Harbir Singh (ed.), *Innovations in Cross-Cultural Management*, p. 206. Copyright © 2000 by Sage Publications, Inc. Reprinted by permission of Sage Publications, Inc.

HOSPITALITY FOCUS

RESOURCE SHARING IN THE DEBSWANA AND BOTSWANA JOINT VENTURE

Debswana Diamond Company Ltd. is a unique equal partnership between the Government of the Republic of Botswana and De Beers Centenary AG (50-50 public/private). The company primarily mines, recovers, and sorts diamonds. In an effort to introduce diversity, Debswana initiated plans for a $31.75 million, 100-room, five-star hotel project, the most ambitious undertaking of its kind in Botswana. The government awarded Debswana a casino and hotel license. It also allocated the diamond company a prime site at the edge of the Chobe Game Park. Debswana believes a luxury hotel at the site will improve quality access to game viewing, create jobs, and provide subsequent downstream economic activity.[7]

Many of the potential advantages of interorganizational relationships are summarized in Table 7.1. These advantages are most easily illustrated through joint ventures, a form of interorganizational relationship that results in a separate, jointly owned entity. Consequently, many of the examples that follow are joint ventures. However, most of the advantages are also available to some degree through the other types of partnerships.

One of the primary advantages of interorganizational relationships is that they allow firms to gain access to particular resources. Examples of resource sharing are easy to find. Disney teamed up with the American Automobile Association (AAA) to provide a Disney-style multipurpose rest area for travelers.[8] Restaurateur Wolfgang Puck partnered with Schwan's Food Company to build his brand in the frozen-food aisles of grocery stores.[9] CBS formed joint ventures with Twentieth Century Fox to develop videotapes and with Home Box Office (owned by Time Inc.) and Columbia Pictures (owned by Coca-Cola) to develop motion pictures.[10] All of these joint ventures by CBS were similar in that they resulted in related diversification and drew on the combined strengths of all joint-venture partners. Another example of resource sharing is found in a joint venture between the government of Botswana and Debswana, a diamond mining company. (See the "Hospitality Focus" boxed section above.)

When two businesses have strengths in different areas, *resource complementarity* occurs. Resource complementarity is helpful in partnerships just as it is in mergers and acquisitions.[11] Complementary skills, in particular, can help increase speed to market. If two companies have strengths in different areas, by combining those strengths, they can save a lot of time in creating or expanding services.

For example, Canyon Capital Realty Advisors invests in a wide range of real estate property types, including retail, entertainment, multifamily, industrial, office, hospitality, land, mobile home, and mixed-use. Canyon Capital furnished a senior bridge loan to Downtown Resorts LLC for a comprehensive renovation of Lady Luck Casino Hotel in Las Vegas. They also made a $15 million mezzanine loan to Brickman Associates for the purchase and prerenovation of Washington, D.C.'s historic St. Regis Hotel from Starwood Hotels & Resorts Worldwide Inc. During the past several years, Canyon Capital has completed eight transactions with Brickman, for a combined transaction value of $410 million. These partnerships give both companies opportunities for return while taking advantage of distinctive competencies and expertise.[12] (See the "Hospitality Focus" boxed section on page 260.)

TABLE 7.1 Potential Advantages of Participation in Interorganizational Relationships

Gain access to a particular resource	Firms form relationships to gain access to a particular resource, such as capital, employees with specialized skills, intimate knowledge of a market, or an excellent location or facility.
Speed to market	Firms with complementary skills, such as one firm that is operationally strong and another that has strong market access, partner to increase speed to market in hopes of capturing first-mover advantages.
Enter a foreign market	Partnering with a local company is often the only practical way to gain new access to a foreign market.
Economies of scale	In many industries, high fixed costs require firms to find partners to expand production volume.
Risk and cost sharing	Many types of partnerships allow two or more firms to share the risk and cost of a particular business endeavor.
Service development Learning	Partnering can provide firms the opportunity to pool skills to develop new services. Interorganizational relationships often provide participants with the opportunity to "learn" from their partners (e.g., human resource management in an unfamiliar country).
Strategic flexibility	Creation of partnerships can provide a valuable alternative to acquisitions, because they do not have to be as permanent. They also require less of an internal resource commitment, which frees up resources for other uses.
Collective political clout	Interorganizational relationships can increase collective clout and influence governments into adopting policies favorable to their industries or circumstances.
Neutralizing or blocking competitors	Through a partnership, firms can gain the competencies and market power that are needed to neutralize or block the moves of a competitor.

Source: Adapted from B. B. Barringer and J. S. Harrison, "Walking a Tightrope: Creating Value through Interorganizational Relationships," *Journal of Management* 26 (2000): 385, with permission from Elsevier.

HOSPITALITY FOCUS

PEETS COFFEE & TEA INC. AND STANFORD UNIVERSITY PARTNERSHIP

In addition to the advantages associated with resource sharing, partnerships can lead to economies of scale through sharing physical facilities, where one firm may not be able to achieve those economies on its own. Peet's Coffee & Tea Inc., a specialty coffee roaster with 136 retail stores, opened its first on-campus branded coffee unit in 1966 at the University of California at Berkeley. A partnership with Stanford University followed one year later. The chain's executive vice president, Bill Lilla, says brand association with colleges and universities raised the concept's image because campus dining programs are traditionally creative, intelligent, and aggressive. He calls the early partnerships with universities a key factor in advancing the brand's growth. Today the company sells its coffee through multiple channels of distribution, including grocery stores; home delivery; office, restaurant, and foodservice accounts; and company-owned and operated stores in six states.[13]

As the Peet's Coffee & Tea Inc., example shows, a partnership provides participants with ample opportunity to learn from each other. Learning is considered to be one of the most important reasons to pursue interorganizational relationships.[14] Teaching restaurant brands how to work in college foodservice is a challenge. At Ohio State University, striking deals to bring in brands and profits has meant steep learning curves for chains. "You have to teach some companies how college foodservice runs, how to get involved in events and the school's calendar," notes an official at Ohio State.[15] The Ohio Union includes brands such as Freshens, Wall Street Deli, Wendy's, and The Steak Escape.

If shared among the partners, the impact of risk and costs can be minimized on any one organization if the venture should prove to be unsuccessful. Consequently, compared to mergers or internal venturing, joint ventures are sometimes considered a less risky diversification option. Partnerships also allow firms to pool their resources for development of entirely new services, which can lead to a higher level of competitiveness.

Because partnerships often have an ending date or can be canceled with a minimum of difficulty, firms may be able to retain their strategic flexibility by deciding whether to continue a particular venture or allocate venture-related resources elsewhere. Partnerships also have political advantages, because companies can combine their clout with respect to influencing government leaders and agencies. Trade groups and associations, such as the Cruise Lines International Association (CLIA), the American Gaming Association, and the International Spa Association (ISPA), provide a voice for various subindustry members offering educational, networking, and in some cases lobbying efforts. The Travel Business Roundtable (TBR), established in the 1990s to educate elected officials about the important economic and social contributions of the travel industry, worked in partnership with the Travel Industry Association (TIA) to support legislative efforts that advance travel and tourism in the United States.[16] (See the "Hospitality Focus" boxed section on page 261.)

Finally, partnerships may be formed as firms try to improve their competitive positions against rivals by locking in exclusive distribution arrangements or by depriving competitors of essential supplies. Premium Ingredients Group, for instance, signed an exclusive distribution agreement with NutraSweet Company to sell aspartame in the United States and Canada.

TIA AND TBR: SUPPORTING LEGISLATION TO ENCOURAGE INTERNATIONAL TRAVEL TO THE UNITED STATES

HOSPITALITY FOCUS

The TIA and the TBR support the Improving Public Diplomacy through International Travel Act. This legislation is aimed at improving America's image abroad by encouraging international travelers to visit the United States. Congressman Sam Farr (D-Calif.) and Congressman Jon Porter (R-Nev.) introduced legislation and were joined by several industry leaders who applauded the efforts by the co-chairs of the Congressional Travel and Tourism Caucus. By authoring this legislation, Representatives Farr and Porter demonstrate the great value in international travel even beyond the jobs and economic value created. "Our national image abroad has seen a steady decline for many years, and it's long overdue that we take active steps to improve it," said Rep. Farr. "I know from my years in the Peace Corps that people-to-people contact is the best way to genuinely understand another culture. With fewer international visitors coming to America, we're missing that crucial link. This bill seeks to improve our image by encouraging foreign visitors to visit Main Street, U.S.A." According to the TIA, travel is one of the few industries that touches all 50 states and contributes to all local economies. The decline in foreign visitors has cost the United States $94 billion in visitor spending, $15.6 billion in tax receipts, $26 billion in payroll, and an estimated 194,000 jobs.[17]

Capital Beverage Group and Isbre Holding Corporation agreed to exclusive distribution of bottled Norwegian spring water in the District of Columbia.[18] These actions can also deter the entry of new competitors.[19] Despite their strategic strengths, partnerships may be limiting, in that one organization has only partial control over the activity and enjoys only a percentage of the growth and profitability that are sometimes created. In addition, partnerships sometimes create high administrative costs associated with developing the multiparty equity arrangement and managing the venture once it is undertaken.[20]

Company culture clashes can erode cooperation between firms and prevent true partnering from taking place. For instance, partnerships between university foodservice and brand restaurants, while potentially profitable, as is the case with Peet's, can be challenging. Teaching corporate restaurant foodservice managers about university culture can frustrate both sides, says the director of dining at Vanderbilt University in Nashville, Tennessee. "They're used to cookie-cutter systems."[21] While learning a different culture can be challenging, chain restaurants bring needed marketing and training to these noncommercial markets.

Another limiting factor is that joint decision making can be slow and result in too many compromises. Also, evidence shows that some types of partnerships may not be desirable in particular environments. Harvard University, the third largest self-operated college foodservice organization, for example, downplays commercial branding in its partnerships with restaurants, preferring to develop its own brands. They offer Starbucks Coffee, for example, but do not permit the chain to provide logo items like cups and napkins.[22] In fact, partnerships may be no more successful than nonjoint ventures, as one researcher discovered when examining joint ventures in the petroleum industry.[23]

Partnerships also entail a risk of opportunism by venture partners. Unfortunately, a stronger venture partner may take advantage of a smaller or less experienced partner, structuring the deal so that the benefits accrue unfairly to the stronger partner. Well-written contracts alleviate the risk of this imbalance but cannot eliminate it. The director of dining services at the University of California at Santa Barbara has had her share of unpleasant partnerships. She experienced one chain that neglected to pay rent or compensate the building contractors and another partner that failed to comply when asked to change a menu item.[24]

As in mergers and acquisitions, organizational fit is important to interorganizational relationships. Lack of organizational fit can reduce cooperation and lead to venture failure. Potential differences among partners range from dissimilar ethics to different languages to disparate managerial techniques to incompatible operating methods.[25] Trust among partners is also critical. If trust breaks down, the venture can fall apart. Also, companies are more likely to form partnerships with firms they trust. Consequently, partners must manage their interorganizational relationships carefully so as not to violate trust.[26]

In summary, while interorganizational relationships have both benefits and drawbacks relative to other strategic options, many firms have found that they are essential to competitive success.[27] Partnerships are an essential form of business in the hospitality industry. Consequently, partnerships of all types are popular, and many types of partnerships, such as joint ventures, are increasing in use.

Stakeholder Management and the Selection of Partners

Managers have limited resources, and one of the most important of these is time. Clearly, managers do not have time to pursue interorganizational relationships with all stakeholders. Consequently, deciding when and with whom to partner are significant managerial decisions. In general, organizations should consider partnering with stakeholders that are strategically important. This means that these stakeholders significantly affect the firm and its future success. Several factors, outlined in Figure 7.2, can increase the strategic significance of a stakeholder, thus making partnering more attractive. One of the most common reasons to partner is to acquire resources, and many of the interorganizational forms that have been described in this section can facilitate resource transfer. One of the most important resources a company may need is knowledge.

Partnerships can facilitate organizational learning. However, stakeholders also become important when they hold formal power, which means that they have a legal or contractual right to make decisions that affect some part of the organization (i.e., regulatory agencies or governments). Hotel developers may need to partner with the government to get business done. However, some industry experts caution that partnering with a government is generally not attractive because there is a distortion of the true asset value for the developer. As Art Buser, president of Lodging Capital Markets—Americas for Jones Lang LaSalle Hotels, notes, "The government gets you into a deal, but usually the developer doesn't get a good return when it exits."[28] A recent effort by the Swiss Federal Institute of Technology in Zurich to preserve

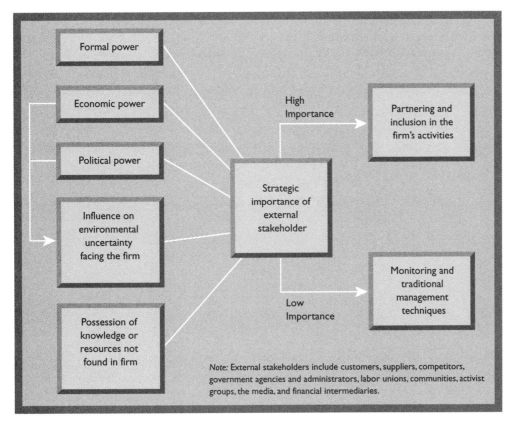

FIGURE 7.2 Strategic importance of stakeholders and the decision to partner

heritage sites in China may show new and promising ways in which partnerships can enhance long-term tourism development. (See the "Hospitality Focus" boxed section on page 266.)

UNCERTAINTY

Another factor that can dramatically affect the strategic importance of a particular stakeholder is its influence on the organizational uncertainty facing the firm.[29] For example, organizations are uncertain of the level of future demand; the price elasticity of demand; the strategic moves of competitors, suppliers, activists, unions, and other key stakeholders; the nature of future government regulations; and the ability to secure adequate resources, whether physical, financial, or human.

Stakeholders that have high economic or political power have more influence on the environmental uncertainty facing a firm. Consequently, arrows are drawn from the economic-power and political-power boxes to the environmental-uncertainty box in Figure 7.2. For example, a customer can quit buying from an organization, or a bank can sever a financial agreement. These are examples of exerting economic power.

Stakeholders with political power have the ability to influence events and outcomes that have an impact on the organization. In one example, some of Wal-Mart's angry competitors

TABLE 7.2 **Examples of Tactics for Managing and Partnering with External Stakeholders**

STAKEHOLDER	TRADITIONAL MANAGEMENT	PARTNERING AND INCLUSION STRATEGIES
Customers	Customer service departments Marketing and marketing research On-site visits 800 numbers Long-term contracts	Involvement on teams to create or refine services Joint planning sessions Joint training/service programs Financial investments Appointments to board (interlocking directorate)
Suppliers	Purchasing departments Encourage competition among suppliers Sponsor new suppliers Threat of vertical integration Long-term contracts	Involvement on design teams for new services Integration of ordering system Shared information systems Coordinated quality control Appointments to board (interlocking directorate)
Competitors	Direct competition based on differentiation Intelligence systems Corporate spying and espionage (ethical problems)	Joint ventures or consortia for research and development, manufacturing, marketing, etc. Alliances to pursue a variety of objectives Trade associations for sharing information and collective lobbying Informal price leadership or collusion (may be illegal)
Government agencies and administrators	Legal, tax, or government-relations offices Lobbying and political action committees Campaign contributions Personal gifts to politicians (ethical problems)	Jointly or government-sponsored research Joint foreign development projects Problem-solving task forces on sensitive issues Appointment of retired government officials to board

TABLE 7.2 (*Continued*)

Local communities	Community relations offices Public relations advertising Involvement in community service Donations to local causes	Task forces to work on special community needs Cooperative training and educational programs Development committees/boards Joint employment programs
Activist groups	Organizational decisions to satisfy demands Public/political relations efforts Financial donations	Consultation with representatives on sensitive issues Joint development programs Appointments to the board
The media	Public/political relations efforts Media experts/press releases	Exclusive interviews or early release of information Inclusion in social events and other special treatment
Unions	Union avoidance through excellent treatment of employees Hiring professional negotiators Mutually satisfactory labor contracts Chapter XI protection to renegotiate contract	Contract clauses that link pay to performance Joint committees on safety and other issues Joint industry/labor panels Inclusion on management committees Appointments to the board
Financial intermediaries	Financial reports Close correspondence Finance and accounting departments High-level financial officer Audits	Inclusion in management decisions requiring financing Contracts and linkages with other clients of financier Shared ownership of projects Appointments to the board

Source: Adapted from J. S. Harrison and C. H. St. John, "Managing and Partnering with External Stakeholders," *Academy of Management Executive* (May 1996): 53. Used with permission of Academy of Management in the format Textbook via Copyright Clearance Center.

SWISS FEDERAL INSTITUTE OF TECHNOLOGY INVESTS
IN CHINA'S CULTURAL HERITAGE

HOSPITALITY
FOCUS

Winner of the Travel + Leisure Global Vision award for cultural preservation, the Swiss Federal Institute of Technology was recognized for preserving an endangered cultural site in China. Founded on the idea that heritage sites can be valuable economic resources, the Institute invested $1.3 million in the Shaxi Rehabilitation Project. At a time when newer, faster, and bigger seem to be the guiding principles of Chinese development, this project appears to be challenging the trend toward modernization in the hopes of preserving tradition.

On the 1,500-year-old Tea and Horse Caravan Trail in the Shaxi Valley, an ancient market village is being carefully restored. The village of Sideng first gained prominence in the seventh century as an important economic nexus for southwest China and Tibet. By the mid-20th century, however, trade was dwindling, and the town's original character was quickly eroding. Thanks to the efforts of the Institute, a Buddhist temple, a theater, two village gates, and many other centuries-old architectural masterpieces from the Ming and Qing dynasties have been restored. The next challenge is developing a sustainable infrastructure to attract tourism dollars to the town.[30]

have convinced communities and governments in several locations in the northeastern United States that Wal-Mart, by causing small businesses to suffer, harms the community more than it helps it. The result has been adverse legislation, causing Wal-Mart to lose several new locations for its stores.[31]

Environmental uncertainty occurs when a firm is unable to predict the actions of external stakeholders and other external influences. One way to understand the role of environmental uncertainty is to imagine a situation in which managers knew everything that would happen with regard to customers, suppliers, unions, competitors, regulators, financial intermediaries, and every other relevant external force for the next year. In such a hypothetical situation, management of the company would be a straightforward task of generating maximum revenues at minimum costs so that profits are maximized. Management is difficult because our hypothetical world does not exist. Managers have to make decisions without knowing how customers, suppliers, and competitors will react. Customers are particularly important, because their actions have so much impact on how the firm will perform. In other words, customers have a large influence on the uncertainty the firm is facing.

While environmental uncertainty often originates in the broad environment (e.g., economic cycles, social trends), organizations feel most of its influence through external stakeholders. For example, gasoline price increases affect consumers' purchasing power. Automobile travel is not the only casualty of rising fuel prices; so are automobile sales and car purchase preferences. These fuel costs also produce a shock in the broad environment of the lodging industry. According to one study, hotels experience a decline in rooms demand when gasoline prices rise.[32] Nevertheless, not all lodging operators need to worry that jumps in gasoline prices will affect their demand levels. The study showed that the effects of gas price changes are magnified in hotels located along highways and outside of major metropolitan locations—in short, those that depend on automobile access.

Establishment of the strategic priority of stakeholders provides direction as to the amount of attention they should be given during the development of strategy. However, prioritizing stakeholders also provides clues concerning the types of strategies that may be appropriate in managing them. Strategically important stakeholders should be seriously considered for partnerships. According to Pfeffer and Salancik, two well-known organizational researchers, "The typical solution to problems of interdependence and uncertainty involves increasing the mutual control over each other's activities."[33] Companies may also want to consider including them in organizational processes, such as including a supplier on a research-and-development team to create a new product. Less-important stakeholders should not be ignored. They should be monitored and managed in more traditional ways.

Buffering versus Partnering

Organizations use two basic postures when managing relationships with external stakeholders. One posture is partnering, and the other involves *buffering* the organization from environmental uncertainty through techniques designed to stabilize and predict environmental influences and, in essence, raise the boundaries. They soften the jolts that might otherwise be felt as the organization interacts with members of its external environment. For instance, the establishment of a director of diversity is often a buffering technique to respond to concerns about opportunity for minorities in the industry. Buffering techniques focus on planning for and adapting to the environment so that the needs and demands of critical stakeholders are met. Traditional stakeholder management techniques include (see Table 7.2 for more examples):

- Marketing research
- Creation of special departments to handle specific areas (e.g., legal, recruiting, purchasing)
- Public-relations efforts
- Financial donations
- Advertising efforts to ensure regulatory compliance

Partnering, the other approach to stakeholder management, requires selecting stakeholders with attractive resources; with high levels of formal, economic, or political power; and/or with a large influence on environmental uncertainty facing the firm. Partnering activities allow companies to build bridges with their stakeholders in the pursuit of common goals, whereas traditional stakeholder management techniques (buffering) simply reduce shocks and facilitate the satisfaction of stakeholder needs and/or demands.

There is much to be learned from the not-for-profit sector on how to facilitate inclusive partnerships. Faced with the dilemma of preserving the environment versus obtaining economic development, many island communities forgo the preservation of their fragile

HOSPITALITY FOCUS

SEACOLOGY: PROTECTING THE ENVIRONMENT WHILE HELPING LOCAL COMMUNITIES

Seacology understands the need to provide a win-win situation to local island communities that allow them to protect the environment, while offering island residents tangible benefits for caring. Island residents are often prone to succumbing to development pressures when faced with a choice between economic prosperity and natural resource preservation. To facilitate mutual benefit, Seacology offers islanders schools, health clinics, and sanitation systems in exchange for legal agreements that prohibit logging, overfishing, and other harmful practices. In Falealupo Samoa, Seacology built a school in exchange for the establishment of a 30,000-acre forest reserve. They constructed a kindergarten in Vuna Village, Fiji in exchange for the establishment of a 4,752-acre forest preserve and two marine protected areas totaling 3,010 acres.

For a $1,000 donation, Seacology also offers travel adventures in which supporters visit project sites along with trips that include land- and sea-based activities such as scuba diving, snorkeling, hiking, and kayaking. Seacology is responsible for preserving roughly 1.8 million acres of marine and island habitat—by devising an inclusive partnering strategy.[34]

environments. One innovative approach to protecting the environment while helping local communities is used by a nonprofit organization called Seacology. (See the "Hospitality Focus" boxed section above.)

Effective Stakeholder Management

It is nearly impossible to be competitive in the lodging industry on a large scale without effective use of interorganizational relationships. Table 7.2 lists examples of traditional stakeholder management techniques as well as partnering techniques, grouped by type of external stakeholder. The rest of this section elaborates on effective management of specific types of stakeholders with an emphasis on the creation of partnerships.

CUSTOMERS

Firms are increasingly trying to include customers more in internal processes or form partnerships with them. Even with the growing recognition that millions of kids between the ages of five and fourteen have direct buying power, estimated at more than $40 billion, many restaurants have not yet learned to value this important stakeholder group by using them in formal product testing.[35] However, chains like Dairy Queen and Red Lobster are involving young people in their design teams. Dairy Queen, eager to improve its status as a snack destination among young people, relied on a special panel of "'tweens" (8- to 12-year-olds) to determine

JONATHAN TISCH, CEO OF LOEWS HOTELS, FOCUSES ON CUSTOMER PARTNERSHIPS

HOSPITALITY FOCUS

Because customers are so vital to organizational success, many firms place their highest priority on satisfying customer needs. Organizations pursue several traditional management tactics to satisfy customers. Among the most important are customer-service departments, marketing research, on-site visits, and service development. Listening to customers is one of the most vital strategies a firm can pursue. In his book, *The Power of We*, Jonathan Tisch, CEO of Loews Hotels, presents his reasons why Loews and other businesses should build partnerships with customers.

According to Tisch, "We've built our success by treating customers as partners." To elaborate on what it means to "treat customers as partners," he has identified three key components:

Communicating from the bottom up: *Businesses must recognize that today's customer isn't content to be merely a passive target of advertising or marketing campaigns. Instead, she actively participates in shaping the popular perception of companies, products, and services through "buzz" and word-of-mouth (positive or negative) perceptions. Companies that want to partner with customers have to change their thinking about marketing from top-down to bottom-up. Rather than trusting in the power of big media to push ideas onto a passive mass audience, they must find ways to generate buzz about their products and services among consumers themselves.*

Focusing on the customer experience: *Companies have traditionally had a product-centric or service-centric view of the marketplace: They concentrated on making excellent products or services, assuming that this would capture the allegiance of customers. Today, this view of competition is simplistic. Most customers don't care about products or services as such; what they care about is the quality of the experience we can help them to enjoy. Partnering with customers demands that companies see the experiences they create through the eyes of customers and find ways to make those experiences as rewarding as possible.*

Linking with customer communities: *Traditional marketing and advertising were oriented to the mass market: The monolithic organization broadcast a message to thousands or millions of individual consumers. Today, more and more companies are recognizing the existence of customer communities—groups of customers who identify with one another, have shared ideas and feelings, and want to help shape their relationship with your business. Partnering with customers includes facilitating the creation of customer communities and making those communities part of your marketing system.*

As Tisch notes, at Loews Hotels, we use all three of these approaches to help turn our customers into partners—people who recognize, trust, and seek out the Loews name whenever they travel.[36]

the Blizzard flavors for the chain, which encompasses more than 5,900 fast-food and frozen-treats outlets.[37] At Red Lobster, after getting initial feedback from children on popular trends and flavors, they developed a variety of items. The dishes are refined based on results from formal product testing with youngsters.[38] Efforts to strengthen linkages with customers often provide significant benefits. (See the "Hospitality Focus" boxed section on page 269.)

SUPPLIERS

Building strong partnerships with key suppliers facilitates competitive advantage and is essential to successful supply-chain management. In fact, recent research has revealed that inefficient management of the supply chain can reduce overall corporate performance.[39] More hospitality firms are discovering that their suppliers can provide knowledge, technical assistance, and joint problem solving.[40] For example, Tyson Foods recently introduced the first of three toolkits, called "foodWISE® – Good For Me,™" for school foodservice operators. The kits provide resources that school foodservice professionals can use in developing wellness policies, such as menu templates, classroom activity guides, and wellness planning tools.[41]

Considering the establishment of strong supplier relationships comes at a time when many firms are downsizing their own corporate purchasing activities and outsourcing key activities to others. Outsourcing allows a firm to leverage its own capabilities by focusing resources on high value-added activities. Scarce management talent and time are not wasted on activities that do not add unique value. In addition, outsourcing provides the potential to reap economies of scale through specialized suppliers.

Outsourcing is often approached as a quick-fix rather than a long-term relationship. Take the owner and general manager of the Charlesmark Hotel in Boston, who used outsourcing to help keep costs down in a tough market. He farmed out sales and marketing, public relations, information technology, maintenance, and some food preparation to outside companies, but he considered this outsourcing to be a short-term solution while his business was getting off the ground in its first year.[42] In contrast, Choice Hotels has developed a web-based system to direct its hotel owners toward preferred vendors of hotel supplies. *Preferred vendors* often provide products or services with special terms or lower prices, in exchange for long-term contracts.

Preferred alliance programs with major vendors are often used as a selling point for franchisees.[43] What distinguishes the more traditional and contractual supplier relationships noted in the Boston hotel example from strong alliances like those developed by many hotel franchisors is that partnering involves technology transfer and training, increased interfirm communication, coordinated quality control, involvement on design teams, and risk sharing. (See the "Hospitality Focus" boxed section on page 271.)

Because of the commitments required to be a true business partner, companies are consolidating by limiting the number of suppliers with which they do business.[44] The partnerships that are likely to last are those where a closer relationship is forged. Strong relationships offer both firms several advantages: Suppliers gain preferential treatment and more market security, while buyers benefit from technological development and better response times.[45] Talking about partnerships between vendors and hotels, Robert Barnard of PKF notes, "Getting the relationship right depends on very careful preparation for the contract and knowing that you've got a good cultural fit. And it's got to be beneficial for both parties." Hoteliers remain wary of outsourced staff who will not necessarily provide the level of loyalty or commitment on which a high-quality establishment relies.[46]

HOSPITALITY FOCUS

HOTEL FRANCHISEES AND PREFERRED VENDOR PROGRAMS

"We want franchisees to have the lowest prices and the widest choice," states a representative from Hilton, when asked about corporate supplier programs. Preferred vendor programs are viewed by some franchisees as a profit center that takes money out of the pockets of franchisees. Choice Hotels has reorganized its preferred vendor program to allow for voting on some vendors by franchisees, and InterContinental Hotel Group works only with a small group of vendors for proprietary items. Balancing the efficiencies of developing a supplier program and also avoiding any hints of improprieties is a challenge for franchisors, particularly when so much money is at stake.

The ChoiceBuys.com portal, for example, is hoping to capture a bigger piece of the $1.5 billion in annual purchases made by the company's independent franchisee hotel owners. Choice Hotels has also begun to resell its hard-won e-commerce expertise to other organizations. Under the PrimarySource.com brand, Choice now offers hotels outside of its franchise base access to the same basic web purchasing system.[47]

In partnerships between foodservice operators and their suppliers, a recent study found that trustworthiness and problem-solving ability were the most critical traits in the relationship. The research, sponsored by the Center for Hospitality Research at Cornell University, also reported that the major barrier to maintaining strong partnerships was the turnover of the vendor representative.[48] Trust becomes particularly critical when a firm builds dependence on a supplier. This situation often surfaces in hotels that rely on vendors to handle their information technology needs. Rapid changes and complexity of information systems in hotel operations make the importance of trust-based supplier relationships all the more important.

COMPETITORS

Competitors pose a difficult stakeholder management problem, because it is often in the best interests of one competitor to cause another competitor to falter. However, to combat increasing levels of global competition and to get a jump on emerging technologies, competitors are joining forces in increasing numbers. In fact, about half of all major alliance deals are among rival firms.[49] They are coming together to form alliances for technological advancement and new-product and new-service development, to enter new or foreign markets, and to pursue a wide variety of other opportunities.[50]

International airlines for some time have been joining forces with competitors to enhance customer service. The underlying motive of some partnerships seems to be to put the remaining firms that are not included in an alliance at a competitive disadvantage. According to one industry analyst, "Regulatory barriers created by firm conduct may be used by groups in the industry as a competitive weapon against other groups."[51] While global alliances are not new, after the industry slump early in the 21st century, U.S. carriers like Delta, Northwest, and

Continental joined together to code-share, allowing customers of partner airlines to earn and redeem frequent flier miles on flights, and airport-lounge members to obtain access to partner lounge facilities.[53] These carriers must still compete on fares and schedules to comply with antitrust laws, and both the U.S. Transportation Department and the Justice Department's antitrust officials have carefully reviewed the alliance. (See the "Hospitality Focus" boxed section above.)

In oligopolies, where a few major rivals dominate an industry, the major firms may cooperate with one another in setting prices. Formal price-setting cooperation among firms is called *collusion*. In the United States and many other countries, collusion is illegal, but companies may still cooperate informally by being careful not to drop prices enough to start a price war. Price wars can damage the profits of all firms in the sector, as demonstrated several times in the airline industry since it was deregulated. Alternatively, some sectors have an established price leader, usually one of the largest companies in the industry, which establishes a pricing pattern that other firms follow.

In some countries and regions, collusion is not illegal, or it is widely practiced despite its illegality. For example, for many years, the Organization of Petroleum Exporting Countries (OPEC) cartel established the price charged for crude oil produced by Middle Eastern countries. Ultimately, the cartel lost some of its power when countries participating in OPEC discovered that great financial rewards were available for individual firms that were willing to violate OPEC agreements.

Working cooperatively with competitors is easier in the hotel industry because of the geographic dispersion of individual properties. Shared resources and cooperative arrangements can be devoted to a particular market, with competition occurring in other areas. The absence of local conflict makes competitor cooperation more effective and eases joint planning, marketing, and development.[54]

GOVERNMENT AGENCIES AND ADMINISTRATORS

Business organizations and governments share many common goals, among them creating a favorable environment for international trade, stable market conditions, a healthy economy, and production of desirable goods and services. Consequently, many organizations form alliances with government agencies and officials to pursue a wide variety of objectives, including alleviating social problems, developing particular parts of cities, or establishing trade policies. Tourism ministries often work cooperatively with hospitality organizations and others to promote a destination or heritage site. (See the "Hospitality Focus" boxed section above.)

Government/business partnerships are widely used outside of the United States, where governments often play a more active role in economic development. One such effort resulted in the formation of the major aerospace company Airbus Industries, jointly owned by aerospace firms from Britain, France, Germany, and Spain. The Japanese Ministry of International Trade and Industry (MITI) targets particular segments of the Japanese industry and provides support for those that are determined to be most closely linked to the growth of the Japanese economy.

The relationship between the Australian Gold Coast City Council and the Gold Coast International Tourism Committee, an association of 18 major destination operators, illustrates the importance of the public and private sectors cooperatively working to market a destination. Promotion of the Gold Coast has relied on formal marketing and informal promotion by chambers of commerce and tourism promotion associations. These efforts are combined with media reports of events and activities, and advertising by real estate developers to complement the relationship between the governmental body and the tourism operators.[56]

Governmental actions can profoundly shape the competitive environment in developing countries. In many instances, the government not only regulates businesses but may also have power through state-owned enterprises. These businesses are quite different from their private-enterprise counterparts, often operating at a substantial loss or with unfair advantages. If we return to the government of Botswana's luxury hotel project mentioned earlier in this chapter, we see that existing hoteliers are critical of the casino project proposed by the half-government-owned Debswana Diamond Company. (See the "Hospitality Focus" boxed section on page 274.)

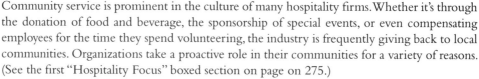

THE GOVERNMENT AND THE DEBSWANA CASINO PROJECT

Existing hoteliers, perhaps worried about the impact of the new complex on their own tourism receipts, were hostile to the Debswana project. The manager of Kasane's The Garden Lodge notes, "This hotel has the potential to destroy the aesthetic value of the boat cruise completely as well as negatively modify the game viewing." Reacting to the criticism, the managing director of the project states, "We are not going to compete with anybody. Why are they so worried? Some of the people who criticize the government for granting us a site within the Chobe National Park are themselves in the park! What exclusive right do they think they have?"[57]

LOCAL COMMUNITIES

Community service is prominent in the culture of many hospitality firms. Whether it's through the donation of food and beverage, the sponsorship of special events, or even compensating employees for the time they spend volunteering, the industry is frequently giving back to local communities. Organizations take a proactive role in their communities for a variety of reasons. (See the first "Hospitality Focus" boxed section on page on 275.)

Community activities are good for employee morale and company image. In addition, healthier and more vibrant communities contribute to better business environments. Other organizations find opportunities to achieve financial or operating objectives while satisfying a need in the local community. (See the second "Hospitality Focus" boxed section on page 275.)

Quasi-public alliances between local governments and business leaders are flourishing across many sections of the United States. For example, the Metro Orlando Economic Development Commission (EDC) represents four central Florida counties. The commission works with government and business leaders to create economic plans and initiatives. With the support of community partners, the EDC has successfully assisted thousands of companies in relocating, expanding, and growing in Metro Orlando. The commission focuses on attracting, retaining and growing targeted industries that have the potential to create high-wage, high-value jobs and to diversify the region's economic base.[58]

Because the hospitality industry can profoundly affect communities and their citizens, not just as an employer but also in altering the physical surroundings and the economics of a location, it is important to involve communities before development begins. Many firms work closely with local organizations not only to support the long-term success of their enterprises, but also to care for the welfare of the local people. For example, the rapid growth of tourism in some communities can result in a shortage of qualified hospitality employees. To address this problem in Scottsdale, Arizona, a partnership was formed between the Hyatt Regency Scottsdale and a community college, city government, school district, and university. The hotel developed an educational program that was instituted at the high school level and leads directly into a two-year associate degree program at the local community college, which transfers to the hotel program at the university.[59] To implement this program, the hotel had to work closely with the school district, and meetings were held regularly for all of the partners

DISNEY GETS TAX BREAKS FOR MANHATTAN DEVELOPMENT INITIATIVES

HOSPITALITY FOCUS

Good relationships with communities and governments can result in favorable local regulation or in tax breaks. For example, the Walt Disney Company received tax breaks and special treatment from the city of New York when the company invested millions of dollars in the development of one of the most crime-filled areas in the city—42nd Street between Times Square and Eighth Avenue in Manhattan. The company constructed a live-production theater, a Disney Store, cinemas, hotels, game parlors, and restaurants.[60] The once-seedy Times Square location now attracts media and entertainment giants like Viacom, Bertelsmann, MTV, and Condé Nast without special tax breaks.

"DINE FOR AMERICA" FUNDS GULF COAST RECOVERY EFFORTS

HOSPITALITY FOCUS

More than 17,000 restaurants—from coffee shops to fine-dining establishments, and from large chains to single-unit independent restaurants—joined "Dine for America" to raise funds for Gulf Coast recovery efforts. A Benefit for the American Red Cross Disaster Relief Fund organized by the National Restaurant Association raised more than $12 million through the nationwide "dine out" day to help those impacted by Hurricanes Katrina and Rita.

The hospitality community also relocated and hired many of the roughly 200,000 displaced hospitality workers who were without jobs after the hurricanes. Restaurants around the country donated a portion of their dinner sales to Share our Strength's Hurricane Katrina Relief Fund. Chefs from New York City and New Orleans joined forces, donating their time and talent to "New Chefs for a New New Orleans," a special fundraising event intended to spur restaurant and hospitality redevelopment in New Orleans. Local and regional raffles, bake sales, and benefits were also evident throughout the country in the aftermath of the hurricanes. While too numerous to detail individually, these and other efforts demonstrate the industry's commitment to community service.[61]

to discuss changes and improvements in the program. The program accomplished its goal of providing qualified and skilled workers to the industry while giving young students an opportunity to explore a career in hospitality.

ACTIVIST GROUPS

Organizations formed with the purpose of advancing a specific cause or causes are called *activist groups*. Activist groups such as The Sierra Club, Greenpeace International, People for the Ethical Treatment of Animals (PETA), the National Association for the Advancement of Colored People (NAACP), the National Organization for Women (NOW), and Mothers Against Drunk Driving (MADD) represent a variety of social and environmental perspectives. *Public-interest groups* (e.g., MADD) represent the position of a broad cross-section of society, whereas *special-interest groups* (e.g., PETA) focus on the needs of specific subgroups. Although these groups are most often seen in an adversarial role relative to the desires of other organizational stakeholders, this does not have to be the case. However, it is difficult for executives to break out of the old mind-set and adopt an attitude of common goal achievement.

As an example, the efforts of public health activists and lawyers to attack the restaurant industry over obesity have led to lawsuits and aggressive name-calling. McDonald's was the target of a lawsuit claiming that the chain was responsible for obesity-related health problems and that fast food, like tobacco, is addictive. McDonald's called the lawsuit frivolous.[62] A spokesperson for the National Council of Chain Restaurants, commenting on the growing movement around healthful menu items and court action, argued, "They've sucked all the money they can out of the tobacco industry, and now they are moving on to other industries. And let's be clear about this: These lawsuits are not about improving public health. It's about making money."[63]

While companies can be the target of criticism from activist groups, businesses that make commitments to important social issues may find it makes good business sense. The NAACP releases its annual Lodging Industry Report Card as a wake-up call for the hotel industry. While many hotel companies have been working to improve diversity within their organizations and utilize minority suppliers, according to the NAACP, the lodging industry overall gets a C when it comes to diversity-related activity. The industry is most responsive in the area of charitable giving, but the greatest challenge is in the area of property ownership, followed by vendor relationships and marketing/communications.[64] The president of the National Association of Black Hotel Owners, Operators and Developers (NABHOOD) has observed that without the NAACP report card, African-American ownership in the industry would not be where it is today.

To adopt a win-win attitude with activist groups, executives should consider potential benefits from partnering activities, especially in situations in which an activist is strategically important. In the case of health, all agree that Americans are getting fatter and that the public-health implications are serious with regard to diabetes, heart disease, and other illnesses that are more likely to occur in overweight people.[65]

One example of such a partnership is the efforts of McCain Foods Ltd. in cooperation with the Alliance for a Healthier Generation. (See the "Hospitality Focus" boxed section in page 277.)

McCain Foods offers 19 products that fit within the Alliance's guidelines, containing fewer than 35 percent calories from fat, 0 grams of transfat, fewer than 10 percent of calories from saturated fat, and fewer than 230 milligrams of sodium. "The Alliance for a Healthier Generation is breaking new ground as a catalyst for ensuring healthier choices for children, and we are eager to support their efforts," states McCain Foods CEO.[66]

As the efforts of McCain Foods USA show, one of the best ways to reduce unfavorable regulation in an industry is to operate in a manner that is consistent with the values of society. Organizations that respond to the widely held positions of public-interest groups on issues such as pollution, fair-hiring practices, safety, and waste management do not need to be regulated. They find themselves in the enviable position of solving their own problems, instead of having a regulatory body of individuals with less experience in the industry dictating how problems will be solved.

McCAIN FOODS, LTD. AND THE ALLIANCE FOR A HEALTHIER GENERATION

HOSPITALITY FOCUS

"We believe that producing healthier products is good for people and good for business," notes the CEO of McCain Foods USA. The multinational frozen-food supplier, McCain Foods, Ltd., has expressed its commitment to support new product development and public education efforts to enhance nutrition in American public schools by offering products that fit a balanced diet and comply with nutrition guidelines set by the Alliance for a Healthier Generation.

The Alliance is a joint initiative of the American Heart Association and the William J. Clinton Foundation. One of its objectives is to work with the foodservice industry to take bold steps that will help kids live healthier lives. It supports schools' efforts to eliminate childhood obesity by putting healthy foods and beverages in vending machines and cafeterias.

Sprawling development and diminishing water and wildlife resources continue to place ski resorts on many environmentalists' blacklists and targets for regulation. But Aspen Skiing Company and more than 150 other ski resorts joined together almost a decade ago in signing the National Ski Areas Association environmental charter to voluntarily make environmental improvements.[67] Today, Aspen Ski Company can celebrate several environmental initiatives, a few of which are listed in the "Hospitality Focus" boxed section on page 278.

Alliances with activist groups can also help companies develop new products or services. The increasing social emphasis on environmental protection has left companies rushing to introduce products that are environmentally acceptable.[68] Examples include environmentally sensitive amenities, programmable thermostats, water-efficient showerheads, and energy-efficient lighting, to name a few.

Public-Interest Groups

Public-interest groups are particularly important in helping organizations avoid conflicts with social values, which can result in unfavorable media and a damaged reputation. For instance, an activist with PETA threw fake blood on the CEO of Yum! Brands as he entered a Kentucky Fried Chicken unit in Germany several years ago.[69] Today, a host of restaurant chains, including Burger King, Hardee's, and Carl Jr., have entered into agreements with PETA to source eggs from suppliers that do not keep their hens in metal cages. Other companies have also adopted humane-purchasing policies as consumer concern about animal welfare continues to increase. Groups such as PETA are experts in the causes they represent. As a result, many companies are limiting their vulnerability to activist pressures and boycotts, by inviting members of public-interest groups to participate in strategic-planning processes, either as advisors or as board members. The policy changes of several restaurant groups to buy meat and poultry that have been humanely raised is receiving unprecedented consumer support and may become a strategic necessity.[70]

ASPEN SKI COMPANY'S ENVIRONMENTAL INITIATIVES

The Aspen Ski Company operates four mountains, three hotels, and fifteen restaurants in Aspen, Colorado. Their environmental programs are designed to reduce the company's impact on the environment through a *sustainability report*, green development, habitat protection and enhancement, on-mountain education, and climate protection or green purchasing efforts. Their goal is to lead the skiing industry toward more sustainable practices. Following are a few of the company's initiatives:[71]

Established the largest solar photovoltaic system in the ski industry.

Became the first ski resort in the United States to be certified to the ISO 14001 standard.

Established the first ski-resort-supported environment foundation (almost $1 million given to local environmental causes).

Built one of the first LEED-certified buildings in the world.

Became the first ski resort to join the Chicago Climate Exchange.

Developed the ski industry's first climate policy.

Launched the first climate change education campaign in the ski industry.

Became the first ski resort to fuel all of its snowcats with biodiesel.

Built a small hydroelectric plant to power a portion of its operations.

Organizations should also consider the needs of special-interest groups, which represent the views of smaller social groups. However, buffering techniques may be more applicable because these groups, by virtue of their smaller social scope, are likely to be less strategically important than are public-interest groups. Both types of activists can also provide an alternative perspective on issues that affect the environment, consumers, minorities, or other interests. This alternative perspective can lead to new ways to solve organizational problems. Another benefit to allowing participation by important public-interest or special-interest groups during planning processes is that there may be fewer obstacles during strategy implementation. The groups involved would be less likely to protest or seek government intervention, allowing firms under some circumstances to gain some degree of immunity from prosecution. This may also result in good public relations and publicity.

THE MEDIA

Not only must an organization assess the potential effects of social forces on its business, but it must also manage its relationship and reputation with society at large. The media act as a watchdog for society. They are a commanding force in managing the attitudes of the general public toward organizations. Executives have nightmares about their companies being the subject of the next 20/20 program or some other news show. A *Dateline* investigation used a

INNOVATIVE TRAVEL MARKETING: COOPERATIVE BARTERING

HOSPITALITY FOCUS

"It is timely to barter in today's economy," says Jody Merl, president of Innovative Travel Marketing, a company that arranges the barter exchange between hotels and media outlets such as television and radio stations. "The opportunity cost for barter is at its lowest because there is so much inventory out there, and [hotel operators] should make that inventory work for them. You can never make up the revenue of a lost room night." According to Merl, barter is a $20 billion industry utilized by 80 percent of Fortune 500 companies.[72]

hidden camera to investigate the cleanliness of America's top 10 fast-food companies. In this TV news program, the 1,000 restaurants they sampled totaled 1,755 critical violations, and 613 restaurants were cited at least once.[73] Inspections by reporters from ABC News found bedbugs and urine stains in hotel rooms.[74] On the other hand, a well-managed media effort can significantly help the image of a firm.

It is rather difficult to pursue an inclusion or partnering strategy in the case of the media. In general, companies will rely on traditional management techniques to deal with this stakeholder. To manage relations with the media, large firms typically employ public-relations experts. The public-relations staff is usually active in releasing information that will place the company in a favorable light, while being careful not to create the impression that the organization is withholding information from the public.

It is not uncommon in the hospitality industry for an owner/operator to build public relations around his or her own name. Wolfgang Puck, the chef known for California cuisine, has put his name on four operations: Puck's casual-dining, Puck special events, Puck catering, and the Puck fine-dining group.[75] Driving the entire engine is Puck, whom some describe as an icon. This high-profile chef spends 50 percent of his time with some form of media, using his television show to establish the Puck brand.

While it is difficult to include the media directly in the organization, and formal partnerships are out of the question in most countries including the United States, managers can make individual reporters feel as though they have a special relationship with the company, thus prompting the reporters to portray the company in a more favorable light. Granting individual interviews to specific reporters, providing early release of information to a limited set of reporters, or treating a few media people to social activities such as luncheons or golf are some of the many efforts that firms make to cultivate the goodwill of the press. Hotel operators who trade room nights for electronic media placement are engaged in a form of cooperative activity called barter. For more than a decade, The Breakers Palm Beach has been using barter as a way to advertise. (See the "Hospitality Focus" boxed section above.)

Images and features found in motion pictures, television, newspapers, and magazines have an important impact on popular culture and consumer interest in tourism destinations. An old television program, "Love Boat," gave consumers an opportunity to think about a cruise every week they tuned in to watch the show. Movies and television familiarize audiences with places and attractions, which is important, because familiarity has been found to be an important factor in shaping consumer decision making. The movie *Braveheart* attracted tourists to Scotland to visit places depicted in the film (although much of the movie was actually filmed in Ireland), according to one study.[76]

Unfortunately, marketers are not likely to have control over how a destination or even a company is portrayed. A 2003 reality television show called "The Restaurant" featured a New York chef, Rocco DiSpirito, as he operated his recently opened Manhattan restaurant, Rocco's. While industry opinion generally held the show to be a ridiculous and sensationalized view of the industry and the owner's handling of staff to be by the "seat of the pants," the restaurant's three-week wait for reservations grew to three months.[77] Clearly, the media can be powerful allies in the hospitality industry.

In some parts of the world, such as Africa and the Middle East, state ownership of media is the rule, while North and South American media outlets are often owned by families.[78] In parts of the world where states provide support, biased reporting and favorable coverage of the incumbent government is more likely. Hence the level of cooperation the hospitality industry can obtain with the media will vary widely around the world.

LABOR UNIONS

Unions are formed to protect and advance the welfare of their members. By bargaining with management as a group, employees believe that they can more effectively gain what may be difficult to get as individuals. Employees believe that they have more power in making requests for higher wages and better working conditions, and that management is more motivated to listen when employees belong to a union.

The labor movement in the United States had its roots in trades (e.g., shoemaking) and crafts (i.e., bakers), but evolved to include manufacturing and service businesses. The American Federation of Labor and Congress of Industrial Organizations (AFL-CIO) is the largest federation of unions in the United States, consisting of 55 national and international unions, representing more than 10 million workers.[79] From 1955, when the AFL and CIO merged, until 2005, the AFL-CIO's member unions represented nearly all unionized workers in the United States, with the goal of improving the lives of working families. However, labor unions have seen a decline in membership.

Union strength in the United States has declined to only 13.2 percent of the workforce, down from 35 percent in the 1950s, with some concerned that unions are losing clout. In the private sector, less than 8 percent of employees are unionized.[80] Industries such as steel and automobiles are seeing the largest declines in unions, while growth is evident in unionizing government employees. Currently, the largest union in the AFL-CIO is the American Federation of State, County and Municipal Employees (AFSCME), with more than 1 million members. While the strength of unions varies from state to state and from country to country, and labor laws are subject to change, some have begun to debate whether unions will prosper or continue to decline.

Hospitality Unions

Union organizing is shifting toward the service sector as unions work to shore up their dwindling membership and strive to revitalize the movement. The hospitality industry is particularly

"THE CHANGE TO WIN" ALLIANCE

Hundreds of working people from around the country came together to create a new labor federation, Change to Win, comprising seven unions. The federation promises to be a lean organization, focusing more than 75 percent of its budget on organizing working people.

Over the course of its daylong founding convention, delegates ratified a constitution and structure, and passed resolutions on organizing, diversity, and politics. Anna Burger was officially designated as chairperson of the new federation, the first time in American history that a woman has headed a labor federation. Edgar Romney was chosen as the secretary-treasurer of the federation, the first time an African-American has headed a labor federation. In addition, workers shared firsthand their struggles to ensure that their jobs pay enough to support a family and that their employers offer quality, affordable health care and reasonable retirement plans.

"May the history books record that on the 27th day of September 2005 in St. Louis, delegates gathered and chose to change not just their unions, but their country," said Anna Burger. "Today we come together, having traveled here on separate roads with our separate proud histories, and our own union's colors, but we are all going in the same direction now. We are on the way to rekindle the American dream. Strategic, smart organizing is our core principle—our North Star."

"Today is a day the labor movement can be proud of," stated Edgar Romney. "We are embarking on a journey together toward a new era, where workers are valued and the economy works for everyone. And for the first time ever, the movement is being led by a woman. We are committed to diversity throughout our ranks, and there is no better place to start than the top."[81]

attractive to union organizers, partly because many jobs cannot be exported or handled offshore, and the jobs are relatively low paying. One well-known union is UNITE HERE, formed in 2004 when UNITE (formerly the Union of Needletrades, Industrial, and Textile Employees) and HERE (Hotel Employees and Restaurant Employees International Union) merged.[82] The union represents employees in hotels, casinos, foodservice, airport concessions, restaurants, apparel and textile manufacturing, apparel distribution centers, and apparel retail. Major union employers include Aramark, Caesar's Entertainment, Harrah's Entertainment, Hilton, Hyatt, Mandalay Resorts, MGM-Mirage, Starwood, Walt Disney World Company, and Wynn Resorts.

Internal dissent within the AFL-CIO in 2005 resulted in UNITE HERE splitting from the federation and joining with the Service Employees International Union (SEIU), the Teamsters, the United Food and Commercial Workers (UFCW), Farm Workers, and the Carpenters Union in a dissident federation known as the Change to Win Coalition.[83] Change to Win is devoted to creating large-scale, coordinated campaigns to rebuild the American labor movement. The primary issue of contention between UNITE HERE and the AFL-CIO was whether to focus on political action (favored by the AFL-CIO) or recruitment to strengthen

UNITE HERE'S "HOTEL WORKERS RISING" CAMPAIGN

According to UNITE HERE's Hotel Workers Rising campaign, thousands of hotel workers in upscale properties across North America are rising up to improve their jobs and secure better lives for themselves and their families. Angela Reid, a bartender at the Glendale Hilton, has worked at the non-union hotel for six years. "I'm fortunate," Angela says, "because I make tips. But until I got active with the union, I didn't realize how badly dishwashers, housekeepers, and others are treated. We have workers at my hotel who haven't had a raise in ten years."

The campaign is designed to draw attention to the many hotel workers—largely minority and immigrant women—who earn poverty wages and must work two jobs to get by. They are concerned that these workers are getting injured on the job because of understaffing and an increase in room amenities like heavier mattresses and linens. Wages for the same jobs vary wildly from city to city, and workers struggle to make ends meet and keep important benefits like health care and retirement plans, as well as their right to organize a union. By standing together, hotel workers are sending this message to the hotel industry: We are determined to make our jobs safer, middle-class jobs on which we can support our families.[84]

union membership (favored by UNITE HERE). The new Change to Win alliance represents 6 million workers and believes that by shifting focus to organizing, conducting joint campaigns, and promoting strategic support among members, the unions will grow. (See the "Hospitality Focus" boxed section on page 281.)

The leadership of UNITE HERE believes that millions of workers want to join unions, and they need help and support in the face of vigorous opposition by employers. According to the union, half of low-paying job categories are in hotels and restaurants.[85] They also note that the more union hotels there are in a city, the more hotel workers are paid. In cities with few union hotels, workers are paid just $7 per hour. In cities with mostly union hotels, that rate more than doubles, to $19 per hour. One initiative of the union is the "Hotel Workers Rising" campaign focused on fair wages and health-care benefits. The campaign targeted hotels in Chicago, New York, and San Francisco, all of which ended up signing collective bargaining agreements. (See the "Hospitality Focus" boxed section above.)

While the potential for cooperation between unions and employers is great, the traditional adversarial relationship has not changed much. A proposed $1 billion, 2,000-room hotel development by Gaylord Hotels ended when local unions in southern California asked that bidding on 50 to 75 contracts be opened only to union shops.[86] In addition, political action is common; for example, local and national politicians may pass ordinances that require employers who do business with a city to recognize unions. Unions are often able to steer major conventions toward or away from certain hotels based on their labor practices. For example, the Informed Meetings Exchange (INMEX), a group affiliated with UNITE HERE, distributes information about the hospitality industry to meeting planners so they can spend their convention dollars with hotel companies that are pro-union.[87] INMEX provides a database rating relationship between hotel owners and workers on its web site of destinations and properties.

UNION RESTAURANT WORKERS PICKET OUTSIDE OF HOLIDAY INN IN TORONTO

HOSPITALITY FOCUS

About a dozen picketers walked the pavement in front of the Holiday Inn in Toronto after the hotel's restaurant was shut down. The 22 beverage and restaurant workers, who are represented by Local 75 of UNITE HERE, say they were locked out after a vote that rejected the company's latest offer. A lawyer representing the hotel in the labor negotiations said the Holiday Inn's contract offer "is consistent with what other hotel employees" in downtown Toronto have negotiated. The workers say their demands are simple: They want to have the same wage as many other unionized hotel workers in the downtown core, and they want a three-year contract. According to the union, restaurant and bar staff at the Holiday Inn make anywhere from just under $10 per hour to $11 per hour. The hourly salary at many of the other unionized hotels for the same positions is about $15. Many of them don't make enough money at their restaurant or bar job to make ends meet and have to take second and third jobs. As a result of the picketing and leafleting and attempts to distract business away from the hotel, a decision was made to close the restaurant, and the employees were issued notices of layoff.[88]

LIVING CONTRACT ENCOURAGES DISPUTE RESOLUTIONS

HOSPITALITY FOCUS

The living contract has allowed study teams made up of line workers and managers at individual hotels to resolve a multitude of departmental and hotelwide problems. The study team approach permits customization of programs among hotels to account for their differences, but still allows them to operate under the citywide contract's mandatory provisions. At the Holiday Inn Fisherman's Wharf, the study team reduced contractual cook classifications in the kitchen from approximately 21 to 7, thereby achieving efficiencies that the hotel had long sought unsuccessfully through bargaining. This partnership helped Hyatt Regency adjust their room inspection process and helped the Hilton manage a complex luggage-handling task.[89]

Multinational firms may also apply pressure to American properties, as was the case for Sodexho to maintain good relations between the parent company and its own unions.[90] Whether it's the banner "Atlanta hotel boycott continues," "Crowne Plaza workers in Secaucus demand: Give us back our vacation & sick days!," "Puerto Rico hotel workers rally," or "Hotel workers from across the city join Holiday Inn picket line," a quick look at news headlines confirms that the contentious nature of union–management relationships still persists for hotels, casinos, and foodservice operators. (See the first "Hospitality Focus" boxed section above.)

Unions are being treated as partners instead of adversaries in some companies with great success. Eleven hotels in the San Francisco area formed a multiemployer bargaining group with the goal of promoting labor–management cooperation and creating a partnership with their workers and the union. They brought this new idea to the union leaders, who agreed that it was time to try a different approach. This partnership began with a joint study to analyze the problems facing hotels in the San Francisco market and resulted in the creation of a "living contract."

Unlike more traditional contracts, the living contract permitted changes after the parties finished negotiations to address unforeseen problems and modify the contract. The contract's primary accomplishment was to foster cooperation between the hotels and the union. It allowed several interest-based study teams to develop solutions to problems facing the industry. In addition, the partnership permitted the hotels and union to revise work rules, create joint training programs, and implement a grievance-mediation program that reduced the traditional formal and costly approach to dispute resolution. This program has dramatically changed the hotel and union relationship from a grievance and arbitration-driven one to a partnership based on finding mutually satisfactory solutions to important problems. (See the second "Hospitality Focus" boxed section on page 283.)

Neutrality Agreements

Traditionally, unions would organize employees in the workforce, but today a new approach focuses on working with the ownership company and management. Unions consider the hotel construction stage as one of the best times to organize.[91] This may seem rather early, since the hotel may not yet have employees, but the union often approaches the hotel to discuss the establishment of a *neutrality agreement*. A hotel signing one of these agreements promises to stay neutral if the union decides to organize the property. The neutrality agreement means that the hotel does not have the right to contest union organization, and the employees do not have the right to vote in a secret ballot to determine whether they wish to be represented. Instead, union recognition is based on a card-check procedure, where the union is recognized once 50 percent of the bargaining unit employees sign a union-authorization card.[92] Both Hilton Hotels and Starwood signed national neutrality agreements with UNITE HERE. The union also secured separate neutrality language in contracts with hotel associations in several major cities, including New York, Chicago, and San Francisco. Not all industry experts consider signing neutrality agreements to be a viable approach, arguing that hotels virtually guarantee that the union will be the bargaining agent for their employees. However, in highly unionized cities, this approach may make strategic sense. The American Hotel and Lodging Association has expressed their position on card-check neutrality. (See the "Hospitality Focus" boxed section on page 285.)

Organizations that succeed in labor–management relationships are starting to see representatives from labor unions as key partners in strategic-planning decisions. In reaching contract agreements, the Hilton–UNITE HERE "Partnership for Future Growth" agreement included promises to work together on growth where it makes strategic and economic sense, and commitments to explore ways to enhance Hilton Hotels' productivity and competitiveness, especially in the area of foodservice and restaurants.[93] Hilton received preferred status as a hotel management company of choice for the union. The president and chief operating officer of Hilton Hotels Corporation noted, "We believe that cooperation and productive dialogue between labor and operators is an important factor in helping keep our industry strong and moving onward and upward."[94]

One of the most effective ways to deal with a union is to avoid unionization, when possible. For example, a unionization effort at a New Orleans hotel was thwarted because its

THE AMERICAN HOTEL AND LODGING ASSOCIATION ON "CARD-CHECK NEUTRALITY"

The American Hotel and Lodging Association (AH&LA) Position on "Hotel Workers Rising" Campaign and "Card-Check Neutrality"

We believe the real reason that UNITE HERE has recently started a new campaign called "Hotel Workers Rising" in major cities is to boost labor's dwindling membership in other parts of the United States. We do not feel that hotel employees in unionized areas should be used by national labor leaders simply to grow their membership numbers in other parts of the United States.

UNITE HERE is pressuring hotel companies to sign "card-check neutrality" agreements that would eliminate the long-standing National Labor Relations Board (NLRB) secret-ballot elections. Instead, these elections would be replaced with "card check," which would allow a union to represent employees as soon as a majority signed a card stating their intention to join a union. Because card checks are conducted out in the open, many employees are either forced into signing the cards or fear being singled out in their workplace if they don't.

Unions are also demanding that employers sign "neutrality agreements," which would prevent the employer from telling their side of the story to employees about unionization and effectively impose a gag order. Hotel employees deserve accurate and truthful information. Both the union and management have a right to present their case so that workers can make an educated decision based on all of the facts.

The hotel industry strongly believes that our employees should have the personal right to determine if they want to join a union. We are not against unionization. We are against the union's decision to eliminate our employees' right to choose. The unionization process should be fair, open, and democratic. It should allow employees to vote by secret ballot in order to protect employees against intimidation. It is their job. It is their life. It should be their choice.

The hotel industry comes to the bargaining table in good faith, wanting to negotiate a contract that is fair to our employees. Hotels are committed to providing its hard-working employees with competitive wages, generous benefits, and affordable health care.[95]

employees were so well treated. Good human resource management would suggest that careful attention to wages and benefits, proactive responses to issues of safety and discrimination, and attention to employee complaints will help diminish the need for employees to seek a more powerful partnership in the form of a union.

Union–management relationships can have several levels of complexity. For example, it is interesting to note that unions also finance hotel projects through their equity-based pension funds and their real estate investment debt funds. The building investment trust of the AFL–CIO has invested millions in hotels through union pension funds, allocating 10 to 15 percent

LANDRY'S RESTAURANT, INC. FILES LATE FINANCIAL STATEMENTS WITH THE SEC.

The court has ordered Landry's Restaurants Inc. to meet with its bondholders, who have demanded the early repayment of $400 million in notes. The restaurant operator, owner of 179 full-service restaurants and two Golden Nugget hotel-casinos, has asked the court to issue a permanent restraining order against the lenders, who demanded the repayment after Landry's delayed filing its 2006 financial statements.

Landry's CEO Tilman Fertitta noted, "I've been in this business for 25 to 30 years—I have been in a lot of battles—but I have never felt so totally trapped in a corner." While attorneys for Landry's compare the bondholders to vultures and sharks, lawyers for the bondholders Post Advisory Group and Lord Abbett Bond-Debenture Fund say the issue is simple business.

The restaurant company notes it has backup financing secured from a bank, but that the funding would cost Landry's $35 million more than its current financing agreement with the bondholders. The alternative financing would cut the company's liquidity by more than $200 million, forcing it to put all development on hold. After reaching a settlement, Landry's will find interest on the notes up 2 percent, costing the firm an additional $8 million annually.[96]

of its assets to hotel financing.[97] The Loews New Orleans Hotel is an example of a project built with labor union pension fund money. The construction jobs were 100 percent union, and Loews agreed not to oppose unionization of the hotel once construction was complete.[98] In these stakeholder roles, unions become financial intermediaries and business partners, a topic we turn to next.

FINANCIAL INTERMEDIARIES

Financial intermediaries consist of a wide variety of institutions, including banks, stock exchanges, brokerage houses, investment advisors, mutual-fund companies, pension-fund companies, and other organizations or individuals that may have an interest in investing in the firm. This list is not exhaustive, and many financial service firms play more than one role.

Trust is especially important in dealing with creditors. Disclosure of financial records helps establish trust, as do timely payments. A delay in filing financial statements with the U.S. Securities and Exchange Commission by Landry's Restaurant Inc. violated the bondholders' covenant and was met with a prompt reaction, as illustrated in the "Hospitality Focus" boxed section above.

Many organizations, in an effort to manage their relationships with creditors and develop trust, have invited creditor representatives onto the board of directors. For instance, at MGM Mirage, one of the largest gaming companies, one of the 11 outside members of the board of directors, Kirk Kerkorian, owns a private investment company called Tracinda Corporation that is the largest stakeholder of MGM Mirage.[99] In some cases, board membership is a loan requirement. This type of involvement allows creditors to know firsthand the financial condition of the company and to have a say in major financial decisions such as acquisitions, restructuring, and new offerings of stock and debt.

Another type of linkage occurs when an organization does business with a company that is represented by the same financial institution. This type of cooperation, which can facilitate contracting and financial transactions, is common among the keiretsu in Japan. Banks and other lenders may also participate as part owners of business ventures of client firms. One of the largest independent management companies, Interstate Hotels and Resorts, operates hotels for REITs, institutional real estate owners, noninstitutional ownership groups, and privately held companies. Their board of directors includes senior officials from Providence Equity, a private equity company, and Lehman Brothers, a financial services firm.

Financial intermediaries are the last of the external stakeholders that will be discussed in this chapter; however, it should be noted that other external stakeholders, of varying importance, exist on a firm-by-firm basis. For example, donors are a key stakeholder in nonprofit organizations. Donors should probably be treated more like customers than anything else. In fact, individuals who donate to charities or religious organizations are forgoing other purchases. Nonprofit organizations should communicate with donors, involve them in the processes of the organization, and create a high-quality service that donors will want to support. In the case of charities, the recipients of goods and services should also be treated as customers.

Managing Partnerships

Much of this chapter so far has dealt with creating successful partnerships with external stakeholders. It is clear that interorganizational relationships are desirable and are becoming increasingly important activities for strategic advantage. Those that promise the most benefit are also likely to present the greatest implementation challenges. Critical attention to the integration of divergent operational and strategic goals of partners is essential for long-term alliance success. For many large hospitality firms, a variety of partnerships are managed simultaneously, as seen in the business transactions of Accor. (See the "Hospitality Focus" boxed section on page 288.)

This section will close with a few comments on how to manage partnerships so that they are likely to succeed. Managers should communicate the expected benefits of the venture to important external and internal stakeholders so they will understand the role the alliance will play in the organization.[100] They should also develop a strategic plan for the partnership that consolidates the views of the partners about market potential, competitive trends, and potential threats. Several additional steps may be used to improve the likelihood of success:

1. Engage in careful, systematic study to identify an alliance partner that can provide the capabilities that are needed. Avoid the tendency to align with another firm just because forming alliances is a trend in the industry.

2. Clearly define the roles of each partner and ensure that every joint project is of value to both.

3. Develop a strategic plan for the venture that outlines specific objectives for each partner.

ACCOR: MANAGING PARTNERSHIPS

Building partnerships is not new to Accor. As part of its business-to-business strategy, the company has developed partnerships with major firms in transportation, telephone and Internet services, financial services, and the foodservice industry. Forming alliances offers the various partners a win-win relationship, in which the strategic goal of enhanced customer satisfaction is accomplished through providing complimentary services. This cooperative model of partnering is based on carefully selecting relationships that have the highest probability of providing potential synergies, or that target the same customer base.

The primary drivers of Accor's joint strategy with its partners are increased market share, cost reduction through shared resources, and brand recognition. The company believes that the hotel brands have increased visibility and can provide faster and easier access to their products and services by having formed these partnerships. Following are a few examples of existing partnerships:

Transportation (Airlines, Railways, and Cars): Accor has a long-term partnership contract with Europcar, the leader in European car rentals, to offer customers convenient travel arrangements. Air France has formed a series of alliances with Accor, including a joint customer loyalty program, a project to develop services for Air France customers, and joint promotional campaigns. In addition, Accor has formed relationships with over 24 airlines through participation in major loyalty programs. French National Railways (SNCF) have a "Train + Hotel" partnership, in cooperation with Accor. Accor also offers easy reservations with other European railways including Thalys, Lyria, and SN.

Communication (Telephone and Internet): Accor has a partnership with Orange WiFi access in France, in which hotel customers enjoy wireless broadband Internet access in hotel lobbies, bars, meeting rooms, and guest rooms. Accor has a partnership with France Telecom that allows customers to book services directly from their cell phones by dialing Orange 711. Also, customers can book rooms on their cell phones thanks to partnerships with SFR and Bouygues Telecom.

Finance (Banks and Credit Card Services): Through a partnership with Visa International, Accor provides privileges and special offers to special groups of card holders. American Express is the partner of Accor for the "Carte Compliments American Express" and the co-branded "Carte Corporate" (with Accor and Air France). Accor, a partner of LCL's Avantage loyalty program, offers program members gift vouchers for use in its hotels and restaurants. HSBC's partnership with Accor allows the bank's premier customers to receive special services from select hotel brands.

Restaurants and Events: Accor owns a 20 percent stake in the restaurant company Courtepaille and maintains a marketing partnership between the restaurants and its economy hotels. Accor also partners with Danone, a global leader in dairy products, to sponsor and promote events such as the Danone Nation's Cup.[10]

4. Keep top managers involved so that middle managers will stay committed.

5. Meet often, informally, and at all managerial levels.

6. Appoint someone to monitor all aspects of the partnership, and use an outside mediator when disputes arise.

7. Maintain enough independence to develop your own area of expertise. Avoid becoming a complete captive of the alliance partner.

8. Anticipate and plan for cultural differences.[102]

This concludes our discussion of strategy implementation through the creation of partnerships and managing relationships with external stakeholders. The next section focuses on another element of strategy implementation: developing functional-support strategies.

FUNCTIONAL-LEVEL RESOURCE MANAGEMENT

Translating corporate and business strategies into specific actions is the responsibility of managers in the various functional areas of an organization. The collective pattern of day-to-day decisions made and actions taken by managers and employees who are responsible for value-creating activities in a particular functional area are called *functional-level strategies*. Functional-level strategies, by being more specific and short-term, help employees understand what they are to do to accomplish the broader long-term aspirations of the corporation. The Pierre Hotel in New York, for example, is a luxury hotel that devised a marketing strategy in the early 2000s to maintain rate integrity and focus on individual versus groups sales with an emphasis on foreign markets.[103] To accomplish this strategy, the hotel relied on major press tours in Europe to promote the hotel.

Similarly, the information technology group at Starbucks worked on providing Internet access to guests to fit with the firm's guest loyalty strategy.[104] Functional-level strategies are about paying attention to details. Some of the most successful companies operate in low-growth, moderately profitable industries and pursue strategies that are not unique. The reason for their extraordinary success is their attention to the details associated with strategy implementation. Organizations are made up of people who interact with one another and with external stakeholders as they perform functions that meet the goals of the organization. Several years ago, researchers found that companies that were most successful in implementing their strategies had created a "pervasive strategic vision" throughout the company, with the full involvement of all employees.[105] In those firms, employees worked as a coordinated system, with all of their separate but interdependent efforts directed toward the goals of the firm. Consequently, each functional area is one piece of a larger system, and coordination among the pieces is essential to successful strategy execution. For example, coordination of the hotel's various functions was essential for the Newark Gateway Hilton when it implemented its guest check-in on the shuttle bus to the hotel. (See the "Hospitality Focus" boxed section on page 290.)

HOSPITALITY FOCUS

NEWARK GATEWAY HILTON: EXPRESS CHECK-IN

The idea for an express check-in service originated with the president of Hilton Hotels. Acting upon this suggestion, the Newark Gateway Hilton formed a cross-functional team representing front office, security, housekeeping, finance, sales and marketing, and reservations. John Luke, vice president of front-office operations and systems, remarked that it was important to involve these departments in particular, so that each area affected by the decision would have some input into the process. After brainstorming for approximately one month, the team developed the Mobile Zip-in Check-in program. With the implementation of this process, overall guest satisfaction has improved.[106]

From a coordinated–systems perspective, well-developed functional-level resource management strategies should have the following characteristics:

- *Decisions made within each function will be consistent with other areas.* For example, if a new hotel marketing promotion is developed, it has implications for reservations in explaining the program, human resources in training staff, and rooms division for costs and operational execution.

- *Decisions made within one function will be consistent with those made in other functions.* Interdependencies and linkages exist among the many activities of a firm. It is common for the decisions made by one department to be inconsistent with those of another department. For example, although they are responsible for most of the primary value-adding activities, marketing and operations frequently advocate very different approaches to the many interdependent decisions that exist between them. Left to their own devices over time, it is likely that marketing will make decisions that implement a differentiation strategy, while operations will implement a low-cost leadership strategy. The finance area also tends to conflict with operations, as operations strives for high service satisfaction and finance seeks to reduce costs.

- *Decisions made within functions will be consistent with the strategies of the business.* For example, if a company is pursuing a low-cost competitive strategy, then the bulk of the activities and resources should focus on cost reduction to improve profitability. It is often difficult to adapt to changes in the competitive environment. Suppose a company is pursuing an aggressive-growth strategy in a healthy business environment. Under those conditions, marketing may pursue market-share increases and revenue growth as its top priority. If the business environment changes—demand slows down and profits are squeezed—then the focus of marketing may have to change to stability and profit improvement over sales-volume increases. Unless prodded by the organization, marketing may be very reluctant to change from its traditional way of doing business.[107]

The rapid success and subsequent decline of the low-cost commuter airline, People Express Airlines, is a good illustration of what can happen when there is inconsistency in tactical decisions across departments or between a generic strategy and functional strategies. In the beginning, every management decision supported low costs: aircraft were bought secondhand, pilots kept planes in the air more hours per day than any other airline, terminal leases were inexpensive, and human-resource policies required cross-training, encouraged high productivity, and rewarded employees with profit-sharing plans. The airline was extraordinarily successful with its strategy, and achieved the lowest cost position in the industry. However, with success, People Express began to alter its pattern of decisions and, over time, drifted from its low-cost strategy. It pursued longer routes, which pulled it into direct competition with the full-service airlines, even though People Express did not have the elaborate reservation systems and customer services to support this strategy. It contracted more-expensive terminal arrangements and purchased new aircraft at market prices. The close-knit, high-performance culture that encouraged an extraordinary work pace in exchange for profit sharing was undermined by rapid growth and too many new faces. Just a few years after its start-up, and within a year of becoming the fifth largest airline, People Express was in serious financial trouble and was forced to sell out to another airline. Some have wondered if JetBlue might go the way of People Express. (See the "Hospitality Focus" boxed section on page 294.)

A *functional-strategy audit* can help determine whether functional strategies are internally consistent, consistent across functions, and supportive of the firm's strategies. Table 7.3 outlines some of the functional areas to be included in a functional audit. The first step is to determine what an organization is doing in each area. Internal consistency is evaluated, as is consistency across functional areas and with the strategies of the organization. The next step is to develop plans to correct any inconsistencies. A functional-strategy audit is especially helpful as an implementation tool for new strategies. You may personally find it useful if you are doing case analyses in a strategic management course. If your instructor requires you to write an implementation section for a strategy you recommend, you can develop your plan, in part, based on the items for each functional area found in Table 7.3.

The collective pattern of day-to-day decisions made and actions taken by managers and employees who are responsible for value-creating activities result in the functional strategies that are used to implement the growth and competitive strategies of the business. The following sections discuss the responsibilities and patterns of decisions made in a few select functional areas, including marketing, human resources, and operations.

Marketing Strategy

One of the most critical responsibilities of marketing employees is to span the boundary of the organization and interact with external stakeholders, such as customers and competitors. Marketing is responsible for bringing essential stakeholder information about new customer needs, projected future demand, competitor actions, and new business opportunities into the organization as an input to plans for continuous improvements, expansions, new technologies, and new products and services.

TABLE 7.3 Conducting a Functional–Strategy Audit

Marketing Strategy

- Target customers—few vs. many, what groups, what regions
- Product positioning—premium commodity, multiuse, specialty use
- Product line mix—a mix of complementary products
- Product line breadth—a full-line offering of products
- Pricing strategies—discount, moderate, premium prices
- Promotion practices—direct sales, advertising, direct mail, Internet
- Distribution channels—few or many, sole contract responsibilities
- Customer service policies—flexibility, responsiveness, quality
- Product/service image—premium quality, good price, reliable
- Market research—accuracy, frequency, and methods for obtaining marketing information

Operations Strategy

- Capacity planning—lead demand to ensure availability or lag demand to achieve capacity utilization
- Facility location—near suppliers, customers, labor, natural resources, or transportation
- Facility layout—floor plans, integration of service activities, grounds, and external services
- Technology and equipment choices—degree of automation, use of computers and information technology
- Sourcing arrangements—cooperative arrangements with a few vs. competitive bid
- Planning and scheduling—standard services or custom, flexibility to customer requests
- Quality assurance—process control, standards, feedback gathering processes
- Workforce policies—training levels, cross-training, rewards, use of teams

Information Systems Strategy

- Hardware—local area network (LAN), mainframe, minicomputer, internal systems, links to Internet
- Software—data processing, decision support, Web management, computer automated design (CAD), computer integrated manufacturing (CIM), just-in-time inventory
- Personnel—in-house experts, subcontracting, or alliances
- Information security—hardware, software, physical location and layout
- Disaster recovery—off-site processing, backup procedures, virus protection and treatment
- Business intelligence—management support, marketing, accounting, operations, R&D, human resources, finance
- Internet—communications, marketing, resource acquisition, research, management

TABLE 7.3 (*Continued*)

Innovation Strategy

- Innovation focus—services, service processes, other applications
- Innovation orientation—leader, early follower, late follower
- Project priorities—budget, quality, creativity, time
- Knowledge creation—training, alliances and ventures, acquisitions, cross-functional teams
- Corporate entrepreneurship—"seed money" grants, time off to develop a venture, management
- support, rewards for entrepreneurs, ideas come from everyone

Human Resources Strategy

- Recruitment—entry-level vs. experienced employees, colleges, technical schools, job services
- Selection—selection criteria and methods
- Nature of work—part-time, full-time, or a combination; on-site or off-site, domestic or foreign
- Performance appraisal—appraisal methods and frequency, link to rewards
- Salary and wages—hourly, piece rate, commission, fixed, relationship to performance, competitiveness
- Other compensation—stock ownership programs, bonuses
- Management compensation—stock awards, stock options, bonuses linked to performance, perquisites, low-interest loans
- Benefits—medical, dental and life insurance, paid leave, vacations, child care, health club
- Personnel actions—disciplinary plans, outplacement, early retirements
- Training—types of training, availability of training to employees, tuition reimbursement

Financial Strategy

- Sources of capital—debt, equity, or internal financing
- Financial reporting—frequency, type, government, shareholders, other stakeholders
- Capital budgeting—system for distributing capital, minimum ROI for investments, payback
- Overhead costs—allocation of overhead costs based on direct labor, machine use, sales volume, activity
- Financial control—system to ensure accuracy of internal and external financial information, audits
- Returns to shareholders—dividends policy, repurchase of stock, treasury stock, stock splits
- Financial targets—establishment of financial targets for functional areas and business units, method of reporting on progress

HOSPITALITY FOCUS

JETBLUE: THE GAP BETWEEN STRATEGY AND EFFECTIVE IMPLEMENTATION

JetBlue, like RyanAir, was founded using Southwest's low-cost airline model. In the words of its founder, David Neeleman, JetBlue looks "to bring humanity back to air travel." Extraordinary growth and success have followed the airline since its start, but by 2005, operational issues were bringing its financial performance down, and the carrier was slow to upgrade operational systems. Adding more planes and routes began to cause growth pains, and union-organizing efforts were attempted. In the first quarter of 2006, the company announced its first-ever losses, due to rising fuel costs and moves into new markets, but cost cutting put the airline back in the black in the second quarter.

By the winter of 2007, the gap between strategy and effective implementation got worse when a JetBlue flight from John F. Kennedy International Airport was delayed on the tarmac in snowy weather for nearly nine hours. Other JetBlue aircraft were also stranded that day, and the lack of system upgrades left the airline unable to juggle flight delays. The reservation and call-center systems were overloaded, and crew scheduling systems failed, leaving crews unable to reroute to their next assignment. CEO David Neeleman said afterward he was "sorry and embarrassed," assuring customers "it will never happen again." But industry insiders believe the JFK debacle was inevitable. "They can't keep running off a legal pad and number-two pencil," observed a longtime industry executive. The system failures that made the situation a nightmare suggested that rapid expansion had outstripped management's ability to execute on its strategy.[108]

Marketing strategy evolves from the cumulative pattern of decisions made by the employees who interact with customers and perform marketing activities. To support growth strategies, marketing identifies new customer opportunities, suggests product opportunities, creates advertising and promotional programs, arranges distribution channels, and creates pricing and customer service policies that help position the company's products for the proper customer groups. If a company pursues a stability or turnaround strategy within one of its businesses, the demands placed on marketing will change. Instead of pursuing growth, marketing may manage a reduction in the number of customer groups, distribution channels, and products in the product line—all in an attempt to focus on the more profitable and promising aspects of the business.

The competitive strategy of the firm also influences marketing decisions.[109] Low-cost competitive strategies require low-cost channels of distribution and low-risk product and market development activities. If demand can be influenced by advertising or price discounts, then marketing may pursue aggressive advertising and promotion programs or deep price discounts to get demand to a level that will support full-capacity utilization and economies of scale within operations, as when the soft drink companies advertise and discount their products. Differentiation strategies require that marketing (1) identify the attributes of products and services that customers will value; (2) price and distribute the product or service in ways that capitalize on the differentiation; and (3) advertise and promote the image of difference.

Human Resources Strategy

In the not-too-distant past, human resources (HR) activities were considered to be more administrative than strategic. However, a shift has taken place.

> *So what is different now? Why are people more important today? What is it about HR issues that bring them into a discussion of strategic management? Part of the answer to these questions has to do with shifting priorities and perspectives about competition and firm advantage. As theories of strategic management turn toward resource-based and knowledge-based views of the firm, where competitive advantage increasingly resides in a firm's ability to learn, innovate, and change, the human element becomes increasingly important in generating economic value.* [110]

James Brian Quinn reinforced this idea by stating that, "with rare exceptions, the economic and producing power of the firm lies more in its intellectual and service capabilities than in its hard assets—land, plant and equipment." [111]

HR managers serve a coordinating role between the organization's management and employees, and between the organization and external stakeholder groups, including labor unions and government regulators of labor and safety practices such as the Equal Employment Opportunity Commission and the Occupational Safety and Health Administration. HR management can play an important role in the implementation of a firm's strategies. [112] Disney is an example of a company that uses training to create a competitive advantage.

The pattern of decisions about selection, training, rewards, and benefits creates a *human resources strategy*. Mature or cost-oriented businesses usually hire employees at the entry level and promote from within to fill higher-level positions. They are more likely to focus rewards on short-range performance goals and to include seniority issues in compensation systems. [113] Firms following turnaround strategies, such as Delta Airlines, have to focus their HR priorities on programs for early retirements, structured layoffs, skills retraining, and outplacement services.

The HR strategies that are in place create a workforce with certain skills and expectations, which then influences the strategy alternatives available for the future. [114] Because of the potential for conflict between existing HR policies and new organization strategies, HR managers play their most strategic role at the point when a major change in organization strategy is necessary. They must anticipate the change in skills and behavior that will be needed to support the strategy, modify the HR practices, and plan for an orderly, timely transition.

Operations Strategy

Operations strategy emerges from the pattern of decisions made within the firm about production or service operations. The task of operations managers is to design and manage the operation so that it can create the products and services the firm must have to compete in the marketplace. An effective operation strives for consistency between its capabilities and the competitive advantage being sought. [115]

Operations managers, like marketing managers, must manage multiple stakeholder interests in their daily decision making. According to Michael Porter, "It's gone from a game of resources to a game of rate-of-progress. Competition today is a race to improve."[116] Speed is often the result of rethinking processes and procedures. While small entrepreneurial organizations may be at a disadvantage relative to larger organizations in developing some of the other competitive weapons, they actually have an advantage when it comes to speed and flexibility.[117] Smaller firms are typically less constrained by large investments in capital equipment. In addition, less bureaucracy often means that changes that are required as a result of new technology can be made in a shorter period of time. This also means that managers are typically closer to their customers and have fewer customers, thus allowing them to really get to know customers and understand their needs. Consequently, many operations managers in larger companies are struggling to be competitive with regard to speed.

The interdependencies among stakeholders can also create difficulties for operations managers. Employees want good wages and benefits, reasonable work schedules, and a safe and pleasant work environment. Communities want industries that will provide stable employment for citizens of the community and add to the tax base. Suppliers want predictable demand for their products and services, and a fair price. Customers want excellent service, quality products, and reasonable prices. However, a change in customer demand can upset schedules with workers and suppliers. A problem with a supplier can create havoc with the quality levels that are intended to serve the needs of customers. A new labor contract or labor shortages can cause cost structures and then prices to go up. In managing these interdependencies, operations managers must be guided by an understanding of business-level strategies.

Every strategy affects operations in ways that have implications for stakeholder interests. For example, growth strategies put pressure on the systems and procedures used to hire and retain customers. Turnaround strategies often target the activities of operations first: line employees are laid off, renovations and new service levels are demanded. Differentiation strategies based on flexibility and high-quality service may require a flexible or temporary workforce, special arrangements with suppliers, and very high levels of training for employees. Major capital investments in new facilities or amenities may depress earnings in the short run, which lowers earnings per share reported to stockholders. How operations managers handle these types of trade-off decisions can have a substantial influence on the firm's performance.

This chapter focused on implementing strategy from two perspectives: looking outward to the environment or inward to the firm's resource capabilities. As discussed in the beginning of this chapter, organizations can look outward to external stakeholders, especially through the formation of interorganizational relationships. Functional-level resource-management strategies, such as those in marketing, human resources, and operations, are another approach to executing on strategy. These approaches are not mutually exclusive, but rather include a range of options that executives may consider when devising implementation plans.

KEY POINTS SUMMARY

• This chapter focused on implementing strategy through external stakeholder management and functional-level resource management.

- Interorganizational relationships are an increasingly popular technique for pursuing strategic objectives.

- One of the most important reasons for forming partnerships is to acquire resources, especially knowledge.

- High priority should be given to stakeholders with a large amount of formal, political, or economic power; stakeholders that have a large impact on the uncertainty facing an organization; and/or stakeholders that possess needed resources. Other stakeholders should not be ignored, but they can be managed with more traditional stakeholder management techniques, with the objective of buffering the organization from their influence.

- Strategies are implemented through the day-to-day decisions and actions of employees throughout the organization. Management's challenge is to create a pattern of integrated, coordinated decisions that meets the needs of stakeholders and fulfills the planned strategy of the organization.

- Strategies are established for functional-level resource areas, such as marketing, human resources, and operations, among others. In each area, employees interact with different stakeholder groups and manage conflicting expectations.

- In managing functional strategies, managers must ensure that decisions within each area are consistent over time, with other functions, and with the stated strategies of the firm.

REVIEW QUESTIONS

1. Returning to Chapter 2 (Table 2.4), review the definitions of the following interorganizational relationships: joint ventures, networks, consortia, alliances, trade groups, and interlocking directorates.

2. What is a tourism cluster? Provide examples of firms in the three sectors of a cluster for a specific tourism destination.

3. What are the major advantages of interorganizational relationships?

4. Do interorganizational relationships have any disadvantages? If so, what are they?

5. What primary factors make some stakeholders more important than others? How should high-priority stakeholders be managed?

6. How do management techniques for high-priority stakeholders differ from those of low-priority stakeholders? Give examples.

7. What can organizations do to ensure that their partnerships are effective?

8. Why does the hotel industry have so many partnerships among competitors? Is this true for other industries? Which ones?

9. What methods can organizational leaders use to effectively manage relationships with local communities, activists, the media, unions, and financial intermediaries?

10. What is a functional-level resource-management strategy? Give an example of how a functional-level resource-management strategy can be used to carry out one of the generic business-level strategies, such as low-cost leadership.

11. What characteristics should well-developed, functional-level resource-management strategies have?

CRITICAL THINKING AND APPLICATION QUESTIONS

1. Select a destination and create a tourism cluster that identifies key players in three types of organizational sectors, including (1) the direct providers of travel services, (2) support services or suppliers to the industry, and (3) tourism development organizations, agencies, and institutions that affect provider firms, support service organizations, and the traveler. Prepare a figure of our tourism cluster similar to the one shown in Figure 7.1 for Costa Rica.

2. Joint ventures are a popular form of partnership in the hospitality industry. Conduct library research on recent joint ventures among hospitality firms. What were the primary reasons for these joint ventures? Were they successful? Why or why not?

3. In your opinion, are unions like UNITE HERE good or bad for the industry? Develop a pro-union argument and an anti-union argument. In small groups, debate the question.

4. Partnering doesn't just happen. For partnerships to flourish with mutual benefit, a lot of hard work is necessary. Search for examples of mutually beneficial and troubled partnerships by reading trade publications and searching news sources. See if you can find examples from various stakeholder groups, such as customers, suppliers, competitors, government agencies, local communities, activist groups, the media, labor unions, and financial intermediaries. Explore the following questions:

   a. What does each partner gain from the alliance or relationship?

   b. Are the partners equally strong? Are their skills complementary?

   c. Are the partners equally committed to the relationship?

   d. How do the partners handle shifts in the value of their contributions overtime?

   e. Is the alliance the only one between the two partners or part of a web of alliances between the same partners?

CHAPTER 8

STRATEGY IMPLEMENTATION THROUGH ORGANIZATIONAL DESIGN AND CONTROL

YOU SHOULD BE ABLE TO DO THE FOLLOWING AFTER READING THIS CHAPTER:

1. Know the key dimensions that describe formal organizational structures, including the degree of specialization, formalization, centralization, and levels of authority.

2. Draw an organization chart to represent the three basic business-level structures and describe the attributes of each structure.

3. Create diagrams of the three types of corporate-level structures used by multibusiness organizations.

4. Understand the role that the lateral (horizontal) organization plays in successful implementation of strategy.

5. Identify the differences between strategic and financial controls, and between feedback and feedforward controls.

6. Describe bureaucratic, clan, and process controls.

7. List the steps companies can take to control organizational crises.

FEATURE STORY

REORGANIZING THE U.S. BUSINESS

Yum! Brands Inc. is aggressively pursuing a growth strategy by building dominant restaurant brands in China, driving profitable international expansion, and improving U.S. brand positions and returns. To execute this strategy, the company is organized into three divisions: Yum! China (including mainland China, Thailand, and KFC Taiwan), Yum! Restaurants International (YRI), and U.S. Brand Building. With more than 34,000 restaurants in more than 100 countries and territories, the company is the world's largest restaurant company in terms of system restaurants. Four of the company's restaurant brands—Kentucky Fried Chicken (KFC), Pizza Hut, Taco Bell, and Long John Silver's—are the global leaders of the chicken, pizza, Mexican-style food, and quick-service seafood categories, respectively.

Based in Shanghai, the Yum! China Division is focused on substantial growth, with more than 2,600 system restaurants. The KFC brand was the first quick-service restaurant chain to enter China, and now has more than 1,800 restaurants in more than 400 cities in mainland China. Pizza Hut was the first and is the number-one casual-dining brand in China, with 250 restaurants in more than 60 cities. In an effort to appeal to local tastes, a Chinese food concept called East Dawning is gaining popularity primarily because of its appealing facilities.

The strategy to drive profitable international growth is the focus of YRI, the largest division of Yum! Brands, with nearly 12,000 restaurants outside the United States (this figure excludes Yum! China Division). Almost all new international restaurants are opened by franchise and joint venture partners in more than 100 countries. Finally, the U.S. business is stable but requires more effort to improve profitability and returns. Pizza Hut, in particular, is in need of better same-store sales and profit growth improvement.

At the end of 2006, the company reorganized its U.S. business by creating a new position called President of U.S. Brand Building and modifying the existing position of

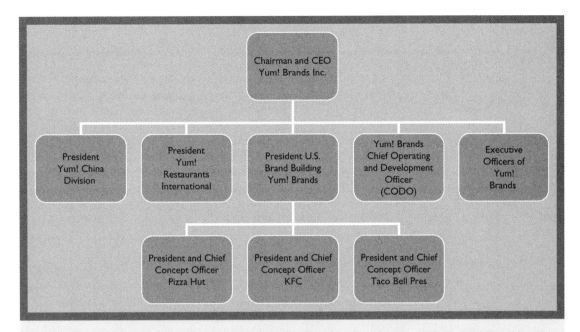

Yum! Brands Chief Operating and Development Officer (CODO). Both of these senior managers, along with the division presidents and executive officers, report directly to the CEO, as the organization chart shows.

Under this new structure, all three domestic brand presidents (Pizza Hut, KFC, and Taco Bell) report directly to the newly created position of President of Brand Building. After the reorganization, the CODO has responsibility for significantly improving systemwide operations and opening new restaurants by working with company leaders and franchisees. The divisional chief operating officers will report to two executives, the CODO and their respective divisional presidents. In the United States, chief development officers will report directly to the CODO. The reorganization in the U.S. business is designed to better leverage Yum! Brands scale and strengthen brand building, operations, and development across its entire domestic portfolio of brands.[1]

DISCUSSION QUESTIONS:

1. Why is the reorganization focused on just the U.S. business and not on the China or International divisions?

2. What are the pros and cons of having the chief operating officers report to both their brand-level president and the chief operating and development officer?

INTRODUCTION

Organizations employ a wide variety of tactics to implement their strategies. In the opening example, Yum! Brands is using a divisional management structure to enhance implementation of its growth strategy. In this structure, the China division and the International division operate as independent enterprises, but they also benefit from having access to capital and other resources of the larger company. In the U.S. division, the company has created three separate brand companies: Pizza Hut, Taco Bell, and KFC.

One element of the corporate strategy is to improve U.S. brand positions and returns, while business-level strategy for Taco Bell includes new product launches, creative promotions, and improved operating systems. The corporate and business-level organization structures can have a powerful influence on the execution of these strategies. Success in accomplishing these and other strategic plans rests on the managers and employees knowing how to get the work done.

An organization that is appropriately organized and has activities, budgets, and programs directed toward the desired objectives will likely succeed in the implementation of strategy. While there were a few hints at how to do this in earlier chapters, this chapter will add a great deal of understanding. It will begin with a discussion of the key building blocks of organizing (e.g., formalization, specialization, and hierarchy of authority), and then explore the various formal structures and how they can be used to support a particular strategic focus. The section closes with a brief commentary on newly emerging organizational structures and the importance of lateral relationships.

The final section of this chapter on implementation reviews control systems. Beyond the traditional measuring and monitoring functions, managers use control systems to overcome resistance to change, communicate new strategic agendas, ensure continuing attention to new strategic initiatives, formalize beliefs, set boundaries on acceptable strategic behavior, and motivate discussion and debate about strategic uncertainties.[2] Therefore, control systems may also be considered "tools of strategy implementation."[3] A discussion of the increasingly important topic of crisis management completes this chapter.

ORGANIZATIONAL STRUCTURES

One of the most important activities associated with strategy implementation is designing a strategy-supportive organization. Because people who have not been involved in the strategy formulation process perform so many activities that take place within organizations, it is essential that their work be designed to deliver on the strategy. It is systems, not smiles, that make excellent customer service. That is, managers need to carefully design the operating systems to enable effective action and to modify those systems as an organization grows or shifts its strategic focus.

Designing an organization involves defining organizational roles, determining reporting relationships, establishing how to group individuals, and creating ways to coordinate employee

CENTRALIZATION AT McDONALD'S

To ensure that all McDonald's restaurants serve products of uniform quality, the company uses centralized planning, centrally designed training programs, centrally approved and supervised suppliers, automated machinery and other specially designed equipment, meticulous specifications, and systematic inspections. To provide its customers with a uniformly pleasant "McDonald's experience," the company also tries to mass-produce friendliness, deference, diligence, and good cheer through a variety of socialization and social control techniques.

The point-of-sale system (POS) is at the core of many current McDonald's innovations like cashless and gift card payment, handheld order takers, and kiosks. The chain's move to cashless payment in the United States was implemented in 12,000 stores that share a common POS platform. Cited as an example of McDonald's standardization, the vice president of information systems noted, "When the decision was made to launch cashless payment across the system in the U.S., the business was able to deploy a standard, integrated solution in record-breaking time." Despite sneers from those who equate uniformity with mediocrity, the success of McDonald's operating structures has been spectacular.[4]

efforts. One element of design is the formal structure of how work is organized. The activities and people within corporations are usually subdivided into departments and groups so that employees may specialize in a limited number of activities and focus on a limited set of responsibilities. The *formal structure* specifies the number and types of departments or groups and provides the formal reporting relationships and lines of communication among internal stakeholders. The purpose of these structures is to coordinate, communicate, and control individual actions to support the strategy, and to facilitate workflow, permit management control, and create doable jobs.

Alfred Chandler was the first researcher to recognize the importance of the structure–strategy relationship.[5] According to Chandler, an organization's structure should be designed to support the intended strategy of the firm.[6] An organization can choose from a variety of structural forms when implementing a chosen strategy. The underlying assumption is that a fit between the strategy and the structure will lead to superior organizational performance, which seems logical but has not been proved conclusively.

Nevertheless, the connection between organizational structure and performance has been supported by research in the restaurant industry.[7] Higher-performing restaurants, defined by growth in unit sales, are less centralized, more formalized, and more specialized. Franchised operations are more formalized, as are companies in the quick-service segment. McDonald's, admired by its supporters and reviled by those who see it as robbing workers of meaningful tasks, is an excellent example of fitting the operating structure to the low-cost-provider strategy it uses to sell food. (See the "Hospitality Focus" boxed section above.)

Several principles or dimensions may be used to characterize an organization's structure. The dimensions, described in Table 8.1, capture the formal arrangements of people, activities,

TABLE 8.1 **Dimensions of Organizational Structure**

DIMENSION	DESCRIPTION
Hierarchy of authority	Formal reporting relationships among levels and across functions and departments. A tall, narrow structure means that there are multiple levels between the CEO and the customer. A flat, wide structure means fewer levels and a wider span of control for managers (more people report to them). A flat structure may be associated with more use of cross-functional, self-managed teams.
Degree of centralization	Refers to where in the structure the decision-making authority lies. A highly centralized structure means that high-level managers make most of the critical decisions. A decentralized structure puts more decision-making authority in the hands of lower-level managers and teams.
Complexity	Describes the number of levels in the hierarchy, the number of units such as departments or teams, and the number of markets served.
Specialization	The degree to which the tasks of the organization are divided into separate jobs. Some organizations have a highly specialized structure, with people focusing on one particular task or function. The advantage is that people can get very good at what they do. Other organizations expect people to be skilled in a number of tasks, which improves scheduling flexibility and teamwork.
Formalization	This might also be called bureaucracy. It describes the extent to which formalized rules, policies, and procedures exist within the organization and the extent to which people actually follow them. A high level of formalization can lead to efficiency but may reduce the flexibility that is sometimes required to satisfy customers.
Professionalism	Refers to the amount of formal education and training possessed by employees and managers. High-technology firms tend to have more professionalism, while firms engaged in agriculture or basic assembly tend to have less-well-educated employees.

Source: R. L. Daft, *Organization Theory and Design* (Cincinnati, OH: South–Western College Publishing, 2001).

and decision-making authority. Each of these dimensions represents an organizational design decision, and these decisions have ramifications with regard to organizational behavior. Conscious decisions are made regarding the degree of *specialization, formalization, centralization,* and *levels of authority* necessary to operate an organization.

Over time, decisions are revisited and organizations are redesigned to accommodate growth and changes in size, environmental complexity, competition, and entry into new or different businesses. When a new strategy is formulated, administrative problems often emerge and performance declines. This situation requires the establishment of a new structure, which leads to performance improvements. Hence, the careful design and redesign of organizations is essential to ensuring that the execution of a strategy is supported by the right system of coordination, communication, and control.

Simple Management Structures

To illustrate this evolution, let's start with a small business. A chef/owner decides to open an upscale restaurant in Buffalo, New York. This fine-dining establishment has a chef/owner who creates the menu, decides on food preparation methods, purchases the ingredients, cooks the meals, and then moves to the dining room to socialize with the guests.[8] In this small organization, little specialization is evident because the owner does many of the tasks necessary to operate the business. The reporting relationships are very informal, as her family and friends work by her side to deliver the meals. No job descriptions or formal performance reviews exist, and everyone in the restaurant is part of a "family."

This type of organization relies on the simplest management structure, the entrepreneurial structure, sometimes called the *owner/manager structure*. This form is common for smaller hotel and restaurant companies. The owner is the top manager, and the business is run as a sole proprietorship. This means that the owner/manager makes all of the important decisions and directs the efforts of all employees.

As this chef/owner builds her reputation, she may need to hire additional kitchen workers to perform specific culinary functions. As the volume of meals served increases, the chef/owner creates departments separating front-of-house service from back-of-house food preparation. She has now doubled the number of departments, increased her staff levels, and increased the level of specialization in the performance of various tasks. She has created levels of hierarchy, hiring a sous chef to supervise the kitchen and a dining room manager to handle guests. Her restaurant's popularity has led to an emerging catering business, requiring even more departmentalizing and specialization. The business is becoming more complex, and this entrepreneur must now create a more formalized structure. Our chef decides that now is the time for her to develop an *organization chart*, a useful tool for showing the various parts of the organization, how they interrelate, and how each position fits into the whole.[9]

Her success leads to careful business analysis and a revised strategy in which she wishes to expand by opening another restaurant in Syracuse, New York, and branching into retail by selling her sauces at a local grocery store called Wegman's. With these moves come increasing levels of hierarchy and complexity, as her organization now serves several markets with multiple units and increasing numbers of employees. Many of the critical decisions in the day-to-day operation of each restaurant and the retail business are now delegated to her subordinate managers, making the organization more decentralized.

To complete our example, after years of success, this small business is now a big business with 15 units in seven northeastern cities and two separate divisions, one for restaurants and the other for retail sales. Our CEO/owner has expansion in her five-year plan, with a desire to diversify into casual-dining restaurants and to move her fine-dining concept into a franchise operation. Along the way, she has altered the organizational structure several times to reflect the evolution in her strategy.

The key point is that managers need to be deliberate about organizational-design choices because they have ramifications on a firm's ability to execute its chosen strategies. For instance, decentralized decision making is likely to encourage innovation and entrepreneurship, whereas a high level of formalization (rules and procedures) will have the opposite influence. Generally speaking, restaurant chains have a fairly high degree of formalization, which supports the operating unit strategies, particularly in the quick-service segment. Also, high levels of professionalism (well-educated employees) may be needed to support a strategy of technical leadership. A surprising feature of many multiunit restaurants is the absence of a specialized research-and-development function, although this pattern is changing, and the function is often considered essential for long-term growth.[10] These are just a few examples of what might happen to the operation of an organization when different decisions are made regarding organizing elements like centralization, formalization, and levels of hierarchy.

As competition increases and the hotel industry matures, hotel strategists have begun to question what should be centralized to corporate headquarters and what could be more effectively executed at the property level. Choice Hotels, for example, evaluated service delivery and then created a more centralized franchise services function to provide more consistency in delivery and a better focus on customer needs.[11] Centralization has often been found to provide cost savings and efficiency. Examples include the consolidation of food and beverage operations into a single prep kitchen that delivers product to several outlets fast and with fewer workers. For some firms, moving sales and marketing out of the hotel and into regional areas has provided a more effective selling model. Accounting activities such as payroll have also become more efficient when handled at a chain's corporate headquarters, as have central reservation systems (CRS) that serve multiple properties. (See the "Hospitality Focus" boxed section on page 307.)

When making decisions about how to structure an organization, it is important to remember the following:

- Structure is not an end; it is a means to an end. The end is successful organizational performance.

- There is no one best structure. A change in organizational strategy may require a corresponding change in structure to avoid administrative inefficiencies, but the organization's size, strategies, external environment, stakeholder relationships, and management style all influence the appropriateness of a given structure. All structures embody trade-offs.[12]

- Once in place, the new structure becomes a characteristic of the organization that will serve as a constraint on future strategic choices.

THE PROPERTY MANAGEMENT SYSTEM (PMS) AT WYNDHAM HOTELS & RESORTS

HOSPITALITY FOCUS

Centralized property management systems (PMSs), also called application service provider (ASP) systems, save hotels money by providing computer-based services over a network. Hotel users access applications that exist off-property, requiring a browser or thin client application instead of a full PC software suite. These systems are often housed in a vendor data center, providing greater reliability and ease of integrating new properties. InterContinental Hotels found that due to their scale, they could save $15,000 per hotel by deploying a centralized system.

When Wyndham Hotels & Resorts shifted from a real estate investment trust (REIT) to a branded hotel operating company and C corporation in the late 1990s, technology purchasing priorities changed. As a REIT, Wyndham wasn't concerned with having a systemwide CRS, and properties relied on seven different project management systems. But as a branded operating company with a desire for seamless connectivity among properties and a CRS, Wyndham began to have difficulty justifying the cost of licensing seven PMSs and developing seven interfaces to a CRS. For Wyndam, it made sense to employ a centralized PMS to which individual properties subscribe on an ASP basis. Wyndham acts as the central ASP of the OPERA PMS by MICROS Systems, loading and configuring software on a single server that is linked to every property in the system. Updates to the server can upgrade all properties overnight, reinvigorating systems in a manner that would take a chain with decentralized, on-property PMSs countless hours of labor.[13]

- Administrative inefficiencies, poor service to customers, communication problems, or employee frustrations may indicate a strategy-structure mismatch.

Business-Level versus Corporate-Level Structures

The various structural forms can be divided into two broad groups: business-level and corporate-level. These groups are consistent in their definitions with the way we have been using the terms business-level and corporate-level in describing strategies. *Business-level structures* are methods of organizing individual business units, which are often called divisions if they are part of a larger corporation. Another way to think of these units is as separate operating companies. If an organization consists of only one operating company, then its business-level structure is its corporate structure. However, as organizations diversify and form multiple operating companies, they encounter the need to create a corporate-level structure to tie these separate companies together. It is interesting to note that a single corporation, like Yum! Brands, could

CORPORATE-LEVEL STRUCTURE AT INTERCONTINENTAL HOTELS AND RESORTS

InterContinental Hotels and Resorts is made up of three operating regions (Europe, the Middle East, and Africa; the Americas; and Asia-Pacific) and a UK-based corporate headquarters. The organization chart shown captures the corporate-level structure.

Corporate headquarters has four main function-based units:

1. *Corporate Services* is responsible for corporate governance, risk management, insurance, internal audits, company secretariat, group legal services, and corporate social responsibility.

2. *Finance and Asset Management* and *Central Shared Services* establish and manage the capital structure for the business, capital allocation processes, communicate financial information, manage corporate income taxes, and provide global IT systems and standardized processing for business transactions. Reservation channels, loyalty marketing programs, and global sales strategy are handled by the Global Brand Services unit.

3. The *Global Human Resources* unit is responsible for attracting, motivating, developing, and retaining their people and improving the organization through developing and implementing company-wide HR strategies, programs, systems, and policies.

```
                        ┌─────────────────────┐
                        │  InterContinental   │
                        │    Hotel Group      │
                        │      Global         │
                        │   Headquarters      │
                        │    Windsor, UK      │
                        └─────────────────────┘
       ┌──────────────┬──────────┴───────┬──────────────────┐
┌──────────────┐ ┌──────────────┐ ┌──────────────┐ ┌──────────────────┐
│InterContinental│ │InterContinental│ │InterContinental│ │ Corporate Centre │
│ Hotel Group   │ │ Hotel Group   │ │ Hotel Group   │ │ Corporate Services│
│ Europe, Middle│ │ The Americas  │ │ Asia Pacific  │ │ Finance and Asset │
│ East and Africa│ │ (Atlanta, USA)│ │ (Singapore)   │ │   Management     │
│ (Windsor, UK) │ │              │ │              │ │  Global Brand    │
│              │ │              │ │              │ │    Services      │
│              │ │              │ │              │ │  Global Human    │
└──────────────┘ └──────────────┘ └──────────────┘ └──────────────────┘
```

The President of the European, Middle East, and Africa (EMEA) unit has responsibility for 639 hotels, constituting approximately 13 percent of hotel operating profit before central costs. This regional executive, like the President of the Americas and the Chief Executive of the Asia-Pacific area, is responsible for the management, growth, and profitability of the portfolio of brands within the operating region. Within each region is an executive committee that includes functional managers in the areas of sales and marketing, information technology, finance, engineering, legal counsel, and human resources, and Chief Operating Officers (COOs) that cover various subregions. For example, in the EMEA region, four COOs are responsible for different aspects of hotel operations: one COO handles the Middle East and Africa and one handles the United Kingdom and Ireland. Two different COOs are responsible for Europe: one handles the Inter-Continental Brand, and the other oversees the Holiday Inn brand family.[14]

have two or more business units using different business-level structures. For example, one unit could be organized according to functional activities like marketing, accounting, and human resources, and another unit could be organized according to geographic markets like the East, West, and Midwest. A corporate-level structure ties the business units together. The "Hospitality Focus" boxed section on page 308 illustrates how a firm designs its operation to run multiple businesses along with the overarching corporate structure.

Types of Business-Level Structures

In the hospitality industry, the basic business-level structures include functional, geographic/customer, and project matrix. Some of the essential characteristics, strengths, and weaknesses of these structures are presented in Table 8.2.

TABLE 8.2 Important Attributes of Basic Business-Level Structures

	FUNCTIONAL	GEOGRAPHIC OR CUSTOMER	PROJECT MATRIX
Organizing Framework	Functional inputs such as marketing, engineering, and manufacturing	Outputs such as types of services or various markets in which they are provided	Inputs and outputs
Degree of Centralization	Centralized	Decentralized	Decentralized with shared authority
Competitive Environment	Tends to work better if the environment is stable and demands internal efficiency or specialization within functions	Works well in a dynamic environment with pressure to satisfy needs of particular customers, markets, or locations	Responds to both internal pressure for efficiency or specialization and external market pressure to satisfy particular needs
Growth Strategy	Supports market penetration well	Useful for market and/or service development	Frequent changes to products and markets

TABLE 8.2 (*Continued*)

Major Strengths	• Economies of scale within departments may lead to efficiency • Allows development of functional expertise and specialization • Best in organizations with few products or services	• Suited to fast change in an unstable environment • High levels of client satisfaction • High coordination across functions • Best in large organizations with several products or markets	• Achieves coordination • Flexible sharing of human resources • Best in medium-sized firms with multiple products
Major Weaknesses	• Slow response time to environmental changes • Hierarchy overload from decisions collecting at the top • Poor coordination across departments • Restricts view of organizational goals	• Lose economies of scale • Some functions are redundant within the organization • Lose in-depth specialization within functions • May lead to poor coordination and integration across locations, customers, or products, depending on the style used	• Dual authority can cause frustration and confusion • Excellent interpersonal skills needed • Additional training required can be expensive • Time consuming due to frequent meetings • Great effort needed to maintain power balance

Sources: R. L. Daft, *Organization Theory and Design* (Cincinnati, OH: South-Western College Publishing, 2001); R. Duncan, "What is the Right Organization Structure? Decision Tree Analysis Provides the Answer," *Organization Dynamics* (Winter 1979): 429–431.

FUNCTIONAL STRUCTURES

The most common way in which companies organize is called a *functional structure* and is based on putting people in groupings or departments based on their shared expertise. Functional structures are organized around the common activities or similar tasks performed by individuals.[15] Hotels are most often functionally structured and usually have marketing, human resources, food and beverage, accounting, and rooms departments, at a minimum. If the hotel is larger in size, it will have other departments, such as engineering, public relations, and convention services. The structure is centralized, highly specialized, and most appropriate when a limited service or product line is offered to a particular market segment and when the needs of external stakeholders are relatively stable.

The functional structure is oriented toward internal efficiency and encourages teamwork and coordination of activities within individual departments or units. It is particularly appropriate in organizations that want to exploit economies of scale, efficiency, and learning effects from focused activities. Small businesses often employ functional structures very effectively (see Figure 8.1). A functional structure can also be effective for a firm pursuing a market-penetration strategy, because organizational scope (i.e., number of products and markets) and customer requirements will be relatively stable over time.

The functional structure is not appropriate in an environment where customer needs are diverse or changing, as when a firm is trying to provide many products or services to many customer groups. The functional structure may result in poor coordination across departments and thus impede the ability of the firm to adapt to changing needs. Over time, the different departments may become insular and focus on departmental goals at the expense of overall organizational goals.[16] Because functional departments concentrate on their own professional or technical activities, it is possible for a department to be high-performing, but the overall hotel to not be. In addition, interdepartmental conflicts easily emerge when people focus exclusively on their own area of skill.

In hotels, it is common for departments to be in conflict over service delivery. The sales team books business, but the rooms division and banquet staff must deliver on the sales promises made to customers. Because of the nature of a functional design, it is not easy to handle interdepartmental communication and coordination. It is unlikely that individual departments are capable of resolving interdepartmental conflicts, and the task of handling these issues falls on the general manager (GM).

Hierarchy overload can lead to decisions piling up at the top of the organization, because most interdepartmental issues fall on the general manger. It is not uncommon for a GM to feel overloaded with problems and decisions. Turnover among GMs has been found to be primarily due to management conflict and problems between the property and owners.[17] One

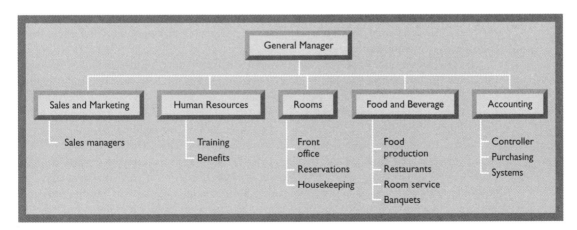

FIGURE 8.1 **Functional structure for a hotel**

way to reduce the problems inherent in this structure is to avoid the tendency to blame other departments and to develop general management skills in the functional managers. Later in this chapter, we will discuss ways in which lateral relationships can help reduce the coordinating challenges faced in functionally designed organizations. The following are examples of problems that can develop across functions in a hotel.

Imagine that the director of sales is under pressure to increase group bookings. Without coordinating with the other hotel departments, here is what might happen:

- Sales might guarantee more rooms for a convention than are actually available, resulting in overbooking, a problem that the front desk and reservations staff will have to handle.

- Sales might book a group that has meeting-room needs the hotel cannot satisfy because of previous commitments. The convention services manager, if consulted, might have avoided this problem.

- Convention services may try to accommodate the meeting needs of the group, but neglect to let food and beverage know of the additional guest needs, causing the coffee service to be missed during a break.

- Finally, the hotel laundry may be unaware of the banquet requirement for clean uniforms with the addition of this new group business and not have the uniforms available.[18]

GEOGRAPHIC AND CUSTOMER-BASED STRUCTURES

In the hotel and restaurant industry, organizations often grow by adding hotels or restaurants in new locations. Corporations that organize on the basis of expanding into new locations are using a *geographic structure*.[19] This form of organizing is common in the hospitality industry, because companies operate in diverse geographic markets. Best Western operates more than 4,200 hotels in 80 countries; Darden Restaurants has 1,700 stores in various locations; and MGM Mirage owns or operates 18 casino properties on three continents. Restructuring of InterContinental Hotels and Resorts into geographic divisions at both the corporate and regional levels, as featured earlier, is an example of a geographic structure and is thought to have streamlined that company.[20]

A firm that expands its business from a regional market base to a national market base may form new units around geographic segments. For example, Pegasus Solutions, Inc., a global provider of hotel reservation technologies, has divided its regional offices to cover North America, Latin America, Europe/Middle East/Africa, and Asia-Pacific/India.[21] A restaurant chain may be divided into units responsible for eastern and western regions (see Figure 8.2a).

If the organization structures its major units around the characteristics or types of customer, it is a *customer-based structure* (see Figure 8.2b). Some firms that pursue growth through market development seek out new customer groups. If sales to a particular new type of customer reach sufficient volume, the organization may reorganize around customer groups. For example, a hotel chain may organize around economy and luxury lodging. A foodservice firm might organize by institutional versus educational clients. Similarly, a microcomputer company might organize its business around home-user, business, academic, and mail-order

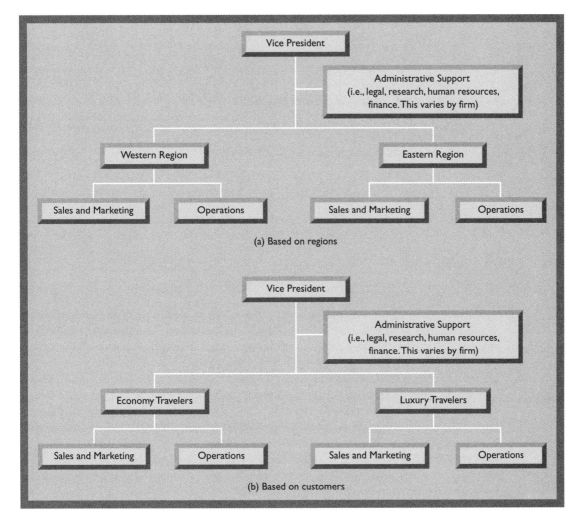

FIGURE 8.2 Geographic- and customer-based structures

customer groups. Or an architectural firm might organize around commercial, hospitality, and residential projects.

When a business organizes around geographic regions or type of customer, it may continue to centralize its production or service operations in one area if economies of scale are significant. If not, then each geographic region or market unit may have its own operations facilities. However, in most cases, at least some administrative functions, such as legal or information technology, are still centralized.

Both the geographic and customer organizational structures have as a major strength their focus on unique needs and customer preferences. The goal is to be responsive to local market conditions. A company that uses a geographic structure is better able to serve the unique tastes and needs of customers in various locations. Unfortunately, there may be little sharing of resources across locations or customer groups and obvious duplication of efforts. The following hotel example illustrates how unique a hotel location can be and how difficult it would be to share these resources. (See the first "Hospitality Focus" boxed section on page 315.)

Geographic and customer-based structures are suited to a fast-changing environment and high levels of customer satisfaction. They are especially appropriate in larger businesses with multiple types of services, and they are helpful if market or service development is the strategic focus. However, economies of scale are lost if operations are separated, and some functions will be redundant across locations. Also, the company loses some of its in-depth functional specialization and coordination across product lines, which can be a problem.[22] Nevertheless, these structures are popular in larger hospitality companies. (See the second "Hospitality Focus" boxed section on page 315.)

NETWORK STRUCTURES

Some organizations, particularly large integrated service organizations, use the network, or "spider's web," structure.[23] The *network structure* is similar to the geographic or customer-based structure, but it is even more decentralized. It represents a web of independent units, with little or no formal hierarchy to organize and control their relationship. The independent units are loosely organized to capture and share useful information. Other than information sharing, however, little formal contact occurs among operating units.

A hotel consortium is a good example of a network in which hotels combine resources in order to establish joint purchasing arrangements and marketing services.[24] Best Western is an excellent example of this type of structure. The company is organized as a nonprofit association of member hotels, providing member services such as a reservation system, marketing, brand identity, facilities design, and training.[25] The services are funded by member fees and dues. One senior leader characterized the network as the "ultimate Jeffersonian Democracy."[26] Other examples of a spider web structure include the top five consortia in terms of number of rooms: Utell/Unirez–Pegasus Solutions Rep. Services, SynXis Corp., Vantis Corp., Supranational Hotels, and InnPoints Worldwide.[27] Incorporating the network service provider as a brand is the approach taken by Leading Hotels of the World, Ltd., the eighth largest consortium, providing global distribution, reservations, and luxury marketing support to five-star independent hotels and hotel groups. (See the "Hospitality Focus" boxed section on page 316.)

MATRIX STRUCTURES

A hybrid structure that combines some elements of functional structures with other forms, discussed earlier, is called a *matrix structure*. For example, a construction company with functional departments could form teams to carry out specific projects. Each team would have individuals from the functional areas reporting to both a project leader and their functional manager. The project-matrix structure is viewed by some as a transition stage between a functional form and other forms, and by others as a complex form necessary for complex environments.[28] Either way, the many stakeholder influences that simultaneously pull an organization toward functional forms and the more diverse geographic, customer, product, or service forms reach an equilibrium in the matrix structure. Project matrix structures are most common in turbulent or uncertain competitive environments where internal stakeholders are highly interdependent and where external stakeholder demands are diverse and changing.[29] Matrix structures can improve communications between groups, increase the amount of information the organization can handle, and allow people and equipment to be used more flexibly.[30]

BRAZIL'S ARIAU TREETOP RESORT

HOSPITALITY FOCUS

"One day the eyes of the whole world will be on the Amazon," Jacques Cousteau supposedly told a wealthy Brazilian lawyer in 1982. "If you build a hotel up in the trees, people will come." And they have come—to Brazil's Ariau Hotel, a 205-room treetop resort. Tarzan's house is one perch in the world's largest treetop resort. With seven cylindrical towers and two lookout towers rising to 130 feet, and three miles of catwalks connecting them through the multilayered mazeway of the rain forest, Brazil's Ariau Hotel dwarfs the more famous tree lodges of Kenya and California.[31]

CARLSON HOTELS WORLDWIDE CENTRALIZES ADMINISTRATIVE STRUCTURE

HOSPITALITY FOCUS

When Jay Witzel took over as president and CEO of Carlson Hotels Worldwide, he was determined to inject more of a customer focus. One of the tools he used to stress customer focus was to change the organization's structure. In his role at Carlson, he is one of seven presidents who oversee different businesses. His responsibility is to lead the global strategies and growth of all of Carlson's hotel operations, which currently includes more than 950 locations in 70 countries. The five brands of Carlson Hotels Worldwide include Regent Hotels & Resorts, Radisson Hotels & Resorts, Park Plaza Hotels & Resorts, Country Inns & Suites By Carlson, and Park Inn hotels. Witzel also oversees the company's cruise company, Regent Seven Seas Cruises, which includes four luxury vessels sailing worldwide itineraries.

Reflecting on his approach to organizing the hotel business, he notes, "The first thing I wanted to do then was take us out of four or five operating companies and move us into one multibranded operating company. Then I wanted to split up the globe." In essence, what he did was increase the power of the central administration over the way business would be conducted, while simultaneously increasing the power of each geographic area to satisfy local needs. "We are going to merge all our brands into Rezidor in Europe," said Witzel, "Rezidor will be responsible for Regent, Radisson, Country Inns & Suites and Park Inns." One of the real advantages of centralization is found in marketing. "Up to this point, sales teams for the different brands have been selling on an individual basis. Now we have a centralized team that sells on behalf of all the brands."[32]

In a matrix structure, the organization is simultaneously functional and product, geographic, customer, or service oriented (see Figure 8.3). Unfortunately, matrix structures can be disconcerting for employees because of the "too many bosses" problem. Power struggles may occur because it is difficult to balance the different lines of authority. Matrix structures require a lot of interpersonal skill because of frequent communications. Meetings can take a lot of time, and it is sometimes difficult to coordinate the many people and

HOSPITALITY FOCUS

BEST WESTERN: A NETWORK STRUCTURE

Best Western was founded in 1946 as an informal referral system among member hotels. Unlike most hotel franchise companies that have a mix of company-owned and franchised units, each property is an independently owned and operated franchise. Best Western, named because it originally had hotels primarily in the Western United States, has a unique business model. The company is a nonprofit association, with each franchisee acting and voting as a member of the association. Hotels renew their membership annually, instead of relying on long-term contracts. In addition, hotels can keep their independent identity, although they must use Best Western signage and identify themselves as a Best Western hotel. The chain charges a rate based on an initial cost plus fees for each additional room in exchange for providing marketing, reservations, and operational support. Today Best Western is the world's largest hotel chain, with 4,200 hotels worldwide in 80 countries, with 19 international affiliate offices and property-direct relationships with another six regions.[33]

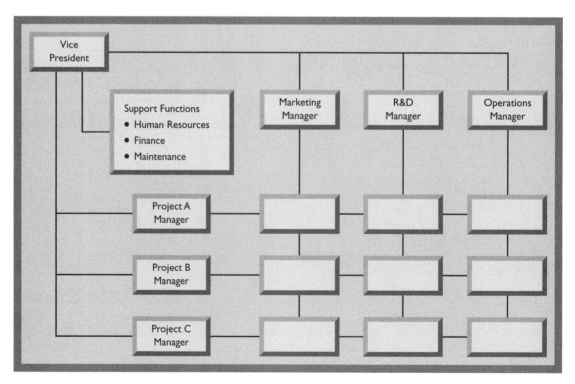

FIGURE 8.3 **The project–matrix structure**

A MATRIX STRUCTURE AT THE TRAVEL INDUSTRY ASSOCIATION (TIA)

HOSPITALITY FOCUS

"Let's invent," said William Norman on the day he began as president and CEO of the Travel Industry Association (TIA). In a discussion of his experience at TIA, Norman describes a system he calls matrix management. Two prominent features—task teams and an unusually free-spirited quarterly staff meeting—capture the essence of how the matrix functions. Norman looks at an organization as "a cross-functional form," or matrix that should have relatively few barriers between traditional departments. TIA's matrix has broken down many old barriers.[34]

CORPORATE RESTRUCTURING OF ORIENT-EXPRESS HOTELS LTD

HOSPITALITY FOCUS

Orient-Express Hotels Ltd. began in 1976 as a division of Sea Containers Ltd., a diversified Bermuda company. Sea Containers was engaged in three main activities: passenger transport, marine container leasing, and leisure-based (hotel) operations. In addition, Sea Containers' other activities include property development and management, publishing, fruit farming in the Ivory Coast and Brazil, and a UK-based travel agency.

In 2000, Orient-Express became a publicly traded hotel company (symbol OEH) focusing on the luxury end of the leisure market, and in 2005, the parent company, Sea Containers, sold the last of its share in the hotel company. Sea Containers is now focused on its passenger transport and marine container leasing businesses.

Orient-Express Hotels Ltd. owns or partly owns and manages 40 hotels, two restaurants, and six tourist trains. The company also partly owns and manages PeruRail in Peru, which operates the Cuzco–Machu Picchu train service used by nearly every tourist to Peru. Under Simon M. C. Sherwood, former president of OEH, regional vice presidents played a large role in the company's operational success. Decentralized in its approach, OEH has only 20 to 25 staff at its corporate headquarters that oversee corporate planning and serve as resources for property managers. "Corporate staff is there to help, not to look over anyone's shoulder. I respect the general managers as businesspeople and give them the autonomy to manage their hotels," noted Sherwood in 2002. In late 2007, the company promoted Paul White to President and CEO (he was formerly CFO). In addition to other promotions, the company eliminated the regional vice presidents and instead put in place eight area managing directors who will continue to run their individual hotels while taking on specific geographic responsibilities. These area managing directors will report to the Vice President of Operations, who was previously the regional Vice President of Africa, Latin America, and Australasia.[35]

schedules. The overall complexity of the structure can create ambiguity and conflict between functional and product managers and between individuals. The sheer number of people that must be involved in decision making can slow the decision processes and add administrative costs.[36] (See the first "Hospitality Focus" boxed section on page 317.)

Corporate-Level Structures

Three general types of structures are used by multibusiness organizations: multidivisional, strategic business unit, and corporate matrix. These structures are used when a company begins to diversify its services, enters unrelated market channels, or begins to serve diverse customer groups.[37] Sea Containers Ltd., for example, is a diversified firm with multiple divisions. These more complex structures are necessary because of the increased coordination and decision making required for handling large and diversified firms. Typically, decision making is decentralized, and the corporate headquarters focuses on coordinating all of its divisions or groups of business through reporting systems and corporate planning. Table 8.3 lists the major characteristics of these corporate-level structures. Following is an example of the restructuring put in place by Orient-Express Hotels Ltd., which began as a division of Sea Containers, Ltd., but now operates as a totally independent business. (See the second "Hospitality Focus" boxed section on page 317.)

MULTIDIVISIONAL STRUCTURES

If an organization has relatively few businesses in its portfolio, management may choose a multidivisional (line-of-business) structure, with each business existing as a separate unit. For example, a multidivisional organization may have a time-share division, a corporate services division, a transportation division, and a gaming equipment division. In this type of structure, a general manager—sometimes referred to as a divisional president or vice president—heads up each of the three divisions. Each division has its own support functions, including sales, accounting/finance, personnel, and research and development. Services that are common to all three businesses are housed at the corporate level, such as legal services, public relations, and corporate research. Divisional activities and overall financial control are monitored by the corporate headquarters.

International strategies are often implemented through multidivisional structures. If an organization chooses to produce and sell its products in Europe, management may form an international division to house those activities, as did Yum! Brands, discussed at the beginning of the chapter. If a firm pursues a multidomestic strategy that involves it in several independent national or regional businesses, management may form a separate division for each business. The multidivisional structure is appropriate when management of the different businesses does not require sharing of employees, marketing resources, or operations facilities.

The *multidivisional structure*, shown in Figure 8.4, has several advantages. By existing as a separate unit, each business is better able to focus its efforts on the needs of its particular stakeholders, without being distracted by the problems of other businesses. Corporate-level management is freed from day-to-day issues and is able to take a long-term, integrative view of the collection of businesses. Corporate executives may monitor the performance of each division

TABLE 8.3 **Distinguishing Characteristics of Corporate-Level Structures**

	MULTIDIVISIONAL	STRATEGIC BUSINESS UNIT	CORPORATE MATRIX
Number of Businesses	Few relative to the other corporate-level structures (but at least two independent businesses)	Many businesses grouped into SBUs based on commonalities such as products or markets	Few or many businesses
Degree of Relatedness	No operational or marketing relatedness required; however, sometimes a low level of relatedness exists	Related businesses are grouped into SBUs, but there may be little or no relatedness across SBUs	Typically very high relatedness is required so that people can be transferred throughout the corporation without significant retraining or frustration
Need for Coordination Across Businesses	Typically low coordination across units; coordination required only to the extent that relatedness exists	Coordination required within SBUs; little or no coordination required across SBUs	Significant coordination required to make the structure work
Expected Synergy	Financial synergy can be achieved; limited operational synergies, only to the extent that units are related and coordinated	Financial synergy available across SBUs; operating synergy may be available within SBUs to the extent that strategies and activities are coordinated	High operational synergies are available; may result in high levels of innovation, cost savings, or a greater ability to serve multiple markets

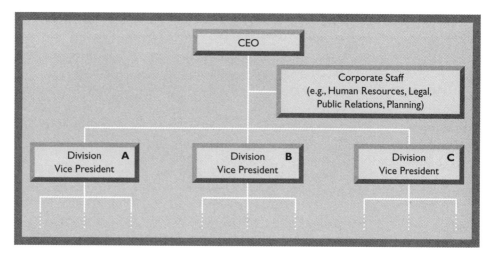

FIGURE 8.4 The multidivisional structure

separately and allocate corporate resources for specific activities that show promise. This can lead to what is referred to as financial synergy. *Financial synergy* can be defined as the value added because of the ability to allocate financial resources to the areas that have the highest potential. The result may be increased returns, reduced risk (variability in earnings), or both.

With the multidivisional structure, it is often difficult to decide which activities will be performed at the corporate level and which will be held within each division. Competition for corporate resources (research, legal, investment funds) may create coordination difficulties among divisions. Also, organizational efforts may be duplicated, particularly when the different businesses within the corporate portfolio are highly related. It may be that shared distribution channels or common-process development could save costs for the two businesses, yet separation in the organization structure discourages cooperation.

A multidivisional structure is well suited to an unrelated-diversification strategy, where there is no attempt to achieve operating synergies through coordinating and combining activities. However, managers sometimes use a multidivisional structure while pursuing a related-diversification strategy. Unfortunately, to exploit operational synergies, managers must structure relationships among businesses and partners in ways that encourage interdependence, and they must manage them over time with shared goals, shared information, shared resources, and cooperative program development.[38] The multidivisional structure makes resource sharing and cooperation difficult, but those two behaviors are necessary for operating synergy to occur.

STRATEGIC BUSINESS UNIT STRUCTURES

When an organization is broadly diversified with several businesses in its portfolio, it becomes difficult for top management to keep track of and understand the many industry environments and business conditions. Management may choose to form *strategic business units* (SBUs), with each SBU incorporating a few closely related businesses and operating as a profit center. Each SBU is composed of related divisions, with divisional vice presidents reporting to the president of an SBU or group.

If an organization becomes very large, it may combine strategic business units into groups or sectors, thus adding another level of management. The Tata Group uses an SBU structure in the management of its 98 separate operating companies, grouped into seven sectors.[39] The SBU structure is illustrated in Figure 8.5.

The SBU structure makes it possible for top management to monitor many businesses at one time. It allows decentralization around dimensions that are meaningful to the business, such as markets or technologies. SBU presidents can encourage the members of the SBU to coordinate activities and share information. The intent of the structure is to provide top management with a manageable number of units to keep track of and to force responsibility for decision making lower into the organization, near the important internal and external stakeholders. Financial synergy is possible through allocating resources to the SBUs that have the greatest potential. Operating synergy is also available within SBUs, because they are formed based on relatedness among businesses. Consequently, financial synergy is available across SBUs, whereas operating synergy is possible only within SBUs. (See the "Hospitality Focus" boxed section on page 323.)

CORPORATE-LEVEL MATRIX STRUCTURES

The *corporate matrix* is the corporate-level counterpart to the matrix structure described earlier (see Figure 8.6). It is a way to achieve a high degree of coordination among several related businesses. Corporate-matrix structures are used when the individual businesses within a corporation's portfolio need to take advantage of resource, information, or technology sharing in order to succeed in their industries. The corporate-matrix structure tries to reach a balance between

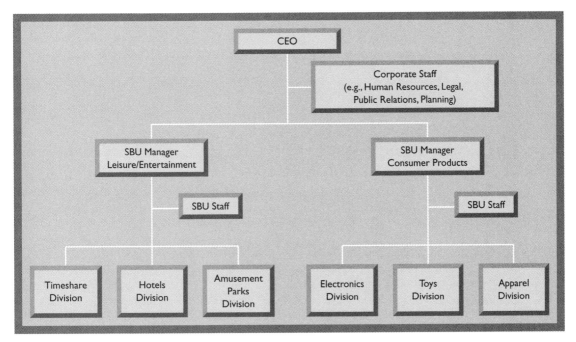

FIGURE 8.5 The strategic business unit (SBU) structure

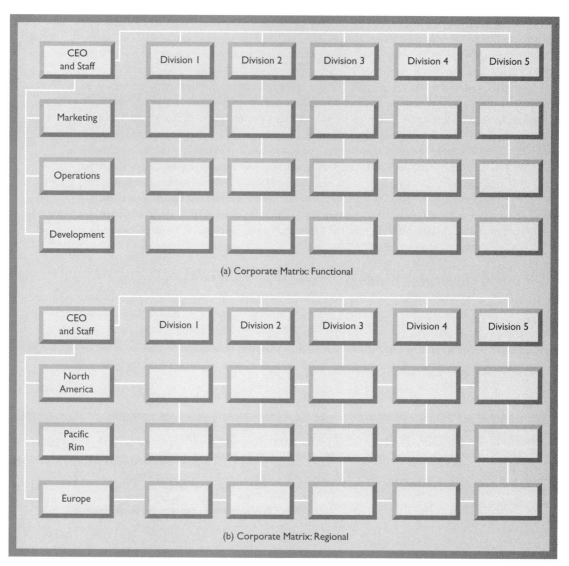

FIGURE 8.6 **Types of corporate matrix structures**

the pressures to decentralize units closer to market and technological trends and the pressures to maintain centralized control to bring about economies of scope and shared learning.

The corporate–matrix structure is particularly appropriate for related–diversification strategies and global strategies. For example, a hospitality firm that has businesses in lodging, gaming, and cruise lines may use a matrix structure to capitalize on economies of scale and capture operating synergies in marketing and distribution, as shown in Figure 8.6. Ideally, the corporate–matrix structure improves coordination among internal stakeholders by forcing managers within related businesses to maintain close contact with one another.

THE STRATEGIC BUSINESS UNIT STRUCTURES (SBUs) AT DISNEY

HOSPITALITY
FOCUS

The Walt Disney Company is a leading producer and provider of entertainment and information, using a portfolio of brands to differentiate its content, services, and consumer products. With a total market value of $71.6 billion, the corporation consists of media networks, studios and entertainment, parks and resorts, and consumer products. Within these SBUs are a wide variety of businesses. In media networks, for example, rests the Disney-ABC television network, ESPN Inc., Walt Disney Internet Group, and ABC-owned television stations, all overseen by presidents.

The leader of the hospitality SBU bears the title of Chair, Walt Disney Parks and Resorts. He oversees a broad range of businesses, including Disney Cruise Line, eight Disney Vacation club resorts, Adventures by Disney, and five resort locations and theme parks. The theme parks and resorts include the Disneyland Resort in California, Walt Disney World Resort in Florida, Tokyo Disney Resort, Disneyland Resort Paris, and Hong Kong Disneyland.

Michael Eisner, CEO for more than 20 years, resigned in 2005 after shareholders expressed a lack of confidence. One year later, Robert Iger was the new CEO, marking a turnaround for Disney. Net income rose 33 percent, and the stock climbed 28 percent. Disney has made significant inroads into the lucrative "tween" market with products like *High School Musical*, a Disney Channel original movie, and the success of various other spinoffs—including music videos, merchandise, Radio Disney promotions, and interactive online feature—exhibited the company's celebrated operational and financial synergies at their finest.[40]

The difficulty of the SBU structure is that operating units, and therefore the customer, are even further removed from top management than in the multidivisional form. As with the multidivisional form, there is competition for corporate financial and staff resources, which may create conflicts and coordination problems. It is important to assign specific job responsibilities and expectations to business presidents, SBU presidents, and the corporate president, or conflicts may occur.

It can help the organization become more flexible and responsive to changes in the business environment, and it can encourage teamwork and participation.[41] Cendant Corporation used a corporate matrix to structure its 60,000-employee conglomerate before divesting the various businesses. During this time, the vice president of human resources was responsible for corporate and business unit human resource functions across the entire organization.[42]

The corporate-matrix form may also be effective in structuring a hospitality company that provides services that are all sold in several nations. A multinational firm may create a matrix structure that groups all products under each national manager and simultaneously groups all nations under each product manager. This type of matrix structure allows the firm to achieve a national focus in its marketing and distribution practices, and it encourages synergies through economies of scale and shared information within each product category.

If we return to Yum! Brands, we see the use of a matrix design in the structure of having divisional Chief Operating Officers report to both the divisional president and their respective brand presidents. The corporate-matrix structure applied to a multinational organization is shown in the bottom half of Figure 8.6.

Transnational Structure

A more complex version of the corporate-matrix structure is the transnational form.[43] Whereas the global-matrix structure organizes businesses along two dimensions, the *transnational structure* organizes businesses along three dimensions: nation or region, product, and function. The transnational form is an attempt to achieve integration within product categories, within nations, and within functions while simultaneously achieving coordination across all of those activities. The transnational form requires three types of managers, who serve integrating roles: (1) country or region managers, who oversee all products and functions performed in their area to maintain a focal point for customers; (2) functional managers, who oversee the activities of a particular function (technology, marketing, or manufacturing) for all products in all nations; and (3) business managers, who oversee all functions and markets supported by a particular service group.[44] When Royal Dutch Shell used a transnational form, its executives often reported to a country, a regional, and a functional head.[45]

The corporate-matrix and transnational structures are plagued by one serious difficulty: sheer complexity may interfere with what they are designed to accomplish. It is difficult to balance the needs of the different functional, national, and product stakeholders. The unusual command structure can create an atmosphere of ambiguity, conflict, and mixed loyalties. The overall complexity and bureaucracy of the structure may stifle creativity and impede decision making because of the sheer number of people who must be involved. Furthermore, the administrative costs associated with decision delays and extra management may overwhelm the benefits of coordination.[46]

This concludes our discussion of the business- and corporate-level structures. Each of the forms contained in this section is a model that provides a general idea of how to structure an organization. With the exception of the simpler forms, it would be unusual to find a firm structured exactly like one of the models in this chapter. Also, it would be unusual to find any two companies structured in exactly the same way. Organizations create their own designs based on their own needs. Also, many companies create hybrid structures that combine elements of two or more of the models discussed in this section, as we saw in the structure of Yum! Brands. It is not uncommon for a company to have one division based on geography and another based on products, with a functional staff at the corporate level.

Earlier chapters discussed the worldwide trends that are leading firms to increased interorganizational relationships. These trends are causing newer organizational forms to emerge. *Modular structures* outsource all of the noncore functions of the organization. The organization is actually a hub surrounded by networks of suppliers. This type of structure allows the firm to minimize capital investments and to focus internal resources on core activities. A second new form is referred to as the virtual type, a group of units from different firms that have joined into an alliance to exploit complementary skills and resources in the pursuit of a common strategic

COASTAL HOTEL GROUP: A BUDDY SYSTEM FOR LATERAL ORGANIZATION

HOSPITALITY FOCUS

Coastal Hotel Group developed a buddy system to help newly acquired properties benefit from the experience and skills of department heads in existing properties. The way the system works, corporate management determines the buddy needs of the acquired property and the training time table. The providing hotel saves payroll costs when the buddy is away, and the new hotel gains knowledge and insights. Before the sharing of skilled workers across hotels, newly acquired hotel staff knew that things could be done better, but they were not seeing it happen. With the buddy system, someone is there to help.[47]

objective. The term *virtual* comes from the computer industry, where computers can be programmed to seem as though they have more memory than they actually have. Paramount Communications, through strategic alliances, positioned itself to exploit as many stages of the entertainment industry as possible. Modular and virtual organizational forms present new management challenges for managers.[48]

THE LATERAL ORGANIZATION

To successfully implement strategy, managers must design the lateral (horizontal) organization carefully. The *lateral organization* consists of the communication and coordination mechanisms that occur across departments or divisions.[49] Building lateral capability enables a company to more flexibly and quickly accomplish organizational objectives by bypassing the movement up through the vertical hierarchy. Recall that the limitation of a functional structure is that it leads to poor coordination among departments, whereas a product-based structure leads to poor coordination across product lines, and the geographic-based structure makes coordination across locations problematic. Lateral linkages allow work to get done at the level in which it occurs, with people communicating directly with those in other departments or divisions, rather than through their managers.

Characterized as working in the "white spaces" between the boxes on an organization chart and across divisional boundaries, the lateral organization, while often unseen, is a key part of organizational structure. In fact, the job of organizing is not complete until both the vertical structures, discussed earlier in this chapter, and the lateral linkages are designed. The more highly differentiated a company is, the more it will need a high level of integration to make the organizational structure function effectively. (See the "Hospitality Focus" boxed section above.)

HOSPITALITY FOCUS

CEO OF STOP AND SHOP ENCOURAGES DIRECT CONTACT WITH HONEST DIALOGUE

Lewis G. Schaeneman Jr., the driving CEO of Stop and Shop Companies, Inc., a large New England grocery chain, brought out the best in his senior management staff by encouraging and soliciting open and honest dialogue. If a department head was not willing to be challenged and questioned by his or her peers, that executive did not survive in this company. Relying on data, Lew would have his senior management team talk and talk and talk about important issues until they had talked them to death and every manager agreed about the direction the firm would be taking. By having candid, open, and continuous senior management conversations, the group built a commitment to implementation and a clear understanding of every department's or division's role in making the corporate strategy a reality. In Lew's words, "We evolved a system of management that empowered ordinary people to do extraordinary things."[50]

Simple Coordinating Mechanisms

Firms can use a variety of lateral coordinating mechanisms, ranging from the simple and informal to the highly structured (e.g., matrix) and complex. *Direct contact* among managers from different departments or divisions is the simplest form of coordination, and it is often based on an informal friendship network. Information often gets shared naturally in these networks, making "who you know" an important component of effective implementation. Meetings and committees are also devices used to help coordinate work. When used strategically, these lateral coordinating processes can be extremely effective. One successful CEO, Lewis Schaeneman, was so effective in using meetings and informal ties with his senior management staff at Stop and Shop Companies, Inc., that most of this team went on to senior executive positions in other firms, having learned how to build cooperative teams. (See the "Hospitality Focus" boxed section above.)

Accenture and other consulting firms were early to develop communities of practice as another way to share information horizontally and network. A *community of practice* is a group of people who share a concern, a set of problems, or a passion about a topic and who deepen their knowledge and expertise in this area by interacting continually.[51] Organizations frequently hold annual meetings and retreats with their general managers to help build commitment and interpersonal relationships as well as to update and inform participants of corporate strategies and new practices.

Teams and task forces bring together individuals from several functions or groups to solve problems or work together to accomplish an overall outcome. *Task forces* are a common form of coordination in hospitality firms; for instance, Accor North America establishes task forces to help develop practices to improve customer and employee satisfaction.[52] Members of these task forces, from different levels and hotels in the region, perform various designated roles, including the role of conscience, who end the meeting by giving constructive feedback to each member of the team. It is not uncommon for Accor to also include an outside consultant on its task force teams.

Formal Integrators

In large firms, boundary-spanning positions are created so that various components of a business fit together and resources are appropriately allocated. These formal integrator positions may be project managers or *knowledge managers*. Whether these positions are chief knowledge officer (CKO), chief learning officer (CLO), director of intellectual assets, or manager of performance, these roles have been developed because of an awareness of the importance of using the ideas of people at every level of the firm and ensuring that opportunities are not missed and that people and projects are coordinated. A *chief knowledge officer* frequently works to ensure the organization can get maximum value from its intangible assets and best practices. Maximizing the return on knowledge investments helps ensure innovation and avoid knowledge loss that often occurs when an organization restructures. Finally, when the need for lateral coordination in a highly differentiated firm is great, the lateral mechanisms discussed may fall short, requiring a formal integrating structure like a matrix. (See the "Hospitality Focus" boxed section on page 328.)

ORGANIZATIONAL CONTROL

From the perspective of top executives, a *strategic control system* is "a system to support managers in assessing the relevance of the organization's strategy to its progress in the accomplishment of its goals, and when discrepancies exist, to support areas needing attention."[53] Scandinavia's SAS Group's huge operating losses in the early 21st century resulting from a misguided strategy provide an example of what happens when managers lose control of a company. The CEO of SAS Group at the time noted, "If you run a business when you lose that much, you simply lose control of it."[54] As mentioned in the introduction to this chapter, top managers use control systems for a variety of important functions, such as:[55]

- Overcoming resistance to change
- Communicating new strategic agendas
- Ensuring continuing attention to strategic initiatives
- Formalizing beliefs
- Setting boundaries on acceptable strategic behavior
- Motivating discussion and debate about strategic uncertainties

Several types of control will be discussed. *Feedback control* provides managers with information concerning outcomes from organizational activities. With feedback control, managers establish objectives and then measure performance against those targets at some later time. *Feedforward control* helps managers anticipate changes in the external and internal environments, based on analysis of inputs from stakeholders and the environment. The learning processes associated with

HOSPITALITY FOCUS

ERNST & YOUNG: CHIEF KNOWLEDGE OFFICER (CKO) ENABLES GLOBAL KNOWLEDGE SHARING.

John Peetz, a partner with Ernst & Young, worked mainly as a consultant, advising clients in fields ranging from the entertainment business to engineering and construction. When he was asked to chair an ad hoc knowledge committee in 1992, Peetz had no idea the assignment would result in a career shift. "We obviously needed a better process for managing intellectual capital and a strategy to match it with the company's overall business objectives," recalls Peetz. Two years later, Ernst & Young named him its first chief knowledge officer (CKO). "We're decentralized, so at first our tax people couldn't imagine any of their knowledge would be of use to auditors, or that auditor information could help consultants and so on," he notes. Peetz was formally charged with the tasks of organizing, capturing, and cataloging the firm's collective knowledge. CKOs like John Peetz actively promote the knowledge agenda within a company, oversee the development of knowledge infrastructure, and facilitate communication and coordination throughout the entire organization.

Today the Ernst & Young Center for Business Knowledge® (CBK) and its network of local centers enable global, firmwide knowledge sharing. They have developed a variety of practices that make it easier for their professionals to leverage the knowledge and insight of their 130,000 employees globally, whether in the office, on the road, or at client sites. Some of these practices include an intranet platform, the KnowledgeWeb (KWeb), which provides portable and Web access to internal and external (vendor-provided) news, analysis, benchmarks, experience, methodologies, and sales and marketing material. Additionally, specialized KWeb tools, such as the Search Engine and Community HomeSpaces, enable consultants to retrieve immediately the content most relevant to their needs. Customized knowledge such as primary and secondary research, analysis, and market and competitive intelligence; financial, economic, and demographic data; literature searches; executive profiles; company overviews, industry trends, and competitive landscapes is shared by more than 200 globally connected consultants in 10 countries.

Ernst & Young Online, the firm's private secure extranet, provides clients with continuous access to Ernst & Young people and knowledge worldwide. Collaborative services and individually tailored content, tools, and resources are also available to clients via this tool. Finally, network coordinators align with specific communities of interest (by region, industry, service line, account, engagement) to connect them with the most relevant information and to advance knowledge within each practice area. By focusing on specific areas of interest, network coordinators drive the acquisition, reuse, and creation of knowledge within those communities and on behalf of the larger organization.[56]

feedforward and feedback control form the basis for changes to strategic direction, strategies, implementation plans, or even the targets themselves, if they are deemed to be unreasonable given current conditions. In addition to feedforward and feedback controls, organizations use a variety of internal controls to encourage behavior that is consistent with the overall objectives of the firm. In this chapter, we discuss three types of behavioral controls: bureaucratic, clan, and process controls. Finally, we conclude with a discussion of crisis prevention and management.

Strategic versus Financial Controls

A brief review of the evolution of organizational control systems will help you understand how they work and why so many of them fail to live up to expectations. Early in the 20th century, the increase in diversified and vertically integrated organizations created the demand for systems that could help top managers allocate time, capital, and human resources where they were most needed. E. I. du Pont de Nemours Powder Company, formed from a combination of previously independent companies, was one of the innovators in this area.[57] DuPont created one of the most enduring systems for controlling diversified businesses. The system was based on *return on investment* (ROI), which was defined as the operating ratio (return on sales) times the stock turn (sales to assets).[58] Sales cancel out, leaving return divided by assets. Using this summary measure of performance for each division, top managers could identify problem areas and allocate capital to the most successful operations and divisions.

Because financial-reporting requirements included figures for income, assets, and sales, managers could easily calculate ROI or related measures from existing data. As the multidivisional form of organization proliferated after 1950, the use of financial measures such as ROI gained wide acceptance and application.[59] In many organizations, they became the only important measure of success. In the words of Roger Smith, past CEO of General Motors: "I look at the bottom line. It tells me what to do."[60]

Unfortunately, organizational-control systems that rely primarily on *financial controls* are likely to have serious problems. The main problem with financial-control systems as a primary basis for control is that high-level managers typically do not have an adequate understanding of what must be done to improve value-adding activities within the organization. According to some control experts, financial-control measures based on accounting data are "too late, too aggregated, and too distorted to be relevant for managers' planning and control decisions."[61] Lateness refers to the long lag times between the organizational transactions and the dates financial reports come out.

The aggregation problem simply means that financial measures based on accounting data do not contain the detail that is necessary to make meaningful improvements to organizational processes. In a study of branded hotels in the United States, the commonly used industry averages of average daily rate (ADR), revenue per available room (RevPAR), and occupancy were found to be distorted by certain markets and price segments.[62] Table 8.4 shows that average RevPARs and ADRs are higher than the typical (modal) hotel's performance levels. The study showed that reliance on aggregate industry averages can lead to overstating ADR and RevPAR and understating occupancy.

Finally, distortions associated with financial information are well documented (e.g., the Enron scandal). Differences in the way financial-control variables are created make meaningful comparisons difficult across departments, divisions, or companies. Also, changes in the way a department, division, or company calculates a variable from one period to the next can cause distortion. Distortion is especially evident in the way inventories, plant, and equipment are valued and in the way overhead costs are allocated to departments and divisions. (See the "Hospitality Focus" boxed section on page 331.)

In addition, accounting-based financial measures sometimes prompt managers to behave in ways that are counterproductive over the long run. For example, financial measures such as ROI discourage investments in long-term research projects because expenses must be paid out

TABLE 8.4 **Performance of Branded Hotels in the Top 25 Markets**

	MEAN (AVERAGE)	MEDIAN (MIDDLE)	MODE (TYPICAL)	PERCENTAGE BELOW THE MEAN
RevPAR				
Rev Par for Top 25 Markets	$52.56	$45	$30	60.30
RevPAR for All Other Markets	$37.73	$33	$26	58.99
ADR				
ADR. for Top 25 Markets	$76.35	$67	$52	61.57
ADR far All Other Markets	$58.93	$54	$47	60.54
Occupancy				
Occ for Top 25 Markets	66.36%	69%	75%	45.73%
Occ for All Other Markets	61.87%	63%	70%	46.64%

Number of observations for top 25 markets = 469,299
Number of observations for all other markets = 1,348,348

Source: C. Enz, L. Canina, and K. Walsh, "Hotel-industry Averages: An Inaccurate Tool for Measuring Performance," *Cornell Hotel and Restaurant Administration Quarterly* 42 (December 2001): 22–32.

immediately, while benefits may not accrue until many financial periods later.[63] Also, managers may cancel services (e.g., turn-down service in the guest room) that appear to be too costly, placing an emphasis on essential services or services that are most efficiently produced. If financial-control information is used as a part of an incentive system to reward managers, then organizations should consider adding back long-term investments such as research and development before calculating ROIs. Another alternative is to create separate accounts for longer-term investment programs that are independent of the rest of the financial-reporting system. (See the "Hospitality Focus" boxed section on page 332.)

Rather than establish a control system based purely on financial controls, top managers should establish a more complete strategic-control system. In the literature on strategic management, some scholars use the term *strategic control* to mean that corporate-level managers become

TRUMP'S FINANCIAL DISTORTIONS MISLEAD INVESTORS

In January 2002, the Securities and Exchange Commission (SEC) pursued its first enforcement action regarding the abuse of pro-forma earnings figures against Trump Hotels & Casino Resorts Inc., now called Trump Entertainment Resorts (TER). The company was charged with making misleading statements in the company's third-quarter earnings release. According to the SEC, Trump committed three separate acts that collectively amounted to misleading investors:

1. Trump's earnings release and the accompanying financial data did not use the term "pro forma," even though the net income and earnings per share (EPS) figures contained in the release significantly differed from such figures calculated in conformity with generally accepted accounting procedures (GAAP).

2. Trump's release expressly stated that its net income and EPS excluded an $81.4 million one-time charge. Not until several days later, however, did an analyst's report unveil that Trump's net income and EPS figures included an undisclosed one-time gain of $17.2 million.

3. Trump's release compared its earnings favorably to analysts' earnings estimates without stating that its figures were non-GAAP, pro-forma figures, whereas the analysts' figures were GAAP. Discounting the pro-forma adjustments would have resulted in a decline in revenues and net income, as well as in a failure to meet analysts' expectations.

The Commission found that Trump Hotels had violated the Exchange Act and was ordered to cease and desist from violating Section 10(b) and Rule 10b-5. By 2004, the company was desperate to reduce its debt load and filed for Chapter 11 bankruptcy. The name change to TER occurred in mid-2005 when the company emerged from Chapter 11.[64]

integrally acquainted with the processes and operations of each of their divisions through sharing of "rich" information and face-to-face contact.[65] This kind of knowledge is necessary so that they can evaluate the performance of each division on the basis of factors that are relevant within their own companies and markets. A corporate manager who relies on this type of control puts less weight on financial controls as a source of information for evaluating division performance. Our use of the term *strategic control* is also based on the idea that financial controls should not be relied on exclusively to evaluate performance. They are one of many types of feedback-control systems that should be in place in an organization. The combination of control systems is what we refer to as strategic control.

Feedback-Control Systems

Any time goals or objectives are established and then measured against actual results, a feedback-control system exists. Feedback-control systems perform several important functions in organizations.[66] First, creating

DEPARTMENT HEADS MAY RESIST COMPLEX COST ALLOCATION PROCESS

The overhead cost allocation process is fairly complex and is not well understood by the lodging industry. The major drawbacks of cost allocation relate primarily to the managers of operating departments and to misunderstandings regarding its use. For example, department heads may not understand the process and may resist it. Department heads may defer discretionary costs such as repairs, or otherwise strive to achieve short-run profitability at the expense of the long-run profitability of the company. Finally, fully allocated department statements are not appropriate for performance evaluation.[67]

specific targets ensures that managers at various levels and areas in the company understand the plans and strategies that guide organizational decisions. Second, feedback–control systems motivate managers to pursue organizational interests as opposed to purely personal interests, because they know they will be held accountable for the results of their actions. This alignment of interests reduces some of the agency problems discussed in Chapter 4. Finally, feedback–control systems help managers decide when and how to intervene in organizational processes by identifying areas requiring further attention. Without good feedback–control systems, managers can fall into the trap of spending too much time dealing with issues and problems that are not particularly important to the future of the firm.

Examples of feedback–control systems are easy to find. Budgets are feedback–control systems because they provide revenue and expense targets against which actual results are measured. For instance, if food costs are set at 31 percent of food sales, and actual food costs are 36 percent, the gap would signal that corrective action might be required. Financial-ratio analysis is another example. Ratios such as ROI or a current ratio are measured against targets that are established on the basis of past performance or in comparison with competing firms. Audits are also a type of feedback–control system because firm conduct and outputs are measured against established guidelines, typically by independent auditors.

Financial audits control accuracy within accounting systems, based on GAAP. Social audits control ethical behavior, based on criteria that are established either totally in-house or in conjunction with activist groups, regulatory agencies, or editors of magazines that compile this sort of information (e.g., *Business and Society Review*). Food safety audits focus on product safety and reducing the possibility of contamination or spoilage. For example, Avendra, a procurement specialist for the hospitality industry, arrives at customer locations like cruise lines and airport concessions to review and check deliveries of goods for proper weights, counts, temperatures, and the condition of all products.[68] (See the "Hospitality Focus" boxed section on page 334.)

Figure 8.7 contains a flowchart of activities for a feedback–control system as it applies to strategic control. The starting point is the strategic management process, beginning with establishment of strategic direction, followed by identification of basic strategies and implementation plans. Objectives are established as a part of the implementation process. Time passes, and eventually these objectives are measured against actual performance. Performance information is then used as feedback to guide the strategic management process, and the cycle continues. The steps in developing a feedback–control system for strategic control, shown in Table 8.5, will now be explained. They include determining broad goals, establishing links between those

TABLE 8.5 **Steps in Developing a Feedback-Control System**

STEP	DESCRIPTION
1. Determine broad goals	If the organization achieves its vision, what will be different? Answer this question from the perspective of the organization and each of its key stakeholders. In other words, what is the organization going to do for each key stakeholder?
2. Establish links between broad goals and resource areas or activities of the organization	Determine which areas are instrumental in achieving each of the broad goals. For instance, if one of the goals is to have the highest level of customer satisfaction, determine which activities, skills, and resources are needed to make this happen. Examples might be customer service, product quality, and pricing. The objective is to identify factors that can be measured.
3. Create measurable operating goals for each resource area or activity	The things that are measured and rewarded are the things that get done. Operating goals are established for each factor that was identified in the last step, including a date by which each goal should be accomplished. Monitoring systems should also be established as a part of this step.
4. Assign responsibility	Each of the goals should be assigned to a specific manager, who is then responsible to make sure it is accomplished.
5. Develop plans for accomplishment	Each manager should develop an action plan for accomplishing each goal, including needed resources (technology, personnel, capital, supplies). Some resources may be available inside the organization, while others will have to be sought through outside contracts, joint ventures, or other forms of interorganizational relationships.
6. Allocate resources	Resources should be allocated to the accomplishment of each goal, as needed.
7. Follow up	At an agreed-upon time, each manager should report on the status of a goal. Following up also means rewarding managers and employees who are responsible for accomplishment of a goal.

HOSPITALITY FOCUS — FOOD SAFETY AUDITS OFFER RESTAURANTS IMPORTANT FEEDBACK

In the restaurant industry, food safety audits usually involve an outside contractor inspecting a facility and verifying that food safety standards are being met. While putting a third-party auditing system into an operation isn't easy to manage or implement, many operations see them as an opportunity to correct sanitation short-comings before local health inspectors' official visits. "When we've done internal audits, it's a little like the fox watching the hen house," notes the senior director of quality assurance and food safety for Sodexho. "Third-party auditors give us unbiased, objective opinions, and we can serve as helpers instead of hindrances."

Feedback is an important element of these audits. "An auditor who doesn't communicate with staff when he or she sees something is wrong is no benefit for us," observes the senior director of quality assurance and food safety for Sonic Drive-In. "Providing recommendations about where we need improvement makes the difference between accomplishing our goals and just getting a score." As the Sodexho director notes, "We get real-time data from our auditors. They can quickly share results with the operations and focus on corrective action."[69]

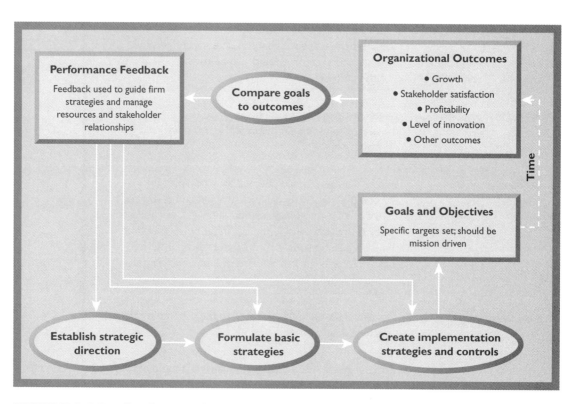

FIGURE 8.7 Feedback controls

goals and resource areas or activities, setting measurable targets for each resource area or activity, and a variety of specific tasks that increase the probability that targets will be achieved.

DETERMINATION OF BROAD GOALS

The first step in developing a strategic-control system is determining what needs to be controlled. One way to determine control factors is to ask, "If we achieve our vision, what will be different?" Robert Kaplan and David Norton have developed an approach to designing a strategic-control system that considers organizational performance from four perspectives: (1) financial, (2) customer, (3) internal business, and (4) innovation and learning.[71]

Each of these performance perspectives has its own set of feedback controls and is linked to particular stakeholder groups. For example, stakeholders who evaluate an organization's performance using financial targets will typically look to ROI, cash flow, stock price, and stability of earnings. Customers evaluate other types of information: pricing, innovation, quality, value, and customer service. From the perspective of internal stakeholders and processes, other performance indicators become important, such as cost controls, skill levels and capabilities, product-line breadth, safety, on-time delivery, quality, and many others. From an innovation and learning perspective, an organization may consider the foundation it is building for the future, such as workforce morale, innovation, investments in research, and progress in continuous improvement.

While Kaplan and Norton's four areas are important and worthy of control, they do not capture everything that is important to a firm's long-term success. The stakeholder perspective of organizations provides a fairly comprehensive view of who is important to a firm. Stakeholders that might be worthy of attention include shareholders, customers, employees and managers, suppliers, local communities, government regulators and taxing agencies, creditors, bondholders, unions, or even particular special-interest groups, among others. A company should not establish control systems for every possible stakeholder, but only for the most important.

Examples of the kinds of broad goals an organization could set on the basis of achieving its vision include "We want to have the highest level of customer satisfaction"; We want to give back to the community through community-service programs"; and "We want to maximize shareholder return." The first goal pertains to customers; the second goal relates to the communities in which the organization operates; and the third goal pertains to shareholders. Following is the broad goal of Four Seasons Hotels, an operator of luxury hotel and resorts that also offers vacation ownership properties and private residences. (See the "Hospitality Focus" boxed section above.)

HILTON HOTELS: FIVE BROAD GOALS FOR DELIVERING VALUE

Hilton Hotels developed a comprehensive approach to delivering value for all stakeholders. At the heart of the approach were five broad goals: delighted customers, loyal team members, satisfied owners and shareholders, successful strategic partners, and involved community. The four primary resource areas, which they called value drivers, were activity areas that directly contributed to success. The areas that together create value for Hilton's constituencies include: Brand management, Revenue maximization, Operational effectiveness, and Value proposition. Brand management, for example, involves promoting and maintaining consistency in the delivery of services and products expected by customers. In the areas of revenue maximization, Hilton implemented flexible, rational pricing, taking into consideration demand elasticities in different segments and local markets.[72]

IDENTIFICATION OF RESOURCE AREAS OR ACTIVITIES

As shown in Table 8.5, the next step in establishing a feedback-control system is to identify resource areas or organizational activities that are key to accomplishing the broad goals identified in the first step. This identification of resource areas or activities should lead to factors the firm can measure, although the measures do not have to be financial in nature. For example, assume that one of the broad goals is to achieve a very high level of customer satisfaction. Specific factors that lead to customer satisfaction may include a high-quality product, excellent customer service, good value (price relative to features and quality), and excellent hands-on training or instructions. These things can be measured by using direct customer surveys or interviews, implementing quality-measurement systems, hiring a research firm, observing repeat business, or conducting competitor-comparison surveys. Notice that the factors identified as important to customers include both resources (a high-quality product) and activities (customer service, training, pricing). (See the "Hospitality Focus" boxed section above.)

Financial measures are appropriate to achieve broad financial goals. Consequently, if a broad goal is a high rate of return for shareholders, as it is in many public corporations, then things such as profitability, debt relative to assets, RevPAR, and short-term cash management should be measured. A study of six major UK hotel groups indicated widespread adoption of techniques to analyze accounting data and relate it to business strategy. In particular, data on real costs and prices, volumes, market share, cash flow, and resource demands are used.[73] Because the things that get measured are often the things that receive attention in organizations, managers need to be sensitive to the needs of stakeholders and make sure that the critical result areas identified reflect the priorities that have been established concerning satisfaction of various stakeholder needs and interests.

Sometimes a factor will need to be evaluated further so that an appropriate resource area or activity can be identified. For example, profitability is a good thing to measure, but what really causes profitability? Managers should analyze what they think are the key drivers of

BALANCED SCORECARD AT HILTON HOTELS

"Hilton Hotels conducted a conjoint study to determine the key attributes on which they were not meeting customer expectations. Overall they discovered that the quality of the guest experience was inconsistent. The study was a catalyst for managers asking whether Hilton was delivering on this standard at all times." Their analysis also showed that a 5 percent increase in customer loyalty at Hilton Hotels (measured as the percentage of customers who indicated they are likely to return to Hilton) in a given year was associated with a 1.1 percent increase in annual revenues the following year at a typical property.[74]

profitability in their industry and establish measures in those areas as well. They may determine that cost control is the primary driver, or they may decide that occupancy is vital. Whichever factors they decide are most important should then become other factors to control. The same sort of thinking applies to quality. What causes high quality? These factors should also be controlled. A balanced scorecard system of measures based on research has been successfully used by several hotel chains. (See the "Hospitality Focus" boxed section above.)

CREATION OF MEASURABLE OPERATING GOALS

Once identified and linked specifically to financial, customer, internal-process, learning, and other stakeholder-driven outcomes, the critical result areas become the objectives that pace strategy implementation. Vision and mission statements include broad organizational goals and lofty ideals that embrace the values of the organization. These ideals can provide motivation to employees and managers; however, they typically provide general, not specific, direction. Specific operating goals or objectives are established in an effort to bring the concepts found in the vision statement to life—to a level that managers and employees can influence and control. As time passes and operating objectives are met, then the broader goals will be met as well, and ultimately the vision will begin to be realized. By specifically linking objectives to the vision, the firm can structure a control system that is strategically relevant.

The terms *objectives* and *goals* capture the same basic concept: they each represent a performance target for an individual, a department, a division, a business, or a corporation. In practice, the term *target* is often used. The important point to remember when using these words is to make sure that people understand how you are using them. In this section, a distinction is made between broad goals and *operating goals*. Unlike the broad goals contained in vision statements, operating goals in key result areas provide specific guidance concerning desired outcomes. Consequently, they are an important part of strategy implementation. Effective operating goals should be high enough to be motivating yet realistic. They should be specific, measurable, and cover a specific time period. They should be established through a participative process and understood by all affected employees.[78]

Goals are established at all levels in the organization. At the corporate level, they encompass the entire organization. At the business level, goals focus on the performance of a particular business

HOSPITALITY
FOCUS

HILTON HOTELS LINKS GOALS TO ITS ANNUAL BUSINESS PLANNING PROCESS

"Property-specific goals are linked to incentive bonuses, performance reviews, merit-based salary increases, and stock-option grants. The result of setting the standard and making sure that everyone understands how those standards are measured is an alignment of actions with goals. People at every level of the organization, from the president to front-line team members, know what is expected of them and how they are doing," noted Dieter Huckestein, the now-retired chairman and CEO of Conrad Hotels and former president of the Hilton Global Alliance[76].

unit. Goals are also developed at the functional level, where they provide functional specialists with specific targets. One of the keys to effectively setting goals is that they must be well integrated from level to level. To connect property-level actions with corporate strategy, Hilton Hotels uses an annual business-planning process. (See the "Hospitality Focus" boxed section above.)

Once the goals and critical results areas are determined, systems for monitoring progress must be put into place. These systems typically involve the accounting, marketing research, and information systems departments, but other departments may be needed. Many larger organizations have an individual or department specifically devoted to strategic planning. If this is the case, then that individual or department typically coordinates the collection of data for monitoring progress.

FACILITATION OF OPERATING GOALS

Goals do not get accomplished on their own. Behind each goal should be a manager with responsibility for making it happen. After managers are assigned responsibility for goal achievement, they should develop plans for accomplishment. Often these plans are evaluated and approved by higher-level managers. Plans should include a list of needed resources such as technology, personnel, capital, equipment, and supplies. Some of these resources may be available inside a department or business unit, whereas other resources might need to be acquired from other units of the organization. The plan might also include resource acquisition from outside the organization through purchases, contracts, joint ventures, or other types of interorganizational relationships. (See the "Hospitality Focus" boxed section on page 339.)

The higher-level managers who assign managers responsibility for achieving a goal should also make sure that required resources are allocated. Then, at the agreed-upon time, the assigned manager should report on progress. Reward systems should be linked to accomplishment of goals. While rewards are usually financial, they do not have to be purely monetary. Besides salary, bonuses, and profit sharing, recognition could include professional advancement, assignment of more responsibility or more personnel, tangible awards, and public recognition.

The purpose of all control systems is to provide information that is critical to decision making. If a control system reveals that something has changed or deviated from expectations, the managers should assess cause and effect in an effort to learn why. This will usually happen when goals and outcomes are compared. For example, assume that a passenger airline has established an operating goal that its planes should be 80 percent full for the first quarter of the fiscal year. At the end of the quarter, performance is at 70 percent, which causes enough concern that managers investigate the matter. They look at other goals that were set in support of the 80 percent goal. They look specifically at marketing and other internal functions. They investigate competitor behavior and look at economic variables. They discover that early indicators suggest a slowdown in the economy. The airline uses this information to revise its performance goals. In this case, an adjustment to the goal was warranted because of factors outside the organization's influence. In other cases, adjustments to operations or marketing might have to be made.

Numerous control systems at multiple levels are necessary to keep an organization and its component parts headed in the right directions. However, they should be integrated so that information can be shared. In other words, information from all parts of the organization should be accessible when and where it is needed to improve organizational processes. To enhance the quantity and quality of organizational learning, comprehensive organizational-control systems should have the following characteristics:

- Information generated by control systems should be an important and recurring item to be addressed by the highest levels of management.
- The control process should also be given frequent and regular attention from operating managers at all levels of the organization.
- Data from the system should be interpreted and discussed in face-to-face meetings among superiors and subordinates.
- The success of the control process relies on the continual challenge and debate of underlying data, assumptions, and strategies.[79]

Feedforward Control

Feedforward control helps managers anticipate what will happen in the external environment so that they can make timely adjustments to organizational strategies and goals. If good feedforward controls are not in place, managers may overlook something important. Good feedforward control

HOSPITALITY FOCUS

MANAGERS "MAKE IT HAPPEN" AT DAVE & BUSTER'S

Discipline means setting standards, being a moral leader, and sharing ownership shift by shift. "Training, setting goals, and then giving [our people] the tools to achieve those goals on the floor is critical to creating a sense of ownership for our hourly team members and managers," said the regional training manager for Dave & Buster's. "Our managers and our shift leaders work together to formulate an operating plan for each shift. They ask, 'What should we focus on today?' By soliciting their input and not relaxing our standards, this allows all of the team members to feel like a bigger piece of the whole and that what they did today at work really matters."[79]

systems are also important because of *environmental discontinuities*, which are major, unexpected changes in the social, economic, technological and political environments that necessitate change within organizations.[80] Environmental discontinuities can also arise from inside the organization, such as the unplanned development of a new product or a problem with labor turnover. Consequently, feedforward control also has an internal dimension.

Environmental discontinuities may lead to changes in the assumptions that underlie the organizational vision, goals, strategies, and, in some cases, organization structure and technology. For example, a merger between two competitors would cause a firm to reevaluate its goals and strategies. A serious problem with labor turnover might cause a firm to improve its wage and benefits plans, which would affect its cost structure. New industry regulations could influence new-product development plans. A shortage of skilled labor could force a firm to reconsider developing a project in that community or locating a store in a given place. Even in stable environments, where environmental discontinuities play a minor role (e.g., production of commodities), feedforward control is essential to learning processes that allow organizations to move toward the accomplishment of their goals.

BUSINESS INTELLIGENCE AND STRATEGIC SURVEILLANCE

In feedforward control systems (see Figure 8.8), information is collected from the internal and external environments, compiled in a usable form, then compared to the premises or assumptions made by the organization. Corporate managers at companies like Starwood, Ashford Hospitality, Merritt Hospitality, Peabody Hotel Group, Interstate Hotels, and Host Marriott rely on business intelligence applications to provide accurate real-time data on the health of their properties and enterprise.[81] The process of collecting information from the broad, operating, and internal environments is called *strategic surveillance*. Information gained through strategic surveillance becomes part of the business intelligence of the firm. *Business intelligence* is sometimes defined as "the collection and analysis of information on markets, new technologies, customers, competitors, and broad social trends."[82] However, a more comprehensive view of business intelligence includes information gained from internal sources and from the feedback-control system. All organizations have a business intelligence system, although some systems are

PEABODY HOTEL GROUP'S BUSINESS INTELLIGENCE SYSTEM AT WORK

Peabody Hotel Group uses business intelligence to create more accurate forecasts based on performance facts that result in greater efficiency and profitability," according to the firm's controller. Their business intelligence tools allow them to access historical and current data immediately. By using data from their general ledger, they can forecast energy costs and other expenses while taking room revenue, occupancy, and other data from property management systems and using it all to build performance reports. Business intelligence systems have gained acceptance among players in the industry such as Hilton Hotels that rely on their own IT staffs, but other small and medium-sized companies such as Concord Hotels and Dolce International work with vendors.[83]

elaborate and formal whereas others may be simple and informal. In many small businesses, the business intelligence system consists of the information absorbed by the owner/manager.

Preliminary efforts to develop business intelligence systems include the creation of management information systems (MIS), decision support systems (DSS), and group decision support systems (GDSS). An MIS requires collection and use of information about products, services, costs, and quality, typically gathered from internal sources. Accounting information systems are a type of MIS. DSS goes one step further in allowing individual or multiple managers to tap into databases and ask novel questions that are not answered through standard reports.[84] For example, Frito-Lay has an enormous DSS that collects sales information from 10,000 salespeople on a daily basis. The system is used by managers to fine-tune product and marketing decisions.[85] Full-scale business intelligence systems are similar to decision support

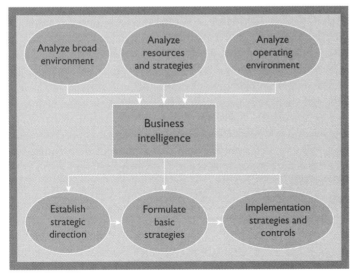

FIGURE 8.8 **Feedforward controls**

systems, except that their scope is comprehensive. They perform the functions of supporting the strategic decision-making and feedback-control processes of the organization, providing early warning signals of threats and opportunities, and tracking the actions and reactions of competitors.[86] (See the "Hospitality Focus" boxed section on page 341.)

A well-developed business intelligence system is a vital part of the strategic management process. Although many hospitality firms have applications that provide data mining and reporting applications within a single system, like a PMS, a true business intelligence system uses a free-standing data warehouse with the ability to capture, standardize, and store information from many separate systems for analysis, graphics presentation, and reporting. This includes data from outside the enterprise such as Smith Travel Research and PKF cost numbers. Information in the system helps managers to identify strengths, weaknesses, opportunities, and threats. Also, the business intelligence system is central to the development and application of organizational resources, which can help an organization develop competencies leading to a competitive advantage. The system is also central to the strategic management activities of establishing strategic direction, developing strategies, and implementing those strategies.

One of the most important functions of a business intelligence system is to compare information collected to the premises, or assumptions, that underlie organization vision, goals, and strategy. This is called *premise control*. Strategic direction and strategies are established based on premises about the organization and its external environment. These premises are assumptions about what will happen in the future, based on current conditions. For example, an organization may plan to expand or multibrand its facilities over a period of five years based on the assumption that interest rates will remain approximately the same. If interest rates change, it could make the planned expansion unprofitable. These types of situations demonstrate the need for premise control. Premise control helps organizations avoid situations in which their established strategies and goals are no longer appropriate.

Premise control has been designed to check systematically and continuously whether the premises set during the planning and implementation process are still valid. Accordingly, premise control is to be organized along these premises. The premises should be listed and then assigned to persons or departments who are qualified sources of information. The sales force, for instance, may be a valuable source for monitoring the expected price policy of the major competitors.[87]

Creating a business intelligence system is a complex and difficult task, made difficult in developing countries, where accurate information is often not readily available. Organizations have to learn to derive their information according to circumstances, relying on line managers in-house for much of what is collected. The sales force can still gather information about competitors' products and can establish informally the level of competitors' sales. Accountants may be able to get some information through the strength of their contacts with banks. In general, successful strategic planning in developing countries relies more on fast feedback than precision of information.[88]

The collection and dissemination of intelligence is loaded with ethical implications. People associate intelligence-gathering activities with spying. In fact, spying agencies such as the Central Intelligence Agency and the old Soviet KGB developed some of the most comprehensive and sophisticated information management systems in the world. Clearly, organizations should always abide by the laws preventing surreptitious activities, but even when laws are not broken, scouting out information on competitors and customers can be laden with ethical implications. Effective information management often means organizing and properly using available information rather than going to extreme lengths to find confidential information.

RESPONSIBILITY FOR INTELLIGENCE MANAGEMENT

Responsibility for collecting and disseminating intelligence information should be assigned deliberately to the appropriate levels, areas, and individuals within the firm. For example, marketing departments are typically responsible for collecting information on consumer tastes and preferences; sales departments manage most of the interactions with customers; middle managers can collect information about union activities; and public relations departments typically deal with the media, special-interest groups, and the general public. These are just a few examples of possible assignments.

Many firms have created a very high-level officer sometimes called the *chief information officer* (CIO) to oversee the collection, analysis, and dissemination of information. Many leading-edge corporations are also experimenting with the creation of special units within their organizations, called environmental scanning or analysis units. These units play a variety of different roles in the organization:

1. *Public policy role.* These units are assigned the task of scanning the environment for early detection of emerging issues that are suspected to be harbingers of widespread shifts in societal attitudes, laws, or social norms.

2. *Strategic planning integrated role.* These units play an integral role in the corporate-wide strategic planning process. The focus is on both the operating and broad environments. Typically, these units are required to prepare an environmental forecast and analysis for the entire corporation, to be distributed to line and/or staff executives during various stages in the planning cycle.

3. *Function-oriented role.* The function-oriented role is just the opposite of the public policy role. While the public policy role means that scanning units search for broad issues, the function-oriented role focuses on only those aspects of the environment that impinge directly on the activities of one function, such as product development or public relations. These units are typically housed within the functional departments of an organization.[89]

In conclusion, feedforward control systems take information collected through the business intelligence system and compare it to the premises, or assumptions, that the organization is using in its strategic management activities. Business intelligence guides the development of strategic direction, strategies, and implementation plans. Top managers are already involved in a continuous process of collecting information, assessing key stakeholders, devising strategies that will satisfy their needs and desires, and delegating duties for stakeholder analysis and management. A good business intelligence system can assist top management in these processes and in identifying external trends that will affect the organization.

Other Types of Controls

The creation of control systems is a vital part of the implementation process. So many types of organizational controls exist that they are difficult to classify, and there is no consensus with regard to definition of terms or titles. Some controls help guide an organization's progress in the accomplishment of its goals. Other controls ensure that reporting is accurate and that organizational processes are accomplished according to predetermined standards. This section describes a group of controls that are closely linked to the functional-level strategies. They include behavioral controls, such as bureaucratic and clan, and process controls. Figure 8.9 demonstrates that these types of control systems are created as a part of implementation planning.

A special set of controls is used to motivate employees to do things that the organization would like them to do, even in the absence of direct supervision. We will refer to them as *behavioral controls*, although other names could be used.[90] Behavioral controls work to encourage employees to comply with organizational norms and procedures. They are real-time in that they influence the employee as the job is being performed. Among the most important of these systems are bureaucratic controls, clan controls, and process controls. We are discussing these particular controls in this chapter because they are particularly relevant to strategy implementation.

BUREAUCRATIC CONTROLS

Bureaucratic control systems consist of rules, procedures, and policies that guide the behavior of organizational members. They are especially appropriate where consistency among employees is important. For example, in an effort to guarantee quality, McDonald's has established standard ways of doing everything from cooking french fries to assembling orders. Rules and procedures outline specific steps for an employee to follow in a particular situation. When a particular problem is routine or arises often, a rule or procedure may be developed so that every employee handles it in the way that is consistent with the organization strategy. Because rules and procedures outline detailed

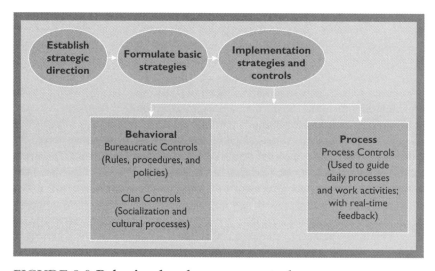

FIGURE 8.9 Behavioral and process controls

actions, they are usually relevant for specific situations. Unusual situations and quickly changing business conditions can make an existing procedure obsolete or ineffective.

A policy is a more general guide to action. Some policies are stated in broad terms and communicate the organization's commitment to a guiding principle. They guide behavior in a general sense only (e.g., equal-opportunity employer), with specific procedures needed to translate that commitment into action. Other policies are more specific. For example, human-resource policies may specify which employees are eligible for training programs or what employee behaviors deserve disciplinary actions. A marketing policy may specify which customers are to get priority, and an operations policy may describe under what conditions an order of supplies will be rejected. The procedures and policies that most companies employ to govern daily activities, such as check approval, price setting, overtime, maintenance, and customer service, are all a form of concurrent control and are intended to ensure consistency of action.

Unfortunately, many companies do not see everyday rules, procedures, and policies as strategic. But because the rules, procedures, and policies guide the decisions and actions of employees, they are a major determinant of how well strategies are implemented. For example, one of the most successful retailers in the United States, The Gap, uses detailed procedures extensively. The Gap replaces most of its merchandise in stores every two months. At that time, all store managers receive a book of detailed instructions specifying exactly where every item of clothing will be displayed. Company procedures also require that white walls be touched up once a week and wood floors polished every three to four days.[91] Gap management believes this level of procedural detail is necessary to achieve consistency and high levels of performance.

It is also possible for policies and procedures to encourage behavior that works against the firm's strategies. For example, rules and procedures may stifle employees from improving processes because they feel rule-bound. Merchandise-return policies that alienate customers can undermine any attempt at a customer-service advantage. Purchasing policies that require bids to be awarded on the basis of price can erode quality. Reward policies often create tensions among interdependent stakeholder groups.

CLAN CONTROL

Clan control is based on socialization processes through which an individual comes to appreciate the values, abilities, and expected behaviors of an organization.[92] Socialization also helps organizational members feel inclined to see things the same way, by espousing common beliefs and assumptions that in turn shape their perceptions. Socialization processes for existing employees take the form of intensive training; mentoring relationships and role models; and formal organizational communications including the vision, mission, and values statements. Clan control is closely linked to the concepts of culture and ethics that were discussed in earlier chapters. (See the "Hospitality Focus" boxed section on page 346.)

Organizations that want to create, preserve, or alter their culture and ethics often use formal and informal orientation programs, mentoring programs, rigorous selection procedures, skills and communications training, and other methods of socialization to instill commitment to organization values. The first step is to define those behaviors that the company finds important, and then stress them in selection, orientation, and training procedures. Some firms select employees on the basis of their existing personal work-related values. Other firms prefer to hire young people and then socialize them toward a required set of values that will support the culture of the organization. Either way, human-resource management systems play an important role in controlling organizational behavior.

CLAN CONTROL AT THE SIMPSON HOUSE INN

The general manager of the Simpson House Inn, a bed-and-breakfast located in Santa Barbara, California, appreciated the power of socialization when she developed training modules that promote understanding, improve staff communication and self-understanding, and enhance self-esteem. She explains the property's philosophy as follows: "Seamless, flawless, gracious service can be given only by people who feel good about themselves and what they are doing, and who are motivated intrinsically by their own competence and sense of personal mission."[93]

PROCESS CONTROLS

Process controls use immediate feedback to control organizational processes. For example, the warning systems built into navigational equipment on an aircraft tell the pilot immediately if the aircraft falls below an acceptable altitude. The systems don't just feed back an aggregate report at the end of the flight telling the pilot how many times the aircraft fell below acceptable standards. That aggregate feedback information might be important for some uses, such as designing new navigational systems, but it would not be useful for the pilot. Within a business environment, real-time feedback is also useful in some instances but would be a disadvantage in others. Real-time financial feedback, for example, would make managing a business much like operating on the floor of the stock market—a frenzy. However, real-time controls in service-delivery environments can be very useful. Returning to Hilton's control system, we see how it relies on process controls. (See the first "Hospitality Focus" boxed section on page 347.)

To summarize this section, strategic-control systems help companies monitor organizational progress toward the accomplishment of goals and encourage human behavior that supports this progress. In many cases, control systems are used to help managers create and monitor organizational changes. Organizational crises are a type of change that requires an immediate response from managers. The final section of this chapter deals with how to prevent and manage crises.

Crisis Prevention and Management

Organizational crises are critical situations that threaten high-priority organizational goals, impose a severe restriction on the amount of time in which key members of the organization can respond, and contain elements of surprise.[94] Crises such as the outbreak of hoof-and-mouth disease in the United Kingdom in 2001 and Hurricane Katrina in the U.S. Gulf Coast in 2005 cannot be avoided, but managers have at least some control over the incidence and resolution of human-induced organizational crises. Examples of these types of crises include

HILTON HOTELS RELY ON SPECIFIC PROCESS CONTROLS

Hilton developed a continuous-improvement process called Situation–Target–Proposal (STP). The STP takes data and helps determine the actions needed to address a problem. In one hotel, for example, the balanced scorecard revealed low scores on guest comment cards. Reviewing the report showed that bath and shower facilities fell into the "fix-it now" quadrant of the scorecard. The staff members thought the problem was due to low water pressure and hence an infrastructure issue. However, a process team investigated the problem, and after taking apart a showerhead, found the problem. When the team removed the unit's centrifugal flow restrictor, the water pressure improved and so did customer satisfaction.[95]

NORWALK STOMACH VIRUS OUTBREAK CAUSES CRISIS ON MANY CRUISE SHIPS

Norwegian Cruise Line, Royal Caribbean, Princess Cruises, Carnival Cruises, Celebrity Cruises, Cunard, and Holland America have all been hit by stomach ailment outbreaks. Even with extensive cleaning, the "Farmington Hill" strain of Norwalk is particularly difficult to eradicate. The virus contaminates surfaces on cruise ships, prompting cruise lines to pull ships out of service long enough to break the cycle of the virus. Cruise lines have learned from the 2002 outbreaks, increasing training and establishing protocols to contain the virus when it appears. Princess Cruises formed six-member Norwalk crews on each ship, who disinfect the cabins of passengers who fall ill. These ships also carry special Norwalk test kits, allowing health workers to identify the virus within hours of someone becoming sick. Previously, tests for Norwalk took days or weeks.

Nevertheless, Norovirus continues to pose problems on cruise ships. In November 2006, more than 700 passengers and crew members aboard Carnival Cruise Lines' *Carnival Liberty* fell ill. As the year ended, another 384 passengers of Royal Caribbean's *Freedom of the Seas* contracted the Norovirus. At the same time, 97 passengers and six crew members of the Princess Cruises *Sun Princess* ship had the virus. In 2007, 17 percent of the passengers (276) aboard the cruise-liner *Queen Elizabeth II* of Cunard Line experienced an outbreak. Throughout the year, numerous cases of Norwalk disease were reported, including Princess Cruises' 79 passengers in April, Royal Caribbean's 200 passengers in May, and Celebrity Cruises' 500 passengers in August.[96]

the massacre in 1984 at a McDonald's in San Ysidro, California, that left 21 people dead and 19 wounded; the shooter who entered a Brown's chicken unit in a Chicago suburb in 1993 and shot seven workers in the head; the disclosure in 2001 that McDonald's had been using oil with a beef extract for cooking its fries; and the Norwalk stomach virus outbreaks aboard various cruise ships. (See the second "Hospitality Focus" boxed section above.)

PROACTIVE CRISIS-MANAGEMENT AT CHEVYS RESTAURANT

When Chevys franchisee Stan Knoles left his suburban Salt Lake City unit on a busy Thursday evening, it seemed like a business-as-usual day. "Surreal" is how he described the scene 30 minutes later. Surrounded by police, cameras, and distraught employees and customers, Knoles was caught in a restaurateur's worst nightmare. He couldn't change the fact that a shooter had run off the street into his restaurant, shot and killed the front-of-the-house manager and a customer, and injured another employee and a customer, before fleeing the scene. But he had to act fast to keep a bad situation from getting even worse.

Knoles called Chevys headquarters in San Francisco and the public relations manager. With the go-ahead from corporate offices, Knoles and the PR manager sat down for a strategy session. The two agreed that their first priority would be the victims—they'd worry about the news cameras later. But even as mangers and employees get on with it, in many cases of restaurant violence the media can often be counted on to dwell on it—only further fixing tragic images in the public's mind. In the wake of the San Ysidro McDonald's killings, headlines like "McMurder," "McMassacre," and "Big Mac Attack" filled the papers.[97]

PHASES OF CRISIS MANAGEMENT

The five phases of *crisis management* include signal detection, preparation/prevention, containment/damage limitation, recovery, and learning.[98] Firms that ignore crises until they are involved in one will spend most of their time in the containment and recovery stages, essentially mopping up the damage. Back in 1984, the vice president of McDonald's advised his people to do the right thing and not worry about legal implications and media attention.[99] He focused on helping the survivors and families of the victims. Management experts advise clients to seize the early hours of a crisis to proactively manage local media, employees, the public, and, in the case of a violent incident, the victims' families. (See the "Hospitality Focus" boxed section above.)

On the other hand, crisis-prepared companies establish early-detection systems and prepare for crises, or even prevent them from occurring (left side of the model). For Keaton Woods, the general manager of the Le Meridian Kuwait, extra food was ordered and hidden in the hotel two weeks before the invasion by Iraqi forces during the Gulf War. Later he protected and provided for his guests and avoided being taken hostage by Iraqi soldiers for four months.[100] (See the "Hospitality Focus" boxed section on page 349.)

Some organizations are crisis prone. Studies conducted at the University of Southern California Center for Crisis Management have identified crisis-prone organizations as those having the following characteristics:

- If these organizations prepare at all, they prepare for only a few of the possible types of crises. Furthermore, their preparations are fragmented and compartmentalized.

- They focus on only one aspect of a crisis, and only after it has already occurred.

CRISIS MANAGEMENT: BEEF EXTRACT USED FOR COOKING
McDONALDS FRENCH FRIES IN INDIA

HOSPITALITY FOCUS

"Vegetarian French Fries in McDonald's India" read the posters made by Amit Jatia and his staff. Amit Jatia's company, Hardcastle Restaurants, owns and manages McDonald's restaurants in India, a country in which half of those eating at a McDonald's are vegetarian. Within hours of the story that McDonald's uses beef extract for cooking fries in the United States, the Indian operator jumped into action. PR specialists and a team of corporate and legal experts were assembled to build a strategy for handling the crisis.

On the same day the story broke, Jatia submitted samples of the fries to leading laboratories in Pune and Mumbai. Tests were quickly done by the Bombay Municipal Corporation and FDA and local political parties. Results were posted in the various outlets and the papers.[101]

- They consider only technical factors (as opposed to human or social) in the cause or prevention of crises.
- They consider few, if any, stakeholders in an explicit fashion.[102]

Safety and security of hotels has become a critical matter for hotel guests and managers. Hotels have become targets of terrorism, as the 2003 attack on the Marriott in Jakarta illustrates. In response to those concerns, some hotel operators have created new security procedures, such as conducting more detailed background checks on their employees. Hilton Hotels now requires customers to show an identification with a picture on check-in, for instance, while Starwood Hotels and Resorts has raised security standards in its parking garages.[103] The Peninsula New York established a crisis management team to focus on the safety and survival of its guests and employees during a crisis.

While many hotels are proactively preparing to handle crises, a study conducted at Cornell University revealed that U.S. hotels had made few changes to their safety and security arrangements in the aftermath of the September 11th crisis.[104] Overall, general managers were not doing a great deal of reevaluation of their security procedures (only 29 percent indicated they had done much), and even fewer were substantially changing their procedures (only 12 percent reported making a great deal of change). When it came to adding employees, about 70 percent of the GMs responded that they had made no additions to their security staff.

With regard to stakeholders, the key questions organizations should ask are: "Who are the individuals, organizations, groups, and institutions that can affect as well as be affected by crisis management? Can the stakeholders who will be involved in any crisis be analyzed systematically?"[105] As in other types of stakeholder management, open communication with important stakeholders is essential to success.

Organizations can take steps to control organizational crises. These activities fall into the categories of strategic actions, technical and structural actions, evaluation and diagnostic actions, communication actions, and psychological and cultural actions. Examples of these types of actions are found in Table 8.6. Above all, organizations have to plan ahead for things

TABLE 8.6 **Crisis Management Strategic Checklist**

Strategic Actions	Communication Actions
1. Integrate crisis management (CM) into strategic planning processes 2. Integrate CM into statements of corporate excellence 3. Include outsiders on the board and on CM teams 4. Provide training and workshops in CM 5. Expose organizational members to crisis simulations 6. Create a diversity or portfolio of CM strategies	1. Provide training for dealing with the media regarding CM 2. Improve communication lines with local communities 3. Improve communication with intervening stakeholders (e.g., police)
Technical and Structural Actions	**Psychological and Cultural Actions**
1. Create a CM team 2. Dedicate budget expenditures for CM 3. Establish accountabilities for updating emergency policies/manuals 4. Computerize inventories of CM resources (e.g., employee skills) 5. Designate an emergency command-control room 6. Ensure technological redundancy in vital areas (e.g., computer systems) 7. Establish working relationships with outside experts in CM	1. Increase visibility of strong top management commitment to CM 2. Improve relationships with activist groups 3. Improve upward communication (including "whistleblowers") 4. Improve downward communication regarding CM programs/accountabilities 5. Provide training regarding human and emotional impacts of crises 6. Provide psychological support services (e.g., stress/anxiety management) 7. Reinforce symbolic recall/corporate memory of past crises/dangers
Evaluation and Diagnostic Actions	
1. Conduct legal and financial audit of threats and liabilities 2. Modify insurance coverage to match CM contingencies 3. Conduct environmental impact studies	4. Prioritize activities necessary for daily operations 5. Establish tracking system for early warning signals 6. Establish tracking system to follow up past crises or near crises

Source: I. I. Mitroff and C. Pearson, "From Crisis Prone to Crisis Prepared: A Systematic and Integrative Framework for Crisis Management," *Academy of Management Executive* (February 1993): p. 58. Reproduced with permission of Academy of Management in the format Textbook via Copyright Clearance Center.

MERRILL LYNCH PLANS AHEAD FOR WORST-CASE SCENARIOS

HOSPITALITY FOCUS

In the 1950s and 1960s, the surest way to get a job at Merrill Lynch was to be an ex-Marine; the place was full of them. Though that is no longer the case, Merrill employees still pride themselves on being good Marines. Like those graduates of Parris Island, they had planned for worst-case scenarios long ago. In 1999, Merrill installed a global-trading platform that meant all of its business was on the same system—and that the system would operate even if part of it went down. And Merrill's chief technology officer, John McKinley, was well versed in disaster planning. The firm had prepared for all kinds of problems: loss of power, loss of water, loss of voice and data communications, loss of an entire building.[106]

that might happen. Because of its planning, Merrill Lynch was up and running when the stock markets reopened six days after the September 11th terrorist attacks. (See the "Hospitality Focus" boxed section above.)

In summary, organizational crises have the potential to thwart organizational efforts toward the accomplishment of goals. However, the Japanese symbol for "crisis" is made up of two characters: one elaborate character symbolizes threats, and one simple character symbolizes opportunities. Crisis-prevention and crisis-management programs represent yet another opportunity for organizations to develop distinctive competencies. Distinctive competencies in these areas may be difficult to detect, because it is difficult to measure, in financial terms, savings from a disaster that does not occur or whose negative effects are reduced. However, as more organizations suffer blows from large crises, it is evident that effective crisis prevention and management is critical to steady long-term performance.

KEY POINTS SUMMARY

- This chapter described the organizational structures and control systems that are used in implementing strategies.

- Centralization, formalization, specialization, and other key dimensions are important to characterizing organizational structures.

- In configuring the relationships among departments in a single business, organizations usually employ one of the following structures: functional, geographic/customer group, product/service group, or project matrix. Each of the structures exhibit strengths, weaknesses, and fit with particular strategic choices.

- The functional form encourages functional specialization and focus, but discourages coordination among functions or departments.

- Geographic or customer structures are grouped by various locations or customer types.
- The project-matrix structure employs a dual-reporting relationship that is intended to balance functional focus and expertise with responsiveness to customer needs. However, it is expensive and may create ambiguity and hinder decision making if managed improperly.
- In structuring relationships among multiple business units, managers attempt to create either independence, so that organizations are unencumbered, or interdependence, to exploit operating synergies.
- Multidivisional and strategic business unit (SBU) structures divide businesses into divisions.
- The multidivisional structure creates the potential for financial synergy as managers allocate financial resources to the most promising divisions; however, the business units are typically so independent and share so few resource similarities that coordination and resource sharing among businesses is difficult. Consequently, operating synergy across divisions is difficult to achieve.
- The SBU structure combines divisions into groups based on commonalities, thus allowing for the creation of operating synergy within an SBU.
- Corporate-matrix structures are intended to exploit economies, learning, and resource sharing across businesses; however, they require extra measures of coordination to avoid divided loyalties, sluggish decision making, and management conflicts.
- Lateral relationships range from simple direct contact, networks, and communities of practice to teams, task forces, and even formal integrators such as knowledge officers. These horizontal coordinating mechanisms are essential for effectively addressing the deficiencies of the vertical structures and for getting work done across departments and divisions.
- Strategic controls consist of systems to support managers in tracking progress toward organizational vision and goals and in ensuring that organizational processes and the behavior of organizational members are consistent with those goals.
- Feedback control provides managers with information concerning outcomes from organizational activities; the information is then used as a basis for comparison with the targets that have been established.
- Feedforward control helps managers anticipate changes in the external and internal environments, based on analysis of inputs from stakeholders and the remote environment.
- The learning processes associated with strategic control form the basis for changes to strategic direction, strategies, implementation plans, or even the goals themselves, if they are deemed to be unreasonable given current conditions.

- Control systems are developed at the corporate, business, functional, and operating levels in a company. These systems should be integrated so that information can be shared. Goals should also be integrated from one level to the next and across the firm.

- Development of a feedback-control system entails determining broad goals based on strategic direction, establishing links between broad goals and resource areas or organizational activities, setting measurable goals for each resource area or activity, assigning responsibility for completion of each goal to individual managers, allowing those managers to develop plans for accomplishment and allocating resources to them, and following up to ensure completion and provide rewards.

- The factors that are to be controlled should reflect the interests of various stakeholder groups inside and outside of the organization.

- Closely related to the functional strategies are a special type of process control that might be called functional controls. These internal systems encourage accuracy in processes and reporting, as well as motivating employees to make decisions and behave in a way that will move the organization in the intended directions. They include behavioral controls such as bureaucratic controls and clan controls, as well as process controls.

- Crisis-prevention and crisis-management systems are a special type of control, specifically designed to prevent major disasters. Organizational crises are critical situations that threaten high-priority organizational goals, impose a severe restriction on the amount of time in which key members of the firm can respond, and contain elements of surprise.

- Companies can take steps to control organizational crises. Crisis-prevention and crisis-management activities fall into the general categories of strategic actions, technical and structural actions, evaluation and diagnostic actions, communication actions, and psychological and cultural actions.

- While the potential for crisis is a threat to an organization, effective crisis prevention and management may also represent an opportunity to develop a distinctive competence.

REVIEW QUESTIONS

1. Describe each of the dimensions of organizational structure. How are they important?
2. Explain how these dimensions change as an organization grows.
3. Use the resources of your college library and interviews in your community to describe each of the dimensions of organizational structure for a local quick-service

and fine-dining restaurant. How and why do the structures differ? Compare the structural dimensions of a Wendy's and a McDonald's. How do the structures differ?

4. For each of the business-level structures presented in this chapter, discuss its strengths and weaknesses and when each structure might be most appropriate.

5. What are the primary differences between the functional structure and the geographic/customer structure? How is a project-matrix structure a combination of the two?

6. Discuss the distinguishing characteristics of each of the corporate-level structures presented in this chapter.

7. How are the multidivisional and SBU structures the same? How are they different? When would one structure be more appropriate than the other?

8. What is the primary purpose of the lateral mechanisms of an organization? When would the different types of lateral mechanisms (e.g., direct contact, teams, task forces, full-time integrator) be more appropriate?

9. What is a strategic-control system? Give examples.

10. Describe the problems associated with traditional accounting-based financial controls. Are they ever appropriate? In what circumstances?

11. What is feedback control? Describe the steps associated with developing a feedback-control system.

12. What is feedforward control? How does it differ from feedback control?

13. What is a business intelligence system? For instance, where does business intelligence come from, and how is it used?

14. What are the characteristics of crisis-prone organizations? Name 10 things companies can do to control organizational crises.

CRITICAL THINKING AND APPLICATION QUESTIONS

1. One of the most important activities associated with strategy implementation is designing a strategy-supportive organization. Contact a hospitality organization and request a copy of its organization chart. Keep in mind that not all organizations are comfortable providing this document, and you may have to contact several firms before one provides you with the document. Examine and identify the structure of this company. What are some of the strengths and weaknesses of this structural form. If you were to change the structure, what would you modify and why? If this firm

grew to twice its current size, what changes in its current organizational form would you recommend? Why?

2. Research the existence of a chief knowledge officer (CKO) or chief learning officer (CLO) in hospitality firms. Do these positions exist in the industry? Are these organizational positions common or rare based on your research? Explain your findings and what it might suggest about the importance of formal organizational leaders responsible for ensuring that the organization maximizes its return on knowledge investments.

3. This exercise gives you an opportunity to design structures for a new resort.

Design: You are establishing a new luxury resort business on a small Caribbean island. Construction of the 200-room resort is under way, and it is scheduled to open a year from now. You decide it is time to draw up an organizational chart for this new venture. Your initial workforce will consist of 150 employees. Draw your organization chart and briefly discuss the rationale for your company structure. Don't forget to include your corporate as well as hotel staff. Keep in mind your differentiation strategy (it is a luxury property) and the jobs you will need to have covered. What services will you provide? What recreation activities?

Redesign: You are into your tenth year of operation. The company is wildly successful. You and your partners own 30 resorts (all fewer than 200 rooms) in a variety of locations in South America, Central America, North America, the Caribbean, and the South Pacific, and the total number of employees is more than 4,000. Draw an up-to-date organization chart focusing on the top two to three levels (corporate structure), and briefly discuss the rationale for your new structure. Keep in mind some of the likely problems you have faced when expanding from one to 30 resorts. Be sure your new structure deals with these growth issues.

Redesign Again: Ten more years have passed. The resorts are now in 50 warm climate locations (not in Alaska or the Far East), and you operate five cruise ships. The fleet of ships offers seven-day cruises to the Caribbean, Alaska, and the Far East. Ships include casinos, live music, dancing, nightclubs, and multiple dining room options. Food is available around the clock in the main dining rooms. A recent customer profile shows that almost 50 percent of the cruise ship customers also stay at one of your resorts. High-rate hotel bookings have been down over the past several seasons as the cruise customer and the luxury resort customer do not always want the same on-land experience. You believe that better coordination is necessary between the cruise and resort businesses. Draw an up-to-date organization chart again focusing on the top two to three levels, but also draw an organization chart for the cruise business level. Be sure your reorganization addresses the coordination challenges you are facing. Be sure to draw both corporate and cruise business-level structures.

CHAPTER 9

STRATEGIES FOR ENTREPRENEURSHIP AND INNOVATION

YOU SHOULD BE ABLE TO DO THE FOLLOWING AFTER READING THIS CHAPTER:

1. Know the entrepreneurial tasks that bring a new venture into existence.

2. Explain the key components of a business plan and the importance of having an end-game strategy.

3. List the most common sources of start-up capital.

4. Identify the major tasks of entrepreneurs during the first year of a new venture.

5. Cite the major reasons why new ventures fail.

6. Define innovation and distinguish among the various types of innovation possible within businesses.

FEATURE STORY

THE AMAZING JOURNEY OF THE IMMIGRANT ENTREPRENEUR

Imagine an immigrant population from India, England, and Africa that arrives in America with suitcases, modest family assets, and the hopes of a better life and education for their children. Motels and hotels provide jobs for all members of a family, as well as a place to live. "When you are an immigrant, it takes a lot of money to buy a business," says Paresh Patel, owner of the Howard Johnson Inn and Suites on Route 17 in Paramus, New Jersey. "So what they do is pool their resources." With the promise of immediate housing and cash flow, the hotel industry was a popular choice for newly arriving Indian entrepreneurs. Families often provided support, and especially financing, for these new ventures.

The flow of Indians into the U.S. hospitality industry began in the 1940s, when a few immigrants bought cheap single-room occupancy hotels in the San Francisco area, according to Mike Amin, a third-generation hotelier and former Chairman of the Asian American Hotel Owners Association (AAHOA). The numbers of immigrants really took off in the late 1970s, when many successful Indians living in Uganda were forced out of the country by political turmoil.

In the beginning, most Indian American hotel owners shared a common Gujarati heritage. While their shared heritage served as a source of cultural and family strength, the journey to prosperity was not easy. Early on, these hoteliers were met with resistance from bankers and insurance companies, some of whom accused the Indian entrepreneurs of conspiring to buy hotels, burn them down, and collect on the insurance. Competitors were not above resorting to racism, with "American owned" motel signs and taunts for those who would purchase lodging from "foreigners." Today the persistence, hard work, and business savvy of these immigrants reveals an American success story. Members of AAHOA collectively own more than 22,000 hotels with 1 million rooms. They hire 800,000 people and own more than one-third of all the hotels in the United States. When you look just at the economy segment, they own 50 percent of the hotels.

What started as small, usually independent economy hotel operations run by husbands and wives or brothers and sisters has been transformed. Kundan and Chanbrakanp Patel bought their first motel in 1980 because Kundan could not find suitable employment as a medical technician. The business was a sound investment that could grow through hard work. According to Kundan, "Indians are hardworking, and you can build up clientele with a friendly air." Now the Patels own several lodging properties.

Hersha Shah and her husband Hasu bought their first hotel in 1984 in Harrisburg, Pennsylvania. In 14 months, the couple had doubled the revenue of the underperforming hotel and were on their way to further acquisitions. Hersha, which means "happiness" in Sanskrit, was responsible for operations, while Hasu worked on development opportunities. Today the company is a publicly traded real estate investment trust (REIT) with sons Jay and Neil Shah playing key leadership roles in the hotel company and their other businesses. The Shah family owns Hersha Hospitality Management, which manages 55 hotels; Hersha Development Corporation, with 16 properties under development; and Hersha Interiors and Supply.

Another Indian American, R. C. Patel, bought his first hotel in Pell City, Alabama, with his brother Mukesh "Mike" more than 20 years ago when he was just 20 years old. The Patels lead the Atlanta-based Diplomat Hotels and hold related businesses, including three banks that specialize in small business financing. These entrepreneurs became the first Asian franchisors in the U.S. industry by purchasing the Budgetel brand in 2007.

Indian Americans have quietly carved out an unparalleled niche within the industry that is growing in size and influence. A new generation of Indian-American hoteliers is emerging, such as Manhattan-based hotelier, Vikram Chatwal, who has created an independent hotel group of luxury boutique hotels, including Time Hotel and The Dream, two of New York's hip hotels. In addition, many Indian American hotel companies have grown in size, welcoming members of their family and establishing sophisticated enterprises such as the Hersha Group and Diplomate Hotel Company.

Other large family enterprises with notable growth include B. U. Patel and sons' Tarsadia Hotels, the Rama brothers of JHM Hotels, the father and son team of Bharat Shah and Mitesh Shah of Noble Investments, Shree Hospitality Group headed by Ravi Patel, and Apple Core Hotels in Manhattan, of which Vijay Dandapani is a partner and chief operating officer. Former AAHOA Chairman Bakulesh "Buggsi" Patel observes that many younger Indian Americans have grown up in the hotel business, and it is now their challenge to transform their parents' assets into better assets. The entrepreneurial journey continues.[1]

DISCUSSION QUESTIONS:

1. What were some of the major challenges early Indian hoteliers faced in America? Do these challenges exist today?

2. What were the primary sources of funding available to Indian entrepreneurs? Do you think these sources of capital have changed over the years?

INTRODUCTION

In the broadest sense of the term, *entrepreneurship* is the creation of new business. It involves recognizing or creating opportunity, assembling resources to pursue the opportunity, and managing activities that bring a venture into existence. Some ventures are complete start-ups, whereas other ventures are pursued within an existing organization. According to Arnold Cooper, widely acknowledged as a pioneer in the study of entrepreneurship: "Entrepreneurial ventures, whether independent or within established corporations, might be viewed as experiments. They test to determine the size of particular markets or whether particular technologies or ways of competing are promising. They have good internal communication and enormous commitment from their key people."[2]

This chapter discusses entrepreneurship, innovation, and growth. The first section discusses independent new-venture creation, including franchising, followed by a section on innovation and entrepreneurship within established firms.

ENTREPRENEURIAL START-UPS

The U.S. economy relies heavily on entrepreneurship as a source of growth and strength. Hundreds of thousands of small firms are created each year. Annually, more than 1 million jobs are created by these firms, while *Fortune* 500 companies are cutting their workforces. Eating and drinking places in America are mostly small businesses, with more than half being sole proprietorships or partnerships.[3] More than half of the private workforce is employed in firms with fewer than 500 employees. These businesses account for about half of the private-sector gross domestic product. Two-thirds of new inventions come out of smaller firms.[4] Nevertheless, entrepreneurship is a high-risk activity.

Entrepreneurs in nations with highly developed economies often complain about how difficult it is to keep a new business going, and they are right. However, entrepreneurial efforts in less-developed economies such as Russia are even more difficult: "An unstable government, an undeveloped legal system, overregulation, a virtually unfathomable taxation system, a pervasive mafia, and an inadequate business structure characterize the maze that Russian entrepreneurs must navigate in their attempts to create successful ventures."[5]

Much of what is found in this book is valuable to entrepreneurs. However, this section looks specifically at aspects of entrepreneurship that are different from other types of strategic planning. The topics include characteristics of entrepreneurs, the entrepreneurial tasks of opportunity recognition or creation, development of a business plan, financing arrangements, venture management through its first year, and common causes of new-venture failures.

The Entrepreneur

Entrepreneurs have been studied for many years, and lists of their characteristics are numerous. Research seeking to identify the specific traits that distinguish entrepreneurs from those who do not start new businesses has been inconclusive, but some evidence exists to suggest that entrepreneurs have a higher need for achievement, a greater tendency to take risks, and a stronger belief that they control their own destiny (internalized locus of control).[6]

A close look at entrepreneurs in the small hotel sector in Scotland revealed that those who survive actively pursue rational business objectives and employ marketing strategies to achieve those objectives. In short, successful entrepreneurs appear to be good strategists, in that they recognize and take advantage of opportunities. Kemmons Wilson founded Holiday Inn in 1952 after a family vacation the previous year in which he became annoyed at the $2-per-child surcharge attached to his bill for each of his five children. He saw the opportunity for a new concept and introduced a chain of hotels that defined the modern hotel era with amenities we now take for granted, such as kids stay for free, air conditioning in every room, free parking, free ice, in-room phones, rates by the room and not the number of people, and high cleanliness standards.[7]

Entrepreneurs are opportunists, but also resourceful, creative, visionary, hardworking, and optimistic. Conrad Hilton got his start in the lodging industry by renting out rooms in his home in New Mexico. Entrepreneurs are independent thinkers who are willing to take risks and innovate. They also tend to be excellent leaders.[8] Above all, they are dreamers:

> *Would-be entrepreneurs live in a sea of dreams. Their destinations are private islands—places to build, create, and transform their particular dreams into reality. Being an entrepreneur entails envisioning your island, and, even more important, it means getting in the boat and rowing to your island. Some leave the shore and drift aimlessly in the shallow waters close to shore, while others paddle furiously and get nowhere, because they don't know how to paddle or steer. Worst of all are those who remain on the shore of the mainland, afraid to get in the boat. Yet, all those dreamers may one day be entrepreneurs, if they can marshal the resources—external and internal—needed to transform their dreams into reality.[9]*

Everyone around her thought Debbi Fields would fail when she decided to start selling her delicious homemade cookies. She founded Mrs. Fields' Original Cookies, a company with more than $100 million in sales and more than 4,000 employees. Not everyone has the internal stamina and drive to be an entrepreneur. Entrepreneurship causes a lot of stress. Disappointments are common. Uncertainty is a constant. However, successful entrepreneurs can also acquire great wealth and personal satisfaction. Harris Rosen bought his first hotel, the Quality Inn on Orlando's International Drive in 1974, just as the oil embargo hit, gas prices jumped sky high, and many Americans altered their summer travel plans. Many of the hotels in Orlando closed, but Harris used initiative to hunt out his customers. He explained the situation in his own words—given in the "Hospitality Focus" boxed section on page 361.

Today Rosen Hotels & Resorts employs more than 3,000 people and operates seven hotels (approximately 5,000 rooms), including the original Quality Inn, and the newest called Rosen Shingle Creek resort. In addition to becoming a successful entrepreneur, Rosen's philanthropic efforts have included the establishment of the Rosen College of Hospitality Management at the

ENTREPRENEUR HARRIS ROSEN MARKETS HIS FIRST HOTEL DURING WIDESPREAD FINANCIAL CRISIS

HOSPITALITY FOCUS

"The vast majority of hotels in Orlando were bankrupt or closed, and here I was buying a hotel in the midst of this chaos, and getting guests to stay at the hotel was very difficult. I remember I used to stand right at the entrance ramp to the hotel and literally pray that somebody would turn in and come on to our property. Just try to draw them in with my mental powers that I might have possessed. It was very difficult to do that, and so very early on after I had acquired the property for a week, I knew that standing there begging for business was not the appropriate thing to do. So I packed a little bag, got out on I-4, and said that I was going to hitchhike to New England where I knew there were dozens and dozens of motor coach operators who came to Orlando. And so I got a ride almost all the way up to New England, kept hitchhiking until finally I got to meet with motor coach companies.

I would strike a deal with the president or the chief operating officer of the company. I had my little business cards, I would ask what rate do they want to stay with us. They would say $8 or $9 or $7; I would write the rate down, the name of the company on the business card, sign my name, and that was the contract. And I probably signed 11 or 12 contracts that way. Some of these guys were so kind—they felt so sorry for me—that they would actually drive me to my next appointment in their buses.

When I finished, what was probably around five days, I literally had enough business to sustain us for that first year. And the truth is that many of those New England motor coach operators remain today as our clients. It was one of those quirks of faith that led me to do what I did. Clearly a ridiculous attempt to market the hotel, but at that moment it was the only opportunity I thought that presented itself for me to get off my chair, go to where the business was, and try to convince people to use our hotel. And it worked very well."[10]

University of Central Florida in Orlando, and the Tangelo Park Pilot Program. Through the program, any child in Tangelo Park (a predominantly African-American community in South Orange County) who graduates from high school is provided a free college education within the Florida state system—thanks to Mr. Rosen.

Entrepreneurial Tasks

The primary tasks associated with a new venture are recognizing or creating an opportunity, developing a business plan, securing start-up capital, and managing the venture through its early stages. (See the "Hospitality Focus" boxed section on page 362.)

METRO RESTAURANT: A NEW VENTURE

In the spring of 1988, Patrick Clark opened an upscale restaurant called Metro in New York City's Upper East Side. He had apprenticed with renowned French chef Michel Guerard and had been chef at Manhattan's Odeon for seven years. He was ready to move from the trendy downtown dining scene to the city's bastion of wealth for his own venture. He had financing, a chic dining room, and a sterling reputation. "Like most chefs, I wanted my own place. I had made my reputation, and I felt the time was right," noted Clark. He found a location on East 74th Street, signed a 15-year lease, and set a budget of $1.1 million. His major investors were three Odeon customers. In addition, he used his own savings and that of his working partners, Clark's assistant and the maitre d' from Odeon. Metro was off and running with an average check of $60. Clark ended his first year of operation with gross income of almost $4 million.[11]

RECOGNIZING OR CREATING AN OPPORTUNITY

Entrepreneurship is often envisioned as a discovery process. *Entrepreneurial discovery* entails channeling resources toward the fulfillment of a market need.[12] For a start-up to be successful, this often means meeting a need better than other companies. In the case of Metro, the reviews were mixed about his concept. While *Gourmet* magazine lauded Clark, and both *Esquire* and the *New York Times* wrote mostly positively about the new concept, the press thought the concept had serious problems. In other cases, success involves creating an entirely new market. (See the "Hospitality Focus" boxed section on page 363.)

As this example illustrates, entrepreneurial discovery may be viewed as the intersection of a need and a solution. There are a lot of unmet needs in the world. For example, we need clean energy, we need a cure for AIDS, and we need to be able to communicate more easily in a wide variety of languages. There are also a lot of solutions for which there may be no need at the present time. Scientists and even common people discover things every day. Human creativity is unbounded. Entrepreneurial activity occurs anytime an entrepreneur is able to link a need to a solution in such a manner that a new business emerges. Opportunities to do this are context specific.

What might be an opportunity today in Ukraine may not be an opportunity at all in the United States today or even in Ukraine tomorrow. This means that entrepreneurial opportunities do not necessarily lie around waiting to be discovered by the serendipitous entrepreneur who stumbles upon them, or even be divined by entrepreneurial geniuses, if any such geniuses exist. Instead, entrepreneurial opportunities are often residuals of human activities in noneconomic spheres and emerge contingent upon conscious actions by entrepreneurs who continually strive to transform the outputs of those noneconomic activities into new products and firms, and in the process fulfill and transform human aspirations into new markets. In other words, before there are products and firms, there is human imagination; and before there are markets, there are human aspirations.[13]

GROVER VINEYARDS: CREATING A BRAND NEW MARKET

HOSPITALITY FOCUS

In the opulent settings of the Taj or the Grand Hotel in Mumbai, sipping the inordinately expensive but shockingly mediocre French wine jarred the otherwise pleasant dining experience, thought Kapil Grover and his father, Kanwal, in the early 1980s. This dissatisfaction inspired the Grovers to try growing, for the first time, French varieties of grapes suitable for wine production in India. More than two decades later, Grover Vineyards has succeeded in developing specialty wines to complement traditionally spicy Indian cuisine.

Grover Vineyards was established in 1988 on 40 acres of land at the foot of the Nandi Hills near Bangalore. The family spent several years experimenting with different types of French grapes and their response to Indian conditions. In 1996, the vintner became a joint venture with Veuve Clicquot, a brand of Paris-based luxury goods giant LVMH Moet Hennessy Louis Vuitton SA. The younger Grover is the director of the company, which now boasts 200 acres of world-class varietals under production. Kanwal is the company's chairman. With their winery, the Grovers undertook one of marketing's most exciting and exhausting challenges: creating a market where one did not previously exist. Today they are India's largest exporter of wine, even selling their wares in France.[14]

DEVELOPING A BUSINESS PLAN

Everything associated with a new venture revolves around a business plan. A *business plan* contains the details of how a new venture will be carried out. Creation of the plan forces the entrepreneur to think through the details of the venture and determine whether it really seems reasonable. Table 9.1 contains a description of the various sections. The executive summary has the primary objective of catching the interest of the reader. This is followed by a description of the proposed business venture; an analysis of the environment; a resource analysis; and functional plans such as a marketing plan, operations plan, and a management plan.

Financial projections are among the most important elements of a business plan, especially for potential investors. Projections determine when financing will be needed and in what quantity, as well as when investors can expect to begin receiving returns. Projections often take the form of *pro-forma financial statements*, including financial statements, balance sheets, and cash-flow statements. Pro-forma statements are forward-looking and difficult to develop because entrepreneurs seldom have good data upon which to base them. But the process of developing pro-forma statements requires research on how much resources will cost and potential margins that might be expected. Pro-forma statements are an excellent way for an entrepreneur to communicate expected financial needs and performance.

Before complex pro-formas are prepared, a simple economic model that focuses on how profit is derived can often help the entrepreneur determine the attractiveness of the business. Figure 9.1 presents the four key variables to consider when determining the viability of a business idea, including contribution margins, volumes, operating leverage, and product/service mix.[15]

The contribution margin is determined by subtracting variable costs from total revenue. When expressed as a percentage of total revenue, a contribution margin tells a manager how

TABLE 9.1 **What's in a Business Plan?**

SECTION	DESCRIPTION
Executive summary	The executive summary contains a brief description of the venture and why it is likely to be successful. It must immediately catch the attention of potential investors and encourage them to read the entire business plan.
Business description	The introduction provides a thorough description of the venture. It should include elements such as where it will be launched, who will be involved, the customers it will serve, and when everything is likely to happen.
Environmental analysis	This section covers the most-relevant characteristics of the external environment in which the new venture will compete. These characteristics often include: • Market analysis (including customer analysis and evaluation of past and expected growth in demand) • Existing-competitor analysis • Supplier analysis • Evaluation of potential substitutes • Discussion of entry and exit barriers and their influence on entering and exiting competitors • Relevant government regulations and regulators • Financial condition of the industry • Availability of funding • Overall economic factors for the host country • Availability of technology • Availability of personnel with appropriate qualifications
Resource analysis	Resource analysis focuses on the special resources the venture already possesses and the resources that will be needed in order to make the venture a success. Such things as personnel, financial capital, equipment, patents and intellectual capital, and physical property are described. The most important resource and the one that should receive the most attention is the entrepreneur(s).
Functional plans	The nature of the venture will determine which functional plans should be included. A marketing plan (how the market will be reached, advertising ideas, distribution strategy, etc.), a management plan (who will be responsible for which activities), and an operating plan are essential. Beyond these, other plans may include research and development, information management strategy, or personnel (training).

TABLE 9.1 (*Continued*)

Financial projections	Good data for projections typically is not available, but potential investors want to have some sense of the potential market size and growth and the projected margins that will be available. Financial projections (pro-forma statements) also help investors understand timing issues, such as when money will be needed, how much will be needed, and when their investment will begin to provide tangible returns.
Implementation schedule	This is a plan outlining the steps that will be taken as the venture unfolds. It provides a time frame for the accomplishment of various activities.
End-game strategy	Potential investors will be interested in knowing at what point they can exit the venture. Other important elements of an end-game strategy from the perspective of the entrepreneur include an executive succession plan and an exit strategy if the venture is not successful or when the venture has concluded.
Risk analysis	All ventures entail risk. Potential investors appreciate a good analysis of risk. This section is also very helpful to the entrepreneur in determining whether to pursue the venture.

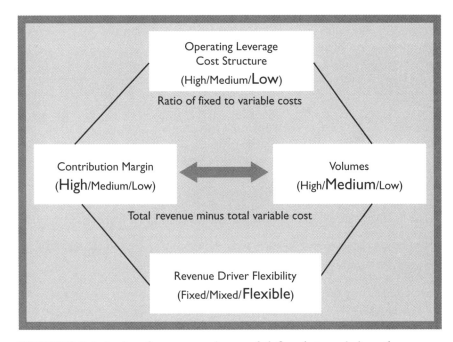

FIGURE 9.1 A simple economic model for determining the attractiveness of a new venture

much is available to pay for fixed costs and profit after variable costs have been paid. The higher the contribution margin, the more attractive the business. Volumes capture the level of business transactions from low to high volume. In a perfect world, a business would have high contribution margins and high volumes, but these two dimensions of profit often work as trade-offs for determining pricing and quality levels. Do we go with a high-priced product with high margins and low volume, or design our business for lower margins and higher volume. The profit model of a fine-dining restaurant may be feasible if the operator can obtain high margins and medium volume, but may become infeasible if the owner has both low margins and low volume.

The operating leverage of the firm is the proportion of total costs that are fixed. A business that has a lower proportion of fixed costs and a higher proportion of variable costs is said to employ less operating leverage. The cost structure of the firm is more desirable if the operating leverage is low. Finally, the product/service mix can be fixed or variable, in which several different services or products can be created to add value. By working with all four of these variables, an attractive business venture would be one with low operating leverage, high margins, moderate to high volumes, and several value-added services for which customers would be willing to pay. If a proposed business has high operating leverage, low margins, volume limits, and a standardized or fixed product mix, then the economic viability of the business may be doubtful.

A fully developed implementation schedule may or may not be included in the initial business plan. However, even when a full schedule is not included, a business plan typically outlines a timeline for major events. Investors are also interested in what might be called an end-game strategy. This is a plan for concluding the venture, transferring control to others, or allowing potential investors to exit the venture with a high return on their investments. It may also include contingency plans in the event the venture does not succeed (i.e., alternative uses or sales potential for acquired resources) and an executive-succession plan in case the primary entrepreneur leaves the venture. Finally, potential investors will be very interested in the amount of risk found in a venture. Rather than sidestepping this issue, it is probably better to include a section that honestly evaluates financial and operating risks.

In most ways, a business plan closely resembles a strategic plan for an existing business. It contains the basic elements of situation analysis (external and internal), strategy formulation, and strategy implementation but there is more emphasis on financing. Also, the perspective from which the two types of plans are written is very different. For instance, strategic plans assume an ongoing business, whereas a new business venture may not be pursued if it is determined to be infeasible. Also, the target audiences of a business plan and a strategic plan are different. Because a business plan will go to potential investors, it must be written in a concise format (no more than 30 to 40 pages), and it must answer the types of questions that potential investors would like to have answered. A strategic plan usually includes a lot more detail in the implementation sections, because it serves as a guide for an existing organization. Potential investors are not interested in as much operating detail as are managers in an existing organization.

SECURING START-UP CAPITAL

Obtaining the financing required to begin a new venture, or *start-up capital*, is probably the most difficult problem facing a potential entrepreneur. As will be demonstrated later in this chapter, not obtaining sufficient capital is one of the biggest causes of failure. Some of the most common sources of start-up capital include commercial banks, personal contacts, venture capitalists, corporate partnerships, investment groups, and business angels (see Table 9.2).

TABLE 9.2 **Potential Sources of Capital for Entrepreneurs in Hospitality**

SOURCE	DESCRIPTION
Commercial banks	Includes asset-backed borrowing, small loans, third-party loan guarantees, leasing, credit cards, and credit lines. Once in a while, a bank will select a venture for funding with very little security, usually based on the track record and credentials of the entrepreneur.
Personal contacts	Family and friends, asset sales
Venture capitalists	Organizations or individuals who evaluate business plans and invest "seed money" in some of them for an ownership interest and other compensation. They expect very high returns on their investments because of the risk they are taking.
Corporate partnerships	Many corporations seek opportunities to invest in new ventures with a high potential payoff. The corporation usually trades money or other resources for an ownership interest.
Investment groups	Wealthy investors or corporations often form investment groups that own most or all of the capital assets associated with a hospitality venture. The operator then pays the investment group for use of the facilities, and the investment group also enjoys the benefits from property appreciation. Real estate investment trusts (REITS) are an example.
Business angels	High-net-worth individuals who invest in entrepreneurial ventures as an opportunity to grow their wealth at a rate higher than a secure investment would provide. Many angels are also interested in providing opportunities to entrepreneurs.
Initial public offerings	These are usually used during a more advanced stage of the venture, rather than at start-up. The venture has existed long enough to provide adequate information that would lead potential investors to believe that it will be highly successful. The IPO basically provides the capital to pursue the venture at a larger scale.

Sources: J. A. Fraser, "How to Finance Anything," *Inc* (March 1999): 32–48; P. DeCeglie, "The Truth about Venture Capital," *Business Startups* (February 2000): 40–47; K. Schilit, "How to Obtain Venture Capital," Business Horizons (May-June 1987): 76–81; J. Freear, J. E. Sohl, and W. E. Wetzel Jr., "Angels and Non-angels: Are There Differences?" *Journal of Business Venturing* (March 1994): 109–123.

HOSPITALITY FOCUS

HUSBAND AND WIFE TEAM ENDURE STRUGGLES TO SET UP NEW RESTAURANT

Yvonne Parker and her husband, Larry, began their restaurant with a dream and $15,000 in start-up capital that they borrowed from friends and family. After the death of her husband, and faced with running their venture on her own, Yvonne made some changes, starting with the restaurant's name—Empire Food became Yvonne's Southern Cuisine. What started as a seven-seater storefront is today a two-floor, 200-seat restaurant. However, reaching this level of prosperity was far from simple. Yvonne's Southern Cuisine was one of the first black-owned businesses in Pelham, New York, and Yvonne was unable to get a bank loan when she needed to expand. Undaunted, she discussed her concerns with her sister, Evelyn Hall, and her brother-in-law, Armel Desir. Given Desir's business sense and Hall's dedication, Parker knew that a partnership with them would help boost the business. With a $150,000 investment in the restaurant, the two family members became partners.[16]

Bank loans result in debt. Personal contacts, such as family financial support in the Indian community or the customers and coworkers of Patrick Clark in his Metro restaurant venture, may be among the most flexible sources of financing because the financiers have a personal interest in the entrepreneur. In the early years of the gaming business in Las Vegas, for example, most of the funding came from the Teamsters Central States Pension Fund because financial institutions steered clear of casino investments.[17] Venture capitalists, corporate partners, investment groups, and business angels may provide loans, receive equity, or own part or all of the property in exchange for the capital they provide. After start-up, if the venture has enough of a track record so that potential investors believe that it will be highly profitable in time, an initial public offering may be pursued.

Some entrepreneurs are able to start with their own financial resources. For example, the first of Colonel Sanders' fried-chicken restaurants was financed with his Social Security check.[18] Anne Beiler (of Auntie Anne's, Inc.) began her first pretzel stand with a $6,000 loan from her in-laws. For larger ventures or once these resources are exhausted, they often turn to a bank. Because of the risks involved, commercial banks are unenthused about financing entrepreneurial ventures unless substantial secured assets are involved. For example, entrepreneurs often mortgage their homes or offer their automobiles, jewelry, or financial investments as loan security. Banks also consider loans more attractive if a wealthy third party is willing to co-sign, thus taking on the financial obligation if the entrepreneur is unable to pay. Occasionally, a bank will make an unsecured loan based on the reputation or credentials of the entrepreneur or on a personal relationship. Restaurants are often considered a bad investment by bankers, who will refuse to finance these ventures because of the low barriers to entry, little collateral value in used restaurant equipment, and the long hours required on-site by owners.[19] (See the "Hospitality Focus" boxed section above.)

Venture Capital

Venture capitalists are another potential source of start-up capital. They are individuals or groups of investors who seek out and provide capital to entrepreneurs who have ideas that seem to have the potential for very high returns. Retail and service businesses began to receive more attention from the venture community in the 1990s, although they typically do not get involved in restaurant investments unless they are larger and more established multiunit operations. Venture capitalists may seek an annual return as high as 60 percent or more on "seed money" for a new venture.[20]

In evaluating business plans, venture capitalists consider the entrepreneur's personality and experience, the product or service characteristics, market characteristics, financial potential, and the strength of the venture team.[21] Financing from a venture capitalist is often combined with capital from other sources, such as banks or private investors. In the restaurant industry, venture capitalists often wait until later stages in the company's life cycle to provide capital. The most common first disbursement is usually provided to companies that are about to expand (called third-stage or mezzanine financing) rather than to provide start-up financing to develop an initial unit.[22] The House of Blues, a restaurant and nightclub concept, used three venture capital firms—Aeneas Group, US Venture Partners, and the Platinum Group—to help finance the building of new units and a merchandising operation.

The restaurant industry has many advantages as an investment target, including its fragmented nature with good growth potential, low risk of obsolescence in products, and the potential for mass distribution. Considering the use of venture capital can also benefit the entrepreneur because of access to large amounts of capital and the ability to obtain management expertise and advice to refine and sustain the start-up.[23] Entrepreneurs who seek financing from venture capitalists should prepare a thorough business plan and answer questions as completely and accurately as possible. They should not expect an immediate decision, embellish facts, dodge questions, hide significant problems, or fixate on pricing.[24]

Corporate Financing and Angels

Entrepreneurs may also turn to corporations to obtain financing. From the entrepreneur's perspective, the chief disadvantage of this form of financing is a partial loss of control and ownership. Large corporations often seek investments in new ventures as a way to obtain new technology, products, or markets. A special type of corporate partnership is the *investment group*. These are groups of wealthy individuals, business owners, or corporations that take an ownership interest in the capital assets of the venture. For example, an investment group may own a hotel and the property on which it stands. The hotel operator pays the group for use of the property. The investment group also receives the benefits from property appreciation. A common example of an investment group is the real estate investment trust (REIT). (See the "Hospitality Focus" boxed section on page 370.)

Another potential source of capital are business angels, wealthy individuals who provide start-up capital to entrepreneurs with promise. Many of them were once entrepreneurs themselves. They sometimes seek high returns, but many of them enjoy investing simply for the sake of helping an entrepreneur, promoting economic development objectives of a region, or advancing the state of technology in an area such as medicine, the arts, or computer technology. The Arab Business Angels Network (ABAN), for example, was conceived by the Young Arab Leaders—a group of accomplished leaders from every sector across the region—and Dubai Holding as a link between entrepreneurs and angel investors. This group acts as a vehicle to promote entrepreneurial endeavors and to build a community of angel investors across the Arab region.[25] Unlike venture capitalists, business angels do not pursue investing full time.

INVESTMENT GROUP GLENMONT CAPITAL MANAGEMENT FINANCES HOTEL PROJECTS

Glenmont Capital Management, LLC, is a privately held real estate investment management firm that deploys equity capital from its existing investment funds to finance hotels with experienced entrepreneurs. The company funds joint venture equity investments in which it can leverage the expertise of its experienced and proven partners who operate the hotels on a day-to-day basis. The funds are derived from institutional and high-net-worth investors. They focus on high-yielding, small to midsize investment opportunities that typically require $5 million to $15 million of equity capital. Glenmont's existing portfolio consists of several million square feet of various hotel, retail, industrial, office, multifamily, land, and other properties around the United States and in Europe.

Recently, this investment group announced a joint venture with American Hotel Development Partners (AHDP), a hotel development company whose principals have years of expertise in managing and operating hotels. The plan is to build a 112-room Candlewood Suites Hotel. Larry Kestin, Managing Principal of Glenmont Capital Management, remarked, "We believe we have identified a growing segment of the hotel market where we can achieve extraordinary returns for our investors, and we have also ventured with a quality group in AHDP, the principals of which we believe are well positioned to take advantage of the opportunities in the market." AHDP's ultimate strategy is to achieve operational stability approximately three years after each hotel is built, at which time and given appropriate market conditions, AHDP would seek to sell such hotels in bulk or individually.[26]

Initial Public Offerings

After a venture has established a record of performance, entrepreneurs or venture capitalists may pursue an *initial public offering* (IPO). An IPO entails selling stock to the public and investors (see Figure 9.2). Assuming a board of directors has been created, the first step is to receive approval from the board to proceed with the IPO. Then an underwriter (investment banker) is selected, and a "letter of intent" is drafted. The letter of intent outlines the financial relationship between the company and the underwriter (e.g., fees) and other conditions of the offering. Attorneys then begin work on a prospectus, being careful to follow guidelines set by the Securities and Exchange Commission. The investment banker will oversee an elaborate due diligence process, which is a thorough examination of the company, its financial situation, markets, customers, creditors, and any other important stakeholders. After a printer is selected for the prospectus and a preliminary prospectus is filed, the underwriter assembles a syndicate of companies that will help sell the IPO to targeted investors. Venture managers and the investment banker then make a series of formal presentations to potential investors. If everything looks positive after these presentations, the final prospectus is printed, the offering is priced, the size of the offering is determined, and the IPO takes place.[27]

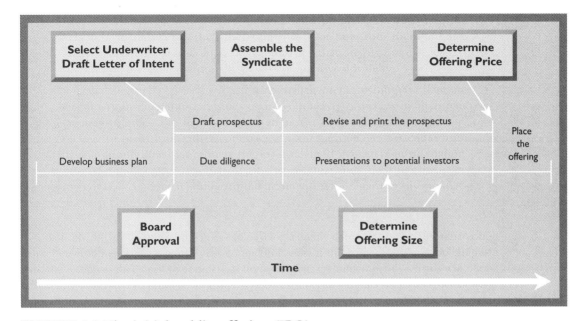

FIGURE 9.2 The initial public offering (IPO) process
Source: This model is based on information found in Nasdaq, "Going Public" (New York: The Nasdaq Stock Market, Inc., 2000).

Krispy Kreme, for example, went public in 2000. The stock ended the first day of trading at $9.25, split adjusted, and in mid-2003 sold for four times that amount. Unfortunately, as sometimes happens with public companies, the amazing success of this relatively small donut operator began to change when rapid growth and accounting problems led to store closings and the termination of franchise agreements.[28]

MANAGING THE VENTURE

The early stages of an entrepreneurial start-up are the most difficult.[29] Some of the major tasks of entrepreneurs for the first year of a venture are outlined in Table 9.3. In the early stages, financing and financial management are difficult problems. Even after the difficult process of securing initial financing, the entrepreneur must still set up a system to manage financial flows and keep records necessary to satisfy venture capitalists, creditors, and the Internal Revenue Service. For those who wish to operate a restaurant or hotel, the uniform systems of accounts provide standardized accounting systems that contain many supplementary operating statements covering budgeting and forecasting. The *Uniform System of Accounts for the Lodging Industry* (USALI) and the *Uniform System of Accounts for Restaurants* (USAR) are designed with the special needs of those industries in mind and permit entrepreneurs to compare their operating results directly with industry standards.[30]

Entrepreneurs often experience cash-flow problems because occupancy rates and other cash flows typically take a while to materialize. Low sales can plague a new venture, especially in the first few months after introduction. Many consumers and businesses wait to see if the new restaurant or hotel receives good reviews. They look for a track record. Without sufficient

TABLE 9.3 **First-Year Agenda for Entrepreneurial Startups**

ACTIVITY	DESCRIPTION
Financial management	Once external funding is obtained, the emphasis becomes establishing systems to track revenues and expenses and control costs. A record-keeping system must be established that will satisfy the demands of investors, creditors, and the Internal Revenue Service.
Marketing	Early marketing efforts may include providing a service to a few customers at a nominal price to establish a track record and gain references. Targeted advertising is also appropriate.
Services development	This includes establishment of a system for collecting feedback from early customers so that services can be improved. Continual improvement is essential.
Resource acquisition	This process begins with site selection and construction of a building, if necessary. The site must also be equipped with necessary machinery, furnishings, information systems, utilities, and supplies. Contracts need to be established with suppliers of raw materials, components, and services.
Process development	The focus is on production and operations management to ensure efficiency and quality. Once again, continual improvement is essential.
Management and staffing	One of the most essential activities is recruitment of motivated, well-trained employees and selection of managers, as needed. This area also includes assignment of responsibilities, establishment of personnel policies, overcoming administrative problems, training, and establishing a compensation system, which may include benefits. The entrepreneur is establishing an organizational culture in this first year. It should support the objectives of the venture.
Legal requirements	The venture will need a legal form (sole proprietorship, partnership, corporation). If employees are hired, the venture will need an Employer Identification Number and will need to collect and pay payroll taxes. Patents and trademarks are sometimes necessary to protect the proprietary technology or brand image of the venture. Other legal requirements vary depending on the nature of the venture, the country and industry in which it is formed.

capital, the venture may fail even if the idea was good and the management skills were present. In the case of the Metro restaurant, as a general downturn in business hit New York City, customer counts were down to about 175 on the weekend and considerably lower during the week. Clark, the chef, concedes that he may not have been in tune with what his Upper East Side clientele wanted, and by the start of his second year in operation, he began trimming his staff and cutting his prices.[31]

One strategy for overcoming resistance is to provide services to the first few customers at a nominal price. Those first customers then become references. Targeted advertising is also helpful, and it requires that the entrepreneur carefully define the target markets. In the case of a restaurant, the menu, hours of operation, location, and service must be aligned with what the customer believes is worth buying. Building a strong and stable customer base is important to early operational success.

Establishing Operations and Site Selection

Another important first-year activity is service development. Entrepreneurs seldom get a service exactly right from the outset. Early consumers will very quickly discover flaws. Entrepreneurs should set up a system that collects feedback from early customers so that services can be improved. Theme restaurants, like the previously bankrupt Planet Hollywood, suffered from low profitability because of the high wages of their entertainers, inflated prices, stagnant menus, and the lack of repeat customers.[32] Continuous improvement is essential, because if the product or service is a success, other firms will quickly imitate it. They may be larger firms with more resources. Therefore, it is important to stay one step ahead of the competition in order to enjoy first-mover advantages.

Many resources need to be acquired at start-up. One of the most important decisions in this regard is site selection. The entrepreneur has to determine a size that is small enough to be cost efficient, yet large enough to take advantage of current and future demand. The site-selection decision is usually made during the development of the business plan, because potential investors will be interested in making sure that a suitable site is available. The site also has to be attractive to personnel who have the skills required for the venture to be a success. It should also be as close as possible to suppliers and customers. If the site does not yet include a suitable building, then construction must be coordinated. Other physical resources that need to be acquired include furnishings, utilities, information systems, and supplies. Contracts need to be established with suppliers of essential materials and services. (See the first "Hospitality Focus" boxed section on page 374.)

In addition to product/service development, process development cannot be neglected. Once a site has been selected, it has to be prepared for service production. The first units of a service are the most expensive to produce. For example, the first meals prepared will take the most time, and the first week of a hotel will be very expensive, as all the bugs are worked out and systems are put in place. Entrepreneurs should pay close attention to process issues, establish a quality-control system, and focus on obtaining supplies at a minimum cost. Costs of production should drop rapidly in the early stages of the service life cycle, consistent with the experience curve presented earlier.

Other production and operations-management issues will present themselves and will require immediate attention. Industry research reveals that on average hotels and restaurants replace two-thirds of their workers annually.[33] With this level of employee turnover, it is important for an entrepreneur to focus on how to retain those service workers who occupy low-skill and low-wage jobs. (See the second "Hospitality Focus" boxed section on page 374.)

ESTABLISHING OPERATIONS TO RENOVATE OLD RESTAURANT

"The kitchen was atrocious," noted Clark when he first began the lengthy renovation necessary to convert the long-standing restaurant called Adam's Rib into the Metro. The kitchen walls and floor needed to be retiled, the dining room required massive work on the ceiling arches to bring it into conformance with city codes, and the costs rose. Furnishings like the Tihany-designed chairs were $240 each, bringing costs even higher.[34]

EMPLOYEES MATTER AT JOIE DE VIVRE HOTELS

Joie de Vivre Hotels was started by Chip Conley, while in his mid-twenties. Now one of California's largest boutique hotel companies, the personality of the hotel and its service process reflect his beliefs and a brand personality that is similar to the California lifestyle experience: fresh, inventive, casual, and grassroots oriented. Employees matter in this company, which boasts a "service is the heart" philosophy that fosters a "participative, empowered and entrepreneurial, dynamically diverse and inclusive environment."

One simple example is how Joie de Vivre handled their service process when they took over management of the Hotel Carlton in San Francisco. The former management didn't like to replace aging vacuums, despite staff complaints. After Joie de Vivre Hospitality took over, the new manager bought a vacuum for each of the 15 housekeepers—and replaces them every year. The new vacuums make a big difference to employees—in performance and morale.[35]

Many entrepreneurial ventures begin with a small group of people; however, successful ventures need more personnel soon. The entrepreneur simply has too much to do. As the venture grows, recruitment and training of personnel and managers become important activities. The entrepreneur has to delegate responsibilities and establish a compensation system, which might even include benefits such as insurance.

As the organization grows, it is important to have a culture in place that supports the objectives of the venture. The culture is established very early through the examples of the entrepreneur and other early employees. For example, if the entrepreneur works hard, a cultural norm that values hard work will be established. If customers are given highest priority, then a customer-oriented culture will emerge. (See the "Hospitality Focus" boxed section on page 375.)

Choosing a Legal Form

Legal requirements are also a major issue during the first year. First, the entrepreneur should decide which legal form the venture will take. In a sole proprietorship, the entrepreneur is the

ENTREPRENEURIAL CULTURE AT HINES COMPANY

Maintaining an entrepreneurial culture is one of the key features of the Hines company, now one of the world's largest real estate organizations in the world. Gerald D. Hines, an engineer from Gary, Indiana, began his entrepreneurial career more than 50 years ago by forming an engineering partnership while taking on development projects on the side. Soon the real estate side of the business became his real passion. Hines's deep appreciation of architecture and his keen eye for design have been handed down to his employees.

He has also inspired employees to adopt his entrepreneurial spirit. When the company wanted to expand into global markets, it assigned each of its U.S. regional partners an area of the world to explore and let them gain financially from projects they brought to the table. Jeff Hines, the founder's son, notes, "If people are good at creating value, they can create a lot of value for themselves as well as the firm. We have a large piece of the pot available to nonfamily members. We think that's a very effective way to operate." Today the Hines portfolio includes more than 1,000 properties, with offices in 16 countries and controlled assets valued at approximately $19.9 billion.[36]

owner and is financially and legally liable for the venture in its entirety. In a partnership, the partners each contribute resources, such as money, physical goods, services, knowledge, and external relationships to the venture. They also share in the rewards. Typically, articles of partnership are drawn up by the partners to define such things as the duration of the venture, contributions by partners, division of profits and losses, rights of partners, procedures for settlement of disputes, and employee management.[37]

A *limited partnership* can be established in which the management responsibility and legal liability of partners are limited, except that at least one partner must be a general partner with unlimited liability. Several forms of limited partnerships exist.[38] A key advantage of a partnership over a corporation is that profits are passed through to partners instead of being taxed at higher corporate rates. Also, the problem of double taxation, in which profits are taxed at the corporate level and then dividends are taxed at the personal level, is avoided.

At this point, the only thing that needs to be added is that one of the advantages of forming a corporation is that the financial risk of a shareholder is limited to the amount invested in the corporation. However, shareholder control over the actions of the company is extremely limited. Also, the tax advantages found in partnerships are lost when a corporation is formed. The only exception is the *S corporation*, formerly called the Subchapter S corporation (from Subchapter S of the Internal Revenue Code), which allows tax advantages similar to what are found in a partnership. However, to qualify as an S corporation, organizations must have relatively few shareholders and must adhere to other strict guidelines.[39] Trademarks or unique processes may need to be protected from competitor infringement. Other legal requirements depend on the nature of the venture and the regulations surrounding it.

This discussion is not intended to be complete, but it does provide a glimpse of what an entrepreneur faces in the first year or so. For any would-be entrepreneurs, it adds a dimension of realism with regard to what it will take to make it through the first year. Entrepreneurs experience a lot of problems. From an external perspective, customer contact is an issue facing more than one-quarter of entrepreneurs.[40] Other major concerns are a lack of market knowledge and problems with market planning. It is interesting to note that most entrepreneurs do not feel that competitors are much of a problem. This point attests to the advantages of being small and introducing a new product or service to the market.

From an internal perspective, the most common issues are obtaining adequate capital and managing cash flow.[41] Management problems are also experienced with inventory control, facilities and equipment, human resources, leadership, organization structure, and accounting systems. For some entrepreneurs, the benefit of brand recognition, economies of scale, training, access to a reservation system, and marketing support make franchising a viable approach to business ownership. In addition, chain affiliation often gives hotel developers an edge with lending institutions.[42]

Franchising

In the United States, lodging industry franchising is a viable way to start a new venture, with around 70 percent of hotels affiliated with a chain, although this percentage is substantially lower in other parts of the world. Franchising is also popular in the restaurant industry, with the greatest number of franchised concepts being in the fast-food industry.[43] Franchising is when two independent companies form a contractual agreement giving one (the franchisee) the right to operate a business in a given location for a specified period under the brand of the other firm (franchisor). Franchisees agree to give the franchisor a combination of fees and royalties, usually in the form of a percentage of unit sales in restaurants or a percentage of room sales in hotels. Also included in these agreements are an advertising contribution paid to the franchisor as a percentage of unit revenues. Hospitality firms engage in what is called *business-format franchising*, which is when the franchisor sells a way of doing business to its franchisees. This form of franchising is in contrast to traditional franchising, in which the franchisor is mostly a manufacturer selling its product through a franchise network, such as car dealerships.[44]

Is franchising less risky than going into business on one's own? While conventional wisdom might say yes, current research suggests that joining a new and small franchise may be more risky than starting one's own business because success depends on the capacity of the franchisor and the other few franchisees to make the entire chain work. The likelihood of failure is lower when one joins an established chain with many units such as Subway, Pizza Hut, IHOP, McDonald's, or Red Lobster. It is important to understand that franchising is not without risks, with one study showing less than 25 percent of companies that offered franchises in the United States were still franchising 10 years later.[45] The Rosenberg International Center of Franchising (RCF) prepares a franchise index quarterly that tracks the market performance of the top 50 U.S. public franchisors. The RCF index represents more than 98 percent of the market capitalization of companies pursuing business format franchising. The index illustrates that even top franchisors can have amazing success and serious failure. (See the "Hospitality Focus" boxed section on page 377.)

Finally, an entrepreneur considering franchising as a method of doing business needs to keep in mind that multiunit franchisee ownership is common in the hospitality industry; for

TOP FRANCHISORS: FAILURE AND SUCCESS STORIES

Benihana Inc., the operator and franchisor of the nation's largest chain of Japanese and sushi restaurants, was the best performer of the RCF 50 index early in 2007. Its market value soared 40 percent as investors bid up its shares following several positive developments. The company announced double-digit total restaurant sales growth and strong company-wide comparable restaurant sales and guest count growth. Later in the same year, Hilton Hotels Corporation topped the RCF 50 index when its stock skyrocketed after being acquired by Blackstone Group LLC in 2007. Hilton gained 39 percent in market value by the end of the third quarter of 2007.

In contrast, quick-serve restaurant operator and franchisor Wendy's International lost almost 20 percent of its market value in the first quarter of 2007. Wendy's reported a 90 percent drop in profits due to lower franchise revenues and losses related to its recently divested chains (Tim Horton's and Baja Fresh Mexican Grills). The company promised major changes, including revitalizing the Wendy's brand, streamlining and improving operations, and new initiatives such as expansion of the breakfast program and the Frescata sandwich product line.

Also at the bottom of the index was Krispy Kreme, the donut maker, which reported poor financial returns, resulting in a stock price plunge of 38 percent in one day. Declining sales and high impairment charges and lease termination costs led to a net loss of $27 million, a much higher loss than the $4.6 million loss the previous year. The donut maker finished the third quarter with a 57 percent loss of market value, making it the worst performer of the index for that quarter.[46]

example, the average McDonald's franchisee in the United States owns three restaurants. The multiunit franchisee will have far more bargaining power in transactions with the franchisor, and hence new entrepreneurs need to consider their long-term ownership strategies. Franchising can be very promising, although there will always be opportunities for entrepreneurs who operate independent hotels or restaurants, in which they can reap substantial store-level profits and leverage prime locations and distinctive service features. Whether franchising or nonchain ownership is the method of operation, a variety of factors can cause failure. Some of these causes of failure are discussed further in the next section.

Causes of Failure

According to both entrepreneurs and venture capitalists, the most common reasons why new ventures fail are internal.[47] Specifically, the number-one reason cited by both groups is lack of management skill. Entrepreneurs often have enthusiasm, optimism, and drive but do not possess

METRO RESTAURANT: WHY IT FAILED

Two years after its promising opening, Metro went out of business. "We did all we could to stay open, but the concept was very expensive to maintain. And the overhead killed us," noted one of Clark's partners. "We were never able to accrue a cash reserve to see us through the slow times." Clark, deemed "a terrific chef" by former *New York Times* critic Ruth Reichl, was unable to save his restaurant venture from failure. He was a chef trained in the French tradition who achieved celebrity status, but he could not turn Metro into a successful new restaurant in the competitive New York market. After his entrepreneurial efforts failed at Metro, he returned to his former role as chef and worked at several restaurants, including the nation's most profitable independent restaurant, Tavern on the Green. Clark died young, and a cookbook in his honor, *Cooking with Patrick Clark,* was published by Charlie Trotter.[48]

the business skills they need to make a venture successful. In addition, entrepreneurs often lack the ability to manage finances effectively. One of the reasons why failure rates are high in the restaurant sector is the ease of entry into the industry. The low barriers make it possible for inefficient operators lacking skill, experience, and capital to enter the industry.[49] A poor management strategy and inappropriate vision are also common problems in failed ventures. These management errors in restaurants can often be seen in the choice of a poor location, poor food or service quality, and mispriced menu items. (See the "Hospitality Focus" boxed section above.)

FAILURE RATES

According to Dun and Bradstreet's *Business Failure Record*, the retail sector, which includes the restaurant industry, and the service sector, which captures the lodging industry, experienced the highest business failure rate. In addition, within the retail sector, which includes food stores and general merchandise stores along with other types of businesses, eating and drinking places have more business failures than any other industry.[50] Although no exact figures are available on restaurant failure rates, experts, executives, and the investment community estimate that they are as high as 90 percent in the United States and West European cities.[51] Failure rates are not tracked by the National Restaurant Association, and statistics appear to vary by the source. Of particular concern to many entrepreneurs in recent years are the highly variable reports on the failure rate of franchise operations. The U.S. Federal Trade Commission's consumer protection director notes, "The most widespread myth is that franchises are a safe investment because they have a much lower failure rate than independent business. In fact, there may be much less of a difference than is commonly thought."[52]

INSUFFICIENT CAPITAL

Many new ventures fail because of a lack of capitalization. New businesses often need a lot of capital at the beginning if they are going to succeed. Without sufficient capital, the venture may fail even if the idea was good and the management skills were present. Many entrepreneurs underestimate how much money is needed to get the business up and running and sustain it while getting a foothold in the market. For example, a business may need to be a particular size to generate enough efficiency to make a profit. Or a venture may fail because not enough people know about a product or service as a result of insufficient advertising. A firm that does not initially have enough financial backing may also assume too much debt too early. Interest payments can divert funds away from more important uses, and the risk of insolvency from not being able to make timely payments is a constant threat. When entrepreneurs feel high levels of financial risk, their behavior may change. They may be less willing to take other risks that are necessary for the venture to continue to progress.

MARKET CONDITIONS

Another common problem is that the service-delivery system is inefficient or ineffective, thus making the venture uncompetitive. Even if a venture has excellent management, sufficient capitalization, and a good service-delivery system, it can still fail if market conditions are not favorable. This is another timing issue. An entrepreneur may launch a new hotel or restaurant right before a downturn in the domestic economy, as Metro was, or in a foreign economy on which the new venture is dependent. Tourism is extremely vulnerable to localized recessions and seasonal demand. For example, some expatriate-owned bars and cafés may even depend on particular nationalities within the already niche tourism market for their success.[53] In these instances, sudden and unpredictable changes in consumer demand can be fatal. The language barrier and ignorance of local customs and regulations can also be sources of failure for expatriates running small businesses.

From an owners' perspective, a variety of factors appear critical to successful hospitality ventures in mass tourist destinations, including:[54]

- Access to sufficient capital
- Sound planning
- Effective financial management
- Management experience
- Industry experience
- Business training
- Use of external advisors
- Overseas experience

Table 9.4 contains a summary of common problems leading to failure of entrepreneurial-ventures. There are many other reasons why a venture can fail, but these are some of the most common. So far, this discussion has focused primarily on entrepreneurial start-ups, but existing organizations also need entrepreneurship. The next section deals with entrepreneurship and innovation in established firms.

TABLE 9.4 **Most Common Sources of Entrepreneurial Failure**

PROBLEM	DESCRIPTION
Management skills	This is perhaps the most common problem. It can be manifest in poor planning, a poor management strategy or ineffective organization, or inadequate financial management. Or an entrepreneur may lack "people skills." Inflated owner egos, poor human resource management, and control issues can stifle a venture.
Lack of adequate capitalization	Many entrepreneurial ventures begin "on a shoestring." They lack the financial backing necessary to be large enough to be efficient or effective in reaching the desired customer. Some organizations may also acquire too much debt too early, which can stifle a new venture.
Service delivery problems	Poor service delivery design can hinder success. Or the venture may depend too much on a single customer group. Timing is also an issue. A hotel, restaurant, airline, or casino may be too early or too late into the market to be successful.
External market conditions	An otherwise outstanding venture may still fail if economic conditions turn sour in a domestic or international economy upon which the new venture depends.

Sources: D. E. Terpstra and P. D. Olson, "Entrepreneurial Startup and Growth: A Classification of Problems," *Entrepreneurship Theory and Practice* (Spring 1993): 19; A. V. Bruno, J. K. Leidecker, and J. W. Harder, "Why Firms Fail," *Business Horizons* (March–April 1987): 50–58.

INNOVATION AND CORPORATE ENTREPRENEURSHIP

Most hotel companies are in the business of "selling sleep" to their customers. I teach our staff that we're in the business of "creating dreams."

—*Chip Conley, CEO Joie de Vivre Hotels*

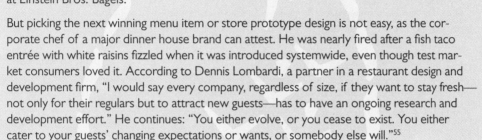

CREATING SUCCESSFUL INNOVATIONS: NOT ALWAYS EASY   HOSPITALITY FOCUS

Chick-fil-A officials reported that it took six years and nearly $500,000 to perfect one menu idea, a chargrilled barbecue chicken sandwich, before rolling the product out systemwide. In contrast, taste panels are created quickly at Einstein Bros. Bagels, as items are tried at three to five stores, and new items reach the marketplace within six months of development. "If you have a great idea and it takes two years to develop and test it, it may not be so interesting anymore," notes the vice president of product research and development at Einstein Bros. Bagels.

But picking the next winning menu item or store prototype design is not easy, as the corporate chef of a major dinner house brand can attest. He was nearly fired after a fish taco entrée with white raisins fizzled when it was introduced systemwide, even though test market consumers loved it. According to Dennis Lombardi, a partner in a restaurant design and development firm, "I would say every company, regardless of size, if they want to stay fresh—not only for their regulars but to attract new guests—has to have an ongoing research and development effort." He continues: "You either evolve, or you cease to exist. You either cater to your guests' changing expectations or wants, or somebody else will."[55]

Entrepreneurial success comes from more effectively accumulating, combining, and directing resources to satisfy a need than other firms can. However, the advantage is not likely to last for long because of competitor imitation.[56] Consequently, continued growth requires continual innovation and entrepreneurship. Some argue that small companies tend to be better at innovation than are large companies. One reason for the difference is that smaller companies are more flexible. They are not as subject to the constraints of a rigid bureaucracy that can stifle creative activity. They also tend to foster more of an entrepreneurial spirit.[57] As Seth Godin notes, "Why didn't Maxwell House create Starbucks?"[58] Others note that large firms have the complementary resources necessary to commercialize an innovation. If the firm has some degree of monopoly power, it can deploy the economies of scale and leverage its better access to capital to invest more heavily in innovations.[59] The Ford Mustang, 3M's Post-It notes, and Apple's iPhone are all examples of commercially successful innovations created within large corporate settings. (See the "Hospitality Focus" boxed section above.)

Corporate entrepreneurship, sometimes called *intrapreneurship*, involves the creation of new products, processes, and services within existing corporations that enable them to grow.[60] The offering of new menu items in restaurants has been accelerating at a dramatic rate (up 31.6 percent since the mid-1990s), although competition and the ease of imitation make these product innovations short-lived.[61] Intrapreneurship is more common in organizations that foster innovation. Consequently, this section begins with a discussion of factors that encourage corporate innovation. Because so much entrepreneurial activity has been directed recently toward communications technology, this section closes with a discussion of the Internet and e-commerce.

Fostering Innovation in Established Firms

Innovation cannot be separated from a firm's strategy or its competitive environment, which means that what we consider to be innovative is defined by the strategic choices a firm makes and the setting in which the firm operates. Innovation is among the top three strategic priorities for senior managers, according to a Boston Consulting Group (BCG) survey of senior executives in leading companies.[62] For 23 percent of the senior managers studied, innovation was their most important priority.[63] Some argue that innovation is the most important component of a firm's strategy, because it provides direction for the evolution of a firm.[64] This view is supported by research that shows innovative firms to be higher performers.[65] Comparisons of total shareholder returns of the most innovative companies compared to their industry peers over a five-year period revealed that innovators outperformed peers by nearly 400 basis points per year.[66]

The invention of a new service, product, process, or idea is often called an *innovation*. For many, invention and innovation are synonymous. However, innovation also includes existing ideas that are reapplied or deployed in different settings for different customer groups. Innovations may be a recombination of old ideas or a unique approach that is perceived as new by the individuals involved.[67] The development of electronic newspapers from around the world delivered to hotel guests on demand is an example of a recombination of the old idea of providing a copy of a local paper to each guest room. Innovation combines invention with commercialization, making it easy to see why innovation and entrepreneurship are so closely linked. Developing a new product or process is not enough; the innovative firm must know how to convert an idea into a service or product that customers want. (See the "Hospitality Focus" boxed section on page 383.)

TYPES OF INNOVATION

Firms innovate in several ways, including business models, products, services, processes, and marketing channels, with either the goal of maintaining or capturing markets or the desire to reduce costs or prices through greater efficiencies. Well-established brands like White Castle or In-N-Out Burger may on the surface look as if they are not innovating, but these brands and others are experimenting with new equipment, prototype and design changes, product sources, and processes.

Innovation can be characterized into different types depending on the nature of the change in knowledge. Innovations are often characterized as *radical innovations* when the knowledge required is different from what exists currently versus *incremental innovations* when the existing knowledge is built on to enable a new product, service, process, or marketing channel. The Heavenly Bed mentioned in Chapter 1 was an incremental product innovation. In contrast, expanding worldwide communication via the Internet is more likely to yield radical innovations for the hospitality industry and the establishment of new business enterprises.

Another distinction developed in the innovation literature categorizes innovations as product versus process innovations. *Product innovations* address final goods or services whereas *process innovations* address how an organization does its business. Westin's development of online retailing to sell the Heavenly Bed was a process innovation for getting beds to customers, but also a new product innovation in the form of selling beds and a channel innovation in retailing hotel items. Finally, the Heavenly Bed has spawned new businesses that help hotels run their

ONITY'S ADVANCE LOCKING SYSTEM: SUCCESS THROUGH EXTENSIVE R&D AND USER FEEDBACK

HOSPITALITY FOCUS

The ADVANCE locking system designed and manufactured for the hospitality industry by Onity was the winner of the prized Platinum ADEX (Award for Design Excellence) award for design sponsored by *Design Journal* magazine. The company was recognized for the lock's revolutionary modular design and unique ergonomic features by a panel of independent experts representing a cross-section of the design industry, including interior and graphic designers, architects, and product and industrial engineers. The new electronic lock was developed with extensive and thorough R&D that included detailed scientific data, as well as feedback from a broad spectrum of hoteliers, guests, and design professionals. The lock offers a range of aesthetic design and operational features.

Onity (formerly TESA Entry Systems) is the world's leading provider of electronic locks, in-room safes, and energy-management solutions, setting the standard for locking doors electronically with installations of more than 3.7 million electronic locks throughout the world. The company was founded in 1941 as a lock manufacturer and is now part of UTC Fire and Security, a business unit of United Technologies Corp. (UTC)— a multibillion-dollar global corporation with a history of technological pioneering. The UTC corporate parent brings to Onity world-class quality processes and R&D resources. Onity's motto is "innovative thinking."[68]

retail arms. In total, the simple introduction of a comfortable, all-white bed in a hotel chain has illustrated how just one innovation can incorporate incremental, product, process, marketing, and supply chain innovations in order to move from idea to commercialization.[69]

BECOMING AN INNOVATIVE ENTERPRISE

Companies are increasing their spending on innovation, yet remain unsatisfied with the return on their investments.[70] Senior executives cite a risk-averse corporate culture, an overly lengthy development period, a lack of coordination within the company, and difficulty choosing the right ideas to commercialize as the most common obstacles to generating a return from their investments in innovation.[71] In addition, researchers have been able to identify several factors that seem to encourage innovation. Some of the major factors that encourage or prevent innovation in established firms are listed in Table 9.5.

A Clear Vision and a Strong Culture

Large corporations that are successful innovators tend to have a clear-cut, well-supported vision that includes an emphasis on innovation.[72] Their cultures support this vision by encouraging people to discuss new ideas and take risks. The organization should not only tolerate failures, but also encourage employees and managers to learn from them.[73] The cultures of service firms like Disney, Southwest Airlines, Starbucks, and Ben and Jerry's illustrate the

TABLE 9.5 Factors Encouraging or Discouraging Innovation in Established Forms

FACTORS ENCOURAGING INNOVATION	FACTORS DISCOURAGING INNOVATION
• Vision and culture that support innovation, personal growth, and risk taking • Top management support and organizational champions • Teamwork and collaboration; a flat management hierarchy • Decentralized approval process • Valuing the ideas of every employee • Excellent communications • Innovation grants and time off to pursue projects • Large rewards for successful entrepreneurs • Focus on learning	• Rigid bureaucracy and conservatism in decision making • Absence of management support or champions • Authoritarian leadership and traditional hierarchy • Difficult approval process • Attention given to the ideas of only certain people (researchers or managers) • Closed-door offices • Inadequate resources devoted to entrepreneurial activities • Harsh penalties for failure • Exclusive emphasis on measurable outcomes

importance of having line-level workers engaged in creating the experience. Innovative cultures also promote personal growth in an effort to attract and retain the best people. Joie de Vivre uses a monthlong sabbatical program for its salaried employees to reflect and nourish themselves, often at one of the company's Balinese resorts. The CEO, Chip Coley, expresses the value in promoting growth this way: "Our base line of business is hospitality, so why not give deserving employees an opportunity to experience the legendary graciousness of the island of Bali?"[74]

The best people also seek ownership, and innovative companies often provide it to them through stock incentives and stock options.[75] This is one way to align the interests of the organization with the interests of talented individuals. Finally, a culture that supports innovation encourages employees and managers to challenge old ideas by instilling a commitment to continuous learning and strategic change. "Past wisdom must not be a constraint but something to be challenged. Yesterday's success formula is often today's obsolete dogma. My challenge is to have the organization continually questioning the past so we can renew ourselves every day," noted Yoshio Maruta, the former chairman of the board of directors of Kao Group, a Japanese diversified consumer products and chemical corporation.[76]

Innovation in services is often characterized as more fluid and evolutionary than product-based innovation, which tends to have more distinct development stages. In hospitality firms, innovation goes hand in hand with implementation because design of a new idea and delivery often occur at the same time. Another key distinction between innovations in services versus manufacturing is that innovation in services is distributed throughout the organization, highlighting the importance of building cultural norms and social controls that support innovation at all levels of the organization.

The norms and values that define the culture are important, because behavior is itself the product in services; that is, what employees do and say in the encounter is far more important for successful innovation.[77] As J. W. Marriott Jr. describes it: "Success is never final." He continually stresses three things: (1) the constant need to improve, to always try to get better; (2) the sharing of best practices across brands (i.e., practices that are invented in one part of the company should be shared with everyone in the company); and (3) always looking for new ideas because customer needs change and competitors improve.[78]

Support at the Top

Rigid bureaucracies can stifle innovation because organizational structures and processes are building blocks for a service culture. Organizations characterized by rules, policies, and procedures that make it difficult for an individual to vary from normal activities can hamper the evolutionary elements of innovation. People who feel as though they cannot or should not vary from established rules are unlikely to be sources of creativity and innovative thought.

Top-management support of innovation is essential, including efforts to develop and train employees with regard to innovation and corporate entrepreneurship.[79] Choice Hotels conducts an annual organization-wide talent review, which includes a mapping of upcoming business initiatives against any possible competency shortfalls by senior executive staff. They use this readiness assessment to determine current leadership capability to pursue new business initiatives.[80] Managers play a vital role in ensuring that employee values fit those of the organization.[81] Because they shape the vision and purpose of the organization, top managers must also serve a disruptive role, making sure that managers and employees don't get too comfortable with the way things are.[82]

Richard Branson, CEO of the Virgin Group (including Virgin Airlines), is an excellent example of a CEO who supports innovation. The overall philosophy of the group is to find areas in which Virgin can provide a better service or product to people than they are currently getting. This philosophy has led the group into a wide variety of hospitality, entertainment, and service businesses.

Philippe Bourguignon, who was hired to transform Club Med, created an innovation-friendly culture, but resigned five years later after disappointing financial results. Nevertheless, he is widely credited with having implemented a turnaround at the company. (See the "Hospitality Focus" boxed section on page 386.)

In addition to top managers, *organizational champions* are important.[83] A champion is someone who is very committed to a project and is willing to expend energy to make sure it succeeds. Two champions are needed. The first is a managerial champion, a person with enough authority in the company to gather the resources and push the project through the administrative bureaucracy. The second is a technical champion. This is an expert with the knowledge needed to guide the technical aspects of the project from beginning to end.

As top managers support innovation, they also have to be careful not to be too dictatorial in their decision making. Authoritarian management can stifle innovation. This type of management is being replaced by networking, teams, and a people-friendly style of management.[84] At Chowking Food Corporation, an Asian fast-food restaurant, new product development involves almost all key departments, not just the head cooks and the research-and-development department. "We are one big team with the president himself heading the product board. All aspects of operations are involved," notes the marketing manager.[85]

HOSPITALITY FOCUS

PHILIP BOURGUIGNON IMPLEMENTS A TURNAROUND AT CLUB MED

Club Med is the most widely recognized holiday company in the world. However, the company became "arrogant with success. It started losing sight of reality," according to Philippe Bourguignon. "The company had never made big profits. But when it started making losses, it decided to raise prices. But when you raise prices you lose clients, so you cut costs. The quality and level of service fails, so more clients are lost. So you raise prices even more. The guests are dissatisfied, the staff is dissatisfied, so you lose more clients and you lose market share."

In an effort to update the company, Bourguignon introduced many new activities to the clubs, including The Flying Trapeze, BMX bikes and climbing walls, and in-line skating to appeal to a new generation. In addition, the company created an Internet department and refocused the Club Med brand, revamped operations, and altered the management culture. Club Med also used acquisitions to expand its market base, including an acquisition of the French tour operator Jet Tours.[86]

Teamwork, Systems, and Incentives

To maintain an adaptive learning atmosphere at all organizational levels, many firms have created self-managed work teams and cross-functional product-development teams, so that multiple perspectives will be brought to problem solving. Teams cut across traditional functional boundaries; a single team might include representatives from engineering, research and development, finance, marketing, information systems, and human resources. These teams are kept small so that they are highly flexible, adaptable, and easy to manage. [87] The management hierarchy in these types of organizations tends to be flat, meaning that there are not a lot of management levels between the customer and the top manager.[88]

The level at which projects are approved is also a key factor in determining support for innovative activities. Some large corporations require that an idea receive approval from five or more managers before any resources are committed to pursuing it. Innovative organizations create project teams that do not report through the traditional lines of authority. Consequently, their work does not have to pass through multiple levels for approval.[89] (See the "Hospitality Focus" boxed secction on page 387.)

Innovation is also more likely to emerge from a company with a culture that values the ideas of every person. Gary Hamel, an expert on innovation, talks about his work with companies in which administrative assistants come up with ideas for multimillion-dollar businesses. He says, "Many companies have succeeded in making everyone responsible for quality. We're going to have to do the same for innovation."[90] Unfortunately, many large companies don't give equal attention to everyone's ideas. They expect researchers or managers to come up with all of the innovations. Along with an egalitarian culture, excellent communications are found in innovative organizations. They encourage communication by having informal meetings whenever possible, forming teams across functions, and planning the physical layout of the facility so as to encourage frequent interaction (they don't let people hide in their offices).[91]

THE GUIDANCE TEAM AT RITZ-CARLTON

HOSPITALITY FOCUS

The Ritz-Carlton Tysons Corner, in affluent northern Virginia, established an innovative program to shift decision making from management to the hourly staff and to eliminate by attrition certain management positions. The initiative began with the executive committee of the hotel changing its name to the "guidance team," to help set the tone for what it hoped to achieve. A mission statement was created and signed by all employees, and special attention was given to keeping everyone, especially the hourly workers, fully informed and consulted every step of the way. After considerable discussion, the hotel staff identified several management tasks for possible transfer to the hourly staff, including forecasting budgets and work scheduling. The results of this initiative were reductions in management costs, lowered employee turnover, increased guest satisfaction, and a more motivated and committed staff.[92]

For corporate entrepreneurship to take place, organizations also have to commit resources, such as people, money, information, equipment, and a physical location.[93] Some companies, such as 3M, even provide seed money in the form of innovation grants. Giving people time to pursue their ideas is also critical. At 3M, a corporate policy that supports internal venturing allows scientists to spend up to 15 percent of their time on personal research projects. The company's Post-It notepads were invented through this program.[94]

Effective rewards systems are also important. Corporate entrepreneurship allows creative people to realize the rewards from their innovative talents without having to leave the company.[95] Innovation should be rewarded through raises, promotions, awards, perquisites, and public and private recognition. While the upside rewards for innovation should be high, the downside penalties for failed innovation efforts should be minimal.[96]

Corporate entrepreneurship can be viewed as an organizational-learning process directed at developing the skills and knowledge necessary to compete in new domains.[97] Organizational learning is at the center of innovative activities. Chapter 4 discussed activities associated with knowledge (1) creation, (2) retention, (3) sharing, and (4) utilization. As was demonstrated in that chapter, outstanding execution of these activities can be a source of competitive advantage leading to superior performance.[98]

Many of the characteristics of innovative companies are found in organizations such as Apple, Google, General Electric, and Walt Disney Company. Table 9.6 lists the most innovative companies by industry, defined as those that are able to innovate consistently over long periods. Topping the list of innovative companies is Apple, for its unmatched understanding of customers (knowing what consumers want before they know themselves), its ability to marry design and technology (with user-friendly devices such as the iPhone, iTouch, and iPod), and its cutting-edge marketing (turning commodities into objects of desire).[99] Google was also recognized for its breadth of new offerings, speed to market, and innovation-supporting culture. The next section discusses the Internet and e-commerce, which have profoundly influenced the hospitality industry and radically shaped innovation within the industry.

TABLE 9.6 The Most Innovative Companies by Industry

Travel, Tourism, and Hospitality	1. Marriott International 2. Virgin Group 3. Hilton Hotels Group 4. Starwood Hotels & Resorts Worldwide 5. Southwest Airline
Entertainment and Media	1. The Walt Disney Company 2. Apple 3. Sony Corporation 4. Google 5. News Corporation
Financial Services	1. Citigroup 2. The Goldman Sachs Group 3. Bank of America Corporation 4. ING Group 5. Fidelity Investments
Consumer Products	1. Procter & Gamble 2. Apple 3. Sony Corporation 4. Johnson & Johnson 5. 3M
Retail	1. Wal-Mart 2. Target Corporation 3. amazon.com 4. Best Buy Company 5. Nordstrom
Technology and Telecommunications	1. Apple 2. Google 3. Microsoft Corporation 4. Cisco Systems 5. AT&T
Top Innovators across All Industries	1. Apple 2. Google 3. Toyota Motor 4. General Electric Company 5. Microsoft Corporation

Source: BCG 2007 Senior Executive Innovation Survey.

The Internet and E-Commerce

We live in an age of expanding worldwide communication. The Internet is a major part of the information revolution. According to Peter Drucker:

> *The explosive emergence of the Internet as a major, perhaps eventually the major, worldwide distribution channel for goods, services, and, surprisingly, for managerial and professional jobs is profoundly changing economies, markets, and industry structures; products and services and their flow; consumer segmentation, consumer values, and consumer behavior; jobs and labor markets.* [100]

Firms use the Internet for e-tailing, exchanging data with other businesses, business-to-business buying and selling, and e-mail communications with a variety of stakeholders. The Web is far more than a productivity tool or a distribution channel. Its most profound impact on business comes from the explosion of new products, new services, new content, new companies, and new organizational forms that have emerged in recent years. [101] (See the "Hospitality Focus" boxed section on page 390.)

In the 1990s, thousands of entrepreneurs started businesses that came to be known as *dotcoms*. These companies would register a domain name on the World Wide Web, typically with a ".com" extension, and begin providing some sort of service over the Internet. Companies spent millions of advertising dollars through many forms of media trying to attract users to their web sites. Computer.com, a help site for novice computer users, was one such firm that actually burned through 60 percent of its funding in 90 Super Bowl seconds. [102]

Early in the Internet craze, the race was not to achieve profits or even revenues, but to attract "eyeballs." The notion was that if a web site could become a favorite for users throughout the world, eventually the business owners would figure out a way to make money from it. The founders of these types of web sites had an inadequate business model for turning eyeballs into profits and cash flow. [103] Eventually, their initial investment capital ran out, and they were left with inadequate cash flow to continue operations. For example, Pets.com, which raised significant venture capital and experienced initial success, failed because the business concept was not sound. [104] Some of these failing dot-coms were bought out. Others like Pets.com went out of business. A few of the most successful dot-coms, like Amazon.com, Google, and Yahoo! have risen to notable success. (See the first "Hospitality Focus" boxed section on page 391.)

A variety of approaches to the Internet have been used. Some dot-coms provide retailing. Many of these dot-com retailers carry no inventory themselves. Rather, they connect buyers and sellers. Other dot-coms provide a service to consumers and sell advertising on their web sites. For instance, Lycos.com has extensive road-map information, and Google.com is a Web search engine. Monster.com is a job-placement service. Some companies use a combined approach. Amazon.com is a retailer that provides extensive services to its users and sells advertising. So how do you make money on the Internet? According to Gary Hamel:

> *Electricity created dramatic productivity gains—and shrank margins. The Net is doing the same. The way for companies to avoid the crunch: Be unique. The collective delusion of the dot-com mob was that clicks could readily translate into customers and revenues. The collective delusion of the Fortune 500 is that productivity gains translate into plumper profits. Any company that plans to make money from "e" must have a Web strategy that creates unique value for customers, confers unique advantages in delivering that value, and is tough to copy.* [105]

HOSPITALITY FOCUS

NEW PRODUCTS AND SERVICES AT GOOGLE INC.

Google Inc. helps people find what they are looking for on the Web, with its primary competitors being Microsoft and Yahoo. The company was founded by two Stanford University students, Larry Page and Sergey Brin, with seed money from angel investors in the late 1990s. Google's initial revenue model focused on revenues from Internet search services and online advertising. The company maintains an index of web sites and other content, and makes this information available free of charge to anyone with an Internet connection. Its automated search technology enables people to obtain nearly instant access to relevant information from its online index. The simple design and usability of the Google search engine has attracted a loyal following among the growing number of Internet users.

In 2000, the company began selling advertisements using a pricing system pioneered by Goto.com, before it was acquired by Yahoo! Delivering online advertising is the primary focus of revenue generation for the company. Businesses use its AdWords program, an auction-based advertising program that lets advertisers deliver relevant ads targeted to search queries or Web content across Google sites and through the Google Network. This product helps clients promote their products and services with targeted advertising. In addition, the third-party web sites that comprise the Google Network use the Company's AdSense program to deliver relevant advertisements that generate revenue. These search appliances are a complete software and hardware solution that companies can implement to extend Google's search performance to their internal or external information.

In 2004, the company had an initial public offering that raised $1.67 billion, making it worth $23 billion. More recently, the company has introduced new products and expanded its initial search and advertising businesses to include web-based e-mail, online mapping, office productivity, and video sharing. Using an acquisitions strategy, Google continues to think about ways in which technology can improve upon existing ways of doing business. In 2006, the company acquired the online video company, YouTube, and JotSpot, a company that has developed a series of online productivity software programs that offer many of the functions of Microsoft Office programs. In March 2007, Google acquired Adscape Media Inc., a company that makes technology to deliver advertising over the Internet for placement within videogames. As Google Inc. continues to expand its business model, exploring new ideas to prototype and new services for its advertisers, the company remains rooted in providing useful and relevant information to millions of users.[106]

Electronic Tourism Markets

Travel is one of the most successful commercial sectors on the Internet, bringing fundamental changes to both airlines and travel agencies. Airlines in particular were aggressive leaders in using the Internet to bypass their product and service intermediaries. With the advent of electronic ticketing in 1995, airlines reduced distribution costs by combining their established national networks and brand awareness with direct Internet sales. Traditional travel agencies

PETS.COM: A FAILED DOT COM

Pets.com, an online business that sold pet accessories and supplies, was launched in 1998, and became the last dot-com to go public before the bubble burst. Purchased by the venture capital firm of Hummer Wionblad in 1999, the company went public in 2000. Like many dot-com businesses, the company aired its first national commercial as a Super Bowl ad at a cost of $1.2 million. It also received awards for its advertising efforts and created a popular mascot, the Pets.com sock puppet that gained cult status in the early 2000s. However, potential consumers discovered that buying pet food at the grocery store was just as easy as buying it on the Internet. Nine months after its IPO, the business was unable to find investors to help it out of its cash bind and liquidated. Pets.com stock had fallen from more than $11 per share in February 2000 to $0.19 on the day of its liquidation announcement.[107]

AIRLINES MOVE TO ONLINE BOOKING

To encourage people to book online, airlines offer numerous incentives. They attract customers to their sites with exclusive Web fares, undercutting the prices offered via Central Reservation Systems (CRSs) and travel agents. They offer mileage bonuses to registered frequent fliers and signing bonuses for travelers joining their loyalty programs. They send their frequent fliers weekly e-mails, offering special fares not available through travel agencies. They broaden the range of online services and information, and make their sites more user-friendly by reducing the number of keystrokes necessary to search and book.[108]

began losing sales not only to airline sites but also to online agencies. Direct online ticketing now accounts for 40 percent of the tickets sold at most airlines.[109] Travelers have discovered that they can obtain direct access to information, lower rates, and other benefits and incentives offered by the airlines. (See the second "Hospitality Focus" boxed section above.)

While airlines were early to take advantage of the Internet, lodging firms have followed their lead, extensively using the Internet as a marketing and sales tool. Electronic tourism products and services have evolved with the advances in Internet technologies, beginning with simple systems that only provided travel information like sightseeing or destination guides or the promotion of hotel products. From these simple systems, the industry evolved by integrating internal databases with the Web, producing more efficient and convenient information management systems. Many hotels and airlines have adopted these integrated Web/database business models, which link the Web to legacy systems such as customer relationship management (CRM) and back-office enterprise resource planning (ERP) systems.[110]

HOSPITALITY FOCUS

A PORTFOLIO OF BRANDS AT EXPEDIA, INC.

Expedia, Inc. is the world's leading online travel company, providing business and leisure travelers with the tools and information they need to research, plan, book, and experience travel. Founded within Microsoft in the mid-1990s, Expedia went public in 1999. Four years later, the firm was purchased by IAC/InterActiveCorp. Two years later, IAC spun off Expedia into a separate publicly traded firm. With more than $17 billion in annual gross travel bookings, Expedia also provides wholesale travel to offline retail travel agents. Expedia's portfolio of brands includes Expedia.com, hotels.com, discount travel web site Hotwire, Expedia Corporate Travel, TripAdvisor—a travel search engine, and Classic Vacations for the luxury travel segment.[111]

The one-stop travel services that permit a customer to complete all travel-related activities by visiting one site, such as Travelocity, require yet another level of cooperative relationships among various players, necessitating the development of strategic alliances. The development of electronic tourism, in which levels of integration and cooperation are both very high, continues to be a challenge, because customer databases and revenue management systems (e.g., hotels, rental cars, and airlines) are not yet fully integrated with the Web reservation systems of cyber travel agencies.

Travel web sites first targeted the airline industry and introduced consumers to heavily discounted e-fares. The hotel industry was next, and year-over-year growth in online lodging revenue has already begun outpacing growth in the overall online travel sector. What started simply as an online alternative to bricks-and-mortar travel agencies, travel web sites have evolved into online merchants. Online travel companies have often been acquired by larger firms that offer many travel products and brands, such as Expedia Inc., Orbitz Worldwide (60 percent owned by Travelport, which also owns the Galileo reservations service), and Travelocity (a subsidiary of Sabre Holdings). (See the "Hospitality Focus" boxed section above.)

Web bookings have put incredible pressure on prices in the lodging industry, because the Internet tends to make pricing transparent. Research at Cornell University has shown that heavy price discounting in hotels did not yield the desired boost in market share or occupancies.[112] Internet intermediaries may be to blame for the reported losses in revenue, as consumers learned that they can get a better price for a hotel room by going to the Internet. To regain control over their product pricing, several hotel companies began to rethink their long-term strategic relationships with third-party Internet distributors. One approach to retaining control over pricing and inventory resulted in alliances among major competitors to create their own web sites, such as the TravelWeb consortium, led by Marriott, Hilton, and Hyatt.[113] TravelWeb was later acquired by Priceline. Another outcome of the proliferation of web sites is that independent hotels are now as easy to book as the chains, creating further competition and challenging the role of tour operators, particularly in resort locations in developing parts of the world.

The Internet has been a key innovation for the travel industry, stimulating remarkable changes in how consumers create and book their travel services. Travel agents were the primary source for packaged (or bundled) travel services before the Internet, while custom packaging is now possible through intermediaries and second-generation web-based technologies (called Web 2.0) that blend communities such as social-networking sites with commercial sites.[114]

Today airlines, hotel chains, car rental, and other travel suppliers offer their products online and through various intermediaries. Intermediaries such as Expedia, travel agencies such as Carlsontravel.com, search engines like Yahoo.com, and even destinations like Lasvegas.com sell packages. Learning to use the Web to help differentiate a hospitality product is essential to leveraging the Internet, and operators are moving from a focus on price to the unique features and bundled services of a product, helping to reduce price transparency.

It is difficult to predict the future of the Internet, but several trends seem apparent. First, the Internet is an increasingly important tool for the exchange of information, goods, and services. Sites like Facebook and MySpace allow consumers to exchange travel information through social networks. Sales via the Internet are increasing at an astronomical rate, with online travel intermediaries expanding their offerings. Businesses are using the Internet as a tool for a wide variety of applications. Second, managers and investors are being much more careful as they design business models around the Internet, making sure that there is some way to use invested resources to generate positive returns. Finally, information technologies are changing at such an amazing rate that the internet is likely to be a source of entrepreneurial ventures for many years to come.

KEY POINTS SUMMARY

- Modern economies rely on entrepreneurship as a source of growth and job creation.

- Entrepreneurship involves the creation of new business. Some ventures are complete start-ups, whereas other ventures are pursued within an existing organization.

- Successful entrepreneurs appear to be opportunists, in that they recognize and take advantage of opportunities. They also have a higher need for achievement, a greater risk-taking propensity, and a stronger belief that they control their own destiny (internalized locus of control).

- Entrepreneurial tasks include recognizing or creating an opportunity, assembling resources to pursue the opportunity, and managing activities that bring a new venture into existence.

- Entrepreneurial activity occurs anytime an entrepreneur is able to link a need to a solution so that a new business emerges. Opportunities to do this tend to be context specific, and they can emerge from anywhere.

- Everything associated with a new venture revolves around a business plan. Creation of the plan forces the entrepreneur to think through the details of the venture and determine whether it is feasible.

- A business plan includes an executive summary; a description of the proposed business venture; an analysis of the environment; a resource analysis; and functional plans such as a marketing plan, operations plan, and a management plan.

- A business plan should include an honest assessment of potential risks and financial projections, which are especially important to potential investors. An implementation schedule or timeline for major events is also included.

- Investors are also interested in what might be called an end-game strategy—a plan for concluding the venture, transferring control to others, allowing potential investors to exit the venture with a high return on their investments, contingency plans in the event the venture does not succeed, and an executive-succession plan in case the primary entrepreneur leaves the venture.

- A simple economic model such as that provided in Figure 9.1 helps an entrepreneur determine the attractiveness of the business. Using key variables such as contribution margins, volumes, operating leverage, and product/service mix, a venture can be evaluated for its profit making potential.

- Obtaining start-up capital is probably the most difficult problem facing a potential entrepreneur. Some of the most common sources of start-up capital are commercial banks, personal contacts, venture capitalists, corporate partnerships, investment groups, and business angels.

- After a venture has established a record of performance, entrepreneurs or venture capitalists may pursue an initial public offering (IPO). An IPO entails selling stock to the public and investors.

- Some of the major tasks of entrepreneurs for the first year of a venture include financing and financial management, marketing, service development, resource acquisition, process development, management and staffing, and satisfying legal requirements.

- Entrepreneurs also need to decide whether to form their new ventures as sole proprietorships, partnerships, or corporations.

- Business-format franchising is a popular and viable approach to new venturing in hospitality firms. While affiliation with a large and established franchisor can be relatively low risk, new entrepreneurs need to keep in mind a long-term ownership strategy and realize that going with smaller new franchisors may be more risky than going into business on one's own.

- The most common reason for the failure of entrepreneurial ventures is lack of management skill. This is sometimes demonstrated by a poor management strategy, inappropriate vision, or an inability to manage finances effectively. Many new ventures fail because of a lack of capital.

- Other factors that can lead to failure are associated with the service itself, such as poor timing. Even if a venture has excellent management, sufficient capital, and a good service, it can still fail if market conditions are not favorable.

- Innovation is a top strategic priority for senior managers. It is often defined as the invention of a new service, product, process, or idea.

- Innovation also includes existing ideas that are reapplied or deployed in different settings for different customer groups. A recombination of old ideas or a unique approach that is perceived as new by the individuals involved are also ways to think about innovation.

- Firms innovate in a number of ways, including business models, services, processes and marketing channels.

- Corporate entrepreneurship, or intrapreneurship, involves the creation of new products, processes, and services within existing corporations. This sort of entrepreneurship is more common in organizations that foster innovation.

- Some of the factors associated with intrapreneurial firms include a well-supported vision that includes an emphasis on innovation and a culture that supports this vision, top-management support, organizational champions, teamwork and collaboration, a flat management hierarchy, a decentralized approval process, respect for everyone's ideas, excellent communications, adequate resources devoted to entrepreneurial activities, a reward system that encourages innovation, and a focus on learning.

- Firms are using the Internet for e-tailing, exchanging data with other businesses, business-to-business buying and selling, and e-mail communications with a variety of stakeholders.

- The hospitality industry extensively uses the Internet, as online travel intermediaries along with others continue to innovate in new travel services and offerings.

- As social networks and new technologies evolve, even more innovations in travel distribution are expected. While it is difficult to predict the future of the Internet, it is clearly an increasingly important tool for the exchange of information, goods, and services.

REVIEW QUESTIONS

1. What is entrepreneurship, and why is it important?
2. What are some of the characteristics of entrepreneurs? Are you that sort of person? Do you know anyone who would be a good entrepreneur?
3. Describe the entrepreneurial tasks.
4. What does a business plan contain? Is a business plan the same as a strategic plan for an existing business? If not, how are they different?
5. What is the difference between business-format franchising and traditional franchising?
6. Is franchising more or less risky than starting one's own business?

7. What are the primary reasons why new business ventures fail?

8. What are some of the typical activities of an entrepreneur during the first year of a venture?

9. Describe the sources to which an entrepreneur can turn for venture capital.

10. How can established firms foster innovation?

11. What are the different business models available to tourism organizations for leveraging the Web? How well do you think the industry is doing at balancing the integration and coordination of databases and Web interface?

CRITICAL THINKING AND APPLICATION QUESTIONS

1. Find a local entrepreneur and interview him or her. Discuss with your classmates what you learned from your interview. Following are some suggested questions:

   • Could you tell me about your early career experiences as an entrepreneur?

   • What were some of your greatest professional successes and failures? What did you learn about being a successful entrepreneur?

   • What advice would you offer students who want to become entrepreneurs? Perhaps you can offer advice about starting up a firm, obtaining capital, moving forward with growth. What should they think about before becoming an entrepreneur? Should they wait? How long? When is the right time to start you own hospitality business?

   • Are entrepreneurs made or born? Do you believe entrepreneurial skills can be taught? If there are key skills that students can develop now, how might they be nurtured in college? business practices with philanthropy?

   • Looking to the future, what is next on your business agenda?

2. You have decided to start your own small hospitality business. Begin by briefly describing the venture and why it is likely to be successful. Before you begin the process of devising a business plan, use the simple economic model shown in Figure 9.1 to determine the profitability of your business. Does your proposed business have high margins? high volumes? product/service variety? low operating leverage? How could you enhance the profitability of your new venture?

3. Identify an example of a recent hospitality innovation. What type of innovation is it? What are the characteristics of this innovation? Are innovations in services different from product-based innovations in manufacturing? How? Give examples.

CHAPTER 10

GLOBAL STRATEGIC MANAGEMENT AND THE FUTURE

YOU SHOULD BE ABLE TO DO THE FOLLOWING AFTER READING THIS CHAPTER:

1. Identify the most popular reasons why companies make foreign investments.

2. Explain multidomestic, global, and transnational strategies for global expansion.

3. Describe the most common expansion tactics used when hospitality firms pursue global opportunities.

4. List the most important criteria when picking an option for international growth.

5. List the most important questions to ask about a potential foreign market.

6. Understand why some nations produce stellar companies in a particular industry.

7. Define cultural intelligence.

FEATURE STORY

THE COFFEE WARS

"As long as we can differentiate ourselves from all others, we will continue to be the leader," claims Howard Shultz, chairman of Starbucks. Aggressive domestic competition appears to be making this position increasingly more difficult. McDonald's entered the gourmet coffee market through an agreement with Green Mountain, offering a high-quality and lower-priced product. Starting in 2008, the fast-food giant began installing coffee bars with baristas in more than 14,000 U.S. locations, further blurring the difference between Starbucks and fast-food rivals. In addition, Dunkin' Donuts continues to offer increasingly sophisticated coffee also at lower prices.

In the United States, the Starbucks experience is becoming increasingly commoditized, according to some experts, making it even more essential that Starbucks continue its international expansion. A plan to slow the pace of new store openings in the United States will enable capital to be redeployed to accelerate international expansion.

Beginning in Japan in 1995, Starbucks now operates more than 4,000 stores internationally in 43 countries. With plans to expand the Starbucks Experience to more customers throughout the world, the company deploys a development strategy that adapts to different markets and responds to local needs. "There are a lot of consistencies about us, but every store is different depending on the neighborhood. You can't take something that is right in one culture and expect it to work in another," notes a Starbucks official.

To ensure that each store works for its local market, Starbucks likes to work with co-operators. It relies on joint ventures, licensing agreements, and company-owned operations as its three primary modes of entry. In establishing joint ventures, the company likes to select partners who know the indigenous culture and market. Starbucks Coffee Japan, for example, is a joint venture between Sazaby League and Starbucks Coffee International, its international subsidiary. Since the opening of its first store in the Ginza district of Tokyo, the venture has expanded rapidly throughout the country and reached 686 stores by March 2007. Rivals are luring away customers, however, and Starbucks has shown negative investment cash flows in Japan for the last five years.

In China, the company bought out its primary local partner Beijing Mei Da Coffee, which was owned by private equity firm H&Q Asia Pacific and other shareholders. Beijing Mei Da opened its first store in Beijing in 1999. As the China market becomes easier to navigate, more companies are moving to take control of their China joint ventures.

Analysts speculate that, "Starbucks at the corporate level probably feels they know better how China works now, and so they can go it on their own." Starbucks continues to focus on emerging nations like India and Russia, with plans to enter India in partnership with Kishore Biyani, founder of the largest publicly traded Indian retailer, and V. P. Sharma, head of the U.S. company's Indonesian franchise. Because foreign direct investment is not yet allowed in the retail sector of India, Starbucks will need to rely on its partners to facilitate entry.[1]

DISCUSSION QUESTIONS:

1. How has rapid expansion in the United States and abroad affected the success of Starbucks?

2. How should Starbucks enter new markets to ensure the Starbucks Experience while adapting to local cultures?

INTRODUCTION

Intense global competition and greater collaboration go hand-in-hand for organizations as they increasingly operate in international markets. As the Starbucks example shows, developing internationally isn't for the faint of heart, but it is for all who are farsighted, notes Jay Witzel, president and CEO of Radisson Hotels and Resorts.[2] When domestic markets begin to show slowed growth, as they have for Starbucks, companies redirect their efforts to international expansion. "New Starbucks Opens in Restroom of Existing Starbucks," a joke headline from the pages of *The Onion*, a satirical online publication, highlights the challenges of growth in saturated markets. "We probably self-cannibalize our stores at a rate of 30 percent per year," notes Howard Schultz, Starbucks founder.[3] Menu expansion may have further blurred the distinction between Starbucks and fast-food providers.

Commoditization of products in domestic markets is one of the catalysts for global expansion. Among the most popular reasons why companies make foreign investments are to (1) search for new markets or better resources, (2) increase efficiency, (3) reduce risk, or (4) counter the competition (see Table 10.1).[4] In a wide variety of industries, corporations are making huge investments in foreign markets because of growth opportunities and the reduction of barriers to entry.

TABLE 10.1 **Primary Reasons Why Firms Make Foreign Investments**

REASON	DESCRIPTION
New markets	As domestic markets become saturated, companies seek to expand their market reach into other countries.
Better resources	Some countries have more-abundant resources than do others. Firms may seek resources such as raw materials, excellent suppliers, trained workers, advanced technologies, well-developed infrastructures, and good financial markets.
Efficiency	Organizations can create economies of scale through increasing production. Also, they can increase efficiency through cutting costs in countries with inexpensive labor. In addition, fixed investments in certain resources can be applied to multiple markets (economies of scope).
Risk reduction	Although global markets are interconnected, their business cycles do not match up perfectly. Consequently, a recession in Europe may not coincide exactly with a recession in Japan or in the United States. By investing in multiple global regions, a company can theoretically reduce volatility in overall corporate earnings.
Competitive countermove	If a major competitor invests in a particular global region, other competitors may feel obliged to do so to protect their own interests. For example, they may fear that one company will develop better resources or achieve more efficiency.

One of the outcomes of increasing internationalization is that countries are economically interconnected at an unprecedented level. In the hospitality industry, the connection between local business demand and the prosperity of foreign economies has always been extremely strong. With the United States, Germany, and the United Kingdom being strong outbound or source markets for travel to many countries, the economics of these countries shape the prosperity of emerging nations and new destinations. Tourism accounts for 6 percent of total world trade and 3 percent of global employment, making it a key international industry.[5]

Given the importance of travel and tourism to globalization, it is not surprising that many hospitality companies were pioneers in global expansion, with international hotel development starting in the late 1940s and early 1950s and McDonald's opening its first overseas restaurants in the Caribbean and South America in the 1960s.[6] InterContinental, Hilton, and Sheraton were early entrants to international development, followed by Holiday

HOSPITALITY FOCUS

THE CHALLENGES OF INTERNATIONALIZATION

There are two primary areas to consider when developing a brand internationally: the size of each market and the type of products. According to Georges Le Mener, former president and CEO of Accor Lodging North America, "With an upscale brand, you can get critical mass without many properties. If it's upscale you want to be in major cities. When developing a budget brand, you need a large number of hotels in a market."

Adding to this analysis, David Martinez of Starwood distinguishes between critical mass in operations and critical mass in brand awareness. He notes that if you are after a boutique market, you can get the job done with a small number of operations.

"We're not going to sprinkle the world with our brands. You need to get a critical mass. We'll look at opportunities wherever they come up, but the danger of doing one to two hotels in a country is that we can't support them," notes Tom Keltner of Hilton Hotels.

Finally, Marriott believes it is easier to take a brand and build under it, than to push up a brand by entering with a product like Courtyard. According to Susan Thronson, a senior executive at Mariott, "We don't want a Courtyard to be the first Marriott hotel in a country."

As these executives' ideas show, there are a variety of factors to consider when devising a global strategy.[7]

Inns (the largest international company in the late 1970s) and Hyatt.[8] North American companies tended to dominate the international hotel scene, but Club Méditerranée and Novotel from France and Trusthouse Forte and Travelodge from the United Kingdom were also large operations in the 1970s. Three restaurant chains have led the way in international expansion: McDonald's, Pizza Hut, and KFC.

Rapid growth and expansion in domestic and international markets dominated the hospitality industry in the 1980s, while consolidation through acquisitions and mergers was a theme in hotels of the 1990s. KFC was the first fast-food company to enter China, back in 1987, and had grown to 200 restaurants a decade later. Now this chain has more than 1,800 restaurants in more than 400 cities in China.[9] In the early years, most international strategies focused on a single product; today large firms are working with a portfolio of brands and sophisticated worldwide consumers, adding levels of complexity to the challenges of internationalization. (See the "Hospitality Focus" boxed section above.)

This chapter begins with a discussion of the global strategies companies can select from to facilitate entry and expansion internationally. Consistent with the underlying themes of this book, the next section describes global stakeholder management and the challenges of managing a diverse workforce. The final section briefly discusses some of the global trends that are likely to be a part of the competitive environment in the future. In this book, you have seen numerous applications of the theory and tools of strategic management to firms based in various countries throughout the world. Nevertheless, significant differences exist among countries and markets, creating strategic and operational challenges for multinationals.

GLOBAL STRATEGIES

Some scholars have argued that global strategic management is "simply the application of strategic management in a larger arena." Others "see the strategic concerns of multinational firms to be intrinsically different from their domestic cousins"; they "point to the historical legacy of international economics and trade theory, to the powerful effects of cultural differences, to the role of exchange rate risk, and to the very different institutional conditions in different countries."[10] Both views are correct. Many aspects of strategic management apply regardless of whether an organization is domestic or international, but internationalization can also lead to increased competition and complex strategic human resource management. Many of the tools you have learned—such as environmental, stakeholder, and resource analysis; creation of strategic direction; and development of control systems—can be directly applied to global firms. However, the complexity of diverse international competitors playing with different goals, strategies, and cost structures can alter the competitive landscape and make it more difficult to compete.

As firms approach international markets, they have several strategic decisions to make. They must formulate an expansion strategy and decide how they plan to enter new markets. We now turn to the various strategies that companies apply as they approach global markets.

Multidomestic, Global, and Transnational Strategies

International expansion is the process of building an expanding operational presence, and the strategies companies use fall into three broad categories: multidomestic, global, and transnational.[11] A *multidomestic strategy* focuses on extensive customization on a country-by-country basis by tailoring the services provided around individual market needs. A high degree of local discretion is given to operators although corporate personnel may provide management skill and operational standards.

Hospitality firms that pursue a multidomestic strategy are responsive to local needs and somewhat independent from the parent company. As organizations expand their reach, they can enjoy benefits such as increased market size, economies of scale, increased opportunities for learning, a larger pool of resources from which to draw, more opportunities to create partnerships, and more advancement opportunities for their managers. This multinational strategy is illustrated by Hyatt International, which relies on local and regional managers' evaluations of local conditions and property-level business plans. Managers throughout the global network

HYATT'S GLOBAL ORGANIZATION

As planning responsibility is shared throughout the global organization, changes in local market conditions can be identified rapidly. When, for example, the complex process of change began to gain momentum in Eastern Europe, details of development opportunities began to emerge instinctively from all parts of Hyatt's global organization. The information came from managers at all levels in the organization who were either witnessing change or gathering market information from talking to business travelers and others with experiential knowledge of what was actually happening.[12]

are encouraged to identify and respond to opportunities, while the corporate office provides coordination and support. (See the "Hospitality Focus" boxed section above.)

Organizations pursuing a *global strategy* standardize what they offer so that it is essentially the same in all markets.[13] A global strategy can result in cost efficiency, global flexibility, and an ability to apply the firm's resources and skills across multiple markets. Researchers explain that a global strategy is appropriate only if:[14]

1. There is a global market segment for a product or service.

2. There are economic efficiencies associated with a global strategy.

3. There are no external constraints, such as government regulations, that will prevent a global strategy from being implemented.

4. There are no absolute internal constraints.

Global strategies are more common in manufacturing industries where products can be produced in a limited number of locations and shipped globally, while sales and marketing operations may exist in many locations. For firms pursuing this strategy, local customization is low, and authority is centralized at the corporate headquarters where most strategic decisions are made.

A *transnational strategy* entails standardized and yet flexible services, seeking both the benefits of global efficiency and local responsiveness. Through cooperation and integration among corporate offices, local operations, and international subsidiaries, a company using this approach seeks to integrate global operations. McDonald's, for instance, has relied on a standardized American concept worldwide, but it has begun to more extensively acknowledge cultural, regional, and national differences, partly because of the criticism of "overarching Americanization" of the world.[15] The difficult task of pursuing this strategy is accomplished through establishing an integrated network that fosters shared vision and resources while allowing individual decisions to be made to adapt to local needs.[16] Four Seasons' strategy can best be described as transnational, as the following excerpts in the "Hospitality Focus" boxed section on page 403 demonstrate.

Organizations that are involved in multiple global markets have advantages available to them in pursuing their strategies. Examples of the many options available for improving competitive position vis-à-vis a global strategy include the following:

THE FOUR SEASONS' TRANSNATIONAL STRATEGY

HOSPITALITY FOCUS

"Four Seasons has done an exceptional job of adapting to local markets. From a design perspective, they are much more clever than other companies. When you sit in the Four Seasons in Bali, you feel that you are in Bali. It does not scream Four Seasons at you," according to David Richey, president of Richey International, a firm Four Seasons and other hotel chains hired to audit service quality.

On the other hand, there are things about the Four Seasons approach that are the same, such as the 270 core worldwide operating standards and the service culture standards noted as follows. The seven Four Seasons service culture standards expected of all staff all over the world at all times are:

- SMILE: Employees will actively greet guests, smile, and speak clearly in a friendly manner.
- EYE: Employees will make eye contact, even in passing, with an acknowledgment.
- RECOGNITION: All staff will create a sense of recognition by using the guest's name, when known, in a natural and discreet manner.
- VOICE: Staff will speak to guests in an attentive, natural, and courteous manner, avoiding pretension and in a clear voice.
- INFORMED: All guest contact staff will be well informed about their hotel, their product, will take ownership of simple requests, and will not refer guests elsewhere.
- CLEAN: Staff will always appear clean, crisp, well-groomed, and well-fitted.
- EVERYONE: Everyone, everywhere, all the time, will show their care for our guests.[17]

- Expanding markets leading to economies of scale. Some companies could not grow large enough to enjoy the lowest possible costs on the basis of domestic demand alone, but expansion into foreign markets can lead to significant increases in demand.

- Transfer of technological know-how through joint ventures (learning from competitors). Joint ventures may provide opportunities to learn new technologies that can lead to significant cost reductions.

- Superior quality through joint ventures. Just as U.S. companies can learn cost-saving technologies through joint ventures, they can also learn how to better differentiate their products through higher quality or some other unique feature.

- Licensing of brands or technologies from abroad.

- Forcing an open, learning mind-set. Companies that attempt to differentiate themselves in the international marketplace must develop an innovative mindset or culture and must be willing to learn from and adapt to a variety of conflicting circumstances. They can then bring what they learn back to the home country and apply it to local businesses.[18]

While world markets provide many opportunities, pursuing these opportunities creates additional costs and risks. Managing businesses in foreign countries can result in additional costs associated with such things as travel, communications (including translation costs), export and import duties and tariffs, transportation of products, advertising, taxes, and fees. In addition, managers may find themselves unable to understand or effectively manage businesses in countries that are unfamiliar to them. This is a good reason why hiring a local manager may be desirable.

Market Entry Tactics

As economies grow and develop, different types of businesses are needed.[19] Increasing demand for hospitality services often reflects the structure of an economy. As an economy develops and companies begin to serve multiple locations in a region and international markets, the demand for services increases and new opportunities emerge. In an early economic phase, a country or region relies mostly on manufacturing and extractive industries dominated by single-location companies. In these economies, hotel demand comes from international business travelers who primarily visit major cities, while domestic business demand is relatively low. Large franchised hotel brands like InterContinental, Starwood, Accor, or Hilton, oriented to overseas visitors, would frequently serve these locations in capital cities.[20] As a country's economy grows and business development leads to nationwide expansion and beyond, more jobs require travel to secondary and tertiary markets. Local and regional hotel companies emerge to service these needs. (See the "Hospitality Focus" boxed section on page 406.)

As an economy makes additional improvements in transportation, such as faster trains, improved roads, and more airline routes, more business travel can be undertaken on day trips. In addition, there is a limit to growth, and in mature markets like the United States, there may be only marginal growth in demand, and in some locations saturation. As various parts of the world evolve economically, the level of competition to provide hotel services will also rise. Marriott International and Starwood both report that half of their new hotels in development are outside of North America, as the largest hotel companies continue their global expansion, as shown in Figure 10.1.

EXPORTING, CONTRACTING, AND DIRECT FOREIGN INVESTMENT

Firms can pursue global opportunities through exporting, contractual arrangements, and direct investments. *Foreign direct investment* occurs when a firm makes a direct investment, defined as

STARWOOD EXPANDS IN INDIA

S tarwood has been quick to respond to India's increased need for lodging, driven by the country's brisk economic growth. "Its exotic landscapes, rich cultural heritage, and booming economy make India one of the world's most vibrant markets and a perfect match for the energy and vitality of aloft hotels," notes Brian McGuinness, Vice President of aloft and element hotels, the lifestyle brand developed by Starwood Hotels. "We're thrilled to bring a bold new lodging alternative to the 'land for all seasons' with the arrival of our two new aloft hotels in Bangalore and Chennai."

In 2007, Starwood aggressively expanded its footprint in this fast-growing market, signing deals to open new hotels in markets throughout India across several of its brands, including two new Sheratons, three new Westins, and these two new aloft hotels. Starwood partners in India, particularly in newly developing submarkets in both major urban centers and secondary cities, have tailored aloft to meet the needs of the Indian market by including an all-day dining restaurant and more space for meetings.[21]

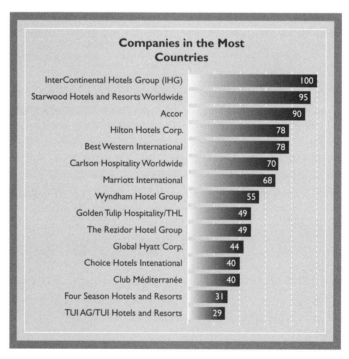

FIGURE 10.1 Global expansion of hotel companies
Source: HOTELS' Giant Survey 2007.

HOSPITALITY FOCUS

McDONALD'S: ADAPTING TO JAPANESE CULTURE

The first McDonald's in Japan was a 50-50 partnership between McDonald's and Den Fujita. He overruled McDonald's American management for the choice of the first site; instead of choosing a suburban Tokyo drive-in, he chose a high-rent location right in the center of Tokyo, which he said would give the little-known McDonald's brand more prestige. He argued that in order for McDonald's to succeed in Japan, it must appear to be a 100 percent Japanese operation. Den Fujita also asked that the spelling of McDonald's be changed to make it easier for the Japanese to pronounce, so it became "Makudonarudo." While McDonald's would not permit deviation from its operating principles, it did permit Fujita more freedom in the marketing arena.[22]

building or acquiring assets in another country. Transferring goods to other countries for sale through wholesalers or a foreign company is *exporting*. Because hospitality firms tend to focus on providing services rather than trading goods, contracting and foreign direct investments are particularly relevant entry tactics.

Strategies in service businesses may vary from what produces success in other industries, as Kurt Ritter, Rezidor SAS's president and CEO, observes: "Big mergers have not shown major economic benefits. Yes, there will be near-term opportunities for takeovers and rebranding, but we believe more in organic growth. Mixing cultures is much harder in the hotel industry than in manufacturing."[23] (See the "Hospitality Focus" boxed seciton above.)

Hotel chains often rely on franchising, joint ventures, management contracts, ownership, and acquisitions to facilitate market entry, while restaurant chains tend to focus on franchising. Following is a summary of the most common expansion tactics in services.

CONTRACTUAL ARRANGEMENTS, SUCH AS:

- *Licensing*. Selling the right to use a brand name in a foreign market. This right typically comes with restrictions that allow the licensing firm to protect its brand image.

- *Franchising*. Similar to licensing, but franchising typically requires more standardization on the part of the franchisee. A foreign firm buys the legal right to use the name, but it may also be required to apply operating methods or use supplies from the franchisor company. Marketing arrangements vary, but a lodging franchisee is typically a part of the companywide reservation system. Also, the franchisee typically contributes to a companywide advertising pool. Both hotels and restaurants use this tactic extensively.

- *Long-term management contract*. A contract between an owner and a management company. The owner agrees to make a payment from the operation's gross revenues to the management company in exchange for running the business with full management responsibility. This is a common hotel tactic for expansion.

FOREIGN DIRECT INVESTMENT, SUCH AS:

- *Joint venture.* Cooperative agreement among two or more companies to pursue common business objectives.
- *Wholly owned subsidiary.* Venture is started from scratch, thus creating a wholly owned foreign subsidiary. These ventures are sometimes called a "green-field investment."
- *Acquisition.* Purchase of a foreign firm or the foreign subsidiary of a foreign or domestic firm.[24]

ENTRY CRITERIA

Among the most important criteria when deciding on an option for international growth are cost, financial risk, profit potential, and control. In general, moving down the list of alternatives from first to last entails greater cost and greater financial risk, but also greater profit potential and greater control. Consequently, these alternatives represent a trade-off between cost and financial risk on one hand and profit and control on the other. Of course, this is a gross generalization. Some of the options, such as joint ventures and acquisitions, are difficult to judge on the basis of these four criteria because the exact nature of the agreement can vary so widely from deal to deal.

   For any international growth decision, these options should be weighed using real data on cost, risk, profit potential, and control, rather than generalizations. Hotel operators tend to rely on more than one of these options, although they may favor a particular approach over others. Accor, for example, has altered its strategy to focus more on growing the company through franchising and management contracts and less on building new hotels.[25] For fast growth, acquisition of regional firms and joint ventures are also popular. The comparatively small Dubai-based Jumeirah Hotels plans for ambitious international growth through management contracts.[26] (See the first "Hospitality Focus" boxed section on page 409.)

International Alliances and Business-Format Franchising

International strategic alliances are an outstanding way to acquire resources, specialized skills, or market knowledge. Resource combinations can lead to increased competitiveness. For example, Starwood will partner with Urbanedge Hotels Private Limited, a joint venture between Citigroup Property Investors and Auromatrix Hotels Private Limited, to develop aloft hotels across India.[27] KFC parent Yum! Brands Inc. and the Russian firm Rostik Restaurants Ltd. opened their first co-branded chicken outlet in Moscow under a joint-venture agreement.[28]

   International franchising can be an extremely profitable tool to accomplish branding and growth. In the beginning, the first to export a business-format franchise model to markets outside of the United States were fast-food franchise powerhouses such as McDonald's and KFC (of parent company Yum! Brands).[29] Now these pioneers of international franchising are

CARLSON HOTELS RELIES ON JOINT VENTURES FOR GLOBAL EXPANSION

Carlson Hotels Worldwide manages the largest portfolio of any international hotel group in India and plans to continue its expansion into key markets in the region including China. To facilitate that strategy, it formed a joint venture with the Lotus Hotel Investment Fund, a new US$1 billion private equity fund. The Lotus Hotel Fund is a Pan Asia specialist hotel fund with a focus on China, India, and Southeast Asia. It targets hotels for both development and rebranding opportunities and partners with global brands like Carlson to operate hotels for them under management contracts. Senior industry professionals with expertise in hotels, Asia, finance, and business development operate the fund.[30]

YUM! BRANDS: AGGRESSIVE FRANCHISING IN CHINA

Yum! Brands opens about three new restaurants each day of the year, making it one of the fastest growing retailers in the world. Its strategy includes building dominant restaurant brands in China and driving profitable international expansion. Its key international brands are KFC, with more than 1,800 units in China, and Pizza Hut, with more than 250 units in this country. KFC is the number-one quick-service restaurant brand, and Pizza Hut is the number-one casual-dining brand in mainland China.

Yum! China Division has more than 2,600 system restaurants, and mainland China is the firm's number-one market for new company restaurant development. The China division showed a 20 percent increase in operating profit by year-end 2007. Yum! Restaurants International (YRI) operates in more than 100 countries outside of China and the United States, reporting more than 10 percent growth in operating profit in 2007. YRI is 85 percent franchisee owned and operated, and these franchisees are responsible for almost all (90 percent) new restaurant development.[31]

as common in many other countries as they are in the United States, and they have been joined by other food concepts, hotels, and most of the major players in all industries that franchise. For many large franchisors today, the question is not where they have franchises, but rather where they do not. (See the second "Hospitality Focus" boxed section above.)

Selection of high-quality franchise partners is one of the most important factors in international markets. Tony Roma's, a Romacorp Inc. brand with the largest number of casual theme restaurants in the world, has found that selection of financially strong, well-established, and operationally experienced franchise partners can make a huge difference between success and failure.[32] Operations expertise is key. (See the "Hospitality Focus" boxed section on page 410.)

TONY ROMA'S SELECTS STRONG FRANCHISE PARTNERS

HOSPITALITY FOCUS

Tony Roma's, with locations in 32 countries and five continents, has franchise partners in every major region of the world. The franchise partners understand the system, understand the guests in their country, and have the resources to provide world-class service on a daily basis. If they do not deliver outstanding experiences everyday, the brand is quickly tarnished, growth stops, and future reentry back into the market is almost impossible. International franchise partners must know what makes customers in their market tick and be able to deliver what they demand and expect from the brand. A quality franchise partner not only strengthens the concept in their country, but also provides a "worldwide billboard" for you're the brand.[33]

As mentioned in Chapter 9, business-format franchising has been a common strategy for domestic expansion in the hospitality industry. In addition to helping create new businesses in a home country, franchising has historically been an important tool for international expansion. In this form of franchising, an ongoing business relationship between franchisor and franchisee includes the entire business concept, not just the product, service, and brand.[34] Marketing strategy, operating manuals and standards, quality control, and continuing assistance and guidance are elements of this type of franchising.

Franchising constitutes an alliance between at least two organizations, where each side benefits from the skill and resources held by (the) other. Independent hotels benefit from the global brand name of the international hotel chain and its reservations system. The franchising firm (foreign) gains quick, often smooth, access to a new market without the risk involved in ownership.[35]

However, franchising is a lower-return strategy compared with equity investments in hotels abroad.[36] A franchise strategy may be more difficult outside of North America because of the lack of infrastructure in some countries. Finding franchisees with good sites to build on is also a challenge in light of regulations restricting hotel property development in Europe and other parts of the world.[37] A certain level of learning skill or absorptive capacity is required of a franchisee to adopt the business concept in the overseas location; studies in hotel franchising have shown that franchising is more likely in developed nations because of the greater likelihood that the global partners possess the needed organizational skills.[38] To help deal with the challenges of developing internationally, chains sometimes develop master franchisees as partners. (See the "Hospitality Focus" boxed section on page 411.)

Master Franchises

Master franchise agreements involve larger franchisees who have the rights to develop in a specific territory. A master franchise is often used in nonstrategic or smaller markets. Curtis Nelson explains the Carlson Hotels' approach to using master franchise arrangements, noting, "Where you are established, where you have critical mass, it makes sense to do it yourself. Those partnerships are less beneficial the more you are established. It's less important to establish a new [master franchise] after you have distribution of a brand."[39] Take Marriott, who doesn't master

THE KEY ROLE OF MASTER FRANCHISEES IN ASIA

HOSPITALITY FOCUS

TT Resources has the exclusive master franchise rights from Gloria Jean's Gourmet Coffees Franchising Corp. for Malaysia, Singapore, Brunei, and Thailand. The five-year agreement allowed it to grant subfranchises for third parties to develop and operate outlets. It may also distribute coffee to hotels, restaurants, and retailers. TT Resources has been a Gloria Jean's franchisee since 1999 for Malaysia, Singapore, and Brunei. It has been a franchisee for Thailand since 2000. Under their master franchise agreement, TT Resources has to open and operate at least 45 stores, which include existing ones, in Malaysia, Singapore, and Brunei. It also has to open at least 25 stores, including existing ones, in Thailand. TT Resources also runs San Francisco Steakhouse, Tai Thong Chinese Restaurants, and Shrooms and Stars Oyster & Sushi Bar.[41]

franchise as much as other hotel chains, and not at all with its Ritz-Carlton brand.[40] Markets dictate whether franchising is used; for example, Marriott relies on franchising in Moscow, but terminated its master franchise agreement with Whitbread in the United Kingdom.

Global competition is also causing firms to reevaluate how they acquire knowledge. "New knowledge provides the foundation for new skills, which in turn can lead to competitive success," according to Andrew Inkpen, an expert on international alliances. "In bringing together firms with different skills, knowledge bases, and organizational cultures, alliances create unique learning opportunities for partner firms."[42] When it comes to international development, the complexity of ownership and franchising rights can make hotel competitors also partners in some settings. To illustrate, at one time Marriott owned the franchising right of Ramada internationally, a Wyndham Hotel Group brand (formerly Cendant), and the Pritzker family of Hyatt Hotels owned the rights to Travelodge in Asia.[43] These relationships and agreements can also shape decisions on which brands are and are not taken international.

INTERNATIONAL MARKET SELECTION

Significant changes in the global environment have created great opportunities for organizations that are willing to take a risk and wait patiently for returns. However, these changes have also created significant challenges. Furthermore, problems in the financial markets of one emerging nation can have ripple effects on financial markets in other emerging nations. Some of the greatest management challenges experienced by firms entering developing countries include:

- Unstable government
- Inadequately trained workers

- Low levels of supporting technology
- Shortages of supplies
- Weak transportation systems
- Unstable currency

Many characteristics must be evaluated when considering a foreign country for investment. Many of them fall within the general areas of the broad environment, including the social environment, the economy, the political/legal environment, and the state of technology. Other characteristics are related to specific industries and markets. Questions concerning each of these factors are listed in Table 10.2. These questions are a useful tool for evaluating a potential country for investment.

The wrong answers to any of the questions in Table 10.2 can make a country less attractive. The following are examples that demonstrate this point:

1. An unstable government can greatly increase the risk of a total loss of investment.

2. An inefficient transportation system can reduce demand because people cannot get to hotels, casinos, or other properties.

3. Inadequate school systems can result in poorly skilled workers, who may not have the ability to work at a high level of quality.

4. A slowly growing GNP could mean that consumer demand will be sluggish.

5. High foreign tax rates can virtually eliminate profits.

6. If the local currency cannot be translated into U.S. dollars, the organization will have a tough time removing profits from the country.

Firms also have to struggle with managing stakeholders that are typically very different—in values, beliefs, ethics, and in many other ways—from stakeholders found in the industrialized countries. However, firms that are first-movers into developing countries may be able to develop stakeholder-based advantages, such as long-term productive contractual and informal relationships with host-country governments and organizations, that followers won't have the opportunity to develop. For example, Spanish firms took huge risks by making major investments in Latin America during the first wave of privatizations, and they are now firmly entrenched in one of the world's fastest-growing regions. According to one large Spanish bank executive with significant investments in Latin America: "It's not a new frontier for Spanish companies because we discovered America in 1492. But it's a growth frontier. It's a financial rediscovery of the Americas."[44]

In North America, the North American Free Trade Agreement (NAFTA) has done much to open up borders and stimulate trade between the United States and its neighbors, Canada and Mexico. In fact, rightly or wrongly, NAFTA is sometimes credited with creating jobs in both Mexico and the United States.[45] After passage of NAFTA, more U.S. chain hotels made their presence felt in Mexico, and other major hotels throughout Mexico expanded and upgraded their facilities.[46] More recently, the Dominican Republic–Central America

TABLE 10.2 Examples of Questions to Ask about a Potential Foreign Market

Social Forces

What currently are the hot topics of debate? How well organized are special-interest groups with regard to the environment, labor, and management issues? Are current policies or behaviors of the organization likely to be offensive in the new host country? What is the attitude of potential consumers toward foreign products/services? Will there be significant cultural barriers to overcome? How difficult is the language? How old is the population? What other differences could cause difficulty for the organization?

The Economy

What is the inflation rate? How large is the gross national product (GNP)? How fast is it growing? What is income per capita? How much impact does the global economy have on the domestic economy? How high is the unemployment rate? What actions does the government take to fuel economic growth? What is the trade balance with the United States? Can the currency be exchanged for the home currency? How high are interest rates? Is the financial sector well organized? How expensive are the factors of production?

Political/Legal Environment

What is the form of government? How much influence does the government have over business? Is the government stable? What is the attitude of the government toward private enterprise and U.S. firms? What is the attitude of the home government toward the foreign government? How high are tax rates compared with the home country? How are taxes assessed and collected? How high are import and export taxes? What is the nature of the court system? Is legal protection available through incorporation or a similar form?

Technology

Is the country technologically advanced? Do schools and universities supply qualified workers? Are the required skills available in sufficient quantity? Are suitable information systems available? Is the infrastructure sound (i.e., roads, transportation systems)? Is an appropriate site available?

Industry Specific

How large is the industry? How fast is it growing? Can it be segmented? How many competitors are there? How strong are they? What is the relative position of industry participants in relation to suppliers and customers? Are substitute products available? What is the primary basis for competition? Is there a possibility of reaching the market through a joint venture?

HOSPITALITY FOCUS

THE DOMINICAN REPUBLIC–CENTRAL AMERICA FREE TRADE AGREEMENT (DR-CAFTA)

"About half our deals in Central America we're doing with either an American company or with American financing," notes Hilton Hotel's vice president of development for Latin America and the Caribbean. One result of the DR-CAFTA agreement is increased financial incentives for investing in the region. As Hilton develops hotels in Latin America, they rely on a franchisor or management company strategy in which they have no ownership presence, and ownership of the properties is a combination of international capital and local entities. Usually the international group will take a majority interest and keep the local partners in the deal for their expertise. For example, two conversions in Costa Rica had the New York–based Caribbean Property Group as the principal owner. Citibank was involved in structuring the deal in Costa Rica and New York.[47]

Free Trade Agreement, called DR–CAFTA, with the countries of Costa Rica, El Salvador, Guatemala, Honduras, Nicaragua, and the Dominican Republic, have also sought to create a free trade area like NAFTA. (See the "Hospitality Focus" boxed section above.)

China, with more than 1 billion potential consumers, will provide much of the growth in demand for tourism as well as consumer products over the next several decades.[48] An open-door policy on the part of the Chinese government has made China the largest recipient of foreign direct investment among developing nations and second among all nations (after the United States).[49] Nevertheless, there are risks and difficulties for foreign firms operating in China. Rising land and building costs will make development choices more critical, even as intra-Asian and domestic travel are poised to grow dramatically. While many Western hotel companies have turned their attention to Asia, many Asian hotel companies continue to prosper. (See the first "Hospitality Focus" boxed section on page 415.)

A common currency (the Euro) and reduction of trade barriers among many European countries have created a more open market of 340 million consumers.[50] Also, differentiation is easier to achieve because organizations can draw freely from the strengths of each nation. Privatization programs in the United Kingdom and elsewhere and a fundamental restructuring of the financial capital markets in countries such as Germany have put a lot more assets into the hands of private citizens.[51] Companies that have businesses in Europe already enjoy the advantages of a typically well-educated workforce, a well-developed infrastructure, a sophisticated level of technology, and high consumer demand—all factors that are associated with First World countries.

Restaurant chains are making strides in Europe, attracted by the size of the market and the consumers' growing interest in American food. For example, Foster's Hollywood restaurants franchisee, Madrid-based Grupo Zena, operates these restaurants across Spain and has found that American-themed casual dining is a natural culinary product for young European consumers who view American food as being like Italian, Chinese, and Korean.[52] Nevertheless, chains are a smaller part of the European quick-service sector, and consumers in different countries have unique preferences. A study of the ways consumers outside of the United States use fast-food restaurants revealed that in France, Germany, and Spain, the sandwich-bakery

ASIAN HOTEL BRANDS HOME INNS AND JIN JIANG INNS PROSPER

HOSPITALITY FOCUS

Founded in 2002, Home Inns is a growing economy hotel chain headquartered in Beijing. With more than 200 hotels in 59 cities across China, the company went public on the NASDAQ in 2006. According to Hu Shengyang, CEO of Shanghai Inntie Hotel Management Consulting, "Every hotel [in the Home Inns chain] had reached a market value of RMB 43 million (about $5.3 million) by the time it went public, while the cost of each was only RMB 5 million ($600,000), 8.6 times the original investment. This is an impossible achievement for traditional hotels." Nevertheless, Home Inns' CEO Sun Jian warns that despite huge market potential, blind investment without market analysis is risky.

The economy hotel subsidiary Jin Jian Inns, of Shanghai-based Jin Jiang International (Group) Co., a leading tourism conglomerate, is also growing. Jin Jiang owns, manages, or franchises more than 270 hotels and inns, with more than 53,000 rooms in China. Besides these two publicly traded companies, unlisted Chinese hotel chains include Motel 168, GreenTree Inn Hotel, 7days Inn, and Hanting Inns. Investment from state-owned capital and domestic private capital complement overseas private equity funds to fuel rapid growth in China.[53]

INCREASING GLOBALIZATION INCREASES COMPETITION FOR MARKET SHARE

HOSPITALITY FOCUS

Global brands, European regional brands, and the independent sector through marketing consortia are all fighting for market share. The industry is being driven by rising travel volumes and rising living standards. Most of these features reflect the increasing globalization that is taking place internationally across all sectors, coupled with the expansion of the tourism industry itself; some are features that are specifically a result of the New Europe.[54]

category is most popular, while the hamburger segment dominates in Great Britain.[55] To successfully enter new markets in Europe, McDonald's has focused on its McCafé concept.

According to a study conducted at the turn of the 21st century by PricewaterhouseCoopers, the hotel sector in Europe has changed faster in the past 10 years than at any time in history. This regional market is the world's largest for hotel inventory, with the most hotels located in the countries of Italy, Germany, France, Spain, and the United Kingdom. With around 75 percent of its hotel inventory unbranded, the industry is still fragmented, although the degree of branding varies by country. The Pricewaterhouse Coopers study made the following observations about the structure of the industry. (See the second "Hospitality Focus" boxed section above.)

Institutional Differences

One of the most important factors to consider when deciding whether to enter a country is the state of its capital markets. Some economies support very well-developed capital markets with very efficient financial transactions, while other economies are less well developed (see Figure 10.2). *Market-centered economies* have well-developed infrastructures, business environments, and external capital markets. Laws and regulations regarding capital markets are well developed and enforced. The capital market is not dominated by either equity or debt as a source of funding. Examples are the United States and the United Kingdom. *Bank-centered economies* also have well-developed infrastructures and business environments. However, capital markets are not as strong as in the United States or the United Kingdom. Banks and other financial institutions play the most significant role in the external capital markets. One of the advantages of this system is that banks are willing to let companies take on higher debt levels, and then are willing to help the borrowers through tough times. Examples of bank-centered economies are Japan and Germany.

In *family-centered economies*, families hold a lot of the stock in large corporations, allowing them control. A pyramidal structure is often used to maintain control.[56] At the lower levels, the parent company holds stock in its subsidiaries. At the next level, different parent companies are linked to a large financial institution. At the highest level, these financial institutions are interconnected through "capital networks and interlocking directorates." A good example of a family-centered economy is France, where about one-third of the largest companies are still managed by their founders or heirs. Other examples are Sweden and Italy. (See the "Hospitality Focus" boxed section on page 417.)

Group-centered economies such as South Korea do not have strong financial systems. Groups of companies manage the use of internal capital as a replacement for external capital markets. This system is sometimes created because only the government is able to borrow abroad. The government then channels borrowed money into particular sectors. Firms in those sectors

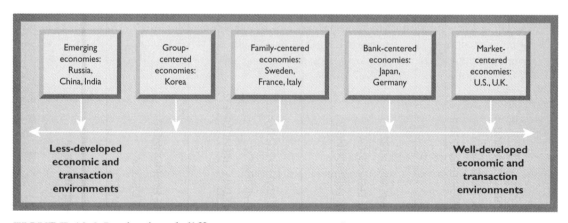

FIGURE 10.2 Institutional differences across countries
Source: R. E. Hoskisson et al., "Restructuring Strategies of Diversified Business Groups: Difference Associated with Country Institutional Environments," in *The Blackwell Handbook of Strategic Management,* eds. M. A. Hitt, R. E. Freeman, and J. S. Harrison (Oxford: Blackwell Publishing, 2001), 444. Used with permission.

THE FRENCH FAMILY-CENTERED ECONOMY AND LAURENT-PERRIER CHAMPAGNE

HOSPITALITY FOCUS

Laurent-Perrier Champagne is one of the world's most esteemed champagne brands and the largest family-owned brand. Making elegant and unique champagnes for nearly 200 years, the house was acquired by the Nonancourt family in 1939. Madame Louise Lanson de Nonancourt purchased the almost-bankrupt company and managed it through World War II. At one point, she hid 100,000 bottles behind a wall, while her sons Maurice and Bernard were members of the French Resistance movement and fought in the war. Sadly, the eldest son, Maurice de Nonancourt, who was expected to run Laurent-Perrier after the war, was killed in the concentration camp of Oranienbourg. The second son, Bernard de Nonancourt, spent several years training at several Champagne houses—including Lanson, which was owned by the family—to learn the business inside out. He took the reins of the family business in 1949, and today serves as Chair of the Supervisory Board. Alexandra and Stéphanie, the two daughters of Bernard de Nonancourt, hold the future of Laurent-Perrier. The two sisters are fully involved in the family business, focusing on strategy and development. They represent the majority shareholders and at some point in the future will assume ownership of the Champagne house.[57]

secure funds from the government, diversify their portfolios, and then recycle capital into other ventures.

Finally, *emerging economies* such as Russia and China historically are dominated by government ownership of the economic enterprise, with very little development of financial capital markets. Some of these economies are now pursuing privatization programs that put economic assets into the hands of private citizens. These programs are experiencing varying levels of success.[58] One notable success story for private enterprise comes from Prince Karim Aga Khan IV, spiritual head of the world's Ismaili Shia Muslims and venture capitalist to the Third World. Through his economic development institutions, he is increasingly taking equity positions in small-scale commercial enterprises, including hotels and lodges in Africa. (See the "Hospitality Focus" boxed section on page 418.)

National Advantages

One of the major advantages of global involvement is that organizations can draw from a much broader and more diversified pool of resources, including human resources, physical resources such as supplies and locations, and technological know-how.[59]

Michael Porter, whose name should now be familiar to you, expanded his analyses of competitive environments to include the global economy. In his book *The Competitive Advantage of Nations*, he developed arguments concerning why some nations produce so many

HOSPITALITY FOCUS

PRINCE KARIM AGA KHAN: VENTURE CAPITALIST TO THE THIRD WORLD

Prince Aga Khan was early to push the idea that the dispossessed could find hope in private economic enterprise. He grasped that government hand-outs and multilaterally funded megaprojects—like those from the United Nations or the World Bank—can often foster dependence in the people they're meant to help. Instead, the Aga Khan's goal is to spur sustainable economic development and individual self-reliance at the grassroots level in South and Central Asia and Africa. Poor countries like Tanzania, Pakistan, and the former Soviet republic of Tajikistan don't otherwise hold much hope of attracting high-profile foreign investors.

The Aga Khan Development Network focuses largely on health care, early childhood and female education, building business opportunities, clean water, farming, and housing. However, tourism is another success story, particularly in Kenya, where the Network's Tourism Promotion Services Ltd. is traded on the local stock exchange. Tourism has been the major generator of foreign exchange—in some cases it has overtaken the traditional foreign exchange earners of tea and coffee. Aga Khan–funded companies have built three lodges in Kenyan game parks and reserves, and hotels in Nairobi and on the Mombasa coast. In 1997–98, the company added three new lodges and a luxury tented camp in Tanzania's fabled Serengeti game reserve and a big hotel on the island of Zanzibar.[60]

stellar companies in particular industries. For example, Germany is the home base for several top luxury-car manufacturers, and Switzerland has many leading companies in pharmaceuticals and chocolate. The United States is the undisputed world leader in the entertainment industry. Porter explains that four characteristics of countries actually create an environment that is conducive to creating globally competitive firms in certain business areas. These four characteristics are:

- *Factor conditions.* Some nations enjoy special endowments, such as uncommon raw materials or laborers with specific skills or training. Often countries with excellent schools or universities that excel in particular areas produce laborers with superior skills. For example, Japan is well known for producing graduates with outstanding quantitative and technical skills.

- *Demand conditions.* If a nation's buyers of a particular product or service are the most discriminating and demanding in the world, then firms must achieve product and service excellence just to survive. Because they are so good, these companies can easily outperform foreign companies that compete in the same industry, even in the home countries of those foreign competitors. For example, American consumers are very discriminating in their consumption of movies and theme parks. Consequently, American entertainment companies are very competitive, even in foreign markets and against home-country rivals.

- *Related and supporting industries*. If suppliers in a particular country are the very best in the world, then the companies that buy from them are at a relative advantage. Firms in related industries that are also global leaders can also help create a nationally based competitive advantage.

- *Firm strategy, structure, and rivalry*. If the management techniques that are customary in the nation's businesses are conducive to success in a particular industry, then the firms in that nation are at a competitive advantage relative to firms from other countries. Another advantage can come from having an industry that attracts the most talented managers in the nation. Finally, if industry rivalry is strong in a particular industry, then firms are forced to excel. This is similar to the argument with regard to discriminating buyers.[61]

Basically, the reason why companies can develop a highly competitive nucleus is that tough market environments create world-class competitors only if the competitors are also endowed with the resources they need to compete. If home markets are uncompetitive, firms will not be sufficiently motivated to produce a quality service or superior product. Greater efficiency and innovation are also found to be benefits of greater competition.[62] However, if home markets are highly competitive but the factors of production, support industries, and human talent are not available, firms will likewise be incapable of producing globally competitive products.

Some firms buy foreign companies specifically to get a foothold in a world-class industry. The logical conclusion from Porter's analysis would seem to be to locate subsidiaries in the nations with the strongest home bases in particular industries. However, he argues that this is sometimes difficult to do. First, it is difficult in some cases for an outsider, a foreign firm, to become an insider. In other words, it may be difficult for a foreign firm to tap into the sources of supply or obtain the highly valued resources that make home-base competitors so successful. Japan, in particular, is a tough nation to penetrate. Second, Porter suggests that it is difficult for the foreign subsidiary in the nation with the natural advantages to influence the parent company long distance.[63]

Porter suggests that firms should take advantage of their own nation's natural-resource advantages. He also recommends that some of the principles that apply to the competitive advantages of nations can be applied in any company that wants to become more competitive in the world economy. Specifically, organizations can seek out the most discriminating buyers, choose from the best suppliers in the world, seek to excel against the most outstanding global competitors, form alliances with outstanding foreign competitors, and stay abreast of all research findings and innovations that are relevant to their core businesses.

GLOBAL STAKEHOLDERS

Global strategic management provides challenges and opportunities that are not found in domestic markets. Stakeholder management is more complicated because of the diversity of people, organizations, and governments involved. However, a more diverse environment offers more opportunities to develop stakeholder-based competencies through effective management and interorganizational relationships. Also, global diversity provides a much larger pool of resources from which to draw.

Stakeholder Management in Foreign Environments

The World Tourism Organization (UNWTO) predicts that global employment in tourism will reach more than 251 million jobs by 2010, or one in every 11 jobs worldwide.[64] As a result, a growing number of countries are developing strategic plans for national tourism. The macroeconomic benefits from both employment and foreign exchange has motivated many countries to explore ways to attract multinational firms while also supporting local and regional enterprises. Emerging destinations in Asia and the Pacific, Africa, and the Middle East are particularly attractive for multinational hospitality firms because of the tremendous growth in tourism, while mature regions such as Europe and the Americas may prove to be more challenging for international development because of market saturation.[65]

Global expansion requires an adjustment in the business definition of the organization. The answer to "Who is being satisfied?" typically is enlarged to include worldwide customers. According to a senior manager at InterContinental, "You have to look to see where there are consumers who have the same needs your brand meets."[66] Answering "How are customer needs satisfied?" may involve relationships with a much broader range of suppliers and partners. When McDonald's entered Europe, it could not find local food processors who could handle the high-volume automated production and cryogenic meat freezing that were essential elements of the company's operations.[67] To solve this problem, McDonald's used its established suppliers, who built facilities in new countries, sometimes with the restaurant chain serving as a partner in these supplier ventures.

Depending on the nature of the venture, any of the stakeholder groups may be enlarged. For example, many global firms are outsourcing some portion of their work to other countries, sending millions of service and knowledge jobs offshore, often to India. At a minimum, all global ventures rely on cooperation from a foreign government; however, most foreign ventures involve many other stakeholder groups as well. These new stakeholders add a new dimension to stakeholder analysis and management. They also increase the need for a state-of-the-art business intelligence system.

OWNERS AND DEVELOPMENT

Stakeholder analysis, a complicated process in domestic environments, becomes even more demanding when companies are significantly involved in countries other than their home countries. Organizations may respond to this complexity by evaluating stakeholders in all countries simultaneously. This process, which requires a high level of information system sophistication, results in a comprehensive view that provides the firm with a global picture and helps high-level managers craft missions, goals, strategies, and implementation plans that are applicable in a global setting. Many hospitality companies instead use a decentralized approach to stakeholder analysis, allowing local managers to manage their own information and customize or modify strategic direction, goals, strategies, and implementation plans.

Development directors play a key role in stakeholder analysis and implementation of an international strategy. While average daily rate is the primary factor in hotel market analysis, owners and franchisors also look at the demand generators, supply in the market, and the price of real estate.[68] What makes development more complex in international settings is the unique cultural differences in various markets.

A study of the role of development directors in hotel expansion revealed that these individuals serve as critical intermediaries between opportunities in the market and the hotel group. The primary responsibilities of development directors include:

- Developing a strategic plan for the designated geographic area
- Establishing a network of productive contacts, such as real estate developers, individual and institutional investors, hotel owners, hotel management companies, municipalities, and governmental development organizations
- Selling the value proposition of the brand, particularly to potential franchisees
- Assisting franchisees with applications and fee payments, and developing relationships with existing local franchisees and owners[69]

Global stakeholder management is even more taxing than analysis. Going global offers many new management challenges. The fact is that Europeans and the Japanese have different views of business and manage differently from American managers, although management techniques are converging.[70] Although there are similarities among countries in specific regions of the world, there are also significant differences. It is a mistake to lump all European countries together, all Asian countries in another bloc, and all African or Middle Eastern countries in their respective groups. In fact, the difference between Indonesia and South Korea is probably greater than that between Japan and the United States.

EMPLOYEE STAKEHOLDERS

Seeing, thinking, acting, and mobilizing in a culturally sensitive fashion is a key skill in global hospitality firms. Management of internal stakeholders such as employees becomes difficult and complex when an organization operates in more than one country or even in different regions of the same country. Take, for example, a manager in Spain. While many practices are the same throughout the country, running a business in Bilbao (Basque) is not the same as doing business in Madrid (Andalusian) or Barcelona (Catalan), because each city reflects different Spanish subcultures as indicated.

Working in different parts of the world takes tremendous human resources know-how and awareness of cultural values. According to researchers who are interested in improving the effectiveness of global managers, *cultural intelligence*, defined as an aptitude that enables outsiders to interpret unfamiliar gestures and actions as though they were insiders, can be acquired.[71] A culturally intelligent person can separate universally human behaviors from those that are rooted in culture or unique to the person, and can effectively discern and respond to dissimilar

HOSPITALITY FOCUS

JUMERIAM HOTELS' TRAINING FACILITY

"We see a huge need for training our future bookkeepers, chefs, waiters, restaurant managers not only in Dubai, but in the world," says Jumeriah Group executive chair Gerald Lawless. The Jumeriah Group is one of the fastest growing luxury hotel chains in the world. Parent company Dubai Holding has expansion plans that include restaurant chains, entertainment parks, and real estate development activities in the Middle East and North Africa. To address training issues in the hotel business, the company has established a company-owned, full-scale hotel management school, The Emirates Academy of Hospitality Management. A four-year curriculum in hospitality management is provided, along with academic association with the Ècole Hoteliere de Lausanne in Switzerland. The school makes training available to students with no obligation to work for Jumeriah. Plans to build a vocational training center are also part of this firm's approach to preparing workers for the growing industry in the region.[72]

cultures. Since the introduction of this idea, training has begun to focus more on cultural adaptation and less on learning the do's and don'ts of a given culture.

Perhaps the biggest challenge to the hospitality industry is developing and training employees, as hotels compete among each other and with other industries for talent. Accelerated growth in Dubai is part of the vision of Sheikh Mohammed bin Rashid al-Maktoum, the ruler of Dubai and prime minister of the United Arab Emirates, to make it the leading commercial and leisure destination in the Middle East. To accomplish this end, Jumeriah Hotels has created its own training facility. (See the "Hospitality Focus" boxed section above.)

Communication can often be a challenge in international settings because of language differences and conflicts between expatriates and local managers and staff. Employees and managers will need new relational skills. The challenges that Four Seasons' managers faced when opening a hotel in Bali, Indonesia, are instructive. (See the "Hospitality Focus" boxed section on page 423.)

Corporate training programs designed to teach operating standards don't always deliver when applied in new cultural settings, but management training can do a lot to help firms cope with global stakeholder management. Companies are sending some of their managers to special training programs to help increase their global awareness and vision. The School of Hotel Administration at Cornell University provides instruction for hundreds of industry professionals from around the world each year through its professional development and general managers programs. The University of Michigan developed an intensive, in-depth five-week program for 21 executives from Japan, the United States, Brazil, Great Britain, and India to help them become global thinkers. The program first made the participants more aware of the differences that existed between them. Then the trainers helped the participants to work out these differences. The training program was so successful that organizers have made the program an annual event.[73] Some South Korean firms have thorough training programs. An example is the use of "culture houses." An employee who will be sent to Germany, for example, is put in a "German house," where the employee is confined until he or she is able to eat, live, and sleep like a German.[74]

CULTURAL CHANGES IN BALI: MANAGING A HOTEL OPENING

Although there were more than 10,000 applicants eager to fill the 580 jobs at the Four Seasons Resort Bali, virtually none of them were able to speak English, and many didn't have any concept about world cuisine and Western customs. The traditional corporate training methods were fairly useless in educating the indigenous population. The gracious and hospitable Balinese people did not need to be taught the concept of service, they just needed it refined. "It was the specifics of Western culture that the native workers needed to learn, like milk goes with cereal, butter goes on toast, and ketchup goes with fries," noted Reny Ratman, director of human resources. Middle management and expatriate staff also had several misunderstandings about compensation and allowances packages. Many of the problems were made more difficult because Indonesians avoid conflict. Senior managers five years after the opening still felt they needed to change their focus and proceed slowly so there is time to learn and overcome differences.[75]

GOVERNMENTS

Government stakeholders are among the most difficult for a global firm to manage. A common approach when entering a new country is to obtain a foreign partner that understands the government system. At a minimum, a firm should hire employees and managers who are natives of the host country and have significant business experience specifically to handle government issues such as regulations and taxes. In the Beijing headquarters of McDonald's, only one American, a Chinese speaker, is on the staff. In Japan, decisions in this large quick-service restaurant chain have been in the hands of locals since the company opened its first store in 1971.[76]

The level of involvement of government administrators and regulators varies widely from nation to nation. For example, in two Egyptian Red Sea resort cities, Hurghada and Sharm El-Sheikhled, overbuilding and underpricing led the Ministry of Tourism and the Red Sea governate to stop issuing licenses for new hotels. According to the ministry, the decision to end hotel development will put a stop to price wars and a deterioration of service quality.[77] "From airports to bridges—things that assist with movement of people—those issues in China are a bit easier because the government is involved. India is more democratic, but as a result, the process takes much longer," according to the senior vice president of development for Four Seasons Hotels.[78]

Why do organizations enter such difficult environments? In a word, opportunity. China is a huge market. As David Martinez, who oversees international growth for Starwood Hotels and Resorts, put it, "China is a big but growing, awakening giant (for American business)."[79] Hotel companies based in the United States continue to see opportunity in developing hotels throughout Asia. The high barriers to entry that can inhibit construction in the United States and Western Europe are less of an issue in many Asian cities, where desirable sites can be found in existing and emerging heavily trafficked business districts.[80] Other countries in the region, such as South Korea and Vietnam, are seeing some of the same forces driving their growth. Starwood Hotels opened its first property in Vietnam, and Ramada International Hotels & Resorts, a division of Marriott International, opened its first hotel in South Korea during the early 2000s.

In summary, global organizations face a much more complicated management task as a result of diversity of stakeholders and resources. However, this diversity provides opportunities with regard to both stakeholder relationships and acquisition or development of resources that domestic companies do not enjoy. The way global firms manage their foreign subsidiaries has much to do with how they manage their resources. Also, firms can learn new technologies and acquire skills and other resources through international alliances.

STRATEGIC MANAGEMENT IN HOSPITALITY FIRMS IN THE FUTURE

Without question, the greatest managerial challenges lie ahead. It is difficult to predict with precision the kind of business environment the next generation of managers will face, but judging from the recent past, it will probably be associated with increasing global complexity and interconnectedness. Major events are also difficult to predict, yet they result in sweeping global changes in the business environment. Regional and global economic booms and busts, terrorism, and political and environmental crises will all shape the performance of the hospitality industry in unpredictable ways. Table 10.3 contains a few of the characteristics that, based on recent trends, might be expected to exist in the business environment of the 21st century.

Globalization and technological innovation are likely to be key factors in the future of hospitality. Large hotel companies will continue to extend their reach, and free markets will enable more capital to move across countries and into developing nations. Restaurant chains have learned a great deal from the groundwork of McDonald's and Yum! Brands on how to go global successfully. Technological innovations will enable the development of new distribution

TABLE 10.3 Strategic Management for the Future

* Increasing levels of global trade and global awareness
* Global and domestic social turbulence
* Increased terrorism and a worldwide effort to eliminate it
* Increased sensitivity to ethical issues and environmental concerns
* Rapidly advancing technology, especially in communications
* Continued erosion of buying power in the U.S. and other economies
* Continued development of third world economies
* Increases in U.S. and global strategic alliances
* Revolution in the U.S. health-care industry
* Greater emphasis on security and crisis management

channels and ways of managing customer relationships. Some predict that we will see fully mobile reservations and sales, location-aware marketing, the outfitting of all front-line staff with mobile devices, automatic transmission of preferences from embedded storage devices, and biometric footprinting of guests.[81] How do you prepare for this future? Advice abounds on how to become ready for what lies ahead; some crucial actions for managers are:

- *Pay global attention* by looking after the global traveler at home and the local traveler abroad and by extending the global reach of your portfolio.

- *Uncover the unexpected* experiences that excite and delight your customers.

- *Invest in your guest* by developing a comprehensive framework for guest interactions.

- *Become agile* by integrating your businesses across business units, brands, and locations into a common business infrastructure for back-of-house and key front-of-house functions, and consider strategic outsourcing opportunities.

- *Rethink revenues* to focus on "return on investment management."

- *Polish your GEMs* to transform front-line staff into "guest experience managers."

- *Extend the experience* before the trip begins and after it ends.[82]

What kind of leaders will be needed to navigate through the business environment of the future? They will be strategic thinkers—people who are willing to break with conventional norms, but at the same time learn from and respect the past. They will be revolutionaries who don't simply seek incremental improvements to existing business systems to increase efficiency, but invent new business concepts.[83] As Bill Gates said of Microsoft, any company can be "two years away from failure."[84] They will be global thinkers, eager to establish relationships with outstanding companies, to obtain the best resources, and to sell in the most advantageous markets, regardless of where they are found. They will be sensitive to the organizational and external environment, realizing that long-term success requires a broad attitude regarding what and who is important. Finally, they will be able to instill in organizational members an urgent sense of vision.

The tools, theories, and techniques found in this book can help you become an effective leader for the 21st century. I encourage you to apply what you have learned to current and future business situations in which you and your organizations are found.

KEY POINTS SUMMARY

- One of the outcomes of increasing internationalization is that countries are economically interconnected at an unprecedented level. Among the most popular reasons why companies make foreign investments are to search for new markets or better resources, increase efficiency, reduce risk, or counter the competition.

- Hospitality firms were pioneers in globalization. From cautious expansion before the 1970s to rapid growth by the early 2000s, international reach continues.

- The strategies companies use for international expansion tend to fall into three broad categories: multidomestic, global, and transnational. A multidomestic strategy entails handling operations country by country by tailoring services around individual market needs.

- Organizations pursuing a global strategy produce one type of service and market it in the same fashion throughout the world.

- Quick-service restaurant firms like McDonald's have relied on a strategy that combines the efficiency of a global strategy with the flexibility of a multidomestic strategy in what is called a transnational strategy.

- The evolving economic structures of countries help explain the stages of hotel development. For example, as a country grows and builds commerce, demand for hotels in secondary markets accelerates.

- Firms must also determine which expansion tactics they will pursue. Common options in hospitality include licensing, franchising, management contracts, joint ventures, wholly owned subsidiaries, and acquisitions.

- Among the most important criteria when deciding on an option for international growth are cost, financial risk, profit potential, and control. Another factor that seems to influence the decision among international growth options is multinational diversity.

- International strategic alliances are an outstanding way to acquire both resources and skills.

- Franchising has been an extremely useful tool for global expansion in hospitality firms. Master franchises involve providing a larger franchisee with the rights to develop a specific territory. This approach to franchising can be particularly useful in developing nations and nonstrategic locations. While risk is lower using this model for global expansion, so are the returns.

- One of the most important factors to consider when deciding whether to enter a country is the state of its capital markets.

- Many characteristics should be evaluated before entering a foreign market. They fall into the areas of the broad environment, including the social environment, the economy, the political/legal environment, and the state of technology.

- Organizations can often draw on the special resources of a country. Companies that operate in countries with uncommon factor conditions, demand conditions, related and supporting industries, or exceptional firm strategies, structures, or rivalry may be at a comparative advantage relative to other global competitors.

- Stakeholder management is more complicated because of the diversity of people, organizations, and governments involved. However, a more diverse environment offers more opportunities to develop stakeholder-based competencies through effective management and interorganizational relationships.

- Tremendous human resources know-how is necessary for those who work in many different parts of the world. Building cultural intelligence, or an aptitude that enables outsiders to interpret unfamiliar gestures and actions as though they were insiders, can enhance managerial effectiveness.

- Development directors perform an important role as intermediaries between market opportunities and hospitality firms. Global diversity provides a much larger pool of resources from which to draw, including human resources; physical resources such as raw materials, supplies, and locations; and technological know-how.

- Finally, future strategic management in the hospitality industry will be influenced by globalization and technological innovations. The future is in your hands. Good luck!

REVIEW QUESTIONS

1. Why were hospitality firms some of the first to internationalize?

2. What are some of the outcomes from increasing global interdependence among companies? Why might a firm want to pursue internationalization?

3. How does the structure of an economy shape international development?

4. How can an organization create more of a global mind-set?

5. What is the role of a development director? Why do so many hotel companies rely on these individuals when expanding into new markets?

6. Why do organizations enter difficult environments? How should a firm enter new markets?

7. Explain the conditions that can lead a nation to produce a disproportionate amount of global leaders in particular industries.

8. Describe the various roles played by foreign-owned subsidiaries. What determines which role they will play?

9. Why is a business-format franchise a popular approach to internationalizing in the hospitality industry?

10. What is the difference between a global and a multidomestic product/market strategy, and what are the advantages and disadvantages of each? Is there a strategy between these extremes?

11. What are the major expansion tactics, and what are the factors that determine which one is the preferred approach?

12. What should a company consider before entering a foreign market?

13. What do you predict will be key innovations in the hospitality industry of the future?

14. What leadership skills will be necessary to successfully manage global firms in the 21st century?

CRITICAL THINKING AND APPLICATION QUESTIONS

1. Write a two- to three-page memo to Starbuck's CEO Howard Schultz with actionable recommendations for how to effectively grow international markets.

2. How might the worldwide need for trained employees in hospitality be filled? Explore the number of hotel schools and programs in various regions of the world and report on the different approaches to development provided by governments, corporate players, and educational (nonprofit) organizations.

3. Three companies are planning a joint venture to build a new hotel and retail shopping complex.[85] The hotel company will develop and manage the property, the construction company will build it, and the bank will arrange the financing. The companies come from three different fictional cultures: Blue, Red, and Green. Each has specific cultural values, traits, customs, and practices. You will play the role of a manager in one of the three companies involved in the joint venture.

    Your instructor will assign you to a company and provide you with additional instructions. You are a manager in the company to which you are assigned. You will attend a cocktail party that opens a series of important business meetings, during which the companies will negotiate the details of the partnership. Your management team includes a vice president and several other managers.

    a. In your assigned company, you will meet with the other student to discuss what your objectives and approaches will be at the cocktail party. Using the description of your culture provided by your instructor, practice how you will talk and behave until you are reasonably familiar with your cultural orientation. Be sure to practice conversation distance, greeting rituals, and nonverbal behavior.

    b. At the appointed time, come to the cocktail party venue. As the cocktail party proceeds, interact with the managers from the other companies. Maintain the role you have been assigned, but do not discuss it explicitly. Notice how other people react to you and how you react to them.

    c. Be ready to discuss your experiences after the cocktail party ends.

CASES

CASE STUDY MATRIX

Case Title	Chapters	Topics Covered	Industry Segment
1 The Fun Ship Experience at Carnival Cruise Lines	2, 4, 5, 7	Vision and Mission Five Forces Competitive Advantage Core Resources Business Level Strategies Corporate Strategy	Cruise Industry
2 Building Capabilities at the Westward Hilton	3, 4, 5, 7, 8	Vision and Mission Five Forces Competitive Advantage Core Resources Business Level Strategies Corporate Strategy Organizational Design and Control Innovation and Entrepreneurship	Ownership Group and Individual Hotel
3 Intercontinental Hotel Group's Entry into China	2, 7, 9, 10	Environmental Analysis Competitive Advantage Core Resources Corporate Strategy Stakeholders and Partnerships Global Strategy	International Chain of Hotels and Partners
4 The Summer of 2006 Union Negotiations: Unite Here's Strategy	3, 4, 5, 7	Vision and Mission Environmental Analysis Competitive Advantage Core Resources Corporate Strategy Stakeholders and Partnerships Organizational Design and Control	Hospitality Union

CASE STUDY MATRIX TABLES CONT...

5 Banyan Tree: Sustainability of a Brand during Rapid Global Expansion	2, 3, 6, 9, 10	Vision and Mission Environmental Analysis Five Forces Corporate Strategy Competitive Advantage Stakeholders and Partnerships Organizational Design and Control Innovation and Entrepreneurship Global Strategy	Regional Chain of Hotels
6 Starwood Hotels and Resorts Brings Aloft to India	2, 5, 6, 7, 10	Environmental Analysis Competitive Advantage Corporate Strategy Stakeholders and Partnerships Innovation and Entrepreneurship Global Strategy	International Chain of Hotels and Brand Introduction
7 The Commoditization of Starbucks	3, 5, 6, 9	Five Forces Competitive Advantage Core Resources Business Level Strategies Corporate Strategy Organizational Design and Control Innovation and Entrepreneurship	Restaurant Industry
8 The Movement of Travel Services Online: Intermediaries and Branded Distribution	2, 4, 6, 7, 9	Environmental Analysis Five Forces Competitive Advantage Corporate Strategy Stakeholders and Partnerships	Online Travel Intermediaries and Travel Suppliers

TOPICS	CASES							
	1	2	3	4	5	6	7	8
Environmental Analysis			x	x	x	x		x
Five Forces	x	x			x		x	x
Vision and mission	x	x		x	x			
Competitive Advantage	x	x	x	x	x	x	x	x
Core Resources	x	x	x	x			x	
Business Level Strategies	x	x					x	
Corporate Strategy	x	x	x	x	x	x	x	x
Stakeholders and Partnerships			x	x	x	x		x
Organizational Design and Control		x		x	x		x	
Innovation and Entrepreneurship		x			x	x	x	
Global Strategy			x		x	x		

CASE NOTE: LEARNING THROUGH CASE ANALYSIS

Strategic management is an iterative, ongoing process designed to position a firm for competitive advantage in its ever-changing environment. To manage an organization strategically, a manager must understand and appreciate the desires of key organizational stakeholders, the industry environment, and the firm's position relative to its stakeholders and industry. This knowledge allows a manager to set goals and direct the organization's resources in a way that corrects weaknesses, overcomes threats, takes advantage of strengths and opportunities, and, ultimately, satisfies stakeholders.

Case analysis typically begins with a brief introduction of the company. The introduction, which sets the stage for the rest of the case, should include a brief description of the defining characteristics of the firm, including some of its outstanding qualities, past successes, failures, and products or services. The industries in which the firm is involved are also identified.

The next section of a case analysis can be either an environmental analysis or an internal resource analysis. Both types of analysis are required before all of the organization's opportunities can be identified.

ENVIRONMENTAL ANALYSIS

An analysis of the external environment includes an industry analysis and an examination of key external stakeholders and the broad environment. Findings are then summarized, with an emphasis on identifying industry growth and profit potential and the keys to survival and success in the industry. Some organizations are involved in more than one industry. Consequently, a separate industry analysis is done for each of the industries in which a firm is involved.

THE BROAD ENVIRONMENT

A complete environmental analysis includes an assessment of the broad environment, including social influences, economic influences, political influences, and technological influences. These areas are evaluated only as they relate to the industry in question. They should be evaluated at the domestic and global levels, if appropriate. Forces in the broad environment may pose threats or provide opportunities.

INDUSTRY ANALYSIS

The first step in industry analysis is to provide a basic description of the industry and the competitive forces that dominate it. Porter's Five Forces are evaluated as follows, along with other relevant issues:

1. What is the product or service? What function does it serve? What are the channels of distribution?

2. What is the industry size in units and dollars? How fast is it growing? Are products differentiated? Are there high exit barriers? Are there high fixed costs? These are some of the forces that determine the strength of competition among existing competitors.

3. Who are the major competitors? What are their market shares? In other words, is the industry consolidated or fragmented?

4. Who are the major customers of the industry? Are they powerful? What gives them power?

5. Who are the major suppliers to the industry? Are they powerful? What gives them power?

6. Do significant entry barriers exist? What are they? Are they effective in protecting existing competitors, thus enhancing profits?

7. Are there any close substitutes for industry products and services? Do they provide pressure on prices charged in this industry?

8. What are the basic strategies of competitors? How successful are they? Are competitors likely to retaliate to competitive moves or countermoves? How rapidly do they respond?

9. Is the industry regulated? What influence do regulations have on industry competitiveness?

10. Are any other external stakeholders important in this industry? Examples might include labor unions, special-interest groups, financial institutions, or local communities.

11. To what extent is the industry global? Are there any apparent advantages to being involved in more than one nation?

The findings of this part of the analysis will help you decide whether the industry is "attractive" (growing and profitable) and worthy of further investment (i.e., time, money, resources). It will also help you identify areas in which the firm may be able to excel in an effort to create a competitive advantage.

STRATEGIC ISSUES FACING THE INDUSTRY

A thorough environmental analysis provides the information needed to identify factors and forces that are important to the industry in which your organization is involved and, therefore, your organization. These factors and forces may be categorized as follows:

1. *Driving forces in the industry*, which are trends that are so significant that they are creating fundamental industry change, such as the opening up of Eastern Europe or networked computer communications. Each industry has its own unique set of driving forces.

2. *Threats*, defined as noteworthy trends or changes that threaten growth prospects, profit potential, and traditional ways of doing business.

3. *Opportunities*, which are important trends, changes, or ideas that provide new opportunities for growth or profits.

4. *Requirements for survival*, identified as resources and capabilities that all firms must possess to survive in the industry. An example in the pharmaceutical industry is "product purity." These factors do not command a premium price. They are necessary, but not sufficient to be successful.

5. *Key success factors*, which are factors firms typically should possess if they desire to be successful in the industry. An example in the pharmaceutical industry is the ability to create products with new therapeutic qualities. This ability may lead to high performance.

Having completed an analysis of the external environment, you are ready to conduct a more specific analysis of the internal organization.

ORGANIZATIONAL RESOURCE ANALYSIS

Understanding industry trends, growth prospects, profit potential, and key strategic issues can help you critique an organization's strategies and evaluate its strengths and weaknesses. For example, what might qualify as a strength in one industry may be an ordinary characteristic in another industry. A good organizational analysis should begin with a general evaluation of the internal organization.

EVALUATION OF STRATEGIC DIRECTION AND THE INTERNAL ENVIRONMENT

The following questions are useful in beginning to assess the internal organization:

1. What is the company's strategic direction, including its vision, business definition, and values? If these factors are contained in a formal mission, share it. If not, you may want to write one. Remember that organizations have a strategic direction even if it is not written down.

2. How has the strategic direction changed over time? In what way? Has the evolution been consistent with the organization's capabilities and planned strategies?

3. Who are the principal internal stakeholders? In particular, who are the key managers, and what is their background? What are their strengths and weaknesses? Are they authoritarian or participative in their management style? Is this appropriate for the situation? What seems to drive their actions?

4. Who owns the organization? Is it a publicly traded company with a board of directors? If there is a board and you know who is on it, is the composition of the board appropriate? Is there an individual or group with a controlling interest? Is there evidence of agency problems? How active are the owners, and what do they value?

5. What are the operating characteristics of the company, including its size in sales, assets, and employees, its age, and its geographic locations (including international operations)? Does the company have any unique physical resources?

6. Are employees highly trained? If a union is present, how are relations with the union?

7. How would you describe the organization's culture? Is it a high-performing culture? Is it supportive of the firm's strategies?

Most instructors also require a financial analysis both to identify financial strengths and weaknesses and to evaluate performance. A financial analysis should include a comparison of ratios and financial figures with major competitors or the industry in which the organization competes (cross sectional), as well as an analysis of trends in these ratios over several years (longitudinal). Financial ratio analysis can provide an indication as to whether the firm is pursuing appropriate strategies. Poor financial trends are sometimes symptoms of greater problems. For example, a firm may discover that administrative costs are increasing at a faster rate than sales. This could be an indication of diseconomies of scale or the need for tighter controls on overhead costs. Financial analysis is also used to indicate the ability of the firm to finance growth. For example, managers of a firm that has very high leverage (long-term debt) may have to be less ambitious in their strategies for taking advantage of opportunities. On the other hand, an organization with a strong balance sheet is well poised to pursue a wide range of opportunities. Strong financial resources are often difficult to imitate in the short term.

ANALYSIS OF RESOURCES AND CAPABILITIES

The foregoing analysis of the internal environment provides an excellent starting point for identifying key resources and capabilities. For example, outstanding resources and capabilities may result from (1) superior management, (2) well-trained employees, (3) an excellent board of directors, (4) a high-performance culture, (5) superior financial resources, (6) effective knowledge-generating processes, or (7) the appropriate level and type of international involvement. However, these potential sources of competitive advantage barely scratch the organizational surface.

You also should evaluate the organization's primary value-chain activities to identify resources and capabilities. These activities include its (8) inbound logistics, (9) operations, (10) outbound logistics, (11) marketing and sales, and (12) service, as well as the support activities of (13) procurement, (14) technology development, (15) human resource management, and (16) administration. In addition, an organization may have (17) an excellent reputation, (18) a strong brand name, (19) patents and secrets, (20) excellent locations, (21) outstanding learning capabilities, or (22) strong or valuable ties (i.e., alliances, joint ventures, contracts, cooperation) with one or more external stakeholders. All of these potential resources and capabilities (and many others) have been discussed in this book. They form a starting point that you can use to help identify the potential sources of competitive advantage. Each company has its own unique list.

It is useful to screen resources and capabilities based on their long-term strategic value. This process entails asking several questions:

- Does the resource or capability have value in the market?
- Is the resource or capability unique?
- Is there a readily available substitute?

Positive answers to the first two questions and a negative answer to the third mean that the resource or capability has the ability to provide a source of competitive advantage. Two additional questions are then asked:

- Do organizational systems exist that allow realization of potential?
- Is the organization aware of and realizing the advantages?

Opportunities can exist if an organization is not taking advantage of sources of competitive advantage, either because it is unaware of them or because systems are not yet in place to take advantage of them. A final question is then asked:

- Is the resource or capability difficult or costly to imitate?

If it is difficult or costly to imitate the resource or capability, it can be a source of sustainable competitive advantage. A final part of this analysis is to determine whether the resource or capability can be applied to multiple business areas. If this is the case, it can be classified as a core competency or capability.

PERFORMANCE EVALUATION

The next step in internal analysis is to describe and critique the organization's past strategies. In critiquing strategies, you will need to describe them in detail, discuss whether they have been successful, and then *evaluate whether they fit with the industry environment and the resources and capabilities of the organization*:

1. What is the company's pattern of past strategies (corporate-level, business-level, international)?
2. How successful has the company been in the past with its chosen strategies? How successful is the company now?
3. For each strategy, what explains success or failure? (Use your environmental and organizational resource analyses to support your answer.)

SUMMARY OF SITUATION ANALYSIS: SWOT

On the basis of your environmental and organizational analyses, you should be in a position to draw some conclusions about the situation your organization is facing, called a situation analysis. Many students will do this by creating lists of strengths and weaknesses, opportunities and threats. Strengths are defined as firm resources and capabilities that can lead to a competitive advantage. Weaknesses are resources and capabilities that the firm does not possess, resulting in a competitive disadvantage. Consequently, each of the resources and capabilities identified during the organizational analysis should be measured against the factors identified in the environmental analysis.

Opportunities are conditions in the external environment that allow a firm to take advantage of organizational strengths, overcome organizational weaknesses, or neutralize environmental threats. Consequently, now that the organizational analysis is complete, you should reevaluate your list of opportunities to determine whether they apply to your organization. You should also evaluate threats to make sure they are applicable to your firm. Threats are conditions in the broad and operating environments that may impede organizational competitiveness or the achievement of stakeholder satisfaction.

DEVELOPING A STRATEGIC PLAN

Your environmental and organizational analyses helped you evaluate the past strategies and strategic direction of the firm, as well as develop a list of strengths, weaknesses, opportunities, and threats. The next step is to make recommendations concerning the strategies the firm may want to pursue in the future. If the firm is not a stellar performer, this should be an easy task. However, even firms that have been highly successful in the past should consider taking advantage of opportunities and should respond to threats. History has taught us that firms that are unwilling to move forward eventually decline.

STRATEGIC DIRECTION AND MAJOR STRATEGIES

You should probably begin your strategic recommendations by focusing on the strategic direction and major strategies of the firm. Based on your earlier analyses, you may want to consider adjustments to the mission of the firm, including its vision or business definition. Determine whether the business definition is still appropriate, given your environmental analysis. Is your dominant industry stagnant? Is it over-regulated? Is competition hurting profitability? Should you consider investing in other industries? If so, what are their defining characteristics? What core competencies and capabilities could be applied elsewhere? What opportunities could be explored that relate to the corporate-level strategies?

The business-level strategy should also be considered. If you determined earlier that the business-level strategy is not as successful as it should be, what adjustments should be made? Could the company have more success by focusing on one segment of the market? Or if the company is pursuing a focus strategy, would broadening the target market be appropriate? If the company is following cost leadership, would a differentiation strategy work better? If differentiation doesn't seem to be working very well, would a cost leadership strategy be better? Finally, would a best-value strategy be the most appropriate?

It is possible that you may want to leave the strategic direction and major strategies alone, especially if the organization has enjoyed recent success. Regardless of whether you altered the direction and strategies, at this point you have now established what you think they should be. The direction and corporate- and business-level strategies provide guidance for fine-tuning an organization's strategies. Each of the recommendations you make from this point on should be consistent with the strategic direction and major strategies of the organization. At this point, it is time to explore strategic opportunities further.

EVALUATION OF OPPORTUNITIES AND RECOMMENDATIONS

Using the strategic direction and corporate- and business-level strategies as guides, strategic opportunities should be evaluated further. These alternatives were generated during earlier analyses. They include opportunities that allow a firm to take advantage of organizational strengths, overcome organizational weaknesses, and neutralize environmental threats. Evaluation of opportunities means much more than simply accepting them on the basis of earlier environmental and organizational analyses. They should also be evaluated based on factors such as the following:

1. *Value added to the organization.* Some alternatives may have high potential for growth in revenues, whereas others may be oriented toward improving efficiency, eliminating problems, taking advantage of organizational strengths, or any of a wide range of other factors. Make sure that you look at long-term value as well as short-term value.

2. *Organizational resources required to implement the alternative.* The actual dollar costs to an organization are often difficult for a student to estimate. However, you should always provide a description of all of the resources needed to carry out the alternative.

3. *The extent to which the alternative fits within the organization.* Base this part of your analysis on such things as whether the alternative takes advantage of current distinctive competencies, the ability of the organization to successfully execute the alternative, and whether the existing culture, management, and resources of the organization will support implementation of the alternative. Make sure to specify whether this alternative is consistent with the current strategic direction of the company or requires new direction.

4. *Risks associated with the alternative.* Consider such things as financial risk, risk to the firm's reputation or its existing strengths, and risk to particular stakeholder groups, such as employees, managers, customers, or suppliers. Part of this analysis should anticipate

the reactions of competitors to the strategy and what could happen if they respond adversely.

5. *Future position.* Will the strategy continue to be viable as the industry and the broad environment undergo their expected changes? Will it provide a foundation for survival or competitive success?

The result of this analysis should be a recommendation or recommendations that the organization should pursue. You may not be required by your instructor to conduct a formal analysis of alternatives based on a standard set of criteria; however, you should still make recommendations concerning changes the organization should make to remain or become competitive and satisfy its stakeholders. Through this entire process, remember that many companies identify areas of strength that are no longer capable of giving the company a competitive edge. What was a key to success yesterday may be a requirement for survival today.

IMPLEMENTATION AND CONTROL

Recommendations should always be accompanied by an implementation plan and basic controls. The following are major questions that should be addressed during this section of a case analysis. Items 7 and 8 relate specifically to control.

1. How do the recommendations specifically address concerns that were identified during the analysis?

2. What will be the roles and responsibilities of key internal *and* external stakeholders in carrying out the recommendations, and how are they expected to respond? What actions should be taken to smooth out the transition period or avoid stakeholder discontent?

3. Does the organization have the resources (funds, people, skills) to carry out the recommendations? If not, how should the organization proceed in developing or acquiring those resources?

4. Does the organization have the appropriate systems, structures, and processes to carry out the recommendations? If not, how should the organization proceed in creating the appropriate systems, structures, and processes?

5. What is the appropriate time horizon for implementing recommendations? What should the organization and its managers do immediately, in one month, in six months, in a year, etc.?

6. What are the roadblocks the organization could encounter while implementing the recommendations (i.e., financing, skilled labor shortages)? How can the organization overcome these roadblocks?

7. What desired outcomes or changes should the organization expect once the recommendations have been implemented? How will the organization know if the recommendations have been successful? In other words, what objectives are associated with your recommendations?

8. What were some of the major assumptions you made with regard to the external environment? Which of these factors, if different from expected, would require an adjustment to your recommendations?

In addition, some instructors require separate functional plans for areas such as finance, human resources, or marketing. Chapter 7 contains information that should help you develop these plans.

Following the implementation section, you may want to update your audience (your instructor or other students) concerning actions the firm has taken since the case was written. If a case update is required, it should center on actions that pertain to the focus of your case analysis. If you do an update, remember that what the organization did, even if it appears to have been successful, may not have been the optimal solution.

A NOTE TO STUDENTS

If you are reading this appendix early in the course, you will have the rest of the semester or quarter to practice the case analysis process and study the chapter readings. If you are reading this appendix later in the course, I encourage you to go back to earlier chapters and refresh your memory concerning the concepts that were covered. Just as this course integrates material you learned during your years of business study, the case analysis process integrates material from all sections of the strategic management course.

Because there is not a standard method for analyzing cases, your instructor may teach a method of case analysis that differs from the approach contained herein. Also, cases can be treated in many different formats, including class discussions (complete with discussion questions to be answered before coming to class), written papers, formal presentations, and class debates. Finally, some cases do not lend themselves to comprehensive analysis. After reading this appendix, check with your instructor for specific instructions and requirements.

CASE 1 THE FUN SHIP EXPERIENCE AT CARNIVAL CRUISE LINES

> *We're perfectly happy to be the Wal-Mart of the cruise industry.*[1]
>
> —Terry Thornton, vice president of
> marketing planning, Carnival Cruise Lines

In July 2005, the 2,974-passenger, 110,000-ton[2] *Carnival Liberty* set sail after being christened by its "godmother," actress Mira Sorvino. Built for $500 million, the ship was the 21st vessel sailing in Carnival Cruise Lines' fleet, giving Carnival more passenger-carrying capacity than any other cruise line in the world. With 800-plus oceanview or balcony staterooms, 22 lounges and bars, four swimming pools, and a spiral water slide, *Carnival Liberty* was a far cry from the *Mardi Gras*, Carnival's first ship, which was a converted transatlantic liner bought in 1972 for $6.5 million. For its part, the *Mardi Gras* seemed to signal an inauspicious beginning for Carnival when the ship ran aground at the tip of Miami Beach on its inaugural voyage—in full view of gawking vacationers. However, as Carnival lore had it, bartenders poured free drinks (including a new rum cocktail that a creative bartender dubbed a "*Mardi Gras* on the Rocks"[3]), passengers had fun, and the spirit of the "Fun Ships" brand was born.

The differences between the *Mardi Gras* and the *Carnival Liberty* symbolized the metamorphosis of the Carnival brand. Today's Carnival was dramatically different than the company that cruise industry pioneer Ted Arison started with secondhand ships and savvy marketing. While North American passenger volume doubled between 1994 and 2004, Carnival's volume tripled. More than 3 million guests sailed Carnival in 2004, the most in the company's history, and a figure representing nearly one out of every three cruisers. For the fiscal year that included 2004, Carnival Corp. & plc, the parent company of Carnival Cruise Lines, reported record net income of $1.85 billion on revenues of $9.73 billion. Nine of Carnival's ships, almost half of the line's available berths,[4] had been launched since 2000. Through the years, Carnival had remained true to its Fun Ships lineage and its goal of providing a good-quality, affordable vacation to mainstream travelers. Nevertheless, company executives wondered whether it was time to set a new course for Carnival, and if so, how best to reinvent the brand without losing its essence.

Written by Robert J. Kwortnik, Jr., who is an assistant professor of marketing at the Cornell University School of Hotel Administration (rjk34@cornell.edu). This case study was written for the purposes of classroom discussion.

THE COMPETITIVE STRUCTURE
OF THE CRUISE INDUSTRY

The birth of the modern cruise industry can be traced to the 1960s, in the wake of the first Boeing 707 flight from New York to Europe in 1958.[5] With a rapidly shrinking transatlantic passenger base, opportunistic shipping companies repositioned their service from transportation to vacation travel. Companies that did not "come about" to cruising soon foundered. At the same time, lines that led the transition, such as Princess Cruises (1965), Norwegian Caribbean Line (1966, now Norwegian Cruise Line, NCL), Royal Caribbean Cruise Line (1969, now Royal Caribbean International, RCI), and Carnival Cruise Lines (1972), paced the industry. Still, the passenger base was relatively small. In 1970, only 500,000 people took a cruise.[6] A cruise was an expensive, formal, and relatively lengthy vacation—7 to 14 days on average—factors that contributed to the product's snobby image and limited appeal. That perception began to change with the 1977 launch of "The Love Boat" TV series, when cruising in all its romanticized glory was popularized to mainstream America. Since then, the industry had grown tenfold to more than 9 million passengers in 2004—an annual growth rate of 8.2 percent, making it the fastest-growing form of leisure travel.[7]

The cruise industry was still young and evolving. Whereas *luxury* brands once held sway (at least in the public's perception), less than 5 percent of current cruise capacity served this market (see Exhibit 1).[8] With the exception of Cunard's behemoth *Queen Mary 2*, luxury lines tended to use smaller ships that carried only a few hundred guests and featured exotic itineraries, gourmet dining, a relatively formal atmosphere, and attentive personal service. Not surprisingly, this attracted a refined, affluent clientele that was comfortable with paying $400 to $900 per person per day. An even smaller segment of the industry was served by *destination* or *specialty* cruise lines that sailed, for example, masted sailing vessels or replica paddle-wheeler ships for river cruises. Roughly one-third of the market, often veteran cruisers, sailed the *premium* cruise lines. These companies offered high-quality service on relatively large ships that typically accommodated 2,000 or fewer guests paying $250 to $450 per person per day. Premium-level cruises featured fine dining, a sophisticated atmosphere (though less formal than most luxury cruises), spa facilities, abundant entertainment, and a wide mix of destinations. Cruising was dominated by brands that served the "contemporary" segment, a clever label used by cruise marketers to describe the mass market. These cruise lines featured ever-larger ships that accommodated 2,000 to 3,400 guests who paid fares ranging from $150 to $300 per person per day. Although not heavy on personalized service, these floating resorts offered an abundance of good and varied food, plenty of activities to satisfy travelers' diverse interests (including shopping, gaming, sports, shows, parties, dancing, movies), and itineraries that visited popular vacation destinations. Competition for the contemporary customer was fierce, particularly between Carnival and RCI. Carnival executives argued, however, that the real competition came from outside the cruise industry in the form of land-based resorts and hotels in sightseeing destinations such as Las Vegas and Orlando.

The competitive structure in the cruise industry changed dramatically around the turn of the 21st century. Price wars and soft demand decimated the budget sector, with brands such as Regal, Premier, and Commodore—"bottom feeders" with older ships—unable to compete with the bigger brands' new ships and attractive prices. Carnival Corp. won a battle with RCI to gain ownership of Princess Cruises in 2003; just five years earlier, Carnival Corp. acquired Cunard Line in a move that sent

Exhibit 1: North American Cruise Lines and Brand Positioning

	SHIPS	DOUBLE OCCUPANCY	MARKET SHARE	MARKET POSITIONING
CARNIVAL CORPORATION				
Carnival Cruise Lines	21	47,908	24.2%	Contemporary
Princess	13	28,820	14.5%	Premium
Holland America Line	12	16,978	8.6%	Premium
Costa Cruises (U.S. market)	2	4,224	2.1%	Contemporary
Cunard Line (U.S.)	2	4,411	2.2%	Luxury
Windstar Cruises	3	604	0.3%	Destination
Yachts of Seabourn	3	624	0.3%	Luxury
TOTAL:	**56**	**103,569**	**52.2%**	
ROYAL CARIBBEAN INTERNATIONAL				
Royal Caribbean International	19	44,108	22.3%	Contemporary
Celebrity Cruises	9	16,118	8.1%	Premium
TOTAL:	**28**	**60,226**	**30.4%**	
STAR CRUISES				
Norwegian Cruise Line	9	16,734	8.4%	Contemporary
Orient Lines	1	826	0.4%	Destination
TOTAL:	**10**	**17,560**	**8.9%**	
OTHER CLIA-AFFILIATED BRANDS				
Crystal Cruises	3	2,960	1.5%	Luxury
Disney Cruise Line	2	3,508	1.8%	Contemporary
MSC Cruises	3	4,410	2.2%	Contemporary
Oceania Cruises	3	2,052	1.0%	Premium
Radisson Seven Seas Cruises	5	2,604	1.3%	Luxury
Silversea Cruises	4	1,356	0.7%	Luxury
TOTAL	**20**	**16,890**	**8.5%**	
GRAND TOTAL	**114**	**198,245**		

Source: Cruise Lines International Association, *2005 Cruise Manual*. Note: CLIA–member cruise lines comprise approximately 95 percent of the cruise capacity marketed from North America.

shockwaves throughout the industry for its symbolic significance as the venerable, upscale 150-year-old British line was scooped up by the American company powered by the Fun Ships. Whereas the cruise market in the 1970s and '80s was served by 30 brands, by 2005 only 10 brands owned by three corporations controlled 90 percent of the market. Carnival Corp. emerged as the largest cruise company in the world, with at least one brand positioned in each of the four main segments. Significantly, Carnival Corp.'s flagship brand had developed a formidable cost-leadership competitive strategy that enabled Carnival to deliver a good-value vacation that attracted price-sensitive cruisers and still produced profit margins in excess of an astonishing 25 percent.

Although Carnival's executives dismissed competitive threats from rival RCI, the two companies had waged a marketing war for years. (In the past, when Carnival and RCI ships would pass each other, RCI's cruise directors would launch a broadside: "There goes the Kmart of the Caribbean."[9]) One battleground involved an expensive game of one-upsmanship with industry "hardware," the ships themselves. The hardware competition became hot starting in 1988, when RCI launched the first purpose-built cruise "mega ship," *Sovereign of the Seas*, which carried 2,250 passengers.[10] Carnival answered in 1990 with the brand's own mega ship, the *Fantasy*, the first of eight sister ships, each carrying 2,052 guests and noted for their six-deck-high, neon-trimmed grand atriums and spiral water slides on the pool deck—both signature Carnival elements. Carnival launched the next volley in 1996 with *Carnival Destiny*, the first 100,000-ton cruise ship, which carried 2,642 guests (although it often sailed with 3,000) and featured one of the largest casinos and spa and fitness centers at sea.

In 1999, though, RCI trumped the field by launching the 137,000-ton, 3,114-passenger *Voyager of the Seas*, the first of five ships in the Voyager class. *Voyager of the Seas* featured amenities such as an ice-skating rink, inline-skating track, a basketball court, a mini-golf course, and a rock-climbing wall that traversed the back of the ship's huge funnel. The latter feature became a signature element for RCI, one that cruisers and travel agents associated with the brand, and that was later added to all the ships in its fleet. RCI also leveraged the design attributes of the new ships in the award-winning "Get Out There" promotions campaign launched in 2000. Featuring the tribal beats of the Iggy Pop song "Lust for Life," fast-paced commercials showed passengers climbing, running, skating, kayaking—but hardly cruising. The campaign was intended to reposition the brand by targeting vacationers who had an "explorer" mindset and by focusing on active and adventurous dimensions of the experience.[11] In June 2006, RCI planned to up the stakes again by launching the 158,000-ton, 3,600-passenger *Freedom of the Seas*, featuring an "aqua environment" on the top deck of the ship with a sports pool, a family water playground (with fountains, water cannons, a lazy river, and a waterfall), a wave pool for surfing, and an adults-only swimming area with hot tubs suspended more than 100 feet above the sea.[12]

Competition among cruise lines involved far more than building bigger ships. Brands jockeyed for position in the consumers' (and travel agents') perceptual space. For example, Carnival continued to emphasize its Fun Ships positioning strategy, while RCI attempted to position as a more sophisticated product. A former RCI executive drew the analogy that the brand was in the "wine and cheese" category, whereas Carnival was in the "beer and pretzels" category.[13] RCI's ship décor and overall atmosphere was described as more tasteful than Carnival's glitzy environment. Critics noted though, that with the Voyager ships ("rather like a mall with a ship built around it"), RCI and Carnival had become similar[14] (see Exhibit 2).

Cruise brands also stepped up the competition with new products and services. For example, Princess Cruises' *Caribbean Princess* sailed in April 2004 with a "Movies Under the Stars" program— the industry's first outdoor theater, with a poolside, 300-square-foot screen. (A Princess executive suggested: "This is our rock-climbing wall."[15]) Just one year later, Carnival answered with "Carnival's Seaside Theatre" on the *Carnival Liberty*.[16] NCL broke from the conventional big-ship dining model

Exhibit 2: Cruise Ship Product Comparison—Carnival and Royal Caribbean

	CARNIVAL *LIBERTY*	RCI *MARINER OF THE SEAS*
Year Built:	2005	2003
Tonnage (GRT):	110,000	142,000
Pax (basis 2):	2,974	3,114
Max Pax (inc. Uppers):	3,700	3,835
Passenger Decks:	13	15
Number of Crew:	1,150	1,185
Officers' Nationality:	Italian	Norwegian
Cruise/Hotel Staff Nationality:	International	International
Entertainment	Bars/Lounges, Casino, Disco/Nightclub, Card Room, Game Arcade, Movies	Bars/Lounges, Casino, Disco/Nightclub, Card Room, Game Arcade, Movies
Spa, Wellness, Fitness	Pool, Full-Service Spa, Sauna, Steam Room, Jacuzzi / Whirlpool, Group Fitness Classes, Weight Machines, Free Weights, Cardio Equipment, Putting Greens, Jogging Track, Volleyball, Shuffleboard, Ping-Pong, Fitness Evaluation, Personal Trainer	Pool, Full-Service Spa, Sauna, Jacuzzi / Whirlpool, Group Fitness Classes, Weight Machines, Free Weights, Cardio Equipment, Mini Golf, Basketball, Jogging Track, Shuffleboard, Scuba Instructions, Golf Simulator, Ping-Pong, Rock Climbing, Fitness Evaluation, Personal Trainer
Children/Teens	Dedicated Children's Center, Outdoor Children's Play Area, Dedicated Teen Center, Teen Programs, Children's Pool, Youth Counselor Staff, Babysitters Available	Dedicated Children's Center, Outdoor Children's Play Area, Dedicated Teen Center, Teen Programs, Children's Pool, Youth Counselor Staff, Babysitters Available
Other Facilities/Services	Elevators, ATM, Beauty Salon, Duty-free Shops, Photo-Processing Shop, Tuxedo Rental, Dry Cleaning/Laundry, Self-Service Laundromat, Concierge Desk, Infirmary/Medical Center, Safe Deposit Boxes	Elevators, ATM, Beauty Salon, Duty-free Shops, Photo-Processing Shop, Dry Cleaning/Laundry, Concierge Desk, Infirmary/Medical Center, Safe Deposit Boxes, Business Services

Source: Cruise Lines International Association, Cruise/Ships, available at: *www.cruising.org/CruiseLines*

in 2000 by introducing the "revolutionary" Freestyle Cruising concept,[17] which featured open seating in its ships' dining rooms. Instead of the traditional requirement that guests choose a dining time, Freestyle Cruising emulated land-based resorts by permitting guests to dine when and with whom they wanted. One year later, Carnival answered with Total Choice Dining, which retained traditional fixed-seating dining in the formal restaurants, but offered a choice of four rather than two dining times. This program was complemented by an array of alternative dining venues, such as specialty supper clubs that required a reservation and fee, sushi bars, and 24-hour pizzerias.[18]

Carnival executives believed that changes in the cruise product and cruise markets had blurred the distinction between brands competing in the contemporary and premium market segments. Research by industry analysts at Bear Stearns supported this view, showing that increasing similarity across brands in the design of new ships and in the services offered had made it difficult for consumers to discern differences between cruise lines.[19] As companies like Carnival and RCI continued to innovate to improve both product and service, and as premium lines like Princess and Celebrity pursued the upper end of the mass market by offering more casual vacation experiences, the markets were converging, as were customers' brand perceptions.

CARNIVAL'S FUN SHIP STRATEGY

Carnival Cruise Lines' early marketing strategy grew out of necessity. The age of the *Mardi Gras* made low fares necessary. At that time, Carnival did not have a national advertising campaign—in fact, no cruise line did. While the onboard product was limited during the lean start-up years, so were customers' expectations, because the cruise product was still relatively new. Bob Dickinson illustrated:

> *Years ago, the ship's gym was small and hidden in the bowels of the ship below the water line. You could barely find it. But nobody cared back then. If you did a vegetarian selection 30 years ago, nobody would have touched it. They wanted meat and potatoes. Everything today is much more elaborate—the fitness centers, the menus, the activities. If people want it, we'll give it to them.*

When Dickinson came on board as Carnival's vice president of sales and marketing in 1973, he set in motion the Fun Ships concept that would serve as the brand's cornerstone. Dickinson adopted the Fun Ships moniker for Carnival after seeing a brochure for the *Boheme*, which Commodore Cruise Lines promoted as the "Happy Ship." Cruise marketing at the time tended to focus on destinations, rather than the ships themselves, and promoted cruising as a high-brow, luxurious experience. Dickinson reasoned that fun was what people really sought in a vacation. By promoting the *Mardi Gras* as a fun-ship experience, Carnival would send a message that was unique in the cruise industry.[20] Perhaps more important, by anchoring the brand with the Fun Ships positioning strategy, Carnival built an unmatched value proposition on the promise of fun—a promise that would direct the company's marketing strategy for at least the next 30 years.

In contrast to the typical cruise customers, a relatively young, middle-class clientele was attracted to the Fun Ships theme. Carnival offered an entertainment experience, with the industry's first full casinos, live music, discos, and wild daytime activities—including belly-flop, beer-chugging, and hairy-chest contests—that were a complete change from the image of cruising as shuffleboard and afternoon tea.

Carnival's hardware, in particular the new ships built in the 1980s, were visual bonanzas, with bright colors and neon lighting unlike anything before seen in a cruise ship (shocking to some ship traditionalists).

Carnival pursued first-time cruisers as part of a concerted market-development strategy. To demystify cruising for the uninitiated, Carnival crafted marketing communications that articulated the Fun Ships image by showing the ships and their entertainment architecture, as well as by featuring guests dining, dancing, playing, swimming, sunning, socializing—*having fun*—at an affordable price. At the heart of the message was new company spokesperson, Kathie Lee Gifford, singing, "In the morning, in the evening, Carnival's got the fun. . . ." Carnival's commercials starring Gifford in 1984 were the first time a cruise line advertised on network television. The Carnival–Gifford relationship continued well into the mid-1990s before giving way to ad campaigns that featured the Beach Boys' tune "Fun, Fun, Fun" and the Cyndi Lauper hit "Girls Just Want to Have Fun." The marketing objective remained the same, however: to introduce vacationers to cruising and reinforce the image of Carnival as the essence of fun.

"Today's Carnival," a label that company executives used to underscore changes in the brand, was different in form, but not necessarily direction, than the Carnival of the past. Carnival's pricing continued to lead the industry, with an average price point per person per day of about $175, compared to an industry average of $235.[21] The ships and onboard product were improved.[22] Driving this change, according to Bob Dickinson, was Carnival's vision: "to consistently provide quality cruise vacations that exceed the expectations of our guests." However, the marketing department was still charged with not overpromising. Instead, Carnival's marketing communications would create reasonable guest expectations—just high enough for them to buy; the product was then designed to deliver more.

Dickinson estimated that only 16 percent of North Americans had ever taken a cruise, leaving a substantial untapped market of prospective customers. As such, Carnival continued to direct its marketing efforts at stimulating primary demand for cruising by converting land vacationers to sea vacationers. Carnival estimated that half of its guests were first-time cruisers, and one-third of repeat cruisers had never sailed Carnival before. Dickinson saw this segment of repeaters as the low-hanging fruit. Because these customers understood cruising and loved the experience, it was only necessary to talk to them about the brand. The challenge, though, was reaching these customers and with the right message. Terry Thornton, vice president of marketing planning, explained:

> We don't touch the customer or control the selling experience directly in most sales transactions—80-percent-plus come through travel agents. We still suffer from the perceptions of when our hardware was not so good and when our product had inconsistencies. Sometimes travel agents don't sell with enough frequency to really know the difference, or haven't been aboard one of our ships in years, even though we offer many opportunities for them to sample the product. Our challenge really is to get a little more credit for the product we're providing.

Carnival had a large field-sales force who called on travel agents, as well as a growing direct-sales effort that included an inbound channel (Carnival.com and 1–800-Carnival) and outbound channel of Personal Vacation Planners (PVPs) who followed up on leads obtained through the inbound channel. PVPs called or e-mailed leads to promote cruise sailings that Carnival's revenue managers identified as having soft demand. However, some people at Carnival worried that these "One-Day Only" sales sent the wrong message. Noted one manager:

> We are struggling with how we want to present the brand. This is a lovely vacation, and even though it's an entry-level product for the cruise industry, it is still expensive relative to most vacation products,

so we don't want customers to perceive our direct marketing as this used-car sales approach. We have been travel agent focused for so long. The direct access is so new to us.

Carnival was careful not to be too aggressive in its direct-sales efforts, especially in marketing to past guests who originally booked through agents. Still, the relationship between Carnival and travel agents had turbulent moments. Some agents, in particular the midsized Internet agencies, began to rebate part of their commission to customers to gain a price advantage in the market—a practice that led to channel conflict. Carnival responded with an advertised-price policy, which meant agents could no longer promote a price lower than Carnival's advertised price. Brenda Yester, vice president of revenue management, commented: "It just became dysfunctional and was degrading the brand. There has to be price integrity in the market. Consumers need to shop for a Carnival cruise and not worry about where they're buying it." Bob Dickinson added: "Many travel agents are just order takers; they are driven by price."

Carnival's target market was broad—consumers 25 to 54 years old who made $40,000 or more per year. The average age of Carnival's customer was 46—only a few years younger than the industry average.[23] Carnival's marketers believed that the product was popular with families, honeymooners, singles, and seniors. Bob Dickinson argued that demographic segmentation was irrelevant for Carnival, because there was no prototypical Carnival customer, except that person who cruised to have fun: "If you have a vacation destination that has a wide bandwidth of choice, you're casting a bigger net, and you're going to get more fish."

CARNIVAL CRUISE LINES' EVOLUTION

Maurice Zarmati, vice president of sales and one of the original employees of Carnival Cruise Lines, had seen the brand evolve considerably:

We started Carnival with one old ship. We've upgraded the product tremendously over the years. For example, we serve lobsters on all the ships at least once during a cruise. We put in alternative bistro dining, supper clubs, and complementary 24-hour cabin service. Guests can buy premium wine by the glass. Recently, we put duvets in the cabins, which would have been unheard of 10 years ago. The quality of food and service, in our estimation, is far better than our competitors. Of course, 15 years ago, our product was not at the standard that it is today....

Carnival executives pointed to inconsistent product quality as one of the blemishes on the brand in the past. Initially, secondhand ships were the issue, but even with new ships, service delivery and food quality were variable. It wasn't until the mid-1990s that Carnival began to focus on people and processes. The "Carnival College" in-house training program was started to offer crew the opportunity to enhance language and other skills. Hospitality training was also introduced to encourage crew to treat cruisers as "guests," not passengers. Terry Thornton provided these examples:

We've tried to focus training on the small things, like greeting guests. If a guest passes a crew member, the guest should be greeted. He should hear, "Good morning, how are you, how was your day at shore," things like that. When we first started this training, we measured how many greetings or similar recognition was offered out of all possible interactions, and it was less than 20 percent. Today, it's 65 to 70 percent.

Another simple service idea, which was implemented fleet-wide in 2002, involved placing mirrors in the crew areas near the exit doors, along with a sign to "Share a Smile." The idea was to remind crew to smile when interacting with guests. Thornton noted: "That's what people want today—to feel comfortable and to be recognized."

In 2005, Carnival offered its first customer-loyalty program in the form of a guest-recognition card. When guests embarked on a Carnival cruise, they received a "Sail & Sign" card that was identification for boarding the ship, a cabin key, and a credit card for purchasing almost anything onboard. The new program gave repeat Carnival cruisers a gold Sail & Sign card that would offer a way for crew members to recognize guests for their patronage and to offer more personalized attention. Bob Dickinson believed that such recognition changed the dynamics of the guest–crew interaction and provided huge "psychic income"—an "emotional stroke" for the guest and at little cost. Terry Thornton added:

The strategy is to push on the product, to continually improve it, because as people come back from their cruises, word-of-mouth promotion is getting stronger and stronger. People really are enjoying the product. Their satisfaction levels are high. They tell their travel agents and tell their friends.

Carnival executives believed that brand perceptions still lagged reality, despite their efforts to persuade consumers and travel agents that "Today's Carnival" was different than the all-out party Carnival of the past. Lingering misperceptions were partly a function of the underselling approach of brand promotion. Vicki Freed, senior vice president of sales and marketing, joined the Carnival sales team in 1978:

We used to have travel agents complain, "How come Carnival doesn't have shampoo in the bathrooms?" This amenity would have been a million-dollar upgrade. We would argue that people come with their own shampoo, but the agents would say, "Go to any hotel and you'll find complementary shampoo!" Well, they were right. The customer has changed—there's a trading-up phenomenon. Now we provide brand-name amenities, and the consumer wants brand names now.

Carnival began to investigate co-branding opportunities for the onboard product, to enhance both the guest experience and Carnival's image. Although Carnival's senior management knew that the cruise line would remain a mass-market product, there was a desire to refine the market—to "push the needle up" to a more discerning consumer. Bob Dickinson remarked:

Just as Las Vegas or Orlando have redefined themselves, we've needed to do so, too. In the early days, in product delivery and in perception, we were like Daytona Beach, Spring Break at sea: a lot of kids, unchaperoned, anything goes, beer-drinking contests, things like that. By the mid-1990s, we reengineered all that. We were the first company in the cruise business to change the drinking age from 18 to 21. We also required anyone under the age of 21 to share a cabin with someone who was at least 25. Those two actions, coupled with strengthening of our Camp Carnival children's program, created the same average age of passenger on Carnival, but the 19-year-old was replaced with a 7-year-old and an early-thirties set of parents. That was a much deeper market.

By design, the Carnival experience was casual and unintimidating rather than upscale. Although the ships had sommeliers who offered expensive wines, Carnival sold far more beer, much of it poolside at $14 for a bucket of four bottles. Though some critics said that the ships were garish, the décor was designed to be "different than people would ever see at home." Maintaining consistency of the brand message was considered vital to Carnival's success. Terry Thornton explained:

It's often misunderstood why we are who we are. And we battle ourselves sometimes. We look at our competitors and it's easy to be fooled into thinking we should be more like them. And then we say, "That's not who we are. That's not what got us here. That's not what our guests like."

Bob Dickinson elaborated:

As we build our ships and as we deal with our customers, we try very hard not to send mixed messages. We try to never use the word gourmet, *though we think our food is as good as or better than anyone else in our market, including companies on the premium end. Still, we're trying not to forget our roots.*

Carnival sought to anticipate what guests wanted in their cruise experience. Even as some things remained constant—the entertainment, casino gaming, dining choices, nightclubs, and bars—Carnival also adapted to trends, offering cigar bars, karaoke, and even airbrush tattoos. In 2005, Carnival introduced the Presidential Wine Club and hosted its first Wine Club cruise later in the year (Dickinson is a noted wine collector and connoisseur). The search for new Fun Ships ideas was an ongoing process. Still, there was the sense within the industry that RCI had grabbed Carnival's wind by launching its adventure-theme *Voyager* ships. Commented Brenda Yester:

Royal Caribbean has had a great run with the "Get Out There" campaign. But it attracts a certain kind of person who may not be attracted to Carnival. The rock-climbing wall is their icon—that's their brand. Our icon is fun—that's our brand.

Carnival was not daunted, however, as it continued to promote its augmented fun image with the biggest media buy in the company's history. With the slogan "Million Ways to Have Fun," the 2005 campaign was intended to build the brand by showcasing product enhancements.[24] New print ads targeted such publications as *Travel & Leisure, Condé Nast Traveler, Vanity Fair, People,* and *Oprah,* marking Carnival's first large-scale push into consumer magazines.

Four television commercials, featuring Bobby Darin's recording of "Somewhere Beyond the Sea," coincided with the print campaign, running on *The West Wing, The O.C., Law & Order,* and *The Amazing Race,* as well as on such cable channels as VH1, A&E, The Travel Channel, and the Food Network. The television commercials were softer, subtler, slower-paced, and more sophisticated than past Carnival ads. For example, one spot showed an older couple having breakfast on the balcony, playing golf on shore, enjoying a massage in the spa, and dancing with servers in the dining room. In another spot, a young couple jogged on the deck of a Fun Ship, worked out in the fitness center, flew on elevated cables during an adventurous canopy tour, and sampled a glass of wine at the bar. Another spot featured a family and child gliding down a Carnival waterslide and a cabin steward placing a "towel animal" on a bed. Each spot closed with a male voice-over: "On a Carnival cruise, at any one moment, there are a million ways to have fun. Carnival. The Fun Ships." Vicki Freed explained the strategy behind the new campaign:

Our other commercials didn't really sell Carnival—they sold the category. We've always taken the high road at Carnival: We'll sell the contemporary category and get our fair share because we're the big brand. But now we want to sell Today's Carnival. And that's what the new commercials hopefully convey—a little more upscale, the food, the service. It's important for us to show that we're not the Kmart of the Caribbean!

Carnival's vice president of marketing services, Christine Arnholt, who was the primary contact with the advertising agency that created the campaign, added:

One of the single most difficult things to do is change perception. Our product has changed so much! And we don't get credit for that in the marketplace. We've been incredibly successful over the years, but from a brand standpoint, there are still these lingering perceptions. Some people hear "Carnival" and think, oh, that's the party ships with all the 20-year-olds. How do you change these perceptions? After all, we are the Fun Ships. We'll always be the Fun Ships.

Underlying these concerns about brand perceptions are more fundamental questions: Who are Carnival's *core* guests, what do they want in a Fun Ship experience, and how should this customer information influence brand strategy in the future?

CASE 2   **BUILDING CAPABILITIES AT THE WESTWARD HILTON**

Sitting in the fashionable Café Lupe, an upscale restaurant owned by the company Peter Green worked for, were the company's owners, investors, and top corporate personnel. Hiller Hotels, a wholly owned subsidiary of the parent Hiller Enterprises, was headquartered in Phoenix, Arizona, with a portfolio of more than a dozen midscale and upscale hotels and three trendy, upscale restaurants. The hotel group was gathered for one of its irregular, informal celebrations of success. As Green, the executive vice president of operations, raised his glass to join in the merriment, he wondered whether his facial expression gave away the feelings he was suppressing. Green was torn—earlier in the day this same group discussed the possibility that the Westward Hilton and Towers, the only property in the Hiller portfolio he had personally ever run as a general manager, might be sold. An inquiry from a REIT (real estate investment trust[1]) as to the property's availability had prompted the discussion.

The Hiller Hotels subsidiary owned and managed all of its hotels, branding them with a variety of different midpriced and upper-priced hotel franchisers. The portfolio had grown over a 12-year period to around a dozen properties at any given time. The number wasn't stable because the corporate strategy was to take advantage of opportunities to buy undervalued, underperforming properties and turn them around. Each hotel was operated as a fully self-sufficient operation. When the opportunity to sell a property at a healthy profit presented itself, Hiller's management team had, in the past, generally taken advantage of the market opportunity. With the exception of a second Phoenix property managed as an independent (unbranded) hotel and acquired in 2006 to be the group's flagship, no property was supposed to be untouchable. Perhaps coincidentally, since Green had moved into his corporate position back in 2004, only one Hiller property had been sold. The portfolio had remained relatively stable, and its owners or investors had never broached selling the Westward. The investors were reaping healthy benefits from the portfolio.

Green knew that Karen Connor, whose money was behind Hiller Hotels, felt as strongly about the Westward and the people who worked there as he did. Connor owned the largest share of Hiller Hotels, as well as a major share of the parent company. Her visibility in the local community as a patron of the arts and civic leader was legendary. While Connor was attached to the Westward, Green also understood that it was impossible for every decision to equally benefit owners, customers, and employees. He knew there were times when decisions would have an obvious ill effect on one group of stakeholders. Was the possible sale of the Westward Hotel one of those decisions? Was he too attached to this particular hotel because he had been its general manager when Hiller bought it out of bankruptcy at the end of 2000? Green's thoughts drifted back nearly 10 years to the year before he arrived in Phoenix.

Written by Cathy A. Enz of Cornell University, David L. Corsun of the University of Denver, and Linda Canina of Cornell University. The case study is adapted from a case written by the authors and published in Case Research Journal. *The names of the organization and its members have been disguised at the request of the owners and investors. The affiliation with the Hilton Brand was not altered.*

PROJECT PERSPECTIVE

Peter Green grew up in the hospitality industry. He worked as a teen in his family's restaurant in Buffalo, New York. Through his twenties and thirties, Green used his restaurant experience to move into the hotel side of the industry, starting out in the food and beverage area. Over the course of about 20 years, he worked his way across the eastern half of the country, gaining the experience required to be a hotel general manager (GM). Prior to joining Hiller, Green had more than five years of experience as a GM. When Hiller hired Green in 2000, he was brought on in a consulting role. Specifically, Green did project work for Hiller in the Midwest, solving previously identified business problems.

Project work gave him an opportunity to view an operation from a very different vantage point from when he was a GM. Being removed from the day-to-day operation, Green was able to see aspects of the business that might be less clear to the manager, who was occupied with running the entire operation. The short-term nature of his project assignments and their focus on specific problems with everything else removed from consideration allowed Green the liberty of a broader, big-picture perspective. He attributed two previous projects and experiences to radically shaping his feelings about the business when he entered the Westward.

The first project was a small Chicago hotel in which the employees were considering unionization. When Green arrived, he found an all-white management staff and an almost all-black employee population and no interaction between the two groups. On his first visit, he went to the cafeteria and listened to employees. Through informal conversations, he learned which issues bothered the employees. The problems were mostly small things, like the quality of employee meals, that could easily be remedied. However, the senior management of the hotel was unaware of these employee issues, because they had separated themselves from employees and formed a tightly knit group. The management never ate in the employee cafeteria and spent very little time in communication with the staff. Green did not make radical changes at this hotel, but he did listen carefully to the employees and spent time with them. In describing this experience, Green said it "taught me that managers devalue others when they overvalue themselves. I discovered the importance of creating a work environment that celebrates, nurtures, and values people. It is important to create a business environment in which every job and every employee is treated with dignity and respect. People want to care, but this work environment forced the workers to hide themselves."

The impact the work environment has on the individual came home to Green one evening when he drove past a schoolyard and spotted one of the hotel's employees playing basketball. As he watched the game, he noticed that this worker, whom Green knew to be slow, uncooperative, and lacking initiative at work, was leading a group of his friends in a fast-paced and cooperative team effort. Green wondered how this person could be so different outside the workplace. Perhaps, he thought, it's because the work environment doesn't give the worker permission to be himself. This thought stuck with Green. Before he left this hotel several months later, new management had been brought in, and the union drive was defeated by a vote of 72–2. Green elected to move on rather than serve as the new general manager, although the job was offered to him.

Green's second experience taught him to truly value the guests' perspective and experiences. Living for 90 days in a hotel plagued with quality problems, Green was a guest of sorts himself, and he spoke with other guests daily. During this assignment, he rediscovered what he knew from childhood about committing to the satisfaction of the guest: "I grew up in the restaurant business, and my parents taught me to be close to the customer. It seems that when you become a manager, you start to focus on how to manage versus how to live a commitment to customers." Rather than viewing guest concerns as problems, he discovered through interaction with customers that one could trust their experiences and get something valuable and satisfying from responding to their concerns. He also noticed that most customers were present in the hotel at very specific times in the morning and evening, and these were the times it was most important for the manager to be available to talk with guests. An everyday commitment to listening to guests was one powerful way of committing to their satisfaction.

These projects gave Green a new way of thinking and feeling about the hotel business. He began to feel his way toward a new management philosophy, but the quality of his personal life was suffering. After a year of living on the road and away from his family, Green wanted a stable position. However, to become a general manager again was not very appealing to him. As a GM, he had grown tired of the frustrations that came with the job. He was tired of the long hours, the constant people problems, and the cyclical nature of the business. In bad times, even when he worked very hard, the overleveraged and overbuilt industry had conspired to make him feel bad about his performance. The main people problems were high turnover and a lack of commitment from staff, who were not invested in what they were doing. He had felt frustration at his inability to get employees excited or committed in the past. Green learned a great deal from the project work that occupied his time, and he also knew he needed to make a change. His children and his wife needed him to be more present in their lives too.

ARRIVING AT THE WESTWARD

The Westward Hilton was bought out of bankruptcy when the previous owner was forced to sell the property. For nearly five years, the hotel had been operating at a loss, and the property and the people who worked in it were depressed. The physical plant was in bad shape, and no capital had been devoted to renovation and upkeep. When Hiller purchased the hotel, Green was given the opportunity to become the Westward's general manager. Mostly because of his desire to settle in one place for a while, he took the assignment. Green also thought he might take advantage of this opportunity to put his evolving management philosophy into practice.

During his first visit to the hotel—prior to becoming GM—none of the managers greeted him. Green was placed in a Towers level suite (one of the three floors of rooms with a private concierge and other special services) with "a lot of stuff." He got chocolates, cheese, and a vast array of amenities, but not a note or phone call from the management. His first impression was that the management of the hotel was not sensitive to what the guest might want, but had automatically assumed that more amenities in the sleeping room would satisfy the customer. "They were thinking more and more stuff rather than sincere and genuine care." Green observed that the Westward's management had a traditional command-and-control style. In addition, their beliefs statement was borrowed from Ritz Carlton Hotels, a chain of highly regarded luxury hotels (see Exhibit 1). In Green's opinion, the hotel was trying to be something it was not, and the beliefs were not genuine.

Green arrived at the Westward with a deep belief that all hotel companies and their managers have a moral obligation to make the work experience a positive one. Throughout his career, he had

Exhibit 1: The Ritz Carlton Gold Standards

THE CREDO

The Ritz-Carlton Hotel is a place where the genuine care and comfort of our guests is our highest mission. We pledge to provide the finest personal service and facilities for our guests who will always enjoy a warm, relaxed, yet refined ambiance. The Ritz-Carlton experience enlivens the senses, instills well-being, and fulfills even the unexpressed wishes and needs of our guests.

MOTTO

We are Ladies and Gentlemen serving Ladies and Gentlemen.

Source: Ritz–Carlton information that is printed by corporate headquarters on a small, laminated card that can be folded and placed in a wallet.

experienced the dark side of the hotel business, in which generations of negative conditioning and abusive behaviors justified managers' willingness to undervalue the people who clean rooms and sweep floors for a living. The managers in Chicago reminded him by their bad example that he must break down these beliefs. Deep inside, after years of experience in the business, he was convinced that caring about employees could be profitable. He said, "I didn't arrive at the Westward with a strategic plan, just a new feeling. My project work taught me to get close to the customer and value the employees. I was determined to start by making a real emotional commitment to the hotel."

THE WESTWARD HILTON AND TOWERS

The Westward Hilton was a 13-story, full-service hotel built in 1992. The hotel tower and attached lobby sat on 8.5 acres on a city block at the southeast corner of Camelback Drive and Northern Avenue in Central Phoenix. The hotel contained approximately 151,000 square feet, occupied by 300 guest rooms, board and conference rooms, executive offices, a fitness center, and the main lobby area. The exterior of the hotel was reflective glass over a structural steel frame. The main lobby area was situated in a single-story, attached building that included the main entrance to the hotel, reception desk, guest services area, a lobby lounge, and a gift shop.

After several years of Hiller's ownership, and substantial renovations, the hotel had 13,000 square feet of flexible meeting space, including 14 salons and three ballrooms. The gift shop was leased month-to-month to a third party. The hotel also included a freestanding 8,000-square-foot restaurant. The interior finish of the lobby area primarily consisted of inlaid terrazzo pavers, a combination of painted drywall and vinyl wall coverings, and recessed and track incandescent lighting. A landscaped courtyard led to the Hilton's outdoor pool, hot tub, and sun deck. Directly off the lobby was a bright and airy Southwestern-style atrium finished in rich earth tones.

Each guest room included a full bath, a king or two queen beds, a chaise lounge and ottoman, a work desk, an armoire, one or two nightstands, and three or four lamps. The standard guest rooms featured 24-hour in-room dining, free cable channels with HBO, a coffee/tea maker, minibar, alarm clock radio, card key access, PC phone line, modem hookup, oversized desk, and complimentary newspaper. Executive business rooms also included a fax/copier machine, inkjet printer, VCR, two private phone lines with speakerphone, and a calculator. The top three Towers floors offered a complimentary Continental breakfast buffet every morning, hors d'oeuvres every evening, exclusive registration and checkout, business services, a cocktail honor bar, and video phone. Morning and evening maid service and nightly turndown service were also provided on these floors.

THE VISION THING

"What does this hotel want to be?" was a critical question for Green. He felt the previous management tried to make the hotel something it was not. But what was this hotel to become? This was clearly a critical question. By imitating the Malcolm Baldrige Award–winning Ritz Carlton Hotels' beliefs, the previous management was not focused on how to position this hotel. For Green's first three or four months, during their meetings, the managers talked unendingly about the successful large convention hotel across the street. This hotel had a lounge and a constant flow of leisure and convention customers. The conversations all seemed to be variations of a "Gee, if we were only like them" theme.

Finally, Green had enough. The turning point came in one staff meeting when he told his staff the following:

Let's not focus on what we are not. Focus on what we are. We don't have to be that hotel. Let's stop wishing we were that and start being this. Look, we are a small hotel—we don't want lots of groups. We should be providing a different product and service to a different customer. Look at all the problems they have. It is a noisy hotel with long lines. Do we want that? No! We can become the number-one corporate FIT (frequent individual traveler) hotel in Phoenix. We are a small hotel, we can be warm and friendly, let's use what we have and make it work. Stop focusing on them. Focus on what we are and what we can become. We are going to take the high-end guest, focus on the FIT through uncompromising superior quality and extraordinary service. We are going to actively listen to guests and employees, anticipate market needs, liberate ourselves from old ways of doing things, and provide a wonderful employee experience.

The job of envisioning a new future for this hotel was made possible by years of capital investments and support from the new owners. Capital was needed to position the hotel above the competition. The repositioning would not have been possible if Hiller's owners had not been willing to invest in fully renovating the hotel with a clean, modern, and comfortable look. Exhibit 2 provides a summary of the capital improvement costs.

The restaurant was redesigned and reconstructed in 2003, three years after the hotel's purchase. The renovation was done at a cost of $2,200,000 (including furniture, fixtures, and equipment). It was expanded from its original structure and leased to an independent restaurant group that raised the visibility and prestige of the food and beverage operation. Green believed the restaurant operation was a powerful tool in repositioning the hotel.

The equal value and appreciation of the interests and needs of owners, customers, and employees was the foundation for the vision creation process, according to Green. Uninterrupted owner support,

Exhibit 2: Renovation and Capital Improvements

YEAR	CAPITAL IMPROVEMENT COSTS
2002	$5,225,622
2003	$3,399,842
2004	$1,260,606

continued affiliation with a well-regarded hotel brand like Hilton, and management with a commitment to guest, employee, and owner satisfaction were essential.

The vision emerged in discussion with the senior management staff, but was not written down initially. According to Green, it was a change in thinking, first and foremost:

> *We were going to become the best corporate hotel positioned at the top end, but I approached this vision by doing three things: living my values, constantly talking about our vision, and modeling the vision every day. The plan was shockingly devoid of systems or procedures. I felt it and was deeply into it. The hotel needed an identity in the minds of the employees, and my job was to bring a deep belief in what this hotel could become to these people. Leadership in my opinion is about believing so deeply that people don't doubt. I was more a Civil War leader than a World War II general. My agenda? Focus and model, focus and model. I just did what seemed right at the time.*

Green's vision of what the Westward aspired to become was the precursor to the formal corporate vision of Hiller Hotels and the foundation for the guiding principles that would follow. It was not until 2007, almost six years later and well into Green's tenure as corporate executive vice president of operations, that he formally fashioned the set of guiding principles that explicitly conveyed the essence of Hiller Hotels and the Westward Hilton. The principles were taught companywide. Managers, upon completing their initial training and orientation, were given a daily planner with a 22-page insert titled "Our Daily Compass: Hiller Hotels, Inc. Guide to Leadership and Management." Among other things, including the corporate vision and mission, the insert included the following guiding principles:

1. Dignity—We value everyone equally and highly.
2. Values—We insist that values like honesty, trust, integrity, respect, and fairness determine our decisions.
3. Focus—We establish priorities and concentrate on doing the most important things first.
4. Achievement—We all give our best effort to ensure team success.
5. Balance—We strive to maintain a balance among employees, customers, and owners.

Back in 2001, Green also arrived at the simple statement, *the friendliest place to visit.* This was a vision that remained with him and came to guide all of the hotels in the portfolio. Green explained the meaning of the vision as follows:

> *In the future, our customers and peers will say that we are the friendliest place to visit. The relationship between our employees and our guests should resemble that of the relationship between two*

friends; this is the hospitality experience we wish to provide. We will achieve this vision when the cus-tomer experiences a total commitment from all of us to the friendliest customer service anywhere.

The mission statement, which followed from the vision, was captured in the phrase "Making people's lives better through business." Green noted that:

We will achieve our vision by making our employees', customers', and owners' lives better.
Employees' lives are made better by treating them with dignity, rewarding and recognizing their contri-butions to our success, and providing a safe, secure, flexible, and fun working environment. Customers'
lives are made better by providing a safe environment, excellent service, friendliness, and that extra
thoughtfulness that makes visiting the Westward like visiting a friend. Finally, we make our owners'
lives better by ensuring that the hotel is a leader in return on investment, [a] positive influence on the
local community, and successful on a long-term basis. We aspire to be a role model for other companies
in the service industry: admired for the support we provide to our employees, the friendly experience we
provide to our customers, and the exceptional rewards and satisfaction we provide to our owners.

Green was determined that his vision would become more than the GM's platitudes, neither acted on by subordinates nor lived by the executive in charge. He wanted to live his principles and pass them on to his management team to help guide their actions. It was his desire that all employ-ees of the Westward share the vision, mission, and principles. He wanted to make being a part of the Westward Hilton a different work experience. For Green, the mutual success of owners and employees depended on the acceptance and practice of the vision. But Green knew that good practice required more than inspiration; it required good strategic thinking.

STRATEGIC PLANNING

"What's possible?" is the question Green used to guide the strategic planning process. He insisted that the major issue for strategic thinking was to focus on what could be. "Identifying and removing the barriers between what is and what's possible" is how he proceeded to develop the plan.

Our strategic plan allowed us to dream, ponder, and wonder what could be. Most planning is from
today forward in a process of increases over a five-year period to get to a point. This is "present-
forward" thinking. In this approach you rely on "the plan" and history to drive your thinking.

In contrast, Green introduced a future-backward thinking approach in which one creates an almost impossible future position and determines what needs to be done to achieve this target.

Our strategic planning forced us to change our operation by setting objectives that seemed impossible.
By thinking about the future and backing into implementation, it was quite clear that we couldn't
get to what is possible by doing what we already were. Future-backward thinking forced the staff to
rethink what they do. This approach could easily backfire if failure to reach the target resulted in get-
ting the crap kicked out of you. Trust was critical and made possible by having all targets and incen-
tives at levels below the strategic plan.

Green did not confuse strategic planning with making budget. There was no penalty for failure.

Sure, there was tension. We wanted to create that. It's okay if they felt like they failed. It's not okay if they felt I felt like they failed. The difference is important. We seduced them into a future, but not at their expense.

Green willingly admitted that he had no idea of how to get the hotel to the possible targets. "All I knew is that we could only achieve these targets if we became more skilled and did things differently."

Reports, forecasts, and analysis were the hallmarks of this strategic thinking system. In housekeeping, for example, daily labor costs were tracked, and scheduling of labor was carefully synchronized with forecasts. To produce loyalty and retention, revenue information was assembled on customer segments, and product/service offerings were bundled to provide a carefully targeted customer with the products she or he desired. Green did not believe in yield management, a system in which pricing is adjusted based on projected occupancy and proximity to the desired reservation date in order to fill the hotel. He believed in establishing relationships with guests and focusing on rates that were consistent and of high value.

After setting a vision and defining the target guest, the Westward's business mix changed with a decrease in group business and an increase in the business transient segment. Mini profit-and-loss statements were created for each department so they could keep track of expenses as each day passed. Green believed that daily accountability versus monthly accountability was a key to enabling the staff to carefully and intelligently manage the business.

CLOSE TO THE CUSTOMER

Even five years later, many employees remembered Green for his vigilance—standing in the lobby Monday through Friday from 7:00 A.M. to 9:00 A.M. when most customers entered or exited the hotel. During his ten-hour-a-week commitment to being close to the customer, he saw and solved problems. Green talked with guests and got a feel for what was and what was not working.

If three or four guests mentioned they didn't get a wake-up call, we could locate and solve that problem quickly. If people needed their bags carried in or employees needed a hand in performing a job, I was there to help. My job was to expedite, to help both employees and customers.

Green accomplished two things by hanging out in the lobby: (1) he had the contact with the customer he so valued and believed in, and (2) he modeled the commitment to guest satisfaction. He also showed employees that he would and could do their jobs and that he was there to help them.

I decided when I arrived at the Westward that I was willing to invest 10 hours of my 50 to 60 hours per week to contact with the guests. The key job of a manager is to lead, to set an example, and to focus on real problems and activities.

Green's actions were important, but getting others to live the vision required improving business practices too. He started by taking the customer comment card questions provided by the corporate staff of Hilton and using them somewhat differently. At the time, the typical approach in the industry was to have customer comment cards in the sleeping rooms, and few customers ever responded. When customers did respond, the hotel or guest mailed the cards directly to the brand's corporate headquarters, where the corporate staff provided a tracking service as part of the fees attached to brand affiliation. Problem issues were then identified, and monthly or quarterly reports were passed back to the GM, management company, or owners of an individual hotel. General managers then chose to send a letter or call the dissatisfied customer and apologize or offer some form of service recovery. Some hotel chains responded from the corporate headquarters, and the individual hotels never received the comment card information.

At the Westward, Green made small but significant modifications in the existing system. First, customers were asked to complete the cards at checkout, substantially increasing the completed responses from 2 to 3 percent when he became GM to 75 percent of all guests. A core of 40 questions was put into 10 sets of four questions, with one set per comment card. The cards were randomly distributed so all 40 questions were responded to by multiple guests. Because they included only four questions, scored on a seven-point scale where 1 = poor and 7 = excellent, the guests completed the cards in 10 to 15 seconds while waiting for their folios to print. The cards were then entered and tracked through the property management system, and reports were created daily. The customer tracking report was provided to management, but also posted in the employee gathering places for all employees to view. A sample of the Daily Guest Comment Report is shown in Exhibit 3. Daily huddles, or brief five- to ten-minute meetings at the beginning or end of a shift, were used to share the survey results with employees. As Green noted:

We had been doing the survey for some time, but didn't realize the quantum improvement in the guest experience until we began sharing the guests' feedback with the people who were actually doing the work. Once we started showing people the results of the survey, they started making changes on their own. The improved scores were a direct reflection of team performance, and they all wanted to succeed. The sharing of information tapped into the employees' basic desire to be whole and good. They wanted to fill the gap, and we did not need a program or process. It was magic. We gave people the information they needed to know, and they did what needed to be done. There was no structure or guide. Just a belief that you give people information and they will set about fixing the problems. People love to close gaps. Evidence of our success lies in the data—96 percent of the guests indicated their intent to return, and the repeat rate was 50 percent.

VALUING OTHERS

Green stated:

Another strong, powerful part of our management philosophy was that you need to be willing to do what you ask of others. You can't expect the people to care anymore than you do. People watch what you do. You lose ground if people can't trust you.

Green spent plenty of his time in the employee cafeteria and in the lobby with customers. These were lessons that his project days had brought home, and he put his learning to the test in his own

Exhibit 3: Guest Comment Daily Report

TODAY'S PERFORMANCE METRICS		PERIOD TO DATE (PTD) PERFORMANCE	
TODAY'S % CARDS/W RM#S = 45.6%		PTD CHECK CUT = 1401	
TODAY'S CHECK OUT = 68		PTD TOTAL CARDS = 549	
TODAY'S TOTAL CARDS = 35		PTD % OF RETURN = 39.2%	
TODAY'S % OF RETURN = 51.5%		PTD RIO CHARGES = 23249	
TODAY'S RIO CHARGES = 1384		PTD RIO PER OCC RM $3.70	
TODAY'S RIO PER OCC ROOM = $4.86			

RETURN AGAIN AS %	TODAY'S TOTAL SCORE	PTD TOTAL SCORE 94·92%	GOAL	DIFFERENCE
CRITICAL SERVICES				
OVERALL RESPONSIVENESS	6.36	6.48	6.50	(0.02)
WILL RETURN AGAIN	6.54	6.64	6.50	0.14
RATE THIS HILTON OVERALL	6.48	6.26	6.5	(0.24)
FRIENDLINESS				
RECEPTION STAFF FRIENDLINESS	6.57	6.51	6.50	0.01
DEPARTURE DESK FRIENDLINESS	NA	6.75	6.50	0.25
LOBBY LOUNGE FRIENDLINESS	4.00	6.19	6.50	(0.31)
OPERATOR FRIENDLINESS	6.50	6.48	6.50	(0.03)
ROOM SERVICE FRIENDLINESS	7.00	6.60	6.50	0.10
BANQUET FRIENDLINESS	NA	6.52	6.50	0.02
TTL	6.25	6.52	6.50	0.02

CAFE TIJERA RESTAURANT			
DINING EXPERIENCE	6.00	6.50	5.96	(0.54)
BREAKFAST F&B QUALITY	NA	6.50	6.27	(0.23)
BREAKFAST STAFF SERVICE	5.50	6.50	5.78	(0.72)
DINNER STAFF SERVICE	6.00	6.50	6.10	(0.40)
DINNER F&B SERVICE	6.67	6.50	6.00	(0.50)
TTL	6.14	6.50	6.03	(0.47)
ROOM SERVICE			
PROMPT SERVICE	7.00	6.50	6.09	(0.41)
FRIENDLY SERVICE	7.00	6.50	6.60	0.10
FOOD-BEVERAGE QUALITY	7.00	6.50	6.44	(0.06)
OVERALL EXPERIENCE	5.83	6.50	6.18	(0.33)
TTL	6.30	6.50	6.33	(0.17)
BANQUET EVENT			
PROMPT SERVICE	6.80	6.50	6.55	0.05
FRIENDLY SERVICE	NA	6.50	6.52	0.02
FOOD-BEVERAGE QUALITY	6.00	6.50	6.27	(0.23)
TTL	6.50	6.50	6.43	(0.07)
TOWERS			
WILL RETURN AGAIN	NA	6.50	NA	NA
TOWERS LOUNGE OVERALL	NA	6.50	6.61	0.11
TTL	NA	6.50	6.61	0.11

Exhibit 3: Guest Comment Daily Report (*Continued*)

RETURN AGAIN AS %	TODAY'S TOTAL SCORE	PTD TOTAL SCORE 94.92%	GOAL	DIFFERENCE
LOBBY BAR				
PROMPT SERVICE	6.33	6.37	6.50	(0.13)
COMFORT & DÉCOR	NA	6.11	6.50	(0.39)
LOBBY STAFF FRIENDLINESS	4.00	6.19	6.50	(0.31)
TTL	5.40	6.22	6.50	(0.28)
RECEPTION				
RECEPTION STAFF FRIENDLINESS	6.57	6.51	6.50	0.01
CHECK-IN EFFICIENCY	6.33	6.45	6.50	(0.05)
DOOR/BELL STAFF ASSISTANCE	NA	6.45	6.50	(0.05)
TTL	6.50	6.47	6.50	(0.03)
DEPARTURE				
FRONT DESK FRIENDLINESS	NA	6.75	6.50	0.25
CHECK-OUT EFFICIENCY	7.00	6.77	6.50	0.27
BELL STAFF PROMPTNESS	6.75	6.52	6.50	0.02
TTL	6.80	6.68	6.50	0.18
SERVICES				
TELE OPERATOR FRIENDLINESS	6.50	6.48	6.50	(0.03)
MAIL-MESSAGE DELIVERY	6.00	6.46	6.50	(0.04)
LAUNDRY-DRY CLEANING	7.00	6.70	6.50	0.20

FITNESS CENTER	7.00	6.05	6.50	(0.45)
TTL	6.50	6.41	6.50	(0.09)
ACCOMMODATIONS				
ROOM CLEANLINESS	5.67	6.45	6.50	(0.05)
ROOM COMFORT & DECOR	6.00	6.61	6.50	0.11
ROOM TV-RADIO QUALITY	6.33	6.09	6.50	(0.41)
PRICE/VALUE OF ROOM	5.00	6.33	6.50	(0.17)
TTL	5.75	6.39	6.50	(0.11)
BATHROOM				
BATHROOM CLEANLINESS	6.25	6.51	6.50	0.01
BATHROOM AMENITIES	7.00	6.48	6.50	(0.02)
PUBLIC BATHROOM CLEANLINESS	6.00	6.38	6.50	(0.12)
TTL	6.29	6.47	6.50	(0.03)
EFFICIENCY				
CHECK-IN EFFICIENCY	6.33	6.45	6.50	(0.05)
CHECK-OUT EFFICIENCY	7.00	6.77	6.50	0.27
TTL	6.50	6.61	6.50	0.11
TOTAL OVERALL REPORT w/o Rio	**6.38**	**6.47**	**6.50**	**(0.03)**
TOTAL OVERALL REPORT	**6.37**	**6.44**	**6.50**	**(0.06)**

NA = Not Available

Exhibit 3: Guest Comment Daily Report (*Continued*)

TOTAL OCCUPIED ROOMS	= 285
CALCARDS WITH ROOM #'s	= 31
TODAY'S CHECK OUT	= 68
TODAY'S TOTAL CARDS	= 35
TODAY'S % OF RETURN	= 51.37%
TOTAL % CARDS W/RM #'s	= 45.59%
TOTAL CAFE TIJERA CHANGES	= 1383.88

	TODAY'S TOTAL COMMENT	1	2	3	4	5	6	7	TODAY'S TOTAL POINTS	TODAY'S SCORE	PTD TOTAL POINTS	PTD TOTAL SCORE	PTD TOTAL COMMENT
EFFICIENT CHECK-IN	3					1		2	19	6.33	303.00	6.45	47
GUEST RM COMFORT & DÉCOR	3					1	1	1	18	6.00	304.00	6.61	46
EXP. OF ROOM FOR PRICE PAID	3				1	1	1		15	5.00	285.00	6.33	45
OVERALL DINING EXP. AT CAFE TIJERA	1						1		6	6.00	143.00	5.96	24
OVERALL RESPONSIVENESS TO NEEDS	11				1		4	6	70	6.36	1433.00	6.48	221
EFFICIENT ROOM SERVICE DELIVERY	1							1	7	7.00	201.00	6.09	33
TV PROG/RECEPTION QUALITY	3						2	1	19	6.33	286.00	6.09	47
BANQUET STAFF FRIENDLINESS	0								0	NA	137.00	6.52	21
RM SERVICE STAFF FRIENDLINESS	1		1					1	7	7.00	264.00	6.60	40
BATHROOM AMENITIES & TOWELS	1							1	7	7.00	311.00	6.48	48
EFFICIENT CHECK-OUT	1							1	7	7.00	318.00	6.77	47
GUEST ROOM CLEANLINESS	3			1				2	17	5.67	613.00	6.45	95
CAFE TIJERA DINNER STAFF SERVICE	1						1		6	6.00	177.00	6.10	29

LOBBY LOUNGE STAFF FRIENDLINESS	2						1	8	4.00	198.00	6.19	32
GUEST ROOM BATH CLEANLINESS	4					3		25	6.25	332.00	6.51	51
ROOM SERVICE F&B QUALITY	2						2	14	7.00	218.00	6.44	34
LOBBY LOUNGE STAFF PROMPTNESS	3				2		1	19	6.33	242.00	6.37	38
RATE THIS HILTON ON OVERALL BASIS	21			3	5	13		136	6.48	1686.00	6.26	289
ARRIVAL-FRONT DESK FRIENDLINESS	7		1			6		46	6.57	384.00	6.51	59
OVERALL ROOM SERVICE EXPERIENCE	6		1			4		35	5.83	247.00	6.18	40
BANQUET STAFF RESPONSIVENESS	5				1		4	34	6.60	144.00	6.55	22
FITNESS CENTER	2					2		14	7.00	116.00	6.05	19
TELEPHONE OPERATOR FRIENDLINESS	6			1	1	4		39	6.50	259.00	6.48	40
MAIL/MESSAGE DELIVERY	4			1	2	1		24	6.00	181.00	6.46	28
CAFE TIJERA BREAKFAST F&B QUALITY	0							0	NA	163.00	6.27	26
DEPARTURE - FRONT DESK FRIENDLINESS	0							0	NA	297.00	6.75	44
PUBLIC BATHROOM CLEANLINESS	2					1	1	12	6.00	217.00	6.38	34
BANQUET F&B QUALITY	3					1	1	16	6.00	163.00	6.27	26
CAFE TIJERA BREAKFAST STAFF SERVICE	2					1	1	11	5.50	133.00	5.78	23
LAUNDRY/DRY CLEANING SERVICES	2				2		2	14	7.00	67.00	6.70	10
CAFE TIJERA DINNER F&B QUALITY	3				1	2		20	6.67	192.00	6.00	32
DEPARTURE-PROMPT BELLMAN ASSIST.	4			1	3			27	6.75	274.00	6.52	42
ARRIVAL-PROMPT BELLMAN ASSIST.	0				3			0	NA	213.00	6.45	33
LOBBY COMFORT & DÉCOR	0							0	NA	275.00	6.11	45
TOWERS LOUNGE OVERALL	0							0	NA	238.00	6.61	36
LIKELIHOOD YOU WILL RETURN	35		1	2	8	24		229	6.54	3641.00	6.64	548
TOTALS WITHOUT CAFE TIJERA	138	0	1	3	4	33	85	880	6.38	13846	6.47	2140

NA = Not Available

hotel. Green's human resource approach was deeply rooted in his belief in the dignity of all employees regardless of position or background. In describing his approach, he said:

Human dignity was the most important principle for managing. My philosophy was that everyone must be treated with respect and given opportunities to learn and grow. A manager's highest priority is to treat her or his employees with dignity. Employees, customers, and owners are all linked together, and excellent service and exceptional facilities are essential to compete, but something more is required to truly win. That something extra is the realization that keeping the customer is entirely in the hands of the employees. Each job and task and each person in the hotel is important and deserving of respect. I believe in nurturing the entrepreneurial spirit in everyone —whether the general manager, valet attendant, kitchen steward, or front desk. All people in the workplace perform better when treated with dignity.

Green realized that in the Phoenix market, good service and quality facilities were a minimum expectation of customers. Excellent service was taken for granted, and the competition could deliver just as easily as the Westward could. Given this competitive environment, the question was, what could the Westward do to attract and retain customers over time? For Green, the answer was to build a strong system of rewards for the employees. "The opportunity for advancement and bettering oneself must be available to each employee. Satisfied employees create satisfied guests, and satisfied guests return and remain loyal."

The philosophy behind the design of the wage and benefit system fit with Green's notion that dignity was important. He said:

Wages had to be competitive and fair, but based on the position held, not seniority. We surveyed the market to determine what fair and competitive wage rates should be. By doing job analysis, we determined the worth of each position and then compensated on the worth of the job. I don't believe in individual performance-based pay because I can't figure out how to accurately measure individual performance. I'm better off not trying to reward performance when there is no good way to measure it. That's why all merit pay was based on the performance of the hotel.

Fifty percent of employee bonuses were tied to customer comment scores. In a simple and understandable bonus system, managers as well as hourly employees, both part-time and full-time, received quarterly bonuses based on customer scores, house profit, and employee turnover.

The details of the bonus plan are shown in Exhibit 4. "Performance appraisal was separate from salary review," Green said. "Discussion of pay and performance together is confusing. Instead, we used performance appraisals to discuss future development and acknowledge contributions."

SELECTION, ORIENTATION, AND TRAINING

Green felt that getting the right people for the Westward culture was the key to implementing the hotel's vision, but an intuitive and values-based process was required.

Exhibit 4: Hiller Hotels Inc. Quarterly Bonus Program for the Westward Hilton

All employees are eligible unless they have had written disciplinary action during the quarter. You must be employed at the end of the quarter to be eligible for a bonus. The base salary on the attached schedule will be used, for any vacant positions, in determining bonuses. Employees hired during the quarter will receive a pro-rated bonus based on the following:

Hired any time during the first month of the quarter 66%

Hired any time during the second month of the quarter 33%

Hired any time during the last month of the quarter 0%

"Bonus Quarters" are as follows:

1st Quarter	December, January, February
2nd Quarter	March, April, May
3rd Quarter	June, July, August
4th Quarter	September, October, November

This is an optional program designed to reward employees for performance above the average. This program may be altered or discontinued at any time at the sole discretion of Hiller Hotels, Inc.

A prerequisite to payment of any bonuses will be the achievement of at least the minimum/maximum levels stated below for all three criteria as follows. Budgeted house profit may be adjusted from published numbers to compensate for unusual or unbudgeted events or material time differences.

	MIN/MAX
Employee turnover (annualized)	37.3%
Customer comment card score	6.25
House profit—1st quarter	$1,380,000
2nd quarter	$1,680,000
3rd quarter	$1,440,000
4th quarter	$1,500,000

Exhibit 4: (*Continued*)

Quarterly bonuses are based on the Hiller triangle as follows:

TRIANGLE STAKEHOLDER	MEASUREMENT
Employee	Employee turnover during the quarter, annualized
Customer	Customer comment card quarterly weighted average score
Owner	House profit

Year 6 Quarterly Bonus Program
Westward Hilton—General Manager

The criteria for receiving bonuses will be as follows:

	LEVEL 1	LEVEL 2	LEVEL 3	LEVEL 4
Employee turnover (annualized)	34.8%	32.3%	29.8%	27.3%
Customer comment card score	6.30	6.35	6.40	6.45
House Profit—1st quarter	$1,430,000	$1,480,000	$1,530,000	$1,580,000
2nd quarter	$1,730,000	$1,780,000	$1,830,000	$1,880,000
3rd quarter	$1,490,000	$1,540,000	$1,590,000	$1,640,000
4th quarter	$1,550,000	$1,600,000	$1,650,000	$1,700,000

The basis for calculation of the bonus will be a percentage of the employee's quarterly base salary as follows:

	LEVEL 1	LEVEL 2	LEVEL 3	LEVEL 4
Employee turnover (annualized)	2.66%	5.66%	8.66%	11.66%
Customer comment card score	2.66%	5.66%	8.66%	11.66%
House profit	2.66%+A	5.66%+A	8.66%+A	11.66%+A

A. 3.25% of the first $50,000 over minimum house profit for the level achieved.

We didn't do anything special. We looked for fit versus skill when we hired people. Did they share our values? After several years, we began to use a management committee consensus-process approach. Mostly, we tried to talk people out of coming to work for us. We were different, and if you couldn't buy into our values, or you didn't want to live with these principles, we didn't want you. Our values were not negotiable. We didn't have a formal orientation either. You picked up the values from everyone in the hotel. It wasn't necessary for top management to tell everyone—the people you worked with told you. We ... saw training as a last resort. Training should be for helping people get over the hump once they've exhausted their own resources. If a person needed a skill, then they were provided training to handle that need. We were committed to filling the gaps, but we don't have a formal training program. We supported cross-training to help build employee opportunities."

In the last couple of years, Hiller invested in the Stephen Covey training on *The Seven Habits of Highly Effective People* to help managers and line employees live the company's vision and were pleased with the results. Peter Green, along with a manager from each property, was certified as a Covey trainer, so they were able to do this training in-house.

COMMUNICATION

Green expressed that "providing information to people is a form of respect. Information not only flows to employees, but from them as well." All employees met once per quarter at a property-wide meeting to discuss and review quarterly results of the hotel. The meeting included a question-and-answer period and the distribution of quarterly bonuses. Department meetings were held once a month, and at daily huddles managers and line employees reviewed customer service issues. Surveys were used to obtain feedback from employees as well as guests and owners. Cross-department task forces were assembled and disassembled quickly to respond to special problems. Plus, the company communicated in many one-on-one, personal ways. Key to all of the information exchange was management's emphasis on listening and praise.

CULTURE

In discussing the culture he and his team created at the Westward and were attempting to inculcate throughout Hiller, Green stated:

We had a family environment and were dedicated to one another and to high levels of customer service. I believed that managers should figure out what employees value and value that. We started to do a back-to-school function for employees, because we knew how important the family and education was for our workers. We invited the families to the party and distributed school supplies. It made everyone feel good. We did a Christmas party too—focused around the family with gifts to all the kids from Santa Claus. I think our culture is strong because we have a sense of community and a sense of purpose outside of the job.

I think we created a business environment where people could be themselves. They wanted to care. In the typical work environment, people must hide their true selves. I think we gave people permission to be themselves, to be different. I think our low levels of turnover were critical to our culture. Lots of people like to argue that low turnover is essential because of the costs, but I think high turnover does more damage because it assaults the culture.

We had a high level of trust and also a level of tolerance and forgiving that I think are unique. We had an older woman in the laundry area who was with the hotel from the beginning who took two 15-minute naps each day. Can you imagine how most hotels would deal with an employee who sleeps on the job? I think we may have less talent, but we leverage it by being stronger as a whole. It's like a basketball team that doesn't have one superstar, but a whole group of average players who together do extraordinary things.

Success helps too. We started to see some dramatic positive results from our efforts at the Westward, and that certainly lifted people's spirits. Good news feeds the emotional psyche. When we got into the Westward, it had good people in it, but the culture was dominated by a traditional command-and-control management that didn't let the hard-working and caring employees contribute the way they could. The culture flourished with our guiding principles, and I don't think management can easily change it. But sure, it could go back to that. You bring in bad management, good people leave, turnover increases, and suddenly the work environment is different. Nothing lasts forever.

BUT DID IT MAKE MONEY?

Living a vision is in the details. "It is a slow and continuous process, and you must stick with it," reflected Green. But the ability to do so with the performance pressures of owners and the demands of customers is an ongoing battle. The results at Westward were dramatic support for the Peter Green vision. For four years, the Westward Hilton performed at or near the top of the Phoenix market, as indicated by its occupancy percentage, shown in Exhibit 6. According to the comparative data from Smith Travel Research, the Westward Hilton outperformed the Phoenix market in 2007, although demand was gradually slipping in the city. Exhibit 6 shows the Hilton's position among its primary market competitors, the luxury and upper upscale chain markets, the Phoenix market, and the Phoenix Central markets. This performance was due in part to the redirection of the hotel's marketing efforts away from groups and more toward transient corporate travelers. According to recent investor reports, the above-average penetration was caused by the hotel's chain affiliation with Hilton Hotels and its highly visible location. Westward Hilton was in the top 10 of all Hilton Hotels, with an increase in profitability of about 273 percent over the 2001–2007 period. House profit increased from the takeover (2001) figure of $1,817,137 to $6,769,482 (2007).

Exhibit 5 shows the changes in guest comment scores and employee turnover. The hotel's revenue per available room (REVPAR, calculated by dividing room revenue by the number of available rooms) rose from a rate of $66.65 in 2001 to a 2007 rate of $122.10. Exhibit 6 shows the Westward's market performance based on data from Smith Travel Research. Exhibit 7 provides income statements for the hotel for the seven years from 2001 to 2007. Exhibit 8 provides additional financial information, including the initial investment and estimated value of the hotel. The current value of the property if sold today is about $65 million. This value is derived from projected 2008 earnings and a terminal capitalization rate of 10.5 percent. The expected average annual asset return on this investment is 12.28 percent, and the expected average annual equity return is 30.23 percent, assuming

Exhibit 5: Guest Comment Scores and Employee Turnover, 2001–2007

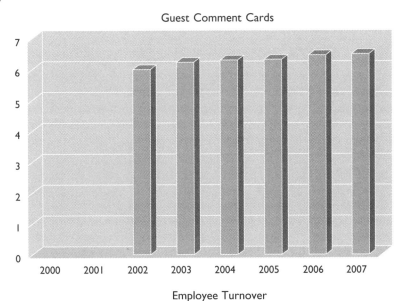

Guest Comment Cards

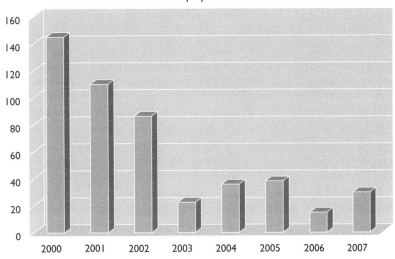

Employee Turnover

a loan-to-value ratio of 60 percent. These returns are the internal rate of return (IRR) on an initial investment of the current value of the property where the property is held through the end of 2016 and then sold at that time. Exhibit 9 reports on returns from other investment opportunities, such as stocks and treasury bills.

Exhibit 6: Phoenix Market Performance, 2001–2007

	OCCUPANCY						
MARKET SEGMENT	**2001**	**2002**	**2003**	**2004**	**2005**	**2006**	**2007**
Westward Hilton	50.2	56.7	62.9	69.4	73.2	73	72.5
Luxury	62.2	62.2	63.8	68.6	71.4	70.9	70.9
Upscale	63.4	63.0	65.6	69.1	72.5	72.4	72.3
Phoenix Market	58.5	57.8	57.8	63.7	67.1	68.2	68.2
Phoenix Central	56.5	57.5	59.2	63.1	66.7	68.2	68.3
Competitive Set	60.5	60.6	62.4	66.6	69.9	70.3	70.3
	ADR						
MARKET SEGMENT	**2001**	**2002**	**2003**	**2004**	**2005**	**2006**	**2007**
Westward Hilton	132.77	130.71	133.18	136.25	147.37	159.33	168.42
Luxury	166.84	155.10	150.08	154.84	165.62	180.04	190.30
Upscale	136.14	127.25	128.17	134.48	145.75	157.96	166.97
Phoenix Market	96.84	92.23	92.66	95.74	102.84	113.28	119.73
Phoenix Central	138.02	131.87	124.25	123.65	129.92	139.32	147.26
Competitive Set	141.98	133.49	130.02	133.46	142.67	154.52	163.33
	RevPAR						
MARKET SEGMENT	**2001**	**2002**	**2003**	**2004**	**2005**	**2006**	**2007**
Westward Hilton	66.65	74.11	83.77	94.56	107.87	116.31	122.10
Luxury	103.72	96.48	95.80	106.17	118.26	127.67	134.83
Upscale	86.34	80.17	84.09	92.98	105.74	114.32	120.75
Phoenix Market	56.67	53.26	53.51	60.97	68.98	77.23	81.69
Phoenix Central	78.04	75.81	73.59	78.08	86.65	95.08	100.57
Competitive Set	85.89	80.88	81.10	88.92	99.73	108.59	114.76

Source: Smith Travel Research

Exhibit 7: Actual Income Before Other Fixed Charges, 2001–2007

Occupancy and ADR :	2001	2002	2003	2004	2005	2006	2007
Occupancy	50.20%	56.70%	62.90%	69.40%	73.20%	73.00%	72.50%
ADR	$132.77	$130.71	$133.18	$136.25	$147.37	$159.33	$168.42
Revenue and Expense:							
Revenues:							
Rooms	$7,298,234	$8,115,326	$9,172,839	$10,354,046	$11,812,295	$12,736,044	$13,370,443
Food	$2,687,639	$2,988,541	$3,377,979	$3,812,969	$4,349,982	$4,690,161	$4,923,784
Beverage	$618,494	$687,740	$777,359	$877,462	$1,001,042	$1,079,326	$1,133,088
Telecommunications	$101,208	$112,539	$127,204	$143,585	$163,807	$176,617	$185,414
Other Operated Departments	$393,587	$437,652	$494,683	$558,385	$637,027	$686,844	$721,056
Rentals and Other Income	$146,190	$162,557	$183,739	$207,400	$236,610	$255,113	$267,821
Total Revenues	$11,245,353	$12,504,355	$14,133,804	$15,953,846	$18,200,763	$19,624,104	$20,601,607
Departmental Costs and Expenses:							
Rooms	$2,260,316	$2,438,349	$2,586,486	$2,823,831	$3,185,133	$3,394,970	$3,522,875
Food	$2,395,260	$2,525,880	$2,770,226	$3,063,138	$3,439,944	$3,669,707	$3,811,297
Beverage	$393,587	$387,635	$395,747	$414,800	$418,618	$412,106	$432,634
Telecommunications	$146,190	$137,548	$127,204	$127,631	$145,606	$137,369	$123,610
Other Operated Departments	$393,587	$400,139	$367,479	$319,077	$345,814	$333,610	$309,024
Total Costs and Expenses	$5,588,940	$5,889,551	$6,247,142	$6,748,477	$7,535,116	$7,947,762	$8,199,439
Total Operated Departmental Income	$5,656,413	$6,614,804	$7,886,663	$9,205,369	$10,665,647	$11,676,342	$12,402,167

Exhibit 7: (*Continued*)

UNDISTRIBUTED OPERATING EXPENSES:

Administrative and General	$1,236,989	$1,325,462	$1,356,845	$1,435,846	$1,619,868	$1,687,673	$1,751,137
Franchise Fees including Marketing Fees	$656,841	$730,379	$825,556	$931,864	$1,063,107	$1,146,244	$1,203,340
Marketing	$258,643	$287,600	$325,078	$239,308	$273,011	$255,113	$267,821
Property Operation and Maintenance	$708,457	$787,774	$791,493	$717,923	$819,034	$883,085	$927,072
Utility Costs	$517,286	$512,679	$551,218	$542,431	$582,424	$608,347	$638,650
Other Unallocated Operated Departments	$0	$0	$0	$0	$0	$0	$0
Total Undistributed Expenses	$3,378,217	$3,643,894	$3,850,190	$3,867,372	$4,357,445	$4,580,462	$4,788,019
Income before Fixed Charges	$2,278,196	$2,970,910	$4,036,473	$5,337,997	$6,308,202	$7,095,880	$7,614,148

MANAGEMENT FEES, PROPERTY TAXES, AND INSURANCE:

Property Taxes and Other Municipal Charges	$269,888	$300,105	$339,211	$382,892	$436,818	$470,978	$494,439
Insurance	$191,171	$212,574	$240,275	$271,215	$309,413	$333,610	$350,227
Total Management Fees, Property Taxes, and Insurance	$461,059	$512,679	$579,486	$654,108	$746,231	$804,588	$844,666
Income before other Fixed Charges	$1,817,137	$2,458,231	$3,456,987	$4,683,890	$5,561,971	$6,291,292	$6,769,482

Exhibit 8: Initial Investment, Estimated Value, and Estimated Returns

Cost of Hotel in 2000	$39,075,000.00
Weighted Average Cost of Capital (WACC)	9.35%
Estimated Sales Price in 2007	$65,082,568.10
Estimated Rate of Return on Asset	12.28%
Estimated Rate of Return on Equity	30.23%

Exhibit 9: Annual Returns

YEAR	STOCKS	T.BILLS	T.BONDS
2001	−11.85%	5.73%	5.57%
2002	−21.98%	1.80%	15.12%
2003	28.41%	1.80%	0.38%
2004	10.70%	2.18%	4.49%
2005	4.85%	4.31%	2.87%
2006	15.63%	4.88%	1.96%
2007	5.48%	4.88%	10.21%

NEW GENERAL MANAGERS ARRIVE

As one subordinate noted, Green had a clear employee emphasis, he was a caring person, and people felt good working for him. This employee indicated that Green was a master at showing interest in people's work. He noticed the small things and acknowledged everyone with a friendly greeting. He fostered a work environment that was informal, responsive, and trusting, not intimidating. The guide for behavior was "do the right thing." His focus was always on the questions: "How does it impact our employees, customers, and owners?" and "Are all three parties taken care of?" He would be a hard act to follow, and for some at the property, the managers who followed Green were simply not up to the task.

Five general managers came and went from the Westward Hilton in the four years after Green moved into his corporate position. While the departures of the managers were for a variety of reasons, Green blamed himself for being too controlling as the executive vice president of operations of Hiller

Exhibit 10: Forecast Income Before Other Fixed Charges, 2008–2016

OCCUPANCY AND ADR:	2008	2009	2010	2011	2012	2013	2014	2015	2016
Occupancy	72.61%	72.50%	72.18%	71.96%	71.74%	71.53%	71.31%	71.20%	71.09%
ADR	$169.76	$172.84	$176.00	$179.29	$182.80	$186.50	$190.38	$194.44	$198.71
REVENUE AND EXPENSE:									
REVENUES:									
Rooms	$13,497,220	$13,721,571	$13,909,504	$14,126,756	$14,360,441	$14,606,993	$14,865,420	$15,159,511	$15,468,835
Food	$4,970,471	$5,053,090	$5,122,298	$5,202,303	$5,288,360	$5,379,155	$5,474,323	$5,582,624	$5,696,536
Beverage	$1,143,832	$1,162,845	$1,178,772	$1,197,183	$1,216,987	$1,237,881	$1,259,781	$1,284,704	$1,310,918
Telecommunications	$187,173	$190,284	$192,890	$195,903	$199,143	$202,562	$206,146	$210,224	$214,514
Other Operated Departments	$727,893	$739,992	$750,127	$761,844	$774,446	$787,742	$801,679	$817,539	$834,221
Rentals and Other Income	$270,360	$274,854	$278,619	$282,970	$287,651	$292,590	$297,767	$303,657	$309,853
Total Revenues	$20,796,950	$21,142,636	$21,432,210	$21,766,959	$22,127,027	$22,506,923	$22,905,116	$23,358,261	$23,834,877
DEPARTMENTAL COSTS AND EXPENSES:									
Rooms	$3,556,278	$3,615,391	$3,664,908	$3,722,150	$3,783,722	$3,848,684	$3,916,775	$3,994,263	$4,075,764
Food	$3,847,436	$3,911,388	$3,964,959	$4,026,887	$4,093,500	$4,163,781	$4,237,446	$4,321,278	$4,409,452
Beverage	$436,736	$443,995	$450,076	$457,106	$464,668	$472,645	$481,007	$490,523	$500,532
Telecommunications	$124,782	$126,856	$128,593	$130,602	$132,762	$135,042	$137,431	$140,150	$143,009
Other Operated Departments	$311,954	$317,140	$321,483	$326,504	$331,905	$337,604	$343,577	$350,374	$357,523
Total Costs and Expenses	$8,277,186	$8,414,769	$8,530,019	$8,663,250	$8,806,557	$8,957,755	$9,116,236	$9,296,588	$9,486,281
Total Operated Departmental Income	$12,519,764	$12,727,867	$12,902,190	$13,103,709	$13,320,470	$13,549,168	$13,788,880	$14,061,673	$14,348,596

UNDISTRIBUTED OPERATING EXPENSES:									
Administrative and General	$1,767,741	$1,797,124	$1,821,738	$1,850,192	$1,880,797	$1,913,088	$1,946,935	$1,985,452	$2,025,965
Franchise Fees - including Marketing Fees	$1,214,750	$1,234,941	$1,251,855	$1,271,408	$1,292,440	$1,314,629	$1,337,888	$1,364,356	$1,392,195
Marketing	$270,360	$274,854	$278,619	$282,970	$287,651	$292,590	$297,767	$303,657	$309,853
Property Operation and Maintenance	$935,863	$951,419	$964,449	$979,513	$995,716	$1,012,812	$1,030,730	$1,051,122	$1,072,569
Utility Costs	$644,705	$655,422	$664,399	$674,776	$685,938	$697,715	$710,059	$724,106	$738,881
Other Unallocated Operated Departments	$0	$0	$0	$0	$0	$0	$0	$0	$0
Total Undistributed Expenses	$4,833,419	$4,913,760	$4,981,060	$5,058,859	$5,142,542	$5,230,834	$5,323,378	$5,428,693	$5,539,464
Income before Fixed Charges	$7,686,345	$7,814,107	$7,921,130	$8,044,850	$8,177,928	$8,318,334	$8,465,502	$8,632,980	$8,809,132
MANAGEMENT FEES, PROPERTY TAXES, AND INSURANCE:									
Property Taxes and Other Municipal Charges	$499,127	$507,423	$514,373	$522,407	$531,049	$540,166	$549,723	$560,598	$572,037
Insurance	$353,548	$359,425	$364,348	$370,038	$376,159	$382,618	$389,387	$397,090	$405,193
Total Management Fees, Property Taxes and Insurance	$852,675	$866,848	$878,721	$892,445	$907,208	$922,784	$939,110	$957,689	$977,230
Income before Other Fixed Charges	$6,833,670	$6,947,259	$7,042,410	$7,152,405	$7,270,720	$7,395,550	$7,526,392	$7,675,291	$7,831,902

Hotels. Even after his promotion to the position of supervising the general managers of several hotels, he was still deeply involved in the life of the Westward. His presence was everywhere in the hotel and remained strong. "I didn't trust it would continue to work. I was not confident in those that followed me, and I was afraid that what we had built would not last." But last it did, and the results continued to be positive.

WHY SELL?

Bringing his thoughts up to the present, Green thought it might be the right time to sell—Hiller had had a good seven-year run at the Westward. However, uncertainty existed about the future. Hotel sales transactions were beginning to drop. In addition, tightening credit and stricter loan underwriting had increased the cost of capital, making it more difficult for a potential buyer to obtain a loan as a result of the collapse of the subprime mortage market. These issues, as well as the possibility of the United States entering a recession, were also on Green's mind. Nevertheless, new products had come on board in the Phoenix market, and the hotel's performance might have peaked.

Phoenix had experienced explosive growth in the late 1990s, and supply growth had continued up through 2003 (see Exhibit 6). Recently, both room supply and demand had begun to fall in the Phoenix market. Growth had been particularly strong within the upper upscale and luxury segments. In 2003, demand for luxury hotels increased by 15.9 percent, while supply increased by 13 percent. In contrast, 2007 showed a 2 percent drop in demand and a .2 percent increase in supply. In the upper upscale segment, 2007 demand was down 1 percent and supply up 1.2 percent from the previous year. Much of the new hotel development had been undertaken by REITs and other public lodging companies, which were establishing or expanding their portfolio or brands, according to E & Y Kenneth Leventhal Real Estate Group's National Lodging Forecast. The overall supply growth in Phoenix in 2007 was .1 percent, after three straight years of negative supply growth. All market segments in the Phoenix area had experienced healthy ADR (average daily rate) and total revenue growth since 2002. The long-term outlook for Phoenix was strong, with its average 300 days of sunshine, good transportation support, natural wonders, and abundance of golf courses.

Hiller Hotels, though, wasn't exactly desperate for the money. The rest of the portfolio was performing well—with the exception of one recently acquired property, all were profitable—and the parent company, which owned and operated a bank and several other businesses, was profitable. Forecasted income before fixed charges for the period 2008 to 2016 is shown in Exhibit 10. Furthermore, all of the Hiller businesses were privately held, with Karen Connor being the majority shareholder in all. Thus, there was little of the short-term performance pressure to which publicly held companies are subject.

Green knew that at their next formal meeting, the seven people in the management/ownership group he was drinking and laughing with now would make a decision that, one way or another, would affect people's lives at the Westward. Perhaps selling would even affect the way Hiller's employees at the other properties would feel about the company. On the other hand, because of his small equity stake in the hotel, Green stood to benefit handsomely from the sale.

Green thought to himself:

My one regret is that I didn't prepare people for this possibility. I don't believe we can protect people; we can only tell them it may not last forever. We should have prepared them. We should have made it clear that this is not forever—it's an investment and we should try to enjoy it for as long as we can. Everyone benefited from being involved with that property—from being part of a place that was so positive. I just worry that selling will catch people flat-footed. We have created such a high trust level that people didn't even ask questions when we had investors visit the property. It embarrasses me that I didn't prepare them.

Green lifted his glass and smiled sadly as he thought of his friends and colleagues at the Westward. He took a long swig of his martini and muttered to himself, "I just don't know for sure what the right thing to do is." He was glad to have the weekend ahead to think about his vote and, if he decided to vote to hold, how he would try to convince the others, especially Connor, to hold the property.

CASE 3 INTERCONTINENTAL HOTEL GROUP'S ENTRY INTO CHINA*

HISTORY OF INTERCONTINENTAL

During the one-month period from June to July 2006, InterContinental Hotels Group (IHG) opened four hotels in China: Crowne Plaza Changshu, Crowne Plaza Fudan Shanghai, Holiday Inn Jasmine Suzhou, and Holiday Inn Seaview Qinhuangdao, adding more than 1,100 hotel rooms.[1] In February 2006, IHG signed six hotels with Chengdu International Exhibition & Convention Group in Sichuang province and four hotels with Shanghai Greenland Group, adding almost 6,000 rooms in China in two weeks.[2,3]

The current goal of IHG is to promote "faster growth by making IHG's brands the first choice for guests and hotel owners."[4] This description is not only a forecast of its future directions, but also a summary of its expansion history. As of December 2007, IHG manages 76 hotels in China, making it one of the largest international hotel chains there. Among these hotels are the following brands: 10 InterContinental hotels, 18 Crowne Plaza hotels, 39 Holiday Inn hotels, and 9 Holiday Inn Express hotels (Exhibit 1).[5] The overall global target of the group is to increase the number of properties in China to 125 by the end of 2008.[6]

InterContinental Hotels Group, formerly Bass PLC, was founded in 1777 by William Bass, when he established a brewery in the English town of Burton-on-Trent. The year 1876 was a landmark year for Bass, when it was recognized as the largest brewery in England. Even more notably, it was also this year that Bass's red triangle trademark became the first trademark to be registered in England. During the 1960s, Bass made two strategic and significant mergers. In 1961, Bass merged with Mitchells & Butler, becoming Bass, Mitchells & Butler. In 1967, Bass, Mitchells & Butler merged with Charrington United Breweries to become Bass Charrington Ltd.[7]

The year 1970 marked Bass's entrance into the world of hospitality, as it purchased about 50 hotels from the oil giant Esso.[8] These hotel holdings became known as Crest Hotels. Renamed Bass

Written by Zhaoping Liu, who is a doctoral student at the Cornell University School of Hotel Administration. This case study was written for the purposes of classroom discussion.

I have benefited from the suggestions from Bin Dai, Chuntian Liu and Zhijun Zhang. Part of "the history of InterContinental" section was revised from the Six Continents case written by Adam Baru, Yinian Hou, Vikas Patel, Bill Spinnenweber, Anjali Talera, and Kem Wilson under the direction of Jeffrey S. Harrison. Lin Kuang and Shenghui Zhou provided some data and references. Special thanks to Cathy A. Enz for her constructive and thoughtful comments.

Exhibit 1: InterContinental Hotels in China by Provinces/Cities and Brands

City/Province	Total Number	Inter-Continental (Upper Upscale)	Crowne Plaza (Upscale)	Holiday Inn (Midscale Full Service)	Holiday Express (Midscale Limited Service)
Beijing	9	1	2	5	1
Changsha	1	0	1	0	0
Changshu	1	0	1	0	0
Chengdu	3	1	1	1	0
Chongqing	3	1	0	2	0
Dalian	1	0	0	0	1
Guangzhou	2	0	0	2	0
Hangzhou	2	0	0	2	0
Harbin	1	0	0	1	0
Hefei	2	0	0	1	1
Hohhot	1	0	0	1	0
Hong Kong	4	2	0	1	1
Huizhou	1	0	0	1	0
Inner Mongolia	1	0	0	1	0
Jinan	1	0	1	0	0
Jiujiang	1	0	0	1	0
Jiuzhaigou	2	1	0	1	0
Macau SAR	1	0	0	1	0
Nanjing	1	0	1	0	0
Qingdao	1	0	1	0	0
Qinhuangdao	1	0	0	1	0
Sanya	3	0	1	2	0
Shanghai	10	1	3	3	3
Shenyang	2	1	0	1	0
Shenzhen	4	1	2	1	0
Suifenhe	1	0	0	1	0

Exhibit 1: (*Continued*)

Suzhou	3	0	1	2	0
Tianjin	3	0	0	2	1
Wuhan	2	0	0	2	0
Xiamen	1	0	1	0	0
Xian	1	1	0	0	0
Yueyang	1	0	0	1	0
Zhanjiang	1	0	1	0	0
Zhengzhou	3	0	1	1	1
Zhuhai	1	0	0	1	0
Total	**76**	**10**	**18**	**39**	**9**

Source: Adapted from InterContinental web site, December 2007.

PLC in the early 1980s, the company's leisure subsidiaries, including its hotel division, "contributed substantially to Bass' growth and profits."[9] In 1988, Bass made the first significant international move into the hotel industry by acquiring the international assets of Holiday Corporation outside the United States, Canada, and Mexico for $475 million.[10]

The year 1989 saw the advent of legislation on the brewing industry through Beer Orders. Through Beer Orders legislation, the government sought to limit the vertical integration within the brewing industry by limiting the number of pubs a brewer could own.[11] Bass's response was to continue to focus on and develop its international hotel business. Therefore, on August 25, 1989, Bass made a monumental decision to purchase Holiday Corporation's flagship Holiday Inn chain for $2.23 billion. Included in this purchase were 1,410 franchised Holiday Inns and 177 company-owned and -managed Holiday Inns.[12]

Founded by Kemmons Wilson in 1952, Holiday Inn quickly grew into the largest lodging corporation in the world. A 1951 road trip to Washington, D.C., with his wife and five children had convinced Wilson of a great need for a brand-name hotel/motel that families could trust anywhere they traveled. Importantly, Wilson was aware of the coming construction of a $76 billion federal interstate highway system and planned to take full advantage by building Holiday Inns alongside it. His foresight paid off as the interstate highway system popularized travel from coast to coast. "It has been said that what John D. Rockefeller did for gasoline and Henry Ford did for automobiles, Kemmons did for lodging: standardizing a product and making it available to the masses at a reasonable price anywhere they went."[13]

When Bass purchased Holiday Inn, the chain was in the midst of a decline due to aged properties and poor services. Additionally, the hotel industry was seeing great growth in budget hotel chains such as Hampton Inn. To counter these issues, Bass began a $1 billion renovation project for the Holiday Inn brand, launched its own budget hotel chain called Holiday Inn Express in 1991 to add a complementary brand in the limited-service segment, and launched its high-end Crowne Plaza Hotels in 1994 to move the group into the upscale market.[14] It entered the profitable U.S. upscale extended-stay segment with the introduction and development of Staybridge Suites by Holiday Inn in 1997.[15]

With the money raised through the sell-off of various retail businesses, Bass outbid Marriott International, Patriot American Hospitality, and Ladbroke Group to acquire the InterContinental hotel chain from Japan's Saison Group for $2.9 billion in 1998. Included in the acquisition were InterContinental's 211 hotels in 77 countries.[16] Thomas Oliver, then chairperson and CEO of Bass's hotel division (Holiday Hospitality), summed up the acquisition well when he said that InterContinental provides an "excellent geographic complement to Holiday Hospitality's current structure and gives us a broader portfolio of brands spanning the midscale and upscale markets around the globe. The purchase . . . is consistent with our strategy of growing Bass's business in markets which offer long-term growth opportunities."[17]

On June 14, 2000, Bass severed its 223-year-old tie to the brewing industry when it entered into an agreement to sell its beer brewing division to Interbrew for $3 billion.[18] Along with Bass's sale came the cessation of its name and, on June 28, 2001, Bass officially became known as Six Continents PLC.[19] On October 1, 2002, Six Continents announced that it would be demerging the group's hotels and soft drinks business, Britvic (to be called InterContinental Hotels Group PLC) from the retail business (to be called Mitchells & Butlers PLC).[20] This separation process was completed on April 15, 2003, and InterContinental Hotels Group PLC (IHG) became a distinct, discrete company.[21]

In December 2003, the midscale extended-stay brand Candlewood Suites was added to IHG's portfolio. The new brand complemented the existing Staybridge brand and increased IHG's U.S. system size by an additional 109 hotels and 12,500 rooms. In April 2004, IHG introduced Hotel Indigo, a hotel brand developed primarily for conversions, to fit a variety of markets in preferred locations. The new brand was designed as a lodging alternative for the traveler seeking a refreshing hotel experience, not just a hotel room.[22]

IHG announced the disposal of 100 percent of its holding in soft drink company Britvic in December 2005. The total proceeds received from the disposal of IHG's entire interest in Britvic were £371 million. The disposal of soft drink assets allowed IHG to focus on being purely a hotel company.[23]

IHG'S EXPANSION INTO CHINA

InterContinental was among the earliest international hotel chains to enter the China market. In 1984, Lido Holiday Inn was opened in Beijing. It was the first hotel managed by an international hotel chain and also the first hotel with the Holiday Inn brand in mainland China. In the same year, Lido opened its executive apartments, which had 1,000 standard rooms and 355 apartments. By the end of the first year, Lido Holiday Inn exemplified outstanding performance by earning a profit. Equally important, Lido became the human resource training base of Holiday Inn, from which it transferred many mid- and high-level managers to other hotels throughout China.[24] In the first 10 years, the revenue of Lido Holiday Inn was ¥1.7 billion, with a profit of ¥1 billion.[25]

By 1990, ten hotels managed by Holiday Inn covered eight major cities in China.[26] In August 2000, the opening of Holiday Inn City Center Shenyang increased IHG's number of hotels in China to 28, making it the largest international hotel operator in the country.[27] In May 2004, 20 years after its first hotel in China, IHG had 26 Holiday Inn Hotels, 15 Crowne Plaza hotels, and four InterContinental Hotels in China.[28]

InterContinental was the first major international hotel chain to launch a Chinese language web site and the first to offer online reservation options to customers who do not use credit cards.[29]

Following is a list of InterContinental's strategic actions in China since the turn of the 21st century:

- In May 2001, the InterContinental Hong Kong was purchased for $346 million in cash. The acquisition strengthened the upscale market position in the Chinese and Asia-Pacific hotel markets. This hotel was the only owned InterContinental brand hotel of IHG in the Asian-Pacific Region.[30]

- In 2003, a central reservation office was launched in Guangzhou, China, to handle Greater China reservations.[31]

- In September 2003, IHG added the first airline alliance in China, Air China, to its loyalty program Priority Club Reward (PCR).[32]

- In February 2004, IHG unveiled its Holiday Inn Chinese language web site, which offers booking facilities in Simplified Chinese.[33]

- In 2004, Holiday Inn Express Zhengzhou was opened, claiming the introduction of the first Holiday Inn Express hotel in Mainland China.

- In April 2006, IHG won five top titles at the China Golden Pillow Awards ceremony.[34]

- In June 2006, InterContinental announced plans to establish the InterContinental Hotels Group Academy in Shanghai, China.[35]

- In August 2006, IHG won the prestigious China Hotel Pioneer Award in Beijing.[36]

- In 2006 and 2007, IHG was named "the top 10 international hotel chains in China."[37]

MARKET SELECTION: WHY CHINA?

THE FAVORABLE SOCIOECONOMIC ENVIRONMENT OF CHINA

China was considered a "forbidden country" prior to 1978 due to its political exclusiveness from Western countries. Before 1978, as a poor, developing country, China did not have hotels of international standards except for a few guest houses that were owned by the Chinese government to host invited guests.[38] By the end of the 1970s, when China first opened its doors to international tourists, lodging was chosen as one of the earliest industries to be opened to foreign investors. The importance attached to the tourism industry was the result of rising demand created by the influx of overseas tourists.[39]

Today, InterContinental's strategy focuses on the biggest markets and segments where scale counts.[40] China, the world's most populous nation and one of the world's fastest growing economies,

Exhibit 2: GDP China (2001–2006)

YEAR	GDP (BILLION RMB)	GROWTH RATE (%)
2001	10,965.5	8.3
2002	12,033.3	9.1
2003	13,582.3	10.0
2004	15,987.8	10.1
2005	18,232.1	9.9
2006	20,940.7	10.7

Sources: Adapted from National Bureau of Statistics of China web site, November 2007.

is definitely a key market for IHG. From 1978 to 2005, China's GDP maintained an average annual growth rate of 9.6 percent.[41] During the past six years, the GDP of China increased from ¥10,965.5 billion in 2001 to ¥20,940.7 billion in 2006 (Exhibit 2).[42,43]

Along with its economic growth, China plays an increasingly important role in the world economy. In 2005, the GDP of China topped those of France and Great Britain, ranking number four in the world. The gaps between China and the top three GDP countries are narrowing. In 2002, China's GDP was 13.9 percent of the United States, 37 percent of Japan, and 71.8 percent of Germany. Four years later, those ratios increased to 20 percent, 60.6 percent, and 91.3 percent, respectively. Between 2002 and 2006, the proportion of China's GDP to the world total grew from 4.4 percent to 5.5 percent.[44]

Joining the World Trade Organization (WTO) further enhanced the openness of China's economy. The WTO director Pascal Lamy has stated that "since its accession to the WTO, China has been the fastest growing trading nation in the world." China has set good examples in many areas in implementing the WTO commitments, and the "Chinese government has substantially reduced barriers to imports."[45] In 1975, the total value of China's exports and imports was $20.64 billion. In 2005, the value increased to $1.42 trillion, with an average annual growth rate of 17.0 percent. China has also instituted a series of favorable policies to attract foreign investment. Between 1990 and 2005, the average annual growth rate of foreign investment in China was 19.7 percent.[46] Take the trade between China and the United States as an example: in 2006, China's exports to the United States were $203.5 trillion, a 24.9 percent increase over the previous year; imports from the United States were $59.2 billion, 21.8 percent higher than that of 2005.[47]

THE STRONG GROWTH OF INBOUND AND DOMESTIC TOURISM IN CHINA

China's open-door policy in 1978 resulted in the rise of international inbound tourist demand, fueling the growth of high-end hotels to meet international standards.[48] The inbound tourism market of China has grown faster than its national economy and has exhibited a high growth rate in all segments.

The openness of China's economy has brought more international business travelers. In addition, the cooperative marketing activities sponsored by the government and tourism firms promoted China's destination image and attracted leisure travelers from all over the world.[49] In seven of the past 10 years, the number of inbound tourists maintained an annual growth rate of more than 10 percent (Exhibit 3).[50]

The domestic travel market did not emerge in China until the 1980s. The increase of personal income and the emergence of a middle class supported the growth of domestic travel. In 1998, the Chinese central government identified tourism as one of the industries with great potential for contributing to national economic growth.[51] The governmental importance assigned to the tourism industry further stimulated the growth of the travel market. The establishment of the "Golden Weeks" policy in 1999—which allows all employees to enjoy three weeklong vacations every year around the Spring Festival, May 1st, and October 1st—was one example of how the government facilitated the dramatic rise in domestic travel demand.[52] Since 1998, domestic travel expenditures have maintained a consistent and rapid growth rate of between 10 percent and 12 percent.[53] In 2006, the domestic tourism income of China was ¥622.97 billion, a 17.9 percent growth over the previous year.[54]

ENTRY MODE SELECTION

Generally, firms choose among exporting, contractual arrangements (licensing, franchising, and long-term management contract), and foreign direct investment (joint venture, wholly owned subsidiary, and acquisition) to expand their businesses across borders.[55] For service-focused hospitality firms, exporting is not highly relevant. For the other two types of entry modes, contractual arrangements enjoy the advantages of low cost and low risk, but limit a firm's control and ability to earn high returns. The wholly owned subsidiary is more complex, often costly, time consuming, and risky, while giving firms greater control and offering opportunities for obtaining above-average returns.[56]

For hotels to enter a new country, franchising, management contracts, and ownership (acquisition, new building, or joint venture) are the three most popular modes. As of September 30, 2007, 67 percent of IHG's profit was from franchised hotels, 22 percent was from managed hotels, and 11 percent was from owned and leased hotels.[57] IHG picked management contracts as the dominant entry mode in China based on its understanding of the local environment.

Before 2003, InterContinental employed three different business models in three major regions. In the midscale lodging brand Holiday Inn, IHG properties were predominantly franchised in the United States. In 2003, 85 percent of rooms in the Americas were operated under license by franchisees. IHG's 2003 annual report announced that "We provide the brand recognition and access to our international infrastructure and marketing to increase revenues at these properties. Our strategy is to own hotels until a brand has achieved critical mass, and then to transfer hotels to the franchise or management model."[58] By June 30, 2007, more than 89 percent of IHG's American hotel rooms were under the franchised mode (Exhibit 4).[59]

In Europe, the Middle East, and Africa (EMEA), the ownership model was frequently used. InterContinental's largest concentration of owned and leased assets was in this region. In 2003, 68 percent of operating profits in EMEA came from owned and leased hotels. IHG claimed that "this puts us in a strong position to benefit from an upturn in the market and from our refurbishment and operational improvements over the past two years. We remain determined to concentrate our owned estate on those properties that are truly competitive and brand enhancing."[60]

Exhibit 3: China's Tourist Market (1995–2006)

YEAR	DOMESTIC TOURISTS (HUNDRED MILLION)	GROWTH RATE %	DOMESTIC TOURISM INCOME (BILLION$)	GROWTH RATE (%)	INBOUND TOURISTS (MILLION)	GROWTH RATE (%)	INBOUND TOURISM INCOME (BILLION $)	GROWTH RATE (%)	TOURISM INCOME (BILLION $)[b]	GROWTH RATE (%)
1995	6.29	—	17.29	—	46.39	—	8.73	—	26.36	—
1996	6.39	1.6%	20.59	19.1%	51.13	10.2%	10.20	16.8%	31.25	18.5%
1997	6.44	0.8%	26.55	29.0%	57.59	12.6%	12.07	18.4%	39.11	25.1%
1998	6.94	7.8%	30.05	13.2%	63.48	10.2%	12.60	4.4%	43.21	10.5%
1999	7.19	3.6%	35.59	18.4%	72.80	14.7%	14.10	11.9%	50.29	16.4%
2000	7.44	3.5%	39.90	12.1%	83.44	14.6%	16.22	15.1%	56.79	12.9%
2001	7.84	5.4%	44.26	10.9%	89.01	6.7%	17.79	9.7%	62.77	10.5%
2002	8.78	12.0%	48.74	10.1%	97.91	10.0%	20.39	14.6%	69.94	11.4%
2003[a]	8.7	−0.9%	43.26	−11.2%	91.66	−6.4%	17.41	−14.6%	61.35	−12.3%
2004	11.02	26.7%	59.21	36.9%	109.04	19.0%	25.74	47.9%	85.95	40.1%
2005	12.12	10.0%	66.43	12.2%	120.29	10.3%	29.30	13.8%	96.58	12.4%
2006	13.94	15.0%	78.32	17.9%	124.94	3.9%	33.95	15.9%	112.32	16.3%

Note: a, The tourism industry was negatively affected in 2003 by an epidemic of Severe Acute Respiratory Syndrome (SARS); b, This column doesn't equal to the addition of domestic tourism and inbound tourism because of the exchange rate used in different years.
Source: Adapted from Yearbook of China tourism statistics, 1996–2007, China Travel and Tourism Press.

Exhibit 4: IHG's Hotel Room Count by Ownership Type, June 30, 2007

	AMERICAS		EMEA		ASIA-PACIFIC	
	ROOMS	%	ROOMS	%	ROOMS	%
Owned and Leased	4,386	1.10	2,569	2.40	693	1.23
Managed	39,594	9.90	38,755	36.18	48,771	86.31
Franchised	356,082	89.01	65,785	61.42	7,041	12.46
Total	400,062	100.00	107,109	100.00	56,505	100.00

Source: Adapted from InterContinental Interim Report, 2007.

Exhibit 5: A List of IHG's Key Disposal Activities (2003–2006)

TIME	HOTELS SOLD	PRICE
July 2003	16 Staybridge Suites in the United States	$185m
Aug. 2003	IC Mayfair, London	£115m
Dec. 2004	13 North American hotels	$450m
Feb. 2005	12 North American hotels	$287m
Mar. 2005	73 UK properties	£1bn
Sept. 2005	ANZ portfolio of 9 hotels	£164m
Sept. 2005	IC Paris	€315m
Mar. 2006	24 Continental European hotels	€352m
July 2006	7 IC hotels in Continental Europe	€634m

Source: Adapted from InterContinental web site, September 2006.

A management-focused business model was widely used in the Asia-Pacific region. By the end of 2003, about 66 percent of IHG's properties in this region were managed under contract. The management mode works very well in the region. Many owners returned to work with InterContinental on additional projects, considering IHG to be a respected partner for new management developments.[61] The proportion of IHG's Asia-Pacific hotels under the management contract category was more than 83 percent by the end of June 2007.[62]

After 2003, IHG implemented the strategy of disposing of hotel assets, focusing on its expertise in hotel management (Exhibit 5).[63] The disposal of hotel assets may somewhat change the trimodel entry framework. Even in EMEA, the owned and leased hotels were not the primary profit generators anymore.[64] Now, franchising and management are the two focused business models popularly used by IHG, which only owned or leased 20 hotels worldwide by September 2007.[65]

THE POPULARITY OF MANAGEMENT CONTRACTS IN CHINA

Overall, franchising is the major business model of IHG. More than 3,300 hotels operating under IHG are franchised.[66] However, franchising is not popularly used in the Asia-Pacific region. Management contracting is IHG's primary entry and operating model in this region. By September 2006, the number of IHG-managed hotels in the Asia-Pacific region was 125 with 37,129 rooms, about 75.8 percent of the total hotels and 80.5 percent of the total rooms (Exhibit 6). In the Asia-Pacific region, IHG only had two owned and leased hotels, about 1.2 percent of the total.[67]

IHG claimed that "statutory and local hurdles stand in the way of franchising."[68] In general, a franchise contract is standardized, with little room for variation, whereas the terms in a management contract are agreed through negotiation between the owners and the management companies. The flexibility of a management contract allows owners and management companies to deal with more complex issues in developing countries with dynamic environments.

Another reason for the popularity of the management contract mode is that China was in great need of expertise in hotel management when international hotel chains first entered China. Because there were almost no formerly trained senior and junior hotel managers on the local human resources market at the time, owners of the tourist hotels in general had to depend on the management teams brought in by the international hotel chains.[69]

In China, management contracting is popular among other international hotel chains as well.[70] Accor and New World Corporation were some of the other major corporations that arranged management contracts in China in the 1980s.[71] Nevertheless, management contracting is not the only model used by international hotel chains in China. For example, Accor entered China's economy hotel market with Ibis Tianjin Hotel, which it owns. Super 8 of Wyndham drove its expansion in China mainly through the franchising model.[72]

The domestic hotel groups own a very large proportion of hotels under their names. The reason for a focus on ownership is that local governments often combined state-owned properties into groups to improve scale and competitiveness.[73] Beijing Tourism Group and Shanghai Jinjiang Group, the top two tourism groups in China, are two examples of previously state-owned operations. Dozens of

Exhibit 6: Three Kinds of IHG Hotels in the Asia-Pacific Region

	OWNED & LEASED		MANAGED		FRANCHISED		TOTAL	
	HOTELS	ROOMS	HOTELS	ROOMS	HOTELS	ROOMS	HOTELS	ROOMS
Number of hotels/rooms	2	693	125	37,129	38	8313	165	46,135
Percentage of total hotels/ rooms	1.2%	1.5%	75.8%	80.5%	23.0%	18.0%	100%	100%

Source: Adapted from InterContinental web site, September 2006.

state-owned hotels in Beijing and Shanghai were assigned to these two groups by city governments.[74] Now, many state-owned hotel groups extend their hotel network by a variety of modes, including signing management contracts, acquisition, and leasing.[75]

To meet the needs of the rapidly growing domestic business travelers and leisure travelers and to speed its expansion in the economy hotel market, IHG has not exclusively focused on management contracting as an entry mode. In April 2007, IHG announced its plans to launch a hotel franchising program for the Holiday Inn Express brand in China.[76]

THE HOTEL INDUSTRY IN CHINA

In 1978, China had just 137 tourist hotels. The economic reform and open-door policy has led to rapid growth in the industry. The first decade after China's open-door policy witnessed the development of primarily luxury and upscale hotels. In 1988, the number of tourist hotels was 1,496, more than 10 times that of 10 years before. In 1998, the number of tourist hotels reached 5,782, more than tripling the volume of 1988 (Exhibit 7). In the 21st century, the hotel industry has continued its expansion. In 2000, China had 6,029 star-rated hotels; in 2006, that number increased to 12,751 (Exhibit 8).[77]

EXPANSION OF INTERNATIONAL HOTEL CHAINS INTO CHINA

In 1979, the Chinese government authorized the building of six hotels in Beijing, Shanghai, Guangzhou, and Nanjing with foreign investment or investment from Hong Kong and Macau, which started the history of foreign-invested hotels in China.[78] In April 1982, the first joint-venture hotel, Jianguo Hotel, which was managed by Hong Kong Peninsula Group, opened in Beijing. In February 1984, Holiday Inn opened its first hotel in Beijing, which claimed the presence of major worldwide hotel chains in China.[79] Sheraton started to manage the Great Wall Hotel in 1985. Some other international hotel chains that entered the China hotel market by 1990 included Hilton, Accor, Shangri-La, New World, Ramada, and Hyatt (Exhibit 9).[80] Most of these hotels were located in popular tourism cities such as Beijing, Shanghai, Xi'an, and Guilin.

With fierce competition in lodging markets in most of the industrialized countries, the international hotel chains realized the importance of developing countries, especially those countries with a huge population base and strong economic growth. Attracted by more favorable policies and the market potential, more international hotel chains entered China for future development.[81] The hotel industry has become an emerging opportunity for international chains as China strives to build its economic activity and participate in free-trade arrangements.[82] In 1987, there were 162 foreign-invested/managed hotels. In 2000, the number increased to 833, an annual growth rate of 13.4 percent.[83] By September 2006, all top 10 worldwide hotel chains have entered the China market: Wyndham had

Exhibit 7: Tourist Hotels of China, 1978–2000

Year	Number of Hotels	Annual Increase	Rooms	Occupancy %
1978	137	—	15,539	—
1979	150	9.5	17,149	—
1980	203	35.3	31,800	—
1981	296	45.8	43,300	—
1982	362	22.3	51,600	—
1983	371	2.5	59,600	—
1984	505	36.1	77,000	—
1985	710	40.6	107740	—
1986	974	37.2	147,500	—
1987	1,283	31.7	184,710	66.3
1988	1,496	16.6	220,165	67.9
1989	1,788	19.5	267,505	57.2
1990	1,987	11.1	293,827	59.4
1991	2,130	7.1	321,116	62.5
1992	2,354	10.5	351,044	67.0
1993	2,552	8.4	386,401	67.7
1994	2,995	17.4	406,280	62.2
1995	3,720	24.2	486,114	58.1
1996	4,418	18.8	594,196	55.3
1997	5,201	17.7	701,736	53.8
1998	5,782	11.2	764,797	51.7
1999	7,035	21.6	889,430	53.4
2000	10,481	49.0	948,185	55.9

Source: Adapted from Yearbook of China tourism statistics, 1979–2001, China Travel and Tourism Press.

Exhibit 8: Star-Rated Hotels in China, 1999–2006

YEAR	NUMBER OF STAR-RATED HOTELS	OCCUPANCY RATE	ROOMS	BEDS
1999	3,856	54.34	524,894	1,024,866
2000	6,029	57.58	594,678	1,144,791
2001	7,358	58.45	816,260	1,533,053
2002	8,880	60.15	897,206	1,729,460
2003	9,751	56.14	992,804	1,887,740
2004	10,888	60.62	1,237,851	2,366,638
2005	11,828	60.96	1,332,200[a]	2,571,700[a]
2006	12,751	61.03	1,459,800[a]	2,785,500[a]

Note: a, Rounding to hundred of rooms/beds.
Source: Adapted from Yearbook of China tourism statistics, 2000-2005, China Travel and Tourism Press; China National Tourism Administration, 2007.

56 hotels including its popular brands Days Inn, Ramada, Super 8, and Howard Johnson; Marriott had 26 hotels with 6 brands; Best Western International had 40 hotels; Accor had 38 hotels; and Starwood had 26 hotels. Those worldwide top 10 hotel chains with less than 10 hotels in China are Global Hyatt Corp., Carlson Hospitality Worldwide, Hilton Group, and Choice Hotels International (Exhibit 10).[84]

The international hotel chains played very important roles in the development of China's lodging industry. The presence of international hotel chains has made tourist hotels in China the first industry to maintain a global service standard. Hou, Xijiu, the previous president of four joint-venture hotels, stated that "in addition to attracting foreign investment, the more important value of joint-venture hotels is that they created the market economy concept, established modern enterprise systems, and enhanced the reform process of the Chinese hotel industry."[85]

COMPETITIVE ANALYSIS OF THE HOTEL INDUSTRY

The performance of star-rated hotels in China varies across different ownership types. In 2006, the occupancy rate of foreign-funded hotels was 65.71 percent, and was 66.34 percent for Hong Kong,

Exhibit 9: Some Overseas Hotel Management Companies in China 1990

NAME	HOTEL
Accor	Novotel Guangzhou Jiang Nan
	Novotel Sightseeing (Guilin)
	Yuanlin (Shanghai)
Hilton	Shanghai Hilton
Holiday Inn	Holiday Inn Lido (Beijing)
	Holiday Inn Downtown (Beijing)
	Holiday Inn Chongqing
	Holiday Inn Dalian
	Holiday Inn City Centre (Guangzhou)
	Holiday Inn Gulin
	Holiday Inn Lhasa
	Holiday Inn Shanghai
	Bell Tower Xi'an
	Holiday Inn Xi'an
Hyatt	Hyatt Tianjin
	Hyatt Xi'an
Inter-Continental[a]	Forum (Shenzhen)
Ramada	Ramada Asia (Beijing)
Sheraton	Great Wall Sheraton (Beijing)
	Sheraton Guilin
	Huating Sheraton (Shanghai)
	Sheraton Tianjin
	Sheraton Xi'an

Note: a, At the time, InterContinental and Holiday Inn were two separate companies.
Source: Adapted from L. Yu, "Hotel Development and Structures in China",
International Journal of Hospitality Management 11, 2 (1992): 106.

Exhibit 10: Number of Hotels in China: Top 10 Worldwide Hotel Chains

NAME	TOTAL ROOMS (2005)	TOTAL HOTELS (2005)	HOTELS IN CHINA (BY 09/08/2006)
InterContinental Hotels Group	537,533	3606	57
Wyndham Worldwide (Formerly Cendant Hotel Group)	532,284	6344	56
Marriott International	499,165	2741	26
Hilton Hotels Corp.	485,356	2817	6
Choice Hotels International	481,131	5897	1
Accor	475,433	4065	38
Best Western International	315,875	4195	40
Starwood Hotels & Resorts Worldwide	257,889	845	26
Carlson Hospitality Worldwide	147,129	922	7
Global Hyatt Corp.	134,296	731	9

Source: Adapted from web sites of the ten hotel chains, September 2006.

Macau, and Taiwan funded hotels. Both were much higher than those of the state-owned, collective, privately owned hotels, and other types (Exhibit 11).[86]

The state-owned hotels (SOHs) are hampered by governance issues. "The complicated relationship among ownership, decision-making power, controlling rights, and rights for residual claims have fundamentally confounded the possibility of any proper corporate governance."[87] For example, some local governments invested in upscale SOHs to enhance the images of the regions or used the hotels as "internal hostels" to facilitate their use by local government officials. The primary political nature of incentive and the double identities of managers both as government officials and business decision makers negatively affect the performance of SOHs when economic efficiency conflicts with political interests.[88]

Performance also differs for hotels operating with different management models. The industry summary of some four-star and five-star hotels in China shows that internationally managed hotels (Int'l) have higher occupancy rates than domestically (Dom.) and independently managed hotels (Indp.). The RevPARs of international five-star hotels was ¥659, or 45 percent higher than that of domestic, and more than twice as much as that of independent hotels (Exhibit 12).[89]

Exhibit 11: Comparison of Performance among Different Ownerships, 2006

OWNERSHIP	NUMBER OF HOTELS	OCCUPANCY RATE %
HongKong, Macau, and Taiwan funded	329	66.34
Foreign-funded	256	65.71
Limited-liability shares	593	64.03
Limited liability	2,278	62.17
State-owned	5,832	60.06
Private-owned	1,871	58.87
Alliance	71	58.72
Collective	902	58.69
Share-holding cooperative	334	58.65
Others	285	58.41
Total	12,751	61.03

Source: Adapted from web site of China National Tourism Administration, November 2007.

Exhibit 12: Comparison of Hotel Performance among Different Management Models, 2005

	5-STAR			4-STAR		
Industry summary	Int'l[a]	Dom.[b]	Indp.[c]	Int'l	Dom.	Indp.
Occupancy %	69.6	69.3	62.6	73.1	68.9	67.6
Average Room Rate	946	657	482	539	417	359
Revenue Per Available Room(RevPAR)	659	455	302	394	287	243
Percentage of RevPAR Compared with Int'l	100	69.0	45.8	100	72.8	61.7

IHG'S COMPETITIVE ADVANTAGE

Scale in Key Markets

Many of IHG's strengths are related to its economies of scale. With more than 3,600 hotels and totals of nearly 126 million stays per year, IHG delivered almost $5 billion in revenue in 2005. It has the number-one loyalty program in the industry and owns the industry's most-visited web site (i.e., Holiday Inn). Moreover, IHG's reservation system receives 22 million calls per year and makes 150 transactions per second. IHG has a global sales team of more than 8,000 representatives. Among the 12 countries that account for 77 percent of the world market, IHG took the top three positions in six of the countries.[90]

In 2006, among the top 10 international hotel chains in China named by the Chinese Tourist Hotel Association, InterContinental was rated number one based on the number of rooms. IHG is larger than other international hotel chains, such as Shangri-La Hotels and Resorts, Shanghai Howard Johnson Hotels and Resorts, Marriott International, Starwood Hotels & Resorts Worldwide, Accor, Conifer, Best Western International, Hilton Group PLC, and China Travel Hotel Management services H.K. Ltd.[91]

IHG had 76 hotels in China by December 2007, maintaining its position as one of the largest international hotel chains in the country. Furthermore, IHG covered China's 35 major cities and has large portfolios in some key cities. For example, IHG has nine hotels in Beijing, the capital of China, and 10 hotels in Shanghai, the largest economic center in China. IHG also has four hotels in Hong Kong, once the "window of China" that connected mainland China with Western countries.[92]

In China, some domestic hotel chains have more hotels and rooms than IHG. The largest domestic hotel group, Shanghai Jinjiang Group, had about 170 hotels by September 2006, about the same number of hotels as IHG's Asia-Pacific Region (IHG had 162 hotels in the Asia-Pacific region by 2005). However, a global comparison of the two groups puts IHG in the dominant position. Jinjiang has fewer hotels, but also lacks global reach because almost all of its hotels are within China. IHG's China hotels get support from their global operation systems, marketing, and loyalty program.

Guanxi—Building Connections: Maintaining Good Stakeholder Relationships

Guanxi is a frequently mentioned word in articles and books on how to do business in China.[93] The two common translations of the word are "connections" and "relationships."[94] Western companies that have business relationships with China have noticed the importance of *guanxi* and have tried to build noninstrumental relationships with key decision makers as well as develop personalized networks of influence.[95]

As an experienced operator in the Chinese market, IHG developed good relationships with local government and industry associations. For instance, IHG is an active player in the China Tourist Hotel Association (CTHA) and joined the survey research of the hotel industry sponsored by CTHA.[96] In

2003, when Beijing was hit by SARS, IHG donated ¥1 million to a local hospital to support the local government's treatment of the epidemic. "We also believe strongly that it is appropriate for IHG to demonstrate our care for the Beijing community, as well as lead in building confidence for the recovery of the Chinese hospitality and travel sector when the time is right," said Mahmood Masood, Regional Vice President of Operations in China, IHG.[97]

Examples of IHG's good relationships with local communities are not rare. The Crowne Plaza Shijiazhuang's community support and fundraising efforts earned it the "Best Community Support Hotel of the Year Award" in 2004. Anna Stackler, the general manager, was recognized as the role model for the hospitality industry by the local labor union.[98]

IHG also developed good relationships with hotel owners in China. To develop a five-star hotel in China's "Wall Street," Beijing Capital Land contacted many major hotel chains and ultimately chose InterContinental. Tang Jun, CEO of the company, said, "We found common language and common enthusiasm."[99] The ability of IHG to develop a good relationship with owners brought it more business. In December 2005, IHG signed an agreement with the Overseas Chinese Town Group to manage the proposed InterContinental Shenzhen. This was the second IHG-managed property from the same owner. "We are glad to be working with InterContinental Hotels Group, with its proven expertise and extensive experience, to seize the emerging opportunities. I have no doubt that having a strong partner with a good understanding of our needs and aspirations will help us ensure that InterContinental Shenzhen will be a big success," said Ren Ke Lei, CEO of Overseas Chinese Town Group.[100]

MANAGING THE BRANDS PORTFOLIO

IHG is pursuing faster growth by making IHG's brands the first choice for guests and hotel owners. IHG's portfolio includes a variety of well-known and popular hotel brands that allow it to respond to most hotel development opportunities (Exhibit 13).[101] The range of IHG's brands allows guests to find a hotel from within the portfolio to meet their needs when they move up and down the hotel brand ladder according to their travel priorities.

IHG entered China with Holiday Inn, providing services that business travelers need, and also offering a comfortable atmosphere for guests to relax. More than half of IHG's China hotels are under the Holiday Inn brand. Later on, the Crowne Plaza was added to accommodate guests in the upscale market. Targeting the small to medium-sized business meetings market, Crowne Plaza Hotels and Resorts claims to be "The Place to Meet." The acquisition of InterContinental added this "first truly international hotel brand in the world" to IHG's Chinese Portfolio and offered services to the upper upscale market. Holiday Inn Express is among the fastest-growing brands in the midscale/limited-services markets, with an average of two new hotels opening worldwide every week. The Express brand entered the China market in 2004, and by April 2007, IHG had opened six Holiday Inn Express hotels and signed nearly 20 management contracts for the brand.[102]

In contrast, domestic hotel groups such as Jinjiang Group held a unibrand strategy. Hotels of different categories targeting various markets used the same Jinjiang brand. Although the establishment of JJ-Inn differentiated it from other Jinjiang hotels, the Jinjiang brand still covers a wide range of hotels from two-star to five-star (Exhibit 14).[103] The inconsistency of hotel quality under the same brand name is thought to cause some confusion among customers.

Exhibit 13: Some of IHG's Lodging Brands

MARKET SEGMENT	THE HOTEL GROUP'S BRANDS	CUSTOMER SEGMENT
Luxury	—	A mix of business and leisure, dependent on location, often with a high proportion of international guests
Upper Upscale	InterContinental	Predominantly International business travelers
Upscale*	Crowne Plaza	Mainly for small-to-medium-sized business meetings
Midscale* (full-service)	Holiday Inn	Predominantly domestic guests, both business and leisure
Midscale* (limited-service)	Express by Holiday Inn (in EMEA and Asia Pacific) Holiday Inn Express (in the Americas)	Predominantly domestic guests who prefer competitive rates and reduced services, both business and leisure
Economy/ Budget	—	Predominantly domestic guests looking for cheapest and most basic hotels

Source: Adapted from InterContinental web site, September 2006.

Exhibit 14: Jinjiang Brand Hotels

	JINJIANG				
BRAND	5-STAR	4-STAR	3-STAR	2-STAR	JJ-INN
Number of hotels	11	29	16	4	110

Source: Adapted from Jinjiang Group web site, September 2006.

Although IHG's brand portfolio created competitive advantages over other hotel chains with undifferentiated brands, IHG didn't cover all market segments. For example, IHG didn't have a luxury brand in its mix. Other international hotel chains, such as Starwood and Marriott, have established their luxury brands in China. The St. Regis Hotel Beijing and St. Regis Shanghai are two luxury hotels from Starwood.[104] Marriott targets key luxury markets in China with its Ritz-Carlton brand. In addition to its Ritz-Carlton hotels in Beijing, Shanghai, and Hong Kong, seven more Ritz-Carlton hotels are scheduled to be opened before 2010 in Beijing, Guangzhou, Shenzhen,

Sanya, Shanghai, Macau, and Hong Kong.[105] In November 2007, Accor's Sofitel Luxury Hotels "revealed its strategic plan to elevate the brand into the premium end of the international luxury hotel market."[106] Having a luxury brand helps enhance the quality and brand image of the whole hotel chain.

Moreover, IHG was not the leading hotel chain in the economy hotel market. For example, Wyndham's economy hotel brand Super 8 had signed 51 franchising contracts in Fujian, Zhejiang, Sichuan, Shandong, Liaoning, and other provinces in China by April 2006.[107] Other domestically developed economy hotel chains such as JJ-Inn and Home Inn had more than 10,000 rooms by the end of 2006.[108]

THE GLOBAL RELAUNCH OF HOLIDAY INN

Perceived as a midscale brand by most consumers in Western countries, Holiday Inn positioned itself as an upscale brand to meet local demand when it first entered China. The first Holiday Inn hotel in China, Lido, was rated a four-star hotel when China implemented the star-rated hotel system.[109] Many hotels managed by Holiday Inn in the 1980s were four-star and five-star hotels (upscale or upper upscale). Guests from the United States were amazed by the gilt and fountains in the lobby and marble in the bathrooms of Holiday Inn hotels in China.

The market positioning as an upscale product was critical to the popularity of the brand when it first entered the Chinese market. The former IHG Asia-Pacific CEO addressed that brand positioning difference as follows: "We came to China in 1984 with purely a Holiday Inn play, and that brand was the main focus. And here it was very much an upscale brand, as opposed to the mainstream Holiday Inns in the United States."[110] Andrew Cosslett, CEO of the InterContinental Hotels Group, explained that "because the ones in Shanghai (China) are newer, the property standard might be a bit higher. Also, owners in China want to push the perceived quality a little higher."[111]

The major reason for Holiday Inn to position itself as an upscale brand was that both Crowne Plaza and the upper upscale InterContinental Hotels brands were not created or purchased by IHG at the time China was eagerly pursuing international hotel chains in the early 1980s. To avoid customer confusion and maintain consistency, some of the high-quality Holiday Inn properties have been rebranded as Crowne Plazas to reduce image confusion. As Holiday Inn is a more powerful brand in the Chinese market, the Chinese translation of the Crowne Plaza keeps the meaning of Holiday Inn. IHG's current brand portfolio has allowed it to assign appropriate brands to a variety of properties, but the global differences between Holiday Inn brands around the world continues to pose challenges for the company. While Holiday Inn in China is a high-end brand, it appeals to a lower segment in Europe, and an even lower one in the United States.

To address this concern and further enhance quality and consistency across its brand portfolio, IHG announced a worldwide relaunch of the Holiday Inn brand family. By redesigning brand signage and the welcome experience, and incorporating refreshed guest rooms and new service promises, IHG's global relaunch program will ensure Holiday Inn's leading position in the midscale hotel market in China and the Asia-Pacific region.[112]

FUTURE

IHG and other international hotel chains are facing many favorable opportunities in China's hotel market:

- As China walks away from a planned economy and moves toward the market economy, more favorable institutional systems will ensure fewer barriers for international hotel chains' expansion in China.[113]

- The economy of China will continue its strong growth. From January to November 2007, the accumulated total retail sale of consumer goods was up to ¥801.95 billion, a 16.4 percent year-on-year rise.[114] During the same period, the accumulated value-added of industrial enterprises (all state-owned enterprises and non-state-owned enterprises with an annual sales income over ¥5 million) rose 18.5 percent over the same period of the previous year.[115]

- China's tourist market maintains its rapid growth. In the first 10 months of 2007, the international tourist arrivals in major Chinese cities increased 13.37 percent over the same periods of 2006.[116] The 2008 Beijing Summer Olympic Games, the World Exhibition Shanghai 2010, and other large events will draw millions of tourists to major cities in China.[117] The United Nations World Tourism Organization (UNWTO) forecasted that China would become the world's leading tourism destination by the year 2020.[118] At the beginning of 2007, the UNWTO revised its forecast to 2015 due to the rapid development of the tourism industry in China.[119]

- The nationwide increase of business and leisure tourists will create the need for hotels in big coastal cities and secondary cities in the mid and west regions. IHG has recognized this great opportunity and included many developing projects in its pipeline. Lodging Econometrics revealed that "hotel development is at a hectic pace—the pipeline for the region has reached new record highs." China is driving the region with 782 hotel (222,591 rooms) projects in the pipeline.[120]

- China is investing heavily in transportation infrastructures: 85,000 km of highway are under construction in China; by 2020, China plans to spend about $250 billion on railway network development.[121]

- The major economy hotel chains are maintaining a high occupancy rate, suggesting a huge potential for IHG's Holiday Inn Express brand, mainly targeting domestic customers.

Other international hotel chains such as Starwood, Accor, and Wyndham are speeding up their expansion into China. Starwood, for example, has more than 16 hotels in the pipeline.[122] Based on Accor's development plan, 10 Ibis hotels will be added to its Chinese list each year starting in 2007.[123] In October 2006, Marriott announced its global growth plan to continue rapid expansion in China.[124]

Domestic brands will also continue their rapid growth and have ambitious plans for expansion. Both JJ-Inn[125] and Home Inn have strategic plans of growing to more than 1,000 hotels in the coming years and are competing for industry leadership.[126] In addition, the top 30 domestic hotel management companies showed a significant increase of hotels and rooms in 2006 over the previous year.[127] As China continues to grow and prosper, competition from both international and domestic hotel chains may threaten the success of future development of IHG brands.

CASE 4 THE SUMMER OF 2006 UNION NEGOTIATIONS: UNITE HERE'S STRATEGY

THE STATE OF THE LABOR MOVEMENT

In North America in 2006, the phrases *organized labor*, *unions*, and the *labor movement* seemed like vestiges from a bygone era—a time when labor leaders like Samuel Gompers, John L. Lewis, George Meany, Jimmy Hoffa, and Lane Kirkland were as well known and powerful as Members of the House of Representatives, Senators, and even Presidents. The labor movement attained its peak of national power when the economy in the United States boomed in the years following World War II. Since that time, the influence of unions in the private sector of American business has steadily declined.

By 2006, the unionization of America's hotel industry was concentrated in a handful of large cities like New York, where more than 80 percent of the City's hotels were unionized. Unions also enjoyed a strong union presence in Chicago, Los Angeles, San Francisco, Boston, and Washington, D.C. Hotel workers, however, traditionally had not been a priority of the American labor movement. Hotel employees were not highly paid, often worked for tips, and did not stay in bargaining unit positions for the duration of their careers. Because union dues are composed of a percentage of employee pay (excluding tips) and because union members who benefit the most are those who stay at the same job for long periods of time, a hotel was not the model employer on which the union movement would theoretically wish to concentrate its efforts. Instead, the union movement focused on heavy labor. In fact, unions had organized more than half of the workforce in manufacturing.[1]

In the 1940s and '50s, the United States was the dominant world producer of heavy manufactured items like automobiles and steel, as well as lighter manufactured items like textiles. These industries, situated for the most part in the Northeast and the Midwest, were heavily unionized.[2] The energy needed to run the plants came from unionized coal mining, while the truck drivers and the longshoremen who moved the product were also predominantly organized. As most of us now know, the days of American dominance in heavy and light manufacturing are long gone. Overall, employment in U.S. manufacturing industries fell by 1.8 million jobs between January 1997 and December 2001, but a disproportionate share of those lost jobs were concentrated among union members, losing nearly 10 percent of its manufacturing-sector membership in that short five-year period.[3] The decline of American manufacturing is reflected in union membership statistics.[4] At its height in the mid-1950s,

Written by David Sherwyn, an Associate Professor of Law at the Cornell University School of Hotel Administration, and Paul Wagner, an Adjunct Professor of Law at the Cornell University School of Hotel Administration, and a Shareholder with the law firm Shea, Stokes, Roberts and Wagner. This case study was written for the purposes of classroom discussion.

organized labor represented about 35 percent of the U.S. workforce.[5] That percentage has declined steadily since that time, to 13.7 percent in 2005. In the private sector today, only 7.8 percent of the private workforce is unionized—the approximate level just before the New Deal.[6]

Although it is beyond our scope to attempt to explain why the U.S. economy has moved away from manufacturing into the embrace of services, labor economists and industrial relations scholars have examined this question in detail. Many scholars attribute some of the shift to globalization. Whereas global trade amounted to approximately one-third of the total world output in the early 1970s, it approached 45 percent in 1995.[7] There has been a 150 percent growth in foreign trade from 1970 to 1997.[8] Pressure of the new global economy has caused domestic organizations to seek lower labor costs abroad, and technological innovation has enabled service-based businesses to outsource labor abroad. According to India's National Association of Software and Service Companies, employment of software developers and call center operators serving clients outside of India increased by 353,000 jobs between 2000 and 2004, reaching a total of 505,000 jobs. Seventy percent of these workers served clients in the United States.[9] This is an example of the trend in many sectors.

At least one industry, however, cannot be relocated or outsourced overseas—the hospitality industry. Put simply, while an apparel manufacturer can have all of its products made in Asia and sold in the United States, a hotel or restaurant serving a domestic clientele cannot move its operations offshore. For this reason, the hospitality industry became a central focus of the labor movement, if not the panacea for its future. One significant challenge stood in the way of the labor movement's increasing focus on the hospitality industry: Would it be able to garner the resources needed to organize this diverse and growing service industry?

THE MERGER OF HERE AND UNITE

The Hotel Employees and Restaurant Employees (HERE) organization had a core membership in a growth industry. Moreover, the union had a very capable, dynamic, and progressive leader, John Wilhelm. But HERE lacked resources—the union simply did not have a lot of money. Meanwhile, UNITE, the successor union to the International Ladies' Garment Workers' Union (ILGWU) and the Amalgamated Clothing and Textile Workers Union (ACTWU), also had a very bright, dynamic leader in Bruce Raynor. In addition, because it owned the Amalgamated Bank of New York, it had substantial resources. The problem for UNITE was declining membership, because it was focused on the apparel and textile manufacturing sectors, which have been in decline for the latter part of the 20th and the early 21st centuries, as discussed briefly and explored in much greater detail by others elsewhere.

On July 8, 2004, UNITE and HERE solved their respective problems by merging to create UNITE HERE. From its inception, UNITE HERE made its priorities clear. The union's web site states: "Organizing the unorganized in our industries is the top priority for UNITE HERE. Over 50 percent of the new Union's national budget will go toward organizing."[10] UNITE HERE declared that it would not organize the old-fashioned way through National Labor Relations Board (NLRB) elections. Instead, the union proclaimed its intent to increase its membership through neutrality agreements and card checks. In order to understand the distinction, both types of union-organizing strategies are explained as follows.

TRADITIONAL ORGANIZING STRATEGIES

Unions use several strategies to organize under the old-fashioned method. Sometimes, unions send their members to apply for jobs with nonunion employers that the unions wish to organize. The applicants' real reason for applying is to organize the other employees. This method, referred to as "salting," has been the subject of a U.S. Supreme Court case in which the Court held that an employer could not terminate a "salter" simply because the real reason the employee joined the Company was to organize it.[11] Another traditional method for organizing is to use current employees to "sell" the union to co-workers. Last, organizers may enter the property and hand out authorization cards or set up picket lines at the entrances and exits to the property.

The National Labor Relations Act (NLRA) sets forth the rules regulating this form of employee organization.[12] Under these rules, before any labor organization can be certified as the exclusive bargaining representative for any group of employees, the employees in that group, called a bargaining unit, vote for or against union representation in a secret-ballot election monitored by the NLRB. In most cases, the NLRB seeks to schedule such an election approximately four weeks after the union initiates the process by filing what is known as a representation certification petition. The time period may be extended if the employer contests the bargaining unit or if other legal issues arise. This approximate four-week period provides both the union and the employer with an opportunity to present their respective positions to the employees.

Under the NLRB rules, a union may request the secret-ballot election only if a minimum of 30 percent of the employees in an appropriate bargaining unit have signed authorization cards. As a practical matter, however, most national unions will not file a petition unless at least 60 percent of the employees have signed cards.[13] To prevail in the election, the union needs a simple majority of those who actually vote, not a majority of those who would be represented in the bargaining unit. Thus, if 50 employees are in the proposed bargaining unit but only 21 vote, the union needs only 11 votes to win. Employers win in the event of a tie.

Both sides are free to campaign prior to the election. The period between the time the petition is filed and the election is held is often referred to as the critical period. During that time, employers may not threaten, interrogate, make promises to, or engage in surveillance of employees. In addition, employers may not solicit grievances or confer benefits. If the employer violates these rules, the NLRB may either order the election to be rerun or issue a bargaining order.[14] Employers may, however, engage in numerous legitimate campaign activities to convince employees to vote against the union.

This is exactly what employers typically do during the critical period, raising issues with the lawful intent of informing employees of their rights and the consequences of voting in favor of the union.[15] One of the key strategies in this regard is to examine what the union is selling and explain to the employees that the costs outweigh the benefits.

One problem for the unions, according to some, is that organized labor does not always have much to sell. For example, Paul Wagner, a member of the management law firm Shea Stokes Roberts & Wagner, and a co-author of this case study, tells the story of an organizing drive in which the union represented to employees that it would demand that the employer implement the union's health insurance plan if it were elected. The union extolled the fact that it would insist that the employer pay 100 percent of the cost of the plan, as opposed to their current plan under which the employees paid a portion of the cost. The employer held a meeting in which it compared the two plans side by side. While the union plan did not feature any upfront costs, the coverage was clearly so inferior that the employees concluded that they were better off with the employer plan and voted against the union. Employers contend that this insurance issue is a typical example of the current state of union organizing: at first the union pitch sounds great, but after close examination, the employees choose not to buy what the union is selling. This is why, employers argue, companies are able to defeat the union in elections.[16] Not surprisingly, unions often possess a very different view of campaigns.

Union advocates claim that during most campaigns, employers illegally threaten, intimidate, and terminate employees who favor the union. According to a 2005 report by the University of Illinois at Chicago's Center for Urban Economic Development, when faced with organizing drives, 30 percent of employers fire pro-union workers, 49 percent threaten to close a worksite if the union prevails, and 51 percent coerce workers into opposing unions with bribery or favoritism.[17] Unions point to the numerous unfair labor practice charges filed against employers as well as anecdotal evidence of outrageous employer behavior. Regardless of whether employers violate the law by intimidating and threatening employees or unions have nothing to sell, one thing is clear: UNITE HERE no longer wishes to organize under the traditional NLRB election rules. In fact, as one HERE organizer stated: "[W]e will never go to an NLRB election again."[18]

The "Change to Win" Organizing Strategy

UNITE HERE is one of a group of national labor organizations to have assembled as part of a novel attempt to shift strategic gears, in particular with respect to organizing. This group is called the "Change to Win" coalition. The unions making up this group include the seven largest and arguably most powerful unions in the United States: UNITE HERE, the Service Employees International Union (SEIU), the International Brotherhood of Teamsters, the Carpenters, United Farm Workers, the Laborers International Union, and the United Food and Commercial Workers (UFCW). As stated on the Change to Win web site, the central objective of Change to Win is "to unite the more than 50 million American workers who work in industries that cannot be outsourced or shipped overseas into strong unions that can win them a place in the American middle class—where their jobs provide good wages, good health care, good pensions and a voice on the job."[19]

The unions forming this group have integrated their organizing programs ("Unite to Win" is UNITE HERE's name for its part in Change to Win) to launch large-scale organizing campaigns, earmarking at least 50 percent of collective resources for organizing drives across the country. The specific goal of these unions is to ban together the critical mass of employees representing the industries that are much less likely to be outsourced overseas. Part of the organizing strategy involves labor-coalition building, with the intent of bypassing traditional organizing drives in favor of larger-scale political and economic pressures exerted on employers to gain alternative means of access to unorganized employees.

As John Wilhelm explains on the Change to Win web site, "what workers in this industry need, what the country needs is a permanent campaign to do in the service sector what we did in manufacturing 70 years ago: transform low-wage work into decent jobs that give people the opportunity to make it into the middle class." These unions seek to accomplish this goal via the nontraditional organizing methods of card-checks and neutrality agreements, described in greater detail as follows.

At a recent Change to Win convention held in Las Vegas, attended by more than 2,000 union organizers, the organization announced a new massive organizing campaign in 35 cities. Operating under the slogan "Make Work Pay," the organizing drive is unique in that it aims to form cooperative cross-union efforts to organize workers in the target cities. One of the primary components of the Make Work Pay campaign is a national campaign led by UNITE HERE to organize workers at a large U.S. hotel chain, including a massive leafleting effort at the company's hotels and community rallies in many cities. Part of the Unite to Win coalition, UNITE HERE's strategy is to organize using card-check neutrality agreements.

NEUTRALITY AGREEMENTS

Although neutrality agreements come in several forms, the common denominator is that employers agree to stay neutral with regard to the union's attempt to organize the workforce.[20] Some agreements simply state that the employer will remain neutral with no other language, whereas other agreements contain more specific provisions.[21] For example, UNITE HERE's standard agreements clearly state that employers "will not communicate opposition" to the union's efforts.[22]

Neutrality agreements commonly provide the union with access to employees in the form of a list of their names and addresses (and sometimes telephone numbers), as well as permission to come onto company property during work hours to collect signed authorization cards. This differs from the guidelines set up by the NLRB and the courts, under which an employer has no obligation to, and may actually be prohibited from, providing the union with such sweeping access to its employees.[23]

Finally, most neutrality agreements also include a card-check provision, which requires the employer to recognize the union if a majority of the bargaining-unit employees sign authorization cards. Under a card-check agreement, the employees do not vote for the union in a secret-ballot election monitored by the NLRB. Instead, the employer recognizes the union if it presents the company with the requisite number of signed authorization cards, at which point the neutrality agreement is no longer needed and expires.

THE EFFECT OF NEUTRALITY AGREEMENTS

Neutrality agreements radically change the landscape of union organizing. One study conducted in the late 1990s examined 170 union campaigns where the employer and the union agreed to neutrality with a card-check provision. With the aid of such agreements, unions prevailed 78.2 percent of the time when they attempted to organize.[24] The authors compared this result to the 46 percent union success rate in contested NLRB elections and concluded that while neutrality with card-check agreements are effective, the results are not nearly as stark as comparing the election result in the private sector to that in the public sector, where unions won 85 percent of the elections in 1995. The authors underestimate the results of their study.

As stated previously, for all practical purposes, no union will petition for an election unless it has more than 50 percent support of the petitioned-for unit. This implies that in those elections that unions lost (54 percent), the unions had majority support at one time and, if there had been a card-check, the unions would likely have been recognized.

The best way to explain this is with an example: Assume that 200 employers are targeted by the same union. One hundred employers sign a neutrality agreement with a card-check and 100 do not. Consistent with prior results, the union successfully organizes 78 of the neutrality employers. The union then attempts to organize 100 employers without neutrality agreements. Of these 100 companies, the employees in 20 companies do not want a union, and because less than 50 percent of the employees sign authorization cards, the union walks away. Of the remaining 80 companies, the union gets more than 50 percent of the employees to sign cards. Under a card-check agreement, *all 80* of these companies would be unionized. Because there is an election, however, the employer tells its story and the union prevails in less than 40 of the elections.

The results of the study would say that neutrality with a card-check yielded a 78 percent union recognition and election yielded a 50 percent union success rate. In fact, however, the election results were actually 40 percent, because 20 companies from which the union walked away do not make it into the election data set. What this means for managers is simple. Assuming there is enough employee interest to warrant an election, the company's chances of becoming unionized are less than 50 percent under the NLRB's election procedures, and nearly guaranteed under a neutrality agreement with a card-check provision. Given these results, it seems clear that employers who want to remain non-union or simply believe that employees should hear both sides of the argument and then vote should refuse to sign a neutrality agreement.

WHY SIGN?

Why would an employer ever accede to a neutrality agreement? The short answer to this question is that the employer will sign a neutrality agreement when it is in the company's best interests. Those that believe that unionization is never in the employer's best interest would likely be puzzled by this argument. There are situations, however, when it is in the employer's best interest to sign a neutrality agreement. First, some municipalities have instituted labor peace agreements that required neutrality in order for employers to obtain building permits or even operate.[25] Second, in the hotel industry, it is not unheard of for a union (or its pension fund) to buy a hotel and make a neutrality agreement a condition for any operator wishing to manage the property. Third, sometimes unions can help an employer staff a property. The last reason to sign a neutrality agreement is because the union is selling something that the employer wishes to buy. For example, in Las Vegas, at least one human resources director contends he could have never opened on time without the help of HERE. Similarly, Southern Bell Corporation (SBC) signed a nationwide neutrality agreement with the communications workers in exchange for that union's agreement to lobby on behalf of SBC with regards to potential antitrust violations.

One important commodity unions have to offer an employer is labor peace. In order to sell peace, the union needs the ability to start a war. In the years leading up to 2006, UNITE HERE forged a strategy that allowed it to wage war against the hotel industry in order to afford the union the opportunity to peddle peace.

A CHANGE IN STRATEGY: SETTING UP THE SUMMER OF 2006

Most of the unionized hotels in the major cities in the United States and Canada are part of an employers' association that bargains as a multiemployer group. The contract that emerges from these negotiations is referred to as an area agreement and covers all the properties in the association. In addition, some properties that are not part of the multiemployer group sign are referred to as "me-too agreements." These agreements simply mean that these associated properties will be bound by the area agreement that was negotiated by the larger chain-style hotels.

Traditionally, the contracts in the major cities expired in different years. Thus, if the San Francisco area agreement was to expire this year, then the Los Angeles agreement would expire the following year and New York would come the year after. In the past, this staggered expiration was acceptable to the union. Because HERE represented properties in all the major cities, it would take too many resources to negotiate on several fronts at the same time. When the hotels were independently owned and operated, however, there was no advantage or disadvantage to negotiating separately each year. As operators developed into large chains, the companies encountered the same issue as the union: it was too cumbersome to juggle multiple negotiations in several cities simultaneously. Thus, the contracts continued to expire in staggered succession.

For the 2006 negotiations, UNITE HERE changed its strategy and sought to have the contracts in several large cities expire simultaneously. In the years before 2006, UNITE HERE either insisted on short contracts or refused to agree to any contract to ensure that in the summer of 2006 there were either expiring contracts or no contracts in New York, Chicago, Honolulu, Los Angeles, San Francisco, Boston, and Toronto. The union succeeded, and the area contracts in all of these cities expired either before or during that summer. Why did UNITE HERE employ this strategy?

According to John Wilhelm, the stated reason for UNITE HERE's strategy was the change in the industry. Wilhelm explained that the union did not want a national labor contract or a standardized wage scale. Instead, the union simply wanted to negotiate with corporate executives and not representatives from each city. While this argument sounds plausible at first, there are some obvious logical flaws. First, to which corporate executives is Wilhelm referring? If it is the director of labor relations, how can this person negotiate in seven places at once? It seems it would be more likely to get that executive to the table if there were not seven negotiations going on at once. Wilhelm cannot believe that CEOs and COOs will come to the table. CEOs and COOs are experts in operations; they hire experts in labor relations to negotiate on their companies' behalf. The union's negotiators are experts in negotiations; they hire people to run their businesses.

Another problem with Wilhelm's explanation is revealed when examining the dichotomy between hotel operators and hotel owners. The corporate executives to which Wilhelm refers work for hotel *operators*, not hotel *owners*, and thus the question arises: who is the party across the table from the union? If it is the owner, then national bargaining makes no sense. If it is the operator, then what role does the owner play? National bargaining seems to be logistically difficult and creates questions and issues that would seem to impede progress. If this is the case, then the question is: why did the union work so hard to get the contracts to expire at the same time?

The answer comes back to labor peace, labor war, and UNITE HERE's priorities. Wilhelm is partially correct when he says the 60-year-old bargaining structure "doesn't work anymore." The development of large chains has seriously hampered the union's threat of labor war in any given city. If New York is on strike and these hotels lose conventions, the New York properties can send their conventions to other properties managed by the same company in another city. While this may not help the owner, that New York owner knows that its time will come where there is peace in New York, but war in another city. Thus, while the 60-year-old structure did not work for UNITE HERE, it worked very well for the hotels. This structure put the union at a serious disadvantage. The question thus arises: did the new structure level the playing field, or did it give the union a substantial advantage?

What UNITE HERE could do was pretty clear. Having seven cities without contracts allowed the union to put a corporate strategy into place. The union could call strikes against one or more operators in all seven cities. These companies could not send all of their conventions to other large cities, because there were so many strikes and the strikes were not against individual properties. Convention-goers, who do not wish to cross a picket line in New York, may not have wished to spend time at the same branded property in Atlanta or Miami. Managers in New York City could not go to Los Angeles to help with Los Angeles' strike because New York City was on strike too. Moreover, the union spent the years before 2006 building up its strike fund. Employees who went on strike knew they would receive union strike pay. This ability to wage war allowed the union to sell peace. The question is: what employers should have to pay for peace: better wages, hours, work rules?

Given UNITE HERE's focus on organizing and the fact that UNITE HERE does not wish to organize with NLRB elections, the goal of the union strategy was to convince the hotels to sign nationwide neutrality agreements. Because neutrality agreements are merely permissive subjects of bargaining (as opposed to mandatory subjects), UNITE HERE could not have insisted that the hotels discuss this form of organizing. The union could, however, package neutrality with lower demands for wage and benefit increases. Hotels were faced with an option: buy peace or go to war.

This complex decision was made more complicated by the question of who is the "hotel." The hotel operator's interests may conflict with those of the hotel's owners. There is good reason why their interests would often conflict. Moreover, different types of hotel owners have different financial interests—short-term real estate investor-owners often have different priorities than long-term hotel owners. Also, the law is simply not clear as to whether an operator can sign a neutrality agreement for another property with another owner. As the hotels prepared for the summer of 2006, they hoped that their management staff would be able to survive a strike, that their sister properties could take care of conventions, and that the union's corporate campaign would not drive guests away.[26]

THE SUMMER OF 2006 NEGOTIATIONS

As the summer of 2006 began, it was clear that the industry would enjoy one of its best summer seasons ever. In fact, the summer would be the industry's best since the summer of 2001. Because both occupancy and average daily rate (ADR) were high, neither the owners nor the operators wanted to endure a strike. As the summer began, the industry did not really know what the union would do. Would it call a strike? Would it attempt to negotiate a national contract? In other words, how would the union operationalize its national strategy? The answer revolved around Hilton and the "me-too agreements."

Hilton:

In each of the seven cities, Hilton Hotels was a member of the multiemployer bargaining unit. The union, as is its right, chose not to have Hilton at the multiemployer bargaining table. As one union official in Chicago said: "we have the good (Hyatt), the bad (Starwood), and the ugly (Hilton)." Hilton was faced with a dilemma. Should it stay strong and negotiate hard, or should it try to get an agreement and avoid war?

Me-Too Agreements:

Traditionally, small operators have little power in bargaining. Sometimes they play a role in negotiations, other times, as stated earlier, they avoid the negotiations and simply sign me-too agreements. Often this decision is based on the company's desire. The company must decide whether to attempt to have input at the bargaining table where, because of its relative size in the multiemployer group, it has very little leverage. Alternatively, it may decide to avoid the time and expense of being part of the process. In 2006, the union added a new factor in the equation. The union approached the smaller operators and informed them that the me-too agreement was a signal to the union. Operators who sign me-too agreements are the union's friends. The union would not strike, disparage, or campaign against me-too signatories. In fact, if there was a strike, not only would the union leave me-too signatories alone, but these properties could actually get the business from properties on strike. The union would endorse these properties on its web site and encourage its members to stay at these properties.

The Large Operators (not including Hilton):

Large hotel operators had two major decisions to make: What should they do with regard to (1) Hilton and (2) the me-too signatories. With regard to Hilton, large operators could either wait to see what happened with Hilton or attempt to negotiate a deal before Hilton. Knowing that the union was pressuring the traditional me-too signatories, the large operators could (1) not get involved in the dispute; (2) offer to give these operators real voice at the bargaining table; or (3) try to convince these operators that they needed to stick together without providing them a real voice.

MAKING CHOICES GOING FORWARD

The strategy of UNITE HERE is now well-known, and key industry players need to react. Obviously, companies do not want a strike, but can they live with a neutrality agreement? What will such an agreement mean to the small operator or the remaining large operators? How will it affect the ability of hospitality companies to manage and flag new properties? How will owners react to a strike over an issue (i.e., neutrality for future properties) that may not affect the current owners? Should these three disparate groups work together, or should they each work to get the best deal?

CASE 5 BANYAN TREE: SUSTAINABILITY OF A BRAND DURING RAPID GLOBAL EXPANSION

Within the next five years, if we play our expansion card right and we manage our growth properly, we have a reasonable, credible opportunity to become one of the top two or three dominant players in a global space which is very niche but nevertheless very global.

—K. P. Ho, CEO

On August 14, 2006, exactly two months after its initial public offering (IPO) listing, Banyan Tree Holdings Limited announced second-quarter results for the period ended June 30. Revenue had more than doubled to S$71.4[1] million, largely due to post-tsunami recovery. Yet the company felt that this was only the beginning and had earmarked part of the IPO proceeds to finance an ambitious expansion plan.

At the core of its business development plan was a proposal to open 21 new resorts[2] over four years, which would span non-Asian territories from Greece to Mexico. CEO Ho Kwon Ping's vision was to "string a necklace [of Banyan Tree properties] around the world." The Asian financial crisis of 1997, the SARS crisis of 2003, and the Indian Ocean tsunami of 2004 had taken their toll on the travel and tourism industry (see Exhibit 1). Although recovery was on the horizon, Ho understood the need to diversify risks across geographic regions, and the IPO provided the finances to venture out of familiar territory.

But two challenges lay ahead for Ho as he considered how the company should manage growth without losing focus on the qualities customers associated with the Banyan Tree brand. First, was the issue of adequate labor and infrastructure to continue delivering a consistent Banyan Tree experience. Second, was the danger of brand dilution if they were to spread themselves too thin and/or venture into locations that could have a negative impact on their brand and their bottom line. For a company established on delivering holistic experiences to guests, it was imperative that the Banyan Tree ethos, culture, and skill set not be lost in the process of growth.

Prepared by Pauline Ng under the supervision of Cathy A. Enz of Cornell University and Ali F. Farhoomand of The University of Hong Kong. This case is not intended to show effective or ineffective handling of business decisions. Banyan Tree is a fast-evolving company, and the case only contains information up to August 2006. It is not to be duplicated or cited in any form without the express permission of the Asian Case Research Centre.

Exhibit 1: Travel and Tourism Industry Trends and Figures

World: Inbound Tourism
International Tourist Arrivals (millions)

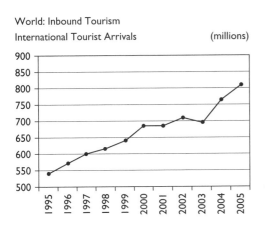

World and regions: Inbound Tourism
International Tourist Arrivals (change, %)

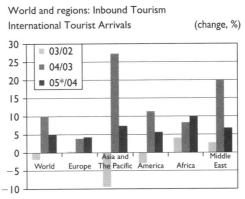

INTERNATIONAL TOURIST ARRIVAL BY (SUB) REGION

| | FULL YEAR | | | | | | | | | | | AVERAGE | | SHARE | |
| | 2000 | 2001 | 2002 | 2003 | 2004 | 2005* | 03/02 | 04/03 | 05*/04 | 05*/04 | 05*/00 | 2000–2005* | 2000 | 2005* |
					ABS (MILLION)			CHANGE (%)		ABS (MILLION)		CHANGE (%)		(%)
World	689	688	709	697	766	308	-1.7	10.0	5.5	42.3	119.2	3.2	100	100
Europe	306.2	395.3	407.4	408.6	425.8	443.9	0.3	4.2	4.3	18.3	47.7	2.3	57.5	54.9
Northern Europe	44.6	42.3	43.8	44.5	48.4	51.8	1.8	8.6	7.1	3.4	7.2	3.0	6.5	6.4
Western Europe	139.7	135.8	138.0	136.1	138.7	141.1	-1.4	1.9	1.7	2.3	1.4	0.2	20.3	17.5
Central Eastern Europe	71.2	74.0	78.1	80.3	89.1	92.3	2.8	11.0	3.6	3.2	21.1	5.3	10.3	11.4
Southern Mediterranean Europe	140.8	143.7	147.6	147.7	149.5	158.8	0.1	1.2	6.2	9.3	18.0	2.4	20.4	19.6
Asia and the Pacific	111.4	118.8	126.1	114.2	145.4	158.2	-9.4	27.3	7.4	10.3	44.3	7.0	16.2	19.3
North-East Asia	58.3	61.0	68.2	61.7	79.4	87.5	-9.6	28.6	10.2	8.1	29.2	8.5	8.5	10.8
South-East Asia	37.8	40.7	42.8	37.0	48.3	50.2	-13.6	30.3	4.1	2.0	12.5	5.9	5.5	6.2
Oceania	9.2	9.1	9.1	9.0	10.2	10.6	-0.9	12.4	3.9	0.4	1.3	2.7	1.3	1.3
South Asia	6.1	5.8	5.8	6.4	7.6	7.9	10.2	18.1	4.5	0.3	1.8	5.4	0.9	1.0
Americas	128.2	122.2	116.7	113.1	125.8	133.1	-3.1	11.2	5.3	7.3	4.9	0.3	18.6	18.5
North America	91.5	86.4	83.3	77.4	85.9	89.4	-7.1	10.9	4.1	3.5	-2.1	-0.5	13.3	11.1
Caribbean	17.1	16.8	16.0	17.0	18.2	19.2	6.5	6.7	5.4	1.0	2.1	2.3	2.5	2.4
Central America	4.3	4.4	4.7	4.9	5.8	6.6	4.2	17.8	13.6	0.8	2.2	8.6	0.6	0.8
South America	15.2	14.6	12.7	13.7	16.0	18.0	7.9	16.2	12.7	2.0	2.8	3.4	2.2	2.2
Africa	28.2	28.9	29.5	30.7	33.3	36.7	4.1	8.4	10.1	3.4	8.5	5.4	4.1	4.5
North Africa	10.2	10.7	10.4	11.1	12.8	13.6	6.6	15.5	6.1	0.8	3.4	6.9	1.5	1.7
Subsaharan Africa	18.0	18.2	19.1	19.6	20.5	23.1	2.8	4.5	12.6	2.6	5.1	5.2	2.6	2.9
Middle East	25.2	25.0	29.2	30.0	35.9	38.4	2.9	19.3	6.9	2.5	13.2	8.8	3.7	4.8

Source: World Tourism Organisation (WTO)   (Data as collected by WTO January 2006)

Source: UNWTO Market Intelligence and Promotion Section, "International Tourism up by 5.5% to 808 Million Arrivals in 2005," January 24, 2006, http://www.unwto.org/newsroom/Releases/2006/january/06_01_24.htm (accessed December 29, 2006).

COMPANY BACKGROUND

LEADERSHIP

Experience from his family's mini-conglomerate business had convinced Ho that any business had to have something proprietary in order for it to be sustainable in the long run. Competing on cost alone had been a successful formula in the 1970s and '80s, but when manufacturing efficiencies and low-cost production had reached its limit, businesses found that they could no longer compete. Bitter lessons had been learned, and Ho believed strongly that proprietary advantages other than costs should form the basis for sustainable competition.

At age 40, Ho set out to build a consumer brand that would be sustainable, not only in Asia, but in the global marketplace. He viewed this as an *imperative for survival* that would become the driving force behind his business. Hotels and resorts became the vehicle for realizing this vision.

Banyan Tree Hotels and Resorts, a subsidiary of the Singapore-based Banyan Tree Holdings Limited, was established in 1992 as a family business with Ho Kwon Ping as the Chairman, his wife, Claire Chiang, as the Senior Vice President of the retail and merchandising arm of the business, and his brother, Ho Kwon Cjan, as the head architect of the company. As a private developer and operator of boutique hotels, resorts, and spas in Asia-Pacific, the company grew in leaps and bounds under the leadership of Ho. Banyan Tree's 250-plus awards and accolades spoke volumes for its success, while Ho had won the 2003 Innovation Award from the Hotel Investment Conference Asia Pacific, the 2005 Entrepreneurship Award from the London Business School, and the 2005 Ernst & Young Singapore, Lifestyle, Hospitality and Retail Entrepreneur Award. (See Exhibit 2 for listing of awards.)

VISION, CORPORATE CULTURE, AND MANAGEMENT TEAM

"I see my role in motivating and inspiring people . . . . A leader is someone who takes people's deepest fears and concerns and anxieties, and transforms these to aspirations and hopes. . . . My colleagues are not necessarily your hotshots, or top software engineers in Silicon Valley. They're people who work in local communities; they have their concerns; they have their normal livelihood issues; they need to raise kids and handle the mundane anxieties of life. And if I can inspire them to have a vision of a better life for themselves and their families, and to be involved in the community and the company which they take pride in, then I think I am doing my work."

—K. P. Ho, CEO

Exhibit 2: Banyan Tree's List of Recent Awards and Accolades

Ernst & Young Entrepreneur of the Year Award

Lifestyle, Hospitality & Retail Entrepreneur of the Year, Singapore 2005

Mr. Ho Kwon Ping

The World's Top 25 2006

Banyan Tree Spa Bangkok

Hotel Spas - Asia & Indian Subcontinent

Banyan Tree Spa Phuket

Hotel Spas - Africa, Middle East & Indian Ocean

Banyan Tree Spa Maldives

Conde Nast Traveller UK Gold List 2006 Best for Rooms

Banyan Tree Bangkok

2006 Singapore 1000/SME 500 Awards

Singapore 1000: Highest Net Profit

Banyan Tree Holdings Pte Ltd.

Singapore International 100 Ranking 2006

Singapore Top 100 International Company
Banyan Tree Holdings Pte Ltd.

Conde Nast Traveller UK

Best Hotel Pool

Banyan Tree Seychelles

Luxury Travel Gold List 2006

Best Overseas Spa

Banyan Tree Spa Phuket

Best Overseas Resort

Banyan Tree Phuket

Best Overseas Golf Resort

Banyan Tree Phuket

Best Overseas Resort

Banyan Tree Maldives

Conde Nast Traveller US 2006 Gold List

World's Best Places to Stay - Asia, Australia & Pacific Nations

Banyan Tree Phuket

2006 T+L 500 World's Best Awards

500 World's Best: Asia

Banyan Tree Phuket

Source: Banyan Tree web site, http://media.banyantree.com (accessed 28 December 2006).

The company's vision was to build on its brands, *Banyan Tree* and *Angsana*, to create a diversified group of niche resorts and hotels in strategic locations throughout the world, which would be complemented by residence and property sales, and spa and gallery operations. The revenue base should ideally be split evenly among property sales, hotels, and fee-based income (such as architectural design fees). Ho was sure that over 14 years, Banyan Tree had nurtured a corporate culture that could successfully take the strengths of the *Banyan Tree* brand beyond Asia-Pacific. These strengths included the corporate social responsibility (CSR) philosophy the Ho family instilled at the outset; Ho's insistence on having a proprietary advantage other than cost, which was to be found in the unique experience associated with the *Banyan Tree* brand; and its Asia-Pacific region staff, who shared the Banyan Tree ethos of CSR and continuously sustaining innovation in an experiential brand.[3]

Core members of the senior management team had been instrumental in the company's development since the inception of the Banyan Tree in 1992. Their multidisciplinary and multicultural mix of skills and experiences contributed significantly in the areas of product innovation, branding, and product/service design, construction, and operations. Of its 5,000 employees, 35 nationalities were represented. Its 40 top managers came from 20 different countries. Ho believed that the mix and diversity of backgrounds, skill sets, and cultures gave Banyan Tree a genuine global perspective and a collective strength and resilience in various environments.

BRANDING

"When I created Banyan Tree, I decided at that time that brand-building had to be one of the most important imperatives of Banyan Tree, perhaps even more so as we are in the hospitality industry."

—K. P. Ho, CEO

The first *Banyan Tree* resort opened in 1994. The brand was targeted primarily at highly affluent travelers wanting a luxury retreat where they would experience romance, intimacy, and rejuvenation. Positioned in the niche resort, hotel, and spa market segment, Banyan Tree pioneered the concepts that have become the signature feature of many of its resorts and spas, including the tropical garden spa and the pool villa. All *Banyan Tree*–branded hotels, spas, and galleries reflect the natural environment, culture, and heritage of their locations.

In 2000, *Angsana*, the sister brand of *Banyan Tree,* was launched. *Angsana* offered a refreshing and contemporary experience reflected through its interior design and spa treatments. Targeted at a younger customer segment than *Banyan Tree*, this brand was associated with youth and revitalization. It appealed to young families, and pricing was typically 20 to 30 percent lower than at *Banyan Tree* resorts.

"Angsana was created to be a broader brand. But we recognized that . . . it would probably be less exclusive than Banyan Tree because it is the more normal, mainstream brand. The Angsana brand was created to precisely compete with the Sheratons of the world, whereas Banyan Tree is very focused."

—K. P. Ho, CEO

Under the name *Colours of Angsana,* the *Angsana* brand also offered an experience that was centred on cultural tourism and soft adventure, often located in off-the-beaten track destinations such as Laos, Sri Lanka, and China. Consisting of a range of boutique resorts and hotels, each was an existing property that had been refurbished with modern adaptations of the indigenous culture and heritage of their respective locations. *Colours of Angsana* debuted in August 2003 in Shangri-la Yunnan, China with the Gyalthang Dzong Hotel.

Through *Banyan Tree* and *Angsana*, distinct customer segments were targeted. The motivation behind this differentiated branding strategy was to expand its customer base while minimizing brand dilution and cannibalism. Furthermore, each brand and product line created cross-selling opportunities, which helped reduce the adverse impact of external events, such as SARS and terrorist bombings. Being located in different countries and having a geographically diverse customer base cushioned the impact of such events. Banyan Tree's experience showed that its brands were capable of being extended to tap into new market segments.

One issue that continuously occupied Ho's mind was how his company should "innovate the product without diluting the brand" and without losing sight of its core values, which defined its corporate culture and CRS commitment. This question was constantly debated at senior management meetings. Contrary to press opinion, Ho advocated that *Banyan Tree* and *Angsana* were neither luxury nor exclusive brands; rather, he likened them to aspirational brands.[4] He was keen to evoke a customer response of, "Yes, it was expensive, but it was really worth it." The association of a memorable experience or emotion to a brand would be the associative value of the brand. Such a response, he thought, could command loyalty and premium pricing. He was convinced that an aspirational brand could continually increase its market reach.

Spas were a valued feature of the resorts and hotels, which were an integral part of this brand experience. The Banyan Tree Spa Academy at Banyan Tree Phuket provided its 500-plus therapists with theoretical and practical training. In addition to having a spa at each of its locations, the company was often approached by other reputable hotel companies to open a *Banyan Tree* or *Angsana* Spa. These opportunities allowed the company to expand its spa business into new markets and promote its brand without incurring capital costs. *Banyan Tree* Spas and *Angsana* Spas each offered distinct product offerings and experiences. *Banyan Tree* Spas offered a more traditional, luxurious environment with a classic design, and the use of natural herbs and spices and more complex techniques as recipes for its treatments. *Angsana* Spas offered a more modern and colorful décor with emphasis on flowers and fruits. *Oberoi Spas by Banyan Tree*, a brand operated under spa management agreements with the Oberoi Group of India, blended the Oberoi tradition of quality with Banyan Tree's spa expertise.

CORPORATE SOCIAL RESPONSIBILITY PHILOSOPHY

"CSR is something that's been very much part of the Banyan Tree ethos. We have not been milking this in a cynical manner because it's now the thing to do. We've always had it as part of our values, we will always espouse it very fervently, and it has now become part of the brand."

—K. P. Ho, CEO

From the outset, the founders were adamant that the company should consider the physical and human environment when making business decisions.[5] Construction projects used designs and techniques that minimized damage to the environment as far as practicable. Where options were available, environmentally friendly methods were adopted, such as installing a biological wastewater treatment system at Banyan Tree Bintan to recycle wastewater for irrigation purposes. Opportunities were actively pursued to support local businesses and communities. Each of its resorts carried out community development and environmental projects.

The Green Imperative Fund was established in 2001 to expand and formalize its environmental conservation and community development efforts. Guests of Banyan Tree and Angsana resorts and hotels were given an opportunity to make a contribution of US$2 or US$1, respectively, for each night they stayed at the resort or hotel. The company would match the guests' contributions, dollar for dollar, to develop the fund. By March 2006, the fund had raised approximately US$1 million. A committee of executive staff members of local origin made recommendations for projects to support. These projects ranged from marine conservation to education and health assistance.

"The people around us recognize that this is a company that looks at issues whether it's dealing with design or the way we hire and train or the materials we use . . . we actually reflect indigenous cultural capital. It is this harnessing of local capital and using it to translate it into our brand attributes— whether it is the way we build or what we stock in our gallery—that I feel makes us stand out."

—Claire Chiang, Senior Vice President Retail and Co-founder

Ho believed that *Banyan Tree* and *Angsana* guests had the purchasing power and consciously chose to utilize that purchasing power to express their value association with those of Banyan Tree. In that sense, CSR was seen as a profitable proposition that won the value of all stakeholders and gained numerous awards for Banyan Tree, which in turn generated brand awareness as Banyan Tree came to be recognized as a company that espoused good CRS practices. As part of the non-cost-based proprietary advantage proposition for sustainable competition, CSR was very much ingrained into the experiential brand value of the company. But up until August 2006, company expansion was mainly concentrated in the developing countries across Asia-Pacific, where CSR practices had an immediate and noticeable impact.

BUSINESS OPERATIONS

Banyan Tree managed and owned interests in upscale niche hotels and resorts usually with 50 to 100 rooms and commanded room rates at the high end of the scale. These included 18 resorts and hotels, 49 spas, 53 galleries, and two golf courses[6] spread across nine countries ranging from Indonesia to the Maldives. As of the end of March 2006, the total number of room inventory was 1,986. The flagship development, Laguna Phuket in Thailand, alone boasted five resorts, five spas, 14 galleries, an 18-hole golf course, and three resort residential developments for private sale, covering 1,000 acres (400 hectares). (See Exhibit 3 for a summary of significant events in the corporate history of Banyan Tree.)

As of June 2006, the activities of the company were divided into six business segments:

- *Hotel Investment*: Revenue was derived from resorts and hotels with ownership interest. This was the largest business segment, accounting for 59.7 percent of the

Exhibit 3: Summary of Significant Events in the Corporate History of Banyan Tree

1984	LRH, a subsidiary of Banyan Tree Holdings, acquires over 550 acres of land on the site of an abandoned tin mine at Bang Tao Bay, Phuket, Thailand.
1987–1992	After extensive rehabilitation of the site, LRH launches Dusit Laguna Resort Hotel and Laguna Beach Resort. LRH begins to market Laguna Phuket as a destination within Phuket. LRH launches a residences/property sales business with the sale of Sheraton Island Villas in Laguna Phuket.
1993	LRH lists its shares on the Stock Exchange of Thailand. Banyan Tree Hotels & Resorts Pte. Ltd., a resort and hotel management company, is established, as well as companies to operate spas and galleries. Sheraton Grande Laguna Phuket and The Allamanda are launched. LRH begins to sell units at The Allamanda.
1994	Banyan Tree Phuket is launched as the first Banyan Tree resort. The resort includes the first Banyan Tree Spa and Banyan Tree Gallery.
1995–1999	Banyan Tree Maldives and Banyan Tree Bintan are launched.
2000	The Angsana brand is launched with the opening of Angsana Bintan and Angsana Great Barrier Reef.
2001	The Banyan Tree Spa Academy is opened. Angsana Maldives and Angsana Oasis are launched.
2002	A strategic alliance with the Oberoi Group of India to manage spas was established. Banyan Tree Seychelles is launched. Laguna Residences, Phuket, Thailand is launched. An additional 450 acres of land is purchased in Bang Tao Bay, Phuket, Thailand for resort and property sales development. Westin Banyan Tree is rebranded to Banyan Tree Bangkok.
2003	The Colours of Angsana product line is established, and Gyalthang Dzong Hotel in Shangri-la, Yunnan, China is launched. Banyan Tree Spa Shanghai is launched. Laguna Townhomes begin sales.
2004	The second Colours of Angsana hotel, Deer Park Hotel, is launched in Sri Lanka.
2005	The third Colours of Angsana hotel, Maison Souvannaphoum, is launched in Laos. The first resort in China, Banyan Tree Ringha, Shangri-la, is established and Thai Wah Plaza, which includes Banyan Tree Bangkok, is acquired.
2006	The first villa-style Banyan Tree resort in China, Banyan Tree Lijiang, and the first resort in the Middle East, Banyan Tree Bahrain, are launched.

Source: Banyan Tree Holdings Limited (26 May 2006) IPO Prospectus, pp. 95–96.

company's revenue in the financial year ended December 31, 2005. The company had majority ownership interests in 10 hotels and resorts as of March 31, 2006.

- *Hotel Management*: Revenue was by way of management, incentive, and other fees received for managing *Banyan Tree* and *Angsana* resorts and hotels. It also included reimbursement of fees received from the sales and marketing services Banyan Tree provided to the resorts and hotels it managed. *Banyan Tree* and *Angsana* resorts and hotels had average room rates of S$601.60 and S$277.00[7] respectively, as of March 31, 2006. Management fees were typically 3 percent of total revenue; incentive fees were typically 10 percent of gross operating profit of the hotel or resort managed; and reimbursement fees were calculated as a percentage of the room revenue. (See Exhibit 4 for the list of hotels and resorts owned and managed by Banyan Tree and Exhibit 5 for room rates of accommodations offered by Banyan Tree Group.)

- *Spa Operations*: Revenue came from the management of spas and royalties received from licensing the use of the *Banyan Tree* brand according to spa management agreements. Spas were often considered by guests as one of the key features at Banyan Tree's resorts and hotels. In 2005, Banyan Tree Phuket won the Crystal Award of "Best Spa in Asia" from SpaFinder's Readers' Poll. Under spa management agreements, royalties were typically 10 to 15 percent of each spa's total revenue. Incentive fees of around 10 to 15 percent of each spa's gross operating profit were also received. *Banyan Tree* spas were located at each of the *Banyan Tree* resorts and hotels, with the exception of *Banyan Tree* Spa at The Westin Shanghai, which was to provide brand exposure in China. *Angsana* Spas could be found in all other resorts managed and/or owned by the company, as well as in other operators' resorts and day spas in Guam, Australia, Hong Kong, Taiwan, and Chiang Mai, Thailand. *Oberoi Spas by Banyan Tree* all operated under spa management agreements in India, Bali and Lombok, Indonesia, Mauritius, and Egypt. Management and incentive fees as a percentage of revenues and gross operating profit, respectively, were received from these operations. Spa treatment prices were based on premium services and branding. Unlike room rates, which were subject to seasonal adjustments, spa treatment prices were not seasonally affected. Each spa had its own pricing structure and offered different packages to increase usage during off-peak hours. (See Exhibit 6 for details of spas.)

- *Gallery Operations*: Revenue was generated from the sale of branded gifts, spa products, indigenous or cultural handicrafts and artifacts, and other souvenirs at Gallery outlets located in resorts, hotels, and many spas. Stand-alone city outlets, such as the one in Singapore, helped promote the company's brands. The *Museum Shop by Banyan Tree* was an affiliate brand of *Banyan Tree Gallery*. The *Museum Shop* offered a unique collection of museum replicas, objects of fine art, ethnic craft arts, apparel and jewelery modeled after pieces displayed in the National Museums of Singapore. There were four *Museum Shop* outlets. In 2003, the *Banyan Tree Gallery* and *Angsana Gallery* received the Pacific Asia Travel Association (PATA) Gold Award for Heritage.

- *Property Sales*: Revenue was derived from the sale of resort residences, primarily in Laguna Phuket. Banyan Tree's policy was to only engage in the development

Exhibit 4: Resorts and Hotels Owned and Managed by Banyan Tree, March 31, 2006

Name of Resort	Location	Number of Available Rooms	Owner	Ownership Interest[5]	Form of Management Arrangement	Year Opened/ Rebranded
Banyan Tree Phuket	Phuket, Thailand	127	LRH[1]	51.8%[6]	Technical assistance	1994
Banyan Tree Maldives Vabbinfaru	Maldives	48	Vabbinvest Maldives Pvt Ltd	96.7%[6]	Management agreement	1995
Banyan Tree Seychelles	Seychelles	47	Banyan Tree Resorts (Seychelles) Limited	30.0%[6]	Management agreement	2002
Banyan Tree Ringha	Yunnan, CHINA	32	Jiwa Renga Resorts Limited	96.00%	Management agreement	2005
Banyan Tree Bangkok	Bangkok, Thailand	197	Thai Wah Plaza	51.8%[6]	Management agreement	2002
Banyan Tree Bintan	Bintan, Indonesia	70	PT. Bintan Hotels	--[8]	Management agreement	1995
Angsana Resort & Spa Great Barrier Reef	Cairns, Australia	64	Manwin Properties Limited[2]	--[7]	Management agreement	2000
Angsana Resort & Spa Bintan	Bintan, Indonesia	113	PT. Bintan Hotels	--[8]	Management agreement	2000
Angsana Oasis Spa & Resort	Bangalore, India	43	Prestige Leisure Resorts Private Limited	--	Management agreement	2001
Angsana Resort & Spa Maldives Ihuru	Maldives	45	Maldives Angsana Pvt Ltd	96.7%[6]	Management agreement	2001
Colours of Angsana - Gyalthang Dzong Hotel	Yunnan, CHINA	47	Gyalthang Dzong Hotel	79.20%	Management agreement	2003
Colours of Angsana - The Deer Park Hotel	Beruwela, Sri Lanka	77	The Deer Park Hotel (Pvt Ltd	--	Management agreement	2004
Colours of Angsana - Maison Souvannaphoum	Luang Prabang, Laos	24	Souvannaphoum Pvt Ltd	--	Management agreement	2005

Exhibit 4: (Continued)

Dusit Laguna Resort Hotel	Phuket, Thailand	224	LRH	51.8%[6]	Managed Externally by Dusit Thani Corporation Limited	1987
Velavaru Island Resort	Maldives	84	Maldives Bay Pvt Ltd	77.40%	Management agreement	2005
Laguna Beach Resort	Phuket, Thailand	252	LRH[3]	25.8%[6]	Jointly managed by LRH and InterPacific Investment Limited [9]	1991
Sheraton Grande Laguna Phuket	Phuket, Thailand	289	LRH[4]	51.8%[6]	Managed Externally by Sheraton Overseas Management Corporation	1992
The Allamanda	Phuket, Thailand	203	Phuket Hotel Limited	--	Technical assistance agreement	1993
Total		1,986				

Notes:

(1) Banyan Tree Phuket is owned by Laguna Banyan Tree Limited, which is 51% owned by TWR-Holdings Limited and 49% owned by LRH.

(2) Reef Services Pty Ltd. has leased the resort from Manwin Properties Limited and unit holders for 10 years commencing on November 1, 2001 and expiring on October 31, 2011.

(3) Laguna Beach Resort is owned by Laguna Beach Club Limited. Please refer to "General and Statutory Information – Subsidiaries and Associated Companies" for ownership details of Laguna Beach Club.

(4) Sheraton Grande Laguna Phuket is owned by Bangtao Grande Limited, which is 100% owned by Laguna Grande Limited, a 100% owned subsidiary of LRH.

(5) This column reflects our effective ownership interests in the companies that own the various resorts.

(6) For details of our ownership interest in this company, see "General and Statutory Information – Subsidiaries and Associated Companies".

(7) LRH, through TWR-Holdings Limited and Laguna Banyan Tree Limited, has a 19.8% interest in Tropical Resorts Limited, which in turn has a direct interest in 100% of the shares of Manwin Properties Limited.

(8) LRH, through TWR-Holdings Limited and Laguna Banyan Tree Limited, has a 19.8% Interest in Tropical Resorts Limited. Tropical Resorts Limited has an effective interest in 49.5% of the shares of PT. Bintan Hotels.

(9) Laguna Beach Resort is co-managed by LRH and InterPacific Investment Limited ("InterPacific"), an unrelated party. A four-person group manages this resort. We receive no management fees for co-managing this resort.

Source: Banyan Tree Holdings Limited (26 May 2006) IPO Prospectus, pp. 105–106.

Exhibit 5: Banyan Tree Resorts' Published Accomodation Rates

BANYAN TREE RESORTS	PUBLISHED RATES
Bangkok, Thailand	Deluxe view suite at THB14,400[1] to presidential suite at THB80,000
Bintan, Indonesia	Valley villa at US$470 to spa pool villa at US$1,450
Lijiang, CHINA	Garden villa at US$400 to deluxe pool villa at US$700
Vabbinfaru, The Maldives	Oceanview villa at US$765 to Vabbinfaru villa at US$1,330
Phuket, Thailand	Deluxe villa at US$580 to two-bed double pool villa at US$2,080
Ringha, CHINA	Tibetan suite at US$310 to Ringha lodge at US$740
Seychelles	Hillside pool villa at €1,010[2] to Independence Pool Villa at €1,610
ANGSANA RESORTS	
Bintan, Indonesia	Superior room at US$181 to two-bed suite at US$388
Great Barrier Reef, Australia	One-bed poolview suite at AUS$370[3] to three-bed beachfront suite at AUS$620
Ihuru, The Maldives	Beachfront villa at US$700 to deluxe beachfront villa at US$770
Bangalore, India	Executive resort room at €140 to Angsana suite at €315
Velavaru, The Maldives	(Rates unavailable on the corporate web site)
COLOURS OF ANGSANA	
Maison Souvannaphoum, Laos	Garden room at US$140 to Laos suite at US$280
Deer Park Hotel, Sri Lanka	Duplex cottage at US$110 to Angsana cottage US$175
Gyalthang Dzong Hotel, Yunnan, CHINA	Deluxe room at US$60 to suite at US$90
Allamanda Laguna Phuket	Junior suite at US$170 to Allamanda suite at US$370

(1) **THB1 = US$0.026 monthly average in August 2006.**
(2) **€1 = US$1.28 monthly average in August 2006.**
(3) **AUS$1 = US$0.76 monthly average in May 2006.**
Source: Banyan Tree web site, www.banyantree.com (accessed January 5, 2007).

and sale of properties where these developments were closely integrated with its resorts and spas. Most buyers resided in Asia-Pacific and Europe. Sales were directly affected by the state of these economies and the state of the property market around the world, and particularly in Phuket. Various local laws also affected construction and ownership rights. For example, under Thai law, foreigners could

Exhibit 6: Banyan Tree's Operating Data for Spas Managed by Banyan Tree

	For the Year Ended December 31 (Unaudited)			For the Three Months Ended March 31 (Unaudited)
	2003	2004	2005	2006
BANYAN TREE				
Number of spas	6	7	9	8
Average rates per hour of use per room per day (S$)	83.00	82.30	87.40	88.80
Average hours of use per room per day	4.40	4.70	3.52	3.86
ANGSANA				
Number of spas	13	18	18	26
Average rates per hour of use per room per day (S$)	64.10	64.50	64.50	68.70
Average hours of use per room per day	2.70	2.40	2.40	2.62
OTHER SPAS				
Number of spas	14	15	15	15
Average rates per hour of use per room per day (S$)	58.30	58.30	60.90	64.40
Average hours of use per room per day	1.70	2.70	3.14	3.32

Source: Banyan Tree Holdings Limited (26 May 2006) IPO Prospectus, p. 60.

own buildings or properties developed on land leased by them, but not the land itself. Hence, foreigners could either lease the property or form a registered company in Thailand to purchase the property. Banyan Tree therefore resolved to offer non-Thai citizens three consecutive 30-year leases as Thai law imposed a maximum of 30 years on each lease. Construction costs in Phuket had increased by 25 percent over the two years up to December 31, 2005.[8] Up to June 2006, the company had sold 470 resort residences at Laguna Phuket, and the average price of each property was Bt16.5 million.[9] Banyan Tree operated a flexible room inventory management policy, whereby unsold properties would remain as part of the resort's available room inventory, thus increase hotel investment revenues. In the past, property sales generated funds to finance future hotel investments.

- *Design and other services*: Revenue came from the provision of design services, office rental income, and income from golf courses. The in-house Design and Planning Division helped choose each site and design the entire resort or hotel, including the architecture, engineering, and interior design. On finalizing the design, the Owners' Project Services Department would establish and monitor a budget for the project, oversee construction, and work with resort and hotel managers to procure furniture, fixtures, and equipment. The in-house Project Division would supervise all renovations, alterations, and extensions. Owners of each resort and hotel would pay all the costs of construction, renovation, and alteration. In addition, a fee equal to a fixed percentage of construction costs for each project and an equivalent fee for construction management were charged to the owner. Banyan Tree strongly believed that maintaining in-house design and construction services ensured advantages of faster design times, better cost and quality control, and consistency in design.

Exhibit 7 provides details of operating profit by business segments; Exhibit 8 provides details of revenue split by business segment and geographic regions; and Exhibit 9 provides a breakdown of the operating expenses of the group. Full-time employee numbers among the business units are shown in Exhibit 10.

Market Positioning

"If you knew that Banyan Tree has won 260 awards, you would say: well, the experience must be good. So, there is a proxy validation for that experience. Then on top of that, there is the word of mouth, which is very important to us. We actually spend very little money on advertising, because for a small group like ours, a strategy of using sort of a broad shotgun approach for advertising doesn't really work."

—K. P. Ho, CEO

To position its brands distinctively, Banyan Tree generally utilized separate distributiovn channels for each brand. For the year ended December 31, 2005, most reservations were made directly through Banyan Tree regional reservation centers, or through the property reservation teams.

The strength of the Banyan Tree brand had enabled the company to attract quality business associates and partners, such as American Express, Citibank, Visa International, MasterCard International, and the Oberoi Group of India. Banyan Tree maintained brand visibility and association with high-end publications in key feeder markets such as *Condé Nast Traveller* and *Tatler* UK. Theme-based signature packages were also promoted through the corporate web site. Membership in The Leading Hotels of the World and Small Luxury Hotels gave Banyan Tree access to high-end customers and provided an endorsement of quality and luxury by association. They also offered the benefits of their worldwide reservations and distribution systems, as well as global marketing programme.

In 2003, the Sanctuary Program was launched as a recognition program that rewarded qualifying guests of *Banyan Tree* resorts with complimentary stays and incentives. The program introduced other Banyan Tree hotels, resorts, and spas to the guests to encourage repeat patronage.

Major international tradeshows, such as the World Travel Market, Internationale Tourismus Börse, and Asean Tourism Forum, were used to promote the Banyan Tree brands and also provided the platform for signing contracts with wholesalers for upcoming travel seasons.

Exhibit 7: Banyan Tree's Operating Profit by Business Segment

| | 2003[1] | | 2004 | | 2005 | | For the Six Months Ended (Unaudited)[1] June 30 2006 |
	Operating Profit S\$ Million	Percentage of Total Operating Profit %	Operating Profit S\$ Million	Percentage of Total Operating Profit %	Operating Profit S\$ Million	Percentage of Total Operating Profit %	Operating Profit S\$ Million
Operating profit(loss)							
Business Segements							
Hotel investment	17.0	41.0	35.1	55.0	2.3	19.3	28.3
Hotel management	2.1	5.1	3.8	6	0.5	4.2	(0.3)
Spa operations	5.1	12.3	6.1	9.6	1.5	12.6	4.4
Gallery operations	0.9	2.2	1.8	2.8	0.3	2.5	0.4
Property sales	22.5	54.2	18.4	28.8	10.9	91.6	21.4
Design fees and others	(8.7)	(21.0)	(7.2)	(11.3)	(5.4)	(44.5)	(2.1)
	38.9	93.8	58	90.9	10.2	85.7	52.1
Other operating profit	0.9	2.2	4.1	6.4	1.7	14.3	N/A
							N/A
Amortization of negative goodwill	1.7	4.0	1.7	2.7	–	–	N/A
	41.5	100.0	63.8	100.0	11.9	100.0	52.1

(1) Banyan Tree Holdings Limited. "Unaudited results for the second quarter ended June 30, 2006", p. 18.
Source: Banyan Tree Holdings Limited (26 May 2006) IPO Prospectus, p. 63.

Exhibit 8: Banyan Tree's Revenue by Business Segment and by Geographic Region

| | 2003[a] | | 2004 | | 2005 | | 2006 | |
| | **Year Ended December 31 (Audited)** | | | | | | **Six Months Ended June 30 (Unaudited)[b]** | |
	Revenue S$ Million	Percentage of Total Revenue %	Revenue S$ Million	Percentage of Total Revenue %	Revenue S$ Million	Percentage of Total Revenue %	Revenue S$ Million	Percentage of Total Revenue %
REVENUES								
BUSINESS SEGMENTS								
Hotel investment	82.3	53.4	133.9	61.2	111.6	59.7	84.7	56
Hotel management	6.8	4.4	9.0	4.1	6.6	3.5	2.5	2
Spa operations	14.3	9.3	16.8	7.7	17.1	9.1	11.3	7
Gallery operations	6.3	4.1	7.8	3.6	6.8	3.7	4.9	3
Property sales	39.3	25.4	44.1	20.1	31.0	16.6	40.9	27
Design fees and others	5.2	3.4	7.2	3.3	13.8	7.4	7.8	5
Total revenue	154.2	100	218.8	100	186.9	100	152.1	100
Other operating income	2.5		5.8		1.7		N/A	
	156.7		224.6		188.6		152.1	

Exhibit 8: (*Continued*)

| | YEAR ENDED DECEMBER 31 (AUDITED) | | | | | | THREE MONTHS ENDED MARCH 31 (UNAUDITED) | | | |
| | 2003[1] | | 2004 | | 2005 | | 2005 | | 2006 | |
	REVENUE S$ MILLION	PERCENTAGE OF TOTAL REVENUE %	REVENUE S$ MILLION	PERCENTAGE OF TOTAL REVENUE %	REVENUE S$ MILLION	PERCENTAGE OF TOTAL REVENUE %	REVENUE S$ MILLION	PERCENTAGE OF TOTAL REVENUE %	REVENUE S$ MILLION	PERCENTAGE OF TOTAL REVENUE %
REVENUES										
GEOGRAPHIC REGION										
Southeast Asia[3]	105.4	68.3	180.2	82.4	142.2	76.1	24.8	71.1	64.4	79.8
Indian Ocean[4]	25.7	16.7	33.8	15.4	32.4	17.3	7.7	22.0	13.4	16.6
Northeast Asia[5]	0.3	0.2	1.0	0.5	2.7	1.5	0.2	0.6	0.6	0.7
Rest of the world[6]	22.8	14.8	3.8	1.7	9.6	5.1	2.2	6.3	2.3	2.9
Total revenue	154.2	100.0	218.8	100.0	186.9	100.0	34.9	100.0	80.7	100.0
Other operating income	2.5		5.8		1.7		0.5		0.6	
	156.7		224.6		188.6		35.4		81.3	

(1) Banyan Tree Holdings Limited. "Unaudited results for the second quarter ended June 30, 2006", p. 17.
(2) LRH's expenses have been consolidated from April 1, 2003.
(3) Thailand, Indonesia, and Singapore.
(4) The Maldives, Sri Lanka, and India.
(5) The CHINA, Japan, Hong Kong, and Taiwan.
(6) Australia, New Zealand, Guam, Morocco, Ireland, Bahrain, United Arab Emirates, South Africa, and Egypt.
Source: Banyan Tree Holdings Limited (26 May 2006) IPO Prospectus, p. 58.

Exhibit 9: Banyan Tree's Operating Expenses

| | Year Ended December 31 (Audited) | | | | | | For the Three Months Ended March 31 (Unaudited) | | | |
| | 2003[1] | | 2004 | | 2005 | | 2005 | | 2006 | |
Operating Expenses	Expenses S$ Million	Percentage of Total Operating Expenses %	Expenses S$ Million	Percentage of Total Operating Expenses %	Expenses S$ Million	Percentage of Total Operating Expenses %	Expenses S$ Million	Percentage of Total Operating Expenses %	Expenses S$ Million	Percentage of Total Operating Expenses %
Operating supplies	20.3	17.6	34.1	21.2	28.9	16.4	4.7	12.4	12.8	23.8
Salaries and related expenses	35.6	30.9	48.4	30.1	59.1	33.5	14	37.1	17	31.6
Administrative expenses	15.2	13.2	22.9	14.2	25.5	14.4	4.7	12.4	4.6	8.6
Sales and marketing expenses	5.6	4.9	8.1	5	9.9	5.6	2.4	6.4	3	5.6
Depreciation of property, plant and equipment	12.2	10.6	15.5	9.7	19.9	11.2	4.5	11.9	5.4	10
Other operating expenses	26.3	22.8	31.8	19.8	33.4	18.9	7.5	19.8	11.1	20.4
Total	115.2	100.0	160.8	100.0	176.7	100.0	37.8	100.0	53.8	100.0

(1) LRH's expenses have been consolidated from April 1, 2003.

Source: Banyan Tree Holdings Limited (26 May 2006) IPO Prospectus, p. 61.

Exhibit 10: Banyan Tree's Full-time Employees by Business Unit and Location

By Business Unit	As of December 31		
	2003	2004	2005
Office and Operations	384	402	476
Resorts and Hotels	2,102	2,085	2,692
Spa Operations	262	311	429
Gallery Operations	49	61	68
Golf	89	89	90
Property Sales	360	414	422
Total	3,246	3,362	4,177

By Location	As of December 31		
	2003	2004	2005
Australia	14	15	18
Indonesia	9	11	11
The Maldives	261	269	365
The Seychelles	3	3	3
Sri Lanka	99	67	68
Guam	10	12	12
Singapore	167	187	211
Thailand	2,683	2,798	3,258
CHINA	--	--	147
Japan	--	--	7
South Africa	--	--	15
Dubai	--	--	35
Egypt	--	--	12
Malaysia	--	--	15
Total	3,246	3,362	4,177

Source: Banyan Tree Holdings Limited (26 May 2006) IPO Prospectus, pp. 137–138.

WHOLESALERS

During the year ended December 31, 2005, most total room revenue was derived from a diversified portfolio of more than 1,000 wholesalers. These preferred partners combined Banyan Tree's product offerings with flights and other holiday components to provide complete vacation packages. Wholesalers were allocated a certain number of available rooms at discount prices for periods between 12 to 18 months. Discounts offered to them ranged from 35 to 40 percent off the standard rack rates. For each of the three financial years of 2003, 2004, and 2005, the percentage of total room revenue derived from wholesalers exceeded 55 percent.[10] Discounts of 15 to 25 percent were also offered to corporate clients and groups.

LOCATIONS

"The locations of hotels we've chosen do give us an advantage because we have generally dared to be very different from other people; we believe in being a prime mover rather than a follower."

—K. P. Ho, CEO

Banyan Tree preferred to be the price-maker rather than a price-taker. It sought locations where the typical industry player would offer room rates as low as one-tenth of what it would charge. On numerous occasions, this strategy worked: at the Maldives, its room rate was four times higher than the competition; it was the first to discover the Seychelles as a five-star location; it was the first to go into Lijiang in China, charging US$400 when the next-highest room rate was US$65. Experience showed that such premium pricing could be enjoyed for between five to seven years before competitors would move in to take market share.

The product and essentially the location had to be excellent to command such prices. In choosing the right location, the following criteria were used: natural beauty; features that were characteristic of a Banyan Tree or Angsana resort or hotel (refer to "Branding" section); potential to achieve high price-to-cost ratios; accessibility; potential market demand; potential to establish a niche position; and the existing basic infrastructure.

"Sanctuary for the senses" was a tagline used to bring together the brands and the location-unique experiences. By leveraging the natural surroundings unique to each location, and adding consistency in the designs, facilities (including spas), ambience (including romance), and services (including warm hospitality) offered, Banyan Tree created strong brand identity and a unique value proposition that was associated with self-indulgence and pampering experiences. Such location-unique experiences included sandbank dining in the Maldives, spa-on-the-beach at Bintan, the Jade Dragon Snow Mountain views from the villas in Lijiang, and staying in a Tibetan lodge at Ringha located 3,200 meters above sea level in Yunnan Province, China.

PRE-IPO STATUS

Since its inception, the company had operated in low-cost environments where it was able to charge for room and spa treatments at the high end of the market. This made for strong operating margins, and revenue grew 41.9 percent from 2003 to 2004, even during difficult industry conditions. (See Exhibit 11 for details of hotel room occupancy rates and room rates for the financial years ended December 31, 2003, 2004, and 2005.) Operating profits also grew 53.7 percent over the same period (refer to Exhibit 7). Profits from hotel operations were 46.1 percent (S\$19.1 million[11]) and 61 percent (S\$38.9 million[12]) of total operating profits in 2003 and 2004, respectively, but dropped to 23.5 percent (S\$2.8 million[13]) in 2005 because of the impact of the Indian Ocean tsunami, which affected hotel occupancy at many of Banyan Tree's resorts. For the year ended 2005, revenue from the Phuket resorts decreased by 40.1 percent year on year, and revenue from the Maldives resorts decreased by 15.7 percent.[14]

Property sales generated more than half the operating profits for the year ended 2003. For the year ended 2005, and with the depression in the hotel segment, profit from property sales represented 91.6 percent of total operating profits. Even with the revival of tourism in the tsunami-affected areas in the first half of 2006, the half-year results fell short of Banyan Tree's target to achieve an even split between property sales, hotels, and fee-based income.[15] For example, two-thirds of earnings from Phuket in the second quarter came from property sales. There was also a geographic imbalance, with two-thirds of revenue derived from Southeast Asia (Thailand, Indonesia, and Singapore) in 2005 (see Exhibit 8). Correspondingly, 3,480 of the 4,177 full-time employees were located at the hotels and resorts in Southeast Asia (see Exhibit 10).

Salaries and related expenses accounted for 33.5 percent of operating expenses in 2005. (See Exhibit 9 for operating costs.) Attracting competent and highly qualified employees was crucial to the business. Local hires were the preferred choice, but expatriate expertise was sometimes necessary in locations that offered an insufficiently qualified workforce. This increased operating expenses. Higher operating costs were experienced in the Seychelles and Australia due to high costs of labor in those locations. Apart from higher salaries, restrictions on the import of food and other goods into the country resulted in higher excise tax in the Seychelles. Other exceptional operating expenses in the Seychelles included the necessity to generate the resort's own electricity.

In the 12 months leading up to the IPO, Banyan Tree had extended its business into other regions outside Asia-Pacific through management agreements in Abu Dhabi and Barbados. It appeared that the strength of its brands gave Banyan Tree a strong negotiating position with potential business associates.

IPO AND THE EXPANSION PLAN

"For us in the tourism industry, expansion into more areas is diversification of risks. . . . We were caught with the tsunami: nine of our hotels were affected. If a tsunami should hit again, hopefully we will be so spread out over the world that only a small portion of our hotels would be hit."

—K. P. Ho, CEO

Exhibit 11: Aggregated Operating Data for Hotels and Resorts in the Banyan Tree Group

Aggregate operating data for the resorts and hotels managed by Banyan Tree and/or in which it had an ownership interest for the periods indicated.

	AS OF OR FOR THE YEAR ENDED DECEMBER 31 (UNAUDITED)			AS OF OR FOR THE THREE MONTHS ENDED MARCH 31 (UNAUDITED)	
	2003	2004	2005	2005	2006
Number of properties	14	15	18	16	18
Average number of available rooms[1]	1,816	1,886	2,024	1,900	1,986
Average occupancy (%)[2]	62.9	69.4	53.3	42.8	67.5
Average room rate (S$)[3]	259.90	273.40	271.60	327.70	340.40
REVPAR (S$)[4]	163.50	189.70	144.70	140.30	229.80
Total revenue (S$ million)	172.8	213.8	171.8	38.7	64.4

Aggregate operating data for the resorts and hotels managed by Banyan Tree for the periods indicated.

	AS OF OR FOR THE YEAR ENDED DECEMBER 31 (UNAUDITED)			AS OF OR FOR THE THREE MONTHS ENDED MARCH 31 (UNAUDITED)	
	2003	2004	2005	2005	2006
Number of properties	12	13	16	16	16
Average number of available rooms[1]	1,303	1,373	1,511	1,387	1,448
Average occupancy (%)[2]	59.6	66.8	54.5	46.9	66.5
Average room rate (S$)[3]	301.20	308.00	309.60	359.60	363.10
REVPAR (S$)[4]	179.70	205.70	168.60	168.60	241.40
Total revenue (S$ million)	131.8	165.8	143.6	33.2	50.0

Exhibit 11: (*Continued*)

Aggregate operating data for the resorts that were operated under the Banyan Tree brand for the periods indicated

	As of or for the Year Ended December 31 (Unaudited)			As of or for the Three Months Ended March 31 (Unaudited)	
	2003	2004	2005	2005	2006
Number of properties	5	5	6	5	6
Average number of available rooms[1]	492	502	540	496	540
Average occupancy (%)[2]	65.9	74.1	65.7	64.0	70.7
Average room rate (S$)[3]	474.50	503.60	482.10	505.80	601.60
REVPAR (S$)[4]	312.80	373.00	317.00	324.00	425.20
REVPAR (S$) (excluding Banyan Tree Bangkok)	467.60	546.40	445.00	461.10	578.90
Total revenue (S$ million)	87.2	109.0	96.6	23.7	32.3
Total revenue (S$ million) (excluding Banyan Tree Bangkok)	68.7	83.9	70.9	16.8	24.1

Aggregate operating data for the resorts that are operated under the Angsana brand for the periods indicated

	As of or for the Year Ended December 31 (Unaudited)			As of or for the Three Months Ended March 31 (Unaudited)	
	2003	2004	2005	2005	2006
Number of properties	5	6	7	7	7
Average number of available rooms[1]	317	394	428	420	413
Average occupancy (%)[2]	52.1	53.1	48.8	42.8	56.3
Average room rate (S$)[3]	246.10	237.40	253.10	282.40	277.00
REVPAR (S$)[4]	128.20	126.10	123.50	120.80	155.80
Total revenue (S$ million)	23.9	32.1	30.1	6.8	8.6

(1) Average number of available rooms means the total aggregate number of rooms available for average occupancy for each day during the relevant period divided by the number of days in that period.
(2) Average occupancy means the number of paid room nights during a period divided by the total number of available rooms during that period, expressed as a percentage.
(3) Average room rate means the total room revenue earned during a period divided by the number of paid room nights for that period.
(4) REVPAR equals average room rate multiplied by average occupancy.
Source: Banyan Tree Holdings Limited (26 May 2006) IPO Prospectus, pp. 19–20.

TIMING

With the turmoil of the Asian financial crisis, the terrorist activities, SARS, and the tsunami (refer to Appendix 1 for details of the impact of these events on the travel and tourism industry), 2006 presented the first opportunity in five years for Banyan Tree to proceed with its long-awaited IPO. Launched on May 26, 2006, the IPO raised S$368.7 million[16] through the sale of 380.1 million shares at S$0.97 each, in the middle of the S$0.87 to S$1.07 range. Critics raised concern that the company had been overvalued and speculated that the share price could take a beating on the first day of trading on June 14. On the first trading day, the closing price was S$0.85.

GEOGRAPHIC EXPANSION

In the IPO document, the company committed to investing S$70 million in new resorts and hotel developments. Banyan Tree planned to increase its geographic presence and diversify its revenue base. Geographic expansion would not only spread out the risks of natural catastrophes, but also reduce the impact of cyclical and seasonal fluctuations in the tourism industry. Strategic expansion was targeted at low-cost locations close to its key customer markets. (See Exhibit 12 for details of its customer mix and Exhibit 13 for a map of Banyan Tree's global presence.) This would give existing customers easier access to Banyan Tree as well as provide reach to affluent customer segments within these operating countries. The ability to command premium rates would be the key consideration in its geographic expansion. It would also allow the company to take advantage of cross-marketing opportunities.

Staff from existing hotels were selected to form pre-opening teams that assisted with training new staff and operational aspects of the new hotels.

Projects in which the company had equity interests were to be financed by cash from operations, loans from financial institutions, and proceeds from the IPO. (See Exhibit 14 for details of proposed investments.)

RESORT EXPANSIONS AND RESIDENTIAL PROPERTY SALES

Apart from plans for new resorts, existing resorts were to be expanded. Several of its resorts had additional land for building new rooms and/or villas, including Chiang Mai, Lijiang, Acapulco, and Cancun. (See Exhibit 15 for details of available landbank.) This was considered to be a cost-effective

Exhibit 12: Banyan Tree's Customer Mix by Country of Residence

	FOR THE YEAR ENDED DECEMBER 31 (UNAUDITED)			FOR THE THREE MONTHS ENDED MARCH 31 (UNAUDITED)
	2003	2004	2005	2006
As a percentage of total room nights				
Europe[1]	25.5%	32.3%	31.2%	46.6%
Americas[2]	4.3%	4.8%	6.3%	6.7%
North Asia[3]	42.0%	38.3%	26.9%	24.5%
South Asia[4]	21.1%	15.1%	22.2%	14.6%
Oceania[5]	5.3%	6.8%	10.1%	5.8%
Others[6]	1.7%	2.6%	2.9%	1.8%

(1) Europe includes the United Kingdom, Germany, France, Switzerland, Russia, and Italy.
(2) Americas includes the United States, Canada, and South America.
(3) North Asia includes Japan, Korea, Hong Kong, China, and Taiwan.
(4) South Asia includes Singapore, Malaysia, India, and Thailand.
(5) Oceania includes Australia, New Zealand, and other Pacific nations.
(6) Others include the United Arab Emirates (UAE), the Middle East, and Saudi Arabia.
(7) This information is based on data provided by our customers as to their country of residence.
Source: Banyan Tree Holdings Limited (26 May 2006) IPO Prospectus, p. 106.

way to increase its revenue base and provide new product offerings without incurring significant new capital expenditure. Cash flow generated from the sale of residence developments would be used to offset investment outlay for resort and hotel developments and expansion of existing resorts and hotels. The value of land surrounding its resorts and hotels were expected to typically appreciate as the resort or hotel matured. This in turn was expected to command higher sale prices of residences.

Plans were in place to commence selling resort residential properties in Lijiang, China and Bangkok, Thailand, toward the end of 2006. In addition, 22 Banyan Tree Double Pool Villas at Banyan Tree Phuket and 28 Pool Villas at Dusit Laguna Resort Hotel, Phuket were due for completion by the end of 2007. These resort villas would be part of the resort's available room inventory and would be available for sale and lease back to the resort. The new Laguna Village residential housing project was underway, and Phase 1 comprised the construction of 36 villas, 28 Laguna Townhomes, and 12 Laguna Residences. These branded residence projects were two years in the making.[17] A new property sales initiative called the Banyan Tree Residences was about to be launched at the time of the IPO. Owners of Banyan Tree villas and resort residences at Banyan Tree Phuket, Banyan Tree Lijiang, and

Exhibit 13: Map of Banyan Tree's Global Presence

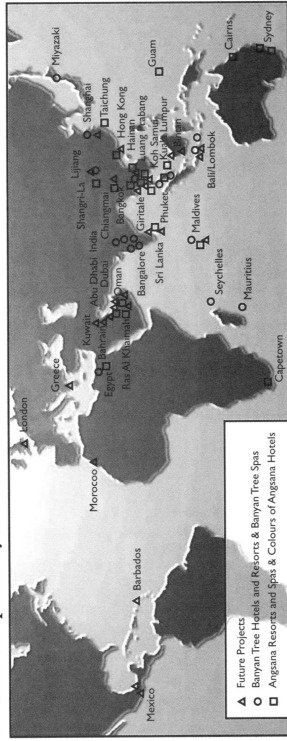

Source: Adapted from Banyan Tree prospectus dated May 26, 2006.

Exhibit 14: Banyan Tree's Planned Capital Expenditure and Proposed Investments in New Resort and Hotel Developments

	Location	Estimated Opening Date	Estimated Project Cost	Estimated BTH Equity Investment[12]	Estimated Investment per Annum		
					2006	2007	2008
			S$ Million	S$ Million	S$ Million	S$ Million	S$ Million
Capital Expenditure							
Angsana Swanee Hotel[1],[13]	Sri Lanka	First quarter 2008	16.7	6.7	0.0	3.2	3.5
Angsana Phuket[2],[13]	Thailand	2008	48.0	24.0	8.0	16.0	0.0
Angsana Velavaru[3]	Maldives	2007	24.3	12.2	9.8	2.4	0.0
Banyan Tree Chiang Mai[2],[13]	Thailand	2009	20.0	10.0	0.0	3.3	6.7
Banyan Tree Ubud[2],[13]	Indonesia	First quarter 2008	25.0	12.5	0.0	6.3	6.2
Banyan Tree Aloofushi[2],[13]	Maldives	2009	30.0	15.0	0.0	9.8	5.2
Banyan Tree Bangkok[4]	Thailand	Fourth quarter 2007 and first quarter 2008	16.8	4.2	3.2	1.0	0.0
Banyan Tree Phuket							
Phase 1 of DoublePool villas[5]	Thailand	Third quarter 2006	31.2	7.8	7.8	0.0	0.0
Phase 2 of DoublePool villas[6]	Thailand	Fourth quarter 2007	30.0	7.5	0.0	7.5	0.0
Sheraton Grande Laguna Phuket[7]	Thailand	Fourth quarter 2006	11.6	0.0	0.0	0.0	0.0

	Country	Expected completion date					
Furnishings, Fittings, equipment and small capital projects		Not applicable	29.0	Not applicable	10.7	9.2	9.1
			282.6	99.9	39.5	58.7	30.7
Investments							
Banyan Tree Lijiang (Phase I)[8],[13]	CHINA	Second quarter 2006	48.3	18.3	18.3	0.0	0.0
Banyan Tree Mayakoba[9],[13]	Mexico	2008	176.5	10.0	2.5	5.0	2.5
Banyan Tree Punta Diamante[10],[13]	Mexico	First quarter 2008	50.0	5.0	0.0	5.0	0.0
Banyan Tree Ras Al Khaimah[11],[13]	UAE	2009	50.0	5.0	0.0	5.0	0.0
			324.8	38.3	20.8	15.0	2.5

(1) This project is to be approximately 40% equity financed and 60% debt financed.

(2) This project is to be approximately 50% equity financed and 50% debt financed.

(3) This project involves the renovation and rebranding of the hotel and is to be approximately 50% equity financed and 50% debt financed.

(4) This project will include the conversion of the low-yielding office floors in Thai Wah Tower II to provide higher-yielding hotel inventory and to provide better banqueting and meeting facilities and will be approximately 25% equity financed and 75% debt financed.

(5) The phase 1 of 22 Double Pool Villas is under construction and will be completed by the third quarter of 2006. It is approximately 25% equity financed and 75% debt financed.

(6) The phase 2 of 30 Double Pool Villas will be commenced in the second half of 2006 and will be completed by the end of 2007. It will be approximately 25% equity financed and 75% debt financed.

(7) The 45-room extension was completed in early 2006, and the room renovations will be completed by the end of 2006. This project is 100% debt financed.

(8) This project is to be approximately 65% equity financed and 35% debt financed.

(9) We have an equity stake of 20% in this project. Our equity contribution is capped at the lower of US$6 million or a 20% stake. We have the option to increase our equity contributions to maintain our share at 20%.

(10) We have an equity stake of 15% in this project, which will be approximately 50% equity financed and 50% debt financed. Our initial equity contribution is capped at US$3.0 million.

(11) We have an equity stake of 15% in this project.

(12) Ignoring minority interests.

(13) These projects involve the construction of a new resort/hotel.

Source: Banyan Tree Holdings Limited (26 May 2006) IPO Prospectus, pp. 81–82.

Exhibit 15: Banyan Tree's Available Landbank as of March 31, 2006

LOCATION	EXPECTED COMMENCEMENT OF SALES	ACREAGE (CURRENTLY DEVELOPING)	ACREAGE (LANDBANK AVAILABLE)
Laguna Phuket	2006	101	228
Seychelles	2006 (under construction)	4	207
Chiang Mai	2007 (Phase 1)	–	93
Lijiang	2006	4	28
Total		109	556

Source: Banyan Tree Holdings Limited (26 May 2006) IPO Prospectus, p. 135.

Banyan Tree Bangkok would enjoy privileges at all Banyan Tree and Angsana hotels, resorts, and spas. Unit owners could expect a guaranteed return of 6 percent per annum for the first six years, and thereafter owners would receive one-third of actual room revenues. Members could also benefit from an exchange program, which would enable unit owners to enter into exchanges with other unit owners on a voluntary basis to visit other resorts within a 30-day period of free usage.

A select group of industry analysts and commentators were keen to remind Banyan Tree that its reliance on property sales to fund the future development of resorts and hotels might backfire.[18] At the same time, other analysts were bullish on Banyan Tree's property sales business and saw it as a good way to reduce investment layouts. As always, there were risks involved when selling residential properties. These included various uncontrollable circumstances other than natural and human-made crises, such as the political instability and foreign ownership laws notably in Thailand, and government restrictions on the sale of residential property in China.

MANAGEMENT ONLY VERSUS OWNERSHIP MANAGEMENT

Apart from developing and selling its own residences, Banyan Tree intended to enter into management agreements to manage premium-serviced residences in selected locations. Such premium-serviced residences would operate under one of its brands. For a Banyan Tree resort or hotel, the company generally had ownership interest dependent on a list of variables such as familiarity, profitability, partners, and so on. For *Angsana* resorts and hotels, it preferred to focus on management agreements.

Management agreements brought the benefit of building brand awareness quickly without huge capital expenditure. For its spa operations, the company planned to expand into new locations through leases, management agreements, and strategic alliances. In addition to stand-alone spas, it was expected that new spas would be opened wherever a new resort or hotel was to be opened. Banyan Tree had to evaluate the benefits and drawbacks of organic growth as opposed to management-only contracts and growth through acquisitions.

COMPETITION IN NICHE MARKETS

Maintaining a niche position as markets matured was an ongoing issue for the company. During the years 2003 to 2005, significant price competition was experienced in the Maldives, Bangkok, Australia, and Bintan in Indonesia. New hotels competed for the same customer segments in locations where Banyan Tree previously had a leader advantage. For example, in 2001, a JW Marriott opened in Phuket in direct competition with Laguna Resorts and Hotels for key market segments, including the corporate meeting market. Shangri-La Hotels and Resorts announced plans to open a resort at the Seychelles in 2007. The rebranding of two existing four-star hotels in Phuket (the Hilton Arcadia in 2004 and the Conrad in 2006) also fueled competition.

Competition usually focused on factors such as room rates, the quality of accommodation and services, brand recognition, convenience of the location, and the quality and scope of other amenities. At the location level, competition depended on political stability, social conditions, market perception, accessibility of the location, local culture, the location's success in promoting itself as a tourist destination, and other macro-level factors.

Apart from competition within a specific location, there was also competition among locations. Following the Bali bombings in 2002, some international travelers opted for Phuket as their alternative vacation destination. However, other locations took preference following the outbreak of SARS in 2003 and the 2004 tsunami.

Typically, Banyan Tree did not compete with large-scale hotel operators, because most of its resorts had fewer than 100 rooms and/or villas. It focused on a niche market in premium resorts and hotels. Banyan Tree's closest competitors were the Amanresorts, COMO Hotels and Resorts, Six Senses Hotels & Resorts, One-and-Only Resorts, and the Four Seasons Resorts. For Angsana resorts and spas, the competitors were different at each location and included the One-and-Only Kanubura, and larger operators such as Shangri-La Hotels.

AMANRESORTS

Amanresorts was named the world's leading international hotel group by the 2006 Zagat Survey of Top International Hotels, Resorts and Spas. Its 18 properties, which spanned 12 countries and four continents, also received individual recognition: Amankila in Bali was rated Asia's top resort and first in the Survey's dining category; Amanpuri in Phuket was awarded the region's top service position; and Amandari in Indonesia was rated the top destination spa.

The focus was on small and intimate hotels (a "less is more" philosophy) with a contemporary design that offered a lifestyle experience in faraway cultures. It indulged the appetite for pampering and appreciation for creativity and elegance. Each resort was different in location, look, mood, and guest experience, with environmentally friendly and aesthetically appealing characteristics. Yet, the intention was to impress an indelible mark on guests.[19] Villas at several locations (Turks and Caicos Islands, Pamalican Island in the Philippines, Jackson Hole, Wyoming, and Marrakech in Morocco) were offered for sale or exclusive rental. Each resort took advantage of the idyllic local surrounding (e.g., open views of rice fields, forest, and mountain peaks at Amandari) and local interior design and furnishing ("ethnicity in design"). Villas typically had swimming pools with untouched beachfronts or garden views.

The trademarks synonymous with the Amanresorts brand were its serene pavilions, infinity pools, and Zen courtyards. These trademarks and the exotic destinations fashioned a loyal following of "Aman junkies."[20] Facilities and services were typical of luxury resorts, including exotic spa treatments, but at its latest resort (the Amanyara in Parrot Cay), guests were provided with a recording studio and a private screening room, which reflected the high proportion of media and music moguls among its guests. Fixtures and fittings were shipped in from Asia; staff were also brought in from other Aman resorts (about half were Filipino), which ensured a consistent Asian-style service. Rates varied from US$650 per person per night for a tent in Aman-i-Khàs to US$10,300 for a four-bedroom ocean villa in Amanyara. The company was privately owned by its founder Adrian Zecha.

COMO HOTELS AND RESORTS

COMO was created by Christina Ong, one of Asia's style icons. Her husband, B. S. Ong, owned five of the Four Seasons Hotels.[21] COMO operated seven resorts ranging from exclusive urban locations (London and Bangkok) to secluded island resorts (the Maldives and Bhutan). The COMO Shambhala (meaning "centre of peace and harmony") spa was a uniquely branded feature that claimed to be a sanctuary for the body, mind, and spirit. At its island resorts, reverence for nature was its focus. At Parrot Cay, a 1,000-acre private island hideaway in the Bahamas, 50 percent of the staff were Asians (Thailand, Indonesia, Java, and Japan). The Asian connection extended to the menu of massages on offer, and therapists came from the treatment's country of origin. World-leading yoga teachers were contracted to provide dedicated retreat weeks. City locations were cool-looking and contemporary, for trendsetters and travelers seeking to be at the center of the action.

SIX SENSES HOTELS AND RESORTS

Established in 1988, the company operated under four brands: *Soneva* offered "luxuries of the highest international standard together with a sensitivity and local feel in design, architecture, and service";

Evason was a five-star resort with a philosophy of "refining experiences"; *Evason Hideaway* offered "a personal environment whilst capturing the essential essence of the *Soneva* brand"; and *Six Senses Spas*, a key element of all Six Senses properties, providing treatments for "balancing senses."[22] The company promoted itself as a resort and spa management and development company employing 2,500 employees. It held equity stakes in most Six Senses–managed resorts.

In creating a memorable experience, focus was on the combination and harmony of the attitude of its employees, the smells, the sounds, the tactile textures, and the pleasing sights that blended together at each resort. Its signature *Six Senses Spas* wsa also operated at third-party resorts. While *Soneva* was in direct competition with *Banyan Tree*, Evason competed with *Angsana* in terms of customer segments. *Soneva* was about creating a unique experience with emphasis on privacy, choice, and tailor-made services. *Evason* was tailored for the family market, with a large kids club and professional Montessori teachers on-site. The intention was to create an overall experience that could be absorbed by all the senses, and to deliver this experience consistently. The company was privately owned and founded by Eton-educated Sonu Shivdasani.

ONE-AND-ONLY RESORTS

One-and-Only was owned by Kerzner International Limited, an international developer and operator of destination resorts, casinos, and luxury hotels. As its brand name suggested, the company was a luxury resorts operator that was committed to offering guests a One-and-Only experience. Each award-winning resort was set in some of the most beautiful locales in the world, and guests experienced the distinctive style and personality of the local culture. Apart from the Bahamas resort, One-and-Only also operated at the Maldives, Mauritius, Dubai, Mexico, and South Africa. On its web site, the company defined the heart and soul of One-and-Only by its core value, which was to "blow away the customer."

FOUR SEASONS RESORTS

The Four Seasons was founded in 1960 and had a presence in major city centers and resort destinations around the world. Appealing to business and leisure travelers, the company had 73 hotels in 31 countries. It claimed to be the first to introduce now-standard items such as bath amenities, terrycloth robes, and hairdryers in North America. Its founder, chairman, and CEO Isadore Sharp said, "We have aspired to be the best hotel in each location where we operate."[23] The company had focused on redefining luxury as a service and claimed to be the world's leading operator of luxury hotels.

As luxury vacation resorts, the company operated 13 unique resort properties worldwide. Its unique selling points included the extra-spacious baths and architectural design, which maximized views, privacy, and enjoyment of the natural surroundings. In-room services included home cooking with a personal chef and customized menu, customized massage and aromatherapy, and in-room exercise equipment on request. Assuming that time was the most precious commodity for guests whether on business or leisure, the company designed its services to make efficient use of guests' time. Other conveniences included a No Luggage Required program for guests who had lost luggage. The Kids "For All Seasons" program offered parents a real vacation. Since 2001, each resort offered spa services. The company had thrived on its philosophy to manage rather than own hotels. In the new millennium, the company announced plans to develop more than 20 new properties around the world located at "exceptional" destination resorts and world financial centers. The expansion was expected to increase its international presence by nearly one-third.

In 1997, the company introduced an extension to its brand: Four Seasons Residential Properties. Such properties provided full and partial ownership of city and vacation homes around the world, including San Francisco, Nevis, Miami, and Punta Mita. Facing a similar predicament as Ho regarding global expansion, Sharp remarked, "It is this quality of service that is so critically important to our guests, and the degree to which we can provide and evolve it, worldwide, is also the degree to which we can differentiate ourselves and stay ahead of the rest."[24]

SHANGRI-LA HOTELS AND RESORTS

The Hong Kong–based company was the largest Asian-hotel group in Asia and the Middle East. It boasted 49 deluxe hotels and resorts in key cities, seven of which were Trader Hotels—a four-star sister brand that was to deliver high-value, midrange, and quality accommodation to business travelers. The Shangri-La branded hotels were five-star venues targeted at the luxury segment. The company announced plans for aggressive expansion with 40 new projects worldwide over four years. Two-thirds of these new developments were located in China, notably in the second-tier cities, and India.[25] Shangri-La was confident that expansion into China would underpin future growth. By the time of the 2008 Summer Olympics, the company aimed to have 37 hotels in China, almost half of its worldwide total.[26] However, unlike Four Seasons, the company's plan was to develop and retain ownership of the new hotels.

Nonetheless, it had also signed management agreements to open hotels in the United States, Canada, and Europe, in prominent cities such as Chicago, London, Vancouver, and Las Vegas. Its cautious approach to overseas expansion translated into smaller hotels (e.g., 140 rooms in Paris, 200 rooms in Chicago, and 147 rooms in Miami), while the average hotel in China featured 420 rooms. To ensure consistency in the quality of service, employees would undergo training for up to 12 months in Beijing, Hong Kong, and Singapore, while the aim of the program was to convey the essence of the Asian culture. Shangri-La's occupancy rate reached a record 73 percent in 2005. By 2010, the company anticipated that 50 percent of its business would come from Asia and China.[27]

POST-IPO AND THE GLOBAL COMPANY

Scanning the competitive landscape, Ho was confident that within five years Banyan Tree could become a dominant player in the small to medium-size (roughly 150 rooms) luxury hotels segment, as no dominant player had emerged so far. However, to reach that position, he had to overcome a few challenges.

Ho claimed that branding had been the key to Banyan Tree's business success and the platform for its global expansion. The company had played its cards right so far. Its future success was dependent on its ability to manage growth while preventing brand dilution. Investors and analysts eagerly awaited more telling results.

APPENDIX I TRAVEL AND TOURISM IN ASIA: 1997–2005

In 1991, the World Travel and Tourism Council (WTTC) claimed that tourism was the world's largest industry.[28] In particular, the Asia-Pacific region was noted to be the fastest-growing tourism region in the world.[29] Between 1980 and 1995, tourist arrivals in the region rose at an annual average rate of 10 percent and 15 percent, respectively, and accounted for 15.2 percent and 19.4 percent respectively of the share of world tourist arrivals. The World Tourism Organization projected that by 2010, Asia-Pacific would surpass the Americas to become the world's second largest tourist region, with 229 million visitors.[30] Fueled by economic growth, an increase in disposable income and leisure time, the liberalization of air transport, and political stability, the worldwide and regional travel and tourism industry looked set to explode in the new millennium. Demographic shifts and changes in lifestyle were having a positive effect on the industry, while technology and the Internet extended global reach for travelers and industry players.

However, the years to follow brought the industry to its knees and accentuated its dependence on international peace, prosperity, and nature's grace. A sequence of crises severely challenged all stakeholders, from airline caterers to hotels to tourist attraction parks, so much so that in its 2003–2004 annual report, the WTTC acknowledged that "Never before have so many issues become entwined and caused a crisis that has lasted so long."[31]

ASIAN FINANCIAL CRISIS, 1997

In mid-1997, a period of economic unrest, which came to be known as the Asian financial crisis, triggered a ripple effect across the Asia-Pacific region and resulted in economic slowdown in other parts of the world. At the macro level, several Asian countries saw sharp reductions in values of currencies, stock markets, and other asset prices. Indonesia, South Korea, Thailand, Hong Kong, Malaysia, Laos, Singapore, and the Philippines saw their currencies dip significantly relative to the U.S. dollar. Businesses went into bankruptcy; millions of people fell below the poverty line; and redundancy levels rose rapidly. The economic crisis also generated political unrest.

Not only did the Asian financial crisis have a lasting effect on international investors who became reluctant to lend to developing countries, but consumers within Asia-Pacific and visitors to the region found that their disposable income was suddenly depleted. Aggravated by a downturn in the U.S. economy, a prolonged global recession ensued. For the travel and tourism industry, the nightmare had just begun.

TERRORIST ACTIVITIES

The series of coordinated terrorist suicide attacks by Islamic extremists on the United States on September 11, 2001 initiated a war on terror by the Bush administration. Military readiness extended to countries such as the Philippines and Indonesia, where internal conflicts with Islamic extremist terrorism was rife. In the days that followed the attacks, and for the first time in aviation history, all non-emergency civilian aircrafts in the United States and several other countries were grounded. Passengers were stranded across the world, and governments issued travel warnings. Even with the reopening of North American airspace, air travel decreased significantly. Air travel capacity was cut back by 20 percent, which exacerbated the ailing U.S. airline industry.[32] Global international arrivals declined by 0.6 percent, marking the first year of negative growth for the industry since 1982.[33]

The series of subsequent direct terrorists' assaults in Bali, Moscow, Mombasa, and elsewhere—and the war in Iraq, which started in 2003—weakened the economy of Asia-Pacific Economic Cooperation (APEC) members and postponed recovery. The direct threat to air travel and destination security resulted in an immediate fall in demand in travel and tourism. For example, the Bali bombings, which resulted in 202 deaths (88 of whom were Australians), saw 40 percent of Australian tourists cancel bookings to Bali.[34] Occupancy rates in large hotels fell from 74.8 percent on October 11 to 33.4 percent on October 19, 2002; a few reported 10 percent occupancy. Accommodation across the board suffered a drastic fall in demand. Terrorist bombings continued through 2003, but as Augusto Huéscar, UNWTO Chief of Market Intelligence and Promotion, said, "These had far less impact than expected as the public seems to have grown accustomed to living in an unsafe world."[35]

SEVERE ACUTE RESPIRATORY SYNDROME (SARS)

The growth in arrival rates at destinations in Asia and the Pacific region in January and February 2003 was short-lived. The emergence of SARS and the Iraq war had widespread consequences in the affected region. Even destinations not directly affected by SARS, such as Australia, Indonesia, Japan, Korea, the Philippines, and Thailand, noted a 10 to 50 percent drop in tourist arrivals.[36] The outbreak of this transmissible new disease, which spread across the globe through routes of international air travel, resulted in 8,100 cases worldwide (although 97.7 percent of the cases were in Hong Kong, China, Taiwan, Singapore, and Canada) and 916 deaths. However, the impact on travel and tourism was crippling. For example, Malaysia, whose tourism industry was the second largest foreign exchange earner that contributed about 7.8 percent of GDP in 2002, reported five incidents of SARS and saw tourist arrivals drop 30 percent and hotel occupancy fall 30 to 50 percent from April 2003 to April 2004.[37] In the same period, airline bookings dropped by 40 percent. It was estimated that 3 million people lost their jobs in China, Hong Kong, Singapore, and Vietnam, where collectively these countries lost US$20 billion in GDP output.[38] The collapse of tourism in the region was caused by induced panic, which convinced travelers that the disease was virulent, rampant, and out of control. All of Asia was viewed as unsafe, and even Chinatowns in other parts of the world were forsaken.

The UNWTO reported positive figures emerging in the second half of 2003, but the recovery was slow. Reflecting on the turmoil of the year, Francesco Frangialli, WTO Secretary-General, said, "The travel industry was affected . . . but it did not collapse. The decline was limited, and in such a hostile environment, this very fact confirms the resilience of tourism, based on the incomprehensible need for travel and leisure that characterizes consumers in post-industrial societies."[39] Through the three difficult years (2001–2003), the UNWTO recorded an increase of 1 percent in international tourist arrivals, which represented an overall increase of 7 million visitors over 2000.

TSUNAMI, DECEMBER 2004

The UNWTO forecasts for 2004 were optimistic, as there were positive signs of economic recovery in the United States, Japan, and Western Europe, and the retreat of SARS and military conflict. At the end of the year, the UNWTO reported "a spectacular rebound of tourism" in all regions.[40] Annual international tourist arrivals worldwide increased by 10 percent to 760 million compared to 2003.[41] Asia-Pacific led the growth with an exceptional increase of 29 percent and received 154 million tourist arrivals. The rebound was fueled by the rapidly growing Chinese outbound market and the revival of the Japanese market. All destinations in Asia posted double-digit growth.

Then the Indian Ocean tsunami on December 26, 2004 dealt another blow to the travel and tourism industry in Asia.

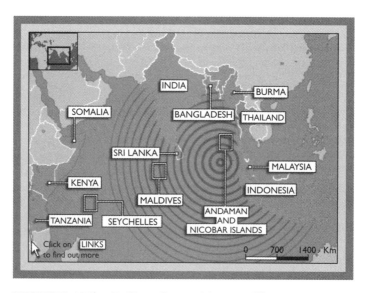

FIGURE 1 **The Indian Ocean Tsunami**[42]

Many of the countries hit by the tsunami were dependent on tourism for their local economies. The WTTC estimated that the tourism and travel industry accounted for 19 million jobs, or 8.1 percent of total employment, in Southeast Asia.[43] In the Maldives alone, tourism provided two-thirds of employment and the most GDP.[44] Within days of the devastation, hoteliers were adamant that they would be open for business within weeks and appealed for travelers to come. But in reality, most of the countries wrote off tourist revenues for 2005.[45] Recovery was slow, with arrivals in August 2005 down by as much as 50 percent and 53 percent in Phuket and Sri Lanka, respectively.[46] For the first six months of 2005, international arrivals to Phuket dropped by 72.7 percent to 0.45 million, compared to 1.66 million arrivals in the same period the previous year.[47]

Despite the challenges of continued terrorist attacks and natural disasters, worldwide annual international tourist arrivals exceeded 800 million for the first time and grew by 5.5 percent year on year.[48] In Asia, average growth was 7 percent with Northeast Asia, Taiwan, and China experiencing double-digit growth. However, the Maldives reported a 39 percent decrease. Arrivals in Indonesia and Sri Lanka fell by 9 percent and 0.4 percent, respectively. The first half of 2005 showed a 6 percent decline in arrivals for Thailand.

Overall, the turmoil and challenges faced by the travel and tourism industry between 1997 and 2005 were short-lived. (See Exhibit 1 for industry trends and figures.) Its resilience to adverse events and crises reinforced speculations of its long-term growth potential. But the experience of those years also highlighted that the industry was extremely vulnerable to short-term shocks, both naturally occurring and human-made. It was against this backdrop that Banyan Tree established its presence in Asia-Pacific.

CASE 6 STARWOOD HOTELS AND RESORTS BRINGS ALOFT TO INDIA

India is becoming the land of opportunity. High and sustainable growth rates, a boom in aviation and real estate, and improving infrastructure—together with easing restrictions on foreign ownership and a wealthier population—have all contributed to the generation of new businesses. Moreover, a huge shortage of rooms and the low quality of existing hotels in most Indian cities have attracted domestic and foreign investors into the hospitality industry.

Starwood Hotels & Resorts Worldwide, Inc.—one of the world's leading hotel and leisure companies—is poised to expand into India. The chain plans to open 50 hotels (approximately 8,000 to 10,000 rooms) by 2010. However, major expansion—at least 25 hotels—will not include its traditional brands, but rather a new select-service brand *aloft*, launched in the United States in 2006.[1] According to aloft's founder, Ross Klein, this brand is suitable for emerging markets and should connect well with other Starwood properties. How successful will it be? The success of the new brand will depend on the ability of Starwood to cope with future developments in the Indian economy. Aggressive expansion by Indian and other international hotel chains will also shape the hoteliers' success. What also remains to be seen is the suitability of the new aloft brand for Indian customers.

THE INDIAN ECONOMY: TRENDS AND OPPORTUNITIES IN THE OVERALL BUSINESS ENVIRONMENT

Thanks to liberalization reforms in the 1990s and recent pro-market-oriented behavior by the Indian government, India has become one of the fastest growing economies in the world and one of the most attractive emerging markets for foreign direct investment (FDI). India's share in the world gross domestic product (GDP) is expected to rise from 6 percent to 11 percent by 2025, not only due to impressive recent growth rates of 9 percent (in 2005–06) and 9.4 percent (in 2006–07), but more importantly due to optimistic forecasts of high sustainable growth around 7 to 8 percent. In contrast, the U.S. share in the world GDP is expected to fall from 21 percent to 18 percent. As such, India may emerge as "the third pole" in the global economy right after the U.S. and China.[2]

Written by Renáta Kosová, who is an Assistant Professor of Strategy at Cornell University, School of Hotel Administration. The author would like to acknowledge extraordinary help and guidance from Professor Cathy Enz and helpful feedback from Professor Daphne Jameson. This case study was written for the purposes of classroom discussion.

The drivers of the Indian economic boom reside in both industrial and service sectors. The industrial sector has rapidly improved over the last five years, with a growth rate of 11.1 percent in 2006–07, where manufacturing itself grew by 12.3 percent. Huge improvements in technology and global competitiveness of manufacturing have also boosted merchandise export growth (about 24 percent on average during 2003–07). Services have been expanding: the average growth rate jumped from 9.8 percent to 11.2 percent between 2006 and 2007, with Trade, Hotels, Transport, and Communication growing by an aggressive rate of 13.0 percent (compared to 10.4 percent in 2005–06).[3] The Indian real estate sector has grown as well. According to Merrill Lynch Co., commercial and residential construction should rise more than four times—from $12 to $50 billion during 2005–10.[4] So, unlike many other emerging markets, especially in Central and Eastern Europe, a single or a few industries do not drive the Indian economy. This promises not only longer growth prospects but also a more stable economy and less sensitivity to short-run structural shocks.

With a booming economy, inflation has almost doubled from 3.9 percent to 6.9 percent between 2006–07, suggesting possible currency depreciation and an increase in interest rates. Paradoxically, however, improved economic conditions and expectations of high sustainable growth rates have led to currency appreciation instead. The Indian Rupee (R) rose against the U.S. dollar (USD) from 46.2 Rs in 2006 (Table 1) to 43.1 Rs by March 2007, and it is expected to further appreciate to 39–41 Rs per $1 in 2008.[5] As a result, in the hotel industry, many U.S.-based chains have switched from pricing in USD to pricing in Rs. This switch is primarily driven by the vision of much higher profits when converted into USD and repatriated back to the United States.

Significant changes have also occurred in Indian government policy with respect to FDI. Most importantly, since 2005, India allows 100 percent foreign ownership in most manufacturing activities and activities involving the development of new housing, commercial properties, hotels, and hospitals,[6] although FDI has so far been slower in the retail than manufacturing sector.

Moreover, very recently, the government has also allowed foreign shareholders to own up to 24 percent in publicly traded real estate companies and is considering removing sectoral caps on foreign ownership across all establishments located in the Special Economic Zones. Such relaxations in the foreign ownership restrictions should not only bring more business opportunities to traditional low-value-added sectors, but should also hopefully increase the trustworthiness of the Indian government and attract investors whose business operations rely heavily on intellectual property (e.g., trademarks, patents, brand names). For these investors, direct ownership and control are crucial when making location decisions.

Higher transparency and overall improvements in the efficiency of financial markets, together with recent developments in the electronic payment infrastructure—the key to facilitating secure and convenient payments—are also bringing more businesspeople and leisure travelers to India.

The welcoming Indian culture, together with good English skills, further attracts foreign investors. Mark Thornton, the managing director and co-head (Asia) of a European venture capital firm 3i Investment Plc., says:

> In some Asian countries, there are cultural barriers which curtail the scope of private equity investment. But in India, people are open-minded, the business processes and capital markets are fine and the private industry is doing well. We are bullish about anything that is to do with growing consumerism in India.[7]

As the average disposable income of Indian citizens rises, so too does the demographic profile of the country, with an increasing proportion of citizens in high- and middle-income categories. According to the 2005 World Wealth Report, the number of people with net financial assets of more than $1 million increased in India by 19.3 percent, which is one of the biggest increases in the world together with the United States, South Korea, and Russia.[8]

TABLE 1 Indian Tourism Indicators and Domestic Pipeline Hotel Statistics

TOURISM INDICATORS	2003	2004	2005	2006
Exchange Rate: *Indian Rupee per 1 USD*	46	44.9	44.5	46.2
Total Number of Arrivals	2,726,000	3.406,623	3,915,324	4,443,893
Arrivals to Major Cities (in %):				
New Delhi	30.8	32.2	32.0	32.10
Mumbai	24.1	25.1	24.9	25.0
Chennai	10.5	10.3	9.9	10
Kolkata	3.7	3.3	3.1	2.9
Expected Domestic Hotel Pipeline across 10 Major Cities by 2011				
Segment	Luxury	First Class	Mid-Market	Budget
New Rooms in Numbers and (%)	12332 (23%)	15924 (30%)	16997 (32%)	8440 (16%)

Source: Adapted from: D. Philip, "Room at the Top," *Tourism* (2007): 31–33.

TOURISM AND THE HOSPITALITY INDUSTRY

Overall economic growth, the rising middle-income class, and the ongoing liberalization of air transportation help stimulate new business opportunities in the tourism and hospitality industry. The number of foreign visitors to India grew by 11 percent and 15 percent, in 2005 and 2006, respectively.[9] Among these, 50 percent represent business travelers. According to *Rankings in Readers Travel Awards*, India was ranked the number-one travel destination in 2007. Moreover, the World Travel and Trade Council (WTTC) expects Indian tourism demand to rise by 88 percent in the period 2004–13. This would make India the third most rapidly growing tourism market after China and Montenegro.[10]

The final numbers will depend on how India succeeds in resolving complex issues, including:

- Inadequate airport and transport infrastructure
- The shortage of hotels and their poor quality
- High taxes
- Bureaucratic visa procedures for foreign travelers

While these issues are major stumbling blocks to India's progress, the Indian government seems to have a serious interest in tourism development. The "Incredible India" and "Brand India" campaigns—that advertise India as a hot tourist destination to consumers (e.g., via the Internet)—have significantly improved tourist arrivals.[11] Moreover, as Steven Rushmore, CEO and Founder of HVS Service International Co., emphasizes, the current boom in Indian tourism is just beginning:

Many Asian countries, especially China and India, are making huge investments in infrastructure such as highways, airports and convention centers, which will further encourage tourism, business and convention travel. In other words, it may be huge now, but it is going to get much bigger.[12]

AIRPORT ARRIVALS

The number of arrivals across all major Indian airports rose by 13.5 percent during 2005–06 (bottom part of Table 1) and even more, by 31.4 percent, in 2007. The air-travel boom, especially in low-fare airlines, such as Jet Airways, Air Deccan, SpiceJet, Go Air, IndiGo, is playing a key role in increasing travel to India. The number of low-cost carriers entering the market is increasing every day, and their presence makes flying accessible also to poorer Indian travelers. These airlines not only offer much cheaper tickets, but they also serve many smaller cities that are often located away from the major hubs and thus are unattractive and unserved by major airlines.

Increasing travel in each city airport, together with high market penetration mostly by low-cost airlines and ongoing industry consolidation, should bring investment to approximately Rs 47,000 crore for the modernization of Indian airports during the next five years.[13] In addition, several new airports in cities near major travel destinations, such as Devanahalli (near Bangalore) and Shamshabad (near Hyderabad), should further improve Indian airport infrastructure.

HOTELS IN INDIA: EXPANSION, COMPETITION, AND MARKET CHALLENGES

The Indian economic boom and substantial growth in business and leisure travel have attracted major international hospitality industry players, including Accor Hotels, Four Seasons, Hilton Hotels Corp., Starwood Hotels & Resorts, and Mariott International, Inc. According to the 2007 HVS International

TABLE 2 **Average Performance of Hotels in India, 2002–2006**

YEARS (NO. OF HOTELS INCLUDED IN THE SURVEY)	2002 (424 HOTELS)	2003 (417 HOTELS)	2004 (484 HOTELS)	2005 (509 HOTELS)	2006 (484 HOTELS)
Rooms per Hotel	63	66	82	81	66
Occupancy Rate (in %)	53.2	54.8	59.7	63.6	64.1
Room Price (in Rs)	2058	2004	2689	3412	3227

Source: Adapted from: "HVS Hotel Services Survey 2007—Part II: Trends and Opportunities in the Indian Hotel Industry."

Hotel Service Survey on India, India currently has approximately 1,980 hotels with more than 100,000 rooms, but there is a huge shortage, by approximately 150,000 hotel rooms. By 2009, current supply should expand by 70,000 to 80,000 hotel rooms across various hotel categories, according to M. N. Javed, Deputy Director-General of the Indian Union Ministry of Tourism. Such investment would bring approximately Rs 52,000 crore.[14]

Major room shortages are especially pronounced in the commercial centers of Delhi, Mumbai, Bangalore, and Hyderabad, but growing tourism has generated shortages in the second-tier cities (e.g., Jaipur, Gurgaon, Pune) too. While average occupancy rates among all Indian hotels are approximately 64 percent (Table 2), in these second-tier cities, occupancy rates have jumped to 75 to 80 percent, and prices have increased by 15 to 20 percent.[15] Consequently, in a 2003 survey by the World Tourism Organization, most travel agents and managers complained that Indian hotels are pretty expensive relative to similar hotels abroad. The tremendous demand growth and the vision to profit from high room rates have encouraged both domestic and foreign investments.

DOMESTIC HOTELS IN INDIA

Indian domestic hotel companies plan to invest approximately $1.01 billion over the next two years in either new hotels or expansions. Major domestic chains, including Indian Hotels, Leela Ventures, EIH (member of the Oberoi group), Kamat Hotels, and Royal Orchid, plan to add approximately 6,500 rooms and 60 new hotel properties across different categories. By 2011, in 10 of the most popular cities, more than 53,000 hotel rooms in total should be added by all domestic hotel companies (Table 1). Out of these, however, only 16 percent are expected to be in the budget category, as most companies see huge profits in filling the large gap between premium five-star and low-quality unbranded hotels. However, good opportunities may also arise in the leisure space as more middle-class Indians start to be ready for family destination resorts built consistently with international standards.

In particular, Hotel Leela Ventures plans to invest $284 million. Founded in 1957 and controlled by the Leela Group, this hotel chain currently operates four deluxe hotels under The Leela Brand in

Bangalore, Goa, Kovalam, and Mumbai, with a total inventory of 1,086 rooms. Its luxurious properties attract both business and leisure travelers.

Indian Hotels Company and its subsidiaries, collectively known as Taj Hotels Resorts and Palaces, are recognized as one of Asia's largest and finest hotel companies. This company is expected to invest almost the same amount, or about $280 million, into new hotel developments. Its properties expand into luxury, leisure, and business categories. Indian Hotels was launched by the founder of the Tata Group, and the first hotel—The Taj Mahal Palace Hotel—was opened in Bombay in 1903. Today Taj Hotels Resorts and Palaces comprises 59 hotels at 40 locations across India, with an additional 17 international hotels in the Maldives, Mauritius, Malaysia, United Kingdom, United States, Bhutan, Sri Lanka, Africa, the Middle East, and Australia.

Another important domestic player, Kamat Hotels plans to invest $82 million into various hotel expansions across India. The company is relatively young, having been incorporated only in 1986, but it is already one of the most successful and best-known Indian hotel and restaurant chains. It offers luxury hotels, budget hotels and restaurants, family leisure and sports clubs, travel business, catering and educational institutions, as well as department stores.

Other large chains, EIH and Royal Orchid, are expected to invest approximately $258 million and $112 million, respectively. Royal Orchid was founded in 1973 as the Baljee Group (rebranded as Royal Orchid Hotels) but soon became one of India's most recognized names in hospitality. The group currently operates nine hotels across four- and five-star business and deluxe categories, with plans for nationwide expansion by 2010. Its first hotel brand, the Royal Orchid Central, Bangalore, won the prestigious Stars of the Industry award (founded by Jonathan Peters and Rayka Rogers) for the Best Business Hotel in 2006. In the same year, its other hotel, Hotel Royal Orchid, Bangalore, won the Best Oriental Restaurant award sponsored by the *Times Food Guide*.

Although domestic chains are aggressive about future expansion, international hotel chains with much deeper pockets (e.g., cash and other resources) are much more ready to bear rising land prices that are already now forcing most domestic hoteliers to upgrade their three- and four-star hotels to the five-star levels.[16]

Currently, hotels in India are categorized into two main types: approved and unapproved. The Indian Ministry of Tourism grants approval to hotels at the initial stage and then classifies them into one of the star categories. This approval status is voluntary, but only approved hotels can obtain various investment incentives, import licenses, and other benefits from the government. Table 2 shows the categorization of hotels during the last five years, and Table 3 shows the average performance in occupancy and prices.[17]

The Hassle Factor

Although the overall business environment is very attractive, investing in India can be quite challenging, as demonstrated by the experience of Sat Pal Khattar, chairperson of the investment group Khattae Holdings Pvt, Ltd.:

> *Very few investments in India are without hassles. For instance, I invested in the Radisson Hotel in Delhi and it took 15 months after the hotel was ready to get a license to open it! In no other country, does one face such hassles. Even with regard to other investments, rules and regulations take a lot of time and it is not always smooth. If there is a possibility of a bureaucrat saying no, the answer will be 'No.'*[18]

TABLE 3 **Starwood's Hotels and Average Performance by Geographic Region, 2006**

Region	No. of Properties	No. of Rooms	Average ADR (in $)	Average Occupancy Rate (in %)	Average RevPAR (in $)
Domestic: North America	450	153,700	185.61[a]	73[a]	135.46[a]
International:			204.33[b]	67.6[b]	138.05[b]
Europe, Africa, Middle East	264	64,600	n.a.	n.a.	n.a.
Asia-Pacific	124	41,800	n.a.	n.a.	n.a.
Latin America	58	12,400	n.a.	n.a.	n.a.
Total Worldwide	896	272,500	191.56[c]	71.2[c]	136.33[c]

Notes: RevPAR: revenue per available room; ADR: average daily room-rates. Average performance indicators calculated using sample of: [a]43 hotels (17,000 rooms); [b]31 hotels (8000 rooms); [c]74 hotels (25,000 rooms).
Source: Adapted from: "Starwood Hotels & Resorts Annual Report, 2006."

Tedious bureaucratic restrictions, arcane business practices, and corruption all contribute to the hassle factor and represent some of the major obstacles to Indian economic development. Hence, financial returns to all enthusiastic investors will depend on future Indian sociopolitical and economic stability. The escalating land and construction prices, infrastructure limitations, and difficulties of doing business—even with a local partner—further complicate entry into the Indian market and make the location choice risky, especially in the hospitality business. "Just because a site is available for a first-class hotel does not mean that it would be the best investment decision for that particular site."[19]

Finding Skilled Labor

One additional challenge is the lack of qualified hoteliers.[20] Skilled managers are aggressively recruited not only by competing hotels but also by other service-oriented businesses (e.g., retail, business process outsourcing, and aviation). The pressure will worsen as more hotels focus on labor-intensive luxury or first-class segments. According to the *HVS International Research Report*, the planned hotel expansions by 2011 in 10 major cities would require more than twice the current level of hotel employment. The biggest hoteliers' shortages are expected in the major cities, Delhi and Mumbai, as well as other tourist destinations like Bangalore, Hyderabad, and Pune. Although most hotels have been adjusting their compensation schemes, hotel wages will have to rise even more. To keep qualified employees, hotels will also have to strengthen their HR and training policies.

In order to fight the tight hoteliers' market, the HVS report emphasizes that the Indian hospitality industry should focus on "improving interface with academia." Most importantly, the report points out that:

> even the relatively well-known hotel schools of India witness negligible involvement from the industry. Complaints about the bad quality and low employability factor of fresh hotel school graduates need to be addressed holistically. Hotel companies, especially those in the luxury segment, need to get together and share industry knowledge with students of accredited schools.

Top business and hotel-management schools in the United States and Europe have begun to acknowledge the lack of high-quality hospitality education, seeing this need as a tremendous opportunity to expand their existing academic programs across all emerging markets, including India, China, the Middle East, and Central Europe. Many of these institutions have not only started to enlarge their existing hotel programs but are considering the establishment of new ones as well.[21]

Cultural Adjustment

Last, but not least, adequate cultural adjustments may also create a challenge. In particular, several changes in foodservice menus will be required to appropriately adjust to the Indian culture. For example, breakfast menus will have to offer a lot of fresh fruits, together with several options of freshly squeezed juices instead of the artificially preserved bottled juices that are typical for American restaurants. In addition, more hot meals and vegetarian menu options will have to be added, because most Indians are vegetarians and traditionally eat less raw food (e.g., salads) than Americans or Europeans.

Moreover, carefully designed food and beverage spaces, as well as meeting spaces, are expected to become even more important as the Indian hotel industry moves toward full-service hotels. Usually, the prefunction spaces were very small and made available only upon request, and thus did not generate a lot of revenues. However, today, most modern hotels are converting these spaces into revenue-generating areas, as demand for big social events such as conferences or business meetings increases also in India and during which the organizers need these previously unutilized areas to host sponsor booths, serve fast refreshments, or organize small receptions.[22]

STARWOOD HOTELS & RESORTS EXPANDS IN INDIA

Starwood Hotels & Resorts Worldwide, Inc. is one of the world's leading hotel and leisure companies, with 871 hotels and 25 resort properties (in 2006), 145,000 employees, and a total of approximately 270,000 rooms in more than 100 countries. Like many other global hotel chains (the expansion plans of these are briefly outlined in Table 4), Starwood is also considering expansion into India in the coming years.

The chain expects to open 50 hotels (approximately 8,000 to 10,000 rooms) by 2010. It will expand not only via its traditional brands—Westin, W Hotel, and St. Regis—but primarily via aloft, the newly launched brand in the select-service category.[23] According to its founder, Ross Klein, this

TABLE 4 **Planned Expansions to Indian Hotel Market by Other International Hotel Groups**

HOTEL CHAIN	PRESENCE IN INDIAN MARKET IN 2006	PLANS FOR FUTURE EXPANSION	TIMELINE
Accor	1 Sofitel (upper-scale) hotel 1 Novotel hotel Since 1997, present via Accor Services (employee benefits, incentives and loyalty programs, expense management)	To develop the following number of new hotels: 100 Formule 1 (budget) hotels 15 Ibis (economy) hotels 2 Sofitel (upper-scale) hotels Expand Novotel and Mercure (midscale) brands In total, plans to add more than 5,000 rooms	by 2011–12
Four Seasons	none	To open one hotel (in partnership with India's Magnus Hotel group)	by 2007–08
Hilton Hotels	9 hotels, franchised through its alliance with Indian real estate development company, EIH (member of the Oberoi group)	To create one of the largest joint ventures with DFL, Ltd. (leading Indian real estate developer) in order to develop and own 50 to 75 hotels and service apartments Launch brands: Garden Inn, Conrad	by 2013
Marriott	6 hotels; 5 brands (1,534 rooms)	To have in total: 21 hotels; 6 brands (5,524 rooms)	by 2010
Sheraton	10 hotels (with Indian Tobacco Co.)	Currently exploring strategies regarding how to expand	n/a
Wyndham	4 hotels; 3 brands	Add 10 new Ramada hotels (1,000 rooms)	first 4 hotels by 2009–10

Source: Table created by the author based on various issues of *STR* and *The Bench Global Hospitality News Reports*.

brand is suitable for emerging markets and should connect well with other Starwood properties. Most hotels in India will be operated via management contracts, and the chain has already established its regional office in Gurgaon.[24]

COMPANY OVERVIEW

Starwood focuses on luxury and upscale full-service hotels and resorts, represented by the following internationally recognized brands: St. Regis Hotels and Resorts, The Luxury Collection, Sheraton Hotels and Resorts, Westin Hotels and Resorts, W Hotels, Le Meridien, and Four Points. The company operates its hotels mostly via management contracts (49 percent) or franchising (41 percent); fewer than 10 percent of hotels are company-owned.

Starwood has almost half of its properties outside North America, but their performance is similar to those in North America (Table 3). As the key to its future success, Starwood's management sees an ability to attract and keep highly qualified personnel and develop new brands, especially in segments with limited presence. Hence, in 2006, Starwood launched two new brands: aloft (select-service hotels) and element (extended-stay hotels).

THE NEW BRAND ALOFT

Aloft is a midpriced select-service brand, developed by Ross Klein, a former senior executive at Ralph Lauren and Polo Jeans, and the current President of Starwood's luxury-brand W Hotels and new Aloft brand. Aloft was officially launched during New York Fashion Week in February 2006. Built on the success of the W Hotel brand, aloft focuses on a new generation of travelers, whom Klein describes as "neo-nomads or road-ready entrepreneurs."[25] He says: "Point-to-point travel can be an isolating experience. After driving for 13 or 14 hours alone in your car, you reach your hotel and are handed a plastic key and put in a cell. We've broken that paradigm."[26]

Aloft follows an American road-trip tradition, but at the same time it offers the latest technology, style, and a social atmosphere. Aloft has loft-like spaces with nine-foot ceilings and corridors with oversized windows to create a bright, airy environment. The loft rooms will have ultra-comfortable signature beds, large stylish bathrooms with oversized walk-in showers, and Bliss-Spa amenities to impress and relax customers. Moreover, each room will combine a high-tech office and entertainment center, offering wireless Internet access and plug-and-play, a one-stop connectivity solution for multiple electronic devices, such as cell phones, MP3 players, and laptops—all linked to a large flat-panel HDTV-ready television.[27] All this in the United States for just an average price of $129 per room. The first U.S. hotels opened in 2008 in Lexington, KY; Minneapolis, MN; Charlotte, NC; Rogers, AR; Green Bay, WI; and Portland, OR; and in areas adjacent to colleges, cultural centers, and airports. Among the first scheduled openings were the airports in Charleston, Philadelphia, and Chicago O'Hare.[28]

SEEING GREEN

Aloft's design incorporates a "see green" program to constantly promote and remind guests to use eco-friendly products and services. "Our vision is to empower each guest to make ecologically-responsible choices and to provide the operators the tools to help reduce our overall impact on the environment," says Brian McGuinness, VP of aloft hotels.

In particular, the focus is outside the hotel: instead of the standard parking lot, there will be an outdoor parklike environment, with a variety of deciduous trees, shrubbery, and a grassy area appropriately named the backyard. A greener environment outside the hotel should help reduce noise pollution and provide guests with an opportunity to relax and take a breath of fresh air. In addition, to keep reminding customers of the benefits of environmentally friendly vehicles, there will be a separate area of parking spots reserved specifically for hybrid cars.

Aloft's eco-friendly approach is also heavily featured inside the hotel. For example, instead of offering the typical bathroom amenity packaging, which usually comes in individual plastic bottles, all aloft bathrooms will use eco-friendly dispensers in the showers. The dispensers will hold shampoo/conditioner and body wash, in order to minimize the use of nonbiodegradable plastic materials. And consistent with recent standards in most hotels, the "see green" program will also allow guests to save water by indicating whether they want to reuse their towels and/or change the linens daily. Moreover, each aloft hotel will have its own laundry facilities, in which Seventh Generation eco-friendly detergent has been established as the brand standard. Finally, the splash pool will be cleaned with Clarity Water Products or Sal-Chlor cleaning agents.[29]

When Starwood Hotels & Resorts executives asked focus groups what they want from new aloft hotels, they heard *convenience, convenience, convenience.*[30] Hence, when it comes to foodservice, aloft is all about grab-and-go. But, as the interviews with focus groups also showed, today's customers desire food options that are not only fast to make, but also healthier. Hence, aloft's expanded Continental breakfast should include, together with top-of-the-line bakery goods, also healthful yogurts, granola and other cereals, as well as some hot meals (e.g., a breakfast burrito, or waffles or pancakes to please family travelers on weekends). In addition, from 11:30 a.m. on, there should be three or four salad choices, several sandwich choices, ice cream and various frozen foods (e.g., personal pan pizza or hot dogs). The hotel bar was carefully designed with the following goal in mind: "Recognizing that guests might want a small bite to eat as they gather for cocktails," says vice president Brian McGuinness. Snacks, pizza, and other light foods with special regional flavors will also be added to the bar fare.

ALOFT BRAND EXPANDS TO INDIA

Aloft hotels were officially launched in India on April 5, 2007, at the Third Hotel Investment Conference South Asia in Mumbai. "We say aloha! to 'the land of all seasons' with the introduction of aloft hotels in India. . . . Aloft will bring style, convenience, and a social atmosphere to the diverse and bustling Indian landscape, offering a fun new way to play and stay to a global community of business and leisure travelers," says Ross Klein, designer of the aloft brand.[31] According to recent company announcements, Starwood should open at least 25 aloft hotels, primarily in the 30 major cities and business centers, within three to five years. The first properties are planned for high-profile locations such as Mumbai and New Delhi, to be followed later in Pune, Bangalore, and Hyderabad. Besides India, by 2009–12, aloft hotels should also open in Brussels, Beijing, Thailand, Singapore, and Australia. Japan, Korea, and Hong Kong should come later, mostly because of higher entry costs into those countries.

But why expand with a completely new brand? According to Malcom Kerr, VP for Acquisitions and Development of aloft Hotels in Asia-Pacific:

> India is one of the fastest growing hotel markets in the world and presents opportunities for aloft. Starwood already has its presence as an international luxury hotel operator in India, and with aloft we expand our reach and prominence into the midmarket segment. While great progress has been made in the introduction of state-of-the-art consumer products in India, there has been no real innovation in the hotel market for years. Aloft hotels will prove to be a market-defining hotel concept in India, and there is no doubt that India is ready for aloft.[32]

Starwood will implement its expansion strategy with financial support from local partners, who should not only help to adjust the product for the Indian market, but also initiate the roll-out of aloft. However, as market surveys show so far, Indians like hot cooked meals, more extensive restaurant service, and extended banquet facilities. Hence, unlike in the United States, Indian aloft will offer a full-service restaurant, and the menu will be expanded by a variety of hot food options and banquet services, provided by a qualified third-party operator. "Aloft will predominantly be a new-build hotel concept designed to provide a 'sassy, refreshing oasis' to recharge our guests. In addition to offering comfort and convenience, the hotels will offer a relaxing social environment," says VP Malcom Kerr.[33]

Starwood also expects that expansion via aloft will be much cheaper than expansion via its other brands. Aloft hotels should have between 130 to 160 rooms, with average costs of $80,000 per room (excluding land costs).[34] It should also be cheaper in terms of staffing: there will be only 45 employees in a 155-unit hotel, which is much smaller than in a full-service or luxury-brand hotel. However, to succeed, the training of those 45 employees will be crucial.[35]

Several questions remain in determining the success of Starwood's expansion of the aloft brand. Will the brand work in India as a new generation of Indian customers emerges? Can Starwood correctly forecast and adjust to future developments in the Indian economy? With the challenges of inflation and rising interest rates, what will the future hold? Will the Indian government continue being cooperative and welcoming to foreign investors? And if not, what can Starwood and other industry players do to increase their bargaining power? As the popularity of Indian market grows, will other global and domestic chains increase their aggressiveness, posing enhanced competitive threats?

Despite all of these possible threats, Starwood executives remain optimistic about the success of aloft in India: "Its exotic landscapes, rich cultural heritage, and booming economy make India one of the world's most vibrant markets and a perfect match for the energy and vitality of aloft hotels," says Brian McGuinness, VP of aloft hotels.[36]

CASE 7 **THE COMMODITIZATION OF STARBUCKS**

> *We desperately need to look into the mirror and realize it's time to get back to the core. I have said for 20 years that our success is not an entitlement, and now it's proving to be a reality.*
>
> —Howard Schultz, Chairman of Starbucks

I s the coffee empire that Starbucks built beginning to fall? In a memo sent to the senior management of the company in February 2007, Howard Schultz warned that Starbucks was in danger of losing its romance and theater, which he believes are fundamental to the Starbucks experience. He noted, "Over the past ten years in order to achieve the growth, development, and scale necessary to go from less than 1,000 stores to 13,000 stores and beyond, we have had to make a series of decisions that, in retrospect, have led to the watering down of the Starbucks experience, and, what some might call the commoditization of our brand."[1] Calling the memo subject "The Commoditization of the Starbucks Experience," Schultz questioned corporate decisions to use automatic espresso machines and eliminate some in-store coffee grinding.[2] He worried that store design decisions to gain scale efficiencies and higher sales-to-investment ratios had turned stores into sterile cookie-cutter properties, without the warmth of a neighborhood café. Streamlining store design was a financial decision, but the result was that stores no longer have the soul of the past.[3] Schultz envisioned the cafés as a "third place" where people gather between home and work and feel some of the romance of the European café, but this feature may have disappeared, to be replaced by a chain store feel versus a neighborhood store. The memo directed to CEO Jim Donald was a call to regain the romance and return to the Starbucks Experience. Schultz illustrated his fear that Starbucks was commoditizing its brand by noting:

> *For example, when we went to automatic espresso machines, we solved a major problem in terms of speed of service and efficiency. At the same time, we overlooked the fact that we would remove much of the romance and theater that was in play with the use of the La Marzocca machines. This specific decision became even more damaging when the height of the machines, which are now in thousands of stores, blocked the visual sight line the customer previously had to watch the drink being made, and for the intimate experience with the barista.[4]*

Written by Cathy A. Enz, who is a professor of strategy at the Cornell University School of Hotel Administration. This case study was written for the purpose of classroom discussion. Special thanks to Adam Baru, Yinian Hou, Vikas Patel, Bill Spinnenweber, Anjali Talera, and Kim Wilson who prepared the "Starbucks Entry into China" case under the supervision of Jeffrey Harrison that was the basis for some of the material in this case. It is not to be duplicated or cited in any form without the copyright holder's express permission.

Other decisions, like the addition of drive-through windows and hot breakfast sandwiches, and Starbucks starts to look like a fast-food chain. As Schultz sees it, "Many of these decisions were probably right at the time, and on their own merit would not have created the dilution of the experience; but in this case, the sum is much greater and, unfortunately, much more damaging than the individual pieces."[5] For example, during fiscal 2007, the Company operated approximately 2,300 drive-through locations and served sandwiches in 4,800 U.S. and 1,600 international stores.[6]

In the United States, almost 80 percent of orders are now consumed outside the store, and 66 percent of company-owned stores sell lunch, further eroding the sense of place. A shifting customer demographic shows that the average income and education levels of Starbucks customers have gone down as well, while the customer base of fast-food giant McDonald's has remained stable.[7] As part of a big push into food, Starbucks sells lunch at more than two-thirds of its company-owned locations in the United States. The loss of coffee aroma, so worrisome for Schultz, is now replaced with the smells of food.

One of the risks of rapid expansion is that the company may be losing its unique identity as it strives for operational effectiveness. "If we just become about products, and not about the people side, I think the experience changes, and changes for the worse," commented Jim Alling, president of Starbucks' U.S. business, in an interview just before the Schultz memo. "We never want to lose sight of where we came from," he noted.[8] The Schultz memo supports this view and notes:

> *While the current state of affairs for the most part is self induced, that has led to competitors of all kinds, small and large coffee companies, fast food operators, and mom and pops, to position themselves in a way that creates awareness, trial and loyalty of people who previously have been Starbucks customers. This must be eradicated.[9]*

Starbucks wants to continue its growth as one of the world's most recognized brands, without losing the uniqueness that has made it so successful. The company, in the past decade, has expanded from 1,000 stores to more than 15,000. But can it continue to charge premium prices and further grow as competition intensifies from fast-food providers like McDonald's and Dunkin' Donuts. Is the Starbucks experience being watered down?

THE McTHREAT

In early 2008, McDonald's announced its intention to install coffee bars with baristas in nearly all of its U.S. locations. Serving cappuccinos, lattes, and a Frappe (similar to Starbucks' Frappuccino) is expected to add $1 billion to McDonald's annual sales of $21.6 billion.[10] Espresso machines will be in view of customers, and McDonald's promises a simple small, medium, and large sizing system rather than the sometimes confusing tall, grande, and venti sizing of a Starbucks cup. Mr. Schultz acknowledged the challenge, noting: "We understand all too well that we have built a very attractive business for others to look at and try and take away. We are up for the defense and we are going to get on the offense."[11]

McDonald's executives contend that they are not challenging Starbucks, but rather the move to espresso drinks is part of catering to evolving consumer tastes. The transition for McDonald's has been in play since the early 21st century. Back in 2001, McDonald's opened its first McCafé in Chicago, a concept it had opened almost a decade earlier in Australia. In 2003, the company began its efforts to rethink the brand through a turnaround strategy called Plan to Win, which included remodeling store interiors by moving to softer lighting and muted colors, along with installing wireless Internet access. This initiative was followed in 2006 with the upgrading of drip coffee to a stronger premium blend.

McDonald's beverage expansion is not limited to coffee. It also plans to add PepsiCo products like Mountain Dew, Lipton green tea, and Red Bull, along with providing flavor shots so customers can create their own drinks like cherry Sprite and vanilla Diet Coke. Coke remains a key partner for McDonalds, and company spokespersons are not concerned about the fast-food chain offering competing beverages.[12]

As for taste, when *Consumer Reports* magazine compared coffee from mega-chains Starbucks, McDonald's, Burger King, and Dunkin' Donuts, a surprising winner emerged. While the tasters found Starbucks coffee to be "burnt," they also reported that McDonald's coffee "beat the rest."[13] It was "decent and moderately strong. Although it lacked the subtle top notes needed to make it rise and shine, it had no flaws." The nickname "char-bucks" may be well earned, according to some consumers, but others contend that people have different tastes and coffee is a matter of taste.

THE BIRTH OF STARBUCKS

Starbucks Coffee, Tea and Spice opened its first store in April 1971 in the Pike Place Market in Seattle, Washington.[14] Its original owners, Jerry Baldwin and Gordon Bowker, had a passion for dark-roasted coffee, which was popular in Europe but hard to come by in America in the 1960s. "They founded Starbucks for one reason: They loved coffee and tea and wanted Seattle to have access to the best."[15] Starbucks stood not only for good coffee, especially dark-roasted coffee, but also for educating its customers about its product.

Jerry, a lover of literature, named the company Starbucks, after the coffee-loving first mate in *Moby Dick*, because it "evoked the romance of the high seas and the seafaring tradition of early coffee traders." The original store did not brew and sell coffee by the cup, but instead offered a selection of 30 varieties of whole-bean coffee.[16] Although Starbucks was bringing high-quality coffee to Seattle, coffee was generally regarded as a commodity item. In Italy, coffee bars serving espresso drinks offered more than great coffee: they provided a great coffee experience.[17] It took the vision of one man to turn coffee from a commodity into an experience. His name was Howard Schultz.

HOWARD SCHULTZ, THE VISIONARY

Howard Schultz came from humble beginnings, growing up in a subsidized public housing project (Bay View Houses) in Brooklyn, New York. His father was a factory worker and truck driver, and his mother worked as a receptionist. He went to Canarsie High School and was able to attend college because of a football scholarship. In 1975, he graduated with a bachelor's degree in communications from Northern Michigan University, becoming the first member of his family to earn a college degree.

After college, he worked as a sales trainee at Xerox and then moved to Hammerplast, a Swedish housewares company, where he rose to vice president of U.S. sales.[18] While he was at Hammerplast, Howard discovered Starbucks, which was a customer of his. After visiting the company and meeting its owners, he knew that he wanted to be part of Starbucks and see it grow nationwide. Baldwin and Bowker hired Schultz as director of retail operations and marketing in 1982.[19]

While traveling through Italy to learn more about the coffee business, Schultz was amazed that the country supported about 200,000 espresso bars, with 1,500 in the city of Milan alone. Convinced that this was the way to get Starbucks to appeal to a greater number of people, he proposed the idea to his bosses. Starbucks sold only coffee beans at the time, but it tested the idea of serving coffee at the new downtown Seattle store in 1984. The test was a great success, but the owners decided not to expand the concept. This disagreement caused Schultz to leave the company in 1985 and start his own coffee-bar company, *Il Giornale*.[20]

IL GIORNALE

Schwartz envisioned bringing the romance of Italian coffee bars to America. To realize this dream, the first *Il Giornale* was opened in April 1986, as a genuine Italian-style coffee bar. Schultz joined forces with Dave Olsen, who had run a successful coffeehouse in Seattle called Café Allegro. Café Allegro was a place where students and professors would hang out, studying philosophy or debating U.S. foreign policy while drinking cappuccinos. It was this type of coffeehouse that Starbucks later became—a gathering place in the neighborhood.[21]

Schultz and Olsen shared a passion for coffee and similar views on how to run a business. Schultz's strengths were communicating the vision, inspiring investors, raising money, and planning for growth. Olsen had a deeper understanding of how to operate a retail café, hire and train baristas, and ensure the best-quality coffee. After adapting their original concept to fit customer needs, such as varying the music from only opera and the move to selling coffee in paper cups to boost carryout business, it was time for expansion. The chain expanded to a second Seattle store and its first international store in Vancouver in April 1987.[22]

SCHULTZ BUYS STARBUCKS

The original owners of Starbucks decided to focus on Peet's Coffee & Tea and put Starbucks, which consisted of six retail stores and a roasting plant, up for sale. Schultz and Olsen raised the $3.8 million and purchased Starbucks in August. They changed the name of all the Il Giornale stores to Starbucks because of its stronger brand name in Seattle and among mail-order customers. In a meeting with employees shortly after acquiring the company, Schultz told the staff:

> *All my life I have wanted to be part of a company and a group of people who share a common vision. . . . I'm here today because I love this company. I love what it represents. . . . I know you're concerned. . . . I promise you I will not let you down. I promise you I will not leave anyone behind. . . . . In five years, I want you to look back at this day and say, "I was there when it started. I helped build this company into something great."*[23]

Schultz had great plans for expansion even then, promising investors that Starbucks would open 125 stores in five years.[24] During the next five years, Starbucks remained a privately held company and expanded its number of stores at a faster pace than planned. With a base of 11 stores in 1987, Starbucks opened 15 stores in 1988 and 20 in 1989. Seeing that their targets were being easily met, Starbucks stepped up their expansion efforts and had 165 stores by 1992. While limited to the Pacific Northwest, Chicago, and parts of California, the strategy was to build customer loyalty through market saturation. The mail-order business helped facilitate this approach by broadening their reach to customers outside their retail locations.[25]

GOING PUBLIC

Schultz took the company public in 1992 to raise capital to fuel growth. Starbucks' managers refused to franchise the stores, because they did not want to jeopardize the quality of their product, and the IPO would provide the additional capital needed to keep pace with their desired growth plans. On June 26, 1992, Starbucks stock was listed on NASDAQ. The offering was priced at $17 per share, but it immediately jumped to $21. The IPO raised $29 million for Starbucks, and by the closing bell the company's market capitalization stood at $273 million. This was only five years after Schultz and Olsen bought the company for $4 million.[26]

With more capital on hand, the company was now positioned to expand—and expand it did. In April 1993, Starbucks opened its first East Coast store in Washington, D.C. The company then moved its efforts to New York and Boston in 1994. Starbucks International was formed the same year, and Starbucks' began to expand its senior management team by hiring confident managers with experience in growing businesses.

Serving as CEO from 1987 to 2000, in July 2000, Howard Schultz showed his commitment to Starbucks' plan to expand globally by stepping down as CEO and assuming the role of chief global strategist. While the company has grown incredibly since he took over, Schultz said, "We're only in the infant stages of what Starbucks is going to be."[27] Turning over the office of CEO to Orin Smith, who later retired in 2005, Schultz was not worried about global expansion, but something did keep him awake at night:[28]

> *What worries me is the question, "How do we maintain our culture, our intimacy with the customer?" What doesn't worry me anymore is how large the market is and how big the prize ultimately can be around the world. I can clearly see the path to how big the opportunity is. The question is whether we can do that and preserve intact, and possibly enhance, the experience the customer has.*

THE VISION AND GUIDING PRINCIPLES

The primary purpose of Starbucks is to roast and sell high-quality whole-bean coffees, a variety of pastries and sandwiches, and coffee-related accessories and equipment. It also sells coffee beans through a specialty sales group and supermarkets. With a vision to establish Starbucks as the most recognized and respected brand in the world, the company has branded its coffee not only through its retail stores and through grocery stores, but it has also licensed its brand for other food and beverage products.

In 1994, Starbucks created a new drink called a Frappuccino®, a cold drink made from ice, coffee, sugar, and low-fat milk. It was a hit, drawing many non–coffee drinkers into the store and increasing sales on hot days. A bottled version is sold in grocery stores through the North American Coffee Partnership, a joint venture between Starbucks and PepsiCo.[29]

To further its brand building, Starbucks formed strategic partnerships to get access to more of its target customers. Such partnerships have made it possible to drink Starbucks' coffee at Nordstrom, at Barnes & Noble, on Holland America cruise lines, and at various hotel chains.[30] In order to offer its products in airports and schools, Starbucks also made strategic alliances with Host Marriott and Aramark.[31]

In 1998, Starbucks launched a partnership with Kraft, a unit of food and tobacco giant Philip Morris, to distribute whole beans and ground coffee to more than 20,000 grocery stores in the United States. Starbucks has a partnership with Nestle's Dreyer's Grand Ice Cream subsidiary to market gourmet ice cream, and partners with Beam Global Spirits to sell coffee-flavored liqueur. Starbucks even expanded into the music industry, partnering with Capitol Records to sell specialized musical compilations in Starbucks stores. The company owns the Seattle's Best Coffee company. Teas produced by its wholly owned subsidiary, Tazo Tea Company, round out the product offerings that are intended to enhance the brand.[32]

Today Starbucks offers coffee, handcrafted beverages, merchandise, fresh food, entertainment, consumer products, and the Starbucks Card.[33] The Starbucks Card is a reloadable stored-value card introduced in 2001. The entertainment products include a selection of music, books, and film from emerging talents. Key strategic relationships in its entertainment business include a relationship with Concord Music Group, which manages the Hear Music record label, and William Morris Agency, which identifies book projects that it can offer in Starbucks' stores as well as provide strategic counsel on opportunities in the entertainment space. Strategic relationships with Apple and AT&T are expected to help enhance the customer experience through the use of Wi-Fi and other in-store technology.[34]

THE STARBUCKS MISSION

With more than 15,000 stores worldwide, Starbucks has fulfilled its vision of being one of the most recognized and respected brands in the world. But has the expansion of its brand into more than 35 countries, with partners in retail segments selling ice cream, teas, CDs, books, and other lifestyle products, taken the company away from its mission? The Starbucks mission is to "Establish Starbucks as the premier purveyor of the finest coffee in the world while maintaining our uncompromising principles as we grow." The guiding principles used to help make decisions include:[35]

1. Provide a great work environment and treat each other with respect and dignity.

2. Embrace diversity as an essential component in the way we do business.

3. Apply the highest standards of excellence to the purchasing, roasting, and fresh delivery of our coffee.

4. Develop enthusiastically satisfied customers all of the time.

5. Contribute positively to our communities and our environment.

6. Recognize that profitability is essential to our future success.

SOCIAL RESPONSIBILITY

The principle of contributing positively to communities and the environment is so important to Starbucks that it works with partners and suppliers to devise sustainable methods for coffee production. In order to minimize its environmental footprint, Starbucks entered a partnership with The Center for Environmental Leadership in Business. Together, they developed guidelines that they believe not only protect their high standards, but also promote the high-quality coffee market. The guidelines are based on the following criteria:[36]

- Quality baselines that are based on maintaining Starbucks quality standards

- Social conditions that are based on conforming to local laws and applicable international conventions related to employee wages and benefits

- Environmental issues based on growing and processing standards that contribute to conservation of soil and water and to biological diversity

- Economics issues that will benefit rural communities by boosting producer income, expanding employment and educational opportunities, and enhancing local infrastructure and public services

Even with the high standards that Starbucks holds itself to, the company faced demands from many social and environmental groups. Environmental activists such as the Organic Consumers Association (OCA) complained about Starbucks' use of milk from cows that have been treated with growth hormones. Starbucks responded to the complaint by offering organic milk for an extra charge.[37]

Social activists in Central America accused Starbucks of abusing poor coffee farmers by paying them low prices for their coffee beans. In an attempt to protect its brand image, Starbucks developed guidelines to pay farmers a premium price if they met certain standards. In 2004, Starbucks paid on average $1.20 per pound ($2.64 kg) for high-quality coffee beans, or 74 percent higher than the commodity market's price during that year.[38] However, some human-rights organizations say this doesn't address the underlying poverty that is "killing coffee farmers and their families." In general, activists suggest, "It's time for Starbucks to share the wealth."[39] In response to these demands, Starbucks encouraged farm groups who sell coffee beans to Starbucks to pay acceptable wages, avoid child labor, and provide acceptable living conditions.[40] They also began initiatives to help provide farmers with access to credit at favorable rates. For example, the company committed $2.5 million through Conservation International's Verde Ventures Fund to assist small-scale farmers in Latin America and Asia.[41]

Starbucks formed a partnership with Conservation International in 1998 to promote environmentally sound methods of growing coffee.[42] Furthermore, Starbucks invested $200,000 to support eco-friendly crops in Mexico in 2003, only to find out that these crops had better taste and greater economic potential.[43] Since then, the company has given an additional $1.5 million to support expansion of the Conservation Coffee™ program in Central America, Peru, and Colombia.

THE STARBUCKS EXPERIENCE

We are not in the coffee business serving people, but in the people business serving coffee. The equity of the Starbucks brand is the humanity and intimacy of what goes on in the communities. . . . We continually are reminded of the powerful need and desire for human contact and for community, which is a new, powerful force in determining consumer choices. . . . The Starbucks environment has become as important as the coffee itself.[44]

—Howard Schultz, Chairman of Starbucks

The Starbucks experience is a combination of an empowering corporate culture that shares the wealth with employees (partners) and in turn creates a unique and personal experience for customers. Schultz believed that in order to build respect and confidence with customers, the company first had to build respect and confidence with the employees.[45] Howard saw this benefit as a part of his core strategy: "Treat people like family, and they will be loyal and give their all. Stand by people, and they will stand by you."[46]

A GREAT WORK ENVIRONMENT

Starbucks has focused on creating a culture in which employees are truly partners—meaning shareholders with a stake in the outcome of the company. Howard Schultz wanted Starbucks to not leave the employees behind as the company became more successful. He saw his father struggle through life working at low-paying jobs where he was treated poorly, and he sought to treat his employees the best he could. He planned to do this by offering a higher wage than other restaurant and retail stores and by offering benefits that weren't available elsewhere. He felt that offering these benefits was a key competitive advantage that attracted more knowledgeable and eager people.

In late 1988, the company began offering health benefits to all full-time and part-time employees, the only company to do so at the time. Then in August 1991, Starbucks started its Bean Stock program, which made all employees in the company eligible for stock options.[47] The purpose of the program was to educate employees on the importance of creating value and profits by linking them to shareholder value.[48]

Management wanted to make sure that the foundation on which it was building the company was linked to everyone in the organization, which would give the company the ability to retain the staff and their values. Schultz believes that a skilled and motivated workforce is an essential element to service quality; in other words, "Satisfied partners create satisfied customers."[49] Starbucks is still one of the few publicly held companies in the country to offer stock options and full health and dental coverage to all its full-time and part-time employees. These policies have contributed to a turnover rate that is well below the industry average.[50]

Since the early days of Starbucks, employees have had a major impact on the direction of the company. Even today, Starbucks' management stands in front of the employees in open forums everywhere the company does business to discuss the previous quarter's result. They discuss openly the plans, decisions, strategies, and concerns of the company. It is part of the Starbucks culture that people are given an opportunity to say what they feel, and what they feel is considered important to management. Howard Schultz recognized the tremendous trust that could be developed when people feel a sense of belonging through their participation in decisions.[51]

CUSTOMER CARE—IT'S PERSONAL

The success of Starbucks demonstrates . . . that we have built an emotional connection with our customers. . . . We have a competitive advantage over classic brands in that every day we touch and interact with our customers directly. Our product is not sitting on a supermarket shelf like a can of soda. Our people have done a wonderful job of knowing your drink, your name, and your kids' names.[52]

—Howard Schultz, Chairman of Starbucks

The key to customer care is the creation of special customer interactions. David Olson, senior vice president of Culture and Leadership Development, puts it this way, "It doesn't matter how many millions or billions of cups of coffee Starbucks serves, if the one you get doesn't suit you. Starbucks has to be able to perform at that level of consistency for the individual automatically, and that's really the promise. We will deliver a drink that suits you every time—and create an experience in the process! The experience must fit the customer."[53]

In an 18-month exploration of the inner workings of Starbucks, a trainer, author, and consultant watched and interviewed Starbucks partners, customers, and senior managers. The analysis led to the writing of a book titled *The Starbucks Experience*, in which five key principles are identified. The author believes that any business can adopt the following five tenets that are reflected in the Starbucks experience:[54]

1. *Make it your own.* A training pamphlet entitled *The Green Apron Book* tells partners to be welcoming, genuine, considerate, knowledgeable, and involved.

2. *Everything matters.* "Retail is Detail."

3. *Surprise and delight.* One example was an advertising campaign in which Starbucks placed regular-sized (magnetic) coffee cups on the tops of taxi cabs and had the drivers give gift cards to individuals who advised them that the cup was there.

4. *Embrace resistance.* Thank customers and recognize their grievances. When employees see that management cares about feedback, they are more likely to care too.

5. *Leave your mark.* Starbucks' social and environmental commitment has led to a separate mission statement to capture the company's belief about doing the right thing for the community.

DIFFICULT ECONOMIC TIMES

Despite a difficult economic and operating environment, Starbucks reported solid financial performance in 2007.[55] Net revenues reached $9.4 billion in 2007, and operating revenues rose by 18 percent to $1.1 billion.[56] Due primarily to increasing costs of products and higher dairy costs, the cost of sales increased to 43.7 as a percentage of total net revenues for the 13 weeks ended September 30, 2007, compared to 41.7 percent in the corresponding 13-week period of fiscal 2006.[57] At the close of the year, Jim Donald, then president and CEO, stated, "Looking ahead, we believe in the global opportunity for Starbucks, and we remain focused on delivering the highest quality beverages and legendary service, while driving innovation and extending the Starbucks Experience to more customers throughout the world."[58]

However, James Walsh, an analyst at Coldstream Capital Management, voiced the following opinion: "Their outlook is pessimistic for 2008. It's going to be a tough year."[59] Of great concern was the slipping stock price. In the prior year, shares in the company fell more than 40 percent in a 12-month period, wiping out roughly $13 billion in market value.[60] After a decade of steady growth, shares of Starbucks' stock traded at $18.38 in contrast to $36.29 in January 2007.

Exhibit 1 summarizes financial ratios for the company in 2007 compared to the industry, sector, and the Standard and Poor's (S&P) 500. Additional financial information is provided in Exhibits 2 to 4 that include the income statement, balance sheet, and cash-flow information for the five-year period from 2003 to 2007.

As 2007 was coming to a close, Starbucks evaluated its plan for fiscal 2008. A total of 2,571 new stores were opened in 2007, bringing the store count to 15,011, but senior leadership was beginning to rethink its U.S. expansion plans. By year-end, Jim Donald proposed adjusting new-store opening

Exhibit 1: 2007 Year-End Financial Ratios

	STARBUCKS	RESTAURANT INDUSTRY	STANDARD & POOR 500
P/E Ratio (TTM)	20.02	29.22	18.23
Quick Ratio (MRQ)	0.51	0.74	1.17
Current Ratio (MRQ)	0.77	0.97	1.69
LT Debt to Equity (MRQ)	0.24	0.86	0.57
Total Debt to Equity (MRQ)	0.48	0.94	0.74
Gross Margin (TTM)	22.92	31.11	44.24
Gross Margin - 5 Yr. Avg.	24.42	30.19	44.28
Operating Margin (TTM)	10.87	13.41	19.53
Operating Margin - 5 Yr. Avg.	11.40	13.58	19.34
EBITD Margin (TTM)	14.96	18.55	23.59
EBITD - 5 Yr. Avg.	15.89	19.27	22.23
Net Profit Margin (TTM)	6.88	7.25	13.23
Net Profit Margin - 5 Yr. Avg.	7.29	8.00	12.81
Return on Assets (TTM)	13.47	8.14	8.86
Return on Assets - 5 Yr. Avg.	13.43	8.50	7.81
Return on Investment (TTM)	22.74	10.74	12.77
Return on Investment - 5 Yr. Avg.	19.90	10.76	11.34
Return on Equity (TTM)	28.81	21.94	21.69
Return on Equity - 5 Yr. Avg.	22.12	21.58	19.44
Revenue/Employee (TTM)	57,113.00	107,759.00	937,101.00
Receivable Turnover (TTM)	36.11	32.39	10.93
Asset Turnover (TTM)	1.96	1.19	0.97

Source: Adapted from Starbucks web site, 2008 and Reuters 2008.

targets to approximately 2,500 net new stores on a global basis in fiscal 2008; approximately 900 company-operated locations and 700 licensed locations in the United States, and approximately 300 company-operated stores and 600 licensed stores in international markets.[61] Operating margins were expected to remain stable in the United States and improve internationally.

Exhibit 2: Income Statements, 2003–2007

	2007	2006	2005	2004	2003
Total Revenue	9,411.50	7,786.94	6,369.30	5,294.25	4,075.52
Total Cost of Revenue	7,215.01	5,866.61	4,771.12	3,981.61	3,061.01
Gross Profit	2,196.48	1,920.34	1,598.18	1,312.64	1,014.51
Total Selling/General/Administrative Expenses	489.25	479.39	361.61	304.29	244.55
Net Operating Interest Expense (Income)	−108.01	−93.94	−76.65	−58.98	−36.9
Total Other Operating Expenses	294.14	253.72	192.53	171.65	141.35
Operating Income	1,053.95	893.95	780.52	606.49	420.85
Net Non-Operating Interest Income (Expense)	2.42	12.29	15.83	14.14	11.62
Income Before Tax	1,056.36	906.24	796.35	620.63	432.47
Total Income Tax	383.73	324.77	301.98	231.75	167.12
Net Income	672.64	564.26	494.37	388.88	265.36

Source: Adapted from 2008 Reuters.

Finally, comparable-store sales growth in 2008 was expected to fall in the range of 3 percent to 5 percent. As data from the first quarter of 2008 came in, revenues were up 17 percent primarily due to the U.S. business, which constitutes more than three-fourths of total net revenue.[62] In contrast, comparable-store sales growth remained flat with a 1 percent increase in the first quarter, driven by the U.S. business, while the international segment (growth of 5 percent) faired better.

As Starbucks prepares for what they believe will be a recession in the United States, they have come to the conclusion that their growth is overseas, and that they can do a better job of delivering on performance. A change of leadership at the top was Starbucks' first step toward stalling Howard Schultz's fear of commoditization of the brand.

STARBUCKS REPLACES ITS CEO

Worries about the state of the U.S. business, rising competition, and the falling stock price motivated the Board of Directors to replace their CEO Jim Donald in early 2008. Jim arrived in 2002 after a career as a grocery executive, but the overexpansion in the United States and the loss of innovation were enough

Exhibit 3: Balance Sheets, 2003–2007

	2007	2006	2005	2004	2003
ASSETS					
Cash and Short-Term Investments	438.69	453.64	307.04	653.01	350.01
Net Receivables	287.93	224.27	190.76	140.23	114.45
Inventories	691.66	636.22	546.30	422.66	342.94
Prepaid Expenses	148.76	126.87	94.43	71.35	55.17
Other Current Assets, Total	129.45	88.78	70.81	63.65	47.40
Total Current Assets	**1,696.49**	**1,529.79**	**1,209.33**	**1,350.90**	**909.98**
Total Net Property/Plant/Equipment	2,890.43	2,287.90	1,842.02	1,551.42	1,447.74
Net Goodwill	215.63	161.48	92.47	68.95	63.34
Net Intangibles	42.04	37.96	35.41	26.80	24.94
Long-Term Investments	279.87	224.90	261.56	302.92	280.42
Other Long-Term Assets	219.42	186.92	72.89	85.56	52.11
Total Assets	**5,343.88**	**4,428.94**	**3,513.69**	**3,386.54**	**2,778.53**
Liabilities and Shareholders' Equity					
Accounts Payable	390.84	340.94	220.98	199.35	168.98
Accrued Expenses	664.29	567.99	474.93	361.84	276.15
Short-Term Debt/Notes Payable	710.25	700.00	277.00	0.00	0.00
Current Portion of LT Debt/Capital Leases	0.78	0.76	0.75	0.74	0.72
Other Current Liabilities	389.42	325.94	253.34	184.34	128.36
Total Current Liabilities	**2,155.57**	**1,935.62**	**1,227.00**	**746.26**	**574.21**
Total Long-Term Debt	550.12	1.96	2.87	3.62	4.35
Deferred Income Tax	0.00	0.00	0.00	21.77	12.54
Minority Interest	17.25	10.74	0.00	0.00	0.00
Other Liabilities	336.82	252.12	193.57	144.68	116.31
Total Liabilities	**3,059.76**	**2,200.44**	**1,423.43**	**916.33**	**707.42**
Common Stock	0.74	0.76	0.77	956.69	959.10
Additional Paid-In Capital	39.39	39.39	129.59	39.39	39.39
Retained Earnings (Accumulated Deficit)	2,189.37	2,151.08	1,938.99	1,444.89	1,058.34
Other Equity	54.62	37.27	20.91	29.24	14.27
Total Equity	**2,284.12**	**2,228.51**	**2,090.26**	**2,470.21**	**2,071.11**
Total Liabilities & Shareholders' Equity	**5,343.88**	**4,428.94**	**3,513.69**	**3,386.54**	**2,778.50**

Source: Adapted from 2008 Reuters.

Exhibit 4: Cash Flows, 2003–2007

	2007	2006	2005	2004	2003
Net Change in Cash	−31.35	138.80	28.76	45.59	33.74
Net Cash-Beginning Balance	312.61	173.81	145.05	99.46	65.73
Net Cash-Ending Balance	281.26	312.61	173.81	145.05	99.46
Net Income	672.64	564.26	494.37	388.88	265.36
Depreciation/Depletion	491.24	412.63	367.21	314.05	266.26
Deferred Taxes	−37.33	−84.32	−31.25	−3.77	−6.77
Noncash Items	45.38	17.13	120.92	99.58	58.02
Changes in Working Capital	159.29	221.94	−28.33	64.18	33.26
Cash from Operating Activities	1,331.22	1,131.63	922.92	862.92	616.12
Capital Expenditures	−1,080.35	−771.23	−643.30	−416.92	−377.98
Total Other Investing Cash Flow Items	−121.60	−69.81	422.68	−336.98	−238.44
Cash from Financing Activities	−171.89	−155.33	−673.83	−66.55	30.76
Foreign Exchange Effects	11.27	3.53	0.28	3.11	3.28
Cash from Investing Activities	−1,201.95	−841.04	−220.62	−753.89	−616.42
Financing Cash Flow Items	89.55	117.37	0.00	0.00	0.00
Net Issuance (Retirement) of Stock	−819.86	−694.80	−950.09	−65.82	31.47
Net Issuance (Retirement) of Debt	558.42	422.10	276.27	−0.72	−0.71

Source: Adapted from 2008 Reuters.

to elicit his departure. Howard Schultz was asked to return to the position he held until 2000. In the role of chairman, he had focused on the company's global strategies and expansion, which now includes a significant and growing presence in 43 countries. As both chairman and CEO, he would now be responsible for the overall strategic direction of the company, with a predominant focus on everything that touches the customer. Schultz expressed his feeling on assuming the position as follows:

> I am enthusiastic about returning to the role of chief executive officer for the long term and excited to lead Starbucks and its dedicated partners (employees) to even greater heights of achievement on a global basis. We must address the challenges we face and we know what has to be done. Put simply, we are recommitting ourselves to what has made Starbucks and the Starbucks Experience so unique: ethically sourcing and roasting the highest quality coffee in the world; the relentless focus on the customer; the trust we have built with our people, and the entrepreneurial risk-taking, innovation and creativity that are the hallmarks of our success.

In a letter sent in February 2008 to customers by the recently appointed new CEO, Howard Schultz reaffirmed his personal commitment to ensuring that guests will be provided with the distinctive Starbucks Experience. Schultz stated that there are no one-shot solutions or overnight fixes; rather, success lies in rigorous execution of the objectives he intends to outline for the company.

> *The position we hold today in our customers' and partners' hearts and souls all around the world is not an entitlement. We must earn the trust of our customers every day—by how we conduct our business, how we treat each other as people and how we act as a responsible corporate citizen. We remain committed to providing health care for all full and part-time partners, executing our best-in-class Corporate Social Responsibility efforts, and encouraging our coffee suppliers to participate in our C.A.F.E. (Coffee and Farmers Equity) practices program in our origin countries.[63]*

TRANSFORMATION AHEAD

First on Schultz's change agenda was realigning the leadership structure to allow the firm to move quickly in the development of new products and initiatives to enhance the Starbucks Experience. In February 2008, a new Starbucks leadership team (see Exhibit 5) was put in place that is directly responsible for executing the Company's transformation agenda. Schultz stated:

> *As the leader of this talented senior executive team, I accept full responsibility for and am totally committed to the in-store customer experience. I will be directly engaged in ensuring a superior experience for our customers. Everything that touches the customer will be a priority. Change will not happen overnight. It will evolve over time, but I ensure you a positive change will occur. I, along with our dedicated partners (employees), will strive to exceed the expectations of our customers every day.[64]*

To introduce the Transformation Agenda, Schultz e-mailed all employees sharing the structural changes.[65] The transformation agenda will include:

- Improving the current state of the U.S. business by refocusing on the customer experience in the stores, new products and store design elements, and new training and tools for the Company's store partners to help them give customers a superior experience

- Slowing the Company's pace of U.S. store openings and closing a number of underperforming U.S. store locations, enabling Starbucks to renew its focus on its store-level unit economics

- Reigniting the emotional attachment with customers and restoring the connections customers have with Starbucks® coffee, brand, people, and stores

- Realigning Starbucks organization and streamlining the management to better support customer-focused initiatives and reallocating resources to key value drivers

Exhibit 5: The New Senior Leadership

Howard Schultz
founder, chairman, president, and chief executive officer

Martin Coles
chief operating officer

James C. Alling
president, Starbucks Coffee International

Launi Skinner
president, Starbucks Coffee U.S.

Peter J. Bocian
executive vice president, chief financial officer, and chief administrative officer

Paula E. Boggs
executive vice president, general counsel and secretary, Law and Corporate Affairs

Dorothy J. Kim
executive vice president, Supply Chain Operations

Chet Kuchinad
executive vice president, Partner Resources

Harry Roberts
senior vice president, chief creative officer

Troy Alstead
senior vice president, Finance and Global Business Operations

Cliff Burrows
senior vice president and president, Europe/Middle East/Africa

Wendy Collie
senior vice president, Licensed Stores and Seattle's Best Coffee

Terry Davenport
senior vice president, Marketing

John Culver
senior vice president and president, Asia-Pacific

Michelle Gass
senior vice president, Global Strategy, Office of the CEO

Peter D. Gibbons
senior vice president, Global Manufacturing Operations

Juan Guerrero
senior vice president, Global Logistics and International Supply Chain Operations

Willard (Dub) Hay
senior vice president, Coffee and Global Procurement

Buck Hendrix
senior vice president and president, Latin America

Lucy Helm
senior vice president, Global Business

Exhibit 5: (*Continued*)

Charles Jemley
senior vice president, Finance, Starbucks Coffee International

Gregg S. Johnson
senior vice president, Global Business Systems Solutions

David Landau
senior vice president, deputy general counsel and chief compliance officer

Cosimo LaPorta
senior vice president, Western Division

Barbara LeMarrec
senior vice president, Operations, Starbucks Coffee International

Katharine Lindemann
senior vice president and general manager, Foodservice

Mark Lindstrom
senior vice president, Western Division

Kenneth T. Lombard
senior vice president and president, Starbucks Entertainment

Gerardo I. Lopez
senior vice president and president, Global Consumer Products

Michael Malanga
senior vice president, Store Development

Jim McDermet
senior vice president, Store Services

Colin Moore
senior vice president and president, Starbucks Coffee Canada

Dave Olsen
senior vice president, Culture and Leadership Development

Denny Marie Post
senior vice president, Global Food and Beverage

Robert Ravener
senior vice president, Partner Resources, U.S. Business

Sheri Southern
senior vice president, Partner Resources, Starbucks Coffee International

Michael Stafford
senior vice president, Organization and Partner Development

Paul Twohig
senior vice president, Eastern Division

Jinlong Wang
senior vice president and president, Greater China

Mark Wesley
senior vice president, Real Estate/Store Development, Starbucks Coffee International

• Accelerating expansion and increasing the profitability of Starbucks outside the United States, including by redeploying a portion of the capital originally earmarked for U.S. store growth to the international business

The 2008 global net new-store opening target was reduced to approximately 2,150 stores, down from the 2,500 stores announced at the end of fiscal 2007 by Jim Donald. This change includes the closure of around 100 underperforming stores domestically and the opening of approximately 75 additional net new stores in international markets. Net new-store openings are expected to be approximately 650 company-operated locations and 525 licensed in the United States and approximately 975 stores in international markets.[66] Already, plans for 2009 include opening 1,000 stores internationally and less than 1,000 locations in the United States. If achieved, that goal would mark the first time the company opened more overseas outlets than U.S. operations.

What remains to be seen is if Mr. Schultz can recapture the Starbucks experience and return the company to its former status as a Wall Street darling. The transformation began with the reorganization of the management team in January 2008, followed weeks later by lay-offs and staff cuts of 600 workers.[67] The staffing cuts were almost all in support positions. The closing of underperforming stores and the slowing of growth in the United States are also strategies Schultz is hoping will improve the future of the company. Schultz contends:

Taken together, these initiatives will help transform Starbucks and drive the Company's enduring success. We know that we can improve our performance by getting back to the essence of what drove Starbucks past success—our passion for the business and a complete focus on the customer and our relationship with our people. In doing so, we will rely on the continued efforts and dedication of our partners all around the world, who have and will continue to contribute so much to the Starbucks success story.

CASE 8 THE MOVEMENT OF TRAVEL SERVICES ONLINE: INTERMEDIARIES AND BRANDED DISTRIBUTION

INTRODUCTION

Since the turn of the 21st century, there has been a relentless shift in the distribution of lodging services to the Internet. That shift has been part of a general migration of travel service shopping and buying to online channels. The trend was initiated in the U.S. leisure travel market by online intermediaries such as Travelocity and Expedia, called online travel agencies (OTAs). These firms rely primarily on the Internet to distribute and package travel services for users. These firms initially offered online shopping and selling of airline service, then expanded to lodging, rental cars, and other destination services. Currently, OTAs provide a variety of travel services à la carte or in packages produced dynamically by customers or prearranged into preset vacation packages. OTA activity and growth caused a channel shift in distribution away from both traditional travel agents and the suppliers. It also caused underlying changes in overall distribution channels.

As travel suppliers, including hotel chains, began to recognize OTAs' incursion into their customer bases, with transaction costs generally higher than a direct customer interaction, they launched their own online activities. These included brand web sites, search engine strategies, and marketing efforts designed to encourage direct, rather than intermediary, online interactions with leisure customers. Coincidently, travel suppliers became increasingly savvy about, and reliant on, online marketing and the effective management of OTAs.

After success in the leisure online travel market, OTAs leveraged their success by expanding into the business market. Leisure sites like Expedia and Travelocity developed sister sites, Expedia Corporate Travel, now Egencia, and Travelocity Business, to serve business travelers. These sites adapted some of the functionality in the leisure sites to serve business needs, including travel budget management, and negotiated rate programs with suppliers.

The online travel agency expansion to the business market intermediated supplier-direct business travel and shifted that business away from traditional travel agents and large travel management

This case was written by Dr. Bill Carroll, Senior Lecturer at the School of Hotel Administration, and Lorraine Sileo, Vice President for Research, PhoCusWright, Inc. The research presented in the case was produced by PhoCusWright and is reprinted here with its permission. PhoCusWright provides global marketplace intelligence, offering an array of qualitative and quantitative research through subscription services, individual reports, and sponsored assignments. Areas of emphasis include consumer travel planning behavior as well as industry segmentation, sizing, forecasting, trends, and analysis. Clients represent all facets of the industry value chain from around the world.

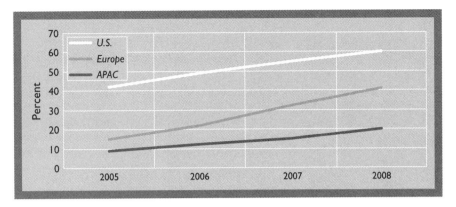

FIGURE 1 **Percent of Travel Revenue Booked Online**
Source: PhoCusWright, Inc.

companies (TMCs), like American Express Travel and Carlson Wagonlit Travel. TMCs are companies that serve primarily the business market with dedicated travel agents, call centers, and web sites. The TMCs serve business clients with oursourced travel management, budget control, negotiated suppler rate programs, and employee travel services.

As a challenge to the OTAs, the TMCs launched their own online efforts. These included migrating travel management and travel booking activity online for their largest corporate customers as a means to protect that customer base and as a convenience and cost-savings step. The TMCs also focused their online service offerings to smaller accounts as a means to grow and protect that customer base from the online travel agencies or, as they are more commonly known, Internet travel management companies (ITMCs).

U.S. online trends were repeated in Europe and Asia with some variations (see Figure 1). However, the existence of large and well-established tour operators and aggregators in Asia and Europe represented a challenge to OTA immediate success in the leisure segment. These operators, like TUI and Thomas Cook in Europe, were long-standing vacation tour operators who were themselves migrating activities online to protect their market positions and serve changing customer buying and shopping behaviors.

European and Asian reliance on traditional travel agents for business bookings and service was also a temporary impediment for business online bookings growth for both major OTAs and TMCs. Despite these differences, online migration of distribution in Europe and Asia is following trends seen in the United States but at a slower rate.

MATURING OF THE U.S. MARKET

In the United States, the travel market is characterized by a relentless migration of business to online channels, albeit at a slowing rate of growth since 2006 (see Figure 2). Growth was driven by both leisure and corporate business segment shifts to online activity and a general growth in travel. In the United States, there is a clear maturing of online channel growth; this online booking saturation caused Internet sales to more closely resemble those of the overall travel market.

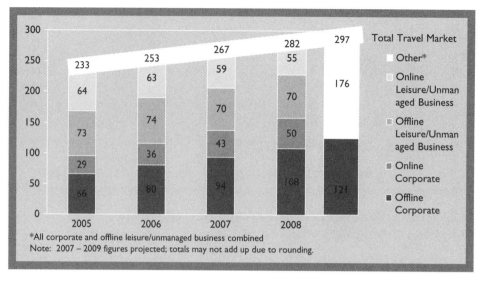

FIGURE 2 U.S. Travel Market Offline/Online Channel/Sector (US$B)
Source: PhoCusWright's *U.S. Online Travel Overview Seventh Edition.*

Maturing of the U.S. online travel market, seen as a flattening of its growth rate, is logical. As more travelers turn to the Web, their demands go beyond securing basic à la carte travel components to creating complex itineraries and service bundles that include air, lodging, car rental, and other services. While OTAs offer packages and packaging, they are often not as well equipped as supplier and tour operator call centers or offline travel agencies to handle complex itineraries or specialized needs. For this reason, online booking in the United States reached a point of natural reliance on offline purchase channels for some portion of U.S. travel customers' demand. Similar maturation trends are expected in Europe and Asia.

Some hotel chains (and OTAs) actually encourage call center contact to boost sales opportunities, recognize customer needs, and increase loyalty. In fact, according to the *PhoCusWright Consumer Travel Trends Survey* (Survey), the percentage of travelers who shopped a supplier web site but purchased by calling the supplier jumped from 32 percent in 2005 to 44 percent in 2007.[1] Some of this increase may be attributable to strategic encouragement of the call center, and some may be the result of consumers bringing their more complex travel needs to the Internet and then resorting to human assistance to supplement the online tools.

THE SPREAD OF ONLINE TRAVEL SERVICES

Airlines have led the way in online growth because of a relatively commoditized travel service, heavy demand for seats, and effective revenue management by a few large carriers. Growth was also spurred by the rise of low-cost carriers (LCCs) that relied heavily on the Internet for low-cost distribution to

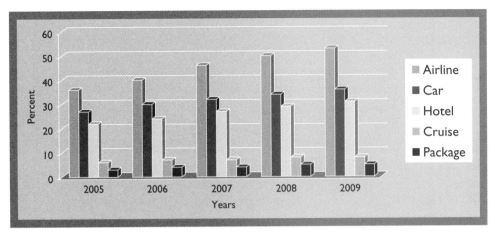

FIGURE 3 Percent of Total Travel Segment Revenue Booked Online
Source: PhoCusWright, Inc.

support their focus on efficiency. The air segment remains the leader of the Internet channel, but it is now just barely ahead of hotels in growth (see Figure 3). Similar patterns of online growth are occurring in Europe and Asia.

Hotel online growth before 2005 came from the early success of OTAs, a countereffort by suppliers to shift bookings to their web sites and away from OTAs, travel agents, and reservations centers. Through 2008, a strong economy drove overall room and online hotel demand and revenue.

Both traditional vacation packaging (TVP) and cruises are small U.S. online segments for several reasons. First, they are a relatively small part of total travel spending. Second, there has been a relatively low penetration of online booking into these segments. Travel packages and cruises are complex and often involve multiple travelers. This requires more human and personalized, call center, and/or traditional travel agent interaction for shopping and booking. In Europe and Asia, the size of package travel is actually larger than in the United States, and the evolution and mix of online travel by segment has been different. In Europe, TVPs rival OTAs for online travel revenue growth.

Online penetration in the cruise segment has been in single digits. This segment is a good example of a hybrid approach to travel purchasing online. Traditional travel agencies and brokers marketed heavily on the Web but lacked online booking capability. Web sites directed travelers to call centers that made the sale. Online agencies and cruise lines had similar marketing processes.

ONLINE AGENCIES VS. BRANDED WEB SITES

In the United States, overall OTA growth was in single digits by 2007, down from over a decade of double-digit growth. Since 2007, growth was driven mostly by the general growth in U.S. travel and rising supplier prices. Transaction growth was, at best, modest as a result of the significant shift to

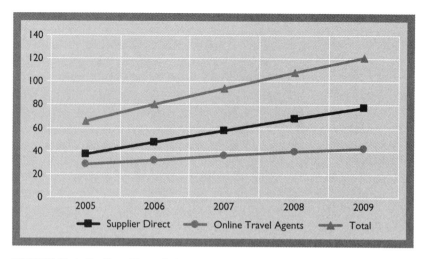

FIGURE 4 Online Travel Agents versus Supplier Direct Online Bookings

online transactions done directly by suppliers for air, car, hotel, and cruise reservations (see Figure 4). OTA packaging for air, hotel, and car reservations was negatively impacted by relatively scarce air availability and tighter controls over hotel rooms by suppliers in key destinations. This was the result of strong travel demand versus supply in both the air and hotel markets, causing inventory availability shifts to direct (lower cost) and away from (higher cost) intermediary channels.

The only major share shift between supplier brand sites and online agencies that differs from these trends has occurred in the package segment. Here, dynamic as well as traditional vacation packaging are included in online figures and, hence, show growth. Dynamic packaging occurs when the consumer self-selects the components of travel service (e.g., combining airline and hotel reservations). OTAs encourage this practice and usually discount the combination purchase. Traditional vacation packages are prearranged and set by the TVP, with limited options for change by consumers.

The true competitive threat to OTAs and an opportunity for suppliers come from other web sites that influenced purchase decisions. According to the survey, search engines are most widely mentioned by those who usually shop online as influential in a travel purchase decision, followed by user review sites (see Figure 5). Deals sites and travel search engines trail behind but are mentioned by one-third and one-quarter of online shoppers, respectively. These influential sites had a profound effect on the use of the Internet to purchase travel. They generated search-based advertising revenue and fees by positional promotion of travel sites for consumers. Consequently, supplier sites and OTAs incorporated search elements (user-generated content in particular) to engage shoppers early in the decision-making process.

For suppliers, search sites represented yet another intermediary cost, but, in fact, made cost-effective marketing channels. For OTAs, search sites represented direct competition because they challenged OTA positional and referral value. Search engines directly monetize top-of-display position with keyword bidding. OTAs must use net rate margins (i.e., the difference between the OTA sell rate and the wholesale price) plus inventory availability as a position "fee" to the OTA.

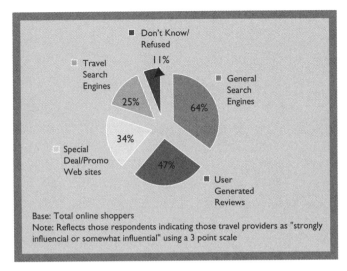

FIGURE 5 Influence of Nontransactional Sites on Travel Purchase Decisions
Source: *The PhoCusWright Consumer Travel Trends Survey Ninth Edition.*

ONLINE HOSPITALITY DISTRIBUTION

As shown in Figure 6, U.S. online leisure/unmanaged business hotel bookings have grown. This growth was driven by an underlying strong economy through 2007 that stimulated rising occupancy and average daily rate (ADR). As discussed following, online booking growth in 2007 was also driven by chain and property efforts to move bookings online as a way to reduce distribution costs and personalize online interactions with guests.

HOTELS RESPOND TO ONLINE TRAVEL AGENCIES

In response to the success of OTAs and as a way to better secure their customer base, hotels, and in particular chains, launched their own online efforts. Bookings on hotel-branded web sites increased as chains invested in direct distribution (see Figure 6). Chains and hotels focused on improving their web site functionality, catering to loyal guests online and providing more flexible reservation cancellation

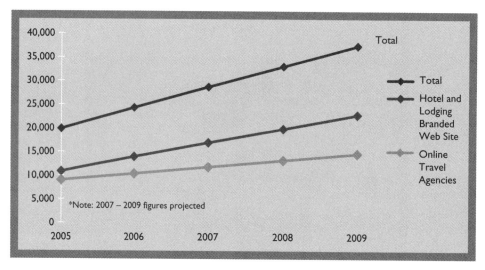

FIGURE 6 U.S. Hotel & Lodging Leisure/Unmanaged Gross Bookings and Channel Growth (US$M)
Source: PhoCusWright's U.S. *Online Travel Overview Seventh Edition.*

and change policies than those of OTAs. Direct online growth was also increased with effective search engine strategies, such as search engine optimization and keyword bidding. Brand site bookings also improved as functionality for group booking was made available.

U.S. OTA revenues grew at a slower pace than hotel-branded web sites (see Figure 6). This was a result of hotel efforts to drive more online direct bookings, a reduction in inventory made available to OTAs due to high occupancies, and the lack of low-cost air inventory for OTA air and hotel packages.

Offline channel revenues stabilized as travel agencies, travel management companies, and hotel reservation centers balanced use of both online and offline channels effectively. For consumers, the balance was based on how they chose to interact with hotels and intermediaries—through a laptop, PC, handheld device, text message, voice, or some other way. For hotels and intermediaries, the balance was determined by the best ways to serve the customer, manage costs, and create long-term relationships with customers using all distribution channels available.

CHAINS' OVERALL DISTRIBUTION CHANNEL SHIFT

Chains can have a significant impact on their branded properties' distribution. That, in turn, can affect their properties' financial performance. Despite relative stability in the online channel mix, there were some fundamental changes in the bookings mix among chains' branded sites, global distribution systems (GDS), display and transaction engines for travel booking, OTAs, reservation centers, and property-direct channels. The migration of booking and shopping to online channels changed the role and reduced the activity level of chain reservation centers. In response, chains used excess capacity to assume property calls, thus allowing property staff to focus more on guest service. Chains also expanded reservations staff activities to include up-selling and cross-selling to raise ADR, on-property spend, and regional (or cluster) occupancy, all while strengthening customer service and attachment. Group sales and booking activities, particularly for small groups, was moved to reservation centers and online to free up local and regional sales forces. Sales staffs were then free to focus on larger groups.

This shift is shown in Figure 7. Chain executives reported that the dominant method of U.S. chain distribution is property direct, which accounted for 47 percent of all room revenue in 2006.[2] Property direct includes walk-up, local and regional sales organizations, phone, and, in some cases, web site distribution. The branded chain web site represents 16 percent of revenue, followed by central reservation system (CRS) reservations at 15 percent. GDS is close behind at 14 percent, followed by OTAs at 7 percent.[3]

Property-direct revenue was expected by chain executives to decline by 2009 because of chains' initiatives to expand activity at central reservation centers. This additional revenue was expected to be distributed between the branded web site and the central reservation centers. GDS revenue was expected to show a modest decline and OTA revenue to be stable.

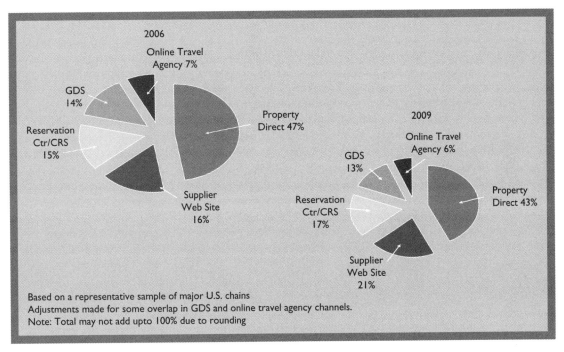

FIGURE 7 Shift in Major U.S. Chain Channel Mix of Reservations
Source: PhoCusWright, Inc.

CONSUMERS PREFER BRAND WEB SITES

In line with the continuing growth in the mix of branded web site revenue, the 2006 PhoCusWright Survey indicated that 47 percent of online travelers who usually bought travel online said they made hotel reservations through a supplier web site. Only 34 percent booked through an OTA. In both cases, however, the percentages barely changed from the previous year, indicating the shift had subsided.

HOTELS IN THE POWER POSITION

Branded web site growth was largely driven by chain property expansion, site enhancements, the migration of group business online, general consumer/user enrichment, and integration of all direct hotel distribution channels. This growth was also spurred by online elements of loyalty programs, on-property packaging, and small group event programs, as well as direct links with corporate customers and their TMCs. Such activities were targeted at reducing distribution costs, raising property revenues, and improving customer relationships.

Hotels grew their branded site revenue through effective control of inventory and price across distribution channels. Investment in brand site functionality and effective search engine strategies directed more users and reservations to hotel sites. OTAs increasingly got hotel inventory only when and where properties needed more volume. Robust economic conditions led to high occupancy and high ADR and prevented even that need from increasing through 2007.

Interviews with chain executives in 2007 found agreement that the packaging of air, car, hotel, and destination services was the purview of intermediaries and not chains. This was despite some major chains providing the functionality to book air and car rental on their sites. Executives expressed a willingness to participate in OTA packaging under reasonable conditions (e.g., acceptable net ADR and duration of stay). They estimated that a relatively small part of their OTA business was derived from packages. Chain executives did express an interest in, and were investing in, property-level packaging as a way to increase on-property spend.

Expanded growth beyond 2006 in online (and direct) bookings coincided with chains' focus on the group marketplace. PhoCusWright estimated that the leisure group market in the United States accounted for 14 percent of hotel room revenue in 2006.[4] Since then, chains have been leading the way in courting this market. Hilton, for example, introduced an online function in 2006 called e-Events that facilitated real-time booking of rooms, event space, and other services for groups using fewer than 25 rooms. Other major chains developed and introduced integrated distribution efforts to support and serve the small-group market with the services of reservations functionality and processing, expanded content, and better integration among branded web sites, reservation centers, and sales forces.

The large-event marketplace also witnessed increased use of online booking and management tools, such as those from Passkey and StarCite. These tools met the needs of event planners by tracking room block use; billing and collecting registration fees; and communicating event information online. These same tools allowed hoteliers to capture more accurate information about guest attachment to events (i.e., through room blocks); tune revenue management systems; and provide better service for guests and planners.

The general need to serve groups, coupled with the decline in reservations center calls, led chains to link their web sites, sales force, and call center operations more closely. For example, some reservations center staff were assigned to small groups and directed to coordinate with sales, while at the same time supporting brand site group-related features.

With the evolution of Web 2.0—the extension of online search and information delivery to higher levels of personalization—hotels viewed distribution channels as more than the traditional means to connect customers with services.[5] Every opportunity to "touch the customer" through a channel became an opportunity to engage that customer, enhance loyalty, and provide service. Examples included Starwood's 2006 redesign of its web site relative for loyalty club members, SPG.com. On this site, guests personalized their relationship with Starwood; searched for redemption options based on points and interests; and received notification of offers based on those interests, all in a media-rich environment.

Other chain examples of Web 2.0 applications included Marriott's adoption of a Really Simple Syndication (RSS) function, where users registered to receive specific promotions on their desktops based on their own predefined conditions. Bill Marriott launched his own blog. Hilton segmented its site with part of its home page devoted to rich social media elements that supported its advertising themes and inspired Hilton-related experience searches. Sheraton allowed guests and others to share their stories and pictures about Sheraton destinations.

ONLINE AGENCIES STRUGGLE IN THE UNITED STATES

OTAs' hotel bookings remained under pressure in the United States from suppliers, travel management companies, search engines, and each other. They are, however, experiencing success in Europe and Asia. In the United States, they have relied on more package sales and independent hotel property inventory.

Solid economics for suppliers (high occupancy and high ADR) stimulated hotel inventory placement in direct and lower-cost intermediary channels. Travel management companies focused on midmarket corporate accounts, an OTA target. TMCs leveraged scale and scope economies, experience, and long-term relationships with suppliers and accounts to secure and serve the midmarket at competitive prices and fees. Still, Internet TMCs like Expedia Corporate Travel did have leverage with smaller accounts and were able to move some small business users from their leisure to their business portals.

OTAs had to fight for their share of both the business and leisure markets. All had low-rate guarantees for hotels. Major OTAs Expedia and Travelocity had reward programs for frequent users—Expedia's Thank You and Travelocity's VIP. Expedia's Hotels.com, a hotel-only web site, dropped its cancellation penalty in 2007 to be more competitive with hotel suppliers. The OTAs also introduced Web 2.0 applications. Both Expedia and Travelocity introduced RSS features in 2006. Travelocity and

Priceline joined My Space, an online group-forming and communications site, with their Gnome and Negotiator characters, respectively. Both Expedia and Travelocity offered users a variety of ways to search for hotels and append additional information about destinations, activities, reviews, and other content. Orbitz launched TLC Traveler Update, which featured user-generated reports about airport activity, including security line wait times, traffic delays, and parking updates.

THE EVOLUTION IN GLOBAL DISTRIBUTION SYSTEMS

Like online travel agencies, global distribution systems like Sabre, Galileo, and Amadeus saw their share of hotel bookings stabilize and revenue growth transaction processing flatten. In part, this was a reflection of stability in the mix of transactions done by TMCs on- and off-line. TMC bookings are typically routed through GDSs. Some hotel bookings were being done directly between TMCs and/or corporations and chains and not through a GDS. In effect, GDSs were being bypassed

More direct connections between chains and TMCs/corporations were reported by chain executives to facilitate rate management; provide better service for corporate travelers; and support travel managers with information for budget management and traveler security. The GDSs had for a long time provided business travel management tools for their travel agency customers for use with their business clients. These were improved. For example, Galileo made significant improvements in the Traversa, its business travel management tool in 2007.

Although they are primarily transaction engines, GDSs became more active in 2006 as marketing platforms. By 2007, all of the major GDSs sold screen positioning: Sabre sold Spotlight, Amadeus sold Instant Preference, and Travelport had Featured Property. These allowed hotels to buy top-of-page position in screens that displayed hotel price and availability information to travel agents. The GDS also sold limited on-screen promotion opportunities, such as Sabre's Promo Spots and Galileo's Headlines, which directed travel agents to on-screen promotional messages by properties.

Paid-for prominent GDS screen positioning made sense for some hotel properties. For example, it provided independent and small chain properties an opportunity to gain visibility with agents by being listed among major (better-known) chain properties. If a property had a specific message to communicate, such as a temporary closing, large event cancellation, or new opening, GDS screen prominence helped. Nearly all hotel executives interviewed in 2007 believed there was a place for GDS pay-for-position programs.

The GDSs also offered rate parity programs for their travel agency users, along with up-sell and promotional opportunities for hotels. In 2007, Sabre introduced its Rate Assured program that guaranteed travel agents the lowest publicly available rates for participating properties. Sabre proactively monitored other distribution channels to ensure hotel partner compliance with the program and create program trust for agents. Sabre also launched Hotel UpSell, which allowed agents to sell (and price) additional services and upgraded rooms more easily for hotel clients. Galileo introduced Complete Pricing Plus in 2007, a program that enabled hotels to return pricing options, such as additional charges for children, cribs, and extra beds. The program also fully disclosed additional taxes, fees, and surcharges.

Consolidation continued through 2008 in the TMC market, as major players like American Express and Carlson Wagonlit Travel attracted more travel agencies as members and went after mid-size accounts while vying among themselves for major corporate accounts. Major TMCs leveraged their advantages over smaller travel agencies and ITMCs through their experience base, operational scale and scope, and long-term relationships with suppliers and corporate accounts. ITMCs did have some advantages with smaller accounts and unmanaged business travelers because they were able to shift OTA leisure experience to business, providing some discount rates and offering access to easy-to-use travel management tools.

In 2007, chain executives indicated that they had no incentive to offer lower rates or better terms and conditions to an ITMC rather than to a TMC, especially if the cost of driving business volume from both was the same. They did feel that relationship circumstances (i.e., a better business deal or incremental volume-driving capability) could influence chain and property decisions in favor of one type of intermediary over the other.

Chain executives expressed interest in sharing more extensive information with TMCs (and possibly ITMCs) if that relationship led to better service for business customers: travelers, arrangers, and managers. Such a relationship could be accommodated with direct connections between the chain (and its hotels) and TMCs and their accounts. Such connections allow the exchange of more detailed information about rates, conditions, services, and customers while supporting travel management reporting.

While transaction costs are a consideration for direct connection by chains, executives expressed more interest in having enhanced services and value for their accounts and travelers. Incremental and loyal business customers are more valuable than modest savings in distribution costs. This strategy may generate more partnerships between brand suppliers and TMCs and ITMCs.

A CHANGED DISTRIBUTION LANDSCAPE

In 2006 and 2007, the two largest distribution companies, Sabre Holdings and Travelport, were privatized and/or reorganized. Sabre Holdings was bought and privatized by Silver Lake and the Texas Pacific Group in December 2006. The Blackstone Group bought Cendant's Travelport in July 2006 and in October 2007 bought Hilton. Both owners reorganized their assets, selling and taking public some of their subsidiaries. In Blackstone's case, the deals may have been more financial than real from an organizational and market value perspective. In May 2007, Blackstone Group spun off Orbitz as a separate entity through an initial public offering.

In 2006, Amadeus changed its primary focus as a distribution portal to become a distribution solutions provider. Expedia, with its ownership of TripAdvisor, took on multiple roles: advisor, travel search engine, and advertising platform for travel services (including hotels), while remaining the world's largest online travel agency. All of these organizational changes signal a changing distribution landscape.

By 2005, search as a marketing tool was transforming the travel distribution landscape for chains and properties. Expedia's TripAdvisor and Travelocity's IgoUgo acquisitions were responses to increasing search use for travel and to the prominence of Google and Yahoo!. These purchases provided the OTAs with another way to reach users who were checking out travel offerings using peer and professional reviews. These sites also provided additional advertising and self-promotion platforms.

Travel metasearch sites, vertical travel service engines, were also evolving as marketing platforms. One of those sites, Kayak.com, bought its rival Sidestep in 2007 to become the largest U.S. travel metasearch engine. In 2008, it was still unclear whether these sites would survive on their own or be acquired (made redundant) by a major search engine like Google or align with OTAs as additional (vertical) travel search and advertising platform.

Distribution service providers (DSPs) also experienced mergers, acquisitions, and partnering. DSPs provide multichannel reservations management, channel price and inventory control, revenue (including channel) management, switch services, search engine marketing and optimization, channel content management, GDS marketing management, and brand site development services.

Starting in 2003, some DSPs became involved in significant merger and acquisition activity. TravelCLICK, initially a hospitality market intelligence and reporting company, acquired iHotelier, an electronic channel distribution management company in 2003. In 2005, TravelCLICK acquired Vantis, a travel reservations and marketing firm; and in 2007, they acquired Blue Square Studios, a web design and search engine optimization company. In 2007, Sabre Holdings bought E-site Marketing to align with its hotel channel management subsidiary, SynXis. In April 2007, Pegasus Solutions acquired Wizcom from Travelport.

What does this rearranging mean for hotel distribution? The dissolution of distribution monoliths like Sabre Holdings and Travelport and the realignment of their subsidiaries with other DSPs have revolved around specific areas:

- Leisure and business travel service promotion display and reservations services
- Travel reservations, booking engines, and related travel agency/TMC service
- Distribution marketing, optimization, and management services and systems

Overall, the DSP evolution has involved the rise of the interactive marketing and advertising agencies, plus marketing platforms and transaction engines. Holding all of this together has been the evolution of a set of companies and applications that were designed to tie together different hospitality systems: property management systems, revenue management systems, central reservation systems, and customer relationship management systems (with channel distribution (see Figure 7).

CONCLUSION

Evolution in travel distribution is certain. How consumers choose to shop for and book travel will change as the technology to do so also changes. Hospitality suppliers will have to respond to that behavior and technology in order to manage their brand, inventory, and service value. At the same time, intermediaries like online travel agencies, travel management companies, traditional travel agencies, search engines, and global distributions will vie for consumer attention and supplier relationships as ways to grow their businesses. How those trends will evolve will differ by major global regions. Understanding the evolution of travel and hospitality distribution will be critical in predicting the future success and roles of both suppliers and intermediaries in serving customer needs.

NOTES

CHAPTER 1

1. V. Barr, "A Plan To Win," *Display & Design Ideas* 18, 4 (April 2006): 32; "Big Mac's makeover," *Economist* 373, 8397 (October 16, 2004): 63–65; "2006 Fact Sheet", corporate web site, http://www.mcd.mobular.net/mcd/90/8/26/ August 2, 2006; "McDonald's Second Quarter Operating Results Fueled by Strong Sales and Margin performance Worldwide," company web site, www.mcdonalds.com/corp/news/fnpr/2006/fpr_072506.html, August 2, 2006; "Strong Comparable Sales Fuel McDonald's Second Quarter Growth," July 24, 2007, www.mcdonalds.com/corp/news/fnpr/2007/fpr_072407.html.

2. J. S. Harrison and C. H. St. John, "Managing and Partnering with External Stakeholders," *Academy of Management Executive* (May 1996): 46–59.

3. "McDonald's Announces Plan to Reduce its Ownership of Chipotle Mexican Grill," company press release, April 26, 2006, www.mcdonalds.com/corp/news/corppr/2006/corp_04262006.html (accessed on August 3, 2006).

4. This is essentially the definition used by Edward Freeman in his landmark book on stakeholder management: R. E. Freeman, *Strategic Management: A Stakeholder Approach* (Marshfield, MA: Pitman Publishing, 1984).

5. C. C. Miller and L. B. Cardinal, "Strategic Planning and Firm Performance," *Academy of Management Journal*, 37 (December 1994): 1649–1665.

6. D. Rigby, "Management Tools and Techniques: A Survey," *California Management Review* 43 (Winter 2001): 139–160.

7. P. A. Phillips, "Strategic Planning and Business Performance in the Quoted UK Hotel Sector: Results of an Exploratory Study," *International Journal of Hospitality Management* 14 (1996): 347–362.

8. P. Sheehan, "Back To Bed", *Lodging Hospitality* 57, 4 (March 15, 2001): 12; "Sleep Study a Design Wakeup Call for Westin," *Hospitality Design* 21, 8 (Nov./Dec. 1999): 3.

9. C. W. Hofer and D. E. Schendel, *Strategy Formulation: Analytical Concepts* (St. Paul, MN: West Publishing, 1978).

10. M. D. Olsen and A. Roper, "Research in Strategic Management in the Hospitality Industry," *Hospitality Management* 17 (1998): 111–124.

11. L. J. Bourgeois III, "Strategic Management and Determinism," *Academy of Management Review* 9 (1984): 586–596; L. G. Hrebiniak and W. F. Joyce, "Organizational Adaptation: Strategic Choice and Environmental Determinism," *Administrative Science Quarterly* 30 (1985): 336–349; M. D. Olsen and A. Roper, "Research in Strategic Management in the Hospitality Industry," *Hospitality Management* 17 (1998): 111–124.

12. T. C. Powell, "Organizational Alignment as Competitive Advantage," *Strategic Management Journal* 13 (1992): 119–134; N. Venkatraman, "Environment-Strategy Coalignment: An Empirical Test of Its Performance Implications," *Strategic Management Journal* 11 (1990): 1–23.

13. Bourgeois, "Strategic Management," 589.

14. L. Smirchich and C. Stubbart, "Strategic Management in an Enacted World," *Academy of Management Review* 10 (1985): 724–736.

15. D. Eisen, "Omni Looks To Extend Presence Through Hotel Alliance," *Business Travel News* 23, 5 (March 20, 2006): 6.

16. H. Mintzberg and A. McHugh, "Strategy Formation in an Adhocracy," *Administrative Science Quarterly* 30 (1985): 160–197.

17. E. Guadalupe-Fajardo, "Westin and W Brands Introduce Retail Catalogue to Sell Heavenly Bed and In-Room, Trendsetting Items," *Caribbean Business* 29, 4 (February 1, 2001): 5; C. R. Schoenberger, "Room for Rent—or Sale," *Forbes* 173, 12 (June 7, 2004): 124–126.

18. H. Mintzberg, "The Design School: Reconsidering the Basic Premises of Strategic Management," *Strategic Management Journal* 11 (1990): 171–196.

19. H. Mintzberg, "Learning 1, Planning 0," 465.

20. J. B. Barney and A. M. Arikan, "The Resource-based View: Origins and Implications," in *The Blackwell Handbook of Strategic Management*, eds. M. A. Hitt, R. E. Freeman, and J. S. Harrison (Oxford, UK: Blackwell Publishers, 2001), 124–188.

21. L. G. Hrebiniak and C. C. Snow, "Top Management Agreement and Organizational Performance," *Human Relations* 35, 12 (1982): 1139–1157; M. A. Hitt and R. D. Ireland, "Corporate Distinctive Competence, Strategy, Industry, and Performance," *Strategic Management Journal* 6 (1985): 273–293.

22. D. Ricardo, *Principles of Political Economy and Taxation* (London: J. Murray, 1817).

23. E. T. Penrose, *Theory of the Growth of the Firm* (New York: Wiley, 1959).

24. Perhaps the first publication to clearly delineate what is now known as the resource-based view of the firm was B. Wernerfelt, "A Resource-based View of the Firm," *Strategic Management Journal* 5 (1984): 171–180. However, no other scholar has contributed more on this view than Jay Barney. See, for example, J. B. Barney, "Firm Resources and Sustained Competitive Advantage," *Journal of Management* 17 (1991): 99–120.

25. Barney and Arikan, "Resource-based View," 124–188; Barney, "Firm Resources," 99–120; J. B. Barney, *Gaining and Sustaining Competitive Advantage* (Reading, MA: Addison-Wesley, 1997); J. S. Harrison et al., "Synergies and Post-Acquisition Performance: Differences versus Similarities in Resource Allocations," *Journal of Management* 17 (1991): 173–190; J. T. Mahoney and J. R. Pandian, "The Resource-based View within the Conversation of Strategic Management," *Strategic Management Journal* 13 (1992): 363–380; B. Wernerfelt, "A Resource-based View of the Firm," *Strategic Management Journal* 5 (1984): 171–180.

26. Barney and Arikan, "Resource-based View," 124–188.

27. Barney, "Firm Resources"; Mahoney and Pandian, "Resource-based View."

28. Barney and Arikan, "Resource-based View," 124–188.

29. J. Huey, "The New Post-Heroic Leadership," *Fortune* (February 21, 1994): 44.

30. J. H. Dyer and H. Singh, "The Relational View: Cooperative Strategy and Sources of Interorganizational Competitive Advantage," *Academy of Management Review* 23 (1998): 660–679.

31. D. Ulrich and D. Lake, "Organizational Capability: Creating Competitive Advantage," *Academy of Management Executive* (February 1991): 79.

32. C. Hosford, "A Transformative Experience," *Sales & Marketing Management* 158, 5 (June 2006): 32.

33. M. Pandya, "Starwood Lodging Moves In," *Business News New Jersey* (September 18, 1996): 17.

34. R. E. Freeman and J. McVea, "A Stakeholder Approach to Strategic Management," in *Blackwell Handbook*, 189–207.

35. This is essentially the definition used in Freeman, *Strategic Management*.

36. Freeman, *Strategic Management*; M. Pastin, *The Hard Problems of Management: Gaining the Ethics Edge* (San Francisco: Jossey-Bass, 1986).

37. Harrison, "Strategic Analysis for the Hospitality Industry."

38. Shangri-La Hotels and Resorts corporate web site, Mission Statement page, http://www.shangri-la.com/aboutus/mission/en/index.aspx (Accessed August 6, 2006).

39. FelCor Lodging Trust corporate web site, Business Strategy page, www.felcor.com/bstrategy.htm (Accessed August 27, 2006); S. McMallen-Coyne, "Development Strategies, Talent Take Center Stage During Upturn," *Hotel & Motel Management* 219, 17 (October 4, 2004): 3.

40. R. H. Woods, "Strategic Planning: A Look at Ruby Tuesday," *Cornell Hotel and Restaurant Administration Quarterly* 35, 3 (1994): 41–57.

41. H. Henzler and W. Rall, "Facing Up to the Globalization Challenge," *McKinsey Quarterly* (Winter 1986): 52–68; T. Peters, "Prometheus Barely Unbound," *Academy of Management Executive* (November 1990): 70–84; M. E. Porter, *Competition in Global Industries* (Boston: Harvard Business School Press, 1986), 2–3.

42. K. H. Zhang, "What Attracts Foreign Multinational Corporations to China?" *Contemporary Economic Policy* 19 (2001): 336; "Foreign Direct Investment–FDI", *BIZCHINA*, Chinadaily.com.cn, www.chinadaily.com.cn/bizchina/2006-10/17/content_710167.htm (accessed October 17, 2006).

43. B. Hu, L. Cai, and R. Kavanaugh, "Chinese and British Hotels: Cultural Differences and Management," *FIU Hospitality Review* 19, 1 (Spring 2001): 37–53.

44. G. Hamel, *Leading the Revolution* (Boston: Harvard Business School Press, 2000).

45. G. Hamel, "The Challenge Today: Changing the Rules of the Game," *Business Strategy Review* 9, 2 (1998): 19–26.

46. J. M. Liedtka, "Strategy Formulation: The Roles of Conversation and Design," in *Blackwell Handbook*, 70–93.

47. H. Mintzberg, *The Rise and Fall of Strategic Planning* (New York: Prentice Hall, 1994).

48. This story comes from actual consulting experience.

49. G. Hamel and C. Prahalad, *Competing for the Future* (Boston: Harvard Business School Press, 1994).

50. K. Kefgen, "The Art and Science of Hospitality," Hospitality Net, http://www.hospitalitynet.org./news.4028309.print (Accessed August 7, 2006).

51. Many of these points come from Liedtka, "Strategy Formulation."

52. Hamel and Prahalad, *Competing for the Future*, 129–130.

53. Trump Entertainment Resorts and Diamondhead Casino Corporation Sign Letter of Intent for Mississippi Casino Development, *Hotel News Resource*, www.hotelnewsresource.com/HNR-detail-sid-22646.html, August 26, 2006.

54. Liedtka, "Strategy Formulation."

55. P. Senge, "Mental Models," *Planning Review* (March/April 1992): 4–10.

56. M. E. Porter, *Competitive Strategy* (New York: The Free Press, 1980).

57. J. Moore, *The Death of Competition* (New York: Harper Business, 1996).

58. Liedtka, "Strategy Formulation."

59. Liedtka, "Strategy Formulation."

60. J. S. Harrison and J. O. Fiet, "New CEOs Pursue Their Own Self Interests by Sacrificing Stakeholder Value," *Journal of Business Ethics* 19 (1999): 301–308.

61. R. Neustadt and E. May, *Thinking in Time: The Uses of History for Decision Makers* (New York: The Free Press, 1986), 251.

62. Hamel, *Leading the Revolution*.

63. "Holiday Inn Founder Kemmons Wilson Dies at Age 90; Wilson Established First Holiday Inn Hotel in 1952," *Bizjournals*, http://bizjournals.bison.com/press/pr2-13-03holidayinn.html, August 28, 2006.

64. The American Hotel and Lodging Association web site 2005 Lodging Industry Profile, www.ahla.com/products_info_center_lip.asp (accessed August 6, 2006); "TIA Fast Facts –Economic Impact," Travel Industry Association, http://www.tia.org/pressmedia/fast_facts_economic.html (Accessed August 25, 2007).

65. P. King, "Major Contractors Experience Boom in Business by Inking School, Healthcare, Multi-site Deals," *Nation's Restaurant News* 37, 26 (June 30, 2003): 130; Compass Group Media section of web site, www.cgnad.com/default.asp?action=category&ID=34&order=datecreated&sort=desc&limit=0 (accessed August 28, 2006).

66. Global Foodservice Industry Profile, *Datamonitor*, July 2006.

67. E. Elan, "Contractors Weigh Tactics for Offsetting Cost Crunch While Updating Offerings, Operations," *Nation's Restaurant News* 40, 26 (June 26, 2006): 109.

68. B, Grindy, "Economic Commentary: A Mid-year Review of the Restaurant Industry," The National Restaurant Association web site 2006, July 20, 2006, www.restaurant.org/research/economy/commentary_20060720.cfm (accessed October 7, 2006); "Increased Restaurant Industry Sales, Employment Growth Predicted in 2007 by National Restaurant Association Economic Forecast," The National Restaurant Association web site 2007, August 6, 2007.

69. C. Walkup, "Sandwich Segment Takes on Fast-Casual Competition with Menu, Décor Updates," *Nation's Restaurant News* 40, 26 (June 26, 2006): 98; B. Thorn, "Chicken Chains Prepare Bird Flu Contingencies, Focus on Operations and Reaching New Markets," *Nation's Restaurant News* 40, 26 (June 26, 2006): 130.

70. M. Prewitt, "Family Dining Makes Room at the Table for Guests Seeking New Flavors," *Nation's Restaurant News* 40, 26 (June 26, 2006): 122.

71. J. Hayes, "Grill-Buffet Leaders Cook up Growth Plans, Tap New Dayparts with Expanded Menus," *Nation's Restaurant News* 40, 26 (June 26, 2006): 148.

72. M. Prewitt, "Dinnerhouses Look to Menu Innovations to Counter Sluggish Guest Traffic and Sales," *Nation's Restaurant News* 40, 26 (June 26, 2006): 104.

73. The American Hotel and Lodging Association web site, *2005 Lodging Industry Profile*, www.ahla.com/products_info_center_lip.asp (accessed August 6, 2006).

74. Carlson Companies web site, About Us: Overview, www.carlson.com/aboutus.cfm (accessed August 6, 2006).

75. Accor company web site, http://accor.com/gb/groupe/activites/hotellerie/activites_hotellerie.asp (accessed September 30, 2003).

76. K. Strauss and M. Scoviak, "Hotels' 325," *Hotels* (July 2006): 38–54.

77. C. A. Enz, "What Keeps You Up at Night?" *Cornell Hotel and Restaurant Administration Quarterly* (April 2001): 2–9.

CHAPTER 2

1. J. Lebkowsky, "Starving in Africa," *World Changing*, January 2, 2006, www.worldchanging.com/archives; "Africa," *Wikipedia*, August 3, 2007, http://en.wikipedia.org/wiki/Africa; "Africa Summary," *Gusto!*, August 3, 2007, www.gusto.com; "UNAIDS Fact Sheet," *World Health Organization 2006*, August 3, 2007, www.unaids.org; "Emergency Relief in Darfur, Sudan," *Relief Web*, August 4, 2007, www.reliefweb.int; *SaveDarfur*, August 5, 2007, www.savedarfur.org; N. King, "Service with a Smile Not Yet a Priority, Say Investors," *Sudan Tribune*, February 18, 2006, www.sudantribune.com.

2. J. S. Harrison, "Strategic Analysis for the Hospitality Industry," *Cornell Hotel and Restaurant Administration Quarterly* 44, 2 (2003): 139–149.

3. K. Hafner, "As the Vision Fades the Indignities Grow," *New York Times*, 4, August 2007, www.nytimes.com/2007/08/04/business/04eyesight.html?.

4. R. L. Tung, "Managing in Asia: Cross-Cultural Dimensions," in P. Joynt, M. Warner, eds. *Managing Across Cultures: Issues and Perspectives* (Albany, NY: International Thomson Business Press, 1996): 233–245.

5. C. Egri and D. Ralston, "Generational Cohorts and Personal Values: A Comparison of China and the U.S.," Research Study, http://faculty-staff.ou.edu/R/David.A.Ralston-1/2.pdf, August 16, 2007.

6. A detailed discussion of generations can also be found on Wikipedia, August 16, 2007, http://en.wikipedia.org/wiki/Generation_Y. The names used to define various groups and the time periods attached to the cohorts are often subject to debate and disagreement.

7. H. Shuman and J. Scott, "Generations and Collective Memories," *American Sociological Review* 54, 3 (1989): 359–381. A detailed discussion of generations can also be found on Wikipedia, August 16, 2007 http://en.wikipedia.org/wiki/Generation_Y.

8. F. Rice, "Denny's Changes Its Spots," *Fortune* (May 13, 1996): 133–134.

9. R. Walsh, "Managing Your Hotel's Online Reputation Takes Time and a Real Commitment," *Hospitality Net*, July 10, 2007, http://www.hospitalitynet.org/news/4032161.search?query=hotel+reputation.

10. A. B. Fisher, "Corporate Reputations," *Fortune* (March 6, 1996): 90; "Top 20 Most Admired Companies," *CNNMoney.com*, March 2007, http://money.cnn.com/galleries/2007/fortune/0703/gallery.mostadmired_top20.fortune/index.html.

11. "New York City Passes Trans Fat Ban: Restaurants Must Eliminate Artery-Clogging Ingredient by July 2008," *MSNBC News Service*, December 5, 2006, (www.msnbc.msn.com/id/16051436; "Transfats 101," *University of Maryland Medical Center*, www.umm.edu/features/transfats.htm; S. Weiss, "Trans Fat Comments Presented by National Restaurant Association at Hearing of New York City Department of Health and Mental Hygiene," *NRA News Release*, October 30, 2006, www.restaurant.org/pressroom/pressrelease.cfm?ID=1330.

12. "The Ten Best Food Trends of 2006 Dateline: Around the Globe," *Epicurious.com*, December 26, 2006, www.epicurious.com/features/news/dailydish/122606; "Consumer and Menu Trends," *NRA Economic Forecast*, December 12, 2006, www.restaurant.org/pressroom/pressrelease.cfm?ID=1348; National Restaurant Association Research Report, 2002, "NRA Survey of Chefs Reveals Top Food Trends Heating Up Restaurant Menus," *NRA in the News*, January 12, 2007, www.restaurant.org/news/story.cfm?ID=545.

13. "What's Hot and What's Not Chef Survey," National Restaurant Association 2006, www.restaurant.org.

14. "Restaurant Industry Facts," National Restaurant Association web site, August 16, 2007 www.restaurant.org/research/ind_glance.cfm.

15. Chuck Williams, founder of the Williams-Sonoma cookware chain, as quoted in Globalgourmet.com, www.globalgourmet.com/food/egg/egg0198/changecook.html.

16. K. Bradsher, "As India Grows Prosperous, Inflation Starts Spiraling," *International Herald Tribune*, February 9, 2007, www.iht.com/articles/2007/02/09/business/rupee.php?page=1.

17. Ibid.

18. "Wynn Macau to Refinance as Venetian Cuts Interest Costs," *Euroweek* 994 (March 9, 2007).

19. A. Batson, "China Trade Surplus Reached Record at $26.91 Billion in June," *Wall Street Journal* (July 11, 2007): A2.

20. K. Walsh, C. Enz, and L. Canina, "The Impact of Gasoline Price Fluctuations on Lodging Demand for US Brand Hotels," *International Journal of Hospitality and Tourism*, 23 (2004): 505–521.

21. V. Chaudhri and D. Samson, "Business-Government Relations in Australia: Cooperating Through Task Forces," *Academy of Management Executive* (August 2000): 19–29.

22. "Italy's Troubled Airline Alitalia Names New Chairman," http://www.chinaview.cn, August 2, 2007, http://news.xinhuanet.com/english/2007-08/02/content_6465022.htm.

23. W. N. Davidson III and D. L. Worrell, "The Impact of Announcement of Corporate Illegalities on Shareholder Returns," *Academy of Management Journal* 31 (1988): 195–200.

24. Adapted from A. Farnham, "Biggest Business Goofs of 1991," *Fortune* (ary 13, 1992): 83.

25. R. Abramson, "Pegasus Gets a Lift From Online Hotel-Reservation Deal," *The Wall Street Journal* (February 12, 2002): B4; J. N. Ader and T. McCoy, "Web Storm Rising," *Lodging Industry* (August 2002): 1; "Orbitz and Travelweb Settle Dispute," *Orbitz Press Room*, Orbitz.com, August 2007, http://pressroom.orbitz.com/ReleaseDetail.cfm?ReleaseID=134378.

26. C. Chisholm, "Top 10 Hotel Technology of the Future," *About.com: Hotels/Resorts/Inns*, August 7, 2007, http://hotels.about.com/od/hiphotels/tp/future_hotels.htm.

27. J. A. Siguaw, C. A. Enz, and K. Namasivayam, "Adoption of Information Technology in U.S. Hotels: Strategically Driven Objectives," *Journal of Travel Research* 39 (November 2000): 192–201.

28. L. Dube, C. Enz, L. Renaghan, and J. Siguaw, "Compcierge Position to Handle Guests' Computer-Related Problems," *American Lodging Excellence: The Keys to Best Practices in the U.S. Lodging Industry* (Washington, DC: American Hotel Foundation, 2001): 199–202; J. Howe, "What the Butler Wired: Do Not Disturb—Unless You've Brought Me Some Floppies," *The Village Voice*, November 10–16, 1999, www.villagevoice.com/news; L. Doup, "Latest Amenity for Upscale Hotels—The Technology Concierge," *South Florida Sun-Sentinel*, December 27, 2003, otel-online.com/News/PR2003_4th/Dec03_TechButlers.html.

29. J. M. Utterback, *Mastering the Dynamics of Innovation* (Boston: The Harvard Business School Press, 1994).

30. The results of a 2007 survey of 2,561 visitors to the Hostelworld.com web site reported on the popularity of traveling with technology, *Photo News Today*, August 7, 2007, www.photonewstoday.com/?p=814.

31. Utterback, *Mastering the Dynamics*.

32. M. McDonald, "European Rail Firms to Link Res Systems, Create an 'Airline-Style Alliance'," *Travel Technology Update*, July 2007, www.atwonline.com/magazine/article.html?articleID=2008.

33. To access the Cornell University Center for Hospitality Research reports, go to: http://www.hotelschool.cornell.edu/research/chr/pubs/reports.

34. K. Reed, "Not Your Father's Magic Bus: LimoLiner Sets Its Sights on Executive Set as it Plies Boston-New York Route," *Boston Globe*, September 12, 2003, www.boston.com/business/globe/articles/2003/09/12/not_your_fathers_magic_bus; "About the Service," *LimoLiner* web site, August 16, 2007, www.limoliner.com/service.html; "Fergus McCann." *Wikipedia*, August 16, 2007 http://en.wikipedia.org/wiki/Fergus_McCann.

35. M. Hitt, R. Duane Ireland, and R. E. Hoskisson, *Strategic Management: Competitiveness and Globalization* (Mason, OH: South-Western, 2005).

36. "Massclusivity," *Trendwatching.com web site*, www.trendwatching.com/trends/MASSCLUSIVITY.htm, August 16, 2007; "5 Star Living," *Trendwatching.com web site*, www.trendwatching.com/trends/5-STAR-LIVING.htm, August 16, 2007.

37. To obtain information from these companies, you can visit their web sites at: www.smithtravelresearch.com/smithtravelresearch and www.hvs.com/Library/Articles.

38. This quote is drawn from a WTO press release on tourism as an instrument of prosperity for Africa, June 2003, www.world-tourism.org/newsroom/Releases/2003/june/angola.htm.

39. E. Hewitt, "Travel Trends 2007: What Globe-Trotters Can Expect over the Next Year," *MSNBC*, January 12, 2007, www.msnbc.msn.com/id/16582299.

40. M. Gladwell, "The Risk Pool: What's Behind Ireland's Economic Miracle and G.M.'s Financial Crisis?" *The New Yorker* 82, 26 (August 28, 2006): 30.

41. Special thanks to Mr. James Quest for providing this comprehensive list of hospitality industries.

42. This section is strongly influenced by M. E. Porter, *Competitive Strategy: Techniques for Analyzing Industries and Competitors* (New York: The Free Press, 1980).

43. This section on competitive forces draws heavily on the pioneering work of Michael Porter. See Porter, *Competitive Strategy*, 1–33.

44. Most of these factors came from Porter, *Competitive Strategy*.

45. W. Zellner, "Airports Feel the Carriers' Pain," *Business Week* (June 9, 2003): 46.

46. Most of these factors came from Porter, *Competitive Strategy*.

47. R. W. Coff, "When Competitive Advantage Doesn't Lead to Performance: The Resource-based View and Stakeholder Bargaining Power," *Organization Science* 10 (1999): 119–133.

48. Most of these factors came from Porter, *Competitive Strategy*.

49. "Growth Slows for Hotels But Rates Remain High," MeetingsNet.com, June 22, 2007, http://meetingsnet.com/associationmeetings/news/growth_slows_hotels_rates_high_062207.

50. R. D'Aveni, "Coping with Hypercompetition: Utilizing the 7S's Framework," *Academy of Management Executive* (August 1995): 45–57.

51. C. Enz, L. Canina, and M. Lomanno, "Hotel Price Discounting Strategies: When Occupancies Rise and Revenues Fall," *Center for Hospitality Research Report* 4, 7 (2004); L. Canina and C. Enz, "Why Discounting Still Doesn't Work: A Hotel Pricing Update," *Center for Hospitality Research Report* 6, 2 (2006).

52. "Blackstone to Acquire Hilton," *Business Travel News Online*, July 4, 2007, http://www.btnmag.com/businesstravelnews/headlines/article_display.jsp?vnu_content_id=1003607209; "Hilton Hotel Corporation to be Acquired by Blackstone Investment Funds," 2007 *Current Press Releases*, July 3, 2007, www.blackstone.com/news/default.asp.

53. J. Millman, "House Advantage," *The Wall Street Journal* (May 7, 2002): A1.

54. Barriers to entry form a major portion of the literature in industrial-organization economics. See J. S. Bain, *Barriers to New Competition* (Cambridge, MA: Harvard University Press, 1956); J. S. Bain, *Industrial Organization*, rev. ed. (New York: John Wiley, 1967); B. Gold, "Changing Perspectives on Size, Scale, and Returns: An Integrative Survey," *Journal of Economic Literature* 19 (1981): 5–33; Porter, *Competitive Strategy*, 7–17; W. G. Shepherd, *The Economics of Industrial Organization* (Englewood Cliffs, NJ: Prentice Hall, 1979). For applications of barriers to entry to competitive strategy, see K. R. Harrigan, "Barriers to Entry and Competitive Strategies," *Strategic Management Journal* 2 (1981): 395–412.

55. Bain, *Barriers to New Competition*; H. M. Mann, "Seller Concentration, Barriers to Entry, and Rates of Return in Thirty Industries, 1950–1960," *Review of Economics and Statistics* 48 (1966): 296–307.

56. Porter, *Competitive Strategy*, 23.

57. "Rapid Expansion of Budget Hotels," *China.Org*, September 2006, www.china.org.cn/english/2006/Sep/180646.htm.

58. B. Z. Posner and W. H. Schmidt, "Values and the American Manager: An Update," *California Management Review* 3 (1984): 206.

59. "Our Values," 2001 *Annual Report*, Four Seasons Hotels and Resorts, 1.

60. "IHG's Priority Club Rewards Program Expands Meeting Rewards Offer," *Hotel and Motel Management Week in Review*, July 3, 2007, www.hotelmotel.com/hotelmotel/article/articleDetail.jsp?id=439455.

61. T. Winship, "View from the Top—The Experts Weigh in on the Future of Travel Loyalty Programs," Loyalty Program News, OAG *Travel Information*, October 27, 2006, www.oag.com/oag/website/com/en/Home/Travel+Magazine/Frequent+Flyer/Loyalty+Program+News/View+from+the+Top+The+Experts+Weight+in+on+the+Future+of+Travel+Loyalty+Programs+27100614.

62. K. Jennings and F. Westfall, "Benchmarking for Strategic Action," *Journal of Business Strategy* (May/June 1992): 22.

63. R. C. Camp, "Learning from the Best Leads to Superior Performance," *Journal of Business Strategy* (May/June 1992): 3.

64. A comprehensive benchmarking study of the lodging industry is available in detail in the following book: L. Dube, C. Enz, L. Renaghan, and J. Siguaw, *American Lodging Excellence: The Key to Best Practices in the U.S. Lodging Industry* (American Hotel Foundation, 2000). Additional articles on specific best practices can be found online at: www.hotelschool.cornell.edu/research/chr/pubs/best/

65. C. A. Enz and J. Siguaw, "Revisiting the Best of the Best: Innovations in Hotel Practice," *Cornell Hotel and Restaurant Administration Quarterly* 44, 6 (2003).

66. "TIA Mission and Objectives," *Travel Industry Association* web site, August 14, 2007, www.tia.org/about/mission.html.

67. Empirical support for this phenomenon is found in K. B. Grier, M. C. Munger, and B. E. Roberts, "The Determinants of Industry Political Activity, 1978–1986," *American Political Science Review* 88 (1994): 911–925; a descriptive review of this problem is

found in I. Maitland, "Self-defeating Lobbying: How More Is Buying Less in Washington," *Journal of Business Strategy* 7, 2 (1986): 67–78.

68. W. R. Scott, *Organizations: Rational, Natural, and Open Systems*, 3rd ed. (Englewood Cliffs, NJ: Prentice Hall, 1992).

69. J. H. Dyer and H. Singh, "The Relational View: Cooperative Strategy and Sources of Interorganizational Competitive Advantage," *Academy of Management Review* 23 (1998): 660–679.

70. B. R. Barringer and J. S. Harrison, "Walking a Tightrope: Creating Value through Interorganizational Relationships," *Journal of Management* 26 (2000): 367–403.

71. A. Inkpen and M. M. Crossan, "Believing Is Seeing: Joint Ventures and Organizational Learning," *Journal of Management Studies* 32 (1995): 595–618.

72. Y. L. Doz and G. Hamel, *Alliance Advantage* (Boston: Harvard Business School Press, 1998).

73. "Blue Coast Hotels, Hilton in Indian JV," *Reuters*, December 16, 2002, http://global.factiva.com/en/arch.

74. Xerox, *Annual Report* (2000), 9.

75. C. Jones, W. S. Hesterly, and S. P. Borgatti, "A General Theory of Network Governance: Exchange Conditions and Social Mechanisms," *Academy of Management Review* 22 (1997): 911–945.

76. Barringer and Harrison, "Walking a Tightrope," 367–403.

77. "About CLIA," *Cruise Lines International Association* web site, August 17, 2007 http://www.cruising.org/about.cfm.

78. P. H. Dickson and K. M. Weaver, "Environmental Determinants and Individual-Level Moderators of Alliance Use," *Academy of Management Journal* 40 (1997): 404–425.

79. J. H. Dyer, P. Kale, and H. Singh, "How to Make Strategic Alliances Work," *MIT Sloan Management Review* 42, 4 (2001): 37–43.

80. R. Verrier, "Disney, Kellogg Seal Honey of a Deal," *Orlando Sentinel* (September 6, 2001): A1.

81. B. Estabrook, "Taking the 'Lug' Out of Luggage," *The New York Times* (September 29, 2002): 7.

82. C. Binkley, "Fairmont Teams Up with Porsche," *The Wall Street Journal* (October 8, 2002): B9.

83. Barringer and Harrison, "Walking a Tightrope," 367–403.

84. J. Pfeffer and G. R. Salancik, *The External Control of Organizations* (New York: Harper & Row, 1978).

CHAPTER 3

1. *Mandarin Oriental Hotel Group Annual Report*, 2006, "Our Mission," *Mandarin Oriental Hotel Group* web site, http://www.mandarinoriental.com/hotel/520000019.asp, (accessed September 6, 2007).

2. L. J. Bourgeois, "Performance and Consensus," *Strategic Management Journal* 1 (1980): 227–248; G. G. Dess, "Consensus on Strategy Formulation and Organizational Performance: Competitors in a Fragmented Industry," *Strategic Management Journal* 8 (1987): 259–277; L. G. Hrebiniak and C. C. Snow, "Top Management Agreement and Organizational Performance," *Human Relations* 35 (1982): 1139–1158; Labich, "Why Companies Fail."

3. S. Nelton, "Put Your Purpose in Writing," *Nation's Business* (February 1994): 63.

4. G. Hamel, *Leading the Revolution* (Boston: Harvard Business School Press, 2000), 246.

5. D. F. Abell, *Defining the Business: The Starting Point of Strategic Planning* (Englewood Cliffs, NJ: Prentice Hall, 1980), 169.

6. Abell, *Defining the Business*, 169.

7. IHG Lodging Brands, company web site, www.ichotelsgroup.com/h/d/6c/1/en/c/2/content/dec/6c/1/en/ob.html (accessed September 10, 2007).

8. "Intercontinental Hotels Group Embarks on Seventh Brand; The Hotel Indigo Brand Created Primarily for Conversions," *Hotel Online*, January 2004, www.hotel-online.com/News/PR2004_2nd/Apr04_IndigoBrand.html.

9. Ibid.

10. Hamel, *Leading the Revolution*.

11. P. F. Drucker, *Management—Tasks, Responsibilities, Practices* (New York: Harper & Row, 1974), 74–94.

12. J. W. Marriott, "To Our Shareholders," Marriott International Inc., Annual Report, 2006, 9–10.

13. Hamel, *Leading the Revolution*.

14. J. S. Bracker, "Delta Airlines," in *Strategic Management: A Choice Approach*, eds. J. R. Montanari, C. P. Morgan, and J. S. Bracker (Chicago: The Dryden Press, 1990), 657–670.

15. Delta Air Lines, *Wikipedia*, http://en.wikipedia.org/wiki/Delta_Air_Lines (accessed September 10, 2007).

16. "About Virgin," corporate web site, www.virgin.com/Companies.aspx (accessed September 10, 2007); "Virgin Group LTD," *Hoover's Online*, July 8, 2003, www.hoovers.com.

17. "A Message from our President," *Royal Caribbean International web site*, www.royalcaribbean.com/ourCompany/messageFromPresident. do (accessed September 10, 2007).

18. J. Betton and G. G. Dess, "The Application of Population Ecology Models to the Study of Organizations," *Academy of Management Review* 10 (1985): 750–757.

19. "Royal Caribbean and the Environment," *Royal Caribbean International web site*, www.royalcaribbean.com/ourCompany/community/ rcAndTheCommunity.do (accessed September 10, 2007).

20. J. Chung, "Au Revoir, Lutece," *Gothamist*, February 11, 2004, http://gothamist.com/2004/02/11/au_revoir_lutece.php.

21. K. Leahy, "As Time Goes By," *Restaurants & Institutions* 117, 9 (June 1, 2007): 51–54.

22. F., Bruni, "Jeans, Yes, but Still Nicely Pressed," *The New York Times*, March 14, 2007, http://events.nytimes.com/2007/03/14/dining/ reviews/14rest.html?ref=dining); K. Leahy, "As Time Goes By," *Restaurants & Institutions* 117, 9 (June 1, 2007); 51–54.

23. "Our Mission, Our Vision, Our Passion," Choice International Hotels web site, www.choicehotels.com/ires/en-US/html/ StrategicPlan?sid=GNle.oE0Hdg2qhg.5 (accessed September 10, 2007).

24. Adapted from C. Enz and D. Corsun, "Living a Vision at Hillerman Hotels," *Case Research Journal, 2004*.

25. "Mission Statement," *Sunland Park Racetrack & Casino Website*, www.sunland-park.com/mission.htm (accessed September 10, 2007).

26. "Wendy's Moves Ahead with New Strategic Plan," *Corporate and Investor web site Wendy's International*, www.wendys-invest.com/ strategic1206/strategicplan.php (accessed September 18, 2007).

27. "Core Values," Marriott web site, www.marriott.com/corporateinfo/culture/coreValues.mi (accessed May 18, 2008).

28. "Our Credo," *Johnson & Johnson web site*, www.jnj.com/our_company/our_credo/index.htm (accessed September 11, 2007).

29. R. Tofel, "Telling a Big Story in a Few Words," *Wall Street Journal*, May 2, 2007; "Our Company," *Johnson & Johnson web site*, www.jnj .com/our_company/our_credo/index.htm (accessed September 11, 2007).

30. "Our Vision," *Royal Caribbean International web site*, www.royalcaribbean.com/ourCompany (accessed September 11, 2007).

31. "About Us," *Starbucks Coffee web site*, www.starbucks.com/aboutus/environment.asp (accessed September 11, 2007).

32. "Vision," Marriott International, Inc., 2002 *Annual Report*, 2.

33. D. J. Isenberg, "The Tactics of Strategic Opportunism, *Harvard Business Review* 65, 2 (March/April 1987): 92–97.

34. This informal study was based on strategic management students' phone calls to corporate reservation systems as part of a classroom assignment.

35. A. Baru, Y. Hou, V. Patel, B. Spinnerweber, A. Talera, and K. Wilson, "Starbucks' Entry Into China," in J. Harrison and C. Enz, *Hospitality Strategic Management: Concepts and Cases* (New York: Wiley, 2005); Starbucks 2006 Annual Report, "Starbucks Corporation," Student Resources web site for Thompson and Strickland, *Strategic Management*, 11th edition, McGraw-Hill, www.mhhe.com/business/management/thompson/11e/case/starbucks-1.html (accessed September 11, 2007).

36. "Salty's Mission Statement," *Salty's web site* www.saltys.com (accessed September 18, 2007).

37. "Company Values," *Starwood Hotels & Resorts World Wide Inc. web site*, July 8, 2003, www.starwoodhotels.com/corporate/company_ values.html (accessed September 18, 2007).

38. E. H. Schein, *Organizational Culture and Leadership* (San Francisco: Jossey-Bass, 1985); E. H. Schein, "The Role of the Founder in Creating Organizational Culture," *Organizational Dynamics* (Summer 1983), 14; P. Selznik, *Leadership in Administration* (Evanston, IL: Row, Peterson, 1957).

39. Clarkson Centre for Business Ethics, *Principles of Stakeholder Management* (Toronto: Rotman School of Management, 1999).

40. I. F. Kesner, "Crisis in the Boardroom: Fact and Fiction," *Academy of Management Executive* (February 1990): 23–35.

41. L. Dube, C. Enz, L. Reneghan, and J. Siguaw, "Disney's Polynesian Resort: A Value-Based Process of Training and Selection," *American Lodging Excellence: The Keys to Best Practices in the U.S. Lodging Industry* (American Hotel Foundation, 1999), 90–91.

42. A. B. Carroll, "A Three Dimensional Model of Corporate Social Performance," *Academy of Management Review* 4 (1979): 497–505.

43. "Souza's Steps Out as a Socially Responsible Restaurant Reducing the Alcohol Footprint in Vermont," *PR.com web site* www .pr.com/press-release/31123 (accessed September 19, 2007).

44. K. Spaeder, "For good CAUSE - 1999 Socially Responsible Franchisee of the Year awards," *Entrepreneur*, July 1999.

45. "McDonald's Social Corporate Responsibility," July 8, 2003, www.mcdonalds.com/corporate/social/index.html; "Ronald McDonald House Charities, September 19, 2007, www.rmhc.org/rmhc/index/programs/ronald_mcdonald_house.html.

46. "Green Convergence: Stakeholders Come Together to Create Sustainable Hotelkeeping Practices," *Hotels* (June 2007): 10–12.

47. "Starwood Capital Group and Barry Sternlicht Unveil Groundbreaking New Hotel Concept: '1' Hotel," *PR Newswire web site*, www .prnewswire.com/cgi-bin/stories.pl?ACCT=109&STORY=/www/story/10-18-2006/0004453948&EDATE= (accessed September 19, 2007).

48. "Green Convergence: Stakeholders Come Together to Create Sustainable Hotelkeeping Practices," 12.

49. "Declaration of Interdependence," *Whole Foods Markets web site*, www.wholefoodsmarket.com/company/declaration.html (accessed September 19, 2007).

50. 33. K. E. Aupperle, A. B. Carroll, and J. D. Hatfield, "An Empirical Examination of the Relationship between Corporate Social Responsibility and Profitability," *Academy of Management Journal* 28 (1985): 446–463.

51. S. Clark, "Corporate Social Responsibility A Marketing Tool for Major Hotel Brands," *HSMAI Marketing Review* 23, 1 (Spring 2006): 42–45.

52. L. T. Hosmer, "Response to 'Do Good Ethics Always Make for Good Business,'" *Strategic Management Journal* 17 (1996): 501; See also L. T. Hosmer, "Strategic Planning as if Ethics Mattered," *Strategic Management Journal* 15 (Summer Special Issue, 1994): 17–34.

53. Hosmer, "Strategic Planning"; D. Schendel and C. Hofer, *Strategic Management: A New View of Business Policy and Planning* (Boston: Little, Brown, 1979).

54. Freeman and Gilbert, *Corporate Strategy*.

55. J. A. Pearce II and F. David, "Corporate Mission Statements: The Bottom Line," *Academy of Management Executive* 1, 2 (May 1987): 109–115.

56. B. Chung-Herrera, C. Enz, and M. Lankau, "Grooming Future Hospitality Leaders: A Competencies Model, *Cornell Hotel and Restaurant Administration Quarterly* (June 2003): 1–9.

57. P. Cobe, "Can Sustainability Be Profitable?," *Restaurant Business* 106, 9 (September 2007); "Conservation," *Aquarium of the Pacific web site*, www.aquariumofpacific.org/conservation/information/C196 (accessed September 19, 2007).

58. Hosmer, *Ethics of Management*.

59. Based on information in Hosmer, *Ethics of Management*.

60. M. Prewitt, "Religion-based Business Models Complicate Operations for Some Chains," *Nation's Restaurant News*, 41, 36 (September 10, 2007): 1, 77; E. Small "The Cult of Chick-fil-A," *Forbes*, July 23, 2007, http://members.forbes.com/forbes/2007/0723/080. html?token=MjAgU2VwIDIwMDcgMTI6NTY6MTYgKzAwMDA%253D; "About S. Truett Cathy," *Chick-fil-A web site*, www.truettcathy.com/about.asp (accessed September 20, 2007).

61. Ibid.

62. J. A. Byrne, "The Best-laid Ethics Programs," *Business Week* (March 9, 1992), 67–69; D. Driscoll, "The Dow Corning Case," *Business and Society Review* 100, 1 (September 1998): 57–64; M. B. W. Tabor, "Ex-Dow Corning Executive Faults Company's Ethics on Implants," *The New York Times*, September 23, 1995, 10.

63. B. McCoy, "The Parable of the Sadhu," *Harvard Business Review* 61, 5 (September/October 1983).

64. "Seneca Gaming Corporation and its Subsidiaries Code of Conduct and Ethics," http://senecagamingcorporation.com/pdf/codeOfEthics.pdf (Accessed October 2, 2007). The entire document can be downloaded at the web site provided above.

65. Ibid.

66. Algar, *Annual Report* (2000), 5.

67. Ibid.

68. E. Thornton, "Japan: Sexism OK with Most Coeds," *Business Week* (August 24, 1992): 13.

69. V. Chambers, *Kickboxing Geishas: How Modern Japanese Women are Changing their Nation* (New York: Simon & Schuster, 2007).

CHAPTER 4

1. "About Us," Ryanair web site, August 17, 2007, www.ryanair.com/site/EN/about.php?page=About&pos=HEAD; "Ryanair," *Wikipedia* August 18, 2007, http://en.wikipedia.org/wiki/Ryanair.

2. R. Grant, *Contemporary Strategy Analysis*, 6th ed. (Malden, MA: Blackwell Publishing, 2008).

3. "Ryanair Full Year Results – 2007 Roadshow Presentation," *Publications on Ryanair web site*, March 31, 2007, www.ryanair.com/site/about/invest/docs/present/quarter4_2007.pdf.

4. Most of these questions are based on J. B. Barney, "Looking Inside for Competitive Advantage," *Academy of Management Executive* 9, 4 (1995): 49–61; R. L. Priem and J. E. Butler, "Is the Resource-Based 'View' a Useful Perspective for Strategic Management Research?" *Academy of Management Review* 26 (2001): 22–40.

5. "Company Overview," Starwood web site, August 26, 2007, www.starwoodhotels.com/corporate/company_info.html.

6. We gratefully acknowledge the intellectual contributions of Michael Porter with regard to the creation and use of value chains. His work deals primarily with a manufacturing setting. In this chapter, we applied many of the same principles to a service environment. For more information, see M. E. Porter, *Competitive Advantage: Creating and Sustaining Superior Performance* (New York: The Free Press, 1985), chap. 2.

7. "New World Wine," *Wikipedia* August 18, 2007, http://en.wikipedia.org/wiki/New_World_wine.

8. K. Maxwell, "Market Research Key to SA Wine Industry's Collective Success - Eminent Academic," WineCoZa, featured June 29, 2006 on *Avenue Vine Wine* News and Information Magazine, June 29, 2006, www.avenuevine.com/archives/001497.html. The academic cited was Dr. Johan Bruwer, a South African academic and convenor of the University of Adelaide's Wine Business Group in Australia.

9. C. Mercer, "'Critters' Prove the Winning Wine Label Formula," Beverage Daily.com, March 22, 2006 www.beveragedaily.com/news/ng.asp?id=66582-wine-label-wine-market-report; "No Critter Wine Review," *NoMerlot.com*, August 18, 2007, www.nomerlot.com/no-critters.html.

10. M. E. Porter, *Competitive Advantage: Creating and Sustaining Superior Performance* (New York: The Free Press, 1985).

11. Y. Yilmaz and U. Bititci, "Performance Measurement in Tourism: A Value Chain Model," *International Journal of Contemporary Hospitality Management* 18, 4 (2006): 341–349.

12. M. A. Hitt, R. D. Ireland, and R. E. Hoskisson, *Strategic Management: Competitiveness and Globalization* (Minneapolis, MN: West Publishing, 1995), 73.

13. L. Canina, C. Enz, and K. Walsh, "Intellectual Capital: A Key Driver of Hotel Performance" *Center for Hospitality Research Report* 6, 10 (2006).

14. L. Dube, C. Enz, L. Reneghan, and J. Siguaw, *American Lodging Experience: The Keys to Best Practices in the U.S. Lodging Industry*, (1999), 95.

15. L. Canina and S. Carvell, "Short-term Liquidity Measures for Restaurant Firms: Static Measures Don't Tell the Full Story," *Center for Hospitality Research Report* 7, 11 (2007).

16. "Land Grab Real Estate Investment Trusts," July 7, 2003, http:hedge-hog.com/sub/reits.html.

17. B. Fearis, "Just Ask the Designer," *Travel Weekly*, UK (July 20, 2007): 30.

18. "Redefining Boutique," *Hospitality Design* 29, 5 (July 2007): 26–27.

19. K. Novack, "Philippe Starck: Style & Design," *Time* 170 (August 2007): 37.

20. L. Anhar, "The Definition of Boutique Hotels," HVS International, *Hospitality Net*, December 2001, www.hospitalitynet.org/news/4010409.search?query=lucienne+anhar+boutique+hotel (accessed August 29, 2007).

21. P. Sheehan, "Seeing Green," *Lodging Hospitality* (July 1, 2007): 22–24.

22. M. Edward, "The Blue Moon Butterfly Effect," *Hotel Interactive*, August 30, 2007, www.hotelinteractive.com/index.asp?lstr=cae4@cornell.edu&page_id=5000&article_id=8753.

23. Ibid.

24. "Fairmont Hotels & Resorts Expands Wind Power Program," *Hotel Interactive*, July 30, 2007, www.hotelinteractive.com/index.asp?page_id=5000&article_id=8228.

25. J. Hogan, "What Are Your Priorities as a Hotel Owner and/or Manager?" *Hotel Online*, March 2002, www.hotel-online.com/Neo/News/PR2002_1st/Mar02_CommonSense.html.

26. S. Finkelstein and D. C. Hambrick, *Strategic Leadership: Top Executives and Their Effects on Organizations* (Minneapolis, MN: West Publishing, 1996), chap. 2.

27. D. Fisher, "Gone Flat," *Forbes Global*, October 15, 2001, www.forbes.com/global.

28. P. Nutt, "Selecting Tactics to Implement Strategic Plans," *Strategic Management Journal* 10 (1989):145–161.

29. N. Byrnes, "The Straight Shooter," *Business Week* (September 23, 2002), 82; "Aramark Completes Merger," Press Release, ARAMARK web site, January 26, 2007, www.aramark.com/PressReleaseDetailTemplate.aspx?PostingID=958&ChannelID=399.

30. C. Handy, *The Age of Unreason* (Boston, MA: Harvard Business School Press, 1989).

31. R. D. Ireland and M. A. Hitt, "Achieving and Maintaining Strategic Competitiveness in the 21st Century: The Role of Strategic Leadership," *Academy of Management Executive* 13, 1 (February 1999): 43–57.

32. Accor Annual Report 2006, www.accor.com/gb/upload/pdf/Ra_2006_gb.pdf.

33. P. M. Senge, "The Leader's New Work: Building Learning Organizations," *Sloan Management Review* 32, 1 (Fall 1990): 7–24.

34. "The Accor Model," July 8, 2003, www.accor.com/gb/finance/strategie.

35. F. Westley and H. Mintzberg, "Visionary Leadership and Strategic Management," *Strategic Management Journal* 10 (1989): 17–18.

36. "Shock Resignation at InterContinental Hotel Group," AsiaTraveltips.com, August 30, 2007, www.asiatraveltips.com/news07/156-PatrickImbardelli.shtml.

37. Dube, Enz, Reneghan, and Siguaw, *American Lodging Excellence*, 86.

38. S. Sjostrand, J. Sandberg, and M. Thyrstrup, *Invisible Management: The Social Construction of Leadership* (London: Thomson Learning, 2001).

39. Sjostrand, Sandberg, and Thyrstrup, *Invisible Management*.

40. D. Hogan "Cultural Tourism . . . on the Rise: Its Popularity Grows as Hoteliers Pursue Those Shrinking Tourist Dollars," *The Daily Courier* (Prescott, June 15, 2003), 1D.

41. "Wendy's Names Interim Chief Executive," *BRANDWEEK*, April 18, 2006, www.brandweek.com/bw/news/restaurants/article_display.jsp?vnu_content_id=1002345876.

42. Ireland and Hitt, "Achieving and Maintaining."

43. Sjostrand, Sandberg, and Thyrstrup, *Invisible Management*, 8.

44. Senge, "Leader's New Work"; C. C. Manz and H. P. Sims, "SuperLeadership," *Organization Dynamics* 17, 4 (1991): 8–36.

45. Senge, "Leader's New Work."

46. Senge, "Leader's New Work"; Manz and Sims, "SuperLeadership."

47. Clarkson Centre for Business Ethics, *Principles of Stakeholder Management* (Toronto: Rotman School of Management, 1999), 3.

48. Senge, "Leader's New Work," 13.

49. L. J. Bourgeois and D. R. Brodwin, "Strategic Implementation: Five Approaches to an Elusive Phenomenon," *Strategic Management Journal* 5 (1984): 241–264.

50. S. Scott, "Like the Big Boys Do It," *QSR Magazine.com*, September 2005, www.qsrmagazine.com/articles/interview/80/nigel_travis-1.phtml.

51. J. G. Michel and D. C. Hambrick, "Diversification Posture and Top Management Team Characteristics," *Academy of Management Journal* 35 (1992): 9–37; S. F. Slater, "The Influence of Style on Business Unit Performance," *Journal of Management* 15 (1989): 441–455; A. S. Thomas, R. J. Litschert, and K. Ramaswamy, "The Performance Impact of Strategy-Manager Coalignment: An Empirical Examination," *Strategic Management Journal* 12 (1991): 509–522.

52. V. Govindarajan, "Implementing Competitive Strategies at the Business Unit Level: Implications of Matching Managers to Strategies," *Strategic Management Journal* 10 (1989): 251–269.

53. K. A. Bantel and S. E. Jackson, "Top Management and Innovations in Banking: Does the Composition of the Top Team Make a Difference?" *Strategic Management Journal* 10 (1989): 107–124; C. M. Grimm and K. G. Smith, "Management and Organizational Change: A Note on the Railroad Industry," *Strategic Management Journal* 12 (1991): 557–562; M. F. Wiersema and K. A. Bantel, "Top Management Team Demography and Corporate Strategic Change," *Academy of Management Journal* 35 (1992): 91–121.

54. A. K. Gupta and V. Govindarajan, "Business Unit Strategy, Managerial Characteristics, and Business Unit Effectiveness at Strategy Implementation," *Academy of Management Journal* 27 (1984): 25–41.

55. B. Brenner, "Tough Times, Tough Bosses: Corporate America Calls in a New, Cold-eyed Breed of CEO," *Business Week* (November 25, 1991), 174–180.

56. S. Weisbach, "Outside Directors and CEO Turnover," *Journal of Financial Economics* 20 (1988): 431–460.

57. J. A. Pearce II and S. J. Teel, "Braniff International Corporation (A) and (B)," in *Strategic Management: Strategy Formulation and Implementation*, 2nd ed. (Homewood, IL: Richard D. Irwin, 1985), 820–838.

58. J. S. Harrison and J. O. Fiet, "New CEOs Pursue Their Own Interests by Sacrificing Stakeholder Value," *Journal of Business Ethics* 19 (1999): 301–308.

59. J. A. Byrne, "How High Can CEO Pay Go?" *Fortune* (April 22, 1996), 100–122.

60. A. Frewin, "Executive Salaries Soar in Hospitality," *Caterer & Hotelkeeper* 196, 4436 (May 25, 2006): 11.

61. J. A. Byrne, "What, Me Overpaid? CEOs Fight Back," *Business Week* (May 4, 1992), 142–148.

62. Byrne, "Overpaid?" 147.

63. A. D. Henderson and J. W. Fredrickson, "Information Processing Demands as a Determinant of CEO Compensation," *Academy of Management Journal* 39 (1996): 575–606.

64. E. J. Zajac, "CEO Selection, Succession, Compensation, and Firm Performance: A Theoretical Integration and Empirical Analysis," *Strategic Management Journal* 11 (1990): 217–230.

65. A. Parlik, "Pay Check," *Restaurants and Institutions* (July 1, 2002), 55–56, 58, 60.

66. Ibid, 56.

67. I. F. Kesner and R. B. Johnson, "Crisis in the Boardroom: Fact and Fiction," *Academy of Management Executive* (February 1990): 23–35.

68. M. Magnet, "Directors, Wake Up!" *Fortune* (June 15, 1992), 86–92.

69. R. Langlois, "Fairmont Hotels: Business Strategy Starts with People," *Canadian HR Reporter* (November 5, 2001), 19–25.

70. M. J. Koch and R. G. McGrath, "Improving Labor Productivity: Human Resource Management Policies Do Matter," *Strategic Management Journal* 17 (1996): 335–354.

71. M. A. Huselid, "The Impact of Human Resource Management Practices on Turnover, Productivity, and Corporate Financial Performance," *Academy of Management Journal* 38 (1995): 635–672.

72. C. A. Enz, "What Keeps You Up at Night? Key Issues of Concern for Lodging Managers," *Cornell Hotel and Restaurant Administration Quarterly* 42, 2 (April 2001): 38–45.

73. W. M. Bulkeley, "The Latest Thing at Many Companies Is Speed, Speed, Speed," *The Wall Street Journal* (December 23, 1994); J. T. Vesey, "The New Competitors: They Think in Terms of 'Speed-to-Market,'" *Academy of Management Executive* (May 1991): 23–33.

74. S. Tully, "The Modular Corporation," *Fortune* (February 8, 1993), 106.

75. J. B. Tracey, "The Strategic and Operational Roles of Human Resources: An Emerging Model," *Cornell Hotel and Restaurant Administration Quarterly* 43, 4 (August 2002): 17–26.

76. B. Talbott, "The Power of Personal Service: Why it Matters What Makes it Possible How it Creates Competitive Advantage," *CHR Reports* (The Center for Hospitality Research Cornell University, July 2006), 7.

77. J. B. Quinn, *Intelligent Enterprise: A Knowledge and Service Based Paradigm for Industry* (New York: The Free Press, 1992).

78. Ibid, 10–11.

79. Based on information from D. Miller, *The Icarus Paradox* (New York: Harper Business, 1990).

80. Based on information from Miller, *Icarus Paradox*.

81. G. G. Dess and G. T. Lumkin, "Emerging Issues in Strategy Process Research," in *The Blackwell Handbook of Strategic Management*, eds. M. A. Hitt, R. E. Freeman, and J. S. Harrison (Oxford: Blackwell Publishers, 2001), 3–34.

82. D. J. Teece, *Managing Intellectual Capital* (New York: Oxford University Press, 2000), 3; see also R. M. Grant, "Toward a Knowledge-based View of the Firm," *Strategic Management Journal* 17 (Special Issue) (1996): 109–122.

83. Teece, *Intellectual Capital*.

84. C. E. Helfat and R. S. Raubitschek, "Product Sequencing: Co-Evolution of Knowledge, Capabilities, and Products," *Strategic Management Journal* 21 (2000): 961–979.

85. K. Kuhn, "US Restaurateur Takes Copycat Chef to Court," *Caterer & Hotelkeeper* 197, 4483 (July 5, 2007): 33; P. Wells, "Chef Sues Over Intellectual Property (the Menu)," *The New York Times*, June 27, 2007, www.nytimes.com/2007/06/27/nyregion/27pearl.html?ex=1188964800&en=c3cc76f4021b676c&ei=5070.

86. Helfat and Raubitschek, "Product Sequencing."

87. Teece, *Intellectual Capital*, 13.

88. D. M. DeCarolis and D. L. Deeds, "The Impact of Stocks and Flows of Organizational Knowledge on Firm Performance," *Strategic Management Journal* 20 (1999): 953–968.

89. Dube, Enz, Reneghan, and Siguaw, *American Lodging Excellence*, 181–182.

90. J. B. Goes and S. H. Park, "Interorganizational Links and Innovation: The Case of Hospital Services," *Academy of Management Journal* 40 (1997): 673–696.

91. W. W. Powell, K. W. Koput, and L. Smith-Doerr, "Interorganizational Collaboration and the Locus of Innovation: Networks of Learning in Biotechnology," *Administrative Science Quarterly* 41 (1996): 116–145.

92. G. Lorenzoni and A. Liparini, "The Leveraging of Interfirm Relationships as a Distinctive Organizational Capability: A Longitudinal Study," *Strategic Management Journal* 20 (1999): 317–338.

93. B. L. Simonin, "The Importance of Collaborative Know-How: An Empirical Test of the Learning Organization," *Academy of Management Journal* 40 (1997): 1150–1174.

94. B. McEvily and A. Zaheer, "Bridging Ties: A Source of Firm Heterogeneity in Competitive Capabilities," *Strategic Management Journal* 20 (1999): 1133–1156.

95. P. Maskell and A. Malmberg, "Localised Learning and Industrial Competitiveness," *Cambridge Journal of Economics* 23 (1999): 167–185.

96. "What Are Patents, Trademarks, Servicemarks, and Copyrights?" The United States Patent and Trademark Office web site, September 4, 2007, www.uspto.gov/web/offices/pac/doc/general/whatis.htm.

97. "History," Carvel Ice Cream web site, September 3, 2007, www.carvel.com/about_us/history.htm.

98. "We'll Have the Fried Chicken,©" Chicagoist, October 26, 2006, http://chicagoist.com/2006/10/26/well_have_the_fried_chicken. php; M. Neil, "Mixing IP with Mmmmmm," *ABA Journal* 93, 5 (May 2007): 15–16.

99. S. Ponsonby-McCabe, "Understanding Brands As Experiential Spaces: Axiological Implications For Marketing Strategists," *Journal of Strategic Marketing* 12 (June 2006): 175–189.

100. J. O'Neill, "Brand and Value," *Lodging Hospitality* (April 1, 2007), 19.

101. G. Khermouch, "The Best Global Brands," *Business Week* (August 6, 2001), 50–57.

102. Walt Disney Company, *Annual Report* (1995), 6–7.

103. "The 100 Top Brands," *Business Week* 4045 (August 6, 2007): 59–64.

104. W. Jiang, C. S. Dev and V. R. Rao, "Brand Extension and Customer Loyalty: Evidence from the Lodging Industry," *Cornell Hotel and Restaurant Administration Quarterly* 42, 4 (August 2002): 5–16.

105. "One-On-One: Hyatt Launches Three New Hotel Brands, Nears E-Folio," *Business Travel News* 24, 10 (May 21, 2007): 3.

106. C. J. Fombrun, "Corporate Reputations As Economic Assets," in *Blackwell Handbook*, eds. Hitt, Freeman, and Harrison, 289–312.

107. J. A. Petrick et al., "Global Leadership Skills and Reputational Capital: Intangible Resources for Sustainable Competitive Advantage," *Academy of Management Executive* (February 1999): 58–69.

108. R. P. Beatty and J. R. Ritter, "Investment Banking, Reputation, and Underpricing of Initial Public Offerings," *Journal of Financial Economics* 15 (1986): 213–232; C. Fombrun and M. Shanley, "What's in a Name? Reputation Building and Corporate Strategy," *Academy of Management Journal* 33 (1990): 233–258; B. Klein and K. Leffler, "The Role of Market Forces in Assuring Contractual Performance," *Journal of Political Economy* 89 (1981): 615–641; P. Milgrom and J. Roberts, "Price and Advertising Signals of Product Quality," *Journal of Political Economy* 94 (1986): 796–821; P. Milgrom and J. Roberts, "Relying on the Information of Interested Parties," *Rand Journal of Economics* 17 (1986): 18–32; G. J. Stigler, "Information in the Labor Market," *Journal of Political Economy* 70 (1962): 49–73.

109. S. Caminiti, "The Payoff from a Good Reputation," *Fortune* (February 10, 1992), 74–77.

110. J. Reese, "America's Most Admired Corporations: What lies behind a company's good name?" *Fortune*, (February 8, 1993): 46.

CHAPTER 5

1. J. Louderback, "The Wynn Wraps Guests in Technology," *PC Magazine*, May 2005, http://findarticles.com/p/articles/mi_zdpcm/is_200505/ai_n13639184 (accessed September 23, 2007); "Investor Relations," *Wynn Resorts web site*, http://phx.corporate-ir.net/phoenix.zhtml?c=132059&p=irol-IRHome (accessed September 22, 2007); *Wynn Las Vegas*, *Wikipedia*, http://en.wikipedia.org/wiki/Wynn_Las_Vegas (accessed September 21, 2007); *Wynn Las Vegas web site*, www.wynnlasvegas.com

(accessed September 23, 2007); "Wynning Pair," *Meeting News* 31 (Supplement) (June 11, 2007): 10; C. Palmeri, "Once and Future Spamalot," *Business Week* 4031 (April 23, 2007): 10.

2. *Wynn Las Vegas web site*, www.wynnlasvegas.com (accessed September 23, 2007).

3. Ibid.

4. H. J. Bryce, *Financial and Strategic Management for Nonprofit Organizations* (Englewood Cliffs, NJ: Prentice Hall, 1987).

5. This discussion of generic strategies draws heavily from concepts found in M. E. Porter, *Competitive Strategy: Techniques for Analyzing Industries and Competitors* (New York: The Free Press, 1980), chap. 2.

6. *Casa Cupula web site*, www.casacupula.com/aboutus2.html (accessed September 24, 2007); *World's Foremost Gay and Lesbian Hotels web site*, www.worldsforemost.com/aboutus.html (accessed September 24, 2007).

7. Porter, *Competitive Strategy*.

8. This discussion of factors leading to cost savings is based, in part, on Porter, *Competitive Strategy*; M. E. Porter, *Competitive Advantage: Creating and Sustaining Superior Performance* (New York: The Free Press, 1985); and R. W. Schmenner, "Before You Build a Big Factory," *Harvard Business Review* 54 (July/August 1976): 100–104.

9. R. Evans, "Le Motel 6, C'est Moi," *Barron's* (April 30, 2001), 20–22; *Accor Hospitality web site*, www.accor-na.com/franchising_info/index.asp; *Motel 6 web site*, www.motel6.com/about; *Etap Hotels web site*, www.etaphotel.com/gb/discovering-etap-hotel/index.shtml (accessed September 23, 2007).

10. "Letter to Shareholders," *JetBlue Airways 2006 Annual Report*, www.shareholder.com/visitors/DynamicDoc/document.cfm?CompanyID=JBLU&DocumentID=1724&PIN=&Page=1&Zoom=1x (accessed September 24, 2007).

11. C. Enz, L. Canina, and M. Lomanno, "Why Discounting Doesn't Work: The Dynamics of Rising Occupancy and Falling Revenue Among Competitors," *The Center for Hospitality Research Report* 4, 7 (2004); C. Canina and C. Enz, "Why Discounting Still Doesn't Work: A Hotel Pricing Update," *The Center for Hospitality Research Report* 6, 2 (2006). For a detailed discussion of pricing strategies and hotel demand, consult the Cornell University Center for Hospitality Research web site at www.hotelschool.cornell.edu/research/chr.

12. L. Canina and C. Enz, "Revenue Management in U.S. Hotels: 2001–2005," *The Center for Hospitality Research Report* 6, 8 (2006).

13. "Reservation System," *Marriott Lodging Development web site*, www.marriott.com/development/europe-middle-east-africa-power-marriott/reservations-systems.mi (accessed October 4, 2007).

14. "Company Overview," *Starwood Hotels and Resorts web site* http://phx.corporate-ir.net/phoenix.zhtml?c=78669&p=irol-hot_about_company (accessed September 23, 2007).

15. As defined by Schmenner, "Before You Build."

16. "About Us," *Le Colonial web site*, www.lecolonialchicago.com (accessed October 4, 2007); L. Bertagnoli, "The Ten-Minute Manager's Guide."

17. L. Bertagnoli, "The Ten-Minute Manager's Guide To . . . Outsourcing Responsibilities," *Restaurants & Institutions* (April 2007), 26.

18. S. Tadelis, "The Innovative Organization: Creating Value Through Outsourcing," *California Management Review* 50, 1 (Fall 2007): 261–277; M. E. Porter, "What Is Strategy?" *Harvard Business Review* 74, 6 (November/December 1996): 61.

19. The same principles apply to "experience effects." In this book, the two terms will be used synonymously.

20. W. J. Abernathy and K. Wayne, "Limits of the Learning Curve," *Harvard Business Review* 52, 5 (September/October 1974): 109–119; Boston Consulting Group, *Perspectives on Experience* (Boston: Boston Consulting Group, 1972); W. B. Hirschman, "Profit from the Learning Curve," *Harvard Business Review* 43, 3 (January/February 1964): 125–139.

21. Porter, "What Is Strategy?" 62.

22. A. Paszton, M. Branningan, and S. McCartney, "ValuJet's Penny-pinching Comes under Scrutiny," *The Wall Street Journal* (May 14, 1996), A2, A4.

23. *The Thomson Future Holiday Forum Report*, www.hospitalitynet.org/file/152001280.pdf (accessed October 4, 2007).

24. Pricewaterhouse Coopers Hospitality Directions European Edition, Issue 14, September 2006.

25. J. Wilson, "Lifestyle Concept Defined by Customers' Needs, Wants," *Hotel & Motel Management*, May 1, 2006, www.hotelmotel.com/hotelmotel/article.

26. R. Grant, *Contemporary Strategy Analysis*, 6th ed. (Boston, MA: Blackwell Publishing, 2008).

27. J. Pine and J. Gilmore, *The Experience Economy: Work is Theatre and Every Business a Stage* (Boston, MA: Harvard Business School Press, 1999).

28. "Company Overview," *Starwood Hotels and Resorts web site*, http://phx.corporate-ir.net/phoenix.zhtml?c=78669&p=irol-hot_about_company (accessed September 23, 2007).

29. Ibid.

30. M. E. Porter, "What Is Strategy?" 61.

31. This statement is borrowed and adapted from the more general work of Jonas Ridderstrale and Kjell Nordstro, m authors of *Funky Business: Talent Makes Capital Dance*. The view expressed is that of the author of this textbook.

32. "Starbucks Chairman Warns of 'the Commoditization of the Starbucks Experience'," *Starbucks Gossip web site*, http://starbucksgossip.typepad.com/_/2007/02/starbucks_chair_2.html (accessed October 4, 2007).

33. P. Nelson, "Information and Consumer Behavior," *Journal of Political Economy*, 78, 2 (1970): 311–329.

34. E. Mansfield, "How Rapidly Does New Industrial Technology Leak Out?" *Journal of Industrial Economics* (December 1985): 217.

35. P. Ghemawat, "Sustainable Advantage," *Harvard Business Review* 64, 5 (September/October 1986): 53.

36. C. W. L. Hill, "Differentiation versus Low Cost or Differentiation and Low Cost: A Contingency Framework," *Academy of Management Review* 13 (1988): 403; See also A. I. Murray, "A Contingency View of Porter's 'Generic Strategies'," *Academy of Management Review* 13 (1988): 390–400.

37. M. K. Starr, ed., *Global Competitiveness: Getting the U.S. Back on Track* (New York: W. W. Norton, 1988), 307.

38. W. E. Demming, *Out of the Crisis* (Cambridge, MA: MIT Press, 1982); L. W. Phillips, D. Chang, and R. D. Buzzell, "Product Quality, Cost Position, and Business Performance," *Journal of Marketing* 47 (1983): 26–43; M. Walton, *Deming Management at Work* (New York: Putnam, 1990).

39. H. Araslli, "Diagnosing Whether Northern Cyprus Hotels Are Ready for TQM: An Empirical Analysis," *Total Quality Management* 13, 3 (2002): 347–364.

40. C. H. Deutsch, "Six Sigma Enlightenment," *The New York Times* (December 7, 1998); reprinted in E. H. Bernstein, *Strategic Management* (Guilford, CT: McGraw-Hill/Dushkin, 2001), 151.

41. "We Encourage Innovation, Accept Accountability and Embrace Change," Annual Report 2001, Starwood Hotels and Resorts Worldwide, Inc., 3.

42. S. Ante, "Six Sigma Kick-Starts Starwood," *Business Week Online* (August 31, 2007), 21, www.BusinessWeekOnline.

43. "Who We Are," 2001 Annual Report, Four Seasons Hotels, Inc., 1.

44. A. Martinez, "The City Life: Hotels with an Attitude," *The New York Times* (August 13, 2001), A16.

45. M. Beirne, "Let It All Hang Out: When Joe Boxer and W Hotels Team Up, It's 'Let's Hear it for the Boys!'" *Brandweek* (December 9, 2002), 32; D. Goetzl, "Starwood's W Hotel Ads Display Interior Motives," *Advertising Age* (September 18, 2000), 13.

46. "Welcome," *Burj Al Arab web site*, www.burj-al-arab.com; "Portfolio," *Jumerirah web site*, www.jumeirah.com/portfolio (accessed October 6, 2007).

47. G. G. Dess and J. C. Picken, "Creating Competitive (Dis)advantage: Learning from Food Lion's Freefall," *Academy of Management Executive* 13, 3 (1999): 100.

48. "The Blackstone Group," Travel Port web site, www.travelport.com/en/about/our_story/blackstone_group.cfm; "Cendant Corporation Completes Acquisition of Orbitz," *Orbitz.Com web site*, http://pressroom.orbitz.com/ReleaseDetail.cfm?ReleaseID=148156; "Commentary: Orbitz' IPO Doesn't Deserve to Fly," *Business Week Online web site*, September 9, 2003, www.businessweek.com/magazine/content/03_39/b3851118_mz020.htm (accessed October 7, 2007).

49. J. Schumpeter, *The Theory of Economic Development* (Cambridge, MA: Harvard University Press, 1934).

50. K. G. Smith, W. J. Ferrier, and H. Ndofor, "Competitive Dynamics Research: Critique and Future Directions," in *The Blackwell Handbook of Strategic Management*, eds. M. A. Hitt, R. E. Freeman, and J. S. Harrison (Oxford: Blackwell Publishers, 2001), 315–361.

51. Predicasts, *Predicasts' Funk and Scott Index, United States Annual Edition* (Cleveland, OH: Predicasts, 1993).

52. All of these trends are well documented in C. M. Grimm and K. G. Smith, *Strategy as Action: Industry Rivalry and Coordination* (Cincinnati, OH: South-Western College Publishing, 1997).

53. I. Peterson, "A New Casino Is Coming," *The New York Times* (April 27, 2003), 41, 46; www.atlanticcityhotelsdirect.com/casinos/borgata_casino_spa.html (accessed July 10, 2003).

54. G. Young, K. G. Smith, and C. Grimm, "Austrian and Industrial Organization Perspectives on Firm-Level Competitive Activity and Performance," *Organization Science* 73 (1996): 243–254.

55. K. G. Smith, C. Grimm, and M. Gannon, *Dynamics of Competitive Strategy* (London: Sage Publications, 1992).

56. Grimm and Smith, *Strategy as Action*, 99.

57. W. Ferrier, K. Smith, and C. Grimm, "The Role of Competition in Market Share Erosion and Dethronement: A Study of Industry Leaders and Challengers," *Academy of Management Journal* 43 (1999): 372–388.

58. H. Lee et al., "Timing, Order, and Durability of New Product Advantages with Imitation," *Strategic Management Journal* 21 (2000): 23–30.

59. R. Abramson, "Pegasus Gets a Lift From Online Hotel-Reservation Deal," *The Wall Street Journal* (February 12, 2002): B4; J. N. Ader and T. McCoy, "Web Storm Rising," *Lodging Industry* (August 2002): 1.

60. P. Ghemawat, *Strategy and the Business Landscape* (Upper Saddle River, NJ: Prentice Hall, 2001).

61. C. Baker, "Vertical Shift," *Airline Business*, October 2002, 64–65.

62. H. Lee, K. G. Smith, and C. M. Grimm, "The Effect of New Product Radicality and Scope on the Extent and Speed of Innovation Diffusion." *Journal of Management* 29, 5, (October 2003): 753–768.

63. J. Gimeno and C. Woo, "Multimarket Contact, Economies of Scope, and Firm Performance," *Academy of Management Journal* 42 (1999): 323–341.

64. Smith, Ferrier, and Ndofor, "Competitive Dynamics."

65. "Electronic Commerce: Legal Issues," *Department of Justice web site*, www.usdoj.gov/criminal/cybercrime/kvd0698.htm#Q5 (accessed October 7, 2007).

66. "Playing a strong hand," The Economist.com, http://www.economist.com/world/britain/displaystory.cfm?story_id=9867876 (accessed October 7, 2007); "A Brief History of Online Gaming," http://kyroslaw.com/articles/online_gambling_law.html; "Out of luck," *Economist* 380, 8487 (July 22, 2006): 61; "Electronic Commerce: Legal Issues," *Department of Justice web site*, www.usdoj.gov/criminal/cybercrime/kvd0698.htm#Q5 (accessed October 7, 2007).

67. Grimm and Smith, *Strategy as Action*.

68. R. A. Nozar, "The House That Steve Built," *Lodging Magazine* (October 2002), 44.

69. K. R. Harrigan, "Strategic Flexibility in the Old and New Economies," in *Blackwell Handbook*, eds. Hitt, Freeman, and Harrison, 98–123.

70. Smith, Ferrier, and Ndofor, "Competitive Dynamics."

71. K. G. Smith et al., "Predictors of Response Time to Competitive Strategic Actions: Preliminary Theory and Evidence," *Journal of Business Research* 183 (1989): 245–259.

72. S. Holmes, C. Dawson, and C. Matlack, "Rumble over Tokyo," *Business Week* (April 2, 2001), 80–81.

73. Smith, Ferrier, and Ndofor, "Competitive Dynamics."

74. Porter, *Competitive Strategy*.

75. Smith, Ferrier, and Ndofor, "Competitive Dynamics."

CHAPTER 6

1. "Group Strategy," *Whitbread Website*, www.whitbread.co.uk/investors/group_strategy.cfm (accessed October 8, 2007); "Premier Travel Inn to Rebrand," *Marketing* (June 27, 2007): 10; N. Paton, "Whitbread Sells David Lloyd to Invest More in Coffee and Hotels," *Caterer & Hotelkeeper* 197, 4479 (June 7, 2007): 8.

2. "Carlson, London Firm Buy U.K.s 45 TGI Friday's," *Nation's Restaurant News* 41, 6 (February 5, 2007): 18.

3. A. D. Chandler Jr., *Strategy and Structure: Chapters in the History of the Industrial Enterprise* (Cambridge, MA: MIT Press, 1962).

4. Domino's Pizza web site, http://phx.corporate-ir.net/phoenix.zhtml?c=135383&p=irol-homeProfile (accessed October 9, 2007).

5. "Domino's Pizza, Inc.," *Hoovers*, http://premium.hoovers.com (accessed October 9, 2007).

6. R. P. Rumelt, *Strategy, Structure, and Economic Performance* (Boston: Harvard Business School, 1974); R. P. Rumelt, "Diversification Strategy and Profitability," *Strategic Management Journal* 3 (1982): 359–369.

7. D. Engber, "Why Do Airlines Go Bankrupt? Delta Can't Keep Up With JetBlue," *Slate Website*, www.slate.com/id/2126383 (accessed September 15, 2005).

8. A. Garber, "Burger Giants Weigh In with More Healthful Menu Ideas," *Nation's Restaurant News* (May 26, 2003): 1, 6; A. Garber, "It's Not Easy Not Being Green," *Nation's Restaurant News* (August 2003): 66; "Salads Plus," *McDonald's web site*, www.mcdonalds.co.uk/pages/eatsmart/saladsplus.html (accessed October 9, 2007).

9. D. Nelms, "Strange Bedfellow," *Air Transport World* (September 1993): 60–65; G. Lafferty and A. van Fossen, "Integrating the Tourism Industry: Problems and Strategies," *Tourism Management* 22 (2001): 11–19; D. Nelms, "Strange Bedfellow."

10. C. Walkup, "McD Pins Global Growth on Upgraded Units, Experience," *Nation's Restaurant News* 41, 31 (August 6, 2007): 1, 6.

11. H. I. Ansoff, *Corporate Strategy: An Analytical Approach to Business Policy for Growth and Expansion* (New York: McGraw-Hill, 1965), 129–130.

12. Ibid, 6.

13. *Tui web site*, www.tui-group.com/en (accessed October 9, 2007).

14. Cendant Corporation, www.cendant.com (accessed August 16, 2003).

15. "TUI AG," *Hoovers*, http://premium.hoovers.com (accessed October 9, 2007); *Tui web site*, www.tui-group.com/en (accessed October 9, 2007); Rumelt, *Strategy, Structure*; Rumelt, "Diversification Strategy."

16. Cendant web site, www.cendant.com (accessed October 9, 2007).

17. K. R. Harrigan, "Formulating Vertical Integration Strategies," *Academy of Management Review* 9 (1984): 639.

18. R. A. D'Aveni and D. J. Ravenscraft, "Economies of Integration versus Bureaucracy Costs: Does Vertical Integration Improve Performance?" *Academy of Management Journal* 37 (1994): 1167–1206.

19. S. Balakrishnan and B. Wernerfelt, "Technical Change, Competition, and Vertical Integration," *Strategic Management Journal* 7 (1986): 347–359.

20. O. E. Williamson, *Markets and Hierarchies: Analysis and Antitrust Implications* (New York: The Free Press, 1975); O. E. Williamson, *The Economic Institutions of Capitalism* (New York: The Free Press, 1985).

21. "Thomas Cook Group, Plc.," *Hoovers*, http://premium.hoovers.com (accessed October 9, 2007).

22. Williamson, *Markets and Hierarchies*, 8.

23. Ibid. 8.

24. B. Klein, R. Crawford, and A. A. Alchian, "Vertical Integration, Appropriable Rents, and the Competitive Contracting Process," *Journal of Law and Economics* 21 (1978): 297–326; Williamson, *Markets and Hierarchies*, 9–10.

25. R. E. Hoskisson, J. S. Harrison, and D. A. Dubofsky, "Capital Market Implementation of M-Form Implementation and Diversification Strategy," *Strategic Management Journal* 12 (1991): 271–279.

26. K. R. Harrigan, "Exit Barriers and Vertical Integration," *Academy of Management Journal* (September 1985): 686–697.

27. A. Spector, "Starwood Cooks Up Joint Venture, Buys 12% Stake in Grill Concepts," *Nation's Restaurant News* (June 4, 2001): 4.

28. D. D. Bergh, "Diversification Strategy Research at a Crossroads: Established, Emerging, and Anticipated Paths," in *The Blackwell Handbook of Strategic Management*, eds. M. A. Hitt, R. E. Freeman, and J. S. Harrison (Oxford: Blackwell Publishers, 2001), 362–383.

29. Information on the strategic arguments can be found in Ansoff, *Corporate Strategy*, 130–132; C. W. L. Hill and G. S. Hansen, "A Longitudinal Study of the Cause and Consequence of Changes in Diversification in the U.S. Pharmaceutical Industry," *Strategic Management Journal* 12 (1991): 187–199; W. G. Lewellen, "A Pure Financial Rationale for the Conglomerate Merger," *Journal of Finance* 26 (1971): 521–537; F. M. McDougall and D. K. Round, "A Comparison of Diversifying and Nondiversifying Australian Industrial Firms," *Academy of Management Journal* 27 (1984): 384–398; and R. Reed and G. A. Luffman, "Diversification: The Growing Confusion," *Strategic Management Journal* 7 (1986): 29–35. The personal arguments are outlined in W. Baumol, *Business Behavior, Value, and Growth* (New York: Harcourt, 1967); D. C. Mueller, "A Theory of Conglomerate Mergers," *Quarterly Review of Economics* 83 (1969): 644–660; N. Rajagopalan and J. E. Prescott, "Determinants of Top Management Compensation: Explaining the Impact of Economic, Behavioral, and Strategic Constructs and the Moderating Effects of Industry," *Journal of Management* 16 (1990): 515–538.

30. Ansoff, *Corporate Strategy*, 130–131.

31. "Darden Restaurants Announces Tender Offer to Purchase RARE Hospitality for $38.15 Per Share: Further Positions Darden as a Leader in the Restaurant Industry," *Darden web site press releases*, http://investor.dardenrestaurants.com/ir_ReleaseDetail.cfm?ReleaseID=260249 (accessed October 10, 2007); "Darden Restaurants Inc.," *Hoovers*, http://premium.hoovers.com (accessed October 9, 2007).

32. A detailed review of this literature is found in R. E. Hoskisson and M. A. Hitt, "Antecedents and Performance Outcomes of Diversification: A Review and Critique of Theoretical Perspectives," *Journal of Management* 16 (1990): 468. More recent evidence is found in P. S. Davis et al., "Business Unit Relatedness and Performance: A Look at the Pulp and Paper Industry," *Strategic Management Journal* 13 (1992): 349–361; J. S. Harrison, E. H. Hall Jr., and R. Nagundkar, "Resource Allocation As an Outcropping of Strategic Consistency: Performance Implications," *Academy of Management Journal* 36 (1993): 1026–1051; J. Robins and M. Wiersema, "A Resource-Based Approach to the Multi-Business Firm: Empirical Analysis of Portfolio Interrelationships and Corporate Financial Performance," *Strategic Management Journal* 16 (1995): 277–299.

33. M. Lubatkin and S. Chatterjee, "Extending Modern Portfolio Theory into the Domain of Corporate Diversification: Does It Apply?" *Academy of Management Journal* 37 (1994): 109–136.

34. M. E. Porter, *Competitive Advantage: Creating and Sustaining Superior Performance* (New York: The Free Press, 1985), 317–363.

35. D. J. Teece, "Economies of Scope and the Scope of the Enterprise," *Journal of Economic Behavior and Organization* 1 (1980): 223–247.

36. B. Gold, "Changing Perspectives on Size, Scale, and Returns: An Integrative Survey," *Journal of Economic Literature* 19 (1981): 5–33.

37. Ansoff, *Corporate Strategy.*

38. M. Beirne, "Four Seasons Puts Luxury into Leisure," *Brandweek* (April 15, 2002): 4.

39. H. Itami, *Mobilizing Invisible Assets* (Cambridge, MA: Harvard University Press, 1987).

40. P. R. Nayyar, "On the Measurement of Corporate Diversification Strategy: Evidence from Large U.S. Service Firms," *Strategic Management Journal* 13 (1992): 219–235; Reed and Luffman, "Diversification," 29–36.

41. A. Zuber, "Accelerated Multibrand Growth Plan Puts Tricon in Driver's Seat," *Nation's Restaurant News* (February 15, 2002): 64; "Multibranding Great Brands," *Yum! web site,* www.yum.com/about/multibranding.asp (accessed October 10, 2007); "Dunkin's Brands to Divest Togo's," *Franchise Times,* www.franchisetimes.com/content/story.php?article=00141 (accessed October 10, 2007); L. Weber, "Multibranding Offers All-in-one Fast-food Eats," *Fastfoodsource.com, Reuters News Service,* www.qsrweb.com/news_multibranding_20303.htm (2003).

42. Annual Report, YUM! Brands Inc., 2002.

43. A. Zuber, "To Market, to Market: Chains Find Strength in Numbers, Use Co-branding as Growth Vehicle," *Nation's Restaurant News,* 5 February 2001, 35.

44. D. B. Jemison and S. B. Sitkin, "Corporate Acquisitions: A Process Perspective," *Academy of Management Review* 11 (1986): 145–163.

45. M. C. Lauenstein, "Diversification—The Hidden Explanation of Success," *Sloan Management Review* (Fall 1985): 49–55.

46. G. R. Jones and C. W. Hill, "Transaction Cost Analysis of Strategy-Structure Choice," *Strategic Management Journal* 9 (1988): 159–172.

47. "Information about Le Meridian," *Starwood Hotels web site,* www.starwoodhotels.com/promotions/promo_landing.html?category=LM_INFO (accessed October 10, 2007).

48. This section and portions of other sections in this chapter were strongly influenced by M. Goold and K. Luchs, "Why Diversify? Four Decades of Management Thinking," *Academy of Management Executive* (August 1993): 7–25.

49. Rumelt, "Diversification Strategy and Profitability," 361. See also Bergh, "Diversification Strategy Research."

50. A few examples of the many studies that demonstrate low performance associated with unrelated diversification are R. Amit and J. Livnat, "Diversification Strategies, Business Cycles, and Economic Performance," *Strategic Management Journal* 9 (1988): 99–110.; R. A. Bettis and V. Mahajan, "Risk/Return Performance of Diversified Firms," *Management Science* 31 (1985): 785–799; D. Ravenscraft and F. M. Scherer, *Mergers, Selloffs, and Economic Efficiency* (Washington, DC: Brookings Institution, 1987); P. G. Simmonds, "The Combined Diversification Breadth and Mode Dimensions and the Performance of Large Diversified Firms," *Strategic Management Journal* 11 (1990): 399–410; P. Varadarajan and V. Ramanujam, "Diversification and Performance: A Reexamination Using a New Two-Dimensional Conceptualization of Diversity in Firms," *Academy of Management Journal* 30 (1982): 380–393. On the other hand, the following studies are among those that support the superiority of unrelated diversification: R. M. Grant and A. P. Jammine, "Performance Differences between the Wrigley/Rumelt Strategic Categories," *Strategic Management Journal* 9 (1988): 333–346; A. Michel and I. Shaked, "Does Business Diversification Affect Performance?" *Financial Management* (Winter 1984): 18–25.

51. Lauenstein, "Diversification"; M. Lubatkin and R. C. Rogers, "Diversification, Systematic Risk, and Shareholder Return: A Capital Market Extension of Rumelt's 1974 Study," *Academy of Management Journal* 32 (1989): 454–465; M. Lubatkin and H. G. O'Neill Merger Strategies and Capital Market Risk," *Academy of Management Journal* 30 (1987): 665–684; M. Lubatkin, "Value-Creating Mergers: Fact or Folklore," *Academy of Management Executive* (November 1988): 295–302; C. A. Montgomery and H. Singh, "Diversification Strategy and Systematic Risk," *Strategic Management Journal* 5 (1984): 181–191.

52. R. S. Attiyeh, "Where Next for Conglomerates?" *Business Horizons* (December 1969): 39–44.

53. "History," www.omnihotels.com/AboutOmniHotels/CorporateInformation/History.aspx (accessed October 12, 2007); "Company Facts, Background Information for TRT Holdings," www.hotelreports.com (accessed August 20, 2003); "TRT Holdings," *Hoovers*, http://premium.hoovers.com (accessed October12, 2007).

54. "About Us," *Tata Group web site*, www.tata.com/index.htm (accessed October 12, 2007); "Tata Group," *Hoovers*, http://premium.hoovers.com (accessed October12, 2007).

55. "History—About Us," www.compass-group.com (accessed August 20, 2003).

56. Hoskisson and Hitt, "Antecedents and Performance Outcomes," 461–509; Shleifer and Vishny, "Takeovers in the '60s."

57. Hoskisson and Hitt, "Antecedents and Performance Outcomes," 461.

58. "Cendant Corporate Press Releases," *Cendant web site*, www.cendant.com/#releases (accessed October 12, 2007).

59. M. A. Hitt, J. S. Harrison, and R. D. Ireland, *Mergers and Acquisitions: A Guide to Creating Value for Stakeholders* (New York: Oxford University Press, 2001).

60. Lubatkin, "Value-Creating Mergers"; J. Pfeffer, "Merger As a Response to Organizational Interdependence," *Administrative Science Quarterly* 17 (1972): 382–394; J. H. Song, "Diversifying Acquisitions and Financial Relationships: Testing 1974–1976 Behaviour," *Strategic Management Journal* 4 (1983): 97–108; F. Trautwein, "Merger Motives and Merger Prescriptions," *Strategic Management Journal* 11 (1990): 283–295.

61. K. Strauss and M. Scoviak, "HOTELS' 325 ranking reveals biggest chains still growing by leaps and bounds," *Hotels web site*, www.hotelsmag.com/archives/2005 (accessed October 13, 2007); K. Strauss, "HOTELS' 325: Special Report, *Hotels* 41, 7 (July 2007): 36; S. Lockyer, IHOP Corp. Serves Up $2.1B Buyout Offer for Applebee's," *Nation's Restaurant News* 41, 29 (July 23, 2007): 1, 6; R. Kline, "Post–Merger Integration in Hospitality," http://hotel-online.com, Spring 1999.

62. "China Merges Nine Airlines into Three," *Weekly Corporate Growth Report*, http://global.factiva.com (accessed October 21, 2002).

63. "Only the Strong Can Survive the Times: Consolidation Is the Wave of the Future," *Nation's Restaurant News* (June 9, 1997): 31; "Lone Star Steakhouse & Saloon," *Hoovers*, http://premium.hoovers.com (accessed October12, 2007).

64. S. Lockyer and R. Ruggless, "Casual-Dining Crisis Takes a Toll on Brand Portfolios," *Nation's Restaurant News* 41, 33 (August 20, 2007):1, 6.

65. L. L. Fowler and D. R. Schmidt, "Determinants of Tender Offer Post-Acquisition Financial Performance," *Journal of Management* 10 (1989): 339–350.

66. M. McDonald, "Brawl at the Mall," *U.S. News & World Report* (March 17, 2003): 37, 63; Lubatkin, "Value-Creating Mergers."

67. T. B. Pickens, "Professions of a Short-Termer," *Harvard Business Review* (May/June 1986): 75–79.

68. One of the most active proponents of the view that mergers and acquisitions create value for acquiring-firm shareholders is Michael Lubatkin (see Lubatkin, "Value-Creating Mergers"). However, he recently reported strong evidence that contradicts his earlier conclusions in S. Chatterjee et al., "Cultural Differences and Shareholder Value in Related Mergers: Linking Equity and Human Capital," *Strategic Management Journal* 13 (1992): 319–334. Other strong summary evidence that mergers and acquisitions do not create value is found in W. B. Carper, "Corporate Acquisitions and Shareholder Wealth," *Journal of Management* 16 (1990): 807–823; and D. K. Datta, G. E. Pinches, and V. K. Narayanan, "Factors Influencing Wealth Creation from Mergers and Acquisitions: A Meta-Analysis," *Strategic Management Journal* 13 (1992): 67–84.

69. K. M. Davidson, "Do Megamergers Make Sense?" *Journal of Business Strategies* (Winter 1987): 40–48; T. F. Hogarty, "Profits from Merger: The Evidence of Fifty Years," *St. John's Law Review* 44 (Special Edition 1970): 378–391; S. R. Reid, *Mergers, Managers, and the Economy* (New York: McGraw-Hill, 1968).

70. M. A. Hitt et al., "Are Acquisitions a Poison Pill for Innovation?" *Academy of Management Executive* (November 1991): 20–35.

71. S. Thurm, "Cisco Says It Expects to Meet Profit Estimate," *The Wall Street Journal* (October 4, 2001): A12.

72. S. Lockyer, "IHOP Corp. Serves Up $2.1B Buyout Offer for Applebee's," *Nation's Restaurant News* 41, 29 (July 23, 2007): 1, 6.

73. S. Wolchuk, S. Lerner, and M. Scoviak, "325 Hotels," *Hotels* (July 2002): 41-42.

74. M. E. Porter, "From Competitive Advantage to Corporate Strategy," *Harvard Business Review* (May/June 1987): 59.

75. L. Canina, "Acquisitions in the Lodging Industry: Good News for Buyers and Sellers," *Cornell Hotel and Restaurant Administration Quarterly* 42, 6 (December 2001): 47–54.

76. M. Hitt et al., "Attributes of Successful and Unsuccessful Acquisitions of U.S. Firms," *British Journal of Management* 9 (1998): 91–114.

77. Hitt, Harrison, and Ireland, *Mergers and Acquisitions*. See also J. B. Kusewitt Jr., "An Exploratory Study of Strategic Acquisition Factors Relating to Success," *Strategic Management Journal* 6 (1985): 151–169; and L. M. Shelton, "Strategic Business Fits and Corporate Acquisition: Empirical Evidence," *Strategic Management Journal* 9 (1988): 279–287.

78. J. S. Harrison, M. A. Hitt, R. E. Hoskisson, and R. D. Ireland, "Resource Complementarity in Business Combinations: Extending the Logic to Organizational Alliances," *Journal of Management* 27 (2001): 679–690; J. S. Harrison et al., "Synergies and Post-Acquisition Performance: Differences versus Similarities in Resource Allocations," *Journal of Management* 17 (1991): 173–190; M. A. Hitt, R. D. Ireland, and J. S. Harrison, "Mergers and Acquisitions: A Value Creating or Value Destroying Strategy?" in *Blackwell Handbook of Strategic Management*, eds. Hitt, Freeman, and Harrison, 384–408.

79. S. Chatterjee et al., "Cultural Differences and Shareholder Value in Related Mergers: Linking Equity and Human Capital," *Strategic Management Journal* 13 (1992): 319–334; D. K. Datta, "Organizational Fit and Acquisition Performance: Effects of Post-Acquisition Integration," *Strategic Management Journal* 12 (1991): 281–297; Jemison and Sitkin, "Corporate Acquisitions."

80. T. H. Brush, "Predicted Change in Operational Synergy and Post-Acquisition Performance of Acquired Businesses," *Strategic Management Journal* 17 (1996): 1–24.

81. F. T. Paine and D. J. Power, "Merger Strategy: An Examination of Drucker's Five Rules for Successful Acquisition," *Strategic Management Journal* 5 (1984): 99–110.

82. D. Kesmodel and D. Ball, "Miller, Coors to Shake Up U.S. Beer Market," *Wall Street Journal* (October 10, 2007): A1.

83. M. L. Sirower and S. F. O'Byrne, "The Measurement of Post-Acquisition Performance: Toward a Value-Based Benchmarking Methodology," *Applied Corporate Finance* 11 (1998): 107–121.

84. Hitt, Harrison, and Ireland, *Mergers and Acquisitions*.

85. This is a private consulting client, and I am not at liberty to disclose the name.

86. F. Vermeulen and H. Barkema, "Learning through Acquisitions," *Academy of Management Journal* 44 (2001): 457.

87. Hitt, Harrison, and Ireland, *Mergers and Acquisitions*, chap. 7.

88. N. Byrnes, "The Good CEO," *Business Week* (September 23, 2002): 80.

89. S. Lockyer, IHOP Corp. Serves Up $2.1B Buyout Offer for Applebee's," *Nation's Restaurant News* 41, 29 (July 23, 2007): 1, 6.

90. These arguments are outlined in M. A. Hitt, R. E. Hoskisson, and J. S. Harrison, "Strategic Competitiveness in the 1990s: Challenges and Opportunities for U.S. Executives," *Academy of Management Executive* (May 1991): 7–22.

91. C. J. Gersick, "Revolutionary Change Theories: A Multi-Level Exploration of the Punctuated Equilibrium Paradigm," *Academy of Management Review* 16 (1991): 10–37; M. I. Tushman and E. Romanelli, "Organizational Evolution: A Metamorphosis Model of Convergence and Reorientation," in *Research in Organization Behavior*, eds. E. E. Cummings and B. M. Staw (Greenwich, CT: JAI Press, 1985), 171–222.

92. J. Peters, "Cosi Chain Seeks Bread, New CEO, Plans Closings," *Nation's Restaurant News* (April 14, 2003): 4; "Cosi Inc. Reports Second Quarter Results," *Cosi web site*, http://phx.corporate-ir.net/phoenix.zhtml?c=131610&p=irol-newsArticle&ID=1038416&highlight= (accessed October 13, 2007).

93. N. A. Wishart, J. J. Elam, and D. Robey, "Redrawing the Portrait of a Learning Organization: Inside Knight-Ridder, Inc.," *Academy of Management Executive* 10 (February 1996): 7–20; J. P. Walsh, "Managerial and Organizational Cognition," *Organization Science* 6 (1995): 280–321.

94. Gersick, "Revolutionary Change Theories"; Tushman and Romanelli, "Organizational Evolution."

95. Gersick, "Revolutionary Change Theories," 22.

96. Gersick, "Revolutionary Change Theories"; Tushman and Romanelli, "Organizational Evolution."

97. J. P. Walsh, "Operators Turn Underperformers into Gems," *Hotel and Motel Management* (March 2001): 1.

98. B. Adams, "IHG Cuts Costs, Maps Brands' Growth Plans," *Hotel and Motel Management* (June 16, 2003): 1.

99. M. Murray, "Amid Record Profits, Companies Continue to Lay Off Employees," *The Wall Street Journal* (May 4, 1995): A1, A6.

100. W. McKinley, C. M. Sanchez, and A. G. Schick, "Organizational Downsizing: Constraining, Cloning, Learning," *Academy of Management Executive* (August 1995): 32.

101. K. S. Cameron, S. J. Freeman, and Aneil K. Mishra, "Best Practices in White-Collar Downsizing: Managing Contradictions," *Academy of Management Executive* (August 1991): 57–73.

102. Adapted from C. Solomon, "Amoco to Cut 8,500 Workers, or 16% of Force," *The Wall Street Journal* (July 9, 1992): A3.

103. J. Brockner et al., "Survivors' Reactions to Layoffs: We Get By with a Little Help from Our Friends," *Administrative Science Quarterly* 32 (1987): 526–541.

104. D. L. Worrell, W. N. Davidson III, and V. M. Sharma, "Layoff Announcements and Stockholder Wealth," *Academy of Management Journal* 34 (1991): 662–678.

105. Bureau of Labor Statistics, "Impact of the Events of September 11, 2001, on the Mass Layoff Statistics Data Series," November 30, 2001.

106. Ibid.

107. "Lone Star Shuts 12% of Chain, Cites Losses: Closure of 30 Steakhouses Clears Way for New Units with Better Economics," *Nation's Restaurant News 40, 13* (March 27, 2006): 1, 9; "CBRL Group Inc.," *Hoovers,* http://premium.hoovers.com (accessed October 14, 2007).

108. M. Taylor and C. Enz, "Voices from the Field: GM's Responses to the Events of September 11, 2001," *Cornell Hotel and Administration Quarterly* 43, 1 (February 2002): 7–20.

109. R. Ward, "September 11 and the Restructuring of the Airline Industry," *Dollars and Sense* (May/June 2002): 16.

110. B. Sternlicht, Chairman/CEO, Starwood Hotels & Resorts, *Hotel Business* (October 21–November 6 2001): 9.

111. D. A. Heenan, "The Downside of Downsizing," *Journal of Business Strategy* (November/December 1989): 18.

112. If you would like to read some of this literature, you can start with Brockner et al., "Survivors' Reactions," and C. Hardy, "Investing in Retrenchment: Avoiding the Hidden Costs," *California Management Review* 29 (1987): 111–125.

113. M. Settles, "Humane Downsizing: Can It Be Done?" *Journal of Business Ethics* 7 (1988): 961–963; Worrell, Davidson, and Sharma, "Layoff Announcements."

114. E. Faltermeyer, "Is This Layoff Necessary?" *Fortune* (June 1, 1992): 71–86.

115. R. E. Hoskisson et al., "Restructuring Strategies of Diversified Business Groups: Differences Associated with Country Institutional Environments," in *Blackwell Handbook of Strategic Management*, eds. Hitt, Freeman, and Harrison, 433–463.

116. R. Ruggless, "Carlson to Divest E-Brands, Focus on Core Concepts," *Nation's Restaurant News* (February 4, 2002): 1.

117. C. Markides, "Consequences of Corporate Refocusing: Ex Ante Evidence," *Academy of Management Journal* 35 (1992): 398–412.

118. J. Higley, "Wyndham Maintains Improvement Course," *Hotel and Motel Management* (July 15, 2002): 4.

119. Hitt, Hoskisson, and Harrison, "Strategic Competitiveness"; R. E. Hoskisson and M. A. Hitt, *Downscoping: How to Tame the Diversified Firm* (New York: Oxford University Press, 1994), 3.

120. Hoskisson and Johnson, "Corporate Restructuring"; Hoskisson and Hitt, *Downscoping*.

121. C. A. Montgomery, A. R. Thomas, and R. Kammath, "Divestiture, Market Valuation, and Strategy," *Academy of Management Journal* 27 (1984): 830–840.

122. C. Goldsmith and A. Raghavan, "Six Continents to Split Businesses," *Wall Street Journal* (March 13, 2003): A5.

123. Hitt, Hoskisson, and Harrison, "Strategic Competitiveness," 7–21.

124. R. L. Daft, *Organization Theory and Design*, 4th ed. (St. Paul, MN: West Publishing, 1992), 94.

125. M. Prior, "Klinger Files for Chapter 11," **WWD: Women's Wear Daily 194, 46 (August 31, 2007): 9.**

126. D. M. Flynn and M. Farid, "The Intentional Use of Chapter XI: Lingering versus Immediate Filing," *Strategic Management Journal* 12 (1991): 63–64.

127. A. Merrick, "Kmart Lays Out Plans to Trim Its Size, Increase Efficiency in Bankruptcy Filing," *The Wall Street Journal* (January 23, 2002): A3.

128. E. Thornton and C. Palmeri, "Who Can Afford to Go Broke?" *Business Week* (September 10, 2001): 116.

129. Flynn and Farid, "Intentional Use."

130. W. N. Moulton, "Bankruptcy as a Deliberate Strategy: Theoretical Considerations and Empirical Evidence," *Strategic Management Journal* 14 (1993): 130.

131. "American Restaurant Group," *Hoovers,* **http://premium.hoovers.com** (accessed October 15, 2007).

132. L. Bushrod, "Little Chef/Travelodge," *European Venture Capital Journal* (April 1, 2003): 1.

133. K. M. Davidson, "Another Look at LBOs," *Journal of Business Strategies* (January/February 1988): 44–47.

134. A good review of these studies, of which there are seven, is found in S. A. Zahra and M. Fescina, "Will Leveraged Buyouts Kill U.S. Corporate Research and Development?" *Academy of Management Executive* (November 1991): 7–21.

135. M. F. Wiersema and J. P. Liebeskind, "The Effects of Leveraged Buyouts on Corporate Growth and Diversification in Large Firms," *Strategic Management Journal* 16 (1995): 447–460.

136. Davidson, "Another Look at LBOs."

137. Davidson, "Another Look at LBOs," 44–45.

138. M. Schwarz and E. A. Weinstein, "So You Want to Do a Leveraged Buyout," *Journal of Business Strategies* (January/February 1989): 10–15.

139. K. Payson, "Harrah's Buyout," *MeetingsNet*, http://meetingsnet.com/corporatemeetingsincentives/mag/meetings_harrahs_buyout (accessed October 15, 2007); "Harrah's Entertainment Inc.," *Hoovers*, http://premium.hoovers.com (accessed October 15, 2007); "Harrah's Gets $15B Buyout Offer from Private-Equity Firms," Fox News.Com, www.foxnews.com/story/0,2933,217036,00.html (accessed October 15, 2007).

140. B. O'Brian, "Delta Air Makes Painful Cuts in Effort to Stem Red Ink," *The Wall Street Journal* (September 10, 1992): B4.

141. J. P. Walsh, "Choice Restructures to Offer Better Service to Franchisees," *Hotel and Motel Management* (February 5, 2001): 1.

142. J. Simoon and T. Fisher, "Vacation Ownership—Reengineering the Financial Platform," *Lodging Hospitality* (May 1998): 14–15.

143. J. M. Graves, "Leaders of Corporate Change," *Fortune* (December 14, 1992): 113.

144. D. Rigby, "Management Tools and Techniques: A Survey," *California Management Review* 43, 2 (Winter 2001): 156.

145. J. F. Bandnowski, "Restructuring Is a Continuous Process," *Long Range Planning* (January 1991): 10–14.

146. P. Hapeslagh, "Portfolio Planning: Uses and Limitations," *Harvard Business Review* (January/February 1982): 58–73.

147. J. P. Shay, "Food-Service Strategy: An Integrated, Business-life-cycle Approach," *Cornell Hotel and Restaurant Administration Quarterly* 38, 3 (June 1997), 36–49; R. A. Kerin, V. Mahajan, and P. R. Varadarajan, *Strategic Market Planning* (Needham Heights, MA: Allyn & Bacon, 1990), 94; J. A. Seeger, "Reversing the Images of BCG's Growth Share Matrix," *Strategic Management Journal* 5 (1984): 93–97.

148. R. G. Hammermesh, M. J. Anderson, and J. E. Harris, "Strategies for Low Market Share Businesses," *Harvard Business Review* (May/June 1978): 95–102; C. Y. Woo and A. C. Cooper, "Market Share Leadership—Not Always So Good," *Harvard Business Review* (January/February 1984): 50–54.

149. J. Schwalbach, "Profitability and Market Share: A Reflection on the Functional Relationship," *Strategic Management Journal* 12 (1991): 299–306.

150. C. W. Hofer and D. Schendel, *Strategy Formulation: Analytical Concepts* (St. Paul, MN: South-Western College Publishing, 1978).

151. P. Aguas, J. Costa, and P. Rita, "A Tourist Market Portfolio for Portugal," *International Journal of Contemporary Hospitality Management* (December 7, 2000): 394–400.

CHAPTER 7

1. The quote at the conclusion of this article is from Bob Voelker, head of the Munsch Hardt Hospitality, Condominium, and Mixed-Use Group, in "Projects Success Can Lie in the Contract's Details." Over the last three years, the Hospitality Group has worked with developers on the W Hollywood hotel and condominiums; B. Voelker, "Projects Success Can Lie in the Contract's Details," *Hardt Kopf & Harr web site*, www.munsch.com/publication.cfm?publication_id=177 (accessed October 19, 2007); You can see video and pictures of this mixed-use development at www.whollywoodresidence.com; B. Voelker, "Coordination between Multiple Developers in Hotel Oriented Mixed-Use Transactions," *Munsch Hardt Kopf & Harr web site*, www.munsch.com/publication.cfm?publication_id=185 (accessed October 19, 2007); B. Voelker, "Luxury Hotel-Centered Mixed Use Projects: Value in the Mix," *Munsch Hardt Kopf & Harr web site*, www.munsch.com/publication.cfm?publication_id=185 (accessed October 19, 2007); "W Hollywood Hotel and Residences," *Western Real Estate Business* 4, 9 (May 2007): 60; "Luxury Micro-Market Hot During Real Estate Cooling Trend," *Los Angeles Business Journal* (April 16–22, 2007): 1, 26; M. Sheckells, "Glamour & Glitz Return to Hollywood," *Options*, www.optionsmag.com (accessed November 3, 2007).

2. J. Crotts, D. Buhalis, and R. March, "Introduction: Global Alliances in Tourism and Hospitality Management," *International Journal of Hospitality and Tourism Administration* 1, 1 (2000): 1–10.

3. J. S. Harrison, "Alternatives to Merger—Joint Ventures and Other Strategies," *Long Range Planning* (December 1987): 78–83.

4. C. Enz, C. Inman, and M. Lankau, "Strategic Social Partnerships for Change: A Framework for Building Sustainable Growth in Developing Countries," in eds. P. C. Earley and H. Singh, *Innovations in Cross-Cultural Management* (Thousand Oaks, CA: Sage Publishing, 2000).

5. P. Dittmer, *Dimensions of the Hospitality Industry*, 3rd ed. (New York: John Wiley & Sons, 2002).

6. R. Kanter, *World Class: Thriving Locally in the Global Economy* (New York: Touchstone, 1995), 325.

7. R. Mukumbira, "Botswana: Debswana Hotel Venture to Go Ahead," *African Business* (June 2003): 49; "About Debswana," *Debswana web site*, http://www.debswana.com/NR/exeres/872AB9D7-852E-47C5-A71D-66B0C43479F8.htm (accessed October 17, 2007).

8. L. Doolittle, "Disney Teams with AAA to Provide Multipurpose Rest Area for Travelers," *Orlando Sentinel* (January 25, 1996): B1.

9. "Schwan Forges Deal with Wolfgang Puck," *Nation's Restaurant News* 40, 36 (September 4, 2006): 50.

10. R. M. Kanter, "Becoming PALS: Pooling, Allying, and Linking across Companies," *Academy of Management Executive* (August 1989): 183–193.

11. J. S. Harrison et al., "Resource Complementarity in Business Combinations: Extending the Logic to Organizational Alliances," *Journal of Management* 27 (2001): 679–690.

12. E. Gilligan, "A Magical Partnership," *Commercial Property News* 21, 5 (March 1, 2007): 32–33; *Canyon Capital Reality Advisors web site*, www.canyonpartners.com/investor/capital/index.html (accessed October 17, 2007).

13. Peet's Coffee & Tea Inc., *Annual Report 2006*, investor.peets.com/sec.cfm?DocType=Annual&Year= (accessed October 17, 2007); Peet's Coffee & Tea, Inc., Press Release, "Peet's Coffee & Tea, Inc. Reports Second Quarter 2003 Result," www.peets.com/abtu/11/4.3.29_newsart.asp (Accessed October 17, 2007); M. Sheridan, "Mutual Attraction," *Restaurants & Institutions* (April 15, 2003): 12–13.

14. A. C. Inkpen, "Strategic Alliances," in *The Blackwell Handbook of Strategic Management*, eds. M. A. Hitt, R. E. Freeman, and J. S. Harrison (Oxford: Blackwell Publishers, 2001), 409–432.

15. M. Sheridan, "Mutual Attraction."

16. "Hundreds of Travel Industry Executives Convene with Lawmakers to Advance International Travel Promotion Act," *Travel Business Roundtable web site*, http://www.tbr.org/newsroom/pr_2007/pr_092607.htm (accessed October 17, 2007).

17. "Farr/Porter Advance Diplomacy Through International Tourism," *Congressman Jon Porter's web site*, http://porter.house.gov/?sectionid=5&sectiontree=3,4,5&itemid=788 (accessed October 17, 2007).

18. "R&D News," *Beverage Industry* 96, 12 (December 2005): 39; "Headlines," **MarketWatch: Drinks** 6, 4 (April 2007): 13–20.

19. B. Kogut, "Joint Ventures: Theoretical and Empirical Perspectives," *Strategic Management Journal* 9 (1988): 319–332.

20. K. R. Harrigan, "Joint Ventures and Competitive Strategy," *Strategic Management Journal* 9 (1988): 141–158; R. N. Osborn and C. C. Baughn, "Forms of Inter-organizational Governance for Multinational Alliances," *Academy of Management Journal* 33 (1990): 503–519.

21. M. Sheridan, "Mutual Attraction."

22. P. King, "Harvard Aims to Give Students a Better Read on Food," *Nation's Restaurant News* (June 30, 2003): 20; M. Sheridan, "Mutual Attraction."

23. D. H. Kent, "Joint Ventures vs. Non-Joint Ventures: An Empirical Investigation," *Strategic Management Journal* 12 (1991): 387–393.

24. M. Sheridan, "Mutual Attraction."

25. P. Lorange and J. Roos, "Why Some Strategic Alliances Succeed and Others Fail," *Journal of Business Strategy* (January/February 1991), 25–30.

26. A. C. Inkpen, "Strategic Alliances"; E. C. Karper-Fuehrer and N. M. Ashkanasy, "Communicating Trustworthiness and Building Trust in Inter-organizational Virtual Organizations," *Journal of Management* 27 (2001): 235–254; R. Gulati, "Does Familiarity Breed Trust? The Implications of Repeated Ties for Contractual Choice in Alliances," *Academy of Management Journal* 38 (1995): 85–112; B. Nooteboom, H. Berger, and N. G. Noorderhaven, "Effects of Trust and Governance on Relational Risk," *Academy of Management Journal* 40 (1997): 308–338.

27. A. C. Inkpen, "Strategic Alliances."

28. J. Walsh, "Partnerships Are Key to Developing Abroad," *Hotel & Motel Management* (June 4, 2001): 40.

29. J. S. Harrison and C. H. St. John, "Managing and Partnering with External Stakeholders," *Academy of Management Executive* (May 1996): 46–50; J. D. Thompson, *Organizations in Action* (New York: McGraw-Hill, 1967); J. R. Lang and D. E. Lockhart, "Increased Environmental Uncertainty and Changes in Board Linkage Patterns," *Academy of Management Journal* 33, 1 (1990): 106–128; A. D. Meyer and G. R. Brooks, "Environmental Jolts and Industry Revolutions: Organizational Responses to Discontinuous Change," *Strategic Management Journal* 11 (Special Issue 1990): 93–110.

30. "Cultural Preservation: Global Vision Awards," Travel + Leisure web site, http://www.travelandleisure.com/globalvision/2006/preservation.cfm (accessed October 17, 2007).

31. J. Perreira and B. Ortega, "Once Easily Turned Away by Local Foes, Wal-Mart Gets Tough in New England," *The Wall Street Journal* (September 7, 1994): B1, B4.

32. L. Canina, K. Walsh, and C. Enz, "Gasoline-price Fluctuations and Demand for Hotel Rooms: A Study of Branded Hotels from 1988 through 2000," *Cornell Hotel and Restaurant Administration Quarterly* 44, 4 (2003).

33. J. Pfeffer and G. R. Salancik, *The External Control of Organizations: A Resource Dependence Perspective* (New York: Harper & Row, 1978), 43.

34. "About Us," *Seacology web site*, www.seacology.org/about/index.html (accessed October 17, 2007); "Community Outreach: Global Vision Awards," *Travel + Leisure web site*, www.travelandleisure.com/globalvision/2006/preservation.cfm (accessed October 17, 2007).

35. L. Lohmeyer, "Chains: Kids' Advice Not Child's Play: Using Youths for Menu Testing Taps Lucrative Niche Market Insights," *Nation's Restaurant News* 23 (June 2003): 49.

36. J. Tisch, *The Power of We: Succeeding Through Partnerships* (Hoboken, NJ: John Wiley & Sons, 2004).

37. L. Lohmeyer, "Chains: Kids' Advice Not Child's Play."

38. Ibid.

39. R. Parker, "Supply Chains Put Market Leaders Ahead of the Pack," *Supply Management* (July 17, 2003): 10.

40. J. Brownell and D. Reynolds, "Strengthening the F&B Purchaser-Supplier Partnership: Actions That Make a Difference," *Cornell Hotel and Restaurant Administration Quarterly* 43, 6 (December 2002): 49–61.

41. J. Pond, "Beyond the Invoice," FoodService Director 18, 8 (August 14, 2005): 12. For a copy of the "foodWISE – Good for Me" kit, call 1-800-24-TYSON.

42. J. Gunn, "Third-party Politics," *Caterer & Hotelkeeper* (February 6, 2003): 24.

43. L. Dube, C. Enz, L. Renaghan, and J. Siguaw, "Cendant Corporation: Developing 'Preferred Alliances' with National Vendors." *American Lodging Excellence: The Key to Best Practices in the U.S. Lodging Industry* (2000): 64–65.

44. R. Bragg and S. Kumar, "Building Strategic Partnerships," *Industrial Engineer* (June 2003): 39.

45. D. McCutcheon and F. Stuart, "Issues in the Choice of Supplier Alliance Partners," *Journal of Operations Management* 18 (2000): 279–301.

46. J. Gunn, "Third-party Politics."

47. D. Carr, "Choice Hotels: Supplies and Demand," *Baseline*, www.baselinemag.com/article2/0,1397,1817352,00.asp (accessed October 17, 2007); J. Higley, "AAHOA Panel Addresses Issues from Different Perspectives," *Hotel & Motel Management 221*, 10 (June 5, 2006): 31–35.

48. J. Brownell and D. Reynolds, "Strengthening the F&B Purchaser-Supplier Partnership."

49. J. R. Harbison and P. Pekar Jr., *Smart Alliances: A Practical Guide to Repeatable Success* (San Francisco: Jossey-Bass Publishers, 1998).

50. J. Hagedoorn, "Understanding the Rationale of Strategic Technology Partnering: Inter-organizational Modes of Cooperation and Sectoral Differences," *Strategic Management Journal* 14 (1993): 371–385; E. R. Auster, "International Corporate Linkages: Dynamic Forms in Changing Environments," *Columbia Journal of World Business* 22 (1987): 3–13; Harrigan, "Joint Ventures and Competitive Strategy."

51. S. Oster, "The Strategic Use of Regulatory Investment by Industry Sub-groups," *Economic Inquiry* 20 (1982): 604.

52. P. Sparaco, "Air France Predicts More Consolidation," *Aviation Week & Space Technology* (December 2, 2002): 2; D. Michaels and S. Neuman, "Global Partners may Get Roiled by Turbulence," *The Wall Street Journal* (December 6, 2002): B1; J. Flottau, "SkyTeam Alliance Courts New Members," *Aviation Week & Space Technology* (October 7, 2002): 3.

53. D. Bond, "Recovery, Phase Two: Majors Change Strategy from Super-sized Alliances to Drinks over the Atlantic, Carriers Top Waiting for the Market to Save Them," *Aviation Week & Space Technology* (September 2, 2002): 24.

54. J. Lewis, *Partnerships for Profit: Structuring and Managing Strategic Alliances* (New York: The Free Press, 1990).

55. "Israeli, Palestinian Tourism Ministries Meet After Long Break," *International Herald Tribune*, www.iht.com/articles/ap/2007/10/16/africa/ME-GEN-Israel-Palestinians-Tourism.php (accessed October 16, 2007); "Israeli, Palestinian Tourism Ministries Re-establish Ties, Set Up Joint Body," *The Jerusalem Post web site*, www.mainejewish.org/page.html?ArticleID=159228 (accessed October 17, 2007).

56. B. Prideaux and C. Cooper, "Marketing and Destination Growth: A Symbiotic Relationship or Simple Coincidence," *Journal of Vacation Marketing* 9, 1 (December 2002): 35.

57. R. Mukumbira, "Botswana: Debswana Hotel Venture to Go Ahead," *African Business* (June 2003): 49.

58. "History," *Metro Orlando Economic Development Commission web site*, www.orlandoedc.com/About%20the%20EDC/history.shtml (Accessed October 18, 2007); B. Kuhn, "Business Growth on the Rise: Central Florida Faces Good News, Bad News Scenario," *The Orlando Sentinel* (January 10, 1994): 24; J. DeSimone, "A Boost for Business," *The Orlando Sentinel* (October 31, 1994): 8; A. Millican, "Want New Industry? House It," *The Orlando Sentinel* (October 7, 1994): 1.

59. L. Dube, C. Enz, L. Renaghan, and J. Siguaw, "Hyatt Regency Scottsdale: A Community-based Hospitality Training Program for High School Students," *American Lodging Excellence: The Key to Best Practices in the U.S. Lodging Industry* (2000): 62–63.

60. F. Rose, "Can Disney Tame 42nd Street?" *Fortune* (June 24, 1996): 95–104.

61. "Restaurant Industry Raises $12 million for Katrina Victims," *QSRWeb*, www.qsrweb.com/article.php?id=905) (accessed October 18, 2007); "Restaurant Industry Hurricane Relief," *StarChefs.com*, www.starchefs.com/community/hurricane/index.shtml (accessed October 18, 2007).

62. S. Leung, "McDonald's See Glimmers of a Return to Its Salad Days," *The Wall Street Journal* (August 1, 2003): B1.

63. M. Prewitt, "Operators Weigh Options over Fat Suits," *Nation's Restaurant News* (July 7, 2003): 1.

64. G. Haussman "NAACP Gives Lodging Industry 'C'," *Hotel Interactive*, www.hotelinteractive.com/index.asp?lstr=cae4@cornell.edu&page_id=5000&article_id=9062 (accessed October 20, 2007).

65. B. Thorn, "The Skinny on Foodservice's Fat Fight: Big Problem Requires Large Helping of Ideas," *Nation's Restaurant News* (July 21, 2003): 34.

66. "McCain to comply with nutrition guidelines set by the Alliance for a Healthier Generation," *Nation's Restaurant News* 41, 28 (July 16, 2007): 40; "For Companies," *The Alliance for a Healthier Generation web site*, www.healthiergeneration.org/companies.aspx (accessed October 16, 2007).

67. K. Kerlin, "Sustainable Slopes," *E: The Environmental Magazine* (November/December 2001): 15.

68. J. J. Davis, "A Blueprint for Green Marketing," *The Journal of Business Strategy* (July/August 1991): 14–17; J. S. Scerbinski, "Consumers and the Environment: A Focus on Five Products," *The Journal of Business Strategy* (September/October 1991): 44–47; Z. Schiller, "At Rubbermaid, Little Things Mean a Lot," *Business Week* (November 11, 1991): 126.

69. "As Environmental Concerns Go Mainstream, Clever Operators Are Joining the Crusade," *Nation's Restaurant News* 41, 40 (October 8, 2007): 23.

70. Ibid., 23.

71. "Environmental Commitment," *Aspen Snowmass web site*, www.aspensnowmass.com/environment (accessed October 20, 2007).

72. G. Haussman, "Barter Biz Plugging Room Sales Shortfall," *Hotel Interactive*, www.hotelinteractive.com/news (accessed August 25, 2003).

73. "Dirty Dining? Dateline's Hidden Cameras Investigate Cleanliness of America's Top 10 Fast Food Chains," *Dateline NSNBC*, www.msnbc.msn.com/id/3473728/ (accessed October 20, 2007). You can visit their web site to see the video and the ranking for each chain.

74. "What's Hiding in Your Hotel Room? Inspections Reveal Bedbugs; Black Light Reveals Urine and More," *ABC News*, (http://abcnews.go.com/GMA/Health/story?id=1507794 (accessed October 20, 2007).

75. A. Spector, "Puck Express Expands through Franchising," *Nation's Restaurant News* (June 11, 2001): 4.

76. H. Kim and S. Richardson, "Motion Picture Impacts on Destination Images," *Annals of Tourism Research* 30, 1 (2003): 216–237.

77. R. Allen, "The Dish on 'The Restaurant': Style over Substance Presents an Unappetizing View of Foodservice," *Nation's Restaurant News* (August 25, 2003): 23.

78. *The World Bank, Building Institutions for Markets: World Development Report 2002* (Oxford, England: Oxford University Press, 2002).

79. "About Us," *AFL-CIO web site*, www.aflcio.org/aboutus (accessed October 21, 2007).

80. D. Whitford, "Labor's Best Hope," *Fortune* (October 29, 2001): 119; C. Wolff, "Hotel Organizing: Down but Not Out," *Lodging Hospitality* (May 1, 2003): 8; K. Maher and T. Audi, "Unions, Casino Workers Seek to Improve Their Odds," *Wall Street Journal Online*, http://online.wsj.com/article/SB119179924417451696.html (accessed October 22, 2007).

81. "Change to Win Founding Convention News," *UFCW web site*, www.ufcw.org/about_ufcw/change_to_win_coalition/index.cfm (accessed October 22, 2007).

82. "UNITE HERE Fact Sheet," *UNITE HERE*, www.unitehere.org/presscenter/factsheet.php (accessed October 21, 2007).

83. P. Sarkar, "Another Loss for AFL-CIO: UNITE HERE Splits to Join Coalition of Dissident Unions," *San Francisco Chronicle*, www.sfgate.com/cgi-bin/article.cgi?f=/c/a/2005/09/15/BUG8OENLEA1.DTL (accessed October 21, 2007).

84. "About the Campaign," *Hotel Workers Rising*, www.hotelworkersrising.org/Campaign (accessed October 22, 2007).

85. "Quick Facts," *Hotel Workers Rising*, www.hotelworkersrising.org/Campaign/profile.php?worker_id=3 (accessed October 22, 2007).

86. R. Katz, "Gaylord Nixes Development on West Coast," **Meeting News** 31, 10 (August 13, 2007): 1–41.

87. You can learn more about INMEX at www.inmex.org.

88. D. Black, "22 Hotel Workers in Wage Fight: Holiday Inn Staff Say They've Been Locked Out After Seeking Parity with Other Union Workers," The Star.com, www.thestar.com/News/article/267191 (accessed October 21, 2007).

89. S. Korshak, "A Labor-management Partnership: San Francisco's Hotels and the Employees' Union Try a New Approach," *Cornell Hotel and Restaurant Administration Quarterly* 41, 2 (April 2000): 14–29.

90. M. Mitchell, "Union Organizing Trends In The Hospitality Industry," *Hospitality Net*, www.hospitalitynet.org/news/4032340.search?query=summer+of+discontent+unite+here (accessed October 23, 2007).

91. C. Wolff, "Hotel Organizing."

92. A. Stokes, R. Murphy, P. Wagner, and D. Sherwyn, "Neutrality Agreements: How Unions Organize New Hotels without an Employee Ballot," *Cornell Hotel and Restaurant Administration Quarterly* 42, 5 (October–November 2001): 86–96.

93. "Hilton, N.Y. Hotel and Motel Trades Council Reach Tentative Agreement: Hilton Also Agrees with UNITE HERE on 'Partnership for Future Growth'," *Hotel Workers Rising*, www.hotelworkersrising.org/News/press_release.php?press_id=108 (accessed October 22, 2007).

94. Ibid.

95. "Hotel Labor Relations," *AH&LA web site*, www.ahla.com/labor/default.asp?ID=33 (accessed October 22, 2007).

96. R. Ruggles, "Landry's Note Holder Fight Underscores Credit Crunch," *Nations Restaurant News* 41, 35 (September 3, 2007): 1, 57.

97. K. Seal, "Union Pension Funds Fill Financing Void for Hotel Projects," *Hotel and Motel Management* (March 6, 2000) 38–40.

98. R. Mowbray, "Looking for the Union Label Never Easier, Thanks to Hotel; Loews Makes Use of Organized Labor," *New Orleans Times-Picayune* (May 9, 2000): C3.

99. "MGM Mirage Board of Directors," MGM Mirage web site, phx.corporate-ir.net/phoenix.zhtml?c=101502&p=irol-board (accessed October 23, 2007).

100. Lorange and Roos, "Strategic Alliances," 25–30.

101. "Strategic Partnerships," Accor web site, www.accor.com/gb/groupe/partenariats/strategiques.asp (accessed July 25, 2008).

102. Adapted from various sources, including P. Burrows, "How a Good Partnership Goes Bad," *Electronic Business* (March 30, 1992): 86–90; G. Develin and M. Bleackley, "Strategic Alliances—Guidelines for Success," *Long Range Planning* 21, 5 (1988): 18–23; Lorange and Roos, "Strategic Alliances"; and J. B. Treece, K. Miller, and R. A. Melcher, "The Partners," *Business Week* 10 (February 1992): 102–107.

103. L. Dube, C. Enz, L. Renaghan, and J. Siguaw, "The Pierre: Maximizing Profitability by Managing the Sales Mix," *American Lodging Excellence: The Key to Best Practices in the U.S. Lodging Industry* (2000): 185–186.

104. A. Liddle, "Operators Chew on Ways to Offer In-store Internet Access," *Nation's Restaurant News* (August 11, 2003): 1.

105. F. W. Gluck, S. D. Kaufman, and A. S. Walleck, "Strategic Management for Competitive Advantage," *Harvard Business Review* (July/August 1980): 154–161.

106. L. Dube, C. Enz, L. Renaghan, and J. Siguaw, "Newark Gateway Hilton: Guest Check-in on the Shuttle Bus," *American Lodging Excellence: The Key to Best Practices in the U.S. Lodging Industry* (2000): 177.

107. R. Hayes and S. Wheelwright, *Restoring Our Competitive Edge: Competing through Manufacturing* (New York: John Wiley and Sons, 1984), 30.

108. "Is JetBlue the Next People Express? As Its Valentine's Day Debacle Shows, Ferocious Growth Can Be Crippling," *Business Week*, www.businessweek.com/magazine/content/07_11/b4025055.htm?chan=search (accessed October 23, 2007); "JetBlue Statement Regarding Operational Impact Today," Press Release JetBlue web site, http://investor.jetblue.com/phoenix.zhtml?c=131045&p=irol-newsArticle&ID=963450&highlight= (accessed October 23, 2007).

109. P. R. Varadarajan and S. Jayachandran, "Marketing Strategy: An Assessment of the State of the Field and Outlook," *Journal of the Academy of Marketing Science* 27 (1999): 120–143.

110. S. A. Snell, M. A. Shadur, and P. M. Wright, "Human Resources Strategy: The Era of our Ways," in eds. M. A. Hitt, R. E. Freeman, and J. S. Harrison, *The Blackwell Handbook of Strategic Management* (Oxford, England: Blackwell Publishers, 2001), 627.

111. J. B. Quinn, "The Intelligent Enterprise: A New Paradigm," *Academy of Management Executive* 6, 4, (1992): 48–63.

112. W. E. Fulmer, "Human Resources Management: The Right Hand of Strategy Implementation," *Human Resource Planning* 12, 4 (1990): 1–10.

113. Ibid.

114. C. A. Lengnick-Hall and M. L. Lengnick-Hall, "Strategic Human Resource Management: A Review of the Literature and a Proposed Typology," *Academy of Management Review* 13, 3 (1988): 466–467.

115. R. Hayes and S. Wheelwright, *Restoring our Competitive Edge*.

116. W. M. Bulkeley, "The Latest Thing at Many Companies is Speed, Speed, Speed," *Wall Street Journal* (December 23, 1994): A1.

117. A. Fiegenbaum and A. Karnani, "Output Flexibility—A Competitive Advantage for Small Firms," *Strategic Management Journal* 12 (1991): 101–114.

CHAPTER 8

1. "Yum! Brands," *2006 Annual Customer Mania Report*; "Yum! Brands Profile," *Yum! Brands web site*, www.yum.com/investors/samsu.asp (accessed November 5, 2007); "Yum! Brands Reorganizes U.S. Business to Power Future Sales and Profit Growth," *Investor News Release Yum! Brands web site*, www.yum.com/investors/news/ir_111606.asp (accessed November 5, 2007).

2. R. Simons, "How New Top Managers Use Control Systems as Levers of Strategic Renewal," *Strategic Management Journal* 15 (1994): 169–189.

3. R. Simons, "Strategic Orientation and Management Attention to Control Systems," *Strategic Management Journal* 12 (1991): 49–62.

4. A. Liddle, **"McD's Global Standardization Strategy Enhanced by Vendor Sale, Chain Says," *Nation's Restaurant News* 40,** 19 (May 5, 2006): 22; R. Leidner, *Fast Food, Fast Talk: Service Work and the Routinization of Everyday Life* (Berkeley: University of California Press, 1993).

5. B. Keats and H. M. O'Neill, "Organizational Structure: Looking through a Strategy Lens," in *The Blackwell Handbook of Strategic Management*, eds. M. A. Hitt, R. E. Freeman, and J. S. Harrison (Oxford: Blackwell Publishers, 2001), 520–542.

6. A. D. Chandler, *Strategy and Structure: Chapters in the History of the American Industrial Enterprise* (Cambridge, MA: MIT Press, 1962).

7. E. Tse, "An Empirical Analysis of Organizational Structure and Financial Performance in the Restaurant Industry," *International Journal of Hospitality Management* 10, 1 (1991): 59–72.

8. This example is drawn from the ideas of E. Nebel, *Managing Hotels Effectively: Lessons from Outstanding General Managers* (New York: Van Nostrand Reinhold, 1991).

9. R. Daft, *Organization Theory and Design*, 8th ed. (Mason, OH: South-Western, 2004).

10. Ibid.

11. Choice Hotels, Letter to Shareholders, http://media.corporate-ir.net/media_files/nys/chh/reports/2001/ch2001ar02.html (accessed September 3, 2003).

12. P. R. Lawrence and J. W. Lorsch, *Organization and Environment* (Homewood, IL: Irwin, 1969), 23–39.

13. D. Gale, "Centralization Offers Advantages, Savings," *Hotels* (April 2006): 53–56; J. Marsan, "One for the Money," *Hotels* (January 2001): 67.

14. "Our Structure," InterContinental Hotels Group web site, www.ihgplc.com/index.asp?pageid=261 (accessed November 7, 2007).

15. A. C. Hax and N. S. Majluf, *The Strategy Concept and Process: A Pragmatic Approach* (Englewood Cliffs, NJ: Prentice Hall, 1991).

16. R. Duncan, "What Is the Right Organization Structure? Decision Tree Analysis Provides the Answer," *Organization Dynamics* (Winter 1979): 429–431.

17. K. Birdir, "General Manager Turnover and Root Causes," *International Journal of Contemporary Hospitality Management* 14, 1 (February 20, 2002): 43–47.

18. This example is drawn from the ideas of E. Nebel, *Managing Hotels Effectively*.

19. M. Davis and D. Weckler, *A Practical Guide to Organizational Design* (Menlo Park, CA: Crisp Publications, 1996).

20. "EMEA Restructure for InterContinental," *Travel Weekly: The Choice of Travel Professionals* (June 23, 2003): 27.

21. Pegasus Solutions, Inc., www.rez.com/products_services/services.htm (accessed November 7, 2007).

22. Duncan, "What Is the Right Organization Structure?"

23. J. B. Quinn, *Intelligent Enterprise* (New York: The Free Press, 1992).

24. A. Roper, "The Emergence of Hotel Consortia as Transorganizational Forms, *International Journal of Contemporary Hospitality Management* 7, 1 (1995): 4–9.

25. Best Western, *Annual Report for 2002*, www.bestwestern.com/aboutus/2002.pdf (accessed September 3, 2003).

26. G. Haussman, "Higgins Out to Be 'Premier' Best Western Pres/CEO," *Hotel Interactive*, www.hotelinteractive.com/news (accessed August 29, 2003).

27. "HOTELS' Consortia 25: Seminal Times for Consortia," *Hotels* (July 2005): 6–7, www.hotelsmag.com/archives/2005/07/consortia-25.asp (accessed November 7, 2007).

28. J. R. Galbraith and R. K. Kazanjian, *Strategy Implementation: Structure, Systems, and Processes*, 2nd ed. (St. Paul, MN: West Publishing, 1986).

29. R. L. Daft, *Organization Theory and Design*, 3rd ed. (St. Paul, MN: West Publishing, 1989), 240.

30. R. C. Ford and W. A. Randolph, "Cross-functional Structures: A Review and Integration of Matrix Organization and Project Management," *Journal of Management* 18, 2 (1992): 267–294.

31. P. Tierney, "The Jungle Booking," *Forbes* (March 10, 1997): 92.

32. "Executive Leadership," *Carlson web site*, www.carlson.com/overview/leadership.cfm (accessed November 7, 2007); first two quotations are from S. C. O'Connor, "Witzel Tapped as Group President at Carlson Hotels," *Hotel Business* (October 21, 2002): 6; third quotation is from B. Serlen, "Carlson Bundles Hotels," *Business Travel News* (June 3, 2002): 3.

33. "Best Western Corporate Fact Sheet," *Best Western web site*, www.bestwestern.com/newsroom/factsheet_countrydetail.asp (accessed November 7, 2007).

34. K. Staroba, "Managing the Matrix," *Association Management* 48, 8 (August 1996): 64.

35. "Management Restructuring at Orient-Express Hotels," *Orient-Express Hotels Website*, www.orient-express.com/web/luxury/releases/4_91252.jsp (accessed November 7, 2007); "Orient-Express Hotels Maximizes Niche Strategy," *Hotels* (May 2002).

36. Ibid.

37. J. Pearce and R. Robinson, *Formulation, Implementation, and Control of Competitive Strategy*, 7th ed. (Boston: McGraw-Hill, 2000).

38. C. W. L. Hill, M. A. Hitt, and R. E. Hoskisson, "Cooperative versus Competitive Structures in Related and Unrelated Diversified Firms," *Organization Science* 3, 4 (November 1992): 501–521.

39. "Our Companies," *The Tata Group web site*, www.tata.com/0_companies/index.htm#business_sectors (accessed November 7, 2007).

40. "The Walt Disney Company," *Conde Nast Portfolio.com web site*, www.portfolio.com/resources/company-profiles/91 (accessed November 8, 2007); "Walt Disney . . . and Other Items of M&A News," *Weekly Corporate Growth Report* (June 2, 2003): 11; B. Pulley, "Disney the Sequel," *Forbes*(December 9, 2002): 106; Walt Disney Company, *Annual Report 2002*.

41. Ford and Randolph, "Cross-functional Structures."

42. Based on information provided by Jo-Anne Kruse, who served as vice president of human resources at Cendant Corporation.

43. C. A. Bartlett and S. Ghoshal, *Managing across Borders: The Transnational Solution* (Boston: Harvard Business School Press, 1989).

44. C. A. Bartlett and S. Ghoshal, "The New Global Manager," *Harvard Business Review* (September/October 1992): 124–132.

45. Davis and Weckler, *A Practical Guide to Organizational Design*.

46. Ford and Randolph, "Cross-functional Structures."

47. L. Dube, C. Enz, L. Renaghan, and J. Siguaw, "Coastal Hotel Group: Employees on Loan for Training with the Buddy System," *The Key to Best Practices in the U.S. Lodging Industry* (Washington, DC: American Hotel and Motel Association, 2001), 76–77.

48. G. G. Dess et al., "The New Corporate Architecture," *Academy of Management Executive* 9, 3 (1995): 7–20.

49. J. Galbraith, D. Downey, and A. Kates, *Designing Dynamic Organizations* (New York: American Management Association, 2002).

50. Personal interviews with Lewis G. Schaeneman (past CEO of the Stop and Shop Supermarket Company) and his senior staff, including Bill Grize, now president and CEO.

51. G. Gregory, "A New Knowledge Management Model," *Information Today* (December 2002).

52. L. Dube, C. Enz, L. Renaghan, and J. Siguaw, "Accor North America: Internal Customer Satisfaction," *The Key to Best Practices in the U.S. Lodging Industry* (Washington, DC: American Hotel and Motel Association, 2001), 36–37.

53. P. Lorange, M. F. Scott Morton, and S. Ghoshal, *Strategic Control* (St. Paul, MN: West Publishing, 1986), 10.

54. M. Pilling, "Getting a Grip," *Airline Business* (October 2002): 34.

55. R. Simons, "How New Top Managers Use Control Systems as Levers of Strategic Renewal."

56. "Our Approach, Knowledge Sharing," *Ernst & Young web site*, www.ey.com/global/content.nsf/US/Knowledge_Management_-_Our_Approach (accessed November 8, 2007); J. Stuller, "Chief of Corporate Smarts," *Training* (April 1998): 28.

57. H. T. Johnson and R. S. Kaplan, *Relevance Lost: The Rise and Fall of Management Accounting* (Boston: Harvard Business School Press, 1987), 10–18.

58. J. F. Weston and E. F. Brigham, *Essentials of Managerial Finance*, 7th ed. (Hinsdale, IL: The Dryden Press, 1985), 154.

59. O. E. Williamson, *Markets and Hierarchies: Analysis and Antitrust Applications* (New York: The Free Press, 1975).

60. A. Lee, *Call Me Roger* (Chicago: Contemporary Books, 1988), 110.

61. Johnson and Kaplan, *Relevance Lost*, 1.

62. C. Enz, L. Canina, and K. Walsh, "Hotel-industry Averages: An Inaccurate Tool for Measuring Performance," *Cornell Hotel and Restaurant Administration Quarterly* 42 (December 2001): 22–32.

63. R. E. Hoskisson and M. A. Hitt, "Strategic Control and Relative R&D Investment in Large Multiproduct Firm," *Strategic Management Journal* 6 (1988): 605–622.

64. D. Heitger, B. Ballou, and R. Colson, "Pro-Forma Earnings," *CPA Journal* 73, 3 (March 2003): 44. "SEC Brings First Pro Forma Financial Reporting Case Trump Hotels Charged With Issuing Misleading Earnings Release," *Securities and Exchange Commission web site*, www.sec.gov/news/headlines/trumphotels.htm (accessed November 13, 2007); "Trump Entertainment Resorts Inc.," *Hoovers*, http://premium.hoovers.com. (accessed November 13, 2007).

65. M. A. Hitt et al., "The Market for Corporate Control and Firm Innovation," *Academy of Management Journal* 39 (1996): 1084–1119.

66. M. Goold and J. J. Quinn, "The Paradox of Strategic Controls," *Strategic Management Journal* 11 (1990): 43–57.

67. N. Geller and R. Schmidgall, "Should Overhead Costs Be Allocated?" In R. Schmidgall, *Hospitality Industry Managerial Accounting*, 4th ed. (Lansing, MI: Educational Institute, American Hotel and Motel Association, 1997).

68. E. Watkins, "What's Coming in Your Back Door?" *Lodging Hospitality* 62, 8 (May 15, 2006): 53–54.

69. E. J. Shea, "Fresh Eyes," *Restaurants & Institutions* 116, 17 (September 1, 2006): 93–94.

70. Four Seasons, *Annual Report for 2002*, www.fourseasons.com, July 2003, www.fourseasons.com/about_us/investor_information/annual_reports.html.

71. R. S. Kaplan and D. P. Norton, "Putting the Balanced Scorecard to Work," *Harvard Business Review* (September/October 1993): 134–147.

72. D. Huckestein and R. Duboff, "Hilton Hotels: A Comprehensive Approach to Delivering Value for All Stakeholders," *Cornell Hotel and Restaurant Administration Quarterly* 40 (August 1999): 28–38.

73. P. Collier and A. Gregory, "Strategic Management Accounting: A UK Hotel Sector Case Study," *International Journal of Contemporary Hospitality Management* 7, 1 (1995): 16.

74. M. L. Frigo, "Strategy and the Balanced Scorecard," *Strategic Finance* (November 2002): 7; Huckestein and Duboff, "Hilton Hotels: A Comprehensive Approach to Delivering Value for All Stakeholders."

75. G. P. Latham and E. A. Locke, "Goal Setting—A Motivational Technique That Works," *Organizational Dynamics* (Autumn 1979): 68–80; M. D. Richards, *Setting Strategic Goals and Objectives*, 2nd ed. (St. Paul, MN: West Publishing, 1986); M. E. Tubbs, "Goal Setting: A Meta-Analytic Examination of Empirical Evidence," *Journal of Applied Psychology* 3 (1986): 474–475.

76. Huckestein and Duboff, "Hilton Hotels: A Comprehensive Approach to Delivering Value for All Stakeholders," 31.

77. R. Carey, "Walking the Talk," *Successful Meetings* (November 2002).

78. Simons, "Strategic Orientation," 50.

79. J. Sullivan, "Planning Best Way to Grow amid Inevitable Change," *Nation's Restaurant News* (January 7, 2002): 16.

80. Lorange, Scott Morton, and Ghoshal, *Strategic Control*, 2–8.

81. J. Troutman, "Hospitality Business Intelligence: Almost Mainstream," *Hospitality Upgrade* (Fall 2006): 170–171.

82. S. Ghoshal and S. K. Kim, "Building Effective Intelligence Systems for Competitive Advantage," *Sloan Management Review* (Fall 1986): 49.

83. Troutman, "Hospitality Business Intelligence."

84. J. P. Stamen, "Decision Support Systems Help Planners Hit Their Targets," *The Journal of Business Strategy* (March/April 1990): 30–33.

85. J. Rothfeder, J. Bartimo, and L. Therrien, "How Software Is Making Food Sales a Piece of Cake," *Business Week* (July 2, 1990): 54–55.

86. J. P. Herring, "Building a Business Intelligence System," *Journal of Business Strategy* (May/June 1988): 4–9.

87. G. Schreyogg and H. Steinmann, "Strategic Control: A New Perspective," *Academy of Management Review* 12 (1987): 96.

88. W. R. Haines, "Making Corporate Planning Work in Developing Countries," *Long Range Planning* (April 1988): 91–96.

89. R. T. Lenz and J. L. Englelow, "Environmental Analysis Units and Strategic Decision-making: A Field Study of Selected 'Leading-Edge' Corporations," *Strategic Management Journal* 7 (1986): 69–89.

90. V. Govindarajan and J. Fisher, "Strategy, Control Systems, and Resource Sharing: Effects on Business Unit Performance," *Academy of Management Journal* 33 (1990): 259–285.

91. R. Mitchell, "Inside the Gap," *Business Week* (March 9, 1992): 58–64.

92. P. McDonald and J. Gandz, "Getting Value from Shared Values," *Organization Dynamics* (Winter 1992): 60–71.

93. C. Enz and J. Siguaw, "Best Practices in Human Resource Management," *Cornell Hotel and Restaurant Administration Quarterly* 41 (February 2000): 48–61.

94. C. F. Hermann, ed., *International Crises: Insights from Behavioral Research* (New York: The Free Press, 1972).

95. D. Huckestein and R. Duboff, "Hilton Hotels: A Comprehensive Approach to Delivering Value for All Stakeholders," *Cornell Hotel and Restaurant Administration Quarterly* 40 (August 1999): 33.

96. E. Perez, "Carnival Unit's Ship Has Norwalk Virus Cases," *The Wall Street Journal* (September 3, 2003): D7.

97. Ibid.

98. I. I. Mitroff, "Crisis Management: Cutting through the Confusion," *Sloan Management Review* (Winter 1988): 19.

99. M. Steintrager, "Lights, Camera, Reaction," *Restaurant Business* (November 15, 2000): 44.

100. K. Woods, "When the Tanks Rolled into Town: A GM's Experience in Kuwait," *Cornell Hotel and Restaurant Administration Quarterly* 32 (May 1991): 16–25.

101. S. Gupte, "McDonald's Averts a Crisis," *Ad Age Global* (July 2001): 134.

102. I. I. Mitroff and C. Pearson, "From Crisis Prone to Crisis Prepared: A Systematic and Integrative Framework for Crisis Management," *Academy of Management Executive* 7, 1 (February 1993): 48–59.

103. R. Terrero, "Hotels Step Up Security: Prepare for Future Events by Training Employees," *Hotel Business* (October 21–November 6, 2001): 15.

104. C. Enz and M. Taylor, "The Safety and Security of U.S. Hotels: A Post–September 11 Report," *Cornell Hotel and Restaurant Administration Quarterly* 43 (October 2002): 119–136; Changes in U.S. Hotel Safety and Security Staffing and Procedures during 2001 and 2002," www.chr.cornell.edu, June 15, 2003.

105. Enz and Taylor, "The Safety and Security of U.S. Hotels."

106. D. Rynecki, "The Bull Fights Back," *Fortune* (October 15, 2001): 132.

CHAPTER 9

1. L. Esposito, "Branching Out," *Hotel Business* 16, 21 (November 7–20, 2007): 34–35,; "Our Team," *Diplomat Hotels*, http://www.diplomatcompanies.com/team.htm#RC (accessed December 4, 2007); "American Hoteliers Make a Difference," *Overseas Indian*, http://www.overseasindian.in/2007/jan/news/2media.shtml (Accessed December 4, 2007); D. Nessler, "Health and Happiness," *Hotel Business* 16, 21 (November 7–20, 2007): 36, 38, 86; L. Melwani, "No More Potels," *Little India*, http://littleindia.com/march2003/No%20More%20Potel%20Motels.htm; Hugh R. Morley, "Like a Rhyme—Motel, Hotel, Patel,

Indian-Americans Own Approximately 35% of All Hotels in U.S.," *The Record*, Hackensack, N.J., Knight Ridder/Tribune Business News, March 6, 2003; Nancy E. Bistritz, "The Evolution of AAHOA," *National Real Estate Investor*, www.nreion-line.com (accessed August 7, 2003); Glenn Haussman, "AAHOA Hails 2002 Triumphs, Sets 2003 Goals," *Hotel Interactive*, April 30, 2003 (accessed August 7, 2003); Kathy Hoke, "Downtown Hotel Opening Just As Owner Had Dreamed," *Business First of Columbus*, September 4, 2000; Melwani Lavina, "Diplomat of Hotels: Indian Hoteliers Step Up," *Welcome to India*, http://206.20.14.67/achal/archive/Jul97/hotel.htm (accessed August 7, 2003).

2. A. M. McCarthy and C. L. Nicholls-Nixon, "Fresh Starts: Arnold Cooper on Entrepreneurship and Wealth Creation," *Academy of Management Executive* 15, 1 (February 2001): 29.

3. D. Milton, "Industry Surveys Restaurants," *Standard and Poor's*, May 8, 2003.

4. P. D. Reynolds, M. Hay, and S. Michael Camp, *Global Entrepreneurship Monitor* (Kansas City, MO: Kauffman Center for Entrepreneurial Leadership, 1999).

5. S. M. Puffer and D. J. McCarthy, "Navigating the Hostile Maze: A Framework for Russian Entrepreneurship," *Academy of Management Executive* (November 2001): 24.

6. K. Wooten, T. A. Timmerman, and R. Folger. "The Use of Personality and the Five-Factor Model to Predict New Business Ventures: From Outplacement to Start-Up," *Journal of Vocational Behavior* 54 (1998): 82–101.

7. M. Brewster, "Kemmons Wilson: America's Innkeeper," *Business Week Online*, October 13, 2004.

8. S. J. Min, "Made Not Born," *Entrepreneur of the Year Magazine* (Fall 1999): 80.

9. L. E. Shefsky, *Entrepreneurs Are Made Not Born* (New York: McGraw-Hill, 1994), 10.

10. S. Pike, "Harris Rosen: Orlando's Hotel Magnate," *Hotel Interactive*, www.hotelinteractive.com/index.asp?page_id=5000&article_id=7874 (accessed June 4, 2007).

11. D. Kochilas, "Manhattan Blues: A Combination of Troubled Times and Wrong Concept Eventually Did Metro In, Despite Rave Reviews," *Restaurant Business*, January 20, 1991.

12. R. Jacobson, "The 'Austrian' School of Strategy," *Academy of Management Review* 17 (1992): 782–807; J. Schumpeter, *The Theory of Economic Development* (Cambridge, MA: Harvard University Press, 1934).

13. S. Venkataraman and S. D. Sarasvathy, "Strategy and Entrepreneurship: Outlines of an Untold Story," in *The Blackwell Handbook of Strategic Management*, eds. M. A. Hitt, R. E. Freeman, and J. S. Harrison (Oxford: Blackwell Publishers, 2001), 652.

14. A. Parmar, "Exposure Wins Indian Vintner Favor," *Marketing News* (October 28, 2002): 6; "Grover Vineyards, Bangalore—Company Profile," *Indian Wines web site*, www.indianwine.com/misc/gorverprofile2004.htm (accessed December 7, 2006); K. Giriprakash, "Grover Vineyards Hopes to Raise Rs 15 cr via Stake Sale," The Hindu Business Line Internet Edition, www.thehindubusinessline.com/2005/11/04/stories/2005110402670200.htm (accessed December 7, 2007).

15. M. Morris, D. Kuratko, and M. Schindehutte, "Towards Integration: Understanding Entrepreneurship Through Frameworks," *Entrepreneurship and Innovation* 2, 1 (February 2001): 35–49.

16. P. Pittershawn and R. Clarke, "Feeding the Soul," *Black Enterprise* 31, 11 (June 2001): 321.

17. S. Lalli, "A Peculiar Institution," in J. Sheehan, ed., *The Players: The Men Who Made Las Vegas* (Reno/Las Vegas: University of Nevada Press, 1997), 1–22.

18. Shefsky, *Entrepreneurs Are Made Not Born*, 20.

19. P. Rainsford and D. Bangs, *The Restaurant Planning Guide: Starting and Managing a Successful Restaurant* (Dover, NH: Upstart Publishing Company, 1992).

20. W. K. Schilit, "How to Obtain Venture Capital," *Business Horizons* (May/June 1987): 78.

21. I. MacMillan, R. Siegel, and P. N. Subba Narasimha, "Criteria Used by Venture Capitalists to Evaluate New Venture Proposals," *Journal of Business Venturing* (Winter 1985): 119–128.

22. B. Hudson, "Venture Capital in the Restaurant Industry," *Cornell Hotel and Restaurant Administration Quarterly* 36, 3 (June 1995): 50–61.

23. Ibid.

24. P. DeCeglie, "The Truth about Venture Capital," *Business Startups* (February 2000): 40–47.

25. "About ABAN," *ARAB Business Angels Network*, www.arabbusinessplan.com/index3.htm (accessed December 10, 2007).

26. "AHDP/Glenmont Capital Joint Venture Commences with Development of First Candlewood Series," *Hotel Interactive*, May 24, 2007, www.hotelinteractive.com/index.asp?page_id=5000&article_id=7817 (accessed December 10, 2007).

27. NASDAQ, "Going Public" (New York: The NASDAQ Stock Market, 2000).

28. R. Walberg, "Enjoy Krispy Kreme's Doughnuts; Skip the Stock," *msn.money*, http://moneycentral.msn.com/content/P106124.asp (accessed December 10, 2007); A. Serwer, "The Hole Story," *Fortune* (July 7, 2003): 53.

29. D. E. Terpestra and P. D. Olson, "Entrepreneurial Start-up and Growth: A Classification of Problems," *Entrepreneurship Theory and Practice* (Spring 1993): 19.

30. To obtain uniform systems of accounts, you can go to the following sources: *Uniform System of Accounts for the Lodging Industry*, 9th ed. (East Lansing, MI: Educational Institute of the American Hotel and Lodging Association, 1996); *Uniform System of Accounts for Restaurants*, 69th ed. (Washington, DC: National Restaurant Association, 1990).

31. D. Kochilas, "Manhattan Blues," 92.

32. S. Campbell, "Prosperity Bodes Well for the Hospitality Industry in the New Millennium," *The Black Collegian* (February 1, 2000): 68–75.

33. P. Dvorak, "Hotelier Finds Happiness Keeps Staff Checked In," *Wall Street Journal* (December 17, 2007): B3.

34. D. Kochilas, "Manhattan Blues," 86–87.

35. "Our Unique Culture", *Joie de Vivre web site*, www.jdvhotels.com/careers/culture_index (accessed December 17, 2007); Dvorak, "Hotelier Finds Happiness Keeps Staff Checked In."

36. C. Perez and J. Hines, "Filling His Father's Shoes," *National Real Estate Investor* 49, 11 (November 2007): 10; "Gerald D. Hines to be Honored by National Building Museum at Washington Gala on June 20, 2000," Press Release, *Hines web site*, www.hines.com/press/releases/05-08-00.aspx (accessed December 14, 2007).

37. D. F. Kuratko and R. M. Hodgetts, *Entrepreneurship: A Contemporary Approach*, 5th ed. (Fort Worth, TX: Harcourt College Publishers, 2001).

38. Interested readers will find a wealth of information on this subject in K. W. Clarkson et al., *West's Business Law*, 7th ed. (St. Paul, MN: West Publishing, 2008).

39. R. L. Miller and G. A. Jentz, *Business Law Today*, 4th ed. (St. Paul, MN: West Publishing, 2007).

40. H. R. Dodge, S. Fullerton, and J. E. Robbins, "Stages of Organizational Life Cycle and Competition as Mediators of Problem Perception for Small Business," *Strategic Management Journal* 15 (1994): 121–134.

41. Ibid.

42. T. Graves, "Industry Surveys—Lodging and Gaming," *Standard and Poor's* (February 6, 2003): 16.

43. D. Milton, "Industry Surveys Restaurants," *Standard and Poor's*, May 8, 2003.

44. F. Lafontaine, "Survey—Mastering Strategy 9 Myths and Strengths of Franchising," *Financial Times* (November 22, 1999): 10.

45. Ibid.

46. "Acquisition News Propels Hilton Hotels to Top of Rosenberg Center Franchise 50 Index," *Hotel and Motel Management Week in Review*, www.hotelmotel.com/hotelmotel/article/articleDetail.jsp?id=475453 (Accessed November 27, 2007); "RCF 50 Index—First Quarter 2007," *Whitmore School of Business web site*, href="http://wsbe2.unh.edu/rcf-50-index-first-quarter-2007 (accessed December 19, 2007).

47. L. Zacharakis, G. D. Meyer, and J. DeCastro, "Differing Perceptions of New Venture Failure: A Matched Exploratory Study of Venture Capitalists and Entrepreneurs," *Journal of Small Business Management* (July 1999): 1–14.

48. D. Kochilas, "Manhattan Blues," 86–87. It is sad to note that Patrick Clark died in February 1998 at the age of 42 while awaiting a heart transplant. *Cooking with Patrick Clark* was published by Charlie Trotter in 1999.

49. W. English, B. Josiam, R. Upchurch, and J. Willems, "Restaurant Attrition: A Longitudinal Analysis of Restaurant Failures," *International Journal of Contemporary Hospitality Management* 8, 2 (1996): 17–20.

50. Dun and Bradstreet Corporation, *Business Failure Record*; Z. Gu and L. Gao, "A Multivariate Model for Predicting Business Failures of Hospitality Firms," *Tourism and Hospitality Research* 2, 1 (2000): 37–44.

51. H. Hubbard, "Putting Your Money Where Your Mouth Is—Restaurants: How to Spot a Hot Investment," *International Herald Tribune* (January 11, 2003): 13.

52. J. Oleck, "The Numbers Game: Failure-rate Statistics Run the Gamut, But Whose Are Right? *Restaurant Business* (June 10, 1993): 86, 91.

53. T. Blackwood and G. Mowl, "Expatriate-owned Small Businesses: Measuring and Accounting for Success," *International Small Business Journal* 18, 3 (2000): 60–73.

54. Ibid.

55. M. Prewitt, "R&D Executives Find Testing New Products, Designs Costly But Necessary," *Nation's Restaurant News* 40, 49 (December 4, 2006): 1, 42; L. Yee, "Bold New Day: Top 400 Chains Keep Innovation on the Menu," *Restaurants and Institutions* (July 15, 2001): 24–28, 32.

56. K. G. Smith, W. J. Ferrier, and H. Ndofor, "Competitive Dynamics Research: Critique and Future Directions," in *The Blackwell Handbook of Strategic Management*, eds. M. A. Hitt, R. E. Freeman, and J. S. Harrison (Oxford: Blackwell Publishers, 2001), 315–361.

57. J. Naisbitt and P. Aburdene, *Re-inventing the Corporation* (New York: Warner Books, 1985).

58. C. Conley, *The Rebel Rules: Daring to Be Yourself in Business* (New York: Fireside Book, 2001).

59. A. Afuah, *Innovation Management: Strategies, Implementation, and Profits* (New York: Oxford University Press, 1998).

60. G. Pinchot, *Intrapreneuring* (New York: Harper & Row, 1985); R. A. Burgelman, "Designs for Corporate Entrepreneurship in Established Firms," *California Management Review* (Spring 1984): 154–166.

61. Yee, "Bold New Day."

62. J. Andrew, H. Sirkin, K. Haanaes, and D. Michael, *Innovation 2007: A BCG Senior Management Survey* (The Boston Consulting Group, Inc., 2007).

63. Ibid, 7.

64. G. Hamel, *Leading the Revolution*, (Boston, MA: Harvard Business School Press, 2000); R. German and R. Muralidharan, "The Three Phases of Value Creation," *Strategy & Business* 22, 1 (2001): 82–91.

65. P. Roberts, "Product Innovation, Product-Market Competition and Persistent Profitability in the U.S. Pharmaceutical Industry," *Strategic Management Journal* 20, 7 (1999): 655–670; M. Subramaniam and N. Venkatraman, "The Influence of Leveraging Tacit Overseas Knowledge for Global New Product Development Capability: An Empirical Examination," In *Dynamic Strategic Resources*, eds. M. Hitt, P. Clifford, R. Nixon, and K. Coyne (Chichester, UK: Wiley, 1999): 373–401.

66. J. Andrew, H. Sirkin, K. Haanaes, and D. Michael, *Innovation 2007: A BCG Senior Management Survey* (The Boston Consulting Group, Inc., 2007), 11.

67. A. Van de Ven, D. Polley, R. Garud, and S. Venkataraman, *The Innovation Journey* (New York: Oxford University Press, 1999).

68. "ADVANCE by Onity Locking Solution Claims Prestigious 2007 Platinum ADEX Award for Design." Press Release on Onity web site, www.onity.com/press-room/#2 (accessed December 11, 2007).

69. C. A. Enz and J. Harrison, "Innovation and Entrepreneurship in the Hospitality Industry," In Roy Wood and B. Brothers, *The Handbook of Hospitality Management* (London: Sage Publishing, 2007).

70. J. Andrew, H. Sirkin, K. Haanaes, and D. Michael, *Innovation 2007*.

71. Ibid, 11.

72. J. B. Quinn, "Managing Innovation: Controlled Chaos," *Harvard Business Review* 63 (May/June 1985): 73–84.

73. Kuratko and Hodgetts, *Entrepreneurship*.

74. C. Conley, *The Rebel Rules*.

75. Naisbitt and Aburdene, *Re-inventing the Corporation*.

76. S. Ghoshal and C. A. Bartlett, "Changing the Role of Top Management: Beyond Structure to Process," *Harvard Business Review* 73 (January/February 1995): 94.

77. R. Lyons, J. Chatman, and C. K. Joyce, "Innovation in Services: Corporate Culture and Investment Banking," *California Management Review* 50, 1 (Fall 2007): 174–191.

78. L. Dube, C. Enz, L. Renaghan, and J. Siguaw, "J. W. Marriott, Jr. Marriott International, Inc.: Overall Best-Practice Individual Champion in Corporate Management," *American Lodging Excellence: The Keys to Best Practices in the U.S. Lodging Industry* (Washington, DC: American Hotel Foundation, 2001).

79. J. A. Pearce II, T. R. Kramer, and D. K. Robbins, "Effects of Managers' Entrepreneurial Behavior on Subordinates," *Journal of Business Venturing* 12 (1997): 147–160.

80. L. Dube, C. Enz, L. Renaghan, and J. Siguaw, "Choice Hotels International: In-House Executive Training and Development," *American Lodging Excellence: The Keys to Best Practices in the U.S. Lodging Industry* (Washington, DC: American Hotel Foundation, 2001): 68–69.

81. R. Lyons, J. Chatman, and C. K. Joyce, "Innovation in Services."

82. Ghoshal and Bartlett, "Changing the Role," 86–96.

83. P. G. Green, C. G. Brush, and M. M. Hart, "The Corporate Venture Champion: A Resource-Based Approach to Role and Process," *Entrepreneurship Theory and Practice* (March 1999): 103–122.

84. Naisbitt and Aburdene, *Re-inventing the Corporation*.

85. "Innovation Key to Success," *Business World*, October 31, 2002.

86. I. Griffiths, "The Accidental Tourist," *The Independent* (September 15, 1999): 1–2.

87. Quinn, "Managing Innovation."

88. Ibid.

89. Ibid.

90. G. Hamel, "Avoiding the Guillotine," *Fortune* (April 2, 2001): 140.

91. Kuratko and Hodgetts, *Entrepreneurship*.

92. L. Dube, C. Enz, L. Renaghan, and J. Siguaw, "The Ritz-Carlton Tysons Corner: Self Directed Work Teams, Job Redesign, and Employee Empowerment," *American Lodging Excellence: The Keys to Best Practices in the U.S. Lodging Industry* (Washington, DC: American Hotel Foundation, 2001).

93. Burgelman, "Designs."

94. "Lessons from a Successful Entrepreneur," *Journal of Business Strategy* (March/April 1988): 20–24.

95. Naisbitt and Aburdene, *Re-inventing the Corporation*.

96. Kuratko and Hodgetts, *Entrepreneurship*.

97. R. Normann, "Organizational Innovativeness: Product Variation and Reorientation," *Administrative Science Quarterly* 16 (1971): 203–215.

98. D. M. DeCarolis and D. L. Deeds, "The Impact of Stocks and Flows of Organizational Knowledge on Firm Performance," *Strategic Management Journal* 20 (1999): 953–968.

99. J. Andrew, H. Sirkin, K. Haanaes, and D. Michael, *Innovation 2007*, 20.

100. P. F. Drucker, "Beyond the Information Revolution," *Atlantic Monthly* (October 1999): 47–57.

101. G. Hamel, "Take It Higher," *Fortune* (February 5, 2001): 169.

102. Salon, "Business As Usual," www.salon.com, May 8, 2000.

103. G. Hamel, "Is This All You Can Build with the Net? Think Bigger," *Fortune* (April 30, 2001): 134–138.

104. "Successful Dot-Com Offers Strategies for Success," Buzzle.com, www.buzzle.com/editorials/10-16-2001-5404.asp (accessed December 31, 2007).

105. G. Hamel, "Edison's Curse," *Fortune* (March 5, 2001): 175.

106. "Google Inc GOOG.O (NASDAQ)," *Reuters*, http://stocks.us.reuters.com/stocks/fullDescription.asp?rpc=66&symbol=GOOG.O (accessed December 31, 2007); "Google Inc.," *Google Finance*, http://finance.google.com/finance?client=ob&q=GOOG (accessed December 31, 2007); "History of Google," *Wikipedia*, http://en.wikipedia.org/wiki/History_of_Google (accessed December 31, 2007).

107. L. Dignan, "The Day Ahead: Can Pets.com's Sock Puppet Save Its Stock?," *ZDnet.co.uk*, http://news.zdnet.co.uk/hardware/0,1000000091,2079355,00.htm (accessed January 1, 2008); "Pets.com," *Wikipedia*, http://en.wikipedia.org/wiki/Pets.com (accessed January 1, 2008).

108. National Commission to Ensure Consumer Information and Choice in the Airline Industry, *Upheaval in Travel Distribution: Impact on Consumers and Travel Agents* (November 12, 2002): 25.

109. M. Shariff, "E-Ticketing Everywhere," *Express computer*, www.expresscomputeronline.com/20071029/market03.shtml (accessed January 1, 2008); "Stats and Facts," *Selfserviceworld.com*, www.selfserviceworld.com/research.php?rc_id=363 (accessed January 1, 2008).

110. J. Joo, "A Business Model and Its Development Strategies for Electronic Tourism Markets," *Information Systems Management* (Summer 2002): 58–69.

111. "Expedia Overview," *Expedia Corporate web site*, http://overview.expediainc.com/phoenix.zhtml?c=190013&p=overview (accessed January 1, 2008); "Expedia Inc.," *Hoovers*, http://premium.hoovers.com.proxy.library.cornell.edu:2048/subscribe/co/overview.xhtml?ID=ffffjrykxfstrxfhrk (accessed January 2, 2008).

112. C. Enz, "Hotel Pricing in a Networked World," *Cornell Hotel and Administration Quarterly* 44 (February 2003): 4–5.

113. M. Rich, "Orbitz to Expand Sales of Rooms in Online Discount-Hotel Market," *The Wall Street Journal* (March 13, 2003): D3.

114. W. Carroll, R. Kwortnik, and N. Rose, "Travel Packaging: An Internet Frontier," *Cornell Hospitality Report* 7, 17 (December 2007).

CHAPTER 10

1. F. Glazer, "NPD: QSR Chains Expanding Globally Must Also Act Locally," *Nation's Restaurant News* 41, 42 (October 22, 2007): 18; D. Roberts, "Starbucks Caffeinates Its China Growth Plan," *Business Week Online* (October 26, 2006): 5; "Starbucks: Is the US Cup Full?" *Drinks Market Watch Datamonitor* (September 2007): 12; S. Holmes, "For Starbucks, There's No Place Like Home," *Business Week* (June 9, 2003): 48; A. Ghosh and S. Chatterjee, "Starbucks to Open in India," *International Herald Tribune*, January 1, 2007, www.iht.com/articles/2007/01/14/bloomberg/sxstarbucks.php (accessed January 3, 2007).

2. J. Walsh, "Patience, Adaptability Help Companies Overseas," *Hotel and Motel Management* 18 (March 2002): 3–4.

3. S. Holmes, "Planet Starbucks to Keep Up the Growth: It Must Go Global Quickly," *Business Week* (September 9, 2002): 100.

4. H. Henzler and W. Rall, "Facing Up to the Globalization Challenge," *McKinsey Quarterly* (Winter 1986): 52–68; T. Peters, "Prometheus Barely Unbound," *Academy of Management Executive* (November 1990): 70–84; M. E. Porter, *Competition in Global Industries* (Boston: Harvard Business School Press, 1986), 2–3; S. Tallman, "Global Strategic Management," in *The Blackwell Handbook of Strategic Management*, eds. M.A. Hitt, R. E. Freeman, and J. S. Harrison (Oxford: Blackwell Publishers, 2001), 464–490.

5. L. Ferguson, "The United Nations World Tourism Organization," *New Political Economy* 12, 4 (December 2007): 557–568.

6. T. Royle, *Working for McDonald's in Europe* (London: Routledge, 2000).

7. K. Strauss, "All Eyes on Asia," *Hotels* 41, 4 (April 2007): 34–40; Walsh, "Patience, Adaptability Help Companies Overseas."

8. D. Litteljohn and A. Roper, "Changes in International Hotel Companies' Strategies," in *Strategic Hospitality Management*, eds. R. Teare and A. Boer (Cassell Educational: London, 1991).

9. "Building Dominant China Brands in Every Category," Yum! Annual Report, 2006, www.yum.com/investors/annualreport/06annualreport/pdf/yum_p01_p07.pdf (accessed January 3, 2007), 2.

10. Tallman, "Global Strategic Management," 464.

11. C.A. Bartlett and S. Ghoshal, "Global Strategic Management: Impact on the New Frontiers of Strategy Research," *Strategic Management Journal* 12 (1991): 5–16.

12. R. Teare, J. Costa, and G. Eccles, "Relating Strategy, Structure and Performance, *Journal of Workplace Learning* 10, 2 (1998): 58–75.

13. K. Ohmae, "Managing in a Borderless World," *Harvard Business Review* 67 (May/June 1989): 152–161.

14. S. P. Douglas and Y. Wind, "The Myth of Globalization," *Columbia Journal of World Business* (Winter 1987): 19–29.

15. R. Smet, "McDonald's: A Strategy of Cross-cultural Approach," *The Journal of Language of International Business* 12, 1 (2002): 11–21.

16. M. A. Hitt, R. D. Ireland, and R. E. Hoskisson, *Strategic Management: Competitiveness and Globalization* (Minneapolis, MN: West Publishing, 1995).

17. R. Hallowell, D. Bowen, and C. Knoop, "Four Seasons Goes to Paris," *Academy of Management Executive* 16, 4 (2002): 10.

18. Some of the options contained in this list were based on information found in Sheth and Eshghi, *Global Strategic Management Perspectives*.

19. "World Development Report 2002 Building Institutions for Markets" (Washington, DC: The World Bank Oxford University Press, 2002).

20. Slattery and Boer, "Strategic Developments for the 1990s."

21. "Aloha! The New Twist in Travel Arrives in India," *Starwood Hotels & Resorts web site*, www.starwoodhotels.com/corporate/company_info.html (accessed January 11, 2008).

22. T. Royle, *Working for McDonald's in Europe: The Unequal Struggle?* (London: Routledge, 2000).

23. "Corporate 300," *Hotels*, 38.

24. H. G. Barkema and F. Vermeulen, "International Expansion through Start-up or Acquisition: A Learning Perspective," *Academy of Management Journal* 41 (1998): 7–26; C.W. L. Hill, P. Hwang, and W. C. Kim, "An Eclectic Theory of the Choice of International Entry Mode," *Strategic Management Journal* 11 (1990): 117–128; C.W. L. Hill and G. R. Jones, *Strategic Management: An Integrated Approach* (Boston: Houghton Mifflin, 1992), 254–259; R. Schmidgall, *Hospitality Industry Managerial Accounting*, 4th ed. (Washington, DC: Educational Institute, American Hotel and Motel Association, 1997).

25. J. Walsh, "Accor Shifts Focus to Franchising," *Hotel & Motel Management* 19(May 17, 2003): 3.

26. K. Strauss, "Hotels' 325: Globalization Has Created a Smaller World and Larger Hotel Portfolios as the Biggest Chains Continue Their Worldwide Expansion Plans, *Hotels*, www.hotelsmag.com/archives/2007/07/sr/default.asp (accessed January 9, 2008).

27. "Aloha! The New Twist in Travel Arrives in India," *Starwood Hotels & Resorts web site*, www.starwoodhotels.com/corporate/company_info.html (Accessed January 11, 2008).

28. "KFC, Russian Chain Debut Co-Brand Outlet, Plan 300," *BNET web site*, http://findarticles.com/p/articles/mi_m3190/is_16_40/ai_n16130374 (accessed January 11, 2008).

29. L. Polly, "International Growth Patterns Remain Strong," *Franchising World* (April 2002): 6.

30. "Lotus Hotel Investment Fund Spurs Carlson Asia Growth," *China Hospitality News*, October 11, 2007, www.chinahospitalitynews.com/2007/10/11/4779-lotus-hotel-investment-fund-spurs-carlson-asia-growth (accessed January 10, 2008).

31. "Full Year 2007 Guidance Update," *Yum! Brands web site*, http://investors.yum.com/phoenix.zhtml?c=117941&p=irol- (accessed January 11, 2008); Yum! Brands 2006 Annual Report.

32. F. Steed, "It's a Small, Small World: Growing Your Brand Globally," *Franchising World* (November/December 2001): 14–15.

33. Ibid.

34. U.S. Department of Commerce.

35. J. F. Preble, A. Reichel, and R. C. Hoffman, "Strategic Alliances for Competitive Advantage: Evidence from Israel's Hospitality and Tourism Industry," *Hospitality Management* 19 (2000): 327.

36. F. Contractor and S. Kundu, "Franchising versus Company-run Operations: Modal Choice in the Global Hotel Sector," *Journal of International Marketing* (1998): 28–53.

37. T. Cruz, "Speed to Market," *Hotels* (February 1998): 40.

38. Contractor and Kundu, "Franchising versus Company-run Operations."

39. J. Walsh, "Franchisors Piece Together Worldwide Master Licenses," *Hotel and Motel Management* (September 17, 2001): 62.

40. Ibid.

41. "TT Resources Bags Deal," *Business Times* (September 16, 2002): 14.

42. A. C. Inkpen, "Learning and Knowledge Acquisition through International Strategic Alliances," *Academy of Management Executive* 12, 4 (1998): 69.

43. Walsh, "Franchisors Piece Together Worldwide Master Licenses; 'Corporate 300'," *Hotels* (July 2003): 37.

44. T. Kamm and J. Friedland, "Spanish Firms Discover Latin America Business As New World of Profit," *The Wall Street Journal* (May 23, 1996): A1, A9.

45. C. J. Whalen, P. Magnusson, and G. Smith, "NAFTA's Scorecard: So Far, So Good," *Business Week* (July 9, 2001): 54–56.

46. P. Alisau, "NAFTA Fuels Growth in Meeting Facilities," *Incentive* (April 1997): 92.

47. B. Serlen, "Hilton Forges Latin America Expansion Front," *Hotel Business* 16, 24 (December 21, 2007–January 6, 2008): 3.

48. L. Kraar, "Asia 2000," *Fortune* (October 5, 1992): 111.

49. K. H. Zhang, "What Attracts Foreign Multinational Corporations to China?" *Contemporary Economic Policy* 19 (2001): 336–346.

50. D. Fairlamb and G. Edmondson, "Out from under the Table," *Business Week* (September 24, 2001): 116–119.

51. A. Spicer, G. A. McDermott, and B. Kogut, "Entrepreneurship and Privatization in Central Europe: The Tenuous Balance between Destruction and Creation," *Academy of Management Review* 25 (2000): 630–649; S. Ogden and R. Watson, "Corporate Performance and Stakeholder Management: Balancing Shareholder and Customer Interests in the U.K. Privatized Water Industry," *Academy of Management Journal* 42 (1999): 526–538; M. Johnson, "Germany Gets a Makeover," *Global Finance* 14, 11 (November 2000): 31–39.

52. L. Hayes, "Love American Style: European Market Embraces US Restaurant Chains," *Nation's Restaurant News* 17 (August 1998): 47–49.

53. "About Jin Jiang," *Jin Jiang web site*, www.jinjianghotels.com/portal/en/ab_ji_ji_view.asp?did=2429 (accessed January 20, 2008); "China's Economy Hotel Business: Is It Too Hot?" *Knowledge@Wharton*, http://knowledge.wharton.upenn.edu (accessed January 20, 2008).

54. L. Hall, ed., *New Europe and the Hotel Industry* (London: Price Waterhouse Coopers Hospitality and Leisure Research, 2000).

55. F. Glazer, "NPD: QSR Chains expanding globally must also act locally," *Nation's Restaurant News* 41, 42 (October 22, 2007): 18.

56. P. Windolf, "The Governance Structure of Large French Corporations: A Comparative Perspective," paper presented at the Sloan Project on Corporate Governance at Columbia Law School, May 1998.

57. Laurent-Perrier Champagne web site, www.laurentperrierus.com/about/biographies.htm (accessed January 29, 2008).

58. R. E. Hoskisson et al., "Restructuring Strategies of Diversified Business Groups: Difference Associated with Country Institutional Environments," in *The Blackwell Handbook of Strategic Management*, eds. M. A. Hitt, R. E. Freeman, and J. S. Harrison (Oxford: Blackwell Publishers, 2001), 433–463.

59. A. McWilliams, D. D. Van Fleet, and P. M. Wright, "Strategic Management of Human Resources for Global Competitive Advantage," *Journal of Business Strategies* 18, 1 (Spring 2001): 1–24.

60. P. Gupte, "Venture Capitalist to the Poor," *Forbes* 31 (May 1999): 58–60.

61. M. E. Porter, *The Competitive Advantage of Nations* (New York: The Free Press, 1990).

62. "World Development Report 2002 Building Institutions for Markets."

63. Porter, *The Competitive Advantage of Nations*.

64. Ferguson, "The United Nations World Tourism Organization."

65. K. Strauss, "Hotels' 325."

66. Walsh, "Patience, Adaptability Help Companies Overseas."

67. T. Royle, *Working for McDonald's in Europe*.

68. J. Walsh, "Market Analysis Determines Brand Location," *Hotel and Motel Management*, (May 19, 2003): 218.

69. L. Altinay and A. Roper, "The Role and Importance of Development Directors in Initiating and Implementing Development Strategy," *International Journal of Contemporary Hospitality Management* 13, 7 (2001): 339–346.

70. M. Muller, "Employee Representation and Pay in Austria, Germany, and Sweden," *International Studies of Management and Organization* 29, 4 (2000): 67–83; R. Calori and B. Dufour, "Management European Style," *Academy of Management Executive* (August 1995): 61–73.

71. P. C. Earley and S. Ang, *Cultural Intelligence: An Analysis of Individual Interactions across Cultures* (Palo Alto, CA: Stanford University Press, 2003).

72. M. Bush, "World Class Hospitality," *Lodging Hospitality* 63, 15 (October 2007): 34–42.

73. S. Tully, "The Hunt for the Global Manager," *Fortune* (May 21, 1990): 140–144; J. Main, "How 21 Men Got Global in 35 Days," *Fortune* (November 6, 1989): 71.

74. M. Maruyama, "Changing Dimensions in International Business," *Academy of Management Executive* (August 1992): 88–96.

75. C. Solomon, "When Training Doesn't Translate," *Workforce* 76, 3 (March 1997): 40.

76. J. Watson, *Golden Arches East: McDonald's in East Asia* (Stanford, CA: Stanford University Press, 1997).

77. "Hotels Halted," *Business Today* (Egypt), August 13, 2003: 11.

78. K. Strauss, "All Eyes on Asia," *Hotels* 41, 4 (April 2007): 34–40.

79. N. Weilheimer, "Starwood Expands Property in China," *Commercial Property News* (June 1, 2003): 3.

80. B. Serlen, "Starwood, Marriott, Hilton Enter or Expand in Asia," *Business Travel News* 24 (March 2003): 15.

81. M. Erdly and L. Kesterson-Townes, Experience Rules: PWC Consulting's Vision for the Hospitality and Leisure Industry, Circa 2010 (New York: PWC Consulting, Transforming Futures Series, 2002).

82. Ibid.

83. G. Hamel, *Leading the Revolution* (Boston: Harvard Business School Press, 2000).

84. G. Hamel, "The Challenge Today: Changing the Rules of the Game," *Business Strategy Review* 9, 2 (1998): 19–26.

85. Special thanks goes to Dr. Daphne A. Jameson of Cornell University, who developed this intercultural communications simulation and has graciously given permission for its use in this textbook.

CASE 1

1. The interview data on which this case study is based were collected in December 2004. In addition to publicly available secondary data sources, interviews of 45 to 90 minutes in length were conducted with 16 Carnival Cruise Lines executives at the company's Miami headquarters before and after my participating in a four-day product experience aboard the Carnival *Fascination*. While onboard the *Fascination*, four of the ship's officers were also interviewed. The data record consists of more than 350 pages of single-space interview transcripts, as well as field notes, photographs, and proprietary cruise documents and records provided by the company.

2. Tons refers to gross registered tonnage (GRT), the volume of space within the hull of a ship, or a ship's total internal capacity (1 vessel ton = 100 cubic feet).

3. Kristoffer Garin, *Devils on the Deep Blue Sea* (New York: Viking, 2005).

4. Cruise ship passenger capacity is measured by the number of lower berths or beds, which is typically two per cabin.

5. See: Roger Cartright and Carolyn Baird, *The Development and Growth of the Cruise Industry* (Oxford, UK: Butterworth Heinemann, 1999); Douglas Ward, *Berlitz Ocean Cruising and Cruise Ships 2005* (London: Berlitz, 2005); and Bob Dickinson and Andy Vladimir, *Selling the Sea: An Inside Look at the Cruise Industry* (New York: John Wiley, 1997).

6. Cruise Lines International Association, *Spring 2005 Industry Overview*, www.cruising.org/press/overview/2.cfm.

7. *Ibid*; and Garin, *Devils on the Deep Blue Sea*.

8. The North American cruise market is estimated to constitute 80 percent of the global cruise market. See: Cruise Lines International Association (CLIA), *Five Year Cruise Industry Capacity Outlook* (New York: CLIA, March 2005); and *Mintel Reports: Cruises – US – April 2005* (Mintel International Group Limited, 2005). Unless otherwise noted, references to the cruise market in this case study refer to the North American market.

9. Garin, *Devils on the Deep Blue Sea*.

10. Passenger carrying numbers are calculated as basis 2 (double occupancy), given that cruise ship cabins typically have two lower berths. Because some cabins also feature pull-down bunks, foldout sofas, or roll-away beds, maximum ship capacity can exceed by 25 percent the basis-2 capacity. Cruise lines frequently report occupancies greater than 100 percent, a statistic that uses the basis-2 capacity. Unless otherwise noted, the basis-2 ship capacity is used here.

11. Cruise News: Royal Caribbean International Receives Top Marketing Honor, www.cruise411.com/cruise_buzz/feature_article.asp?article_ID=360 (accessed August 10, 2005).

12. Royal Caribbean International press release, "Freedom Is—Where the Ocean Comes to Play," www.royalcaribbean.com/pressroom (accessed August 3, 2005).

13. Dickinson and Vladimir, *Selling the Sea*, p. 174.

14. Ward, *Berlitz Ocean Cruising and Cruise Ships*, p. 128.

15. Heidi Sarna, "Movie Stars under the Stars Just One of New Ship's Perks," *Travel Weekly*, April 19, 2004, p. 16.

16. Carnival Cruise Lines News Release, "New Carnival Liberty to Feature Massive 270-Square-Foot Outdoor TV Screen," May 20, 2005, www.carnival.com/CMS/Articles/liberty_led.aspx (accessed August 3, 2005).

17. NCL News, "Norwegian Cruise Line Announces Next-Generation Newbuild Featuring New "Freestyle Cruising," April 14, 2000, www.ncl.come/news/pr/pr000414a.html (accessed August 10, 2005).

18. "Carnival's Total Choice Dining—Cruising's Most Comprehensive Dining Program," July 15, 2005, Virtual Press Kits, www.carnival.com/CMS/Articles/dining_virtual2.aspx (accessed August 10, 2005).

19. Rebecca Tobin, "Report: Ships Need Brand-aid," *Travel Weekly* (June 7, 2004): 1, 58.

20. Dickinson and Vladimir, *Selling the Sea*, p. 32.

21. Sources: Author's calculations based on published Carnival cruise fares and the CLIA 2005 Cruise Market Profile available at www.cruising.org.

22. Ward, *Berlitz Ocean Cruising and Cruise Ships*.

23. Industry averages are from CLIA; Carnival averages are from Carnival sources.

24. Carnival Press Release, "Carnival to Launch New Multimillion-Dollar Ad Campaign Designed to Convey Product Enhancements," December 6, 2004, www.carnival.com/CMS/Articles/new_adcampaign.aspx, (accessed August 17, 2005).

CASE 2

1. Real estate investment trusts are corporations that pay no income tax on their earnings (similar to a mutual fund) so long as they pay 95 percent or more of their profits to shareholders. REITs provide the advantages of corporate ownership to shareholders but also offer tax advantages. As a result, REITs have become very attractive to many investors.

CASE 3

1. InterContinental, News release, September 24, 2006, www.ihgplc.com.

2. Ibid.

3. Ibid.

4. InterContinental, Strategy page, August 13, 2006, www.ihgplc.com/aboutus/strategy.asp.

5. InterContinental, December 17, 2007, www.ichotelsgroup.com/h/d/6c/1/en/hotel-directory/china.

6. InterContinental, News release, September 9, 2006, www.ihgplc.com.

7. J. P. Pederson, ed., *International Directory of Company Histories*, Vol. 38 (Detroit, MI: St. James Press, 2001).

8. D. Atkinson, "Bass to Sell Crest Group to Concentrate on Holiday Inns," *The Guardian* (London), March 1, 1990.

9. S. Butler, "Bass Pays 55 M [Pds] for Four Holiday Inn Hotels," *Financial Times* (London), May 22, 1987.

10. D. Churchill, "Bass Buys a Holiday Inn Hotel Chain for 475 M," *Financial Times* (London), September 16, 1987.

11. Six Continents, History Page, November 15, 2002, www.sixcontinents.com/aboutus/history.htm.

12. G. Strauss, "Holiday Inns Sold; Britain's Bass to Buy Chain for $2.23 B," *USA Today*, August 25, 1989.

13. K. Wilson and R. Kerr, *Half Luck, Half Brains: The Kemmons Wilson Holiday Inn Story* (Nashville, TN: Hambleton-Hill, 1996).

14. Pederson, ed., *International Directory*.

15. InterContinental, History page, August 13, 2006, www.ihgplc.com/baoutus/history.asp.

16. A. Yates, "Bass to Snap Up Inter-Continental with Pounds 1.7 bn Offer," *The Independent* (London), February 21, 1998.

17. C. Seward, "Holiday Inn Parent Buying Luxury Chain," *The Atlanta Journal and Constitution*, February 25, 1998.

18. A. Clark, "Bass Falls to Interbrew," *The Guardian* (London), June 15, 2000.

19. A. Osbourne, "End of an Era as Bass Name Makes Way for Six Continents," *The Daily Telegraph* (London), June 28, 2001.

20. Hotel Business, November 15, 2002, www.hotelbusiness.com/links/archive/archive.

21. InterContinental, History page, August 13, 2006, www.ihgplc.com/baoutus/history.asp.

22. Ibid.

23. Ibid.

24. E. Zheng, "Lido Fengcai," *China Entrepreneur*, Issue 3, 1994.

25. X. Ren, "Beijing Lido Hotel," *Foreign Investment in China*, July 1995.

26. L. Yu, "Hotel Development and Structures in China," *International Journal of Hospitality Management*, 11, 2 (1992).

27. InterContinental, News release, September 10, 2006, www.ihgplc.com.

28. InterContinental, News release, September 9, 2006, www.ihgplc.com.

29. Ibid.

30. InterContinental, News release, September 10, 2006, www.ihgplc.com.

31. Ibid.

32. Ibid.

33. InterContinental, News release, September 9, 2006, www.ihgplc.com.

34. InterContinental, News release, August 13, 2006, www.ihgplc.com.

35. InterContinental, News release, August 13, 2006, www.ihgplc.com.

36. InterContinental, News release, September 9, 2006, www.ihgplc.com.

37. China Tourists Hotels Association, November 24, 2007, www.ctha.com.cn/zuixinzixun/content.asp?newsid=2973.

38. J. Zhao, "Overprovision in Chinese Hotels", *Tourism Management*, 10, 1 (1989).

39. L. Yu, "Hotel Development and Structures in China," *International Journal of Hospitality Management*, 11, 2 (1992).

40. InterContinental, Strategy page, August 13, 2006, www.ihgplc.com/aboutus/strategy.asp.

41. National Bureau of Statistic of China, November 25, 2007, www.stats.gov.cn/tjsj/ndsj/2006/html/B0203e.htm.

42. National Bureau of Statistics of China, Statistical Communique of the People's Republic of China on the 2000 National Economic and Social Development, September 24, 2006, www.stats.gov.cn/tjgb/ndtjgb/qgndtjgb/t20060227_402307796.htm.

43. National Bureau of Statistic of China, November 26, 2007, www.stats.gov.cn/tjgb/ndtjgb/qgndtjgb/t20070228_402387821.htm.

44. National Bureau of Statistic of China, November 26, 2007, www.stats.gov.cn/tjfx/ztfx/sqd/t20070918_402433210.htm.

45. World Trade Organization, November 26, 2007, www.wto.org/english/news_e/spp133_e.htm.

46. National Bureau of Statistic of China, November 26, 2007, www.stats.gov.cn/tjsj/ndsj/2006/html/B0203e.htm.

47. National Bureau of Statistic of China, November 26, 2007, www.stats.gov.cn/tjgb/ndtjgb/qgndtjgb/t20070228_402387821.htm.

48. L. Yu, "Hotel Development and Structures in China."

49. G. He, ed., *Research on Tourism as a New Growth Point for the National Economy* (Beijing: China Tourism Publishing House, 1999).

50. China National Tourism Administration (CNTA), *The Yearbook of China Tourism Statistics*, 1996–2007 (Beijing: China Travel and Tourism Press, 2007).

51. G. He, ed., *Research on Tourism.*

52. Ibid.

53. China National Tourism Administration (CNTA), *The Yearbook of China Tourism Statistics*, 1999–2007 (Beijing: China Travel and Tourism Press, 2007).

54. China National Tourism Administration (CNTA), November 26, 2007, www.cnta.gov.cn/news_detail/newsshow.asp?id=A20071023110273962782.

55. J. Harrison and C. Enz, *Hospitality Strategic Management: Concepts and Cases*, (Hoboken, NJ: John Wiley & Sons, 2005).

56. M. Hitt, R. Ireland, and R. Hoskisson, *Strategic Management* (Mason: South-Western, 2003).

57. InterContinental, "IHG in China," November 2007.

58. InterContinental Annual Report, 2003, p.10.

59. InterContinental Interim Report, 2007, p. 6.

60. InterContinental Annual Report, 2003, p.12.

61. Ibid.

62. InterContinental Interim Report, 2007, p. 11.

63. InterContinental, Financial page, September 2006, www.ichothelgroup.com.

64. InterContinental Interim Report, 2007, p. 8.

65. InterContinental, "IHG in China," November 2007.

66. Ibid.

67. InterContinental, Financial page, September 2006, www.ichothelgroup.com.

68. InterContinental Annual Report, 2003, p.14.

69. L. Yu, "Hotel Development and Structures in China."

70. Beijing Hotel, December 16, 2007, news.bjhotel.cn/hotelnews/html/J7111/200702/10103585.html.

71. L. Yu, "Hotel Development and Structures in China."

72. Accor and Super 8 web sites, November 2007.

73. China Tourists Hotels Association, Z. Zhang, "Operation and Management Analysis of Foreign Funded and Joint Venture Hotels in China," September 16, 2006, www.ctha.com.cn/zuixinzixun/content.asp?newsid=1135.

74. Beijing Tourism Group, www.btg.com.cn; Shanghai Jinjiang Group, www.jinjianghotels.com.cn, November, 2007.

75. Ibid.

76. InterContinental, November 24, 2007, www.ihgplc.com/index.asp?PageID=116&NewsID=1788.

77. CNTA *The Yearbook of China Tourism Statistics*, 1999–2007.

78. China Tourists Hotels Association, Z. Zhang.

79. Ibid.

80. L. Yu, "Hotel Development and Structures in China."

81. R. Pine, "China's Hotel Industry," *Cornell Hotel and Restaurant Administration Quarterly*, 43, 3 (2002).

82. L. Yu and H. Gu, "Hotel Reform in China."

83. China Tourists Hotels Association, Z. Zhang.

84. Hotel web site, September 2006.

85. China Tourists Hotels Association, Z. Zhang.

86. CNTA *The Yearbook of China Tourism Statistics*.

87. F. Tang et al., "Ownership, Corporate Governance, and Management in the State-owned Hotels in the People's Republic of China," *Cornell Hotel and Restaurant Administration Quarterly*, 47, 2 (2006).

88. Ibid.

89. China Tourist Hotels Association, *China Hotel Industry Study 2006* (Beijing: China Travel & Tourism Press, 2006).

90. InterContinental, Strength page, August 13, 2006, www.ihgplc.com/aboutus/strengths.asp.

91. China Tourists Hotels Association, August 22, 2006, www.ctha.org.cn/zuixinzixun/content.asp?newsid=1954.

92. InterContinental, December 17, 2007, www.ichotelsgroup.com/h/d/6c/1/en/hotel-directory/china.

93. J. Kivela and L.F. Leung, Doing business in the People's Republic of China, *Cornell Hotel and Restaurant Administration Quarterly*, Volume 46, Issue 2.

94. InterContinental, "IHG in China," November 2007.

95. J. Child and Y. Lu, *Management Issues in China*, Volume II (New York: Routledge, 1996), p. 70.

96. China Tourist Hotels Association, China Hotel Industry Study 2006.

97. InterContinental, News release, September 10, 2006, www.ihgplc.com.

98. InterContinental, News release, September 9, 2006, www.ihgplc.com.

99. Rednet. com, September 3, 2006, http://house.rednet.com.cn/html/2006/02/07/HOUSEHTML20060207102220-1.html.

100. InterContinental, News release, September 9, 2006, www.ihgplc.com.

101. InterContinental, Strength page, August 13, 2006, www.ihgplc.com/aboutus/strengths.asp.

102. InterContinental, November 24, 2007, www.ihgplc.com/index.asp?PageID=116&NewsID=1788.

103. Jingjiang Hotels, August 23, 2006, www.jinjianghotels.com/portal/cn/ab_ji_ji.asp?did=884.

104. StarWood Hotels, September 26, 2006, www.starwoodhotels.com/stregis/index.html.

105. Wall Street Journal, December 17, 2007, http://online.wsj.com/public/article_print/SB119680945098713628.html.

106. Smith Travel Research, November 24, 2007, http://str.hsyndicate.com/news/4033831.html.

107. Super 8 China, www.super8.com.cn/cn/about_us.htm.

108. China Tourist Hotels Association, November 24, 2007, www.ctha.com.cn/zuixinzixun/content.asp?newsid=2972.

109. E. Zheng, "Lido Fengcai," *China Entrepreneur*, 3, 1994.

110. "InterContinental Group to more than Double China Hotels by 2008," Asia Intelligence Wire, July 18, 2006.

111. "Saturday Interview with Andrew Cosslett," *The New York Times*, July 1, 2006.

112. Hotel online, November 7, 2007, www.hotle-online.com/News/PR2007_4th/Oct07_HIRelaunch.html.

113. China National Tourism Organization, November 26, 2007, www.cnta.gov.cn/news_detail/newsshow.asp?id=A2007 115956223578241.

114. National Bureau of Statistics of China, December 15, 2007, www.stats.gov.cn/english/newsandcomingevents/t20071212_402451565.htm.

115. National Bureau of Statistics of China, December 15, 2007, www.stats.gov.cn/english/newsandcomingevents/t20071213_402451902.htm.

116. China National Tourism Administration, December 15, 2007, www.cnta.gov.cn/news_detail/newsshow.asp?id=A20071213132264814667.

117. T. Lam and M. X. J. Han, "A Study of Outsourcing Strategy: A Case Involving the Hotel Industry in Shanghai, China," *International Journal of Hospitality Management*, 24, 1 (2005).

118. United Nations World Tourism Organization, September 29, 2006, www.mahaon.net/newsroom/Releases/2003/september/china.htm.

119. China insight, December 15, 2007, www.chinainsight.info/june2007/june2007_china_travel_destination.htm.

120. Hotel Online, November 6, 2007, www.hotel-online.com/News/PR2007_4th/Oct07/AsiaConstruction.html.

121. InterContinental, "IHG in China," November 2007.

122. Starwood Hotels, September 26, 2006, www.starwoodhotels.com.

123. Accor, www.accorhotels-asia.com.

124. Smith Travel Research, October 25, 2006, http://str.hsyndicate.com/news/4029204.html.

125. JJ-Inn, December 17, 2007, www.jj-inn.com/COMPANYINFO/intro.aspx

126. China Hotels Research-Online, December 17, 2007, www.chr-online.com/zhuanti/2007bjdh.htm.

127. China Tourist Hotels Association, November 24, 2007, www.ctha.com.cn/zuixinzixun/content.asp?newsid=2972.

CASE 4

1. B. E. Kaufman, *The Origins and Evolution of the Field of Industrial Relations in the United States* (Ithaca, NY: ILR Press, 1993).

2. Ibid.

3. K. Bronfenbrenner and R. Hickey, "Winning is Possible: Successful Union Organizing in the United States—Clear Lessons, Too Few Examples," *Multinational Monitor* 24, 6 (2003).

4. P. T. Osterman, T. A. Kochan, et al., *Working in America: A Blueprint for the New Labor Market* (Cambridge, MA: MIT Press, 2001).

5. Ibid., 46.

6. B. T. Hirsch and A. D. Macpherson, Union Membership and Coverage Database from the Current Population Survey, 2004. The Union Membership and Coverage Database from the CPS is updated on the web at www.unionstats.com. The updated statistics of Hirsch and Macpherson's work may be found here. See also www.bls.gov/news.release/union2.t03.htm.

7. Osterman and Kochan, et al., 62.

8. G. Garrett, "Globalization and Government Spending around the World," *Studies in Comparative and International Development* 35, 4 (2001).

9. J. Bhagwati, A. Panagariya, and T. N. Srinivasan, "The Muddles over Outsourcing," *The Journal of Economic Perspectives* 18, 4 (2006).

10. www.unitehere.org

11. *N.L.R.B. v. Town & Country Elec. Inc.*, 516 U.S. 85 (1995).

12. *See* www.nlrb.gov/nlrb/legal/manuals/rules/act.asp for the full text of the NLRA.

13. Interview with Richard Hurd, professor of labor relations, Cornell University School of Industrial and Labor Relations, on June 28, 2001. Frankly, this is a conservative estimate based on conversations the authors have had with union officials over the past seven years. Some assert that the percentage of employees the union considers supporters (based on authorization card signatures) is between 75 and 90 percent.

14. A bargaining order is an NLRB mandate requiring a company to "cease and desist from their unfair labor practices, to offer reinstatement and back pay to the employees who had been discriminatorily discharged, to bargain with the union on request, and to post the appropriate notices." *National Labor Relations Board v. Gissel Packing Co.*, 395 U.S. 575, 585 (1969).

15. Employers typically raise some or all of the following issues, based in part on advice from counsel and from their unique circumstances, industry, and employee demographics:

Whether unions can guarantee increased pay, benefits, or anything else

How collective bargaining really works

What happens when strikes are called or picketing is conducted

What it costs to be a union member in terms of dues and initiation fees; where that money goes; how it is used, and by whom

Whether the union's leaders are trustworthy and capable

The employer's record of responsiveness to employee issues

The fact that employees will be paying someone to do what they may have been able to do (represent themselves) for free

Whether the organizing drive has actually been beneficial in the sense that it has called attention to problems that need to be addressed whether the union is there or not

Whether the employer should make management changes (because an organizing drive seems to have been triggered by a perceived lack of leadership)

16. Surveys of union organizers and employees who have been through NLRB election campaigns seem to confirm this trend at least indirectly. *See*, for example, American Rights at Work survey (2006) and survey reported by Bronfenbrenner and Hickey, "Winning Is Possible."

17. www.americanrightsatwork.org/press/press.cfm?pressReleaseID=33

18. M. Hughlett, "Hotel Worker's Union in St. Paul, Minn., Plans New Tack (sic) in Organizing," Hotel Online, June 20, 2001, www.hotel-online.com/neo/news/2001_June_22/k.SPH.993243589.html (quoting Jaye Rykunyk, head of HERE Local 17).

19. www.changetowin.org

20. While most agreements define neutrality, the definitions vary widely. Most Communication Workers of America, United Auto Workers, and USWA agreements define neutrality as "neither helping nor hindering" the union's organizing effort, yet still allow employers to communicate facts to the employees. A different approach is apparent from the HERE agreements that prohibit the employer from communicating any opposition to the union. Less-typical definitions declare that management will make an affirmative statement to their employees that it welcomes their choice of a representative. See A. E. Eaton and J. Kreisky, "Union Organizing under Neutrality and Card Check Agreements," *Industrial and Labor Relations Review* 55, 1 (2001), pp. 42–59.

21. Agreements may state that (1) the employer will not attack or demean the union; (2) the employer will not refer to the union as a third party; (3) the parties will strive to create a campaign free of fear, hostility, and coercion; (4) the parties will campaign in a positive manner; (5) the parties will keep their statements pro-company or pro-union; and (6) the employer will not state that it is corporate policy to avoid unionization. See: Eaton and Kreisky, p. 9.

22. Eaton and Kreisky, p. 8.

23. *Lechmere, Inc. v. NLRB*, 502 U.S. 527 (1992). *See also*: Phelps Dodge Corp., 177 NLRB 531 (1969).

24. Eaton, p. 15.

25. *See Aeroground, Inc. v. City and County of San Francisco*, N.D. Cal., No. C-01-1628VRW, injunction granted July 9, 2001. Where the city established a labor peace rule that required any employer that leased, subleased, contracted, or subcontracted with SFO to agree to a card-check authorization procedure with any union that initiated a representation request. The union also had to register with the airport director.

26. Employers do hope that either Congress or the Courts will strike down neutrality agreements. Section 302 of the Labor Management Relations Act prohibits unions and employers from giving each other a "thing of value." The reason for this prohibition seems clear. The drafters of the law did not want unions and employers to exchange favors so that their loyalty was to each other at the expense of the employees. While there is limited case law on what the term of *thing of value* means under Section 302, it seems that the term covers fairly minor "deals."

In *U.S. v. Schiffman*, the question before the court was whether the request for a reduced room rate constituted a thing of value and thus violated Section 302. In that case, a union official who represented a bargaining unit at a Hyatt property in Florida requested that an Atlanta Hyatt provide the official with a room rate that was almost 50 percent less than Hyatt's corporate rate. The court found that the room-rate reduction was a "thing of value" and that the requested favor violated Section 302.

Similarly, in *U.S. v. Boffa*, the court found that an employer unlawfully provided a thing of value when it provided a union official with the use of a car without charge for a four-month period. This seemingly broad definition of "thing of value" in Section 302 is consistent with the judicial interpretation of the same term when it is found in other statutes.

Based on these cases one could argue that a neutrality agreement constitutes a thing of value. Indeed, neutrality agreements almost always require the employer to provide at least four things could be characterized by the courts as things of value: (1) access to the hotel's premises so the union can speak to the employees, (2) a list of employees (often with addresses), (3) a card-check provision, and (4) exclusivity to one union. If any of those are benefits that constitute a thing of value, the typical neutrality agreement would violate Section 302 of the LMRA.

Armed with these arguments, the employees of Heartland Industries in Ohio sought to have a neutrality agreement signed by their employer declared unlawful. These employees did not, however, prevail. In *Patterson v. Heartland Industrial Partners, LLP*, 225 FRD 204 (ND Ohio 2004), the Northern District Court in Ohio, relaying the Third Circuit's reasoning in *Hotel Employees Local 57 v. Sage Hospitality*, 3rd Cir. 299 F. Supp 2d 461 (2004), ruled that the neutrality agreement was not a "thing of value" under Section 302, and accordingly granted the defendants' summary judgment motion dismissing the action. The agreement at issue in that case provided that the employer would cooperate with the union during its organizing campaign by providing the union with employee names and addresses and access to the workplace, and a pledge to not speak negatively about the union. The agreement also described terms of a first contract in the event that the union's campaign was successful.

The Patterson case does not end the legal debate over neutrality agreements, and there is a chance that the current NLRB (made up of a majority of George W. Bush appointees) or the conservative-leaning Supreme Court could, in fact, make neutrality agreements unlawful in the future. In addition, there have been two bills before Congress that seek to legislate card-check recognition. The Secret Ballot Protection Act mandates an NLRB-supervised secret-ballot election in all union-organizing campaigns, while a competing bill championed by the AFL-CIO, the Employee Free Choice Act, would require the Board to certify a union as the bargaining representative through a card-check process. The latter proposed Act also provides for mandatory mediation and arbitration.

CASE 5

1. S$1 = US$0.63 monthly average in August 2006.

2. This figure was revised to 26 by August 2006.

3. An "experiential brand" is defined as a brand that emphasizes "The experience customers can have surrounding the purchase, use or ownership of a good" or service. B. J. Pine and J. H. Gilmore *The Experience Economy* (HBS Press, 1999), 17.

4. An "aspirational brand" is defined as one that a consumer segment has exposure to and wishes to own/experience, but for economic or supply reasons cannot; the product/service associated with the brand has certain positive characteristics to the consumer, and there is a fair probability that at a certain point in the future, the consumer can own/experience it. Wikipedia, http://en.wikipedia.org/wiki/Aspirational_brand (accessed January 5, 2007).

5. Banyan Tree Group web site, www.banyantree.com/greenimperative/index.htm (accessed January 5, 2007).

6. IPO Document, p. 3.

7. S$1 = US$0.61 monthly average in March 2006.

8. IPO Document, p. 53.

9. Bt1 = US$0.027

10. IPO Document, p. 51.

11. S$1 = US$0.57 annual average in 2003.

12. S$1 = US$0.59 annual average in 2004.

13. S$1 = US$0.60 annual average in 2005.

14. IPO Document, p. 51.

15. G. Warden, "Inside Asia: Banyan Tree Hit by Another Wave," *The Edge* Singapore, October 9, 2006.

16. S$1 = US$0.63 monthly average in May 2006.

17. G. Warden, G., "Inside Asia."

18. Ibid.

19. Amanresorts web site, www.amanresorts.com (accessed January 5, 2006).

20. B. Fearis, "The 'Aman Junkies' Get a New Fix in Caribbean," *The Observer*, April 16, 2006.

21. "Best of the Best: Spas," Robb Report, www.robbreport.com/Articles/Leisure/Relaxation-Rejuvenation/Best-of-the-Best-Spas .asp (Accessed January 5, 2007).

22. Six Senses Hotels & Resorts web site, www.sixsenses.com/corporate/document/company_profile.pdf (accessed January 5, 2007).

23. Four Seasons Hotels & Resorts web site, www.fourseasons.com/about_us/aboutus_10.html (accessed January 5, 2007).

24. Ibid.

25. A. Klan, "Shangri-La Hotels Look to China, India for Growth," *The Australian*, May 11, 2006.

26. "Shangri-La Begins Aggressive Expansion," *Financial Times*, February 27, 2006.

27. A. Klan, "Shangri-La Hotels."

28. E. Harsha and E. Chacko, "Positioning a Tourism Destination to Gain a Competitive Edge," *Asia Pacific Journal of Tourism Research*, 1997, www.hotel-online.com/Neo/Trends/AsiaPacificJournal/PositionDestination.html (accessed December 20, 2006).

29. A. Singh, "Asia Pacific Tourism Industry: Current Trends and Future Outlook," *Asia Pacific Journal of Tourism Research*, 1997, www. hotel-online.com/Neo/Trends/AsiaPacificJournal/AsiaPacificTourismOutlook_1997.html (accessed December 20, 2006).

30. A. Singh, "Asia Pacific Tourism Industry."

31. World Travel & Tourism Council, "Annual Report," 2003, www.wttc.org/aboutWttc/pdf/Progress%20%20Priorities%202003.pdf (accessed December 21, 2006).

32. "September 11, 2001 Attacks," *Wikipedia*, http://en.wikipedia.org/wiki/September_11,_2001_attacks (accessed December 21, 2006).

33. J. Wilks and S. Moore, "Tourism Risk Management for the Asia Pacific Region: An Authoritative Guide for Managing Crises and Disasters," *APEC International Centre for Sustainable Tourism*, Asia-Pacific Economic Cooperation, 2004, p. 12.

34. J. Wilks and S. Moore, "Tourism Risk Management," p. 48.

35. UNWTO Market Intelligence and Promotion Section, "UNWTO World Tourism Barometer Rising, Iraq and SARS Influences Not Yet Overcome," October 29, 2003, http://unwto.org/facts/wtb.html (accessed December 29, 2006).

36. J. Wilks and S. Moore, "Tourism Risk Management," p. 9.

37. Ibid.

38. Ibid, p. 20.

39. UNWTO Market Intelligence and Promotion Section, "Global Troubles Took Toll on Tourism in 2003, Growth to Resume in 2004," January 27, 2004, http://unwto.org/facts/wtb.html (accessed December 29, 2006).

40. UNWTO Market Intelligence and Promotion Section, "Spectacular Rebound of International Tourism in 2004," October 27, 2004, http://unwto.org/facts/wtb.html (accessed December 29, 2006).

41. UNWTO Market Intelligence and Promotion Section, "International Tourism Obtains Its Best Results in 20 Years," February 2, 2005, http://unwto.org/facts/wtb.html (accessed December 29, 2006).

42. BBC News, "At-a-Glance: Tsunami Economic Impact," March 22, 2005, http://news.bbc.co.uk/1/hi/business/4154277.stm (accessed December 29, 2006).

43. BBC News, "Tsunami Resorts 'Ready in Weeks'," January 8, 2005, http://news.bbc.co.uk/1/hi/uk/4156775.stm (accessed March 24, 2006).

44. BBC News, "Tourism Revival Key for Maldives," February 7, 2005, http://news.bbc.co.uk/1/hi/world/south_asia/4237389.stm (accessed March 24, 2006).

45. BBC News, "UN Holds Emergency Tourism Summit," January 31, 2005, http://news.bbc.co.uk/1/hi/business/4222077.stm (accessed March 24, 2006).

46. Travel Video Television News, "Tsunami Recovery: More Than One Year On," March 13, 2006, http://travelvideo.tv/news/more. php?id=8256.

47. IPO Document, p. 85.

48. UNWTO Market Intelligence and Promotion Section, "International Tourism up by 5.5% to 808 Million Arrivals in 2005," January 24, 2006, http://unwto.org/facts/wtb.html (accessed December 29, 2006).

1. "We Expect at Least 25 aloft Hotels in India within 5 Years," *Express Hospitality*, 2006.

2. J. Butler, "Why We're Building Hotels in India Like Crazy!" Hospitality Lawyer, December 28, 2006.

3. "Hotels in India—Trends and Opportunities," *HVS Hospitality Services Report*, 2007.

4. Butler, "Why We're Building Hotels in India Like Crazy!"

5. "Hotels in India—Trends and Opportunities."

6. However, foreigners cannot buy already existing buildings or undeveloped land. See, Butler, "Why We're Building Hotels in India Like Crazy!"

7. "Global Funds Eye Indian Realty Pie," *Business Standard/Bvom*, September 19, 2007.

8. Butler, "Why We're Building Hotels in India Like Crazy!"

9. Government of India statistics, see D. Philip, "Room at the Top," *Tourism* (2007): 31–33.

10. "Hotels in India—Trends and Opportunities."

11. Ibid.

12. Ibid.

13. India follows the British measurement system, where 1 crore = 100 lakhs and 1 lakh = 100,000 Rs.

14. Chennai, "Hotel Sector May See Rs 52,000-cr Investment," *Businessline*, April 12, 2007; and "Hotel Chains to Pump in US$ 1 Billion in 2 Years," *Economic Times*, March 29, 2007.

15. Ibid.

16. Philip, "Room at the Top."

17. Part II: "Trends and Opportunities in the Indian Hotel Industry," *HVS Hotel Services Survey 2007*.

18. Chennai, "India is Exciting, but Not Without Hassles," *Businessline* (July 4, 2006): 1.

19. "Hotels in India—Trends and Opportunities."

20. S. Gupta, "Hotels without Hoteliers!," *HVS International Research Report*, October 2005.

21. G. Stoller, "Hotel Schools are in With Inn Crowd," *USA Today*, January 7, 2008.

22. "Hotels in India—Trends and Opportunities."

23. "We Expect at Least 25 aloft Hotels in India within 5 Years."

24. *Starwood Hotels & Resorts Annual Report, 2006*; and P. Chandrasekhar, "Starwood to Set up 50 Hotels in India by 2010." March 6, 2007.

25. D. Eisen, "Lofty Expectations for Starwood's aloft Brand," *Business Travel News* (March 20, 2006): 18.

26. R. Feitelberg, "Ross Klein to Steer Starwood's aloft," *WWD* 190, 76 (October 10, 2005): 20.

27. *Starwood Hotels & Resorts Worldwide, Inc.*, Business Wire Press Release, "Starwood Hotels Introduces Its New Lifestyle Brand—aloft Hotels—at the 2007 Hotel Investment Conference in South Asia," April 5, 2007.

28. *STR News*: "Charleston One of the First Cities to Live ★ Life ★ aloft[(SM)]," August 2006. For the complete list of cities with future openings and the expected dates, see www.starwoodhotels.com/alofthotels/hotels/index.html.

29. Starwood Hotels & Resorts Worldwide, Inc., Press Release, "aloft Sees Green," September 2006.

30. D. DeFranco, "Feeding the New Breed of Traveler," *Lodging Hospitality* 63, 5 (April 1, 2007): 24–28.

31. "Starwood Plans aloft for Mumbai, India," *Hotel Motel Management* (Week in Review), April 10, 2007.

32. "We Expect at Least 25 aloft Hotels in India within 5 Years."

33. Ibid.

34. *Starwood Hotels & Resorts Worldwide, Inc., Press Release*, "Lofty Hospitality: Starwood Coming with Westin, aloft to India," 2007.

35. S. Shellum, "Lofty Ambitions, an Interview with Starwood," *Hospitality & Travel News*, June 19, 2007.

36. *Hotel Development News & Trends*, "aloft Hotels Coming to India," December 20, 2007.

CASE 7

1. Taken from Howard Schultz, February 14, 2007 memo to senior management, Wall Street Journal Online, online.wsj.com; and Starbucks Gossip web site, http://starbucksgossip.typepad.com.

2. J. Adamy, "Starbucks Chairman Says Trouble May Be Brewing," *Wall Street Journal*, February 24, 2007.

3. Taken from Howard Schultz, February 14, 2007 memo to senior management; and Starbucks Gossip web site.

4. Ibid.

5. Ibid.

6. Starbucks Corp. (SBUX), *Reuters*, http://stocks.us.reuters.com/stocks/fullDescription.asp?symbol=SBUX.O (accessed February 22, 2008).

7. B. Tancer, "Brewing Battle: Starbucks vs. McDonald's," *Time* Magazine, January 10, 2008, www.time.com/time/business/article/0,8599,1702277,00.html?iid=sphere-inline-sidebar (accessed February 23, 2007).

8. Adamy, "Starbucks Chairman Says Trouble May Be Brewing."

9. Taken from Howard Schultz, February 14, 2007 memo to senior management; and Starbucks Gossip web site.

10. J. Adamy, "McDonald's Takes on a Weakened Starbucks," *Wall Street Journal* (January 7, 2008): A1.

11. Adamy, "McDonald's Takes on a Weakened Starbucks."

12. Ibid.

13. "McDonald's Tops Starbucks in Coffee Taste Test," Newsmax.com, http://archive.newsmax.com/archives/ic/2007/1/29/102949.shtml (accessed January 29, 2007).

14. Portions of this case were derived from "Starbucks' Entry into China," which was prepared for the first edition of this textbook. Special thanks go to Adam Baru, Yinian Hou, Vikas Patel, Bill Spinnenweber, Anjali Talera, and Ken Wilson, who wrote that case under the supervision of Jeffrey S. Harrison.

15. H. Schultz and D. Jones Yang, *Pour Your Heart into It: How Starbucks Built a Company One Cup at a Time* (New York: Hyperion Press, 1997), 29.

16. Schultz and Jones Yang, *Pour Your Heart into It*, 32–33.

17. Schultz and Jones Yang, *Pour Your Heart into It*, 52.

18. S. Holmes, D. Bennett, K. Carlisle, and C. Dawson, "Planet Starbucks," *Business Week* (September 9, 2002): 100–106.

19. Alan Liddle, "Howard Schultz," *Nation's Restaurant News* (January 1995): 184.

20. Liddle, "Howard Schultz."

21. Schultz and Jones Yang, *Pour Your Heart into It*, 81–86.

22. Ibid, 84–89.

23. A. Thompson and A. Strickland, "Starbucks," In *Strategic Management: Concepts and Cases*, 11th Edition, McGraw Hill, This case is online at http://www.mhhe.com/business/management/thompson/11e/case/starbucks.html

24. Schultz and Jones Yang, *Pour Your Heart into It*, 90–108.

25. Ibid, 110–115.

26. Ibid, 180–185.

27. S. Hume, "Howard's Blend," *Restaurants and Institutions* (July 1, 2000): 45.

28. "Eyes Wide Open: Starbucks Has Enjoyed All the Financial Success Howard Schultz Could Have Hoped for, Yet His Worst Nightmares Also Have Materialized," *Restaurants and Institutions*, February 20, 2008.

29. N. D. Schwartz, "Still Perking after All These Years," *Fortune* (May 24, 1999): 203–207.

30. History of Starbucks, Press Release, www.starbucks.com.

31. Reuters Limited, www.starbucks.com.

32. "What We Are All About," *Starbucks Corporate web site*, www.starbucks.com/aboutus/overview.asp (accessed February 23, 2008).

33. "Company Fact Sheet," *Starbucks Corporate web site*, www.starbucks.com/aboutus (accessed May 18, 2008).

34. Starbucks Refines Its Entertainment Strategy," *Starbucks Corporate web site*, Press Release, http://investor.starbucks.com/phoenix. zhtml?c=99518&p=irol-newsArticle&ID=1134789&highlight= (accessed May 18, 2008).

35. "Starbucks Mission Statement," *Starbucks Corporate web site*, www.starbucks.com/aboutus/environment.asp (accessed February 22, 2008).

36. Starbucks, "Fiscal 2001 Annual Report," 17.

37. P. E. Barnes, "Business," *Business & Economic Review* (July–September 2002): 27.

38. "Premium Prices and Transparency," *Starbucks Corporate web site*, www.starbucks.com/aboutus/bizofcoffee.asp (accessed February 23, 2008).

39. Organic Consumer's Association, May 21, 2002, www.organicconsumers.org (accessed November 16, 2002).

40. Holmes et al., "For Coffee Growers, Not Even a Whiff of Profits," *Business Week*, 9 (September 9, 2002).

41. "Access to Affordable Credit," *Starbucks Corporate web site*, www.starbucks.com/aboutus/bizofcoffee.asp (accessed February 23, 2008).

42. Holmes et al., "Planet Starbucks," 100–106.

43. www.hoovers.com/premium/fin_tables/5/0,2152,15745,00.html (accessed October 29, 2002).

44. J. A. Michelli, *The Starbucks Experience* (New York: McGraw-Hill, 2007), 28.

45. Business Source Premier, "Interviews with Howard Schultz: Sharing Success," *Executive Excellence* (November 1999): 16.

46. Schultz and Jones Yang, *Pour Your Heart into It*, 127.

47. Ibid, 123–135.

48. Ibid, 133–136.

49. Business Source Premier, "Interviews with Howard Schultz," 16.

50. B. McDowell, "The Bean Counters," *Restaurants & Institutions*, (December 15, 1995): 40–45.

51. Business Source Premier, "Interviews with Howard Schultz," 16.

52. Michelli, *The Starbucks Experience*, 12.

53. Ibid, 15.

54. Ibid, 16, 48, 93, 112, and 153.

55. "Starbucks Reports Strong Fourth Quarter and Record Full Year 2007 Results," Starbucks web site, http://investor.starbucks.com/ (accessed February 24, 2008).

56. "Annual Report 2007," *Starbucks web site*, http://investor.starbucks.com/.

57. "Starbucks Reports Strong Fourth Quarter and Record Full Year 2007 Results," Starbucks Website.

58. Ibid.

59. "Starbucks Cautious on 2008, Sees Recession Likely," *Reuters*, January 30, 2008, www.Reuters.Com/Article/Businessnews/Iduswn as851720080131?Feedtype=Rss&Feedname=Businessnews&Pagenumber=3&Virtualbrandchannel=0) (accessed February 23, 2007).

60. "Starbucks Cautious on 2008, Sees Recession Likely," *Reuters*.

61. "Starbucks Reports First Quarter Fiscal 2008 Results," Starbucks Website.

62. "Starbucks Reports First Quarter Fiscal 2008 Results," Starbucks Website.

63. Howard Schultz Letter to Customers, February 21, 2008, Starbucks web site, www.starbucks.com/aboutus/pressdesc.asp?id=815 (accessed February 24, 2008).

64. "Starbucks Unveils Leadership Structure to Execute Transformation of Company," Starbucks web site, http://investor.starbucks. com/ (accessed February 24, 2008).

65. "Howard Schultz Transformation Agenda Communication #7," Starbucks web site, www.starbucks.com/aboutus/pressdesc. asp?id=832 (accessed May 18, 2008).

66. "Starbucks Reports First Quarter Fiscal 2008 Results," Starbucks web site.

67. "Starbucks Realigning, Cutting 600 Jobs," *The Business Journal of Milwaukee*, February 22, 2008, http://milwaukee.bizjournals.com/ milwaukee/stories/2008/02/18/daily48.html.

CASE 8

1. S. Steinbeck, *PhoCusWright Consumer Travel Trends Survey*, 9th ed., PhoCusWright, Inc., May 2007.

2. As part of the PhoCusWright online travel overview published in 2007, more than 30 travel industry senior executives responsible for distribution decisions were interviewed.

3. Note that adjustments were made to account for minor overlap between GDS and online travel agencies.

4. D. Connolly, "Groups and Meetings: Market Opportunity Defined," PhoCusWright, Inc., January 2007.

5. C. E. Green, "The Travel Marketers Guide to Social Media," HSMAI Marketing Review, Winter 2008.

GLOSSARY

A

absorptive capacity The ability of a firm to recognize the value of new information, assimilate it, and apply it to commercial ends

accounting controls Ensure that the financial information provided to internal and external stakeholders is accurate and follows generally accepted accounting practices (GAAP)

acquisition An organization buys a controlling interest in the stock of another organization or buys it outright from its owners

acquisition premium The percentage amount paid for shares of stock above their market value before the acquisition announcement

activist groups Organizations formed with the purpose of advancing a specific cause or causes; public-interest groups represent the position of a broad cross section of society, whereas special-interest groups focus on the needs of smaller subgroups

administration Support activities of the value chain consisting of general management activities, such as planning and accounting

agency problem Exists when top managers attempt to maximize their own self-interests at the expense of shareholders

aggressive strategy These firms use every available resource in an effort to overwhelm rivals, thus reducing the chance that any countermove will be effective

alliance An arrangement between two or more firms that establishes an exchange relationship but that has no joint ownership involved

analyzer strategy Occupies a position between a prospector strategy and a defender strategy; firms attempt to maintain positions in existing markets while locating growth opportunities on the fringes

antitrust laws Established by governments to keep organizations from getting large and powerful enough in one industry to engage in monopoly pricing and other forms of noncompetitive or illegal behavior

average daily rate (ADR) A commonly used measure of hotel performance; ADR is the average daily rate per rented room, or the mean price charged for all hotel rooms sold in a given period

avoidance strategy Competitive strategy in which a firm avoids confrontation completely by focusing on a particular niche in the market in which other firms have little interest

B

backsourcing When firms bring an outsourced service or good back in-house, often because costs have begun to rise in contrast to the primary benefit of outsourcing

backward integration (upstream) A type of vertical integration that involves a firm acquiring its suppliers

bank-centered economies Banks and other financial institutions play the most significant role in the external capital markets

bargaining power Economic power that allows a firm or group of firms to influence the nature of business arrangements for factors such as pricing, availability of products or services, purchase terms, or length of contract

barriers to entry Obstacles that make it difficult for a firm to enter a given market

barriers to imitation Barriers intended to prevent existing competitors from imitating sources of cost savings or differentiation

basic research Activity associated with pushing back the boundaries of science as we know it

behavioral controls A special set of controls used to motivate employees to do things that the organization would like them to do, even in the absence of direct supervision; they include bureaucratic controls, clan control, and human resources systems

benchmarking A tool for assessing the best practices of direct competitors and firms in similar industries, then using the resulting "stretch" objectives as design criteria for attempting to change organizational performance

best-value strategy A firm pursues elements associated with cost leadership and differentiation simultaneously

board of directors In publicly owned companies, a group of individuals who are elected by the voting shareholders to monitor the behavior of top managers, therefore protecting their rights as shareholders

boutique hotels Sometimes called "design hotels" or "lifestyle hotels," they differentiate themselves from larger chain or branded hotels by their intense focus on the physical space through the design of their facilities

broad environment Forms the context in which the firm and its operating environment exist, including sociocultural influences, global economic influences, political/legal influences, and technological influences

buffering Techniques designed to stabilize and predict environmental influences and therefore soften the jolts that might otherwise be felt as the organization interacts with members of its external environment

builder-type culture Growth is the primary goal in the organization

bureaucratic control Rules, procedures, and policies that guide the behavior of organizational members

business angels Wealthy individuals who provide start-up capital to entrepreneurs

business definition A description of the business activities of a firm, based on its products and services, markets, functions served, and resource conversion processes

business-format franchising A popular form of franchising in hospitality firms; this approach to franchising involves a franchisor selling a way of doing business to its franchisees

business intelligence The collection and analysis of information on markets, new technologies, customers, competitors, and broad social trends, as well as information gained from internal sources

business-level strategy Defines an organization's approach to competing in its chosen markets

business-level strategy formulation Pertains to domain direction and navigation, or how businesses should compete in the business areas they have selected; sometimes these strategies are referred to as competitive strategies

business-level structures Methods of organizing individual business units, which are often called divisions if they are part of a larger corporation

business plan A plan that contains the details of how a new venture will be carried out

business process reengineering Involves the radical redesign of core business processes to achieve dramatic improvements in productivity cycle times and quality

C

capital intensity The extent to which the assets of an organization are primarily associated with plants, equipment, and other fixed assets

capital requirements Costs associated with starting a business

causal ambiguity When the factors responsible for competitive performance are difficult to discern; one of the reasons that intangible capabilities are difficult for competitors to imitate is that it is difficult to determine exactly how the source of capability was created

CEO duality Occurs when the CEO also chairs the board of directors

change-style leadership The CEO formulates strategy and then plans the changes in structure, personnel, information systems, and administration required to implement it

Chapter 11 A legal filing under the Federal Bankruptcy Code of the United States; allows an organization to work out a plan or arrangement for solving its financial problems under the supervision of a federal court

chief executive officer (CEO) Common title for the highest-ranking manager in a firm

chief information officer (CIO) A high-level manager who oversees the collection, analysis, and dissemination of information

chief knowledge officer (CKO) An organizational position responsible for ensuring that the organization can get maximum value from its knowledge, intangible assets, and best practices

clan control Socialization processes through which an individual comes to appreciate the values, abilities, and expected behaviors of an organization; closely linked to the concepts of culture and organizational ethics

co-optation Drawing resources from other firms to achieve stability and continued existence

code of ethics Communicates the values of the corporation to employees and other stakeholders

codified knowledge Knowledge that can be communicated completely via written means

collaboration strategy Firms combine resources in an effort to gain a stronger resource position; various forms of interorganizational relationships can lead to collaboration

collaborative-style leadership The CEO works with other managers to create a strategy; participants are then responsible for implementing the strategy in their own areas

collusion Formal price-setting cooperation among firms

commander-style leadership The CEO formulates strategy and then directs top managers to implement it

community of practice A group of people who share a concern, a set of problems, or a passion about a topic and who deepen their knowledge and expertise in this area by interacting continually

competitive advantage Exists when a firm has a long-lasting business advantage compared to rival firms that is a significant edge over the competition; usually this means that the firm can do something competitors can't do or has something competitors lack

competitive convergence Exists when companies make similar strategic choices, compete closely, and become alike or indistinguishable from each other

competitive dynamics The moves and countermoves of firms and their competitors

competitive strategies See *business-level strategies*

competitive tactics Techniques firms use—such as advertising, new product launches, cost-reduction efforts, and quality improvements—to win market share, increase revenues, and increase profits at the expense of rivals

concentration A corporate-level strategy in which the firm has virtually all of its resource investments in one business area

conglomerate A large, highly diversified firm

consortia Specialized joint ventures encompassing many different arrangements; consortia are often a group of firms oriented toward problem solving and technology development, such as R&D consortia

control systems Systems used to measure and monitor firm activities and processes, as well as motivate or encourage behaviors that are conducive to desired organizational outcomes; the tools of strategy implementation

copyright Literally "the right to copy" an original creation and constitutes a set of exclusive rights to the use of an idea or information

core activities The primary activities in a firm's value chain; for a hotel, these activities might include site development and construction (by local owner), marketing and sales (by brand, regional office, and property), service delivery and operations (i.e., check-in, check-out, and in-room services at property level and by management company), service monitoring and post stay service enhancement.

core competency A resource or capability that meets the conditions of being valuable, unique, nonsubstitutable, or difficult to imitate; if it can also be applied to more than one business area, it is also called a *capability*

core knowledge Scientific or technological knowledge that is associated with the actual creation of a product or service

core values The underlying philosophies that guide decisions and behavior in a firm; also called organizational values

corporate entrepreneurship Involves the creation of new business ventures within existing corporations

corporate-level distinctive competencies Derived from the ability to achieve shared competitive advantage across the business units of a multibusiness firm

corporate-level strategy formulation Refers primarily to the selection of business areas in which the organization will compete and the emphasis each area is given; also includes strategies for carrying out the corporate-level strategy

corporate matrix structure The corporate-level counterpart to the project matrix structure described earlier; organizes businesses along two dimensions, such as product and function

corporate raiders Organizations and individuals who engage in acquisitions, typically against the wishes of the managers of the target companies

cooperative partnerships See *consortia*

craftsman-type culture Quality is the primary driver of the corporate culture

creative destruction The inevitable decline of leading firms because competitors will pursue creative opportunities to eliminate the competitive advantages they hold

crescive-style leadership The CEO encourages lower-level managers to formulate and implement their own strategic plans, while still filtering out inappropriate programs; *crescive* means marked by gradual spontaneous development

crisis management Processes associated with preventing, detecting, or recovering from crises

cultural intelligence An aptitude that enables outsiders to interpret unfamiliar gestures and actions as though they were insiders; it can be acquired

culture An evolving set of shared beliefs, values, and attitudes that help shape how a social group thinks, sees, acts, and reacts to various events and situations

cultural-style leadership The CEO formulates a vision and strategy for the company and then works with other managers to create a culture that will foster fulfillment of the vision

customer-based structure Organization structures its major units around the characteristics or types of customer

D

defender strategy A conservative strategy intended to preserve market share

deliberate strategy Implies that managers plan to pursue an intended strategic course

differentiation Requires the firm to distinguish its products or services on the basis of an attribute such as higher quality, more innovative features, greater selection, better service after sale, or more advertising

diseconomies of scale Occur when a firm's larger size causes it to have increased unit costs often resulting from added administrative costs and confusion associated with bigger bureaucracy

diversification Occurs when a firm expands its business operations into new products, functions served, markets, or technologies

divestiture A reverse acquisition; business assets are sold off or spun off as a whole business

domestic stage of international development Organizations focus their efforts on domestic operations, but begin to export their products and services, sometimes through an export department or a foreign joint venture

dominant design A de facto standard, process, or product architecture that dominates a product category or industry

dot-coms Internet-based businesses; the name comes from the fact that many of these businesses have an Internet address that ends in. com, as in Amazon.com

downscoping Involves reducing diversification (refocusing) through selling off nonessential businesses that are not related to the organization's core competencies and capabilities

due diligence Involves a complete examination of a merger or acquisition, including such areas as management, equity, debt, sale of assets, transfer of shares, environmental issues, financial performance, tax issues, human resources, customers, and markets

E

EBITDA Earnings before interest, taxes, depreciation, and amortization

e-commerce Describes business dealings that are electronically based, such as e-tailing (retailing through the Internet), exchanging data, business-to-business buying and selling, and e-mail communications

economic dependence Occurs when stakeholders rely on an organization to provide economic resources such as a salary, interest payments, tax revenues, or payment for goods and services supplied to the firm

economic environment Influences and trends associated with domestic or global economies, such as economic growth rates, interest rates, the availability of credit, inflation rates, foreign exchange rates, and foreign trade balances

economic perspective Defines the purpose of a business organization as profit maximization

economic power Derived from the ability to withhold services, products, capital, revenues, or business transactions that the organization values

economic stake Competitive moves by one firm affect other firms in the industry, which may incite retaliation or countermoves; in other words, competing firms have an *economic stake* in one another

economies of scale Cost savings that occur when it is more efficient to produce a product in a larger facility at higher volume

emergent strategy Implies that the existing strategy is not necessarily planned or intended, but rather a result of learning through a process of trial and error

emerging economies Economies that have historically been dominated by government influence, with poorly developed financial capital markets; some of these economies are now pursuing privatization programs that put economic assets in the hands of private citizens

employee stock ownership plan (ESOP) Reward system in which employees are provided with an attractive method for acquiring stock in the companies where they work

enactment The perspective that firms do not have to submit to existing environmental forces because they can influence their environments

enterprise strategy Joins ethical and strategic thinking about the organization; it is the organization's best possible reason for the actions it takes

entrenchment Occurs when managers gain so much power that they are able to use the firm to further their own interests rather than the interests of shareholders

entrepreneurial discovery Entails channeling resources toward the fulfillment of a market need; the intersection of a need and a solution

entrepreneurial tasks Recognition or creation of an opportunity, creation of a business plan, securing start-up capital, and actual management of the start-up through its early stages

entrepreneurship The creation of new business

entry barriers Forces that keep new competitors out, providing a level of protection for existing competitors

environmental determinism The perspective that the most successful organization will best adapt to existing forces; in other words, the environment "determines" the best strategy

environmental discontinuities Major, unexpected changes in the social, economic, technological, political, or internal environments that necessitate change within organizations

environmental uncertainty A result of not being able to predict precisely what will happen with regard to the actions of external stakeholders and other external influences; results in organizational uncertainty

exit barriers Costs associated with leaving a business or industry

experience goods Goods for which it is difficult to determine product characteristics in advance of consumption

exporting Transferring goods to other countries for sale through wholesalers or a foreign company

external environment Stakeholders and forces outside the traditional boundaries of the firm; they can be divided into the broad and operating environments

F

fad A cultural blip, it's what's "hot" but fades fast and doesn't return

family-centered economies Families hold a lot of the stock in large corporations, giving them a lot of control

feedback control Provides managers with information concerning outcomes from organizational activities

feedforward control A system that reacts to changes and helps managers anticipate changes in the external and internal environments, based on analysis of inputs from stakeholders and the environment

financial controls Based purely on financial measures such as ROI

financial intermediaries A wide variety of institutions—including banks, stock exchanges, brokerage houses, investment advisors, mutual fund companies, pension fund companies, and other organizations or individuals—that may have an interest in investing in the firm

financial risk The risk that a firm will not be able to meet its financial obligations and may eventually declare bankruptcy

financial strategy Primary purpose is to provide the organization with the capital structure and funds that are appropriate for implementing growth and competitive strategies

first-movers Firms that stay at the forefront of technological advances in their industries

five forces of industry competition Forces that largely determine the type and level of competition in an industry and, ultimately, the industry's profit potential; they include customers, suppliers, entry barriers, substitute products or services, and rivalry among existing competitors

fixed costs Costs associated with plants, machinery, or other fixed assets

focus strategy A firm targets a narrow segment of the market through low-cost leadership, differentiation, or a combination of low cost and differentiation

food contractors Provide restaurant services to commercial, industrial, university, school, airline, hospital, nursing home, recreation, and sports center institutions; the institution may provide the facilities and personnel for these operations; examples of contractors include Aramark Corporation, Compass Group, and Sodexho Alliance

Foreign Corrupt Practices Act (FCPA) A response to social concern about bribes paid by U.S. companies to foreign government officials; it defines the "rules-of-the-game" for U.S. companies when they operate in foreign countries

foreign direct investment Occurs when a firm makes a direct investment, defined as building or acquiring assets in another country

foreign exchange rates The rates at which currencies are exchanged across countries; this is a major source of uncertainty for firms operating in foreign countries

foreign trade balance A measure of the relative value of imports to exports from one country to another

formal power Occurs when stakeholders have a legal or contractual right to make decisions for some part of an organization

formal structure Specifies the number and types of departments or groups and provides the formal reporting relationships and lines of communication among internal stakeholders

forward integration (downstream) A form of vertical integration in which a firm expands to control the distribution of its products or services, usually through ownership

franchising A licensing strategy in which two independent companies form a contractual agreement giving one (the franchisee) the right to operate a business in a given location for a specified period under the other firm's (franchisor) brand; franchisees agree to pay fees and royalties, and they may also agree to make advertising contributions as a percentage of unit revenues

full-service restaurants Restaurants that offer eat-in service, expansive menus, and prices that range from low to high; these restaurants are divided into three segments: family, grill-buffet, and dinner houses

functional-level strategy The collective pattern of day-to-day decisions made and actions taken by managers and employees who are responsible for value-creating activities within a particular functional area

functional-level strategy formulation The details of how functional resource areas—such as marketing, operations, and finance—should be used to implement business-level strategies and achieve competitive advantage

functional strategy audit Through evaluation of functional-level strategies on the basis of internal consistency, consistency across functional areas, and the extent to which each functional strategy supports the overall strategies of the firm

functional structure A business-level structure organized around the inputs or activities that are required for producing products and services, such as marketing, operations, finance, and R&D

G

generic business strategies A classification system for business-level strategies based on common strategic characteristics

geographic and customer-based structures A business-level structure organized around geographic locations or customer types serviced

global integration The process through which a multinational organization integrates its worldwide activities into a single world strategy through its network of affiliates and alliances

global product/market approach Companies use one product design and market it in the same fashion throughout the world

global resource advantage A source of competitive advantage resulting from the ability of a global organization to draw from a much broader and more diversified pool of resources

global stage of international development The organization has become so global that it is no longer associated primarily with any one country

gross operating profit (GOP) The difference between operating revenue and expenses, or income after undistributed operating expenses; GOP is calculated by subtracting total undistributed operating expenses from total operated departments income

group-centered economies Groups of companies manage the use of internal capital as a replacement for external capital markets

H

hierarchy overload Leads to decisions piling up at the top of the organization, because most interdepartmental issues fall on the general manager

horizontal integration Involves acquisition of an organization in the same line of business

hospitality Defined in the Oxford English Dictionary as the reception and entertainment of guests, visitors, or strangers with liberality and goodwill

hospitality industry A group of businesses that welcome travelers and guests by providing accommodation, food, and/or beverages

hostile acquisition An acquisition that is not desirable from the perspective of the managers of a target company; unexpected acquisition announcements typically are considered hostile

human resource management Support activities of the value chain associated with human-based activities such as recruiting, hiring, training, and compensation

human resources strategy The pattern of decisions about selection, training, rewards, and benefits

hypercompetition A condition of rapidly escalating competition

hypothesis development and testing Organizations should test their decisions to see if they are appropriate or likely to be successful; hypothesis development is a creative process, whereas hypothesis testing is an analytical process

I

inbound logistics Primary activities of the value chain that include activities associated with acquiring inputs that are used in the product

industries A group of organizations that compete *directly* with one another to win customers or sales in the marketplace

industry consolidation Occurs as competitors merge

industry life cycle Portrays how sales volume for a product category changes over its lifetime, from the introduction stage through the commodity or decline stage

industry revolutionaries Firms that invent business concepts

industry supply chain The sequence of activities in an industry from raw materials extraction through final consumption

information systems strategy Plan for using information systems to enhance organizational processes and strategy

inimitable resources Resources that are possessed by industry participants but are difficult or impossible to completely duplicate

initial public offering (IPO) Entails sale of stock to the public and investors

innovation A new idea, a recombination of old ideas, or a unique approach that is perceived as new by the individuals involved; innovation is the combination of both invention and commercialization

intangible relatedness Occurs any time capabilities developed in one area can be applied to another area

intangible resources Organizational assets that are difficult to quantify, such as knowledge, skills, abilities, stakeholder relationships, and reputations

integrative knowledge Knowledge that helps integrate various activities, capabilities, and products

intelligent opportunism The ability of managers at various levels of the organization to take advantage of unanticipated opportunities to further intended strategy or even redirect a strategy

interlocking directorate Occurs when a director or executive of one firm sits on the board of a second firm or when two firms have directors who also serve on the board of a third firm

internal controls A set of controls that firms use to guide internal processes and behaviors; specifically, behavioral, process, and accounting controls

international expansion The process of building an expanding operational presence; this can lead to global resource advantages

international stage of international development Exports become an important part of organizational strategy; operations and marketing are tailored to the needs of each country

interorganizational relationships A term that includes many types of organizational cooperation or partnerships

intrapreneurship Corporate entrepreneurship, or the creation of new business ventures within existing corporations

investment group This is a special type of corporate partnership; these are groups of wealthy individuals, business owners, or corporations that take an ownership interest in the capital assets of a venture

J

joint venture An entity that is created when two or more firms pool a portion of their resources to create a separate jointly owned entity

K

keiretsu A special type of network form, common in Japan, which is organized around an industry and works in much the same way as other networks; however, firms in a *keiretsu* often hold ownership interests in one another

knowledge economy Refers to the importance of intangible people skills and intellectual assets to developed economies

L

lateral (horizontal) organization Refers to the horizontal communication and coordination mechanisms that occur across departments or divisions, such as direct contact, teams, task forces, a community of practice, and integrator positions

learning curve Demonstrates that the time required to complete a task will decrease as a predictable function of the number of times the task is repeated

L.E.E.D. (Leadership in Energy & Environmental Design) A set of standards for environmentally sustainable construction developed by the U.S. Green Building Council (USGBC) in 1998

legal perspective Ethical behavior is defined as legal behavior

leverage A measure of a firm's long-term or total debt relative to its assets or equity; a common measure of financial risk

leveraged buyouts (LBOs) Private purchase of a business unit by managers, employees, unions, or private investors

licensing Selling the right to produce and/or sell a brand-name product, often in a foreign market

limited partnership A business form in which the partners' management responsibility and legal liability are limited

liquidity A measure of a firm's ability to pay short-term obligations

liquidity ratios A financial metric that is used to help determine an organization's ability to pay short-term debt obligations

low-cost leadership strategy A firm pursues competitive advantage through efficient cost production; also called cost leadership

M

management company In the hotel industry, management companies run the operation of a hotel; they may also be a franchisor and/or owner; examples include Interstate Hotels and Resorts, Tharaldson Enterprises, and Westmont Hospitality

management contract A contract between an owner and a management company in which the owner agrees to make a payment from the operation's gross revenues to the management company in exchange for running the business with full management responsibility

market-centered economies Economies with well-developed infrastructures, business environments, and external capital markets

market development Involves repositioning a product or service to appeal to a new market

market penetration Competing with a single product or service in a single market

marketing and sales Primary activities of the value chain associated with processes through which customers can purchase the product and through which they are induced to do so

marketing strategy Plan for collecting information about customers or potential customers and using this information to project future demand, predict competitor actions, identify new business opportunities, create products and services, and sell products and services

master franchise agreements Involve larger franchisees who have the rights to develop in a specific territory; a master franchise is often used in nonstrategic or smaller markets

matrix structure A hybrid structure that combines some elements of functional structures with other forms

mental model A view of how the world works; mental models should include an understanding of both the internal and external organizations and the interaction between the two

merger Occurs when two organizations combine into one; acquisitions are the most common type of merger

mission statement Defines what the organization is and its reason for existing; often contains all of the elements of strategic direction—including vision, business definition, and organizational values

monopoly An industry in which one firm is the only significant provider of a good or service

multidivisional corporate-level structure A corporate-level structure in which each business exists as a separate unit reporting to top management

multidomestic product/market approach Entails handling product design, assembly, and marketing on a country-by-country basis by custom-tailoring products and services around individual markets' needs

multimarket competition Firms compete in multiple markets simultaneously

multinational stage of international development The organization has marketing and production facilities throughout the world

N

network A hub-and-wheel configuration with a local firm at the hub organizing the interdependencies of a complex array of firms

network structure   A business-level structure in which operating units or branches are organized around customer groups or geographic regions

neutrality agreement   A hotel signing one of these agreements promises to stay neutral if the union decides to organize the property; the neutrality agreement means that the hotel does not have the right to contest union organization, and the employees do not have the right to vote in a secret ballot to determine whether they wish to be represented

newly industrialized economies (NIEs)   Countries that have recently experienced high levels of growth in real gross domestic product

O

objective   Represents a performance target for an individual, a department, a division, a business, or a corporation

occupancy   A commonly used measure of hotel performance; occupancy is calculated by dividing the number of rooms sold by the number of rooms available and multiplying by 100

offshoring   When a company outsources to a supplier in a foreign country

oligopoly   An industry characterized by the existence of a few very large firms

operating environment   Consists of stakeholders with whom organizations interact on a fairly regular basis—including customers, suppliers, competitors, government agencies and administrators, local communities, activist groups, unions, the media, and financial intermediaries

operating goals   Established in an effort to bring the concepts found in the vision statement to a level that managers and employees can influence and control

operations   Primary activities of the value chain that refer to transforming inputs into the final product

operations strategy   Emerges from the pattern of decisions made within the firm about production or service operations

organizational champions   Someone who is very committed to a project and is willing to expend energy to make sure it succeeds

organizational control   The processes that lead to adjustments in strategic direction, strategies, or the implementation plan, when necessary

organizational crises   Critical situations that threaten high-priority organizational goals, impose a severe restriction on the amount of time in which key members of the organization can respond, and contain elements of surprise

organizational culture   The system of shared values of an organization's members

organizational ethics   A value system that has been widely adopted by members of an organization; often used interchangeably with the term *organizational values*

organizational fit   Occurs when two organizations or business units have similar management processes, cultures, systems, and structures

organizational governance   How the behavior of high-ranking managers is supervised and controlled; for example, the board of directors is responsible for ensuring that managerial behavior is consistent with shareholder interests

organizational scope   The breadth of an organization's activities across businesses and industries

organizational structure   Reporting relationships and the division of people into groups, teams, task forces, and departments within an organization

organizational values   The underlying philosophies that guide decisions and behavior in a firm; also called core values or organizational ethics

outbound logistics   Primary activities of the value chain related to storing and physically distributing a final product to customers

outsourcing   Contracting with another firm to provide goods or services that were previously supplied from within the company; similar to subcontracting

owner/manager structure   In this form, the owner is the top manager, and the business is run as a sole proprietorship

P

Pacific Century   Refers to a forecast that the world's growth center for the 21st century will shift across the Pacific Ocean to Asia

partnership   A business form in which the partners each contribute resources and share in the rewards of the venture

patent   Legal protection that prevents other companies from using a firm's innovation

performance-based compensation plan   Reward system in which compensation varies depending on the success of the organization

pioneer-type culture   The emphasis is on new product and new technology development

political environment   Influences and trends associated with governments and other political or legal entities; political forces, both at home and abroad, are among the most significant determinants of organizational success

political power   Comes from the ability to persuade lawmakers, society, or regulatory agencies to influence firm behavior

political strategies   All organizational activities that have as one of their objectives the creation of a friendlier political climate for the organization

preferred vendors   Often provide products or services with special terms or lower prices, in exchange for long-term contracts

premise control   Use of information collected by the organization to examine assumptions that underlie organizational vision, goals, and strategies

process controls   Use immediate feedback to control organizational processes

process innovations   Change in the ways things are created and delivered; the use of new methods, materials, techniques, or equipment

product/market structure   A business-level structure that organizes activities around the outputs of the organizational system, such as products, customers, or geographic regions

product- or service-based structure   A business-level structure organized around the outputs of the organization system

product/service development   Introduction of new products or services related to an existing competence of the firm or development of truly new-to-the-world products not related to the core business of the firm

product/service differentiation   Attributes associated with a product or service that cause customers to prefer it over competing products or services

product innovations   Change that yields a new product or service, a new or novel final good or service

pro-forma financial statements   Forward-looking income statements, balance sheets, and cash flow statements that are based on predictions of what will happen

profitability ratios   A common measure of overall financial success; they provide a barometer for management with regard to how well strategies are working, and they may also provide warning of downward trends and thus the need for more-dramatic changes; external stakeholders pay critical attention to profitability ratios, as they are a primary determinant of share prices, the ability to repay loans, and future dividends

project matrix structure   A hybrid business-level structure that combines some elements of both functional and product/market structures

prospector strategy   An offensive strategy in which firms aggressively seek new market opportunities and are willing to take risks

public-interest groups   Represent the position of a broad cross section of society

Q

quick-service restaurants   Eat-in or take-out operations with limited menus, low prices, and fast service; these restaurants are commonly called fast-food or fast-service

restaurants; examples include McDonald's, Burger King, KFC, and Taco Bell

R

R&D/technology strategy   Plan for developing new products and new technologies

radical innovations   Major innovations that influence more than one business or industry

radical restructuring   Major changes to a firm's direction, strategies, structures, and plans

reactor strategy   Describes firms that don't have a distinct strategy; they simply react to environmental situations

real estate investment trusts (REITs)   A corporation or trust that has at least 75 percent of its investments in real estate; REITs do not pay income tax so long as they pay back to shareholders 95 percent or more of their profits

reengineering   A restructuring approach that involves the radical redesign of core business processes to achieve dramatic improvements in productivity cycle times and quality

related acquisitions   Occur when the acquiring company shares common or complementary resources with its acquisition target

related diversification   Diversification that stems from common markets, functions served, technologies, or products and services

relational ability   The ability to interact with other companies; can increase a firm's ability to obtain and transfer knowledge

religious perspective   Religious teachings define appropriate behavior

reputation   An economic asset that signals observers about the attractiveness of a company's offerings based on past performance

resource-based approach to strategic management   Considers the firm as a bundle of resources; firms can gain competitive advantage through possessing superior resources

resource complementarity   Occurs when two businesses have strengths in different areas

resource procurement   Support activities of the value chain related to the purchase of inputs for all of the primary processes and support activities of the firm

restructuring   Involves major changes to an organization's strategies, structure, and/or processes

retaliation strategy   A firm threatens severe retaliation in an effort to discourage competitors from taking actions

retrenchment   A turnaround strategy that involves tactics such as reducing the workforce, closing unprofitable plants, outsourcing unprofitable activities, implementing tighter cost or quality controls, or implementing new policies that emphasize quality or efficiency

return on investment (ROI)   The operating ratio (return on sales) times the stock turn (sales to assets)

revenue per available room (RevPAR)   A commonly used measure of hotel performance; RevPAR is calculated by dividing total revenue by the number of hotel rooms available for sale

S

S corporation   Formerly called the Subchapter S corporation, this corporate form allows tax advantages in the United States that are similar to those associated with a partnership

salesman-type culture   These firms are excellent marketers who create successful brand names and distribution channels and pursue aggressive advertising and innovative packaging

search goods   Products that a consumer can inspect in advance of purchase

second-movers   These firms have a deliberate strategy of rapidly imitating the innovations of competitors; they enjoy many of the same benefits without all of the R&D costs

segmentation   A subgroup of people or organizations that share characteristics in common

servicemark   The same as a trademark but distinguishes services versus products

situation analysis   Analysis of stakeholders inside and outside the organization, as well as other external forces; this analysis should be conducted at both the domestic and international levels, if applicable

Six Sigma   A philosophy based on minimizing the number of defects found in a manufacturing operation or service function

social responsibility   The duty of an organization, defined in terms of its economic, legal, and moral obligations, as well as discretionary actions that might be considered attractive from a societal perspective

social stake   Occurs when a stakeholder group not directly linked to the organization is interested in ensuring that the organization behaves in a manner that it believes is socially responsible

sociocultural environment   Influences and trends that come from groups of individuals who make up a particular geographic region

special-interest groups   Groups formed to focus on the needs of specific subgroups

spin-off   A type of divestiture in which current shareholders are issued a proportional number of shares in the spun-off business

stakeholders   Groups or individuals who can significantly affect or are significantly affected by an organization's activities

stakeholder approach to strategic management   Envisions the firm at the center of a network of constituencies called stakeholders; firms can gain competitive advantage through superior stakeholder management

start-up capital   The financing required to begin a new venture

steward   A leader who cares deeply about the firm, its stakeholders, and the society in which it operates

strategic business unit (SBU) structure   A multidivisional structure in which divisions are combined into SBUs based on common elements they each possess

strategic control   Refers to a combination of control systems that allows managers excellent control over their firms

strategic direction   Pertains to the longer-term goals and objectives of the organization; this direction is often contained in mission and vision statements

strategic fit   Refers to the effective matching of strategic organizational capabilities

strategic flexibility   A firm can move its resources out of declining markets and into more prosperous ones in a minimum amount of time

strategic-group map   Categorizes existing industry competitors into groups that follow similar strategies

strategic intent   A vision of where an organization is or should be going; similar to the strategic concept of vision defined previously

strategic leadership   Generally refers to leadership behaviors associated with creating organizational vision, establishing core values, developing strategies and a management structure, fostering organizational learning, and serving as a steward for the firm

strategic management   A process through which organizations analyze and learn from their internal and external environments, establish strategic direction, create strategies that are intended to move the organization in that direction, and implement those strategies, all in an effort to satisfy key stakeholders

strategic planning process   The formal planning elements of strategic management that result in a strategic plan; this process tends to be rather rigid and unimaginative

strategic reorientation   A significant realignment of organization strategies, structure, and processes with the new environmental realities

strategic surveillance   The process of collecting information from the broad, operating, and internal environments

strategic thinking   A somewhat creative and intuitive process that leads to creative solutions and new ideas

strategy   (1) a pattern that emerges in a sequence of decisions over time or (2) an organizational plan of action that is intended to move a company toward the achievement of its shorter-term goals and, ultimately, toward the achievement of its fundamental purposes

strategy formulation   The process of planning strategies, often divided into the corporate, business, and functional levels

strategy implementation   Managing stakeholder relationships and organizational resources in a manner that moves the organization toward the successful execution of its strategies, consistent with its strategic direction

structural inertia   Forces at work to maintain the status quo; they may include systems, structures, processes, culture, sunk costs, internal politics, and barriers to entry and exit

subcontracting   Acquiring goods and services that used to be produced in-house from external companies

substitute products/services   Products or services provided by another industry that can be readily substituted for an industry's own products/services

support activities   In a firm's value chain, the activities that enable the company to function and to provide the core activities; examples include human resources, maintenance, information technology, accounting, and purchasing

sustainability   The idea of providing for current needs without sacrificing the needs of future generations

sustainable competitive advantage   Exists when a firm enjoys a long-lasting business advantage compared to rival firms

SWOT analysis   A tool strategists use to evaluate Strengths, Weaknesses, Opportunities, and Threats

synergy   Occurs when the whole is greater than the sum of its parts

T

tacit knowledge   Knowledge that is difficult to articulate in a way that is meaningful and complete

tangible relatedness   Means that the organization has the opportunity to use the same physical resources for multiple purposes

tangible resources   Organizational assets that can be seen, touched, and/or quantified, such as plants, money, or products

technological environment   Influences and trends related to the development of technologies both domestically and internationally

technology   Human knowledge about products and services and the way they are made and delivered

technology development   Support activities of the value chain associated with learning processes that result in improvements in the way organizational functions are performed

thinking in time   Recognition that the past, present, and future are all relevant to making good strategic decisions

top management team (TMT)   Typically a heterogeneous group of three to ten top executives selected by the CEO; each member brings a unique set of skills and a unique perspective

tourism clusters   Geographic concentrations of competing, complementary, and interdependent firms that work together to provide the tourism experience

trade association   Organizations (typically nonprofit) that are formed by firms in the same industry to collect and disseminate trade information, offer legal and technical advice, furnish industry-related training, and provide a platform for collective lobbying

trade barriers   Factors that discourage international trade, such as tariffs and import quotas

trademark   Legal protection that prevents other companies from making use of a firm's symbol or brand name

traditional approach to strategic management   Analysis of the internal and external environments of the organization to arrive at organizational strengths, weaknesses, opportunities, and threats (SWOT), which form the basis for developing effective missions, goals, and strategies

transaction cost economics   The study of economic transactions and their costs

transaction costs   The resources used to create and enforce a contract

transnational structure   A corporate-level structure that organizes businesses along three dimensions: nation or region, product, and function

travel and tourism industry   A variety of interrelated businesses that provide services to travelers; the tourism industry includes a broad range of businesses such as airlines, bars, cruise lines, car rental firms, casinos, entertainment firms, hotels, restaurants, travel agents, timeshares, tour operators, and recreational enterprises

trends   Usually capture long-term changes or movements that are substantial to the society and last

triad regions   Three dominant economic regions in the world; namely, North America, Europe, and the Pacific Rim

turnaround strategies   Sometimes called *retrenchment*; can involve workforce reductions, selling assets to reduce debt, outsourcing unprofitable activities, implementation of tighter cost or quality controls, or new policies that emphasize quality or efficiency; turnaround can occur at the corporate level of a company or on a property-by-property basis

U

Uniform System of Accounts   These standardized industry accounting systems provide many supplementary operating statements covering budgeting and forecasting; the Uniform System of Accounts for the Lodging Industry (USALI) and the Uniform System of Accounts for Restaurants (USAR) are designed with the special needs of the industry in mind and permit comparisons with industry standards

U.S. Sentencing Guidelines (USSG)   Compulsory guidelines courts must use to determine fines and penalties when corporate illegalities are proven

universalist perspective   Appropriate behavior is defined by the question: "Would I be willing for everyone else in the world to make the same decision?"

unrelated acquisitions   Occur between companies that don't share any common or complementary resources

unrelated diversification   Diversification that is not based on commonality among the activities of a corporation

utilitarian perspective   The most appropriate actions generate the greatest benefits for the largest number of people

V

value chain   A representation of organizational processes, divided into primary and support activities that create value for the customer

venture capitalists   Individuals or groups of investors that seek out and provide capital to entrepreneurs

vertical integration   Exists when a firm is involved in more than one stage of the industry supply chain; a firm that vertically integrates moves forward to become its own customer or backward to become its own supplier

vision   Expresses what the organization wants to be in the future

vision statement   A forward-looking statement of what a firm wants to be in the future; an ideal and unique picture of the future

visionary leadership   Pertains to envisioning what the organization should be like in the future, communicating the vision, and empowering followers to enact it

W

whistle-blower   An employee or manager who reveals wrongdoing; an attempt to force the organization to cease a behavior that society finds unacceptable or to incorporate a practice that is in keeping with a new social value, if value changes in society are not voluntarily incorporated into a firm

wholly owned foreign subsidiary   A business venture that is started from scratch; sometimes called a greenfield investment

INDEX